OXFORD READIN

PLATO 1

Published in this series

Other volumes are in preparation

PLATO 1

Metaphysics and Epistemology

Edited by

GAIL FINE

OXFORD
UNIVERSITY PRESS

OXFORD

UNIVERSITY PRESS

Great Clarendon Street, Oxford OX2 6DP

Oxford University Press is a department of the University of Oxford.
It furthers the University's objective of excellence in research, scholarship,
and education by publishing worldwide in

Oxford New York

Athens Auckland Bangkok Bogotá Buenos Aires Calcutta
Cape Town Chennai Dar es Salaam Delhi Florence Hong Kong Istanbul
Karachi Kuala Lumpur Madrid Melbourne Mexico City Mumbai
Nairobi Paris São Paulo Singapore Taipei Tokyo Toronto Warsaw

and associated companies in Berlin Ibadan

Oxford is a registered trade mark of Oxford University Press
in the UK and certain other countries

Published in the United States
by Oxford University Press Inc., New York

Introduction and Selection © Oxford University Press 1999

British Library Cataloguing in Publication Data

Data available

Library of Congress Cataloging in Publication Data

Plato / edited by Gail Fine.
(Oxford readings in philosophy)
Includes bibliographical references.
Contents: [v.] 1 Metaphysics and epistemology—[v.] 2 Ethics,
politics, religion & the soul.
1. Plato. 2. Philosophy, Ancient. I. Fine, Gail. II. Series.
[B395.P516 1999]
185—dc21 99-13233 CIP

ISBN 0–19–875206–7 (Pbk)

1 3 5 7 9 10 8 6 4 2

Typeset by Best-set Typesetter Ltd., Hong Kong
Printed in Great Britain
on acid-free paper by
Bookcraft Ltd
Midsomer Norton, Somerset

PREFACE

This is one of a pair of volumes on Plato: its companion discusses ethics, politics, religion, and the soul. Their aim is to introduce the reader to just some of the important dialogues and issues; I hope the interested reader will be encouraged to pursue the study of Plato further. In keeping with the aims of the Oxford Readings in Philosophy series, all the selections are relatively recent: the earliest appeared in 1970.

Though each volume is self-contained, they are closely related. This reflects the fact that Plato believes there are deep connections between areas of philosophy that are sometimes studied in relative isolation. For example, he takes failure in the elenchus—his method of cross-examining interlocutors—to indicate not only a failure of knowledge but also a moral failure. He takes the notion of goodness to be central not only to ethics and politics but also to metaphysics and epistemology. His metaphysical and epistemological views, as well as his views of human psychology, ground many of his ethical and political views. Indeed, one might speak of the metaphysical, epistemological, and psychological bases of his ethical and political views. Hence much of the material in Volume 1 grounds the material in Volume 2. But many of the articles in Volume 2 also illuminate issues discussed in Volume 1.

Since these volumes are not comprehensive, the Introductions fill in some gaps; hence they discuss some issues to which no article neatly corresponds. They also situate the articles within a broader context. However, space limitations obviously preclude a full and thorough discussion. Footnotes make suggestions for further reading, as does the Bibliography.

Though most of the articles are previously published, some of them have been revised—sometimes in minor, sometimes in major, ways—for inclusion in these volumes. I warmly thank those authors who kindly and promptly revised previous work to suit the needs of these volumes. All the articles have been lightly copy-edited so as to bring them more into conformity with OUP house style. For example, in many cases the style of footnote references has been altered; references to ancient texts have been largely brought into conformity with LSJ; American spelling and usage have been changed to British. However, complete conformity to OUP house style has not been attempted or achieved.

References to Plato, throughout these two volumes, are to the Stephanus pages (e.g. *Apology* 29b). This pagination derives from the edition of Plato published by Henri Estienne in 1578 ('Stephanus' is the Latinization of 'Estienne').

In making my selections, I have had the benefit of advice from many people. I should particularly like to thank Christopher Shields and Christopher Taylor. I have also had helpful advice from Stephen Everson and Lindsay Judson, and from several referees for Oxford University Press. Peter Momtchiloff, of OUP, has been extremely helpful and patient over a long period; and I thank him too for suggesting the project in the first place. Angela Griffin, who joined the project more recently, also deserves thanks. Kate Woolfitt was a gracious and efficient research assistant and prepared the name indexes for the text. Margaret Matthews, of Wadham College, Oxford, and Lisa Patti, of Cornell's Society for the Humanities, provided valuable secretarial assistance. I am especially indebted to Lesley Brown and Terry Irwin, both of whom endured numerous conversations about the tables of contents, and provided helpful comments on the Introductions.

Work on these two volumes was partly supported by a fellowship from the National Endowment for the Humanities, by a Keeley visiting fellowship from Wadham College, Oxford, and by a fellowship at Cornell's Society for the Humanities. I warmly acknowledge their support.

CONTENTS

INTRODUCTION

GAIL FINE

I. THE EARLY DIALOGUES

1. The Elenchus and Socrates' Disavowal of Knowledge

In the early dialogues[1] Socrates often asks the 'What is *F*?' question: for example, 'What is piety?' in the *Euthyphro*; 'What is courage?' in the *Laches*; 'What is friendship?' in the *Lysis*; 'What is temperance?' in the *Charmides*. The interlocutor thinks it's easy to answer Socrates' question, and he readily does so. Socrates then questions him further, and he answers 'as it seems to him'. Eventually, despite the interlocutor's initial self-confidence, he is caught in contradiction. This is Socrates' *elenctic method* (*elenchein*; to cross-examine, test, or refute). In the *Euthyphro*, for example, Euthyphro suggests that (1) piety is what he is now doing,

---

[1] I count the following as early dialogues: *Apology, Crito, Euthyphro, Charmides, Laches, Lysis, Hippias Minor, Ion,* and *Protagoras*; I count the *Gorgias, Meno, Hippias Major, Euthydemus,* and *Cratylus* as transitional dialogues; the *Phaedo, Symposium, Republic,* and *Phaedrus* as middle dialogues; the *Parmenides, Theaetetus, Timaeus, Critias, Sophist, Politicus (Statesman), Philebus,* and *Laws* as late dialogues. The dates of some of these dialogues are disputed. For discussion of chronology based on stylometry, see L. Brandwood, *The Chronology of Plato's Dialogues* (Cambridge: Cambridge University Press, 1990); Charles M. Young, 'Plato and Computer Dating', *Oxford Studies in Ancient Philosophy*, 12 (1994), 227–50. (The dating of the dialogues, however, does not depend solely on stylometry. Other factors—such as Aristotle's testimony, features of style not capturable by stylometry, and views about Plato's development—also play a role.)

The early dialogues are also sometimes called the Socratic dialogues on the ground that they represent the thought of the historical Socrates. Some who favour this view think that, in the early dialogues, Plato himself accepts the views of the historical Socrates. On this interpretation, the early dialogues present the views both of the historical Socrates and of Plato at one point in his career. For this view, see Gregory Vlastos, *Socrates, Ironist and Moral Philosopher* (Cambridge: Cambridge University Press, 1991). For criticism of this view, see Charles Kahn, 'Did Plato Write Socratic Dialogues?', *Classical Quarterly*, 31 (1981), 305–20; 'Vlastos' Socrates', *Phronesis*, 37 (1992), 233–58; and *Plato and the Socratic Dialogue: The Philosophical Use of a Literary Form* (Cambridge: Cambridge University Press, 1996).

prosecuting the wrongdoer.[2] He then agrees that (2) piety is some one thing, the same in all cases, and that (3) there are other sorts of piety than prosecuting the wrongdoer. (1)–(3) conflict; hence at least one of them must be false. Typically, as here, the interlocutor decides that the proposed definition, (1), is false;[3] he then suggests another one, but is again caught in contradiction.

This procedure raises a problem, which Gregory Vlastos, in 'The Socratic Elenchus' (Chapter I), calls *the problem of the elenchus*: it looks as though all that has been discovered is a contradiction among various propositions. Yet a specific proposition is singled out for rejection. The fact of contradiction shows that not all the claims the interlocutor assents to are true; but it doesn't, by itself, allow us to know which proposition(s) to reject. Why, then, do Socrates and the interlocutors reject a specific proposition?

They would be justified in doing so if they *knew* that the retained propositions were true. In the sample elenchus just described, for example, they would be justified in rejecting (1) if they *knew* that (2) and (3) were true, and that (1)–(3) were mutually inconsistent.[4] However, this solution seems to be unavailable; for Socrates claims to lack knowledge, and he thinks his interlocutors lack it too.[5] The problem of the elenchus is therefore closely related to *Socrates' disavowal of knowledge*, an issue Gregory Vlastos discusses in 'Socrates' Disavowal of Knowledge' (Chapter II). In addition to seeming to preclude a solution to the problem of the elenchus, Socrates' disavowal of knowledge raises yet another difficulty: for sometimes Socrates claims to have moral knowledge.[6] Yet it seems inconsistent to disavow knowledge, on the one hand, and to claim to have it, on the other.

[2] There is dispute about whether this definition specifies a token action (Euthyphro's prosecuting his father on a particular occasion), or a low-level type (prosecuting one's father, or a wrongdoer). See A. Nehamas, 'Confusing Universals and Particulars in Plato's Early Dialogues', *Review of Metaphysics*, 29(1975), 287–306; and H. Benson, 'Misunderstanding the "What is F-ness?" Question', *Archiv für Geschichte der Philosophie*, 72 (1990), 124–43; repr. in Benson (ed.), *Essays on the Philosophy of Socrates* (New York: Oxford University Press, 1992).

[3] The definition is not always rejected. In the *Laches* (197a–c), for example, the definition under consideration (that courage is wisdom) is retained, and the view that lions are courageous (a belief about examples) is rejected. Nor is it always a definition that is tested. In the *Crito*, for example, a practical question (whether Socrates should flee from prison) is investigated.

[4] It doesn't in general follow that if one knows that *p*, and *p* implies *q*, one knows that *q*. However, in this case, the conflict among the various propositions is so clear that it seems reasonable to assume that if one knows that (2) and (3) are true, one will know that (1) is false. To say that knowledge that (2) and (3) are true is sufficient justification for rejecting (1) is not to say that it is necessary.

[5] *Ap.* 21b–d7; *Euthphr.* 5a3–c8, 15c11–16a4; *Chrm.* 165b5–c1, 166c7–d6; *La.* 186b8–187a8, 200e1–2; *Ly.* 212a4–7, 223b4–8; *Grg.* 509c4–7.

[6] It is important to be clear that the relevant question here is whether Socrates has, or takes himself to have, moral knowledge in particular. In the early dialogues he explicitly claims to know a moral truth only once, at *Ap.* 29b. It is disputed whether he implicitly claims to have moral knowledge elsewhere. Vlastos thinks he does, but not everyone agrees.

Various solutions to the problem of the elenchus, and various explanations of precisely what Socrates' disavowal of knowledge amounts to, have been proposed. Here are some of them:

1. Socrates and his interlocutors don't use the elenchus to do anything more than detect inconsistencies; the crucial step of rejecting a specific proposition is never taken. Vlastos discusses and criticizes this solution in 'The Socratic Elenchus'. In his support, it can be noted that even if this solution deals satisfactorily with some cases, it doesn't deal satisfactorily with all of them. In the *Crito*, for example, the elenchus is used to arrive at the conclusion that Socrates should remain in prison rather than flee.

2. Socrates' disavowal of knowledge is insincere, perhaps because he wants to get the interlocutor to figure matters out for himself. In 'Socrates' Disavowal of Knowledge', Vlastos ably criticizes this solution.

3. Socrates' disavowal is less complete than it is sometimes taken to be. It is sometimes suggested, for example, that although he claims not to know the definitions of the virtues in question, he takes himself to know at least some of the other propositions on which he relies. Vlastos suggests this view in 'Socrates' Disavowal of Knowledge', although it is not his only or main suggestion. A difficulty for this view is that Socrates seems to believe that if one doesn't know what F is—that is, if one doesn't know a definition of F—then one doesn't know anything at all about F (see e.g. *Meno* 71a).[7]

4. Socrates uses 'know' in two different senses, or thinks there are two kinds of knowledge. This is Vlastos's main solution to the problem of the disavowal of knowledge in 'Socrates' Disavowal of Knowledge'.[8] He argues that Socrates implicitly distinguishes between knowledge as certainty, on the one hand, and elenctic knowledge, on the other, and, in some cases, claims to have elenctic knowledge and disclaims only knowledge

---

[7] It is disputed whether this principle is assumed in all of the early dialogues. In *Socrates and the State* (Princeton: Princeton University Press, 1984), ch. 8, R. Kraut argues that Socrates accepts it in the *Meno* but not in the *Apology*. In 'Socratic Intellectualism', *Proceedings of the Boston Area Colloquium in Ancient Philosophy*, 2 (1986), 275–316, A. Nehamas argues that Socrates never accepts it. See also G. Vlastos, 'Is the "Socratic Fallacy" Socratic?', *Ancient Philosophy*, 10 (1990), 1–16; a revised version of this paper appears as chapter 3 in his *Socratic Studies*, ed. M. F. Burnyeat (Cambridge: Cambridge University Press, 1994). The issue is also discussed in J. Beversluis, 'Does Socrates Commit the Socratic Fallacy?', *American Philosophical Quarterly*, 24 (1987), 211–23; H. Benson, 'The Priority of Definition and the Socratic Elenchus', *Oxford Studies in Ancient Philosophy*, 8 (1990), 19–65. (The phrase 'Socratic fallacy' is due to P. T. Geach, 'Plato's *Euthyphro*: An Analysis and Commentary', *Monist*, 50 (1966), 369–82. It is disputed whether the pattern of reasoning he so labels is actually fallacious.)

[8] It is not, however, the solution to the problem of the elenchus suggested in 'The Socratic Elenchus', for which see below.

conceived as certainty.[9] In the main Vlastos suggests this solution, not as one that is explicitly defended in the text, but as the best explanatory hypothesis of the fact that (as Vlastos thinks) Socrates both avows, and disavows, knowledge.[10] However, he seems to think that the *Apology*'s distinction (at e.g. 20d6–e1 and 23a–b4) between human and divine wisdom provides explicit textual support for his view. For, Vlastos thinks, human wisdom is the same as elenctic knowledge, and divine wisdom is the same as knowledge conceived as certainty; since Socrates claims to have human wisdom but to lack divine wisdom, he claims to have elenctic knowledge but to lack knowledge conceived as certainty.

There are at least three questions one should try to answer in evaluating Vlastos's solution: (*a*) Is it true that Socrates claims to have moral knowledge? If so, how often and where? (*b*) If Socrates both avows and disavows moral knowledge, is Vlastos's hypothesis the best explanation of this fact? (*c*) Is the distinction between human and divine wisdom the same as the distinction between elenctic knowledge and knowledge as certainty?[11]

5. Socrates disavows all (moral) knowledge; yet he none the less rejects a specific proposition, and is justified in doing so. For, contrary to what's been assumed so far, one doesn't need to *know* that (say) (2) and (3) in our sample elenchus are true, and conflict with (1), in order to be justified in rejecting (1). Socrates would be justified in proceeding as he does if he had, or took himself to have, *true beliefs* with some justification (where, however, the justification falls short of knowledge).[12] One objection to this view is that the early dialogues don't explicitly distinguish knowledge from true belief. However, one can rely on distinctions one doesn't explicitly draw.

[9] Vlastos thinks that some of Socrates' disavowals of knowledge concern elenctic knowledge; for example, in his view Socrates doesn't claim to have even elenctic knowledge of definitions. For different versions of the view that Socrates distinguishes various senses of 'know', or kinds of knowledge, see C. D. C. Reeve, *Socrates in the* Apology (Indianapolis: Hackett, 1989), ch. 1; and P. Woodruff, 'Plato's Early Theory of Knowledge', in S. Everson (ed.), *Companions to Ancient Thought*, i: *Epistemology* (Cambridge: Cambridge University Press, 1990), 60–84.

[10] See n. 6.

[11] For criticism of Vlastos's view, see T. H. Irwin, 'Socratic Puzzles', *Oxford Studies in Ancient Philosophy*, 10 (1992), 241–66: 247–51.

[12] For this view, see esp. T. H. Irwin, *Plato's Moral Theory* (Oxford: Clarendon Press, 1977), ch. 3; and *Plato's Ethics* (Oxford: Oxford University Press, 1995), ch. 2. I also defend this view in 'Inquiry in the *Meno*', in R. Kraut (ed.), *Cambridge Companion to Plato* (Cambridge: Cambridge University Press, 1992), ch. 6. See also William J. Prior, 'Plato and the "Socratic Fallacy"', *Phronesis*, 43 (1998), 97–113. For criticism of this view, see Vlastos, 'Socrates' Disavowal of Knowledge' (Ch. II in this volume); A. Nehamas, 'Meno's Paradox and Socrates as a Teacher', *Oxford Studies in Ancient Philosophy*, 3 (1985), 1–30; Beversluis, 'Does Socrates Commit the Socratic Fallacy?'

I take (5) to be an entirely satisfactory solution to the problem of the elenchus. That is, one can in fact be justified in rejecting a given proposition even if one doesn't *know* that the propositions with which it conflicts are true. In 'The Socratic Elenchus' Vlastos defends a version of this view. In particular, he argues that Socrates is justified in rejecting proposed definitions, because he is justified in taking himself to have true, and consistent, moral beliefs; hence, if the beliefs of an interlocutor conflict with one of Socrates' beliefs—as the belief in the proposed definition does— then Socrates is justified in rejecting the proposed definition.[13]

However, this may not be an adequate solution to the problem raised by Socrates' disavowal of knowledge. For, contrary to (5), Socrates at least once explicitly claims to have some (moral) knowledge.[14]

2. The 'What is F?' Question and Socratic Forms

We have seen that Socrates is dissatisfied with the answers he receives to his 'What is *F*?' questions. But why is he dissatisfied, and what sort of answer does he want? Some answers are rejected because they are too narrow. Courage, for example, cannot be defined as 'standing firm in battle', since it can be displayed in other sorts of cases (*La.* 191c–e). Some answers are rejected because they are too broad. Courage, for example, cannot be defined as 'standing firm in battle', since not all cases of standing firm in battle are courageous.[15] A correct answer, then, must preserve coextension: it must be true of all and only the cases of the virtue in question.

In addition to preserving coextension, a correct answer must explain the nature of the virtue in question. In the *Euthyphro* (10–11), for example, Socrates says that although 'piety' and 'being loved by all the gods' are coextensive, the latter is none the less an inadequate answer to the question 'What is piety?'. For being loved by all the gods is an accidental property (*pathos*; 11a8) of piety, whereas Socrates wants to know its nature or essence (*ousia*, 11a7; cf. *Men.* 72b1; *Phd.* 65d13). The essence of piety is 'that very form by which (*hō(i)*) all pious things are pious' (6d10–11), something that 'is the same in every [pious] action' (5d1). Being loved by all the gods isn't that by which all pious things are pious;

---

[13] Vlastos's view is criticized by R. Kraut, in 'Comments on Gregory Vlastos, "The Socratic Elenchus"', *Oxford Studies in Ancient Philosophy*, 1 (1983), 59–70. (Irwin defends a different version of Vlastos's sort of view: see previous note.)

[14] See n. 6.

[15] Hence the very same answer can be both too narrow (if it fails to capture enough of the relevant instances) and too broad (if it captures some incorrect cases).

on the contrary, the fact that a thing is pious explains why the gods love it.[16]

The fact that the answer to a 'What is *F*?' question is supposed to explain the nature of *F*-ness, and why *F* things are *F*, suggests that Socratic definitions are better viewed as real than as nominal definitions. That is, they don't aim to articulate ordinary usage, or to explain the meaning of '*F*', in the sense of explaining how competent speakers of the language use '*F*'. Rather, they aim to specify what *F*-ness really is: its essence or nature.[17]

According to *Euthyphro* 6d10–11, a correct definition specifies a form (*eidos*) or idea (*idea*). Socratic forms are therefore the referents of correct answers to 'What is *F*?' questions. The form of piety, for example, is the one thing in virtue of which all pious things are pious, and reference to it explains why pious things are pious. Socratic forms are explanatory essences: the form of piety is the nature or essence of piety, what piety really is; and something is pious if and only if, and precisely because, it has the form of piety in it. Since it is some one thing, the same in all cases of piety, it is a universal, in the Aristotelian sense of being a one over many.[18]

Here it is useful to distinguish between a *realist* and a *semantic* conception of universals.[19] On the realist conception, universals are genuine properties that, as Plato puts it, 'carve at the natural joints' (*Phdr.* 265e1–2; cf. *Plt.* 262a–b); on the semantic conception, universals are the meanings of terms. On the view we have been considering, Socratic forms are not meanings; rather, they are universals conceived as genuine properties of things.

---

[16] For further discussion of the 'Euthyphro problem', see the Introduction to Volume ii, and the references given there.

[17] For the classic distinction between real and nominal definitions, see Locke, *An Essay concerning Human Understanding*, III. iii, III. vi, III. x, IV. vi. xii. 9. The realist view of Socratic definitions is defended by T. Penner, 'The Unity of Virtue' (Vol. ii, Ch. III); Irwin, 'The Theory of Forms', (Ch. V in this volume); see also his *Plato's Moral Theory*, ch. 3, and *Plato's Ethics*, chs. 2 and 10; G. Fine, 'Forms and Causes: Plato and Aristotle', in A. Graeser (ed.), *Mathematics and Metaphysics* (Bern: Haupt, 1987), 69–112. The meaning view is defended by Vlastos, in 'The Unity of the Virtues in the *Protagoras*', in *Platonic Studies*, 2nd edn. (Princeton: Princeton University Press, 1981), 211–69: 252 ff; 1st pub. in *Review of Metaphysics*, 25 (1972), 415–58; and in 'What did Socrates Understand by his "What is *F*?" Question?', in *Platonic Studies*, 410–17.

[18] See Aristotle, *de Interpretatione* 17ᵃ38–ᵇ1. In 'The Unity of Virtue' Terry Penner denies that Socrates is searching for essences or universals. However, he uses 'essence' and 'universal' differently from me. I agree that Socrates is not searching for essences or universals in Penner's sense.

[19] For this distinction, see D. M. Armstrong, *Universals and Scientific Realism*, 2 vols. (Cambridge: Cambridge University Press, 1978); H. Putnam, 'On Properties', in *Philosophical Papers*, i (Cambridge: Cambridge University Press, 1975), 305–22; 1st pub. in N. Rescher (ed.), *Essays in Honor of Carl G. Hempel* (Dordrecht: Reidel, 1970).

However, Socrates doesn't tell us very much about these forms or universals. In particular, he doesn't take a stand, one way or the other, on the issue of whether they are separate—that is, can exist whether or not the corresponding sensibles do, so that the form of justice, for example, could exist even if there were no just people, actions, or institutions.[20] Nor does he say whether they are observable, or can be defined in observational terms.[21]

II. THE TRANSITIONAL DIALOGUES

1. The Meno and the Theory of Recollection

We asked above how Socrates can inquire if he doesn't already have knowledge.[22] Plato himself explicitly raises this question in the *Meno*, by considering the 'paradox of inquiry' (80a–d):[23]

(1) For all x, either one does, or one does not, know x.
(2) If one knows x, one can't inquire into x.
(3) If one doesn't know x, one can't inquire into x.
(4) Therefore, for all x, inquiry is impossible.

This argument is valid if 'know' is used univocally throughout; and (1) seems to be a harmless instantiation of the Law of the Excluded Middle. Hence the soundness of the argument turns on the truth of (2) and (3). Is there a sense of 'know' such that, if it is assumed in (2), (2) is true? Is (3) true if it uses 'know' in the same way? How does this sense of 'know', or how do these senses of 'know', compare with Socrates' use of 'know' in the early dialogues?

---

[20] For this account of separation, see my 'Separation', *Oxford Studies in Ancient Philosophy*, 2 (1984), 31–87.

[21] These claims about Socratic forms are controversial. For example, Vlastos, *Socrates*, 66, argues that Socratic forms are not observable. (I discuss Vlastos's views further in 'Vlastos on Socratic and Platonic Forms', in T. Irwin and M. Nussbaum (eds.), *Virtue, Love, and Form* (Edmonton, Alberta: Academic Printing and Publishing, 1992), 67–83.) In 'The Theory of Forms' (see also *Plato's Moral Theory* and *Plato's Ethics*), by contrast, Irwin argues that Socratic forms are observable, or are definable in observational terms. In *The Ascent from Nominalism* (Dordrecht: Reidel, 1987), T. Penner argues that Socrates is a nominalist about universals; that is, he doesn't think there are any such things as universals.

[22] As we have seen, Socrates claims knowledge of one moral truth in *Ap.* 29b; it is sometimes thought that elsewhere he claims to have further moral knowledge. However, even if this controversial view is right, he doesn't claim to know all the propositions on which he relies in the elenchus; nor does he claim to know the answers to the questions he asks.

[23] I discuss the paradox of inquiry in 'Inquiry in the *Meno*'. See also N. P. White, 'Inquiry', *Review of Metaphysics*, 28 (1974–5), 289–310; Nehamas, 'Meno's Paradox and Socrates as a Teacher'.

Socrates replies to the argument by conducting a sample elenchus with a slave, about a geometrical problem. In doing so, he shows how the slave can make progress towards the truth: for though the slave lacks knowledge, he has, and relies on his, true beliefs (85b–d). In just the same way, someone who doesn't know the road to Larissa can none the less arrive there successfully, if she has true beliefs about the route (98a–c). Knowledge is therefore not necessary for inquiry; true beliefs will do. This reply rejects premiss (3) of the paradox. We can reject premiss (3) once we see that lacking knowledge needn't mean lacking all beliefs; it needn't be tantamount to total ignorance, which might well preclude, or at least impede, inquiry. It also suggests that, at least in the *Meno*, Plato favours the fifth solution to the problem of the elenchus considered above: one can inquire into something, and make progress towards the truth, even if one lacks all knowledge of it (so long as one has (true) beliefs).

Is it just a remarkable fact that the slave, and all of us, can make progress towards the truth, and that, when faced with contradictions among our beliefs, we tend to favour the true ones over the false ones? Plato thinks not. He explains that we can make progress in this life, because we once knew in a previous life, though this knowledge is now forgotten. This is Plato's theory of recollection. It is introduced here to defend Plato's rejection of (3) of the paradox of inquiry; hence it also defends the early dialogues' assumption that one can inquire even if (like Socrates and his interlocutors) one lacks knowledge. Hence, though the theory of recollection goes beyond the Socratic dialogues, it supports them by explaining one of their central assumptions.[24]

Though Plato distances himself from some aspects of the theory of recollection in the *Meno*,[25] he defends it more fully in the *Phaedo*; he also discusses it in the *Phaedrus*. In 'Platonic Recollection' (Chapter III) Dominic Scott considers various aspects of the theory of recollection, as it is presented in these three dialogues.[26] One important question Scott raises is this: is the theory of recollection meant to explain concept formation? (If so, the theory of recollection looks somewhat Kantian; hence Scott calls this position K.) Or is it only meant to explain how we can move from

---

[24] Plato's appeal to prior knowledge suggests some sort of innatist theory. For discussion of the theory of recollection in connection with innatism, see J. M. E. Moravcsik, 'Learning as Recollection', in G. Vlastos (ed.), *Plato*, i: *Metaphysics and Epistemology* (New York: Doubleday Anchor, 1971), 53–69; D. Scott, *Recollection and Experience* (Cambridge: Cambridge University Press, 1995), ch. 1.

[25] *Meno* 86b–c.

[26] For discussion of the theory of recollection in the *Phaedo*, see also J. L. Ackrill, '*Anamnēsis* in the *Phaedo*', in E. N. Lee, A. P. D. Mourelatos, and R. M. Rorty (eds.), *Exegesis and Argument* (Assen: Van Gorcum, 1973), 177–95; D. Gallop, *Plato:* Phaedo (Oxford: Clarendon Press, 1975), notes ad loc.; D. Bostock, *Plato's* Phaedo (Oxford: Clarendon Press, 1986).

beliefs (a stage at which we already have at least some concepts) to know-ledge? (Scott labels this position D, because a story in Herodotus about Demaratus provides an image for this view of recollection.) Though it is often thought that Plato uses recollection to explain concept formation, Scott argues that he does not do so; in his view, Plato uses it only to explain how we move from belief to knowledge.[27] By the time of the *Phaedo* rec-ollecting involves recollecting forms. Hence, on Scott's view, we don't need to recollect, or know, forms in order to have beliefs or, therefore, in order to learn language or have concepts.

I suggested above that earlier dialogues seem to assume that knowledge differs from true belief. But it is not until the *Meno* that Plato explicitly defines knowledge and distinguishes it from true belief. At *Meno* 98a Plato—giving what may be the first explicit account of knowledge in Western thought—proposes that knowledge is true belief plus an *aitias logismos*, an explanatory account.[28] This is an early version of the still-familiar (though hardly uncontroversial) view that knowledge is justified true belief: one knows *p* if, and only if, one believes *p*, *p* is true, and one has adequate justification for believing *p*.[29]

In the *Meno* Plato doesn't say what counts as adequate justification for knowledge. But in the *Phaedo* he tells us that forms are *aitiai*: causal or explanatory factors (100a ff.). Putting the *Meno* and *Phaedo* together, we may infer that, in order to have knowledge, one must have an explana-tory account that mentions forms; more precisely, knowledge-conferring accounts are definitions of forms. As we have seen, this is also the view suggested in the early dialogues—although, as we shall see, the early and

[27] See also my 'The Object of Thought Argument: Forms and Thoughts', *Apeiron*, 21 (1988), 105–46. In *Plato's* Phaedo, ch. 6, Bostock allows that the *Meno* explains how one progresses from belief to knowledge; but he thinks that the *Phaedo* explains initial concept acquisition. It is important to see that one need not accept the 'Demaratus analogy' in order to accept Scott's view that recollection explains, not concept formation, but one's ability to progress from belief to knowledge.

[28] *Aitia* can mean cause, explanation, or reason; *logismos* means reasoning.

[29] In 'Socrates and the Jury: Paradoxes in Plato's Distinction between Knowledge and True Belief', *Proceedings of the Aristotelian Society*, suppl. vol. 44 (1988), 177–91, esp. 186–8, M. F. Burnyeat argues that Plato is defining or explicating not knowledge but understanding; he also argues that a *logos* is not a justification but an explanation. See also Nehamas, 'Meno's Paradox', esp. 24–30. In his reply to Burnyeat, ibid. 193–206, J. Barnes argues (in my view, rightly) that Plato is discussing knowledge, and holds that adequate justification *consists in* having a certain sort of explanation.

The view that Plato here defines knowledge as justified true belief is also sometimes rejected on the ground that he says that true beliefs *become* (*gignetai*; 98a6) knowledge when they are tied down by an *aitias logismos*; he is sometimes taken to mean that they are no longer true beliefs, just as, when an acorn becomes an oak tree, it is no longer an acorn. However, 'become' need not have this force: when I become stronger, I am still me; similarly, when true beliefs become justified, they are still true beliefs, which now constitute knowledge.

middle dialogues seem to have somewhat different views of the nature of forms.

According to the *Meno*, knowledge is a type of true belief: it is true belief that is adequately justified. It follows that one can have knowledge and true belief about at least some of the same things; indeed, every time one knows *p*, one also has a true belief that *p*. Yet it is often thought that, in the middle dialogues and *Timaeus*, Plato accepts *the Two Worlds theory*, according to which knowledge and belief actually exclude one another: one can't know and have beliefs about any of the same things. More particularly, Plato is sometimes thought to hold that knowledge is restricted to forms, and belief to sensibles: if one knows, one knows a form (and nothing else); and, if one has a belief, it is about a sensible object (and nothing else). There are no beliefs about forms, and there is no knowledge of sensibles. On a weaker version of this view, Plato holds that one can have beliefs about both forms and sensibles, but not knowledge about sensibles.

In defining knowledge as a type of true belief, the *Meno* avoids the Two Worlds theory. Moreover, Plato explicitly allows knowledge of sensibles: he mentions both Meno and the road to Larissa as examples of things one might know.[30] If Plato, in the middle and later dialogues, endorses the Two Worlds theory, then his theory of knowledge undergoes a dramatic change.

2. *The* Cratylus

The main topic of the *Cratylus* is the nature of names. Hermogenes initially defends the view that they are conventional, whereas Cratylus initially defends the view that they are natural; Socrates argues against them both. Hence it is unclear what position, if any, he favours. But on one interpretation, although he doesn't completely accept either view as formulated, he does accept elements of them both. He thinks that names are conventional in so far as it is a matter of convention that in English we use 'horse' to name horses, whereas, in Greek, *hippos* is used instead; what particular sounds one uses to constitute a name for a thing is a matter of convention. In another sense, however, he denies that names are conventional, and accepts a version of the view that they are natural: there is a natural correctness to names in so far as 'horse', for example, 'carves at the natural joints' in a way in which 'toeble' (i.e. whatever is a toe or a table) does not; names are naturally correct to the extent that they demarcate the natures of things.

[30] *Meno* 71b, 97a–c. In 'Meno's Paradox', however, Nehamas argues that these are analogies rather than examples.

Socrates argues that if we were to accept the sort of convention-alism that Hermogenes favours, according to which whatever name we choose for a thing is correct simply because of our choice, we would be committed to the Protagorean view that 'what things seem to each person to be like, that is also what they are like' (386c4–5).[31] Socrates, by contrast, believes that there is a way the world is that is independent of our beliefs about it; and names are correct to the extent that they correctly describe the nature of their nominata. This seems to be one point of the long etymological section: Socrates analyses names into associated descriptions, to see whether those descriptions are true of their referents. In fact, he seems to think that names just are disguised descriptions.[32]

It is sometimes thought that in various dialogues—including the *Craty-lus*, *Euthydemus*, middle dialogues, and *Theaetetus*—Plato accepts seman-tic or logical atomism, according to which names are mere tags for things. As G. E. L. Owen puts it in 'Plato on Not-Being' (Chapter XVII), 'Words are given their purchase on the world by being used to name parts of it, and names, or the basic names to which others are variously reducible, are simple proxies for their nominees' (p. 435). In 'Identity Mistakes: Plato and the Logical Atomists' (Chapter XV) John McDowell also suggests that Plato, in some phases of his career, might favour logical atomism.[33] On the view of the *Cratylus* that I suggested above, however, the *Cratylus* seems to reject semantic atomism: for, rather than treating names as simple proxies for their nominees (that is, as mere tags that lack descriptive content), it treats them as disguised descriptions.

Socrates seems to assume that our names are by and large correct; as he puts it, they preserve an outline (*tupos*, 432e6; cf. 431c–433b) of the natures of things. This is another way of explaining why, or another way of putting the point that, by and large, we have and rely on true beliefs, which is why we can all make progress in inquiry. Hence the *Cratylus* defends a view that is also defended in the early dialogues and *Meno*, since, in these latter dialogues, Socrates assumes that, when faced with a contradiction among one's beliefs, interlocutors tend to favour the true ones over the false ones. Irwin discusses this aspect of the *Cratylus* in 'The Theory of Forms' (Chapter V). In 'Language and Reality in Plato's *Cratylus*' (Chapter IV) J. L. Ackrill provides a synoptic reading of the dialogue as a whole.

[31] I discuss Protagoreanism further below, in connection with the *Theaetetus*.
[32] I defend this view in 'Plato on Naming', *Philosophical Quarterly*, 27 (1977), 289–301.
[33] McDowell's discussion centres on the *Theaetetus*' account of false belief; I discuss this below.

III. THE MIDDLE DIALOGUES

1. The Theory of Forms

According to Aristotle,[34] Plato agreed with Socrates that, since knowledge is possible, there must be definitions of universals; he also says that Plato took these universals to be forms. So in Aristotle's view both Socratic and Platonic forms are universals that are posited to be the basic objects of knowledge and definition. But Aristotle believes that Plato differed from Socrates in some ways. For, he says, Plato accepted the Heracleitean view that, since sensibles are always changing, there is no knowledge of them; since knowledge is possible, forms must be non-sensible objects that are not in flux. Aristotle believes that both Plato's Heracleiteanism and his view that forms are non-sensible distinguish Plato from Socrates. He also claims that, unlike Socrates, Plato separated forms or universals from sensible particulars. Aristotle sides with Socrates here, claiming that separation is responsible for the difficulties in Plato's theory of forms (*Metaph.* 13.9, 1086^{b}6–7).

What sort of flux or change is at issue here? Typically when we think of change, we think of the *succession of opposites*. To say that something undergoes succession of opposites is to say that it is F at t_1, but ceases to be F and becomes not F at some later time t_2. For example, I was fat before I went on a diet, and then I became thin. Commentators have discussed various sorts of succession in connection with Plato. For example, there is *Moderate Heracleiteanism* (MH), according to which objects at every moment undergo succession of opposites in some respect or other. There is also *Extreme Heracleiteanism* (EH), according to which objects at every moment undergo succession of opposites in every respect.[35]

---

[34] Aristotle was Plato's pupil for twenty years, and he is a valuable source of information about Plato's views. I discuss his reliability in *On Ideas: Aristotle's Criticism of Plato's Theory of Forms* (Oxford: Clarendon Press, 1993). For a contrasting view, see H. F. Cherniss, *Aristotle's Criticism of Plato and the Academy* (Baltimore: Johns Hopkins University Press, 1944; repr. New York: Russell & Russell, 1962); Kahn, *Plato and the Socratic Dialogue*, ch. 3. Aristotle discusses the origins of Plato's theory of forms, and contrasts it with Socrates', in three key passages in the *Metaphysics*: 987^{a}29–^{b}8; 1078^{b}12–32; 1086^{a}37–^{b}1. I discuss these passages in 'Separation' and in *On Ideas*, ch. 4.

Aristotle thinks that the views expressed by the character Socrates in the early dialogues represent the thought of the historical Socrates, which he distinguishes from the thought of Plato (whose views he thinks are presented in the middle and late dialogues). My discussion reflects this fact.

[35] In addition, things can come into or go out of existence. There is also Weak Heracleiteanism, according to which each object changes in some respect at some moment or other. I shall not discuss these sorts of flux separately here.

In addition to the succession of opposites, there is also the *compresence of opposites*. Standing firm in battle is both courageous (in some circumstances) and not courageous (in others); returning what one owes is both just (in some circumstances) and not just (in others) (*Rep.* 331c). Plato and Aristotle both take this to be a type of 'change'.[36]

Which of these various types of change does Plato have in mind in arguing for forms?[37] Each of them has its advocates. My own view is that Plato never believed that the sensible world is in EH.[38] Moreover, although he believes that the sensible world, or various items in it, undergo MH, and that that distinguishes sensibles from forms, which are wholly unchanging, that is not the sort of change he appeals to in arguing that there are forms. Rather, in arguing for forms, he appeals to compresence rather than to any sort of succession.[39]

One crucial passage here is *Phaedo* 74b–c, a passage sometimes thought to inaugurate the middle dialogues' allegedly distinctive theory of forms. Plato argues as follows:[40]

[36] In *Theaetetus* 152d2–e9, for example, Plato counts cases of compresence, along with cases of succession, as all alike illustrating the thesis that 'nothing ever is, but things are always coming to be (*gignetai*)' (152e1); both compresence and succession are types of 'flux and change' (152e8). For Aristotle, see *EN* 1134[b]24–1135[a]5. To say that Plato and Aristotle use the language of change in discussing compresence is not to say that they take compresence to be a type of succession; nor is it to say that they are confused about the nature of change. It is only to say that they use 'change' in a broad sense that includes both compresence and succession. Given this broad use of 'change', we cannot tell from the mere use of the language of change whether compresence or succession is at issue.

[37] I shall not ask here which sort of change Aristotle thinks Plato has in mind. I discuss this in *On Ideas*; see esp. ch. 10.

[38] For the view that Plato takes the sensible world to be in Extreme Heracleitean flux, and appeals to that fact in arguing for forms, see F. M. Cornford, *Plato's Theory of Knowledge* (London: Routledge & Kegan Paul, 1935), 99–101; Cherniss, *Aristotle's Criticism of Plato and the Academy*, 211–18 (cf. 'The Relation of the *Timaeus* to Plato's Later Dialogues', in R. E. Allen (ed.), *Studies in Plato's Metaphysics* (London: Routledge & Kegan Paul, 1965), 339–78: 349–60); and R. Bolton, 'Plato's Distinction between Being & Becoming', *Review of Metaphysics*, 29 (1975), 66–95: 76–7. The strongest evidence for Extreme Heracleiteanism in the middle dialogues is *Phd.* 78d10–e4. For cogent criticism of the view that this passage adverts to Extreme Heracleiteanism, see Vlastos, *Socrates*, 69–71; he interprets the passage in terms of MH. See also Irwin, 'Plato's Heracleiteanism', *Philosophical Quarterly*, 27 (1977), 1–13, who defends an interpretation in terms of compresence. It is also sometimes thought that *Ti.* 49–52 adverts to Extreme Heracleiteanism. For discussion, see Owen, 'The Place of the *Timaeus* in Plato's Dialogues', *Classical Quarterly*, NS 3 (1953), 79–95; repr. in Allen (ed.), *Studies in Plato's Metaphysics*, 313–38, and in *Logic, Science, and Dialectic*, ed. M. Nussbaum (Ithaca, NY: Cornell University Press, 1986), 65–84; D. Zeyl, 'Plato and Talk of a World in Flux: *Timaeus* 49a6–50b5', *Harvard Studies in Classical Philology*, 79 (1975), 125–48; M. L. Gill, 'Matter and Flux in Plato's *Timaeus*', *Phronesis*, 32 (1987), 34–53. I discuss Extreme Heracleiteanism in the *Theaetetus* below.

[39] See G. E. L. Owen, 'A Proof in the *Peri Ideōn*', *Journal of Hellenic Studies*, 77 (1957), 103–11; repr. in *Logic, Science, and Dialectic*, 165–79. See also Irwin, 'The Theory of Forms'.

[40] There are numerous difficulties in interpreting this argument. For some discussion, see Irwin, 'The Theory of Forms', and Nehamas, 'Plato on the Imperfection of the Sensible World'

(1) Equal 'sticks and stones, sometimes, being the same, appear equal to one, unequal to another' (74b8–9).

(2) On no occasion 'did the equals themselves ever appear unequal to you [i.e. Simmias], or equality inequality' (74c1–2).

(3) 'Therefore those equals [i.e. the equal sticks and stones], and the equal itself, are not the same' (74c4–5).

On the interpretation that I favour of this notoriously difficult argument, (1) means that any sensible equal is both equal and unequal; for example, this stick is equal in length to that one (both are three inches), but unequal in length to this other one (which is five inches). (2) claims that the form of equal can't be both equal and unequal. (3) infers that the form is different from sensible equals. Plato means, I think, that it is neither observable nor definable in observational terms; it is not to be identified with such things as equal sticks and stones, nor is it definable in terms of such things. On this view, the passage appeals, not to succession, but to comprescence.[41]

Though Plato's example is phrased in terms of sensible particulars— equal sticks and stones—it is important to be clear that he thinks that sensible properties (such as three inches) are also equal and unequal. That is, not only is this stick both equal (to that one) and unequal (to this other one); but three inches is also both equal and unequal, in the sense that some three-inch things are equal, whereas others are unequal.[42] Hence not only is the form of equality not identical to or definable in terms of sensible particulars, but neither is it identical to or definable in terms of sensible properties.

Notice that the conclusion of the argument is only that forms are *not the same* as sensibles. Are forms not only *different* from sensibles, but also— as Aristotle and many others believe—*separate* from them? That is, does Plato believe that the form of *F* could exist whether or not any *F* sensible things exist? *Phaedo* 74b–c certainly doesn't imply that forms are separate from sensibles. And in fact, although separation is usually thought to be one of the distinguishing features of Platonic, as opposed to Socratic, forms, Plato never (in my view) explicitly argues, or even says, that forms

(Ch. VI in this volume). I assume (controversially) that 'appears' means 'evidently is' (assuming a suppressed participle); I also assume (somewhat less controversially) that 'the equals themselves', 'equality', and 'the equal itself' all refer to the form of equality.

[41] Plato also discusses comprescence in *Hp.Ma.* 289a2–c6, 293b5–e5; *Phd.* 100 ff.; *Smp.* 210e5–211a5; and *Rep.* 479a5–b10, 523–5.

[42] This point is rightly emphasized by Irwin, in 'The Theory of Forms'. As we have seen, the early dialogues also take properties to suffer comprescence: endurance is both courageous and not courageous, in so far as sometimes it is courageous to endure, whereas at other times it is not.

are separate, in the sense just explained. However, this doesn't mean that
he didn't take forms to be separate, and in 'Separation and Immanence in
Plato's Theory of Forms' (Chapter VII) Daniel Devereux defends the view
that forms are separate.

Even if forms are separate, they could none the less be immanent in sensibles. That is, even if the form of beauty could exist whether or not sensible beautiful things exist, it could also, quite consistently with that, exist
in, be a property of, sensible things. However, although separation allows
Plato to believe this, it is often thought that he didn't believe it. On this
view, which Devereux defends, Plato believes that, in addition to sensibles
and forms, there are also immanent characters and, when something is
beautiful, it participates in the form (as Plato puts it), but the form itself
isn't immanent in it; rather, the corresponding immanent character is in it.

Plato thinks not only that the sensible world and the world of forms
differ, but also that the former is imperfect, the latter perfect. How exactly
is the sensible world imperfect? According to what Alexander Nehamas,
in 'Plato on the Imperfection of the Sensible World' (Chapter VI), dubs
the approximation view, the idea is that sensible Fs aren't really or truly
F; they only approximate to being F.[43] Nehamas argues, against this view,
that Plato believes that sensible F things really are F; Helen, for example,
really is beautiful. Her imperfection consists, not in her not being beautiful at all, but in various other facts.[44] For example, according to Nehamas,
she is accidentally beautiful rather than essentially so; her beauty is
incomplete (that is, he explains, attributive or relational); and she is both
beautiful and not beautiful (since she is beautiful compared to me, but not
compared to the form of beauty).[45]

We have seen that Plato claims that, although sensible equals are both
equal and unequal, the form itself cannot be both equal and unequal. Why

[43] Nehamas may describe the imperfection view in more than one way. On one account, the
view is that no sensible triangle, for example, is really triangular; and no sensible beautiful thing
is really beautiful. Sensible triangles are approximately triangular, but they aren't actually triangular; Helen approximates to being beautiful, but isn't actually beautiful. On a second
account, the view is that no sensible thing is superlatively F. On this account, Helen could be
genuinely beautiful; it is just that she could in principle be even more beautiful. (Of course, in
some cases, if something is F, it can't be more F. For example, if something is straight, it can't
be more straight than it is. But some genuinely beautiful things, for example, could in principle
be even more beautiful.)

[44] However, in 'Self-Predication and Plato's Theory of Forms', *American Philosophical Quarterly*, 16 (1979), 287–306, he seems to argue that only the form of F is F. This seems to endorse
one version of the approximation view.

[45] It is worth asking whether these various distinctions are equivalent. It is also worth asking
whether all sensible Fs are imperfectly F in all these ways. For example, (actual physical) snow
is essentially cold; yet it is presumably imperfectly cold, compared to the form of coldness. For
more on the notion of incompleteness, see esp. Owen, 'A Proof in the *Peri Ideōn*'; for discussion, see my *On Ideas*, esp. ch. 11.

does he believe this? In *Phaedo* 95 ff. Plato lays out the criteria for an adequate explanation, and he argues that, if something is *F* and not *F*, it can't be the one form of *F* by which all *F* things are *F*. If, for example, we want to explain why something is beautiful, we shouldn't, in Plato's view, say that it is 'by having a bright colour or shape or anything else of that kind' (100c9–d2); rather, we should favour the 'safe' *aitia*, according to which something is beautiful if and only if it participates in the form of beauty. Having expounded the safe *aitia*, Plato then introduces a second, 'more subtle', sort of *aitia*. In 'The Theory of Forms' T. H. Irwin discusses Plato's criteria for adequate explanations. In 'Separation and Immanence in Plato's Theory of Forms', Devereux discusses some aspects of the subtle *aitia*. In 'The Double Explanation in the *Timaeus*' (Chapter XVI) Steven Strange discusses Plato's views on explanation in both the *Phaedo* and the *Timaeus*.

One issue it is important to consider here is the following. *Aitia* can mean both 'cause' and also 'reason' or 'explanation'. When Plato says that forms are *aitiai*, does he mean that they are causes, or that they are reasons or explanations? Both answers seem to lead to difficulties. A cause, at least as it is generally understood nowadays, is usually thought to be a sufficient condition for bringing about change. But, it is often thought, forms can't be causes in this sense. Some commentators have therefore argued that forms aren't causes, but explanatory factors. For the notion of an explanation isn't restricted to causal contexts; for example, we can ask why $2 + 3 = 5$. This has an explanation in terms of number theory and addition, but no cause or change is involved; the explanation is non-causal. Yet if forms are meant to be only non-causal explanations, the structure of this part of the *Phaedo* seems to be quite odd, for Plato claims to be discussing the causes of coming to be and ceasing to be, of generation and destruction; and in explaining such things, we do introduce causes.

Aristotle takes the first horn of the dilemma: he assumes that forms are causes, and criticizes Plato on this score. Others have endorsed the second horn, arguing that forms are explanations or reasons of a wholly non-causal sort. There is a middle ground. On one account of causation, it is a relation between events; and on one account of events, they are ordered triples consisting of an object, a property, and a time. So, for example, John's throwing the stone at t_1 causes the window to break at t_2. The cause, on this account, is the first event. But one constituent of this event is a property, in this case the property of throwing. Forms, on one account, are properties. So perhaps, even if forms aren't causes, in the sense of being sufficient conditions for bringing about an event, they are causally relevant, by being constituents of events. To be sure, Plato invokes forms to explain more than cases of change; they are also relevant in non-causal contexts. But they can be causally relevant in some contexts, without themselves being causes in the sense of being sufficient conditions for bringing about change.[46]

In any case, Plato believes that, if it is to fulfil its explanatory function, the form of F can't be both F and not F. To say only so much leaves open the possibility that it is neither F, nor not F (just as rocks, for example, are neither sighted nor blind). However, Plato seems to think that the form of F is F, but not also not F; the form of equal, for example, is equal, but not also unequal. More generally, Plato takes forms to enjoy *Self-Predication*:[47] any form of F is itself F.

Self-Predication can seem absurd. For example, if the form of equal is equal, it must be equal to something. But what could it be equal to? It can't be equal to another form of equal for, in Plato's view, there is at most one form for any given predicate: this is his *Uniqueness Assumption*. Nor can it be equal to everything, or merely to some things. If, for example, it is equal in length to y, which is three inches, and also to z, which is ten inches, then it is, impossibly, both three inches and ten inches in length. But if it isn't equal to anything, it isn't equal at all.[48] Or again, how could the form of large be large? Surely, if something is large, it must have a size? Yet all forms are incorporeal. Plato explores some of these questions in the first part of the *Parmenides*.

Why might Plato accept Self-Predication? On one view, he does so partly because he confuses identity and predication, which leads him to conflate the form of F's being self-identical with its being predicatively F.[49] On another view, he thinks that we can understand the meaning of the word 'F' only if there is something that perfectly exemplifies F-ness. Since in some cases the sensible world doesn't contain perfect samples, there must be another world—the world of perfect forms—that does contain them.[50] On both of these views, the form

---

[46] I defend this view in 'Forms as Causes'. Aristotle discusses forms as *aitiai* in *Metaph.* 1. 9; *de Generatione et Corruptione* 2. 9. For contemporary discussion of the issue, see G. Vlastos, 'Reasons and Causes in the *Phaedo*', *Philosophical Review*, 78 (1969), 291–325; repr. in Vlastos (ed.), *Plato*, i, and in *Platonic Studies*; J. Annas, 'Aristotle on Inefficient Causes', *Philosophical Quarterly*, 32 (1982), 311–26; R. Bolton, 'Plato's Discovery of Metaphysics: The New *Methodos* of the *Phaedo*', in J. Gentzler (ed.), *Method in Ancient Philosophy* (Oxford: Clarendon Press, 1998), 91–111.

[47] For a general discussion of various interpretations of Self-Predication, see J. Malcolm, *Plato on the Self-Predication of Forms* (Oxford: Clarendon Press, 1991). The term 'Self-Predication' was introduced into contemporary literature by Vlastos, in 'The Third Man Argument in the *Parmenides*', *Philosophical Review*, 63 (1954), 319–49; repr. in R. E. Allen (ed.), *Studies in Plato's Metaphysics* (London: Routledge & Kegan Paul, 1965).

[48] See Owen, 'A Proof in the *Peri Ideōn*'.

[49] Owen suggests this view in 'Notes on Ryle's Plato' (Ch. XI in this volume).

[50] For this view, see Owen, 'A Proof in the *Peri Ideōn*'; Bostock, *Plato's* Phaedo. For criticism of this view, see Irwin, 'The Theory of Forms'.

of F is a perfect particular or sample. It is then either not a property or universal at all; or else it is, impossibly, both a universal and a particular.

These views assume that Plato takes the form of F to be predicatively F in roughly the way in which sensible particulars are F; the form of large, for example, is (on this view) large in virtue of its size. As we have seen, this view leads to absurdities. According to a more charitable interpretation, Plato takes the extensions of predicates to be broader than we ordinarily do, so that the form of large is large, not in virtue of its size, but by being the explanatory property of largeness—that in virtue of which large things are large. We routinely count many different kinds of thing as being just (not only people but also actions, institutions, laws, and so forth). Perhaps Plato extends the scopes of predicates even further, so that the property in virtue of which F things are F is itself F—in the same sense of 'F' though in a very different way from the way in which sensible particulars are F.[51] On this interpretation, forms can be self-predicative even if, like the forms in the early dialogues, they are properties or universals rather than particulars.[52] Nor does this interpretation involve Plato in confusing identity and predication, or in taking forms to be perfect paradigms, acquaintance with which is necessary for understanding the meanings of words.

In addition to being self-predicative, forms are paradigms or standards (*paradeigma*).[53] It is disputed precisely what is involved in forms being paradigms. On one view, the form of large (for example) is a paradigm by being the largest thing there is. On an alternative, the form of F is a paradigm or standard in the sense that, in order to know whether something is F, one must know, and refer to, the form of F. It could fulfil this role by being the explanatory property in virtue of which F things are F. Something is large, for example, if and only if, and precisely because, it is suitably related to the form of large: as Plato sometimes put it in the middle dialogues, if and only if it participates in the form. On this view, the form of large can be a paradigm without having to be the largest thing there is, indeed, without having any size at all.

---

[51] I defend this interpretation of Self-Predication in *On Ideas*. See also S. Peterson, 'A Reasonable Self-Predication Premise for the Third Man Argument', *Philosophical Review*, 82 (1973), 451–70.

[52] Indeed, the forms countenanced in the early dialogues themselves seem to enjoy Self-Predication: see *Prt.* 330c3–e2, where justice is said to be just, and piety pious; *Hp.Ma.* 291d1–3; and, possibly, *Euthphr.* 5d1–5; *Ly.* 217c–e.

[53] *Rep.* 500e3, 540a; *Prm.* 132d2; and (by implication) *Ti.* 28–9. The claim that forms are paradigms is also made in the early dialogues: *Euthphr.* 6e4. It is worth mentioning that nowhere in the *Phaedo* does Plato call forms paradigms.

On the account suggested so far, forms are posited for metaphysical and epistemological reasons: they are the basic explanatory entities, and so they are the basic objects of definition and knowledge. It is sometimes thought that they are also posited for semantic reasons. On one version of this view, the form of F just is the meaning of the word 'F'; on another version of this view, though the form of F isn't the meaning of the word 'F', it must exist if the corresponding term is to be meaningful.[54]

One passage sometimes appealed to on behalf of the view that forms are posited for semantic reasons, or that forms are meanings, is *Republic* 10, 596a6–7, which is generally translated as follows: 'We are, I suppose, in the habit of positing some one form for each group of many things to which we apply the same name'.[55] It is often thought that this passage says that there is a form corresponding to every general term; it might then seem reasonable to assume that forms just are the meanings of general terms. However, this passage need not commit Plato to the view that there is a form corresponding to every predicate: perhaps Plato is using 'name' in the *Cratylus*' technical sense, such that 'n' counts as a name only if it denotes a real property or kind and reveals the outline of its essence.[56] On this reading, *Rep.* 10 posits forms only where there are real properties, which accords well with Plato's claim elsewhere (*Phdr.* 265e1–2; cf. *Plt.* 262a–b) that (unlike every general term) forms 'carve at the natural joints'. On either interpretation, the passage articulates some version of a *One over Many Assumption*: the assumption, namely, that, there is one form of F corresponding to, or over, the set of F things. However, the relevant version of the assumption differs on the two interpretations.[57]

The second interpretation of *Rep.* 10 accords better than does the 'meaning view' with the fact that the other considerations we have looked at on behalf of forms are metaphysical and epistemological. These considerations conceive forms as genuine properties; yet genuine properties and meanings are quite different sorts of thing. For example, the

---

[54] For the view that forms are meanings, see Bostock, *Plato's* Phaedo. For the view that they must exist if words are to be meaningful, see N. P. White, *Plato on Knowledge and Reality* (Indianapolis: Hackett, 1976).

[55] J. A. Smith, in 'General Relative Clauses in Greek', *Classical Review*, 31 (1917), 69–71, suggests an alternative translation: 'We are, as you know, in the habit of assuming [as a rule of procedure] that the Idea which corresponds to a group of particulars, each to each, is always one, in which case [*or*: and in that case] we call the group, or its particulars, by the same name as the *eidos*' (brackets in the original). On this translation, the passage says nothing about the range of forms.

[56] See *Cra.* 386a ff., and my 'Plato on Naming' and *On Ideas*, ch. 8.

[57] The precise formulation of any one over many assumption Plato accepts is disputed, and the formulation just given is deliberately vague. For discussion of the assumption in connection with the Third Man Argument (on which, see further below), see S. Marc Cohen, 'The Logic of the Third Man' (Ch. X in this volume).

words 'unicorn' and 'phlogiston' are meaningful; they can be defined. But they don't pick out genuine features of reality; they aren't genuine properties. If forms are real properties, they can't without confusion be meanings too.

The question whether forms are meanings or genuine properties is related to the question how many forms there are. If forms are meanings, then there are forms corresponding to every meaningful general term. If, on the other hand, forms are real properties that 'carve at the natural joints', then there are forms only where there are real properties. On yet a third view, the middle dialogues posit forms in even fewer cases: for predicates like 'just' or 'large' but not for predicates like 'man'.[58] It is true that Plato focuses on such forms in the middle dialogues; it is also true that his main argument for forms in the middle dialogues (the Argument from Compresence) posits forms only in such cases. However, *Rep.* 10 mentions a form of table, yet nothing is both a table and not a table. Still, this passage is peculiar in various ways; and one might argue that even if there is some sort of form of table, it is not the sort of form for which Plato argues elsewhere in the middle dialogues.

Whether or not the middle dialogues restrict the range of forms to predicates like 'just' and 'large', Plato is plainly more generous in some of the later dialogues: for example, the *Timaeus* has a form of fire, and the *Philebus* has a form of man and one of ox. Does he countenance such forms all along? Or do the late dialogues have a new argument for forms, as they are conceived in the middle dialogues, an argument that posits more forms than the middle dialogues do? Or do the late dialogues have a new conception of the nature of forms altogether?

2. *Knowledge, Belief, and Forms*

At the end of *Republic* 5 Plato offers his longest explanation, in the middle dialogues, of how knowledge differs from belief; he also argues that the possibility of knowledge requires the existence of non-sensible forms. It is often thought that this passage defends the Two Worlds theory described above. In 'Knowledge and Belief in *Republic* 5–7' (Chapter VIII), however, I argue that he defends only the more moderate view that, to know anything, one must know forms; but, once armed with such knowledge, one can know other things as well. Forms are therefore the *basic*, but not the *only*, objects of knowledge.

Plato's opening premisses include the claims that knowledge is of, or is set over, what is; that belief is set over what is and is not; and that

---

[58] For this view, see Owen, 'A Proof in the *Peri Ideōn*'.

ignorance is set over what is not. 'Is' (*esti*) can be used in various ways: veridically (to indicate that something is true); predicatively (to indicate that something is *F*, for some property *F*); existentially (to indicate that something exists); or for identity (to say that *x* is identical to something). With this point in mind, consider Plato's claim that knowledge is of what is, and that belief is of what is and is not. Is this the uncontroversial claim that knowledge but not belief implies truth? Or does Plato mean that one can only know about something if it exists (so that you and I can't know anything about Socrates, since he no longer exists), whereas if one has a belief, it is about what both exists and does not exist? (But what would it be for something to both exist and not exist?) Or does he mean that one can only know *x* if it is *F*—that is, if it has some specific property or properties—and that, if one has a belief, it is about something that is *F* and not *F*? Or is Plato confused about these different uses or senses of 'is'? We saw above that Self-Predication is sometimes thought to rest on a confusion between identity and predication; it is sometimes thought that the argument in *Rep.* 5 rests on confusing various senses (or uses) of 'is' as well. Indeed, it is sometimes thought that Plato was confused about this until the *Sophist*.[59]

In *Rep.* 5 Plato distinguishes knowledge from belief, and in some way correlates knowledge with forms and belief with sensibles. In *Rep.* 6–7, in the famous images of the Sun, Line, and Cave, he goes further: it now emerges that there are two kinds of knowledge (intelligence (*nous*) and thought (*dianoia*)), and two kinds of belief (confidence (*pistis*) and imagination (*eikasia*)). He also tells us how to move from a lower to a higher epistemic condition. I discuss these three images in 'Knowledge and Belief in *Republic* 5–7'. In 'The Form of the Good in Plato's *Republic*' (Chapter IX) Gerasimos Santas discusses the Sun and the Divided Line; his focus is on the form of the good, which he relates not only to Plato's metaphysics and epistemology, but also to his ethics and politics.

On one interpretation, Plato distinguishes among cognitive conditions by reference to their special objects. On this view, one has intelligence if and only if one is confronted by a form; one has imagination if and only if one is confronted by a shadow; and so on. However, this view runs into various difficulties. For example, forms seem relevant to both sorts of knowledge. Or again, Plato says that the philosopher who descends to the

[59] For an interesting discussion of Plato on being in general, which also discusses *Republic* 5 in particular, see L. Brown, 'The Verb "to be" in Greek Philosophy: Some Remarks', in S. Everson (ed.), *Companions to Ancient Thought*, iii: *Language* (Cambridge: Cambridge University Press, 1994), 212–36. This paper should be read in conjunction with her 'Being in the *Sophist*: A Syntactical Enquiry' (Ch. XVIII in this volume). See also C. Kahn, 'Some Philosophical Uses of "to be" in Plato', *Phronesis*, 26 (1981), 105–34.

cave will know the shadows (520c); so not everyone who looks at shadows has the lowest form of belief.

On an alternative interpretation, which I defend in 'Knowledge and Belief in *Republic* 5–7', Plato instead distinguishes among cognitive conditions by reference to the kind of reasoning each involves. On this view, one has imagination when one uncritically accepts conventional beliefs, whatever they are about. This is the stage Plato believes most people are in (515). One has confidence when one learns to make certain discriminations among one's beliefs, though one still lacks the sort of justification necessary for knowledge. This is the condition Socrates takes himself to be in in the early dialogues: he thinks his beliefs are better justified than are those of his interlocutors, but not that they are justified enough to constitute knowledge. One has thought when one uses assumptions (*hupothesis*, 'laying down') to justify various conclusions, although at this stage the assumptions are not sufficiently justified to constitute the highest form of knowledge. This is the stage at which Plato seems to place himself in the *Phaedo* and *Republic*. In the *Phaedo*, for example, Plato uses the hypothesis that there are forms in order to justify the belief that the soul is immortal. The hypothesis that there are forms is justified to some extent; we have seen, for example, that *Phaedo* 74b–c argues that there are non-sensible forms. But the justification is incomplete. In order to have a more complete justification, and so to achieve the highest form of knowledge, intelligence, one must be able to interrelate various assumptions so as to achieve a synoptic understanding of reality as a whole, in terms of the form of the good.

On this interpretation, the Sun, Line, and Cave aren't committed to the Two Worlds theory. Moreover, Plato has a holistic account of knowledge: knowledge is essentially systematic, and one's epistemic condition improves as one can suitably interrelate more and more.

Earlier we considered semantic atomism, the view that names are mere tags for things. This semantic view is generally taken to go along with an epistemological view: that one can learn the meanings of words, or know an entity, in isolation; knowledge, that is, is also conceived of atomistically. On some versions of this view, knowledge consists in direct acquaintance with the thing known, rather than in any sort of articulated account.[60] If, however, Plato has the holistic conception of knowledge just described, then he at least doesn't think acquaintance is sufficient for knowledge. Rather, knowledge requires understanding and explanation; and one

---

[60] For the connection between semantic atomism and atomism about knowledge, see Owen, 'Notes on Ryle's Plato', 365; McDowell, 'Identity Mistakes: Plato and the Logical Atomists' (Ch. XV in this volume).

knows more as one can explain more.[61] Nor does he seem to think that
genuine knowledge is atomistic; rather, to know any given entity, one must
know its relations to other things. As one understands more relations, one's
cognitive condition improves; but some interrelating is necessary for any
sort of knowledge at all.

We have seen that, for Plato, one has the best sort of knowledge only
when one understands how things are related to the form of the good.
Relating things to the form of the good, Plato believes, involves seeing
what they are good for. This, in turn, suggests that Plato takes reality to be
a teleological system, and the best sort of knowledge involves a grasp of
the teleological structure of things. Santas discusses some aspects of Plato's
teleology in 'The Form of the Good in Plato's *Republic*'; so too does Steven
Strange, in 'The Double Explanation in the *Timaeus*'.[62]

One issue Santas raises about the form of the good is this: Plato claims
that the form of the good is the cause or reason (*aitia*) of the knowability
of the forms and of their being or essence (or reality: *ousia*) (508c–509d).
But how exactly is the form of the good the cause or reason of these things?
Above we considered the *Phaedo*'s claim that forms are *aitiai*. We saw that
there are difficulties if Plato means that forms, all by themselves, bring
about change; but, as we also saw, it is not clear that Plato needs to be so
understood. Does the causal or explanatory role of the form of the good
suggest otherwise?

In attempting to explain precisely what sort of cause or explanation the
form of the good is, Santas introduces a distinction between two sorts of
property or attribute that forms have: what he calls their *ideal* and *proper*
attributes.[63] An ideal attribute is a property a form has in so far as it is a
form; for example, every form has the ideal attribute of being everlasting.
A proper attribute is a property a form has in so far as it is the particular
form it is; for example, the form of goodness has goodness as a proper
attribute. It is sometimes thought that Plato isn't clear about this distinction, and that this lack of clarity leads him into various errors. For example,
surely a sane craftsman would aim to replicate only the proper attributes
of the relevant model? Yet, it has been argued, the craftsman who creates
the cosmos in the *Timaeus* aims to replicate the forms' ideal attributes as

[61] This leaves open the possibility that acquaintance is necessary for knowledge. I don't think
that is Plato's view, but I can't defend that claim here.

[62] See also J. Lennox, 'Plato's Unnatural Teleology', in D. O'Meara (ed.), *Platonic Investigations* (Washington: Catholic University Press of America, 1985), 195–218.

[63] For this distinction, see also G. E. L. Owen, 'Dialectic and Eristic in the Treatment of Forms',
in G. E. L. Owen (ed.), *Aristotle on Dialectic* (Oxford: Clarendon Press, 1968), 103–25; repr. in
Logic, Science, and Dialectic; G. Vlastos, 'The "Two-Level" Paradoxes in Aristotle', in *Platonic
Studies*, 323–34.

well by, for example, trying to make the universe as everlasting as possi-ble.[64] Is Plato's divine craftsman therefore mad? Santas considers whether this is so, along with related questions that centre on the distinction between ideal and proper attributes.

IV. THE LATE DIALOGUES

1. The Parmenides *and the Later Theory of Forms*

In the first part of the *Parmenides* Plato raises various objections to a theory of forms. The objection that has received the most attention is the so-called Third Man Argument (TMA).[65] The TMA alleges that some theory of forms is vulnerable to a vicious infinite regress: if there is even one form of F, there are infinitely many of them. This violates Plato's Uniqueness Assumption, according to which there is at most one form for any given predicate. The regress goes roughly as follows. Each form is a *one* over many; that is, whenever many things are F (for some predicates 'F'), there is one form in virtue of which they are F. Consider the set of sensible large things. According to the One over Many Assumption, there is then one form of large—call it the form$_1$ of large—over them. As we have seen, forms are Self-Predicative; the form of large, for example, is itself large. Hence we may form a new set of large things, one consisting of the members of the original set, along with the form of large. The One over Many Assumption tells us that there is a form of large over this set. This can't be the form in the set (i.e. the form$_1$ of large). For, or so the TMA alleges, nothing is F in virtue of itself: this is the so-called *Non-Identity Assumption*.[66] Hence there must be another form of large—call

---

[64] D. Keyt, 'The Mad Craftsman of the *Timaeus*', *Philosophical Review*, 80 (1971), 230–5.

[65] So-called because Aristotle describes an argument that he calls the Third Man, and this argument is generally thought to be the same, from the logical point of view, as the argument Plato describes. See Aristotle, *Peri Ideōn*; *SE* 22; *Metaph.* 7. 13. However, whereas Aristotle describes a regress of *men*, Plato describes a regress of *large*. I discuss Aristotle's account of the Third Man in *On Ideas*, ch. 15. The classic discussion of the TMA in recent times is Vlastos, 'The Third Man Argument in the *Parmenides*'; his view is summarized by S. Marc Cohen, in 'The Logic of the Third Man' (Ch. X).

[66] In Vlastos's original formulation, the premiss says that 'If anything has a certain character, it cannot be identical with the Form in virtue of which we apprehend that character. If x is F, x cannot be identical with F-ness': hence the label 'Non-Identity'. Notice that Non-Identity, the claim that nothing is F in virtue of itself, is quite different from a claim defended in the middle dialogues, that forms are different from sensibles; hence the difference assumption of the middle dialogues does not commit Plato to the Non-Identity Assumption of the TMA. Nor does sepa-ration—the claim that the form of F can exist whether or not F sensible particulars exist—so commit him.

it the form$_2$ of large—which is the form of large in virtue of which the members of our new set of large things are large. By Self-Predication, the form$_2$ of large is large. We can now form yet another set of large things, one consisting of the members of the previous set, along with the form$_2$ of large. By the One over Many, there must be a form of large over this set which, by Non-Identity, must be non-identical with anything in the set— and so on *ad infinitum*, and in violation of Uniqueness.

In 'The Logic of the Third Man' (Chapter X) S. Marc Cohen discusses the TMA in detail. As he reconstructs it, it is valid. The question then is whether Plato is committed to all of its premisses. We have seen that he accepts Self-Predication. But is he committed to the One over Many premiss and to Non-Identity? If so, he is vulnerable to the TMA. If not, why not? And if not, why does Plato raise the argument at all?

The TMA is just one argument considered in the first part of the *Parmenides*. The reader is encouraged to consider other arguments raised there. How exactly do they go? Are they, either in fact or in Plato's view, good criticisms of any views to be found in the middle dialogues? Do later dialogues revise the theory of forms in response to the criticisms? If so, precisely how?[67]

Different views on these issues have been held. Vlastos, for example, believes that Plato's objections are 'a record of honest perplexity': though they are in fact devastating to the middle dialogues' theory of forms, Plato couldn't figure out their underlying basis; he therefore didn't know how to reply and so didn't do so.[68] Another view agrees with Vlastos that Plato didn't revise his theory of forms in response to the objections, but it suggests a different reason: that Plato had no need to do so, since he correctly sees that the objections are not good ones.[69] Yet others have thought that Plato rightly took the objections to be good ones, and so revised his theory of forms in their light.[70] Of course, one might think that different dialogues respond in different ways; or that some but not all of the objections are, or are taken by Plato to be, good ones.

---

[67] Some of the other arguments in the first part of the *Parmenides* are briefly discussed by Vlastos, in 'The Third Man Argument'; see also M. L. Gill's introduction to *Plato:* Parmenides (Indianapolis: Hackett, 1996). For a detailed discussion of the argument at 133c–134c, which Plato refers to as 'the greatest difficulty', see S. Peterson, 'The Greatest Difficulty for Plato's Theory of Forms: The Unknowability Argument of *Parmenides* 133c–134', *Archiv für Geschichte der Philosophie*, 63 (1981), 1–16.

[68] This view is defended by Vlastos, in 'The Third Man Argument'.

[69] This view is defended by Cherniss, in *Aristotle's Criticism of Plato and the Academy*.

[70] This is Owen's view. See esp. 'The Platonism of Aristotle', *Proceedings of the British Academy*, 51 (1965), 125–50; repr. in *Logic, Science and Dialectic*, 200–20, though the same point is made, more briefly, in many of his articles; see e.g. 'Dialectic and Eristic', 112 n. 2; 'Plato on Not-Being', 256; 'A Proof in the *Peri Ideōn*'.

It is sometimes thought that in order fully to understand the arguments
in the first part of the *Parmenides*, and in order to understand how Plato
responds to them, one must understand the second part of the *Parmenides*.[71] So, for example, we have seen that Plato is sometimes thought
to accept Self-Predication because he is confused about the difference
between identity and predication. The second part of the *Parmenides* is
sometimes thought to distinguish between identity and predication. If one
accepts this view, one might infer that Plato took Self-Predication to be
the guilty premiss in the TMA, in which case he presumably abandoned
it. In 'Notes on Ryle's Plato' (Chapter XI) G. E. L. Owen defends this view.
He also provides a general guide to the second part of the *Parmenides*,
whose interest extends far beyond the concerns of the first part of the
Parmenides.

Another dialogue it is especially important to consider in connection
with the *Parmenides*' criticisms of a theory of forms is the *Timaeus*. There
is dispute about its relative chronology. In 'The Place of the *Timaeus* in
Plato's Dialogues' G. E. L. Owen argues that the *Timaeus* was written
before the *Parmenides*. On this view, the *Timaeus* of course doesn't *respond*
to the *Parmenides*' criticisms; and so one wouldn't be surprised if, as Owen
believes, it has the same theory of forms as the middle dialogues do. More
usually, however, the *Timaeus* is taken to post-date the *Parmenides*.[72] On
this view, it becomes pressing to know whether the *Timaeus* has the same
theory of forms as the middle dialogues do. If it does, then presumably
Plato, at least in the *Timaeus*, didn't revise the theory of forms in the light
of the *Parmenides*' criticisms. This might be because he didn't know what
if anything to do in response, or because he (rightly or wrongly) took the
criticisms to be ineffective. If, on the other hand, the *Timaeus* has a different theory of forms from the middle dialogues, then one might infer that
Plato took at least some of the *Parmenides*' criticisms to be good ones, and
so revised the middle dialogues' theory of forms in some way.[73]

Other late dialogues have also been thought to respond in one way or
another to the *Parmenides*' criticisms. For example, it has been argued
that the *Sophist* rejects Self-Predication, though it has also been argued
that it retains it.[74] The *Sophist* has also been thought to revise the middle

---

[71] This view has recently been forcefully defended by C. Meinwald, *Plato's* Parmenides (New
York: Oxford University Press, 1991). See also her 'Good-Bye to the Third Man', in Kraut (ed.),
Cambridge Companion to Plato, 365–96.

[72] For discussion, see Brandwood, *The Chronology of Plato's Dialogues*; and my 'Owen's
Progress', *Philosophical Review*, 97 (1988), 373–99.

[73] For this view, see S. Waterlow, 'The Third Man's Contribution to Plato's Paradigmatism',
Mind, 91 (1982), 339–57.

[74] Owen, in, for example, 'Plato on Not-Being', 256, seems to suggest that the *Sophist* rejects
Self-Predication; for, in his view, Self-Predication rests on confusing identity and predication,

dialogues' theory of forms by arguing that forms are not, after all, entirely exempt from change.[75] There is also dispute about the status of Self-Predication, and the related view that forms are paradigms, in the *Philebus*.[76] It has also been argued that at least some of the late dialogues abandon realism about universals altogether.[77] The reader is invited to consider the late dialogues with this question—among others—in mind.

Doing so, however, is complicated by the fact that it is not always clear when or whether forms are being considered. The *Philebus*, for example, discusses things that are genuinely one, and do not come to be and perish (15a); but it is not clear whether these are forms. Or again, it develops a fourfold ontology, comprising limit (*peras*), unlimit (*apeiron*), the mixture of the two, and the cause of the mixture. It is not clear where, if anywhere, forms fit into this scheme; yet one's decision here will affect one's view of the nature of forms in the *Philebus*.[78] On one view, Plato says that *everything* has *peras* and *apeiron* in it, in which case the units mentioned at 15a do so. But in the middle dialogues forms are said to be simple and partless (*Phd.* 78c–80b). So are the *Philebus*' units not forms, as they were conceived in the middle dialogues? Or can something be simple, in the middle dialogues' sense, even if it has *peras* and *apeiron* in it?

2. *The* Theaetetus

The main question asked in the *Theaetetus* is: 'What is knowledge?' Plato

---

but the *Sophist* clearly distinguishes between them. See also 'Notes on Ryle's Plato' (Ch. XI in this volume). For the view that the *Sophist* retains Self-Predication, see G. Striker, *Peras und Apeiron* (Göttingen: Vandenhoeck & Ruprecht, 1970), 37; R. Heinaman, 'Self-Predication in the *Sophist*', *Phronesis*, 26 (1981), 55–66.

[75] For a recent discussion of this issue, see L. Brown, 'Innovation and Continuity: The Battle of Gods and Giants, *Sophist* 245–249', in Gentzler (ed.), *Method in Ancient Philosophy*, 181–207.

[76] For some discussion, see Striker, *Peras und Apeiron*. Owen, 'The Place of the *Timaeus*', n. 33, claims that the *Philebus* abandons paradigmatism.

[77] At the end of '*Sumplokē Eidōn*', *Bulletin of the Institute of Classical Studies*, 2 (1955), 31–5; repr. in *Studies in Plato's Metaphysics* and *Plato*, i, J. L. Ackrill says that *Parmenides* 135b suggests that Plato took himself to be revising, rather than rejecting, the theory of forms; but, Ackrill thinks, 'we might find it more natural to say that he jettisoned the theory'. He goes on to say that, in the *Sophist*, Plato is no longer sure that forms should be conceived as they were in the middle dialogues, as 'ethical ideals' and as 'metaphysical objects of intuitive and perhaps mystical insight', though Plato is sure that 'there must be fixed things to guarantee the meaningfulness of talk, fixed concepts—the meanings of general words'. If forms are now just concepts or meanings, then they cannot without confusion also be genuine properties.

[78] John Cooper discusses this fourfold ontology in 'Plato's Theory of the Human Good in the *Philebus*' in Vol. ii, Ch. XV. See also Striker, *Peras und Apeiron*; J. C. B. Gosling, *Plato:* Philebus (Oxford: Clarendon Press, 1975); J. M. E. Moravcsik, 'Forms, Nature, and the Good in the *Philebus*', *Phronesis*, 24 (1979), 81–104; and C. Meinwald, 'Prometheus's Bounds: *Peras* and *Apeiron* in Plato's *Philebus*', in Gentzler (ed.), *Method in Ancient Philosophy*, 165–80.

considers three main answers: that it is perception (151d–186e); that it is true belief (187a–201c); and that it is true belief plus a *logos* or account (201d–210d). Each of these answers seems to be rejected; hence the dialogue, like many of the early dialogues, seems to end in *aporia*, at a loss.

Plato doesn't discuss the view that knowledge is perception in isolation. Rather, he links it to two other views: Protagoras' measure doctrine (that a man is the measure of all things) and a Heracleitean flux doctrine (that all things change). At 160d he says that these three theses 'come to one'.

In 'Knowledge and Perception: *Theaetetus* 151d–184a' (Chapter XII) Myles Burnyeat outlines two main ways of reading this part of the *Theaetetus*, which he calls Reading A and Reading B.[79] Both readings agree that Plato denies that knowledge is perception. But according to Reading A, Plato accepts Protagoreanism, as well as an extreme version of Heracleiteanism, if they are restricted to perception and the sensible world, and not extended to forms and the meanings of words. For Reading B, by contrast, Protagoreanism and Heracleiteanism are introduced solely in order to provide dialectical support for Theaetetus' definition, and we cannot infer, from this part of the *Theaetetus*, that Plato accepts any version of them; more strongly, he rejects them, even as applied to the sensible world.

Protagoreanism is initially introduced as a solution to the Problem of Conflicting Appearances. In Plato's example (153d–154b), the wind appears cold to the one who shivers, but not to the one who doesn't. The Protagorean infers that the wind is cold to the first person, but not to the second; he sanctions an inference from how things appear to one, to how they are (to one). Eventually Plato extends Protagoreanism from sensible appearances to all appearances whatsoever, so that any belief whatsoever is true to the one who believes it. Sometimes, however, Protagoras is said simply to hold that all beliefs are true. Which does he mean? Focusing on the first formulation, Burnyeat, among others, takes Protagoras to be a relativist who believes that no propositions are flat out true, or true *simpliciter*; rather, all propositions are true only to, or for, those who believe them. On an alternative interpretation—which Aristotle, among others, seems to favour—Protagoras is an infallibilist: he believes that all beliefs are true *simpliciter*.[80]

[79] Though Readings A and B are two leading interpretations of this part of the *Theaetetus*, they do not exhaust the interpretative options.
[80] See Aristotle, *Metaph.* 4. 5. Burnyeat defends a relativist interpretation of Protagoras not only in his chapter in this volume ('Knowledge and Perception: *Theaetetus* 151d–184a', Ch. XII), but also in 'Protagoras and Self-Refutation in Plato's *Theaetetus*', *Philosophical Review*, 85 (1976), 172–95. I defend an infallibilist interpretation in 'Conflicting Appearances: *Theaetetus*

In order to resolve this dispute, one should ask which of these two interpretations best explains why Plato takes the three theses to be so intimately connected: is relativism or infallibilism better connected to Theaetetus' definition of knowledge as perception, or to a Heracleitean flux doctrine? One should also look at Plato's refutation of Protagoras (169–171; cf. 177c–179d). Does he seem to be arguing against relativism or infallibilism? At several crucial junctures Plato drops the qualifier 'to one' on which the relativist insists. If he is arguing against relativism, he seems to beg the question against him; however, dropping the qualifier is legitimate in an argument against infallibilism. So one might take this as evidence in favour of infallibilism.[81] Yet if Protagoras is an infallibilist, we need to ask why Plato sometimes includes the qualifier.

In 181–3 Plato argues against Extreme Heracleiteanism. On one view, he argues only that *not everything* can be in Extreme Heracleitean flux. Proponents of this view differ over what escapes this sort of flux: forms, or meanings, or the offspring posited by the theory of perception considered earlier in the *Theaetetus*.[82] On an alternative interpretation, 181–3 argues that *nothing* can be in Extreme Heracleitean flux. Those who favour this view sometimes infer that Plato now rejects the middle dialogues' view that the sensible world is in Extreme Heracleitean flux.[83] However, as we have seen, it is disputed whether Plato ever took the sensible world to be in Extreme Heracleitean flux.

In 184–6 Plato presents his final refutation of the claim that knowledge is perception. He argues, in brief, that knowledge requires grasping truth; one can grasp truth only if one grasps being; since perception cannot do this, it is not knowledge. On one view, to grasp being is to grasp that an object, *x*, is something or other; it is to grasp *x* as being *F*, for some *F*. On this view, 'is' is predicative. On another view, to grasp being is to grasp that

153d–154b', in C. Gill and M. McCabe (eds.), *Form and Argument in Late Plato* (Oxford: Clarendon Press, 1996), 105–33; in 'Protagorean Relativisms', in J. Cleary and W. Wians (eds.), *Proceedings of the Boston Area Colloquium in Ancient Philosophy*, 7 (Lanham, Md.: University Press of America, 1996), 211–43; and in 'Plato's Refutation of Protagoras in the *Theaetetus*', *Apeiron*, 31 (1998), 1–34. For further discussion of the self-refutation argument, see S. Waterlow, 'Protagoras and Inconsistency', *Archiv für Geschichte der Philosophie*, 59 (1977), 19–36. The position I call 'infallibilism', Burnyeat calls 'subjectivism'.

[81] In 'Protagoras and Self-Refutation in Plato's *Theaetetus*', Burnyeat argues that the fact that Plato drops the qualifier doesn't vitiate his argument against relativism. I discuss his argument in 'Relativism and Self-Refutation: Plato, Protagoras, and Burnyeat', in J. Gentzler (ed.), *Method in Ancient Philosophy*, 137–63.

[82] Cornford, *Plato's Theory of Knowledge*, thinks Plato argues that forms and meanings escape Extreme Heracleitean flux, but that the sensible world undergoes it. J. McDowell, *Plato: Theaetetus* (Oxford: Clarendon Press, 1973), notes ad loc., thinks Plato argues that the offspring countenanced in the theory of perception escape Extreme Heracleitean flux.

[83] See e.g. Owen, 'The Place of the *Timaeus*'.

something (really, objectively) exists. In 'Plato on Sense-Perception and Knowledge (*Theaetetus* 184–186)' (Chapter XIII) John Cooper considers both interpretations but, in the end, favours the second. In 'Observations on Perception in Plato's Later Dialogues' (Chapter XIV) Michael Frede defends the first interpretation.[84]

The claim that knowledge is not perception sounds familiar from the middle dialogues. So one might think that, in affirming it, Plato is reaffirming his earlier view. However, this is far from clear. For in claiming that knowledge is not perception he is (on one interpretation) arguing only that perception is not knowledge, if perception is taken to be below the judgemental threshold. This leaves open the possibility (although it does not imply) that perceptual beliefs can constitute knowledge. Yet when, in the middle dialogues, Plato denies that knowledge is perception, he means that perceptual beliefs do not constitute knowledge. Since perception is understood differently in the two contexts, the *Theaetetus* is neither reaffirming nor rejecting the middle dialogues' view; it addresses a different issue.[85]

Having rejected the view that knowledge is perception, Plato next asks whether it is true belief. Instead of discussing this question directly, however, he embarks on a lengthy discussion of whether false belief is possible. The suggestion seems to be that if knowledge is true belief, it is difficult to see how false belief is possible, yet surely it is; hence, there is a difficulty in taking knowledge to be true belief.[86] Plato also discusses the paradox of false belief in the *Cratylus*, *Euthydemus*, and *Sophist*. In the *Euthydemus* and *Theaetetus* no explanation of how false belief is possible is endorsed. The *Cratylus* offers a brief account; but it is not until the *Sophist* that Plato offers a full and, according to many, satisfactory account. It is sometimes thought that this is because it wasn't until the *Sophist* that Plato saw how to accommodate false belief.

Why might he have been unable to accommodate false belief earlier? On one view, the explanation is that he was confused about 'is': speaking falsely is saying what is not (the case); but Plato confused this with the claim that speaking falsely is saying nothing. Saying nothing, however, is not speaking at all; hence allegedly false statements aren't genuine state-

---

[84] The first view is also defended by M. F. Burnyeat, in 'Plato on the Grammar of Perceiving', *Classical Quarterly*, NS 26 (1976), 29–51; cf. *The* Theaetetus *of Plato* (Indianapolis: Hackett, 1990), 52–65. These two interpretations do not exhaust the available options.

[85] I defend this view in 'Plato on Perception', *Oxford Studies in Ancient Philosophy*, suppl. vol. (1988), 15–28. Burnyeat, 'Plato on the Grammar of Perceiving', and Cooper, 'Plato on Sense–Perception and Knowledge' (Ch. XIII), argue that the *Theaetetus* rejects the middle dialogues' view of perception.

[86] I defend this view in 'False Belief in the *Theaetetus*', *Phronesis*, 24 (1979), 70–80. Burnyeat, *The* Theaetetus *of Plato*, also seems sympathetic to it.

ments. On another (related) view, the explanation involves his alleged commitment to logical or semantic atomism, or to views naturally associated with it. For it is sometimes thought that Plato at one stage believed not only that names were mere tags for things, but also that sentences are mere names, or strings of names. As Owen puts it in 'Plato on Not-Being', 'Thus falsehood at its simplest, for instance in the presence of the falsifying situation, becomes as vacuous as calling "Stetson!" when Stetson is not there, or pointing at vacancy.'[87]

In 'Identity Mistakes: Plato and the Logical Atomists' John McDowell considers the extent to which, in the *Theaetetus*, one of the puzzles of false belief rests on logical atomism. Even if one concludes that some or all of the puzzles rest on logical atomism, however, one might deny that, in the *Theaetetus*, Plato is committed to that view. For, as we have seen, in the *Theaetetus* he introduces the puzzles of false belief as puzzles that arise for anyone who (unlike himself) takes knowledge to be true belief. Once we are clear about the dialectical structure of this part of the *Theaetetus*, we can see that Plato isn't committed to the assumptions on which the puzzles rest.

In 201a–c Plato offers a direct refutation of the claim that knowledge is true belief: the members of a jury might have the true belief that Jones committed the crime, but only an eyewitness could know that he'd done so. Hence true belief isn't sufficient for knowledge. Here, as in the *Meno* (and as elsewhere too, on some views of the matter), Plato again assumes that there can be knowledge and true belief about at least some of the same things; he also assumes that one can know items in the sensible world, not just forms.[88]

Having argued that knowledge is neither perception nor true belief, Plato wonders whether it is true belief plus a *logos*. This sounds like the view favoured in earlier dialogues, so it is surprising that the dialogue seems to end in *aporia*, at a loss. One possibility is that, despite the seeming *aporia*, Plato hints that he continues to believe that knowledge is true belief plus a *logos*. An alternative is that he hints at a new account of knowledge. Yet another possibility is that the *aporia* is genuine: Plato is no longer sure whether to accept his earlier account, yet neither does he have an alternative in view.[89]

---

[87] Page 435 below. The passage quoted in the text begins with 'Thus'. I quoted the preceding sentence above, when I first introduced semantic atomism in connection with the *Cratylus*. Owen therefore seems to think that semantic atomism implies the difficulties about falsehood. Notice that in n. 42 of his paper Owen suggests that the *Cratylus* anticipates the *Sophist*'s explanation of falsehood. This is somewhat odd, since he thinks that the *Cratylus* precedes the *Theaetetus*, and that the *Theaetetus* accepts semantic atomism and so cannot explain falsehood.

[88] This passage is discussed by Burnyeat, in 'Socrates and the Jury'.

[89] I defend the first view in 'Knowledge and *Logos* in the *Theaetetus*', *Philosophical Review*,

In dialogues generally taken to post-date the *Theaetetus* Plato defends what has been called 'the interrelation model of knowledge'.[90] On this view, knowing something involves knowing its place in a relevant scheme; to know a given mathematical theorem, for example, one must know its place in a general system of mathematics. We might say that on this view knowledge is true belief plus *several logoi*. This might seem to differ from the view that knowledge is true belief plus a *logos*. However, it may be doubted whether, in saying that knowledge is true belief plus a *logos*, Plato ever meant to commit himself to the view that true belief could become knowledge by the simple addition of a single sentence. We have seen, for example, that the *Republic* favours a holistic account of knowledge: the best sort of knowledge is synoptic. If, in dialogues before and after the *Theaetetus*, Plato favours something like the interrelation model of knowledge, then perhaps he favours it in the *Theaetetus* as well. Notice that, on this view, Plato is very far from the sort of epistemological atomism described earlier.

3. Being, Not-Being, Explanation, and Method in the Late Dialogues

We have seen that perhaps the *Theaetetus*, and more clearly other late dialogues, continue to favour a holistic view of knowledge. There are also other ways in which one might compare the epistemology of the late dialogues with that of earlier dialogues. For example, we have seen that, in the *Phaedo*, Plato offers two explanatory schemas: the safe and subtle *aitiai*. Both invoke forms, and both seem to reject material explanations; though material factors are in some cases necessary conditions for an event or state of affairs to occur, they are not themselves genuinely explanatory (*Phd*. 99a–d). In the *Timaeus* Plato reflects further on the nature of explanation in general, and on the explanatory role (if any) of material factors; he now seems to take them to be joint causes of at least some phenomena, rather than mere necessary conditions.

The *Timaeus* also develops the teleological ambitions of the *Phaedo* and *Republic* more fully. As we have seen, in the *Republic* Plato claims that unless one knows the form of the good, one can't have the best sort of knowledge. It is clear why it might be thought that one can't fully understand the virtues without understanding their relation to the good; but Plato also claims that one can't know *anything* fully or purely unless one

88 (1979), 366–97. For discussion of various views, see A. Nehamas, '*Epistēmē* and *Logos* in Plato's Later Thought', *Archiv für Geschichte der Philosophie*, 66 (1984), 11–36.

[90] See esp. the *Sophist*, *Politicus*, and *Philebus*. Some of the relevant passages are discussed by Nehamas, '*Epistēmē* and *Logos*'.

knows the form of the good. This claim suggests some sort of cosmic teleology; though some such view is hinted at in both the *Phaedo* and *Republic*, it is only in the *Timaeus* that Plato develops it. Steven Strange explores
these and other issues about explanation and teleology in 'The Double
Explanation in the *Timaeus*'.[91]

The *Philebus* takes some empirical disciplines to constitute genuine
knowledge, if of an inferior sort. If one thinks the middle dialogues and
Timaeus defend or assume the Two Worlds theory, then one might think
that the *Philebus* abandons it.[92] It has also been argued that the *Philebus*
takes the elenchus, familiar from the Socratic dialogues, to be the route to
philosophical knowledge.[93] What about dialogues in between? Do they,
as Vlastos, for example, believes, ascribe a more limited role to the
elenchus?[94] Or do they too believe that elenchus can take one all the way
to knowledge? Here it is relevant to consider both the hypothetical
method, discussed in, for example, the *Meno* and *Phaedo*, and also the
method of collection and division, discussed especially in the *Phaedrus*,
Sophist, *Politicus*, and *Philebus*.[95]

Questions can also be raised about possible revisions in ontology. We
considered some of these above, in asking about the fate of the middle dialogues' theory of forms in the light of the *Parmenides*' criticisms; but other
issues are also relevant. For example, in the middle dialogues sensibles
are said to be between being and not being, and to belong to the realm of
genesis (becoming) rather than to the realm of *ousia* (being); the same
claims are made in the *Timaeus*. Yet the *Sophist* seems to count sensibles
as *onta*, as things that are. Hence one might think that the *Sophist* is more
sympathetic to the sensible world than the middle dialogues and *Timaeus*
are. However, it is not clear whether there is a genuine contradiction
here. For example, the *Sophist* might mean that sensibles are among the
entities that exist, whereas the middle dialogues and *Timaeus* might use

---

[91] See also David Sedley's 'The Ideal of Godlikeness' (Vol. ii, Ch. XIV).

[92] For a defence of the view that the *Timaeus* doesn't assume the Two Worlds theory, see D.
Frede, 'The Philosophical Economy of Plato's Psychology: Rationality and Common Concepts
in the *Timaeus*', in M. Frede and G. Striker (eds.), *Rationality in Greek Thought* (Oxford: Clarendon Press, 1996), 29–58. In 'Plato's Theory of Human Good in the *Philebus*' (Vol. ii, Ch. XV)
John Cooper discusses the *Philebus*' ranking of various types of knowledge. Of course, there is
no difference between the middle and late dialogues on this score if, as I have suggested, not
even the former are committed to the Two Worlds theory.

[93] See Donald Davidson, 'Plato's Philosopher', in Irwin and Nussbaum (eds.), *Virtue, Love,
and Form*, 179–94.

[94] See 'Elenchus and Mathematics', in *Socrates*, 107–31.

[95] Irwin briefly discusses the method of hypothesis in 'The Theory of Forms'. For discussion
of collection and division, see J. L. Ackrill, 'In Defence of Platonic Division', in O. P. Wood and
G. Pitcher (eds.), *Ryle: A Collection of Critical Essays* (Garden City, NY: Doubleday Anchor,
1970), 373–92; repr. in *Essays on Plato and Aristotle* (Oxford: Clarendon Press, 1996).

'is' incompletely, to mean that sensibles are not (purely or fully) F, since they are both F and not F; unlike forms, they suffer compresence of opposites.[96]

Here again, then—as with Self-Predication and as in *Republic* 5—a crucial issue in Plato turns on his understanding of being (*einai*), a topic discussed in detail only in the *Sophist*. Early on in the *Sophist* Plato rehearses a number of problems about not-being or what is not, including a problem or problems about the possibility of false statement and of false belief (237–40). A false statement can be construed as saying what is not; a false belief can be construed as believing a false statement. Yet the Presocratic philosopher Parmenides had argued that what is not cannot be spoken or thought of.

Having raised various puzzles about what is not, Plato proceeds to argue that there are also difficulties about being, or what is; he suggests that, as Owen puts it in 'Plato on Not-Being', 'any light thrown on either being or not-being will equally illuminate the other' (p. 422). Owen dubs this the 'Parity Assumption'. Plato then attempts to solve the puzzles about not-being, as well as those about being.

There is considerable dispute, however, about how he does so. F. M. Cornford, for example, argues that Plato's main explorations of being and not-being focus on the existential use of the verb; the copula is irrelevant.[97] J. L. Ackrill, by contrast, argues that Plato distinguishes between existential, predicative, and identity senses or uses of 'is'.[98] In 'Plato on Not-Being' Owen argues that the *Sophist* doesn't isolate a special existential sense or use of the verb, or indeed any other senses or uses of the verb—not because he confuses them, but because doing so would be irrelevant to his purposes in the dialogue. On Owen's view, however, Plato does distinguish between identity and predication *statements*. Owen argues that the central concerns in the *Sophist* are problems of reference and predication, not existence. He thinks that these, in turn, are associated with incomplete uses of the verb 'to be'; they don't require any isolation of a complete, existential sense or use.

A possible difficulty with Owen's view is that, as Lesley Brown argues in 'Being in the *Sophist*: A Syntactical Enquiry' (Chapter XVIII), it is not clear how to formulate the distinction between complete and incomplete

---

[96] For discussion of this issue, see Owen, 'The Place of the *Timaeus*'; Fine, 'Owen's Progress'; M. Frede, 'Being and Becoming in Plato', *Oxford Studies in Ancient Philosophy*, suppl. vol. (1988), 37–52; A. Code, 'Reply to Michael Frede's "Being and Becoming in Plato"', 53–60. Though the *Timaeus* may well postdate the *Parmenides*, it may well antedate the *Sophist*.

[97] Cornford, *Plato's Theory of Knowledge*.

[98] 'Plato and the Copula: *Sophist* 251–59', *Journal of Hellenic Studies*, 77 (1954), 1–6; and '*Sumplokē Eidōn*'; both repr. in *Plato*, i.

uses of the verb. She argues that Owen's understanding of that distinction is defective, and that complete and incomplete uses of the verb are far closer than they have generally been thought to be. She agrees with Owen, however, that Plato doesn't solve the various problems of being and not being by distinguishing between complete and incomplete senses or uses of 'to be'; indeed, her view reinforces that part of Owen's claim. However, despite agreeing with Owen about this, she follows quite a different route to the view, with the result that the *Sophist*'s landscape looks quite different at various stages along the way.

However we understand the details of Plato's solutions to the various problems of being and not-being, it is generally agreed that his account of false statement involves the view that statements are structured wholes; they don't consist of mere strings of names (*Sph.* 262). Owen believes that earlier dialogues take statements to be strings of names; hence, on Owen's view, in the *Sophist* Plato breaks free from that view. On another view, Plato was never committed to the view that statements are strings of names, or to the semantic atomism that goes along with that view; although the *Sophist*'s explanation of how false statements and beliefs are possible is clearer and more complete than earlier discussions are, this isn't because Plato was confused earlier. On this, as on several other issues we have explored, it seems to be generally agreed that the late dialogues are clear on some issue or other; the more controversial question is the extent to which this clarity involves rejecting earlier views.

I

THE SOCRATIC ELENCHUS[1]

GREGORY VLASTOS

I

In Plato's earlier dialogues[2]—in all of them, except the *Lysis, Euthydemus,* and *Hippias Major*—Socrates' enquiries display a pattern of investigation whose rationale he does not investigate. They are constrained by rules he does not undertake to justify. In marked contrast to the 'Socrates' who speaks for Plato in the middle dialogues, who refers frequently to the 'method' ($\mu \acute{\epsilon} \vartheta o \delta o \varsigma$) he follows (either systematically[3] or for some parti-

© Gregory Vlastos 1983. Reprinted with permission from *Oxford Studies in Ancient Philosophy*, 1 (1983), 27–58.

[1] An earlier draft of this essay was delivered as one of a series of lectures, 'The Philosophy of Socrates', under the Gifford Trust at the University of St Andrews in the winter and spring terms of 1981. A later draft was presented at a meeting of the American Philosophical Association on 29 Dec. 1982. An abstract of that draft was published in the *Journal of Philosophy*, 79 (1982), 711–14. I am deeply indebted to my friend Richard Kraut, who served as commentator at that meeting, for his exceedingly acute and suggestive critique of my paper. I trust he will soon put into print his own, highly original, interpretation of the Socratic elenchus.

[2] The chronological order of those works of Plato which I accept as authentic (not materially different from that generally recognized in recent Platonic scholarship) is as follows:

(1) The earlier dialogues (listed in alphabetical order): *Apology, Charmides, Crito, Euthydemus, Euthyphro, Gorgias, Hippias Major, Hippias Minor, Ion, Laches, Lysis, Menexenus, Protagoras, Republic* 1. I take the *Lysis, Euthydemus,* and *Hippias Major* to be the latest of these (see the appendix below), falling between the *Gorgias* (which I take to be the only one of the earlier dialogues to precede this trio) and the *Meno,* which I take to mark the point of transition from the earlier to the middle dialogues. I group the first book of the *Republic* with the earlier dialogues: Socratic elenchus (which, as I argue in the appendix, is dropped in *Lysis, Euthydemus,* and *Hippias Major*) is practised there as vigorously as anywhere in the corpus.

(2) The middle dialogues (listed in probable chronological order): *Cratylus, Phaedo, Republic* 2–10, *Symposium, Phaedrus, Parmenides, Theaetetus.*

(3) The later dialogues (also in probable chronological order): *Timaeus, Critias, Sophist, Politicus, Philebus, Laws.*

[3] 'Our customary method' (*Rep.* 10, 596a5–7); 'the dialectical method' (*Rep.* 7, 533c7), which has been explained (533b2–3) as the only 'method which endeavours in every case to apprehend concerning each thing what it really is'.

cular purpose in a special context[4]), the 'Socrates' who speaks for Socrates
in Plato's earlier dialogues never uses this word[5] and never discusses his
method of investigation. He never troubles to say why his way of searching is the way to discover truth or even to say what this way of searching
is. He has no name for it. 'Elenchus' and the cognate verb, *elenchein* (to
refute, to examine critically, to censure), he uses to describe,[6] not to baptize,
what he does; only in modern times[7] has 'elenchus' become a proper name.
So the 'What is *F*?' question which Socrates pursues elenctically about
other things, he never poses about the elenchus, leaving us only his practice of it as our guide when we try to answer it ourselves. Lacking his
definition of it, ours can only be a hypothesis—a guess. And we may guess
wrongly.

I guessed wrongly twenty-five years ago in the account of the elenchus
I put into my *Introduction to the* Protagoras,[8] and so have others before or
since. Here is the one in the article 'Dialectic' by Roland Hall in the *Encyclopedia of Philosophy* (New York, 1967): 'The Socratic elenchus was
perhaps a refined form of the Zenonian paradoxes, a prolonged cross-
examination which refutes the opponent's original thesis by getting him to
draw from it, by means of questions and answers, a consequence that contradicts the thesis.' This comes close, but still makes three mistakes. Obviously wrong is the suggestion that Socrates gets the opponent to draw the
consequence that contradicts the thesis. It is Socrates who draws it; the
opponent has to be carried to it kicking and screaming. Less obviously and

---

[4] The 'methods' he has followed in working out the tripartite analysis of the soul (*Rep.* 4, 435d). Cf. also the description (without use of the word *methodos*) in *Phd.* 99d4–100b4 of the method he is to follow in the final argument for the immortality of the soul.

[5] The word *methodos*, used often in dialogues of the middle period and almost as often in those of the later period (see s.v. *methodos*, Leonard Brandwood, *A Word Index to Plato* (Leeds: Maney, 1976)), created by Plato (its first occurrence in preserved Greek is in the *Phd.*, 79e3, 97b6), is itself an expression of the intensity of its creator's new-found interest in method. It is important terminological coinage, strangely overlooked by Lewis Campbell in his discussion of 'Plato's Technicalities' (in *The* Sophistes *and* Politicus *of Plato* (Oxford: Oxford University Press, 1957), pp. xxiv ff.), which he locates primarily in the later dialogues.

[6] And this in great profusion. There are dozens of uses of the noun and the verb in Plato, a majority of them in the earlier dialogues, as a look at Brandwood, *A Word Index to Plato*, will show.

[7] Perhaps no earlier than its use for this purpose by George Grote in *Plato and the Other Companions of Socrates*, 1st edn. 3 vols., (London: Murray, 1865) (all my references to this work throughout this paper will be to vol. i of the 1st edn.) and by Lewis Campbell in his *The* Sophistes *and* Politicus *of Plato*. It was used for the same purpose by Henry Sidgwick soon after ('The Sophists', *Journal of Philology*, NS 8 (1872)), no doubt under the influence of Grote and Campbell, to whose work he refers.

[8] *Plato's* Protagoras, trans. Jowett, rev. M. Ostwald, ed. with introd. by G. Vlastos (Indianapolis: Bobbs-Merrill, 1956). I have revised some of the views I express in that introduction. Its most serious error is its misinterpretation of the elenchus (on which, see pp. 51–4 below) and, consequently, of the profession of ignorance.

more seriously wrong is the assimilation of the elenchus to Zeno's dialectic, from which it differs in a fundamental respect: Zeno's refutands are unasserted counterfactuals:

> *If* there are many things, they must be both infinitely many and finitely many.

> *If* there is motion, then the swiftest cannot overtake the slowest: Achilles will never catch up with the tortoise.

Socrates, on the other hand, as we shall see below, will not debate unasserted premisses—only those asserted categorically by his interlocutor, who is not allowed to answer 'contrary to his real opinion'.

A third mistake is the notion that the consequence which contradicts the thesis is drawn *from* that thesis, that is, deduced from it. The notion is an invention of Richard Robinson. In his *Plato's Earlier Dialectic*[9] Robinson had maintained that Plato 'habitually thought and wrote as if all elenchus consists in reducing the thesis to a self-contradiction' (28). If that were true, Socrates' procedure would have been as follows: when the answerer asserts p, Socrates would derive not-p either directly from p or else by deriving from p some further premisses which entail not-p—in either case deducing not-p from p 'without the aid of any extra premiss' (ibid.). The trouble with this picture is that what it pictures is not in our texts.[10] There are some thirty-nine elenctic arguments by Robinson's count in Plato's earlier dialogues (ibid. 24). Not one of them exhibits this pattern. The premisses from which Socrates deduces not-p generally do not include p; and even when they do, there are others in the premiss-set, elicited from the interlocutor without any reference to p and not deducible from it.

If Socrates thought he proved what, according to Robinson, Plato 'habitually wrote and thought' he did, Socrates would have believed he was producing the strongest possible proof of the falsehood of p: there can be no stronger proof of the falsehood of a thesis than to show that it entails its own negation. What Socrates in fact does in any given elenchus is convict p not of falsehood but of being a member of an inconsistent premiss-set; and to do this is not to show that p is false, but only that either p is false or that some or all of the premisses are false. The question then

---

[9] (1st edn. Ithaca, NY: 1941; 2nd edn. Oxford: Clarendon Press, 1953.) My references are to the latter. In spite of this and other mistakes, this is an admirable book, which served me as a model of exegesis in my earlier Platonic studies. See the tribute to it in my review of Harold Cherniss, *Collected Papers*, ed. L. Tarán, *American Journal of Philology*, 89 (1978), 537–43: 538.

[10] As pointed out by Paul Friedländer and Harold Cherniss at the time: for the references, and for my discussion of the textual evidence, cf. my review of Cherniss cited in the preceding note.

becomes how Socrates can claim, as I shall be arguing he does claim in 'standard elenchus',[11] to have proved that the refutand is false, when all he has established is the inconsistency of *p* with premises whose truth he has not undertaken to establish in that argument: they have entered the argument simply as propositions on which he and the interlocutor are agreed. This is *the* problem of the Socratic elenchus, and it is spirited away in the account given by Robinson in 1941 and 1951 and repeated in the *Encyclopedia* article in 1967.[12] I shall be returning to this problem in due course.

Let me then suggest a more defensible description:

> Socratic elenchus is a search for moral truth by adversary argument in which a thesis is debated only if asserted as the answerer's own belief, who is regarded as refuted if and only if the negation of his thesis is deduced[13] from his own beliefs.

Elenchus is first and last *search*. The adversary procedure which is suggested, but not entailed, by the Greek word—which *may* be used to mean 'refutation', but also 'testing', or still more broadly 'censure, reproach'—is not an end in itself. If it were, Socrates' dialectic as depicted in the earlier dialogues would be a form of verbal jousting—'eristic'[14]—which it is not,

---

[11] This term will be explained at the start of Sect. II below.

[12] And still being repeated: 'One of the commonest forms [of elenchus] is to argue that a given statement leads to a self-contradiction, in other words to two statements which are mutually contradictory' (G. B. Kerferd, *The Sophistic Movement* (Cambridge: Cambridge University Press, 1981), 65, with a footnote citing Robinson as authority).

[13] The intended force of the argument is deductive throughout; resort to *epagoge* is no exception, for in its Socratic use this is not true induction: see Vlastos, Introd. to *Plato's* Protagoras, p. xxix and nn. 18 and 45.

[14] As misconceived by G. Ryle in his description of 'the Socratic Method' (article on Plato in P. Edwards (ed.), *Encyclopedia of Philosophy* (New York: Macmillan and Free Press; London: Collier Macmillan, 1967), 317) and also in his *Plato's Progress* (Cambridge: Cambridge University Press, 1966), 119, where the elenctic arguments in Plato's earlier dialogues are represented as 'specimens of eristic contests'. The misconception is abetted by a blatant disregard of the 'say what you believe' requirement (to be discussed below), which is ignored even in the admirable essay by Paul Moraux, 'La Joute dialectique d'après *Topiques VIII*' (in G. E. L. Owen (ed.), *Aristotle on Dialectic* (Oxford: Oxford University Press, 1968), 277 ff.: 297–300)—an incomparably more exact discussion of the topic, which notes carefully some other points of difference between Socratic elenchi and Aristotle's 'dialectical jousts'. Similar disregard of that requirement accounts for other conflations of Socratic dialectic with eristic, beginning with G. Grote: he makes no mention of it in his discussion (*Plato and the Other Companions of Socrates*, 531) of 'the real contrast' between Socrates and the *outré* eristics in the *Euthydemus*. This is what makes it possible for him to say that in the *Protagoras* Socrates is 'decidedly more Eristic' than the sophist (ibid. 535): he is using 'eristic' with culpable looseness to mean 'contentious'. Contentiousness in argument is indeed one of Socrates' failings (for which Plato, in retrospect, gently reproaches him; *Tht.* 167d–168c). But in spite of such personal lapses on the part of its human instrument, elenchus remains in principle a method of searching for truth, which eristic is not, but only a method (or set of methods—a whole bag of tricks) for winning arguments, regardless of whether or not you take what you are arguing for to be true (cf. the excellent

because its object is always that positive outreach for truth which is expressed by words for searching (ἐρευνῶ, διερευνῶ), inquiring (ζητῶ, ἐρωτῶ, συνερωτῶ), investigating (σκοπῶ, διασκοπῶ, σκέπτομαι, διασκέπτομαι). This is what philosophy *is* for Socrates. When he thinks of being silenced by the civic authorities, he imagines them saying to him

(T1) ... you shall no longer engage in this search nor philosophize ... (*Ap.* 29c)

where the 'nor' is epexegetic. Equivalently, for Socrates to philosophize is to 'examine'—he searches by examining: were he to go to Hades, he says, he would go on

(T2) ... examining and searching there as I have been doing with people here. (*Ap.* 41b)

What is he searching for? For truth, certainly, but not for every sort of truth—only for truth in the moral domain. If we wanted to know what is the wholesale price of olive oil on the Piraeus market, Socrates would not propose that elenctic argument is the way to find out. Nor yet for, say,

What is the right diet for a patient with a fever?

What is the side of a square whose area is twice that of a given square?

What conditions must be satisfied by a true answer to a 'What is *F*?' question?

There is no reason to suppose that Socrates thinks that truths in the domain of the practical *technai* or of mathematics or of logic are to be ascertained by elenctic argument. He never says or implies anything of the kind. My last two examples are meant to be provocative. The mathematical one, of course, is from the interrogation of the slave boy in the *Meno*. In the 'Socrates' of this passage Plato has already taken a giant step—the doctrine of 'recollection'—in transforming the moralist of the earlier dialogues into the metaphysician of the middle ones. The interrogation is laid on to support that doctrine—to help Meno 'recollect' it (81e–82a).

description of it in Kerferd, *The Sophistic Movement*, 62–3, and *Euthd.* 272a–b, cited in n. 26 below), while for elenchus the aim of 'coming to know what is true and what is false' is paramount (*Grg.* 505e; cf. *Chrm.* 166c–d and also *Grg.* 458a, cited in n. 27 below). (For Aristotle's recognition of 'saying what one believes' in Socratic dialectic, see *Top.* 160ᵇ19–22: the answerer is not just 'maintaining a position for the sake of argument, but saying what he believes'; though Socrates is not named, the examples show that the reference is to Socrates' arguments with Callicles and Polus in the *Gorgias*.)

Elenchus is used to correct mistakes[15]—its proper, purely negative, use in philosophical dialect as conceived in Plato's middle dialogues[16]—but not to discover, still less prove, the proposition which constitutes the true solution to the problem.[17] As to the last example, it does, of course, refer to the unreconstructed Socrates of the earlier dialogues.[18] But note that he does not elicit from his interlocutors the logical conditions for the right answer to a 'What is *F*?' question: he produces them entirely on his own initiative, tells the interlocutors what they are, and requires them to comply, never inviting elenctic argument on whether or not they are the right conditions. Thus when he tells Laches that the definition of 'courage' must cover all of the agreed-upon cases of courageous conduct, he does not ask, 'Do you agree?' but only 'Do you understand?'[19] And this is generally true. The interlocutor is never shown as having dissenting views about the logical pattern to which a good definition should conform—views which need to be refuted by elenctic argument before the search can start. He is shown as all at sea on the topic, too confused to have any opinions at all, needing instruction on its very rudiments, which Socrates is only too willing to provide. He offers it encountering not opposition but incomprehension.[20] The logical truths governing definition, and the still more abstract ones,

---

[15] *Men.* 83b–e.

[16] *Phd.* 85c, 101d–e, 107b; *Rep.* 8, 534b–e.

[17] The method of discovery in this passage is not elenctic but maieutic (though the midwife metaphor is not used here, as it is not in any dialogue prior to the *Theaetetus*). The Socrates of this passage sees the boy getting the answer 'not by learning it from me' (82b), but by 'himself recovering knowledge from himself' (86d), which is what Socrates says of his interlocutors in the *Theaetetus*: they 'have learned nothing from me but have themselves discovered for themselves' the sought-for truth (150d6–7). I agree with Myles Burnyeat (see his 'Socratic Midwifery, Platonic Inspiration', *Bulletin of the Institute of Classical Studies* (University of London), 24 (1977), 7–15) that the midwife metaphor is a Platonic invention: his argument for this thesis I consider conclusive. I would also agree with him that midwifery and recollection are distinct metaphors which should not be conflated. Even so, they have in common the fundamental notion, expressed in each of the two texts I have cited, that the true propositions which are discovered in the interrogation of the interlocutor by Socrates *do not come from Socrates* but from the interlocutor ('recollected' by the latter in the *Meno*, 'brought forth' by him in the *Theaetetus*)—a notion which is not expressed or even hinted at in any of the earlier dialogues.

[18] *La.* 191e–192b; *Euthphr.* 5d, 6d–e, 11a6–b1; *Hp.Ma.* 287c ff.; *Men.* 72a6 ff. (Though this last passage occurs in a transitional dialogue, its place in that dialogue antecedes the introduction of the theory of recollection; paralleling closely the specifications which a correct definiens must meet in the *Euthyphro*—cf. *Men.* 72c6–d1 with *Euthphr.* 6d9–e6—that is, clearly, a faithful reproduction of the definitional doctrine of the earlier dialogues.)

[19] 191e11. Same question in *Men.* 72d1.

[20] Thus when Hippias says 'there is no difference' between 'What is the beautiful?' and 'What is beautiful?', he is not represented as propounding an erroneous doctrine which calls for refutation—only as exhibiting pitiful incapacity to understand the very meaning of those questions (287d–e).

like the principle of non-contradiction,[21] are never treated as elenctic theses.[22] Only moral truths are so treated.

For 'moral' Socrates has no special word. But neither does he have any difficulty indicating that what he is searching for is truth in the moral domain:

> (T3) Our argument is over no chance matter but over *what is the way we ought to live*. [The same phrase, in the identical words, in *Grg.* 500c3–4]. (*Rep.* 1, 352d)
>
> (T4) Of all inquiries, Callicles, this is the noblest—about those things on which you reproached me: *what sort of man should one be, and what should one practice* and up to what point, when he is young and when he is old. (*Grg.* 487e–488a)
>
> (T5) For the things we are disputing are hardly trivial, but, as one might say, those which to come to know is noblest and not to know most base. For their sum and substance is just this: knowing, or not knowing, *who is happy and who is not*. (*Grg.* 472c–d)

These are the questions Socrates attacks by the elenctic method, and he treats them as new questions, never investigated before by the right method, so that what the wise men of the past have or haven't said about them becomes a matter of indifference. When he is talking with you he wants to know your answer. If you quote some wise man's answer—as Polemarchus does in *Republic* 1—he will discuss it as your answer, expecting you to defend it as yours. That you do not yourself have high credentials will not trouble him. He may even count it an advantage. As a partner in the search he welcomes

> (T6) . . . anyone of you I happen to meet at any given time . . . (*Ap.* 29d)
>
> (T7) . . . anyone, young or old, citizen or foreigner. (*Ap.* 30a)

His is the aggressive outreach, the indiscriminate address to all and sundry, of the street evangelist. If you speak Greek and are willing to talk and reason, you can be Socrates' partner in searching, with the prospect that truth undisclosed in countless ages might be discovered here and now, on this spot, in the next forty minutes, between the two of you.

For success in this enterprise two constraints must be observed. The first is to refrain from speechifying, to give short, spare, direct, unevasive

---

[21] Thus Socrates never feels that he has to *argue* that when his interlocutors run into contradiction they suffer logical disaster. The principle of non-contradiction is never so much as stated (as it is in the middle dialogues: *Rep.* 4, 436e–437a), to say nothing of its being defended or justified.

[22] For the view that the conditions of a successful definition are not themselves subject to elenctic argument I am indebted directly to Paul Woodruff. See his excellent remarks on the dependence of 'definition-testing arguments' on 'key premises supplied by Socrates himself' which 'govern the form and content a definition must have to be acceptable . . . On which matter Socrates is an authority . . .' (*Plato:* Hippias Major (Oxford: Blackwell, 1982), 137–8).

answers to the questions put to you. In a cooperative endeavour for mutual enlightenment this is self-explanatory. Not so is the second—the 'say what you believe' constraint:

(T8) By the god of friendship, Callicles! Don't think that you can play games with me and answer whatever comes to your head, contrary to your real opinion (παρὰ τὰ δοκόῦντα) . . .[23] (Grg. 500b)

(T9) My good man, don't answer contrary to your real opinion (παρὰ δοξαν), so we may get somewhere.[24] (Rep. 1, 346a)

(T10) If you agree with these things, Crito, watch out that you are not doing so contrary to your real opinion (παρὰ δόξαν). (Cri. 49c–d)

To Protagoras, who had just said in reply to Socrates' question, 'But what does it matter? Let it be so for us (ἔστω ἡμῖν), if you wish', Socrates says:

(T11) I won't have this. For it isn't this 'if you wish' and 'if you think so' that I want to be refuted, but you and me. I say 'you and me' for I think that the thesis is best refuted if you take the 'if' out of it. (Prt. 331c)

Why should Socrates object to iffy theses? Hypothetical premises had always been legitimate not only in disputation, but even in the most stringent of all forms of argument as yet discovered in Greece: mathematical proof. It is standard in Greek geometry, where indirect proofs (as for example in Euclid 1. 5) employ an unasserted premiss, prefaced by the word Protagoras had just used: ἔστω, 'let this be so'. Zeno, whose dialectic had become classical by this time—Aristotle calls him 'the inventor of dialectic'[25]—had practised systematically the thing Socrates forbids: each of his paradoxes investigates the contradictory consequences of its counterfactual premiss. Why should Socrates ban this modality of philosophical argument? He doesn't say. I suggest he has three reasons.

First, to test honesty in argument. In eristic, where the prime object is to win,[26] one is free to say anything that will give one a debating advantage. In elenchus, where the prime object is to search for truth, one does

---

[23] Cf. also what he had said to Callicles earlier at 495a, and also Euthd. 286d, 'Dionysodorus, are you saying this for the sake of talking—to say something outrageous—or do you really believe that no human being is ignorant?'

[24] For the same requirement in the argument with Thrasymachus, see also 337c: here τὸ φαινόμενον in ἀποκρίνεσθαι τὸ φαινόμενον ἑαυτῷ replaces the more usual τὸ δοκοῦν or τὰ δοκοῦντα, and Socrates' apparent willingness to waive the rule at 340c1–2 is ironical, as is made clear by Socrates' reiterating the requirement at 350e5, though here again he resigns himself, as a pis aller, to Thrasymachus' saying he will ignore it.

[25] Diogenes Laertius 9. 25, and 29.

[26] Cf. the description of eristic sophia: 'prowess in verbal contest and in the refutation of whatever is said, regardless of whether it is false or true' (Euthd. 272a–b).

not have that option. One must say what one believes—that is, what one thinks true—even if it will lose one the debate.[27]

Second, to test one's seriousness in the pursuit of truth.[28] Seriousness can be feigned. One can put on a solemn face, a grave voice, shamming an earnestness one does not feel. But if one puts oneself on record as saying what one believes, one has given one's opinion the weight of one's life. Since people consider their opinions more expendable than their life, Socrates wants them to tie their opinions to their life as a pledge that what they say is what they mean.

A further reason comes from that other dimension of the elenchus to which I have made no allusion so far. It is highlighted in the *Apology* where Socrates' 'search' is, at the same time, a challenge to his fellows to change their life, to cease caring for money and reputation and not caring for what should be for everyone the most precious thing of all—what one is:

> (T12) ... and if one of you says ... he does care, I will not let him go nor leave him, but will question and examine and refute him; and if he seems to me not to have the virtue he says he has, I shall reproach him for undervaluing the things of greatest value and overvaluing trivial ones. (*Ap.* 29e)

Socrates is not always so inquisitorial and censorious. But those who know him best realize that the elenchus does have this existential dimension—that what it examines is not just propositions but lives. Says Nicias, an old acquaintance of Socrates, to Lysimachus, a new one:

> (T13) I don't think you realize that he who comes closest to Socrates in discussion, even if he should start discussing something else, will find himself unavoidably carried round and round in argument until he falls into giving an account of himself—of the way he is living now and the way he has lived in the past. And when he does, Socrates will not let him go until he has done a thorough job of sifting him. (*La.* 187e6–188a3)

Thus elenchus has a double objective: to discover how every human being ought to live *and* to test that single human being that is doing the answering—to find out if *he* is living as one ought to live. This is a two-in-one operation. Socrates does not provide for two types of elenchus—a philosophical one, searching for truth about the good life, and a therapeutic

---

[27] Socrates says to Gorgias: 'I am one of those who would gladly be refuted if what I say is not true', adding that if Gorgias does not share this sentiment, further debate would be pointless (458a–b).

[28] Note the connection Socrates sees between 'saying what you believe' and seriousness in argument at T8 above, which continues: 'Nor must you think of me as playing games. For you see what the argument is all about—and is there anything about which even a man of little sense could be more serious than about this: what is the way we ought to live' (*Grg.* 500b–c; cf. T3 above). The same connection of the rule with seriousness in argument is made at *Rep.* 1, 349a, and is implied in the remark to Dionysodorus quoted above, n. 23.

one, searching out the answerer's own life in the hope of bringing him to the truth. There is one elenchus and it must do both jobs, though one or the other will be to the fore in different phases of it. From this point of view, too, the 'say what you believe' rule makes sense. How could Socrates hope to get you to give, sooner or later, an account of your life, if he does not require you to state your personal opinion on the questions under debate?

This will also explain why on some occasions Socrates is willing to waive the rule. So, for example, when the interlocutor is losing the debate, sees disaster ahead, and tries to spare his battered ego further mauling by shifting from combatant to bystander. This happens to Protagoras shortly after the passage quoted as T11 above. By this time he has lost two arguments. At the start of the third this exchange ensues:

(T14) s. Do you believe that one who acts unjustly may act temperately in so acting?

PRT. Socrates, I would be ashamed to agree to that. But most people would agree.

s. Shall I address my argument to them, or to you?

PRT. Argue first against that view of the multitude, if you wish.

s. It makes no difference to me, provided you do the answering. For what I chiefly examine is the proposition. But the consequence may be that I the questioner and you the answerer will also be examined. (*Prt.* 333b8–c9)

When Protagoras was looking for the same kind of shelter earlier on by hedging his answer with 'if you wish', Socrates had blocked the move, indicating that Protagoras had already taken a stand and would be held to it: his ego was now on the line, as in elenchus it must, for otherwise Socrates would be left with a proposition detached from a person willing to predicate his life on it, and this Socrates would refuse, as in fact he did refuse at the time. Once that is settled, Socrates is willing to make concessions, as a *pis aller* and under protest, so that the argument may go on: Protagoras is allowed to save face by handing his part over to that faceless surrogate 'the multitude'. For the same reason Socrates lets the same thing happen again, and on a bigger scale, later in the dialogue, where Socrates directs his argument for the impossibility of acrasia to the same notional answerer, 'the multitude', dragging along Protagoras as a make-believe ally (352e ff.). At the end of that debate we see that Socrates takes the consequence to be that Protagoras has been 'examined' after all, compelled to confess that *his* thesis—not just that of the 'multitude'—has been shown to be 'impossible' (360e).

II

Because it is allowed the waywardness of impromptu debate, elenctic argument may take any number of different routes. But through its motley variations the following pattern, which I shall call[29] 'standard elenchus', is predominantly preserved:

(1) The interlocutor asserts a thesis which Socrates considers false and targets for refutation.
(2) Socrates secures agreement to further premisses, say q and r (each of which may stand for a conjunct of propositions).[30] The agreement is *ad hoc*: Socrates argues from q and r, but not to them.
(3) Socrates then argues, and the interlocutor agrees, that q and r entail *not-p*.
(4) Thereupon Socrates claims that *not-p* has been proved true, p false.

The main alternative to this pattern is 'indirect' elenchus—so called[31] because here the refutand may be used as a premiss in its own refutation, hence Socrates is not himself committed to the truth of the whole of the premiss-set from which he deduces the negation of the thesis. All he could reasonably claim to accomplish by this means is to expose contradiction within the interlocutor's premiss-set. To establish the falsehood of the thesis he must turn to standard elenchus.[32] Here, and here only, we con-

---

[29] Because it is Socrates' main instrument of philosophical research. With a single major exception (*Prt.* 352d–358a), it is the only form of argument he uses not merely to expose contradiction in his opponent's beliefs, but to establish substantive doctrines of his own, such as the following (the list is not meant to be exhaustive): that the just man will not harm enemies (*Rep.* 1, 335); that the just ruler rules not in his own interest but in that of his subjects (*Rep.* 1, 338c–347d); that justice is more profitable than injustice (*Rep.* 1, 347e–354a); that to teach men justice is *ipso facto* to make them just (*Grg.* 460a–c); that it is better to suffer wrong than to commit it and better to suffer deserved punishment than escape it (the great argument to be discussed below); that the good and the pleasant are not the same and pleasure should be pursued for the sake of the good, not vice versa (*Grg.* 494e–500a); that in matters of justice we should follow not 'the many' but 'the man who knows' (*Cri.* 47a–48a); that the poet versifies and the rhapsode recites by a kind of madness, not by craft (*Ion*); that piety and justice, temperance and wisdom are interentailing (*Prt.* 329e–333b); that pious action is god-loved because it is pious, not pious because it is god-loved (*Euthphr.* 9d–11a).

[30] I use two variables, though one would suffice, with a view to the special case, to be discussed below, where the interlocutor has the option of welshing on just one of the agreed-upon premisses.

[31] I follow Robinson's terminology (*Plato's Earlier Dialectic*, 22 ff.), ignoring those things in his discussion of 'indirect' elenchus (irrelevant to my main argument in this paper) with which I disagree.

[32] See e.g. how indirect elenchus is used to rough up Polemarchus, discrediting in his eyes the ultra-respectable definition of justice as 'rendering to each what is due' (*Rep.* 1, 331e) by showing that when joined to other admissions of his it has bizarre consequences (that 'in all things justice

front what I called earlier on 'the problem of the Socratic elenchus'. Here there can be no question of taking the aim of the elenchus to be only to show the interlocutor that *he* must consider his thesis false if he chooses to stick by his further admissions. So personal and contingent an outcome would not begin to satisfy Socrates' drive for universally valid results:

(T15) For I think that we should all be contentiously eager to come to know what is true and what is false about the things we assert; for it is a common good for all that this should be made evident. (*Grg.* 505e)

(T16) Or don't you think that it is a common good for practically all mankind that how each thing is should be made evident? (*Chrm.* 166d)

What Socrates must do—and what, I shall be arguing, he is convinced he does—is to prove *p* not just false *for the interlocutor*, but *false*. If he cannot hope to do this by standard elenchus, he cannot hope to do it at all.

My discussion of standard elenchus will focus on points (2) and (4). This is how I can best set in historiographic perspective the interpretation of the elenchus I am defending in this paper. At these two points I am departing sharply from each of the leading lines of past interpretation, represented respectively in the two works of nineteenth-century scholarship which are the landmark studies in the field: Eduard Zeller, *Philosophie der Griechen*,[33] and George Grote, *Plato and the Other Companions of Socrates*.[34] I am going against Zeller at point (2), against Grote at point (4). Since Grote's Socrates is incomparably more interesting than Zeller's and, in my view, much closer to the truth, I shall have more to say of the relation of my Socrates to Grote's than to Zeller's.

The claim I am making at point (2) is that the premises $\{q, r\}$ from which Socrates deduces that negation of the opponent's thesis are logically unsecured within the argument: no reason has been given to compel agreement to them. Socrates does, of course, have reasons for q and for r. But he does not bring them into the argument. He asks the interlocutor if he agrees, and if he gets agreement he goes on from there. So in elenctic argument the question of referring to some court of last appeal for settling philosophical disagreement does not arise. In particular there is no appeal

is useless in their use, useful when they are useless' (333d), that 'the just man is a kind of thief' (334a–b)), keeping standard elenchus in reserve until it is needed to establish the Socratic thesis that the just man will not harm enemies (335b–c). Similarly, Euthyphro's first definition is attacked by indirect elenchus (6e–8a), and standard elenchus is then brought in to prove the doctrine, so fundamental for Socrates' rational theology, that pious action is god-loved *because* it is pious (9d–11a).

[33] The volume entitled *Sokrates und die Sokratiker*, 5th edn. (Leipzig, 1922; repr. 1963). My references will be to the Eng. trans. of the 3rd German edn., by O. J. Reichel (repr. New York: Russell & Russell, 1962).

[34] Above, n. 7.

to what Aristotle takes to serve this purpose: none, on one hand, to those self-evident truths which are for Aristotle the foundation of all demonstrative argument;[35] and none, on the other, to what he calls τὰ ἔνδοξα—what is worthy of belief because it is believed 'by all or by most or by the wise'—which constitutes for Aristotle the foundation of dialectical argument.[36] Socrates spurns both. He never tells the interlocutor that he must grant *q* or *r* because they are self-evident truths nor yet because they are the most generally accepted opinion on the topic. To self-evidence there is no appeal at all by anyone in Plato's earlier dialogues.[37] To common belief, there is, but not by Socrates. It is Polus who appeals to it in the *Gorgias*, only to find Socrates rejecting it out of hand. When Polus says

(T17) Socrates, don't you think you've been refuted already when you say things with which no one would agree? Just ask any of these people here . . . (*Grg.* 473e)

Socrates stands on his previously expressed conviction that the only opinion which matters in an argument is that of the arguers themselves:

(T18) If I cannot produce one man—yourself—to witness to my assertions, I believe that I shall have accomplished nothing . . . Neither will you, I believe, if this one man—myself—does not witness for you, letting all those other people go.[38] (*Grg.* 472b–c)

---

[35] Demonstration (ἀπόδειξις) proceeds from premises which are 'primary' (πρώτων), i.e. induce conviction 'through themselves and not through some other things (τὰ μὴ δι' ἑτέρων ἀλλὰ δι' αὑτῶν ἔχοντα τὴν πίστιν) (*Top.* 100ᵃ27–b2; cf. *APo.* 64ᵇ34 ff., *Phys.* 193ᵃ4–6).

[36] The premises of dialectical reasoning are 'those which are believed by all or by most or by the wise and, of these, by all or by most or the most distinguished and most reputable' (*Top.* 100ᵃ29–ᵇ23).

[37] Norman Gulley appears to hold that there is *implicit* appeal to self-evidence: 'while the initial logical aim of the Socratic *elenchus* is to reveal a contradiction in a respondent's views, its further aim is to establish as the contradictory of the respondent's initial thesis a proposition presented as so obviously true that the respondent is driven to abandon his thesis' (*The Philosophy of Socrates* (London: Macmillan, 1968), 43–4). If this statement is taken at face value, it is surely false: thus in the *Gorgias* in each of Socrates' major arguments against Gorgias, Polus, and Callicles, the contradictory of their thesis is a paradox—not at all likely to strike the sponsor of the refutand as 'obviously true', no matter how it is 'presented' to him. Thus in Socrates' second argument against Polus the contradictory of Polus' thesis is that it is better to suffer injustice than to commit it and better to submit to punishment than to escape it; that Socrates should expect that his argument would make this proposition look 'obviously true' to Polus is unlikely, to say the least: after Socrates has 'proved' it, its immediate consequences (480a–d) still strike Polus as 'outrageous' (ἄτοπα; 480e1). If we revise the claim (as we probably should in the light of other things Gulley says on pp. 42–3), taking it to mean that when the interlocutor is confronted with the inconsistency of his thesis with the agreed-upon premises the latter will strike him as more 'obviously true' than the former, the claim, though more plausible, is still unacceptable: the obviousness of one or more of the premises is irrelevant to the logic of the argument. Socrates does not argue, 'concede that your thesis is false because the agreed-upon premises are more "obviously true" than it'; even if those premises *were* obvious, their obviousness would not be a premiss in the argument.

[38] For Socrates' rejection of the appeal to common opinion, see also *La.* 184e, *Cri.* 46d–47d.

At this point the Socrates of Plato's earlier dialogues is at loggerheads with Xenophon's:

(T19) Whenever Socrates himself argued something out he proceeded from the most generally accepted opinions (διὰ τῶν μάλιστα ὁμολογουμένων), believing that security in argument lies therein. Accordingly, whenever he argued he got much greater assent from his hearers than anyone I have ever known. And he said that Homer made Odysseus 'the safe speaker' [*Od*. 8. 171] because he was able to conduct his arguments from what is believed by mankind (διὰ τῶν δοκούντων τοῖς ἀνθρώποις).[39] (*Mem*. 4. 6. 15)

If we were to believe this, what would we do with those doctrines of the Socrates of Plato's earlier dialogues that go dead against 'the most generally accepted opinions' of his time and shock its common sense: that it is better to suffer injustice than to commit it; what one should never harm one's enemy, never return evil for evil; that happiness is not the reward for virtue, but virtue itself; that virtue and knowledge are the same so that to known the good and fail to do it is impossible? And what would we do with the profession of ignorance?[40] If Socrates had 'proceeded from the most generally accepted opinions whenever he argued something out' he could

---

[39] Since what Xenophon is calling here 'the most generally accepted opinions' and 'what is believed by mankind' is the very thing Aristotle would call τὰ ἔνδοξα, Socrates' philosophical method, as understood by Xenophon, would be congruent with the method which Aristotle *contrasts* with the Socratic. He says that the accomplished dialectician will argue not only (*a*) 'peirastically', keeping within the questioner's role in argument, content to do no more than 'exact an account' (λόγον λαβεῖν) from his interlocutor, without expounding and defending positive views of his own, but also (*b*) 'as one who knows' (ὡς εἰδώς), going into the answerer's role, 'rendering an account' (λόγον ὑπέχοντες) to 'defend a thesis (φυλάξωμεν τὴν θέσιν) from the most generally accepted views' (δι' ἐνδοξοτάτων) (*SE* 183[b]2–6: he is recalling the distinction he had established between διαλεκτικοί and πειραστικοί λόγοι in the opening paragraphs of the treatise, 165[b]3–6). It is at just this point that he makes his famous reference to Socrates: 'and this is why [i.e. because he adhered to role (*a*)] Socrates put questions and gave no replies; for he confessed that he had no knowledge' (*SE*. 183[b]7–8). Thus Xenophon's Socrates is at loggerheads with Aristotle's no less than with Plato's. Xenophon's Socrates would be doing regularly (and does frequently in the *Memorabilia*) what Aristotle does not represent Socrates as doing at all. (Aristotle need not be understood as denying to Socrates the willingness, often attested in Plato (*Prt*. 336c, 338c–d; *Grg*. 449b, 462a–b, 504c), to 'reply', no less than 'ask'. He is content to ignore this in the present, all too brief, allusion to Socrates, probably because he had failed to understand (as have so many others after him) that Socrates *could* vindicate positive theses of his own in adversary argument *without* welshing on his confession of ignorance and *without* invoking *endoxa* as a court of last resort.)

[40] I am not suggesting that there is some obviously true interpretation of this extremely perplexing feature of Socrates' thought (which I reserve for separate discussion in a later paper). [*Editor's note*: This later paper appears in this volume as Ch. II.] But it is certainly Socratic, attested not only by Plato and Aristotle but by many other creditable witnesses—in fact by all of our ancient authorities who address the question. Hence no interpretation of the elenchus will stand if it cannot be sustained in full consistency with his profession of ignorance. I count it a merit of the present interpretation that it is both logically and textually independent of my particular interpretation of the profession of ignorance, but is none the less perfectly consistent with the latter—indeed, provides the foundation for it.

not have argued for those paradoxes,[41] nor could he have professed to
know nothing—as he, in fact, does not in Xenophon: in Xenophon's
Socrates there is no profession of ignorance, no interdict on harming the
enemy,[42] and the identity of virtue with happiness and of knowledge with
virtue are blurred and flattened out—the paradoxes become commonplaces. So at point (2) of my account of the elenchus the conflict between
Plato's testimony and Xenophon's is unnegotiable, and the gravest fault
in Zeller, great historian though he was, is that he fudged an issue[43]
which called for a firm decision for one of his two major sources against
the other. He thereby bequeathed to the historians that followed him—
most recently Guthrie[44]—an impossible reconciliation of irreconcilable
data. To accept, as Zeller did, Xenophon's description of Socrates' method
of argument in T19 above,[45] is fatal to the elenchus. And so we see in Zeller,
and now again in Guthrie, the elenchus disappear without a trace.[46] It is
not argued out of their account of Socrates' philosophical method. It just
drops out.

[41] That Socrates uses endoxic premisses for all they are worth should go without saying. But
without *some* contra-endoxic premisses how could he hope to get contra-endoxic conclusions?
Consider *Rep.* 1, 335b–c, arguing by standard elenchus for a thesis (cf. above, n. 32) which goes
against the grain of Greek morality where doing evil to one's enemies is on a par with doing
good to one's friends ('belongs to the same character' (τοῦ αὐτοῦ ἤθους; *Top.* 113ª3–4), says Aristotle, the same *admirable* (ἐπιεικοῦς; 113ª13) character); and doing good to friends is a star
endoxon (*Top.* 104ª22). The argument starts with *endoxa*—when horses (or dogs) are harmed
they are made worse in respect of equine (or canine) excellence—and then moves by analogy
to the premiss that when men are harmed *they* are made worse in respect of their 'human excellence'—which would be as counter-intuitive for the Greeks as it would be for us (does stealing
a man's wallet make him 'worse in respect of human excellence'?). Equally contra-endoxic is
the next premiss, that 'justice is human excellence', if understood to mean (as it must for the
purposes of the argument) that justice is not merely *a*, but *the* human excellence.
[42] Quite the opposite: Xenophon's Socrates explicitly endorses the traditional view (*Mem.* 2.
6. 35).
[43] By a curious sort of inadvertence: nowhere in his book is there a sign of his even having
noticed this conflict, nor yet the conflict between Aristotle and Xenophon on the same issue
(above, n. 39).
[44] W. K. C. Guthrie, *A History of Greek Philosophy*, iii: *The Fifth Century Enlightenment*, and
iv: *Plato: The Earlier Period* (Cambridge: Cambridge University Press, 1969, 1975). Certified by
the Cambridge imprint, this is now the standard reference work throughout the world for all
non-specialists and, often enough, for specialists as well.
[45] Zeller quotes it without dissent and takes Socrates' philosophical method to consist
in 'deducing conceptions from the common opinions of men' (*Sokrates und die Sokratiker*,
121–2).
[46] No discussion whatever of elenchus by Zeller, ibid., ch. iv ('The Philosophical Method of
Socrates') or Guthrie, *A History of Greek Philosophy*, iii. 425–9, and iv, *passim*. The disappear-
ance is more surprising in Guthrie since he, unlike Zeller, takes Plato to be 'the chief, and
Xenophon only an auxiliary source of knowledge of Socrates as a philosopher' (iii. 350) and
since, moreover, the two major studies of Socrates' method of enquiry that had appeared in
English during Guthrie's lifetime—Robinson's in 1941 and 1951, Gulley's in 1968 (nine years
before the publication of vol. iv of Guthrie's *History*) had put the elenchus at the centre of their
interpretation of Socrates.

III

Now for point (4) in my analysis of standard elenchus: the most novel of my proposals.[47] I must begin with the position I had reached in earlier Socratic studies—the extreme opposite of the view I wish to defend now. Explicitly in that brief introduction to the Protagoras of 1956 to which I alluded above[48] and implicitly in an essay 'The Paradox of Socrates', written around the same time,[49] I had maintained that Socrates never meant to go beyond (3) in his elenctic arguments—that their object was simply to reveal to his interlocutors muddles and inconsistencies within themselves, jarring their adherence to some confident dogma by bringing to their awareness its collision with other, no less confident, presumptions of theirs.[50] This interpretation had a mighty precedent in the work of that great Victorian student of Greek antiquity, whose multi-volume *History of Greece* (1851) and three-volume *Plato* (1865) are, in my opinion, still, all in all, the finest contributions ever made in any language to their respective themes. Unlike Zeller, Grote saw with the utmost clarity how central was the elenchus to Socratic enquiry as depicted in Plato's earlier dialogues, how central it had to remain in our picture of

[47] My interpretation of standard elenchus, taken as a whole, and applied rigorously, conceived as the only rational support Socrates offers his moral doctrines, has no clear precedent in the scholarly literature, to my knowledge. Its affinities are with views like those of Norman Gulley (*The Philosophy of Socrates*, 37 ff.) and Terence Irwin (*Plato's Moral Theory* (Oxford: Oxford University Press, 1977), 37 ff.; *Plato: Gorgias* (Oxford: Oxford University Press, 1979), *passim*), which also recognize that the elenchus has positive, no less than negative, thrust, aiming to bring argumentative support to Socrates' affirmative views. One of my differences with Gulley has been noticed above. My main difference with Irwin arises over his view that 'not all [of Socrates'] positive doctrines rely on the elenchus; some rely on the analogy between virtue and craft' (*Plato's Moral Theory*, 37). I see no sound reason for putting this analogy outside of the elenchus; all of the arguments which draw conclusions from that analogy are pure elenctic arguments. A further disagreement arises over alleged constraints which, according to Irwin, Socrates 'normally' imposes on what the interlocutor can or can't say in arguing against him ('normally the interlocutor is not allowed this freedom [to reject counter-examples which refute his definition]'; *Plato's Moral Theory*, 39). The textual evidence appears to be that Socrates *always* allows—indeed requires—the interlocutor to say anything he believes, if he believes it.

[48] n. 8.

[49] *Queen's Quarterly*, 64 (1957), 496–516; repr. in G. Vlastos (ed.), *The Philosophy of Socrates* (New York: Doubleday, 1971).

[50] This is Plato's picture of 'the sophist of noble lineage' in *Sph*. 230a–e, whose service to his interlocutors is simply therapy ('purgation') by enhanced self-knowledge: their dogmatism is battered as they are made aware of conflicts within their own system of beliefs (the identification with Socrates is tightened up in the back-reference to the passage at 268b–c: 'we set him down as having no knowledge'); it should be noted that nothing is said to make this 'purgative' art a sub-division of eristic, *pace* Lewis Campbell ('*The* Sophistes *and* Politicus *of Plato*', 191) and others: see F. M. Cornford, *Plato's Theory of Knowledge* (London: Routledge, 1935), 177–82. No one would doubt that this is an authentic, if partial, representation of Socrates: this is the Socrates who destroys the conceit of wisdom (*Ap*. 21b–23b). But Plato never says this is all Socrates was, as he would have been, if the account of the elenchus I have given at that time were correct.

Socrates if we were to put any faith at all in Plato's testimony, and how valuable a contribution to human thought its relentless polemic against dogmatism would be, even if it were only the negative instrument Grote thought it.[51]

So while that picture of Socrates in my earlier work was very much a minority view, it did not put me in bad intellectual company, and its foundation in Plato's depiction of elenctic argument in his earlier dialogues seemed secure: how could Plato be telling us, I used to ask myself, that his Socrates undertakes to prove to his interlocutors that their theses were false and his true, if all he shows Socrates doing is proving the inconsistency of his interlocutors' theses with other, unargued-for, concessions of theirs? But neither was that picture trouble-free. It left me with this question: if that were all Socrates had expected of the elenchus—exposure of inconsistencies in his interlocutors—where did he find positive support for those strong doctrines of his on whose truth he based his life? If the elenchus, his only line of argument, gave those doctrines no rational grounding, what did? Grote had not been troubled by that question because he found it possible to believe that Socrates' own positive convictions and his critical assaults on those of others ran on separate tracks: 'the negative cross-examination and the affirmative dogmatism are two unconnected operations of thought; the one does not lead to, or involve, or verify the other' (*Plato*, i. 292). I could not. I could not reconcile myself to Grote's missionary of the examined life, who was a dogmatist himself. And there were certainly textual grounds too for uneasiness with the picture, as critics started pointing out.[52] So I began to lose my enthusiasm for it. But it is one thing to become disgruntled with a picture, quite another to liberate oneself from it by discovering the textual evidence that destroys the picture. That evidence I could not get from my critics because they did not have it themselves. I had to discover it for myself.

The crucial text is

(T20) Has it not been proved (ἀποδέδεικται) that what was asserted [by myself] is true? (*Grg.* 479e)

Here Socrates says in so many words that he has done what Grote and I had maintained he never did in an elenctic argument: he says he has 'proved' his thesis true. Grote had certainly gone over that sentence in the *Gorgias* many times, and so had I, and so had scores of others. But it had

---

not hit anyone between the eyes.[53] Let us see what it means when read in its own context.

The argument starts half a dozen Stephanus pages back, where Socrates presses the question: if one were forced to choose between inflicting injustice on another person and suffering it oneself, which would be the better choice—the better for oneself, the chooser? Polus takes the first option. His thesis is

(p) To commit injustice is better than to suffer it.

Socrates defends what he takes to be the logical contradictory,

(not-p) To suffer injustice is better than to commit it.

Attacking in standard elenctic fashion, he gets Polus to agree to a flock of further premises, only one of which need be recalled here:

(q) To commit injustice is baser ($α\overset{\prime}{\iota}σχιον$) than to suffer it,

while all the rest can be bundled up in a single gather-all conjunct r, whose contents need not concern us. Socrates argues, and Polus agrees, that q and r entail not-p. When this result is reached, Socrates tells Polus, in the words I just cited, that the Socratic thesis, not-p, has been 'proved' true, that is, that p has been proved not just inconsistent with q and r, as it of course has, but proved false.[54]

Why had Socrates' perfectly clear-cut words in T20 been ignored? Why had I ignored them myself? Because I had scaled them down, even while reading them, discounting them as a careless overstatement. I would not have done so if I had noticed that it is not only here, in the last gasps of the debate, that Socrates claims he can prove not-p true: he makes the very same claim in different words several pages back, at the start of the debate. Recall what he had told Polus in T18 above: 'If I cannot produce one man—yourself—to witness to my assertions, I believe that I shall have accomplished nothing . . .'. Conceding that 'almost all men would agree with you, Athenians and foreigners' (472a), he had declared

---

[53] There is no comment on it in Dodds's or Irwin's commentary, and no reference to it in Gulley, though it should have been a star text for all three.

[54] Socrates' other two descriptions of the result (*Grg.* 479c4–5, 480b2–5) go no further than pointing out the demonstrated inconsistency between Polus' thesis and the premises to which he has agreed. (The reader should bear in mind that throughout this paper I set aside all questions relating to the logical validity of the arguments by which Socrates undertakes to refute his opponents' theses in specific elenchi. For this whole aspect of Socratic dialectic I would refer to G. Santas, *Socrates* (London: Routledge, 1979), with whose detailed analyses of Socratic arguments I find myself in very substantial agreement.)

(T21) But I, a single man, do not agree; for *you do not compel me*, but produce a multitude of false witnesses against me, trying to drive me from my property, the truth (ἐκ τῆς οὐσίας καὶ τοῦ ἀληθοῦς). (*Grg.* 472b)

How do you 'compel' your adversary to affirm what he denies? In an argument your only means of compulsion are logical. *So to compel Polus to 'witness' for not-p Socrates would have to give Polus a logically compelling proof that p is false.* Thus already in 472b, seven Stephanus pages before asserting at T20 above that he has 'proved' his thesis true, Socrates is announcing that this is exactly what he is going to do. So when he says at T20 that he has done it, this can't be a slip. Thus, *pace* Grote, ex-Vlastos, and who knows how many others, there can be no doubt that this long argument against Polus, elenchus in its standard form, which in point of logic has done no more than demonstrate inconsistency within the premissset $\{p, q, r\}$, Socrates takes to prove that p is false, not-p true. And in one of his statements we see him claiming by implication that he can do the same in all of his elenctic arguments against all comers:

(T22) But I know how to produce one witness to my assertions: the man against whom I am arguing. (*Grg.* 474a5–6)

The claim he makes here is perfectly general: whenever he is arguing elenctically with anyone against any thesis in the domain of morals, Socrates 'knows' how to make his adversary 'witness' to its contradictory: that is how to prove to him by elenctic argument that his thesis is false.

This brings us smack up against what I had called, near the start of this essay, '*the* problem of the Socratic elenchus': how is it that Socrates claims to have proved a thesis false when, in point of logic, all he has proved in any given argument is that the thesis is inconsistent with the conjunction of agreed-upon premises for which no reason has been given in that argument? Could he be blind to the fact that logic does not warrant the claim? Let me frame the question in the terms of the metaphor that runs through the passage: compelling a witness to testify against himself. Suppose the following were to happen: a witness gives testimony p on his own initiative and then, under prodding from the prosecuting attorney, concedes q and r, whereupon the attorney points out to him that q and r entail not-p, and the witness agrees that they do. Has he then been compelled to testify that p is false? He has not. Confronted with the conflict in his testimony, it is still up to him to decide which of the conflicting statements he wants to retract. So Polus, if he had had his wits about him, might have retorted: 'I see the inconsistency in what I have conceded, and I must do something to clean up the mess. But I don't have to do it your way. I don't have to concede that p is false. I have other options. For example, I could decide that p is true and q is false. Nothing you have proved denies me this alternative.'

And why shouldn't Polus in that crunch decide to throw q instead of p to the lions? How strongly he believes in p we have already seen: he thinks it absurd of Socrates to deny it when almost all the world affirms it.[55] For q, on the other hand, he has no enthusiasm. He may have conceded it only, as Callicles observes later, 'because he had been ashamed to say what was in his mind' (*Grg.* 482e2). Why shouldn't Polus then jettison q with the feeling 'good riddance'? He would then have come out of the elenchus believing that doing injustice is better and *nobler* than suffering it; his latter state would have been worse than the first. Couldn't this always happen? Whenever Socrates proved to his interlocutors that the premisses they had conceded entailed the negation of their thesis, why couldn't they hang on to their thesis by welshing on one of the conceded premisses? Surely Socrates would be aware of this ever-present possibility. Why then is he not worried by it? Because, I submit, he believes that if that wrong choice were made he would have the resources with which to recoup the loss in a further elenchus. This, I am suggesting, is his general view: if you disappointed him by denying q instead of p, he would be confident that he could start all over again and find other premisses inside your belief system to show you that you haven't got rid of the trouble—that if you keep p, it will go on making trouble for you, conflicting as much with these other premisses as it did with q and r before. Can it be shown from the text that Socrates has this confidence? I want to argue that it can.

For a start let us observe what happens in the *Gorgias*: there Callicles enacts the part Polus might have played if he had chosen to retract q instead of p. Polus was worsted in the argument, says Callicles, only because he had conceded q, which he should not have done, and would not have done if he had been less squeamish: if he had had the fortitude to admit that to do injustice is nobler than to suffer it, he would have escaped unscathed (482d7–e2). Is Socrates stymied when that happens? Not on your life. He sheds no tears over the loss of q. He extracts a new premiss-set from Callicles and, sure enough, this new set contains all the premisses Socrates needs to deduce not-p all over again. But what if a super-Callicles should arise to repudiate those new premisses from which Socrates derived not-p? Is there evidence that Socrates would not be fazed even then, or even by a super-super-Callicles after him? Does our text attest Socrates' belief that no flesh-and-blood antagonist will ever turn up without always carrying along, in his own system of belief, a baggage of premisses from which he can be 'compelled' to 'testify' against p? I want to argue that it does so in two remarks which, taken in conjunction, yield clear evidence that Socrates believes this very thing.

The first is one of the things he says to Polus before their argument begins:

> (T23) . . . I believe that I and you and the rest of mankind believe that committing injustice is worse than suffering it . . . (*Grg.* 474b)

What in the world could Socrates mean by saying that Polus and the multitudes who agree with Polus 'believe' the opposite of what they assert? There is one—and, so far as I can seen, only one—way of making sense of the remark: we must understand Socrates to be using 'believe' in that marginal sense of the word in which we may all be said to 'believe' innumerable things that have never entered our heads but are none the less *entailed* by what we believe in the common or garden use of the word. Let me call the latter 'overt', the former 'covert', belief.[56] Thus, if I believe overtly that Mary is John's sister and that John is Bill's grandfather, I may be said to believe covertly that Mary is Bill's great-aunt, even if I have never thought of that fact—indeed, even if I do not have a word for 'great-aunt' in my vocabulary. Or, to take a less trivial example, if I believe that a given figure is a Euclidean triangle, then I believe covertly the proposition which is so surprising when we first learn it in geometry, that the figure's interior angles sum to two right angles. Here then is something Socrates might wish to express by saying that Polus & Co. 'believe' not-p, even while they insist that p is what they do believe—namely, that they have certain beliefs (of the ordinary, overt sort) which entail not-p. This gives us a lucid sense for what Socrates might be saying in our text: he is not declining to take Polus & Co. at their word when they insist that p is what they believe; taking their word for this he is telling them that along with their (overt) belief in p they have also certain other (overt) beliefs which entail not-p: in this sense they do (covertly) believe not-p.[57]

---

[56] This terminology was suggested to me by David Gauthier. Alternatively, we might speak of 'explicit' and 'tacit' belief.

[57] Cf. *Ion* 539e: to Ion, who had just said that it pertains to the rhapsode's art to judge *all* passages in Homer, including those which depict the work of different craftsmen, Socrates replies, 'Surely you do not say "all"', Ion (οὐ σύ γε φής, ὦ Ἴων, ἅπαντα). Or are you so forgetful?' The reference is to 538b, where Ion had conceded that the rhapsode's art is different from the charioteer's and, further, that if it is a different art, it is knowledge of different things. Taking admissions *q* and *r* to entail not-*p*, Socrates feels entitled to tell Ion at 539e that he 'says' not-*p*, in the face of the fact that Ion says *p*. He does the same thing to Callicles by prolepsis at *Grg.* 495e: anticipating that Callicles will make admissions which entail the negation of the identity of the pleasant with the good (on which Callicles is 'insisting'; 495b8), Socrates feels entitled to declare that 'Callicles does not agree with [that identity] when he shall take the right view of himself'.

Now consider what Socrates says to Callicles in part (*b*) of the little speech that forms the curtain-raiser to their debate:

(T24) (*a*) ... don't be astonished that I should say these things [which he has been upholding against Polus]. My love, philosophy, is the one you must stop from asserting them. It is she, my friend, who asserts these things you hear from me, and she is much less unstable than are other loves. For the love of Callicles says now one thing now another, while philosophy always says the same thing ...

     (*b*) So you must either refute her saying those very things that I was saying—that to commit injustice and to do it with impunity is the greatest of evils—or, if you leave this unrefuted, then, by the dog, god of Egypt, *Callicles will disagree with you, Callicles,* and *will dissent from you your whole life long.* (*Grg.* 482a–b)

What could Socrates mean by saying that if Callicles cannot refute the Socratic thesis then, in spite of his scornful rejection of it, it will remain in him as a source of lifelong internal dissension? How will it remain in him at all, if he repudiates it absolutely? Surely, in the same way in which Polus is said in the preceding text to 'believe' the thesis he repudiates: in virtue of believing certain other things which, unbeknown to him, entail that thesis. Thus Callicles is being told that if he cannot refute the Socratic thesis (and he is not being encouraged to think he can), he will *always*—his 'whole life long'—believe propositions which entail it. Here we have conclusive evidence for what I suggested above: Socrates is convinced that when he shows his interlocutors the inconsistency of their thesis with the conjunction of premises to which they have agreed, they will *never* succeed in saving their thesis by retracting conceded premises: if they try to save it in this way, they will be bound to fail; fail they must, if regardless of which conceded premises they choose to retract, there will *always* be others in their belief system which entail the Socratic thesis.

Socrates then is making a tremendous assumption. Stated in fullest generality, it comes to this:

(A) Anyone who ever has a false moral belief will always have at the same time true[58] beliefs entailing the negation of that false belief.

That he is counting on the truth of this proposition is implied unambiguously if we assume—as we surely may—that what Socrates is saying at T24(*b*) he would also say about any of the theses he refutes in elenctic

---

[58] At this point the formulation of assumption A in the abstract published in the *Journal of Philosophy* (cf. above, n. 1) is amended by the addition of the word 'true'. This is required to block an unintended consequence of the unamended formula, drawn to my attention by Richard Kraut's interpretation of that formula.

arguments. We could not have derived this result from T23 just by itself. For while this shows Socrates' assurance that 'Polus and the rest of mankind' who have the false belief *p* none the less have true beliefs entailing its negation, it does not show that Socrates is convinced that they will *always* have such beliefs. That this is his conviction becomes entirely clear in T24(*b*). But it shows up also, though less saliently, in T22 and its associated texts, T18 and T21. For why should Socrates come to his elenctic arguments confident that he can produce as 'witnesses' for his own thesis those very persons who deny it, unless he were assuming that if his thesis is true those who assert its contradictory are always harbouring true beliefs which countermand their denial of his thesis?

If this is what Socrates assumes, why does he not argue for it? Because A is a meta-elenctic statement.[59] To support it Socrates would have to engage in meta-elenctic enquiry. And this, as I indicated in the opening paragraph of this paper, Socrates never does in Plato's earlier dialogues. In every one of them prior to the *Meno* Socrates maintains epistemological innocence, methodological naïvety. He assumes he has the right method to search for moral truth, but never attempts to justify that assumption. *A fortiori* he never attempts to justify the assumption on which his confidence in the constructive efficacy of the method is predicated. This is not to say that the assumption is arbitrary. He does have a reason for it. A proves true in his own experience. It never fails. Every time he tangles with people who defend a thesis he considers false and he looks for true premises among their own beliefs from which he can deduce its negation the needed premises are in place: they are always where they should be if A is true. So he has this purely inductive evidence for the truth of A.

Here we come within sight of the solution of 'the problem of the elenchus'. To reach it we need only note that from assumption A Socrates could infer with certainty that any set of moral beliefs which was internally consistent would consist exclusively of *true* beliefs; for if it contained even a single false belief, then, given A, it would contain beliefs entailing the negation of that false belief. We know how highly Socrates prizes the

---

[59] That is why I ignored it in my account of standard elenchus at the start of Sect. II above. It *should* be ignored in the analysis of the logical structure of any given elenctic argument. A is not a premiss in the argument, nor does Socrates ever suggest that it is. The remarks from which I have teased it out are *obiter dicta*. The interlocutor would be perfectly justified if he were to ignore them as pure Socratic bluster: he has been given no reason why *he* should think them true. That is why A has been brought in only to explain *why Socrates himself believes* that to prove the inconsistency of the thesis with the agreed-upon premisses is *ipso facto* to prove that, if the thesis is false, no one can affirm it without generating contradiction within his own system of belief.

consistency of his own set of moral beliefs. The self-consistency of his own position is the only reason he gives Callicles for identifying his own theses—so presumptuously it would seem—with those of 'philosophy': she 'always says the same'; by implication, so does Socrates too.[60] At the conclusion of that speech to Callicles he elevates consistency to a supreme desideratum in his own search for truth:

> (T25) As for myself, I would rather that my lyre were out of tune, or a choir I was training, and that the greater part of mankind should dissent from me and contradict me, than that I should be out of tune with my own single self and contradict myself. (*Grg.* 482b7–c3)

For years he has been striving for just this, constantly exposing the consistency of his beliefs to elenctic challenge, ready to root out any belief, however attractive in itself, which if allowed to stand would disturb the coherence of the system as a whole. So this is where he now finds himself after all those years of searching: of all the sets of moral beliefs competing for acceptance in elenctic argument, only one has shown up in his own experience that meets this desideratum—his own. All others, when tested for consistency, have failed. So he has evidence—as before, inductive evidence[61]—for a further assumption,

> (B) The set of moral beliefs held by Socrates at any given time is consistent.

---

[60] Cf. also *Grg.* 490e10–11: Socrates assures Callicles that he, unlike Callicles, always says 'the same things about the same things'. No one should be misled by his retrospective remark at the dialogue's end (527d): 'we never think the same about the same things'. As Dodds (*Plato: Gorgias*) remarks ad loc., 'this reproach applies of course to Callicles only, but Socrates politely includes himself'. For similar use of the first-person plural—'we' ironically substituted for 'you'—cf. *Euthphr.* 15c8–9: 'Either we were wrong when we agreed before, or, if we were right then, we are wrong now' (as the context shows, 'we' in its last occurrence refers exclusively to Euthyphro); *Chrm.* 175b6–7: 'We have admitted that there is knowledge of knowledge, although the argument said "No" ' (it had been Critias who argued for 'knowledge of knowledge'; it was Socrates who produced the 'argument that said "No" '); *La.* 194c: 'Come, Nicias, and, if you can, rescue your friends who are storm-tossed by the argument' (only Laches had been 'storm-tossed'; Socrates, sailing very smoothly, had rebutted each of Laches' definitions). The irony in *Grg.* 527d is transparent: Callicles had been convicted of numerous inconsistencies, Socrates of not even one.

[61] The consistency of the set is being inferred from its track record in Socrates' own experience: in all of the elenctic arguments in which he has engaged his set has never been faulted for inconsistency—a very chancy inference: the results of elenctic argument are powerfully affected by the argumentative skill of the contestants; since that of Socrates vastly exceeds that of his interlocutors, he is more effective in spotting beliefs of theirs which entail the negation of their theses than are they when trying to do the same to him; so his undefeated record need not show that his belief-set is consistent; it may only show that its inconsistencies have defied the power of his adversaries to ferret them out. Socrates could hardly have been unaware of this unavoidable hazard in his method. This must contribute to the sense of its fallibility which, I believe, is the right clue to his profession of ignorance.

And, as has just been shown, B in conjunction with A entails that Socrates' belief-set consists exclusively of true beliefs.

This last move yields the missing piece required for the solution of 'the problem of the elenchus'. The puzzle arises over Socrates' claim at (4) in the above analysis of standard elenchus: when he has shown that not-*p* follows from *q* and *r*, whose truth his argument has done absolutely nothing to support, why should he want to claim that through his argument not-*p* 'has been proved true'? What makes him think it has? The answer is in assumptions A and B, which entail

(C) The set of moral beliefs held by Socrates at any given time is true,

from which it follows that *q* and *r* are true, since Socrates has agreed to them. Hence Socrates would feel justified in making the claim at (4): to show that a proposition follows from premises which are true *is* to prove that proposition true.

Imagine now Plato writing Socratic dialogues with *his* mind full of epistemological worries. Under the influence of a certain Cratylus he had become convinced that there can be no knowledge of the sensible world because it is all in flux,[62] and this has left him wondering how there could be any knowledge of anything at all. The Socrates he brings to life in dialogue after dialogue, disclaiming *he* has knowledge, none the less searches indefatigably for moral truth, confident that it is findable, and in the most unlikely of all places—in the minds of those misguided, confused, wrongheaded people whose souls he seeks to improve. The question 'How could this be true?', which never disturbs Plato's Socrates, never stops disturbing Plato. For years he sees no answer to it.[63] Then, one day, he becomes convinced of something Socrates would have thought fantastic—that every person's soul had existed long before birth, had gone through many previous births into different incarnations, and had thus, in some mysterious

---

[62] Aristotle, *Metaph.* 987a32 ff., with comment ad loc. by W. D. Ross, *Aristotle's* Metaphysics (Oxford: Oxford University Press, 1924).

[63] We can pinpoint the time of his life at which this question became so insistent in Plato's mind that he put it into the centre of his depiction of Socrates' practice of standard elenchus: the time when he wrote the *Gorgias*, on which I follow the widely held view that it is one of the latest of Plato's earlier dialogues (the best case for this view is in Irwin's commentary on the *Gorgias* (*Plato:* Gorgias, 4–8); for a contrary opinion, see Charles Kahn, 'Did Plato Write Socratic Dialogues?', *Classical Quarterly*, 31 (1981), 305 ff.). Though the elenchus is practised in all of the dialogues which precede the *Gorgias* (except the *Apology* and *Menexenus*), only in the *Gorgias* is Socrates made to give utterance to that flock of *obiter dicta* which reveal the assumptions on which he predicates his confidence that the elenctic method establishes truth and falsehood.

way, acquired knowledge about *everything*,[64] and this knowledge was now in every soul in the form of true covert beliefs. Would not that have struck Plato as answering the question Socrates had never pursued: how could it have happened that each and every one of his interlocutors did have those true beliefs Socrates needs to refute all of that person's false beliefs? That wildest of Plato's metaphysical flights, that ultra-speculative theory that all learning is recollecting, is understandable as, among other things, an answer to a problem in Socratic elenchus. Could this be why, when Plato adopts it, he puts it into Socrates' mouth?[65]

APPENDIX

The Demise of the Elenchus in the *Euthydemus*, *Lysis*, and *Hippias Major*

It does not seem to have been noticed in the critical literature that these three dialogues, each of which has been frequently thought (on the strength of miscellaneous criteria) to fall late within the earlier dialogues,[66] have a common feature which distinguishes them from all of the other dialogues in this group: abandonment of adversary argument as Socrates' method of philosophical investigation. The theses which are seriously debated in these dialogues are not contested by the interlocutor; Socrates himself is both their author and critic.

---

[64] 'The soul being immortal and having had many births, and having seen everything both in this world and in Hades, *there is nothing it has not come to know*' (*Men.* 81c5–7). It should be emphasized that there is not the slightest evidence of Plato's acceptance of this extraordinary doctrine prior to the *Meno* and, especially, in view of what was said in the preceding note, no evidence of his acceptance of it in the *Gorgias*. The eschatological myth with which the *Gorgias* concludes is a purely moral tale, without epistemological content of any sort.

[65] This essay is the outcome of discussions of the elenchus in seminars at Berkeley, Toronto, and St Andrews. An earlier draft was circulated among friends and several of them responded with comments. Though I cannot thank them all by name, I must mention those among them whose criticisms prompted some specific correction: Julia Annas, Myles Burnyeat, Jim Dybikowski, Michael Ferejohn, Alvin Goldman, Charles Kahn, Ian Kidd, Richard Kraut, Jonathan Lear, Alexander Nehamas, Richard Rorty, Jerry Santas, Friedrich Solmsen. My greatest debt by far is to Burnyeat for a discussion which enabled me to clarify the argument in Sect. III. But neither he nor any of the aforenamed should be presumed to agree with any of the views I have expressed.

[66] On the *Euthydemus*, writes Guthrie (*A History of Greek Philosophy*, iv. 266), 'the prevailing opinion [reviewed in H. Keulen, *Untersuchungen zu Platon's* Euthydemus (*Klass. Philol. Stud.*, xxvii (Wiesbaden: Hanassowitz, 1971)] is that [it], like the *Meno*, was written after the earlier Socratic dialogues and the *Protagoras*, but before the great central group'. On the *Lysis*, see esp. the useful review of work on this dialogue in V. Schoplick, *Der platonische Dialog* Lysis (Augsburg: Blasaditsch, 1969; diss. Freiburg, 1968), supporting the conclusion that the *Lysis* is closely related to the *Euthydemus* and probably comes before the *Meno* but after the *Gorgias*. The case for the *Hippias Major* as a transitional dialogue is argued strongly by John Malcolm ('On the Place of the *Hippias Major* in the Development of Plato's Thought', *Archiv für Geschichte der Philosophie*, 50 (1968), 189 ff.) and by Paul Woodruff (*Plato*: Hippias Major, 175–9).

Euthydemus

Prevented by the eristic clowning of the two sophists from using elenctic refutation against them, Socrates does the serious business of the dialogue in a protreptic discourse to young Cleinias. In this discourse the only theses investigated by Socrates are introduced, argued for, examined, and amended by himself in the didactic style of the middle dialogues, where the interlocutor is a yes-man, who may ask questions and occasionally raise objections, but never puts up sustained resistance to a Socratic thesis. In this dialogue the interlocutor, a teenager, is docility itself. When he does contribute something of his own (to everyone's surprise), it is to anticipate the very thing that is needed to round out Socrates' thought (290b–d). A further way in which Socrates breaks with the modalities of elenctic argument is to ground his doctrine in a proposition—the universal desire for happiness—which he presents as uncontestable in principle: to question it, he says, would be 'ridiculous' and 'senseless' (278e4–5). Such a move is never made in any preceding dialogue; there everything is contestable.

Lysis

Here again there is no elenchus at all against anybody—not even *pro forma* and for comic effect, as in the *Hippias Major*. In the initial encounter with Hippothales what the love-crazed youth gets is not a refutation (he has proposed no thesis) but a dressing-down. When the investigation gets under way Socrates proposes all the theses which are discussed and refutes all the theses which are refuted. There is no contest. When Socrates proposes a thesis the amiable teenagers (whose strong point is good manners and good looks, not brains) go along; when he turns against it they are surprised (215c, 218d), but immediately fall in with Socrates' new move and tag along.[67]

Hippias Major

After regaling Hippias with fulsome compliments whose irony is lost on the sophist, the 'What is *F*?' question is sprung. Socrates makes sport with Hippias' ludicrously inept answers (they are the goofiest definitions in the corpus) while trying to get him to grasp what is called for in a definition (cf. above, n. 20) and then cashiers him as sponsor of discussable answers to the 'What is *F*?' question. The definitions which are evidently meant to be taken seriously—'the fitting' (293dff.), 'the useful' (295cff.), 'that which pleases through eyesight or hearing' (297eff.)—are all put forward by Socrates, encountering no resistance from Hippias, and are refuted by Socrates' *alter ego*—that vulgar, hubristic 'relative' of his, who terrorizes him and even threatens to thrash him for his stupidity. It is as if Plato were saying: my Socrates has now come to see that elenctic refutation of others is not worth much; it is his own self-criticism that he must meet to make progress towards the truth.

Thus in these three works, all of which must precede the *Meno*, for none of them anticipate its metaphysical, epistemological, and methodological novelties, Socrates ditches the elenchus. It is a reasonable conjecture that it is Plato himself who has now lost faith in the elenchus and extricates his Socrates from it, allowing him to move out of it quietly, without comment, without saying that he is doing so, and *a fortiori* without explaining why.

II

SOCRATES' DISAVOWAL OF KNOWLEDGE

GREGORY VLASTOS

In Plato's earliest dialogues,[1] when Socrates says he has no knowledge, does he or does he not mean what he says? The standard view has been that he does not. What can be said for this interpretation is well said in Norman Gulley's *Philosophy of Socrates*:[2] Socrates' profession of ignorance is 'an expedient to encourage his interlocutor to seek out the truth, to make him think that he is joining with Socrates in a voyage of discovery' (p. 69). More recently the opposite interpretation has found a clear-headed advocate. Terence Irwin in his *Plato's Moral Theory*[3] holds that when Socrates disclaims knowledge he should be taken at his word: he has

Reprinted with permission from *Philosophical Quarterly*, 35 (1985), 1–31. © The Editors of *Philosophical Quarterly*.

[1] I divide Plato's dialogues into three groups: (I) *Elenctic*: these are the earliest. I believe, but shall not argue on this occasion, that in these Plato re-creates (in scenes which are mostly fictional) the moral philosophy (method *and* doctrines) of the historical Socrates. I list them in alphabetical order: *Apology, Charmides, Crito, Euthyphro, Gorgias, Hippias Minor, Ion, Laches, Protagoras, Republic* 1 (classifying the first book of the *Republic*, down to 354a11, with the preceding, regardless of the time at which it was written, because it satisfies brilliantly the same criterion). (II) *Transitional*: *Lysis, Hippias Major, Euthydemus*, dialogues in which the method of those in (I) is discarded while their moral doctrines are preserved. I argue for this classification in 'Socratic Elenchus', *Oxford Studies in Ancient Philosophy*, 1 (1983), 25–59: 57–8, Ch. I in this volume. To this essay, to which the present one is a companion piece, I shall be referring by the abbreviation 'SE.' (III) Dialogues of Plato's *middle period*, beginning with the *Meno*: here both method and doctrines are Plato's. In present-day Platonic scholarship there is massive agreement on the dialogues in (III) and on most of those in (I). But there is wide disagreement on which should go into (II) because miscellaneous criteria are employed which yield conflicting results.

For all practical purposes the 'Socrates' of this paper is the protagonist of the works in (I). Those who deny that Plato at any time in his life wrote dialogues which aim to re-create his teacher's philosophizing are at liberty to think the 'Socrates' of all the dialogues a Platonic fiction maintaining consistency within each of those three groups. My argument will not be damaged if they do.

[2] (London, 1968.) Hereafter I shall refer to this work only by the author's name.

[3] (Oxford, 1977.) Hereafter *PMT*. My debt to this book is very great. Nothing I have ever read on Socrates' philosophy has done more to sharpen up my own understanding of it. Only those who are strangers to the ethos of scholarly controversy will see anything but attestation of high esteem in my continuing critique of *PMT* here and in a parallel essay, 'Happiness and Virtue in Socrates' Moral Theory', *Proceedings of the Cambridge Philological Society*, forthcoming (and also in *Topoi*). [*Editor's note*: This essay appears as Ch. IV in Volume ii.]

renounced knowledge and is content to claim no more than true belief (pp. 39–40).

I shall argue that when each of these views is confronted with the textual evidence each is proved false: there are texts which falsify the first, and others which falsify the second. How could this be? These views are proper contradictories: if either is false, must not the other be true? Not necessarily. If Socrates is making appropriately variable use of his words for "knowing"[4] both views could be false. I shall argue that this is in fact the case, proposing a hypothesis which explains why Socrates should wish to do just this.[5] I shall review the relevant evidence (Section I), develop the hypothesis (Section II), exhibit its explanatory power (Section III), and meet objections (Section IV).

I

The first interpretation is virtually ubiquitous. It has even captured the dictionaries. *Webster's* gives this entry under "irony":

> (T1) A pretence of ignorance and of willingness to learn from another assumed in order to make the other's false conception conspicuous by adroit reasoning — called also 'Socratic irony'.

The *OED* gives the same explanation for the 'etymological sense' of "irony":

> (T2) Dissimulation, pretence; especially [of] ignorance feigned by Socrates as a means of confuting an adversary (Socratic irony).

"Pretence" is the key word here. Socrates is dissembling, though for excellent reasons. To the pedagogical ones adduced by Gulley might be added Socrates' interest in manœuvring his interlocutors into the answerer's role, so he may keep the questioner's for himself. Aristotle attests this use of the disclaimer:

> (T3) . . .Socrates asked questions but gave no replies: for he confessed (ὡμολόγει) he had no knowledge. (*SE* 183ᵇ6–8)

---

[4] The verbs ἐπίσταμαι, εἰδέναι, γιγνώσκειν, ἐπαΐειν, and their cognate nouns, if any; the adjective σοφός, and the noun σοφία, which is used as interchangeable with ἐπιστήμη (as e.g. at *Ap.* 23a7: here ἐπιστήμη could have been substituted for σοφία *salva veritate*, as it in fact is at 19c6).

[5] This proposal breaks with previous interpretations (with all of those known to me), including an earlier one of mine (in my introduction to *Plato's* Protagoras, trans. Jowett, rev. M. Ostwald, ed. G. Vlastos (New York, 1956), pp. xxx–i), where I conflated two distinct claims: that Socrates renounces certainty (which is true) *and* knowledge (which is false). Gulley fell into the same trap. He assumed that his (perfectly valid) critique of the second claim also disposes of the first.

But Aristotle is not implying that the disclaimer was a pretence.[6] His wording strongly suggests the opposite.[7] The same suggestion is conveyed by a writer of Socratic dialogues contemporary with Plato's:

(T4) I had no knowledge I could teach the man to improve him, but I thought that by associating with him I could improve him through my love. (Aeschines Socraticus, *Alcibiades*; frag. 10C Dittmar)

In Plato the only character who says that Socrates is feigning ignorance is Thrasymachus:

(T5) When he heard this he gave a great sardonic horselaugh and said: 'Heracles! This is Socrates' customary feigning (εἰρωνεία).
    I had predicted this—I had told the people here that you would not want to give answers and would dissemble (εἰρωνεύσοιο) and would do anything but answer if you are questioned.' (*Rep.* 1, 337a3–7)[8]

But Socrates does not agree, nor does anyone friendly to him. If we were to believe Thrasymachus, we would have to do so without support from any of our earliest sources.

And we would have much explaining to do. How could Socrates be dissembling—saying what he does not believe—when his own first rule in elenctic dialogue is "say what you believe"?[9] And how would we account for the pretence in circumstances in which it cannot be meant to bring the interlocutor into the answerer's role? So, notably, at the conclusion of the debate with Callicles. Why should Socrates say *then*, 'I do not assert the things I say as one who knows' (*Grg.* 506a3–4), and again three pages later, after declaring that his theses have now been 'bound and clamped

---

[6] Quite the contrary: as Gulley notes (p. 62), Aristotle cites Socrates as one who argues without having knowledge of the subject under discussion—not ὡς εἰδώς, but 'peirastically' (*SE* 183ᵃ39 ff.). Cf. my discussion of this point in 'SE', 42–3.

[7] ὡμολόγει (in past imperfect: "he used to confess"). For "pretended" or "feigned" Aristotle would have written προσεποιεῖτο: he uses this verb repeatedly in his discussion of the εἴρων in *EN* 1127ᵇ10 ff. (and προσποίησις in 1108ᵃ21) and in *MM* 1193ᵃ28 ff. (note also the use of ὁμολογεῖν in contrast to προσποιεῖσθαι in the description of the ἀληθευτικός, *EN* 1127ᵃ25, τὰ ὑπάρχοντα ὁμολογῶν). For Aristotle Socrates is indeed an εἴρων, but *not* for disavowing knowledge: nowhere does he bring the profession of ignorance under the 'disclaimer of prestigious qualities' which he ascribes to Socrates *qua* εἴρων.

[8] Here εἰρωνεία clearly means "dissembling". It is given this sense in the translations by Cornford, Lindsay, and Robin, but is mistranslated as "irony" in the ones by Bloom, Grube, Shorey, possibly because the conceptual difference between *irony* and *dissembling* is not observed: the intention to deceive, built into the meaning of the latter, must be absent from the former ("What fine weather!", said while it is raining cats and dogs, is not meant to fool anybody). εἰρωνεία straddles this difference, hence Plato may use it for either dissembling (as here and sometimes elsewhere: *Sph.* 268b–c; *Laws* 908e) or irony (as quite clearly in *Smp.* 218d6 and *Grg.* 489e1–3, less clearly in *Ap.* 37e, *Smp.* 216b4).

[9] *Cri.* 40c–d; *Prt.* 331c; *Rep.* 337c, 346a, 350a; *Grg.* 495a, 500b. And see the discussion of this rule in 'SE', 35–8.

down by arguments of iron and adamant' (508e–509a), why should he then add,

(T6) But as for me my position (λόγος) is always the same:[10] I do not know how these things are. (*Grg.* 509a4–6)[11]

If the disavowal is false, why dish out the falsehood at this late moment in the debate?

But we have not yet reached the strongest evidence that the disavowal is sincere. It comes in the *Apology*. Chaerephon had asked at Delphi: 'Is there anyone wiser than Socrates?' And the oracle had said, 'No.'

That answer, Socrates tells the jury, plunged him into prolonged perplexity:

(T7) When I heard this I kept thinking: 'What on earth does the god mean? What is he hinting at? For I am aware of being wise in nothing, great or small. What then could he mean by saying that I am wise?' (*Ap.* 21b2–5)

Could Socrates have said *to himself*, "I am aware of being wise in nothing," if he thought it untrue? The same question arises again a few lines later as Socrates narrates the outcome of his first encounter with a victim of conceit of knowledge:

(T8) As I was going away from this man I reasoned to myself that I am indeed wiser than he. It is unlikely that either of us knows anything noble or good. But he, having no knowledge, thinks he knows something, while I, having none, don't think I have any. (*Ap.* 21d2–6)

What would we make of that narrated soliloquy on the hypothesis that Socratic ignorance is feigned? Is the narrative meant to be fact or fiction? If fiction, Socrates is lying to the judges, to whom he had promised, just a moment earlier (20d): 'Now I shall tell you the whole truth.' If fact—if the story is meant to be true—then Socrates would have had to believe that he had performed an unperformable speech-act, namely, that he had knowingly dissembled to himself.

Let us then consider the alternative hypothesis—that 'Socrates claims no knowledge for himself . . . He allows both his interlocutors and himself

---

[10] The λόγος at 509a4 is not the thesis he has defended against Callicles (to these he refers by ταῦτα at a5, as previously at 508e6 and subsequently at 509b1), but his disavowal of knowledge (cf. οὐδὲ εἰδὼς λέγω at 506a3–4 with λόγος ὅτι οὐκ οἶδα here). Nor is λόγος being used here to mean "argument" (so translated by Irwin; *Plato: Gorgias* (Oxford, 1979)); Socrates disavows knowledge here and at 506a3–4, but does not argue for the disavowal.

[11] This disavowal, so unqualified on the face of it, Gulley (p. 69) dismisses by a complicated exegetical manœuvre, borrowed from E. R. Dodds (*Plato's Gorgias* (Oxford, 1959), 541). For my critique of it, see my retort to Dodds in 'Afterthoughts on the Socratic Elenchus', *Oxford Studies in Ancient Philosophy*, 1 (1983), 71–4: 71.

true beliefs without knowledge.'[12] If so, how is it that what he keeps search-ing for throughout his life is not true belief, but knowledge?

> (T9) I think we should be contentiously eager *to know* what is true and what is false about the things we discuss . . . (*Grg.* 505e4–5)
>
> (T10) For the things we are debating are . . . things which *to know* is noblest, not *to know* most base. For their sum and substance is this: *to know* or not *to know* who is happy and who is not. (*Grg.* 472c6–d1)

If after decades of searching Socrates remained convinced that he still knew *nothing*,[13] would not further searching have become a charade—or rather worse, for he holds that virtue 'is' knowledge: if he has no know-ledge, his life is a disaster, he has missed out on virtue and, therewith, on happiness. How is it then that he is serenely confident he has achieved both?[14]

In any case, there is a familiar text where Socrates says flatly that he knows a moral truth:

---

[12] *PMT* 40–1. Though Irwin's is the only argued-out defence of this view in the scholarly lit-erature, I have the impression that it is widely shared. It is conceded in Myles Burnyeat's 'Exam-ples in Epistemology: Socrates, Theaetetus and G. E. Moore', *Philosophy*, 52 (1977), 381–98: 384 ff.; the concession, incidental to his discussion of the 'Socratic Fallacy', is not argued for on its own account. It is as marginal (and more hesitant) in G. Santas, *Socrates* (London, 1979), 119 ff. and 311 n. 26. To Irwin's argument I cannot do detailed justice. Constraints of space allow me no more than two rejoinders and a more general reflection: (1) While his thesis is a perfectly reasonable conclusion from the texts he cites, that textual base is incomplete: missing from it are a series of texts (also unnoticed by Burnyeat and Santas) where Socrates, though stopping short of asserting explicitly that he has moral knowledge, nevertheless implies it unambiguously (T12–T17 below). (2) I shall argue that the texts which have been dubbed 'the Socratic Fallacy', which he cites in support of his view, are in fact inconsistent with it. (I shall expound (1) at length, devoting to it the rest of the present section. (2) must await my discussion of 'the Socratic Fallacy' in Sect. III.) (3) I surmise that Irwin and those who agree with him are conflating the claim to knowledge with the claim to certainty, as Gulley and I did earlier on (cf. n. 5 above). Once one comes to realize that Socrates can avow knowledge on the basis of nothing better than fallibly justified true belief (as I shall be arguing he does: Sect. II below) one is less likely to dismiss or bypass those texts in which Socrates says or implies that he has knowledge on the strength of nothing better.

[13] 'Absolutely nothing' is the clear import of T7 and T8, whose force has been blunted past all recognition in scholarly comment on it, as e.g. in Eduard Zeller, *Sokrates und die Sokratiker* (Eng. trans. of the 3rd German edn. by O. J. Reichel (repr. New York, 1962), 124; I have added the reference marks): '[a] Socrates really knew nothing, or to express it otherwise, [b] he had no developed theory and no positive dogmatic principles.' Who would have thought that a serious philosopher might have said [a] and *meant* [b]? Similar emasculations of Socrates' avowal of ignorance abound in the scholarly literature; for a fair sample, see the exposition of what W. K. C. Guthrie terms 'the ignorance of Socrates' in *A History of Greek Philosophy*, iii: *The Fifth Century Enlightenment* (Cambridge, 1969), 422 ff.

[14] His avowals of epistemic inadequacy, frequent in the dialogues, are never paralleled by admission of moral failure; the asymmetry is striking. He will face the last judgement confident that 'he has never wronged man or god in word or deed' (*Grg.* 522d); he is convinced that 'he does no wrong to anyone' (*Ap.* 37b3–4). That he does not say he *knows* this (as Irwin observes; *PMT* 294) is no objection: being convinced of *p* is consistent with knowing *p*. As for happiness,

(T11) ... but that to do injustice and disobey my superior, god or man, this I *know* to be evil and base. (*Ap.* 29b6–7)

This single text, if given its full weight, would suffice to show that Socrates claims knowledge of a moral truth. Irwin denies it any weight on the ground that it is so exceptional,[15] which, of course, it is,[16] but not as much so as he and others have thought it.

Consider what Socrates says to Callicles when their debate is about to start:

(T12) I *know* well that if you will agree with me on those things which my soul believes, those things will be the very truth. (*Grg.* 486e5–6)[17]

To grasp the import of this text for the hypothesis that Socrates is claiming to have knowledge of moral truth we must take account of what he aims to achieve in elenctic argument and how he goes about achieving it within the framework of a standard elenchus.[18] His aim, he says, is to compel his interlocutors to 'witness against themselves',[19] i.e. to induce them to see that the falsehood of their theses is entailed by propositions presently embedded within their own system of belief—propositions they themselves consider true. To achieve this aim he figures out what premisses they will accept which will enable him to contrive the contradiction[20] and

no scene recorded in the secular literature of the West portrays more compellingly serenity and even cheerfulness *in extremis* than does the death scene in the *Phaedo* (117b3, c4), which is admissible as evidence of Socrates' personal qualities: here, as also in Alcibiades' speech in the *Symposium*, the personal character of Socrates survives his transformation into a mouthpiece of Platonic philosophy.

[15] *PMT* 58. He gives no other reason for dismissing it.

[16] This is indeed the only place in Plato's earliest dialogues where Socrates avows flatly, without resort to indirection of any sort, that he *knows* a moral truth. Why this should have happened so rarely is an important question to which my hypothesis supplies an answer (in Sect. IV below).

[17] Inexplicably (but perhaps not unpredictably: cf. n. 12 (3) above) there is no confrontation of this text in *PMT* nor yet of the ones I shall be citing after it in the present section (T13–T17): none of them are listed in the book's (commendably full) index locorum; their relevance to Irwin's thesis is ignored.

[18] For my analysis of 'standard elenchus' (the usual form of elenctic argument in Plato's earliest dialogues), see *SE* 38 ff. I indicate there (n. 47) [p. 51 above] briefly some differences between Irwin's understanding of Socrates' use of elenchus and mine. Since they do not affect materially our differences on my present theme I simplify by ignoring them.

[19] For the references and comment see *SE* 48–50. [pp. 54–6 above]

[20] 'The art of elenchus is to find premises believed by the answerer and yet entailing the contrary of his thesis' (Richard Robinson, *Plato's Earlier Dialectic* (Oxford, 1953), 15). To "believed" add "and admitted". For if the answerer were to conceal his true opinion Socrates would be stymied: he can only refute theses to which the interlocutor will own up (cf. n. 9 above). Hence Socrates' joy at meeting in the person of Callicles an adversary whose convictions are at the farthest extreme from his own *and* who can be counted on to blurt them out. Here Socrates will find 'the stone by which they test gold' (486d4). What this touchstone will test will be Socrates'

70   GREGORY VLASTOS

secures their acceptance by *ad hoc* agreement. Let *p* be an interlocutor's thesis which Socrates considers false, and let *q* and *r* be the premises on which agreement is reached. Does Socrates, for his part, believe that *q* and *r* are true? In standard elenctic argument there can be no doubt of this: it follows from Socrates' conviction that the contradiction does more than expose inconsistency within the interlocutor's beliefs—that it *refutes* his thesis, as we can see, for instance, when Polus is told that the argument which faulted him 'proved true' the Socratic thesis against his (*Grg.* 479e8). Socrates could not have said this unless he were convinced that *q* and *r*, which are shown to entail not-*p*, are themselves true. Would he be prepared to say that he *knows* they are true? Just this is what we learn from T12: if Callicles will agree on *q* and *r*, he (Socrates)[21] 'knows well' that *q* and *r* will be true. How so? What makes Socrates think he knows this? And what does he mean by saying he does? These are highly relevant questions. They will be answered in due course (n. 43 below). For the present let us be content to get no more than this out of T12: Socrates is claiming to *know* that the premises to which he expects Callicles will agree are true.

Now if Socrates is assuming he knows that those premises are true, we may infer that he is also assuming he knows that the conclusions, validly deduced therefrom, are true. This inference seems safe enough. But let us not take it for granted. Is there textual evidence that Socrates makes the latter assumption? There is: for when his argument has rebutted *p*, Socrates feels entitled to assert that not-*p* has thereby 'been made manifest',[22] or, equivalently, that the interlocutor now 'sees' that this is the case.[23] To say this is altogether different from saying that the interlocutor has now come to believe not-*p*, which could have happened[24] for epistemically weightless reasons—because he was cajoled or bullied or just worn down. It is to claim

---

assumption that even the most misguided and depraved man will still carry in his own soul a residue of truth which can be shown to entail the negation of his perverse views. This is why Socrates can tell Callicles: 'in your agreement and mine consummation of truth will be already attained' (487e6–7).

[21] Without implying that Callicles does so too. From "*A* knows that *p* and *B* agrees that *p*" it does not follow that *B* knows that *p*; and Socrates has not said that beliefs of his will be true *only* if Callicles agrees: in "if you will agree" he names a sufficient, not a necessary, condition. To serve Socrates as a 'touchstone' (cf. the preceding note) Callicles needs no knowledge; his true beliefs suffice. At no point in their debate does Socrates credit Callicles with knowledge. In 'you have *knowledge* and *goodwill* and outspokenness' (487a2–3) the mockery is as palpable in the first as in the second of the words I have italicized.

[22] ἐφάνη φαίνομαι, in its non-dubitative sense of "come to light", "become manifest": LSJ (*sub verbo* φαίνω, passive, B1), for which its use in mathematical argument might be cited: Democritus B155 (= Plutarch, *de Commun. Notit.* 1079e): φανεῖται τὸ τοῦ κυλίνδρου πεπονθὼς ὁ κῶνος: 'will manifestly have got the properties of the cylinder' (so Cherniss translates).

[23] Cf. my 'Afterthoughts on the Socratic Elenchus', 71–2.

[24] *If* it did. It might not: Callicles may be right in saying that 'many' find Socrates unpersuasive (*Grg.* 513c5–6).

that he has now been given *good reason* to believe that *p* is false. And to say this is to make a knowledge-claim, if we give to "knowledge" its minimal sense of "justified true belief".[25] But is there evidence that Socrates is aware of making such a claim—that *he* would be prepared to say that the elenctic refutation of *p* has put the interlocutor in the position of *knowing* that *p* is false, and not-*p* is true? There is. We see him saying as much on two occasions.

The first comes at the conclusion of his argument against 'the multitude' in the *Protagoras* which establishes that wrong action (ἁμαρτάνειν) comes about not because the agent is 'overcome by pleasure', as his adversaries had maintained, but because of his ignorance of the good. Socrates then proceeds to tell them that, in view of what his argument has shown,

(T13) You yourselves, surely, know (ἴστε που) that wrong action done without knowledge is done because of ignorance (ἀμαθίᾳ). (*Prt.* 357d7–e1)

In saying that *they* know this he is implying that *he* knows it, for if he did not he would have no reason for saying that they do.

Here is the second occasion: Thrasymachus' brazen claim that justice is no virtue and injustice no vice, for justice is 'stupidity' and injustice 'sound counsel', is attacked by a standard elenctic argument (*Rep.* 348c2–350c11), which concludes:

(T14) Therefore, the just man has been revealed to us to be good and wise, the unjust to be ignorant and bad. (*Rep.* 350c10–11)

Then, a Stephanus page later, without any intervening strengthening of the argument for that conclusion, Socrates remarks:

(T15) ... for injustice is ignorance—no one could still not know this (οὐδεὶς ἂν ἔτι τοῦτο[26] ἀγνοήσειεν). (*Rep.* 351a5–6)

---

[25] I shall be arguing that elenctically justifiable true belief makes good sense of what Socrates is claiming to have when he avows knowledge. Irwin too holds (*PMT* 37 ff.) that the true beliefs he allows Socrates are supported by elenctic argument (cf. n. 18 above). Even so, he denies that in Socrates' view they constitute knowledge. This is the crux of our dispute. This is not whether "justified true belief" is an acceptable sense for "knowledge" in standard uses of the term (which nowadays most philosophers would deny) but rather whether Socrates (*a*) does avow what *he* understands by his words for "knowledge", whatever that may be, and (*b*) in so doing has in view nothing stronger than "justified true belief". In the case of (*a*) the evidence I am presenting here, never previously confronted in its entirety (especially texts T12–T17), should be conclusive. In the case of (*b*) I am content to argue for just that; but if a case could be made for giving Socrates' conception of knowledge the benefit of something stronger ('belief which tracks truth' as expounded by R. Nozick, 'Knowledge', *Philosophical Explanations* (Oxford, 1982)) I would welcome it; I cannot now see that it could be.

[26] I take the referent to be the immediately preceding clause, ἐπειδήπερ ἐστὶν ἀμαθία ἡ ἀδικία, which may now be regarded as known ('no one could still not know it') because it follows directly from the long argument at 348c2–350c11, whose conclusion was asserted categorically (ἀναπέφανται; 350c10) and is now regarded as agreed (διωμολογησάμεθα; 350d4).

—that is to say, now everyone would know it: *a fortiori*, so would Socrates.

There are two more passages where Socrates lets on that he has knowledge without actually saying so. The first comes late in the *Gorgias*, when the fight against Callicles has been won and Socrates is engaged in mopping-up operations. He tells a parable. A sea-captain who has brought his passengers safe to port after a perilous journey muses on whether or not he did them a good turn by bringing them back alive. His thoughts take a Socratic turn. He reasons that if one of them had been suffering from 'a grave and incurable' physical ailment, to him safe return would have been no boon. Nor would it, the captain reflects, to one afflicted with an equally grievous illness of the soul, 'which is so much more precious than the body'. Then Socrates adds:

> (T16) He *knows* that for a wicked man it is better not to live, for he must needs live ill. (*Grg.* 512b1–2)

This sea-captain is Socrates' creature. His thoughts and reasonings are what Socrates says they are.[27] So for Socrates to say that the sea-captain knows that for an incurably wicked man death would be better than life is as good as saying that he, Socrates, knows this.

The same admission is made in the *Crito*, where we meet the same doctrine that just as life would not be worth living in a disease-ravaged, ruined body so neither would it be worth living with a comparably damaged soul. Here this is expounded by Socrates himself *in propria persona*—from 47d7 to 48a3 he speaks in direct discourse—and simultaneously imputed to a mysterious figure who is described only as 'the one, if there is one, who knows' (*Cri.* 47d1–2):

> (T17) About the just and the unjust, o best of men, we should consider not what the many but what the man who *knows* shall say to us—that single man and the truth. (48a5–7)

Who *is* this man? Like the sea-captain of the parable he is a construct of the argument. Socrates would have no ground for imputing knowledge about anything to either figure unless he were convinced that he himself had that knowledge. If he did not believe *he* knows what he says *they* know, his saying that they do would be a fraud.

Thus Socrates' disavowal of knowledge is a paradox. He makes it frequently, explicitly, emphatically: and its sincerity cannot be doubted, for what he tells others he also tells himself in the inmost privacy of self-

---

[27] And most certainly believes to be true: cf. *Grg.* 505a–b and *Cri.* 47d–e, where Socrates speaks directly, without resort to a notional mouthpiece.

scrutiny where he is not preparing a face to meet the faces he will meet but facing up to what he is. But when we go through our texts dispassionately, without initial *parti pris*, we see first (T9, T10) that knowledge, not true belief, is what he keeps searching for, and then, if we keep looking as carefully and imaginatively as we should, we can satisfy ourselves that Socrates is himself convinced that he has found what he has been looking for: knowledge of moral truth he avows openly in T11, programmatically in T12, by clear implication in T13 and T15, through notional proxies in T16 and T17. Can we make sense of this behaviour? I want to argue that we can.

II

Let us reflect on our own use of the terms "know" and "knowledge". That they are all-purpose words, used to mean quite different things in different contexts, is a commonplace in present-day philosophy. But there is one aspect of this commonplace which is seldom noticed and when first noticed may even look like a paradox: there are times when we readily say, in a given context, that we know something, while in a sufficiently different context we would be reluctant to say we know it and might even prefer to deny that we do, and this without any sense of having contradicted ourselves thereby. Consider the proposition "Very heavy smoking is a cause of cancer". Ordinarily I would have no hesitation in saying that I know this, though I have not researched the subject and have not tried to learn even the half of what could be learned from those who have. Now suppose that I am challenged, "But *do* you know it?" Sensing the shift to the stronger criteria for 'knowing' the questioner has in view, I might then freely confess that I don't, adding perhaps, "If you want to talk to someone who does, ask N"—a renowned medical physiologist who has been researching the problem for years. By saying in this context, "he knows, I don't", I would not be implying that I had made a mistake when I had previously said I did know—that what I should have said instead is that all I had was a true belief. The conviction on whose strength I had acted when I gave up smoking years ago had not been just a true belief. I had reasons for it—imperfect ones, to be sure, which would not have been nearly good enough for a research scientist: in his case it would be a disgrace to say *he* knows on reasons no better than those. But for me those reasons were, and still are, good enough 'for all practical purposes'; on the strength of those admittedly imperfect reasons I had made one of the *wisest* decisions of my life.

I submit that along roughly similar lines—the parallel is meant to
be suggestive, not exact—we may look for our best explanation for the
extraordinary fact that, without evincing any sense of inconsistency or
even strain, Socrates can deny, and does habitually deny, that he has knowledge while being well aware that he does have it. To resolve the paradox
we need only suppose that he is making a dual use of his words for
knowing. When declaring that he knows absolutely nothing he is referring
to that very strong sense in which philosophers had used them before
and would go on using them long after—where one says one knows only
when one is claiming certainty. This would leave him free to admit that
he does have moral knowledge in a radically weaker sense—the one
required by his own maverick method of philosophical inquiry, the
elenchus. This is the hypothesis to which I referred at the start. I shall
explain it further in the present section and shall proceed to argue for it
in detail in the next.

I start with a passage that gives good insight into the conception of
knowledge acceptable to Greek philosophers around this time:

(T18) SOCRATES. Not long ago you agreed that knowledge and belief are not the
same.
GLAUCON. How could any man of sense identify that which is infallible
(ἀναμάρτητον) with that which is not infallible?
SOCRATES. You are right. (*Rep.* 477e)

Is Plato[28] really saying that to qualify as knowledge a cognitive state must
possess infallibility? That is how his own word comes through all the standard translations. But considering how strong a view we would be imputing to him if we were really to understand him to be saying that this is what
distinguishes knowledge from true belief, let us make sure that we are not
doing so on the strength of a tendentious translation. The Greek word
could be used to mean not "inerrable" (that which cannot be in error), but
only "inerrant" (that which is not in error). We can see Plato elsewhere
using the word in each of these ways: in the latter, when Theaetetus tells
Socrates, in striking contrast to what Glaucon had told him in our present
text, that true belief (δοξάζειν ἀληθῆ) is ἀναμάρτητον[29]—not in error (*Tht.*
200e); in the former, when Socrates asks Thrasymachus if rulers are

[28] The reader may be reminded that I take the 'Socrates' of Plato's middle dialogues to be a
mouthpiece for what Plato thinks at the time of writing, when he is no longer re-creating his
teacher's philosophizing (n. 1 above; and cf. n. 14 *sub fin.*).

[29] Correctly translated "free of mistakes" by John McDowell (Oxford, 1973). What Theaetetus means we can see from the immediate follow-up, 'and all that results from it is admirable
and good', which, as McDowell observes ad loc. 'is best understood in the light of *Meno*
96d5–97c11', i.e. that for the right guidance of action true belief is as good as knowledge.

ἀναμάρτητοι—incapable of error (*Rep.* 339c1).[30] Can we be sure that the latter, not the former, is the way ἀναμάρτητον is being used in our present text? We can. Plato is laying down a criterion for distinguishing knowledge from belief as such—hence from true, no less than false, belief. Inerrancy could not serve this purpose: if a belief is true, it is no less inerrant than is knowledge.[31] "Infallible" then must be what Plato means. So he is maintaining that we know that *P* is true only when we possess the very highest degree of certainty concerning the truth of *P*.

On first hearing, this notion is forbiddingly intractable. One hardly knows how to come to grips with a conception which endows secular knowledge with infallible certainty. We can make better progress by outflanking the position, explaining why the conception which is being denied makes excellent sense—is indeed the one we live by all the time. What would be meant by saying that our everyday knowledge is fallible? Without essaying any deep epistemology, it will suffice for present purposes to hold that one has fallible knowledge that *P* is true if the following conditions are fulfilled:

(1) One believes *P* on evidence *Q*;
(2) *P* is true and *Q* is true;
(3) *Q* is reasonable evidence for *P*;
(4) But *Q* does not entail *P*: *Q* could be true and *P* false.[32]

Let "*P*" stand for "I locked the door when I left the house this morning". Do I know this? I would not hesitate to say so. Is my claim to know it infallible? Obviously not. Why not? Because the evidence, *Q*, does not entail the truth of *P*. Let *Q* be, as is often the case, just my memory of having turned the key in the lock as I went out of the door. The truth of *Q*[33]

---

[30] This has to be the sense if Thrasymachus is to sustain his definition of "justice" as "the interest of 'the stronger'" *and* maintain that to obey the 'stronger' is (always) just (339b7–8). For given the latter, then, were the ruler (*qua* 'stronger') to issue a mistaken order, to obey it would be just, yet also unjust, since it commands the doing of something contrary to the 'stronger's' interest. To avoid this contradiction Thrasymachus' definition of "justice" must be buttressed up by the assumption that *qua* 'stronger' the ruler is *incapable of error*: infallible.

[31] When the ambiguity is thus resolved there is, obviously, no contradiction in Plato's saying in T18 that true belief is not ἀναμάρτητον and saying in *Tht.* 200e that it is.

[32] I have laid down sufficient conditions for fallible knowledge: where "knowledge" = "justified true belief", "fallible knowledge" = "fallibly justified true belief", i.e. true belief whose justification falls short of certainty because it rests on evidence which constitutes reasonable grounds for the belief but does not guarantee its truth. In saying that such knowledge is fallible one is not saying that one may be mistaken in believing what one knows to be true (which would be nonsense: "I know *P*" entails "*P* is true", as Socrates recognized; *Grg.* 454d), but only that one may be mistaken in claiming to know this, i.e. in claiming that one has reasonable evidence for that belief and that the belief is true.

[33] i.e. the fact that I do have this memory, which may, or may not, be veridical.

certainly does not entail that of *P*: my memory, usually reliable, goes wrong at times. This could be one of those times. Is it then reasonable to believe *P* on evidence as insecure as that? Yes, entirely reasonable. For suppose the contrary. Suppose that I insisted on stronger evidence. I could get it, for example, by phoning a neighbour to try the door or, better still, by rushing back to check the door myself. Would this be a reasonable thing to do? It would not: the benefit of the strengthened evidence would not be worth its cost: there is greater utility in living with the risk that *P* might be mistaken than in going to the trouble it would take to reduce the insecurity of its evidential base. There are circumstances when it *would* be reasonable to do that. Suppose there had been many burglaries in my neighbourhood and that a priceless Picasso was hanging in the living room in plain view of anyone entering the house. Then it would be reasonable to go to enormous trouble to raise my certainty that the door was locked. But since nothing much is in jeopardy if *P* is false, I am well content to claim that I know *P* on nothing better than my recollection. If I were not content to live with such deflation of the demands for certainty I would, quite literally, go mad: I would join the compulsive hand-washer, who will not accept the fact that he has scrubbed his hands with Hisofex just ten minutes ago as a good reason for believing that they are now free from deleterious germs. The willingness to live with fallible knowledge is built into the human condition. Only a god could do without it. Only a crazy man would want to.

We can now confront the alternative conception of knowledge that led a great philosopher to accept infallibility as its hallmark. Clearly, he did not mean to cover cases like the ones in my example. These he would dismiss as kitchen stuff. His paradigm cases would be precisely those in which it is plausible to claim that the security gap between *Q* and *P* cannot arise. In Aristotle these may be the ones where in his view no *Q* distinct from *P* is required—propositions which, as he puts it, 'are known through themselves':

> (T19) It is of the nature of some things to be known through themselves; of other
> things to be known through things other than themselves. (Aristotle,
> *APr.* 64ᵇ34–6)

All of the first principles of a science (its ἐπιστημονικαὶ ἀρχαί) are of this sort: propositions 'true and primary, which produce conviction not through other things but through themselves' (*Top.* 100ᵇ1–2). For Aristotle just to understand (or 'think', νοεῖν) such propositions is to be satisfied of their truth:

(T20) About such things it is impossible to be deceived: we either think them or not (ἀλλ' ἢ νοεῖν ἢ μή) ... to think them is [to possess] the truth. (Aristotle, *Metaph.* 1051ᵇ31–1052ᵃ1)³⁴

If we start with propositions of this sort, making them the 'first principles' (*archai*) of our demonstrations, and move beyond them only by steps of necessary inference, every proposition in the sequence will satisfy the infallibility criterion: for any *P* in that ordered system—be it one of its 'immediate' first principles or one of the necessary derivations therefrom—the claim that *P* is true could go wrong only if we fail to understand what we are saying or what follows necessarily from it. Here every *P*, as Aristotle likes to emphasize, is a necessary statement:

(T21) If something is the object of unqualified knowledge, it is impossible for it to be otherwise (τοῦτ' ἀδύνατον ἄλλως ἔχειν). (Aristotle, *APo.* 71ᵇ3–4)³⁵

Statements of this sort no argument could induce us to take back:

(T22) He who has unqualified knowledge must be immovable by persuasion (ἀμετάπειστον εἶναι). (Aristotle, *APo.* 72ᵇ3–4)

In Plato too the essentials of this conception of knowledge are maintained, though reached by a different route, for Plato's attitude to mathematics, the model science of the age, is so different.³⁶ For Aristotle the first principles of that science are self-certifying. Not so for Plato, who regards the axiom-sets of geometry and number theory as mere 'hypotheses' and the mathematician as 'dreaming about reality' so long as

³⁴ Aristotle is not appealing to self-evidence as a psychological state, i.e. to the feeling of certainty, but to insight—that understanding of essence which he takes to be encapsulated in the first principles of an axiomatized science (cf. the quotation from Burnyeat in the next note *sub fin.*) I failed to make this clear in 'SE' when ascribing to Aristotle the view that the premisses of all demonstrative science are self-evident truths. Though "self-evidence" is a close counterpart of Aristotle's phrase "known δι' αὐτοῦ (from which our term "self-evident" seems to derive via the Latin *per se notum*), it may be best to avoid it lest it suggest a psychological process which Aristotle does not have in view.

³⁵ Cf. M. Burnyeat, 'Aristotle on Understanding Knowledge', in *Aristotle on Science: The Posterior Analytics, Studia Aristotelica*, 4 (1981), 97–139: 111: 'To understand a theorem you must understand [that] ... it is necessary because it is demonstrable from prior principles which are themselves necessary ... because they are *per se* predications expressing a definitional connection (*Pr. An.* 74ᵇ5–12 with I, 4). What is required is a predication *AaB* where either *A* belongs in the definition of *B* or *B* belongs in the definition of *A*'.

³⁶ I have in view the definitive position in the middle books of the *Republic*: *not* the transitional one displayed in the *Meno*, where he borrows from the geometricians the 'hypothetical method of investigation' (ἐξ ὑποθέσεως σκοπεῖσθαι; 86e), offers no critique of mathematics, and draws the distinction between knowledge and true belief (97e–98a) without reference to the 'unhypothesized first principle' of the *Republic* (510b7, 511b6) and without appeal to an ontology of eternal forms.

his demonstrations have no greater security at their base.[37] That is where Plato's dialectician must take over, treating the primitives of mathematics as mere 'stepping-stones' and 'springboards' to 'the first principle of all',[38] which is itself certain and confers certainty on everything grounded on it.[39] So for Plato too, as for Aristotle, knowledge consists of propositions which are 'secure and unshakeable' (*Ti.* 29b7) and differs from true opinion in its 'unmovability' by countervailing argument:

> (T23) [Knowledge] is immovable by persuasion, while [true belief] can be changed by persuasion. (Plato, *Ti.* 51e4)

And for him too, as for Aristotle, if *P* is known to be true, then *P* is necessarily true: his whole epistemology is built on the restriction of what is known to what is necessarily true. This is the unavoidable consequence of his cardinal metaphysical doctrine that the subject-matter of bona-fide knowledge consists exclusively of eternal forms—entities, all of whose properties, locked into their definitions, are as immune to contingency as are the truths of logic and mathematics.

In taking this position Plato and Aristotle were not disporting eccentric views. They felt they were articulating the philosophical consensus of their age. Says Aristotle:

> (T24) We all believe that what we *know* could not be otherwise (μηδ᾽ ἐνδέχεσθαι ἄλλως ἔχειν). (*EN* 1139ᵇ19–21)

That Plato too speaks for what he takes to be a consensus shows in the way he brings up the infallibility criterion in the snatch of dialogue quoted above. If he had anticipated resistance he would have had Socrates introduce it, Glaucon demur, and Socrates argue down Glaucon's objection. What he does instead is to have Glaucon state it, and Socrates accept it unquestioningly. The mode of presentation is that of a truth so obvious that no reasonable reader could be expected to gainsay it.

The antecedents of this view can be discerned a generation or more before Socrates, in the dawn of metaphysics in Greece, when epistemol-

---

[37] 'We see that they are dreaming about being and cannot have a wide-awake vision of it so long as using hypotheses they leave them unshaken, unable to give an account of them' (533b8–c3). Contrast the description of the same people—unphilosophical mathematicians—in the *Euthydemus*, which, in common with most scholars, I have been dating before the *Meno* ('SE', 57–8) [pp. 61–2 above]: 'they discover being' (ἀνευρίσκουσι τὰ ὄντα; 290c3).

[38] τὴν τοῦ παντὸς ἀρχήν; *Rep.* 511b6–7.

[39] I take this to be the implication of the dialectician's going ἐπ᾽ αὐτὴν τὴν ἀρχὴν ἵνα βεβαιώσηται; 533c–d: so long as one does what mathematicians do, proving their theorems from primitives which are themselves ungrounded, all one can claim is that one's system has internal consistency, and only 'by force of habit can this be called "knowledge"' (534d); bona-fide knowledge is reached when, and only when, 'doing away with hypotheses, one reaches the first principle to find certainty there'.

ogy, still in its infancy, is not yet a fully articulated discipline and its doctrines are set forth in oracular prose (as in Heraclitus) or in poetic form
(as in Parmenides and Empedocles). To illustrate from Parmenides: his
implicit acceptance of indubitable certainty as the prerogative of the
philosopher's knowledge shows up in the fictional guise of divine revela-
tion in which he presents his metaphysical (and even his physical) system.
His treatise is the notional discourse of a goddess who reveals to him 'the
unshaken heart of well-rounded truth' (ἀληθείης εὐκυκλέος[40] ἀτρεμὲς ἦτορ;
b1, 29), i.e. a doctrine that is undisturbable by objections ('unshaken') and
systematically complete ('well-rounded'). The appeal is throughout to critical reason, not to faith; the goddess does not say "Close your eyes and
believe", but "Open your mind and attend to the 'strife-encompassed refutation'[41] I offer". But the hierophantic trappings of the argument attest the
certainty its author attaches to its conclusion. Even considerably later, in
the materialist Democritus, Socrates' contemporary, the conviction that
genuine knowledge must possess certainty persists. Unlike his predecessors, Democritus has the gravest misgivings that such knowledge can be
attained. He even seems to deny that it can:

> (T25) In reality we know nothing, for truth is in the depths. (Democritus, frag.
> B117 DK)

But this despairing conclusion does not express rejection of the dogma
that knowledge entails certainty. It attests the dogma. Had Democritus
glimpsed the possibility of fallible knowledge, he could not have drawn
such a conclusion from his conviction that:

> (T26) . . . in reality we know nothing with certainty (ἡμεῖς δὲ τῷ μὲν ἐόντι οὐδὲν
> ἀτρεκὲς συνίεμεν). (Democritus, frag. B9 DK)

From "We know nothing with certainty" he could not have inferred "In
reality we know nothing" except on the tacit premiss "In reality we know
only what we know with certainty".

I shall use "knowledge$_C$" to designate knowledge so conceived, using the
subscript as a reminder that infallible certainty was its hallmark. Now
whatever Socrates might be willing to say he *knows* in the domain of ethics
would have to be knowledge reached and tested through his own personal
method of inquiry, the elenchus: this is his only method of searching for
moral truth.[42] So when he avows knowledge—as we have seen he does,

---

[40] I follow the latest editor, M. Schofield (in G. S. Kirk, J. E. Raven, and M. Schofield, *The Presocratic Philosophers* (Cambridge, 1983), 242): a difficult decision in favour of εὐκυκλέος, though the alternative reading, εὐπειθέος, has strong attestation, and is accepted by some editors.

[41] I follow Schofield's translation of πολύδηριν ἔλεγχον, ibid. 248.

[42] *Pace* Irwin, *PMT* 37 and 39; cf. 'SE', n. 47.

rarely, but unmistakably—the content of that knowledge must be propositions he thinks elenctically justifiable.[43] I shall, therefore, call it "elenctic knowledge", abbreviating to "knowledge$_E$".

Socrates could not have expected his knowledge$_E$ to meet the fantasti-
cally strong standards of knowledge$_C$. No great argument should be needed
to show this. In elenctic inquiry nothing is ever 'known through itself' but
only 'through other things' and there is always a security gap between the
Socratic thesis and its supporting reasons. And the general reason Socrates
has for the truth of any particular thesis of his is that it is elenctically viable:
it can be maintained consistently in elenctic argument, while its denial
cannot. This, in the last analysis, is the Q for every proposition, P, in the
domain of ethics which Socrates claims to know; his reason in each case
is, at bottom, twofold:

$Q(a)$ P is entailed by beliefs held by anyone who denies it;
$Q(b)$ not-P is not entailed by beliefs held by Socrates who affirms it.

The claim is trebly insecure. For, to begin with, even if $Q(a)$ were true, all
it would prove is that Socrates' interlocutors happen to have beliefs which,
unbeknown to themselves, entail the Socratic thesis which they dispute—
a very remarkable fact indeed, if fact it is, but what would it show? It could
not begin to show that those beliefs are true.[44] But *is* $Q(a)$ true? What could

---

[43] This is what Socrates would understand by saying he 'knows' the moral truth in T11 above,
since the only reason he could offer is that the claim is justifiable by elenctic argument. So too
by saying at T12 he 'knows well' that the premises on which he can get Callicles to agree are
true: they are propositions he would stand ready to justify by elenctic argument if Callicles were
to dispute their truth. This is evidently the sense of "you know" at T13, i.e. it has been demonstrated to you by elenctic argument. So too *mutatis mutandis* at T15, T16, T17. And see the
comment on T28(b) (= T6) in n. 48 below.

[44] To show this, $Q(a)$ would have to be strengthened to

$Q(A)$ P is entailed by *true* beliefs held by anyone who denies it,

which is equivalent to the proposition I formulated more fully in 'SE' (52) [p. 57 above] as
assumption "A" (the 'tremendous' assumption):

   (A) Anyone who ever has a false moral belief will always have at the same time true beliefs
         entailing its negation.

The other assumption I gave Socrates in 'SE' (55) [p. 59 above] is:

   (B) The set of moral beliefs held by Socrates at any given time is consistent.

B is equivalent to $Q(b)$ above. I have scaled down A to $Q(a)$ in response to helpful criticism
from my friends Thomas Brickhouse and Nicholas Smith (their paper, presented to my Berkeley seminar in the summer of 1983, will be published in the next issue of *Oxford Studies in
Ancient Philosophy*). [*Editor's note*: This paper appeared as 'Vlastos on the Elenchus', *Oxford
Studies in Ancient Philosophy*, 2 (1984), 185–95.] It is now clear to me that inductive evidence
(extrapolation from past experience in elenctic practice) which is available to Socrates for $Q(b)$
is not available to him for $Q(A)$; all he can hope to justify from that source is, at most, $Q(a)$.
$Q(A)$, thus unsupported and unsupportable within the elenctic dialogues, must await the metaphysical grounding it will be given by Plato in the *Meno*: transmigration and the theory of recollection ensure that true beliefs entailing the negation of every false belief are innate in the
soul.

be Socrates' evidence for that? Simply his own experience in elenctic practice. What would that prove? Suppose $Q(a)$ had turned out true in a thousand elenchi; it might still turn out false in the thousand and first. And is $Q(b)$ true? Can the elenchus prove it true? Elenchus is not a computer into which sets of propositions can be fed to have their consistency checked with mechanical accuracy. It is a human process, a contest, whose outcome is drastically affected by the skill and drive of the contestants. So if Socrates wins all the arguments this may only show that he is the better debater. It could not show that there is no inconsistency within his own set of beliefs—only that, if there is, no opponent has managed to spot it.

Socrates could not have been unaware of this uncertainty, built into his instrument of research, which infects all its findings. That he is not so blind shows up in remarks he makes from time to time. So, for example, in this aside to Critias:

> (T27) How could you think that I would refute you for any reason but the one
> for which I would refute myself, fearing lest I might inadvertently think I
> know something when I don't know it? And this, I say, is what I am doing
> now, examining the argument chiefly for my own sake, though no doubt
> also for the sake of my friends. (*Chrm.* 166c7–d4)

Since by "to know" Socrates here is referring directly to what he seeks to achieve by elenctic inquiry, the fear he is voicing is that he might think true theses which have fared well in past elenctic inquiry but are in fact false. In saying that this fear fuels his elenctic searching he reveals his haunting sense of the insecurity of knowledge$_E$—his awareness that in respect of certainty it is the diametrical opposite of knowledge$_C$.

There is a further respect in which Socratic knowledge is poles apart from knowledge$_C$: it is full of gaps, unanswered questions; it is surrounded and invaded by unresolved perplexity. But this does not trouble Socrates. He does not find it debilitating, but exhilarating, as well he may, for what he needs to make his method work is not completeness but consistency within that set of elenctically testable beliefs which constitute his knowledge$_E$. At no time does his method require of him that he produce himself the answers to the questions his interlocutors fail to find. The task it sets him is to refute bogus ones, and this he does by eliciting from them the beliefs which generate the negation of their false answers. So if an inquiry should run into *aporia*, he can reckon the exercise not total failure but incomplete success. Nothing has transpired to show that the unfound answer is unfindable, nor yet to invalidate the fragmentary truths unearthed along the way and shake his claim that in their case he does have knowledge$_E$.[45]

---

[45] Scrutiny of any of the aporetic dialogues should satisfy anyone that *en route* to the eventual *aporia* Socrates produces elenctic justification of important theses whose truth is unaffected by the eventual failure to find the answer to the "What is *F*?" question.

So this is the hypothesis: in the domain of morals—the one to which all of his inquiries are confined—when he says he knows something he is referring to knowledge$_E$; when he says he knows nothing—absolutely nothing, 'great or small' (T7)—he refers to knowledge$_C$; when he says he has no knowledge of a particular topic he may mean *either* that in this case, as in all others, he has no knowledge$_C$ and does not look for any *or* that what he lacks on that topic is knowledge$_E$ which, with good luck, he might still reach by further searching.

III

If this hypothesis were true it would explain the most perplexing feature of Socrates' epistemic stance.[46] It would show how he could, and should, have wanted to say that *after he had proved* his theses true he still did not 'know' if they are true. We see him doing so in the case of that central doctrine of his for which he does battle in the *Gorgias*, first against Polus and then, at greater length and from different premisses, against Callicles: that to suffer injustice is always better than to do it:[47]

> (T28) (*a*) . . . these things have been clamped down and bound by arguments of iron and adamant . . .
> (*b*) (= T6 above) But as for me my position is always the same: I do not know how these things are. (*Grg.* 508e6–509a5)

At (*a*) Socrates implies that he has proved his doctrine true; earlier on, in his argument against Polus, he had not hesitated to *say* he had:

> (T29) Has it not been proved that what was asserted [by myself] is true? (*Grg.* 479e8)

Is Socrates then welshing in part (*b*) of T28 on what he had just said to Callicles in its part (*a*) and more explicitly to Polus in T29? Is he retract-

---

[46] And the most distinctive—unparalleled in the whole of the philosophical literature of the West (no other major philosopher ever puts himself in the position of saying "I have proved, but do not know, that *p* is true"); unparalleled also in any post-elenctic Platonic dialogue, even the *Theaetetus*, where Plato's Socrates simulates Socratic ignorance in its most extreme form ('I question others but make no assertion about anything myself [cf. T3 above], for there is no wisdom in me' (150c5–6): even there Plato never puts Socrates in the position of saying he doesn't know a proposition for which he has produced uncontested, apparently conclusive, proof; thus, when Socrates reaches the conclusion that knowledge is to be found not in sense-perception but 'in what goes on when the soul occupies itself by itself with being' (*Tht.* 187a4–6), he is not made to reiterate his total disavowal of knowledge; he does not turn around and say he doesn't know what, to all appearance, he has just shown that he has come to know.

[47] A corollary of his rejection of the *lex talionis* which he and others feel separates him irreconcilably from the established morality: cf. *Cri.* 49c10–d5 with *Grg.* 481c1–4.

ing his claim to have proved—and thus shown that he knows—that his doctrine is true? On the proposed hypothesis this quandary does not arise: what he disclaims in T28(*b*) and, implicitly, claims in T28(*a*) and T29 are altogether different things: implying that he has knowledge$_E$,[48] he denies that he has knowledge$_C$.[49]

He had made the same disclaimer of knowledge$_C$ a little earlier in the *Gorgias*, in a context where he availed himself of both the opposing uses of "know" within a single paragraph of Plato's text:

(T30) ... we should all be contentiously eager to know [= know$_E$][50] what is true and what is false about the things we discuss ... [So] if it appears to any of you that what I admit to myself is not the truth, you must interrupt and refute me. For I do not assert what I assert as one who knows [= knows$_C$] ... (*Grg.* 505e4–506a4)

When the critical terms are disambiguated in this way we can see not only what Socrates means to say but why he should want to say it at this juncture when it is clear to everyone that he has won the debate. He says in the *Apology* (23a3–4) that those who witness his dialectical victories would 'think him wise [= wise$_C$] in those things in which he refutes others'—a natural enough impression they might derive from seeing him maintain over and over again his record as undefeated champion of the elenchus ring. So in our present passage in the *Gorgias*, marking a moment at which he has given a stunning demonstration that he does have knowledge$_E$ of the truth of his theses, he has special reason to warn his hearers that he does not have knowledge$_C$, thereby underlining the sincerity and urgency of his desire to entertain objections: if he allowed his hearers to believe that he was speaking as one who has knowledge$_C$ his professed interest in hearing criticism would ring hollow.

Similarly we could go through all the texts in Plato's elenctic dialogues

[48] That this is all he meant to claim in T29 can be inferred from the fact that elenctic argument was all he had offered by way of support for the theses he had 'proved' true. That this is what he means at T28 is even clearer: to continue the citation (509a5–7): 'but of all those I have encountered, none has proved capable of speaking otherwise without making himself ridiculous [i.e. by being shown to have beliefs which contradict his assertion], as happened just now'. He is saying: the only proof I can offer for my doctrine is that all those who have opposed it in elenctic argument have been defeated in that argument. Since that result does not entail the truth of his doctrine but does constitute, in his view, reasonable evidence for it, he is perfectly justified in disclaiming knowledge$_C$ and claiming knowledge$_E$ of its truth, as he does, by implication, at T16 above, where his proxy, the philosophical sea-captain, 'knows' (= knows$_E$) that persistent wrongdoing would be so ruinous to one's happiness that the wrongdoer would be better off dead than alive.

[49] Straining to catch this sense Robin slips into overtranslation: οὐχ οἶδα at *Grg.* 509a5 he renders "je ne sais pas d'une science certaine".

[50] That this is the sort of knowledge to which he is referring is clear from the fact that elenctic argument is the method by which it is being sought; cf. T26 above.

in which "know", "knowledge", "wise", "wisdom" occur—all of those I cited earlier and all those others I have had no occasion to cite—resolving their ambiguities in the same way. So understood, all of those statements will make sense. Socrates will never be contradicting himself by saying, or implying, that he both has and hasn't knowledge, for he will not be saying or implying that he does and doesn't have knowledge$_E$, or that he does and doesn't have knowledge$_C$, but only that he does have knowledge$_E$ and does not have knowledge$_C$. Thus his avowal of ignorance will never generate practical inconsistency or doctrinal incoherence. When he tells the interlocutor that he has no knowledge he will not be violating the "say what you believe" rule of elenctic debate, for he will not be feigning ignorance: he does believe with full conviction, with utter sincerity, that he has no knowledge$_C$.[51] Nor will he be endangering his doctrine that "Virtue is knowledge" when this is read, as it should be, "Virtue is knowledge$_E$".

Moreover, the hypothesis explains why Socrates should make, not the avowal of knowledge$_E$, but the disavowal of knowledge$_C$ his front before the world, his epistemic manifesto as it were: only once, it will be remembered (T11 above), does he say in so many words that he knows a moral truth. In all the other texts that go the same way he avows knowledge by indirection, as if, after shouting "I don't know" he would only whisper "and yet I do". The hypothesis motivates this asymmetry. If knowledge$_C$ is what everyone expects of you as a philosopher and you are convinced that you have none of it, not a smidgen of it, you would naturally have reason to advertise your ignorance and admit your knowledge inconspicuously, almost furtively.

I now proceed to a more complex exhibition of the explanatory power of the hypothesis—its dissolution of the so-called 'Socratic Fallacy', much puzzled over in recent discussions.[52] These have centred on passages where Plato makes Socrates assert

(A) If one does not know what the F is,[53] one cannot know if F is truly predicable of anything whatever,[54]

[51] Since the elenchus is Socrates' sole access to moral knowledge.

[52] I broach this question in the present essay (most reluctantly, for constraints of space will allow a mere skeleton of the argument, to be fleshed out in a future publication [*Editor's note*: 'Is the "Socratic Fallacy" Socratic?', *Ancient Philosophy*, 10 (1990), 1–16; repr. in *Socratic Studies* with minor changes and some additional notes]) because if I ignored it the defence of my view against Irwin's (cf. n. 12 (2), above) would limp: his derives good support from what is now widely regarded as the right solution to the puzzle: cf. Burnyeat, 'Examples in Epistemology', Santas, *Socrates*, and Paul Woodruff, *Plato: The* Hippias Major (Indianapolis, 1982), 140 (I forgo further references to contributions to this issue: these three, along with Irwin, *PMT* 39–41, suffice for my present purpose).

[53] Or the form or essence of F which a Socratic definition is expected to disclose.

[54] (A) is asserted in post-elenctic dialogues, the *Lysis* and the *Hippias Major* (which I have classified as 'transitional': n. 1 above) for two values of F: for *philon* in the *Lysis* (at the very

which, Peter Geach argued in a famous paper,[55] has a corollary,

(B) It is useless to try to discover what the *F* is by investigating examples of it.

That (B) is false I take for granted. And no one would have found it more
embarrassing than would the Socrates of the elenctic dialogues,[56] if he had
thought it true: what he does in *La.* 190e–193c is a *locus classicus* of searching for a definition by means of examples. So this is the puzzle: how could
Socrates have searched for definitions by that means if he accepted (A)?
How could he have sought to come to know what the *F* is by investigating examples of it, if he believed that when he did not know it he could
not know if it is truly predicable of those examples, i.e. could not know if
they are genuine *F*s or bogus ones? Irwin's answer (*PMT* 40–1) is in
essence: Accepting (A), Socrates can evade its self-defeating consequences
because although (by (A)) he cannot *know* if *F* is predicable of examples
while using them to search for its definition, he may none the less have
true beliefs about them: true beliefs *sans* knowledge will suffice. Let us call
this proposal the 'sufficiency of true belief' interpretation of the Socratic

end of the dialogue, when the search for the *F* has failed) and for *kalon* in the *Hippias Major*
(at the start of the search for the *F*, 286c–e, and then again at its end to lament its failure, 304d–e
(= T31 below)). It is widely assumed that (A) is also asserted in elenctic dialogues: in the
Charmides (for *F* = *sōphrosyné*, 176a6–8); in the *Laches* (for *F* = "virtue", 189e5–190b1); in the
Euthyphr. (for *F* = "piety", 6e, 15c). I submit that this assumption is unfounded. In the first two
of these passages (A) is not asserted *in full generality* (which is the crux of the puzzle): neither
of them say that if one does not know the *F* one can't know if *anything whatever* is *F*. Full generality we do get in the third, but for a different proposition,

(C) If one knows what the *F* is, one can know if *F* is truly predicable of anything whatever.

As Santas has pointed out (*Socrates*, 116–17), what is laid down as a necessary condition in (A)
is only said to be a sufficient condition in (C). Thus the catastrophic consequence in (A) is not
envisaged in (C), which says only that if we did know the *F* we would be in a position to know
about any *x* if it is *F*: a fortunate position indeed, but by no means a necessary one (thus in the
Crito Socrates has no trouble ascertaining that escape would be unjust without invoking any
definition of "justice" or "injustice"), while the box into which (A) puts us is paralysing (fancy
not knowing that even acting justly is *kalon* just because we have no definition of that predicate!). The fourth passage (*Euthyphr.* 15c) is a spin-off from the third: if Euthyphro *had* acted
with knowledge of piety (which he foolishly thought he had: 4e, 15d–e), he and Socrates would
know that his action was pious—which is not to say that this sufficient condition of pious action,
which Euthyphro had not met, is a necessary one.

[55] 'Plato's *Euthyphro*: An Analysis and Commentary', *Monist*, 50 (1966), 369–82; repr. in *Logic
Matters* (Oxford, 1972)—a paper which has proved powerfully and fruitfully provocative. (A)
and (B), taken from his paper, have been rephrased.

[56] I have been writing, and shall go on writing, 'Socrates' in this paper to refer to the protagonist in part (I) of the Platonic corpus (the numbering as in n. 1 above), ignoring his name-
sake in parts (II) and (III) *except* for purposes of advertising the contrast with either the
"Socrates" in (III) (which became salient in Sect. II: cf. n. 28 above) or with the "Socrates" in
(II) (which has idled so far, but now comes alive: the contrast between the "Socrates" in (I) who
is committed to the elenctic method of investigation, searching for knowledge$_E$, and the Socrates
in (II) who has abandoned the *elenchus* and therewith the conception of knowledge as know-
ledge$_E$ is vital to the proposed solution of the 'Socratic Fallacy'. cf. nn. 60 and 65 below).

view ('STB' for short).[57] Will it solve the puzzle? It would indeed *if* it squared with the textual evidence, as its sponsors have believed. But it does not.

Consider:

> (T31) He[58] will ask me if I am not ashamed to dare speak of the *kalon*[59] when elenctic refutation makes it so evident that I do not even know what on earth the *kalon* itself is. [a] 'And how will you know,' he will say, 'if someone has produced a *kalon* speech or any other *kalon* action whatever, when you don't know the *kalon*? [b] And if this is to be your condition, do you think you are better off alive than dead?' (*Hp.Ma.* 304d5–e3)

Part (*a*) of this text—plainly an instantiation of (A) above—is, of course, consistent with STB.[60] But look at part (*b*): Socrates' critic tells him that if this is to be his condition—that of not knowing if any action whatever is or is not *kalon*—he might as well be dead: his life is worthless. We know what the one thing is that would make life worthless for Socrates: forfeiture of virtue.[61] Thus Socrates' critic is telling him that to be in the condition of not knowing if any particular action is *kalon* is tantamount to moral bankruptcy. He is implying that if Socrates were deprived of such knowledge his practical moral judgements would be at sea: he would be unable to make correct moral choices in his daily life and thus could not act virtuously—could not be *kalos*, i.e. a just, wise, brave, temperate, pious man. Can *this* be squared with STB? Clearly not. If STB had been Socrates' view, then in the absence of knowledge that anything is *kalon*, he would fall back on true beliefs to the same effect[62] and the disaster in (*b*) would be unintelligible. Clearly then the STB solution of the puzzle will not do: it is inconsistent with a text which the sponsors of that solution take to be genuinely representative of the views of Socrates as expounded in

---

[57] Accepted (independently of Irwin) by Burnyeat, by Santas, *Socrates*, and by Woodruff, *Plato: The* Hippias Major, 140.

[58] Socrates' philosophical *alter ego* represented as a relentless, bullying critic—the comic mask Plato wears to distance himself from his beloved teacher, to whose moral doctrine he still adheres while rejecting the elenctic method by which it had been established.

[59] Literally "beautiful", doing double duty by serving also as a moral predicate—indeed as the most general predicate of moral commendation (variously translated as "honourable", "noble", "admirable", "fine").

[60] Irwin (*PMT* 39, 284) cites it as evidence for STB, which would be perfectly right *if* we were entitled to assume that what is true for Socrates in this post-elenctic dialogue (cf. n. 1 above; for argument, see 'SE', 57–8 [pp. 61–3 above]) would have been also true for him earlier, in the elenctic ones, which we are not: the sequence of texts T11–T17, discussed in Sect. I above, in which Socrates (by implication) avows moral knowledge, includes texts (to be cited in the next but one paragraph in the text above) which are irreconcilable with T31(*a*), as I shall be pointing out.

[61] *Cri.* 47d–48a; *Grg.* 512b1–2 (= T16 above).

[62] As the upholders of STB assume, apparently failing to discern that the assumption flies in the face of T31, which states that (*a*) knowledge of the *F* is a necessary condition of knowing that anything is *F* and (*b*) if one cannot *know* that anything is *F* one is damned (I have italicized "know": no room is left for true belief as a viable alternative).

Plato's earlier dialogues. We must look elsewhere for a solution. The hypothesis of the dual use of *to know* in the elenctic dialogues opens the way to one.

Alerting us to the ambiguity in "know", it tells us that if the question "Is (A) true?" had been put to Socrates in the elenctic dialogues it would have required further specification. He would have needed to be told how he should read "know" in (A). Should he read it as "know$_C$"? If so, (A) turns into

   (A$_C$) If one does not know$_C$ what the F is, one cannot know$_C$ if F is truly predicable of anything whatever.

Or should he take it in the alternative sense, reading it as

   (A$_E$) If one does not know$_E$ what the F is, one cannot know$_E$ if F is truly predicable of anything whatever.[63]

How would he have responded to each of these questions? For the Socrates of the elenctic dialogues, who has renounced knowledge$_C$ lock, stock, and barrel, (A$_C$) would be *vacuous*:[64] he has no interest in knowing$_C$ anything, so why should he be at all concerned about the fact that if he did not know$_C$ the definitions of his moral terms, he would not know$_C$ if any of them are truly predicable of any actions or persons? But now suppose, alternatively, that he had read (A) in the sense of (A$_E$). In that case he would have declared it *false*. Thus at T11 above he 'knows' (= knows$_E$) that he can predicate "evil" and "base" of "doing injustice and disobeying his superior", though no definition of either predicate has been assayed and there is no good reason to believe that if it had been it would have met with greater success than had any of those pursued in dialogues of elenctic search. Again, at T15, though no definition of "ignorance" is anywhere in sight, he says that everyone who followed his argument should know (= know$_E$) that "ignorance" can be predicated of "injustice". Thus once the critical verb has been disambiguated, (A) is trouble-free for the Socrates of the elenctic dialogues: innocuous if read as (A$_C$), false as (A$_E$). On either reading it is a paper tiger.[65]

---

[63] I disregard two other permutations:

(A$_C$E) If one does not know$_C$ what the F is, one cannot know$_E$ etc.
(A$_E$C) If one does not know$_E$ what the F is, one cannot know$_C$ etc.

The consequents, respectively those of (A$_E$) and (A$_C$), tell us nothing new about what Socrates can know or wants to know.

[64] Though no doubt true for all he knows (or cares) to the contrary.

[65] The same argument will apply *mutatis mutandis* to the twin of (A), namely

(A*) If one does not know what the F is, one cannot know if anything whatever is truly predicable of F (*Men.* 71a–b and 80d–e; *Rep.* 354c),

IV

So far the hypothesis earns its salt. But two big questions still remain. The first arises over the fact that when Socrates heard that report from Delphi he was *surprised*. Why so, on this hypothesis?[66] Why should he not have thought the tribute well deserved? Not all of his elenctic searches had failed. On some absolutely fundamental things he had struck gold. He had come to know—know$_E$—things which 'to know is noblest, not to know most base: who is happy and who is not'.[67] Why then should he feel perplexed at the oracle's declaration that no man was wiser than himself? In none of the texts I have reviewed is there even a glimmer of the answer. Fortunately there are two more, both of them from the context of the oracle story and its aftermath: when undertaking to explain away his public image as 'wise man', Socrates confesses that on this score the public had not been altogether wrong:

disarming it in exactly the same way: confronted with it in the elenctic dialogues, Socrates would have declared it *vacuous* if read as

> (A*$_C$) If one does not know$_C$ what the F is, one cannot know$_C$ if anything whatever is truly predicable of F,

false if read as

> (A*$_E$) If one does not know$_E$ what the F is, one cannot know$_E$ if anything whatever is truly predicable of F.

(A*), like (A), is never asserted in the elenctic dialogues: *pace* Irwin (*PMT* 294) it is not in *Prt*. 361c2–6, where the required *generality* is lacking. Its only occurrence in the corpus, apart from the *Meno*, is in *Rep*. 354c: tacked on at the end of book 1, this cannot belong to the composition which precedes it, for what it says (if I don't know what justice is I cannot know if it is a virtue) implicitly contradicts T15, where 'no one could not know that injustice is ignorance' and so, by implication, no one could not know that justice is knowledge and, therefore (350b5) virtue. (I have anticipated here the fuller treatment of the 'Socratic Fallacy' I shall be publishing before long, where I shall also be calling attention to a momentous development in the post-elenctic dialogues which explains much that happens there: Plato's immersion in mathematical studies which take him to the frontier of mathematical research in his time (an interest which floods the *Meno* but pre-dates it, showing up fleetingly in the *Hippias Major* (303b7–c1): the first clear indication in the corpus that Plato is now abreast of advanced mathematics) and arguably motivates the abandonment of the *elenchus*, inevitable casualty of a shift to a mathematical model for knowledge.)

[66] I shall waste no time on the easy answer "because he thought there would be others with much higher credentials": it founders on the brilliant triumphs Socrates scores (e.g. in the *Protagoras*, where he is still *young*; 314b, 317c, 361e) over those most highly reputed for their 'wisdom' throughout Greece. If Chaerephon had not expected some such answer as the one he got he would not have asked his question. So *he* could not have been greatly surprised. Why should Socrates? (*Pace* Burnet's gloss on *Ap*. 21a5, we get no light on our question from the report in Diogenes Laertius (2. 65) that Aristippus had been drawn to Athens from far off Cyrene 'by Socrates' fame': Diogenes' authority is excellent (Aeschines of Sphaettus), but he gives no indication of the relative time-frames.)

[67] T10, abbreviated.

(T32) I came by this reputation, O Athenians, only by a sort of wisdom (διὰ σοφίαν τινά). What sort of wisdom? Exactly that sort which is, no doubt (ἴσως), human wisdom (ἀνθρωπίνη σοφία). It looks as though (κινδυνεύω) in this I am really wise (τῷ ὄντι . . . σοφός). But those of whom I spoke just now[68] are wise in a wisdom that is more than human (μείζω τινὰ ἢ κατ' ἄνθρωπον σοφίαν)—I don't know how else to speak of it (ἢ οὐκ ἔχω τί λέγω). (Ap. 20d6–e1)

Here Socrates admits in so many words what I have been hypothesizing all along: that he can use "wisdom" (and "knowledge") to refer to either of two radically different cognitive achievements, one of which Socrates dares claim to have while disclaiming the other. And that this "human wisdom" of his, which he openly avows here, could only be knowledge_E follows from the fact that the elenchus had been his only way of seeking it. He goes on to offer Delphic certification of his claim to have such knowledge:

(T33) It looks as though the god is really wise and that what he is saying in this oracle is this: human wisdom is worth little or nothing. By referring to this 'Socrates' he seems to be using my name as an example, as if he were saying, 'That one of you, O men, is wisest, who, like Socrates, has understood that in relation to wisdom he is truly worthless (οὐδενὸς ἄξιός ἐστι τῇ ἀληθείᾳ πρὸς σοφίαν)'. (Ap. 23a–b4)

Now he is denigrating his 'human wisdom'—saying that in comparison with true wisdom, that of the god who 'is really wise'—his own is worthless. Why so? Isn't this our riddle all over again? If 'the unexamined life is not worth living by man' (Ap. 38a5–6) and the elenchus is its examining, why shouldn't Socrates think the knowledge that issues from it man's most precious possession? Why then should he be saying that it is 'worth little or nothing'? Conversely, shouldn't he be debunking the alternative which, by his own description of it, is beyond man's reach, denouncing it as a will o' the wisp, a mirage, product of the extravagant aspirations of deluded metaphysicians and word-happy sophists?

If Socrates had been an epistemologist this, surely, would be the line he would have had to take. His commitment to the elenctic method would have left him no other choice: it would have called for a head-on collision with the prevailing paradigm of infallible, unrevisable, 'unpersuadable' grasp of necessary truths, and a reasoned defence of a new model of fallible, provisional, corrigible knowledge. But the Socrates of this paper is no epistemologist. He is a moralist pure and simple who practises moral inquiry but never inquires into the theory of moral inquiry.[69] He is as

[68] Natural philosophers (18b–19d7) and sophists (19d8–20c7): cf. sophos at 19c6 and then again at 20a3.
[69] For argument to this effect, see 'SE', 27–8 and 53. [pp. 36–7 and 58 above.]

innocent of epistemology as of metaphysics. He is no Dewey, led to the renunciation of the quest for certainty[70] by an 'instrumentalist logic', no Wittgenstein, impelled in that direction by a critique of language. Our Socrates lacks the conceptual machinery that would be needed to dismantle the established paradigm and erect a new one in its place. When he peers at the abyss that yawns between knowledge$_C$ and knowledge$_E$ he measures the distance not in analytic but in religious terms. He broods on it in the spirit of traditional piety which counsels mortals to 'think mortal'—to keep within the limits of the human condition:

(T34) Cleverness is not wisdom (τὸ σοφὸν δ' οὐ σοφία). And not to think mortal thoughts (τό τε μὴ θνητὰ φρονεῖν), is to see few days. (Euripides, *Bacchae* 395-7)

(T35) Being mortal, I think mortal thoughts: I am not senseless (θνητήν, φρονοῦσαν θνητὰ κοὐκ ἀγνώμονα). (Sophocles, *Trachiniae* 473)

In this, as in so many other ways, he is poles apart from both Plato and Aristotle. Their philosophic outreach wilfully defies the limits of mortality. Transcendence of finitude is the heart of Platonic mysticism. In Aristotle too this faith lives, though rarely voiced. In the *Metaphysics*, calling this science, provocatively, 'divine knowledge' (θείαν τῶν ἐπιστημῶν; 983ᵃ6), he protests the venerable dogma that 'human nature is in bondage', denied that most sublime of cognitive achievements by the 'jealousy of the gods'. In the *Nicomachean Ethics* his rejection of the dogma is more defiant and explicit:

(T36) We should not heed those who counsel us that, being men, we should think human, and being mortals, we should think mortal. But we ought, so far as in us lies, to make ourselves immortal (καθ' ὅσον ἐνδέχεται ἀθανατίζειν), straining every nerve to live in accordance with the highest thing in us. (*EN* 1177ᵇ31-4)

Socrates too strains every nerve to live in accordance with the highest thing in us. But this he takes to be elenctic reason—a poor thing, but man's own. Resigned to think human, he thinks with all his might: with the zest, tenacity, honesty, and daring of Socratic elenchus.

Now, I suggest, we can understand why Socrates is startled by Delphi's accolade. He can hardly bring himself to believe that his own understanding of the good life, chancy, patchy, provisional, perpetually self-questioning, endlessly perplexed as it is, should have any value at all in the eyes of the god who enjoys the unshaken heart of well-rounded truth— the perfect security, the serene completeness of knowledge$_C$. So he goes out into the world, searching high and low for something better. The search fails. He is then left with the conviction he expresses in T33: low as his own

---

[70] 'The Quest for Certainty' had been the title of John Dewey's Gifford lectures.

moral insight must rank by the god's absolute standards, it is still superior to any alternative open to man and earns the god's praise because it is humble. Drained of all epistemic presumption, aware of his own ignorance, he knows$_E$ that he has no knowledge$_C$.

But there is a further question: if that is the point of his "I don't know"— the shortfall in certainty that afflicts man's cognitive achievements at their best—why didn't he say so? Why should he choose to signal it only through an unresolved ambiguity? The question concerns linguistic conventions. Would contemporary speech patterns have tolerated so devious a form of communication? On this I could discourse at length. In Heraclitus, Sophocles, Euripides ambiguous utterance is a favourite form of pregnant speech. I must content myself with one example: T34, τὸ σοφὸν δ' οὐ σοφία. Since the articular neuter adjective is in Greek idiom precisely equivalent to the cognate abstract noun, what Euripides is saying, put into literal, unmanipulated English, is just 'Wisdom is not wisdom'—a blank self-contradiction at which translators balk: they can't swallow what is said in the Greek, so they doctor it up: 'The world's wise are not wise' (Gilbert Murray), 'Cleverness is not wisdom' (Dodds), and so forth. The Greek poet feels no such block. He flings his sentence at the audience, sure that no one in it will fail to catch on instantly, understanding τὸ σοφὸν to refer to the μὴ θνητὰ φρονεῖν displayed in that brash, sneering, jeering, smart-alecky rationalism of Pentheus, the extreme opposite of 'wisdom' in that other sense of the word represented by Teiresias—reverent acceptance of the ancestral faith whose rejection by Pentheus will spell his doom. Couldn't the poet have said this more plainly? Obviously he could. Who would suppose that to contrive a metrical equivalent of δεινότης οὐ σοφία would have strained the resources of Euripidean prosody? But such gain in lucidity would have been poetic loss. If its paradox were defused where would be the wonder stirred in us by its oxymoron? Far better that he should have thrown the burden of disambiguation upon us.

If you say, "But Socrates is a philosopher, not a poet", I would remind you of what a maverick philosopher he is: a teacher who shuns didacticism, believing that moral truth has a dimension which eludes direct expression—a depth best revealed not by instruction but by provocation. For that purpose he invented the figure of speech which still bears his signature in the dictionaries. I did not gloss those entries on "Socratic irony" in *Webster's* and the *OED* when I cited them at the start. Had I done so I would have pointed out that they refer us only to the simplest uses of Socratic irony. Only in these is it a figure in which what is said is simply not what is meant. In Socrates' most powerful uses of it the irony is more complex: in these Socratic sayings what is said both is and isn't what is meant. So, certainly, in that other invention of his which still bears his name in common speech: Socratic teaching. He teaches saying he is not teaching. What he says is what he means if to teach is to impart to a learner truth already known to oneself. It is not what he means if to teach is to trigger in a learner an autonomous learning process. As instrument of Socratic teaching this irony is best left unresolved. Its purpose is not, as Kierkegaard would have it, to 'deceive [the learner] into the truth'.[71] It is to tease, mock, perplex him into seeking the truth. When the profession of ignorance is used for the same purpose its irony is likewise best left unexplained. In telling himself he has no wisdom Socrates has no need to explain. In telling others he doesn't want to. He taunts them to ponder what he is hinting at by using words that do and don't say what he means.[72]

---

[71] 'One can deceive a person about the truth, and (remembering old Socrates) one can deceive a person into the truth. Indeed when a person is under an illusion, it is only by deceiving him that he can be brought into the truth' (quoted by Walter Lowrie, *Kierkegaard* (Princeton, 1938), 248).

[72] My warmest thanks are due to the University of St Andrews for inviting me to give a series of Gifford lectures, allowing me to devote them to the philosophy of Socrates. The effort to meet that challenge led me to rethink my favourite philosopher from the ground up. The present paper is a partial outcome of this project, which is still in progress. I present here thoughts I have voiced in different forms on different occasions: in Gifford lectures at St Andrews in 1981; in Howison lectures at Berkeley in 1984; in *ad hoc* lectures at the National Center for the Humanities in North Carolina in 1980 and 1981; in papers to seminars in Berkeley in 1983 and in Cambridge in 1984. I have learned more than I could acknowledge from friends who have responded to those thoughts: principally Myles Burnyeat and Alan Code, from whom I have learned the most; but also Ian Kidd, Jonathan Lear, Geoffrey Lloyd, Alexander Nehamas, David Sedley, Dory Skaltsas, and Harold Tarrant. I also thank the editor of the *Philosophical Quarterly* for giving me the benefit of comments by an anonymous referee. None of those I have thanked may be presumed to agree with views I have defended.

III

PLATONIC RECOLLECTION

DOMINIC SCOTT

In three of his dialogues Plato advanced the claim that what we call learning is actually the recovery of knowledge from a previous existence. At birth we suffer total amnesia, in the sense of losing all awareness of our previous knowledge, while retaining the capacity to retrieve it later on. But there is currently some disagreement about just when the amnesia begins to dissipate and whether, for some people, it ever does. Did Plato think that eventually everyone starts to recollect, or that some people remain amnesiac till the day they die? Who recollects, and exactly what is recollected? In this article I shall discuss two radically different interpretations about the scope of this theory and argue in favour of one of them.

According to some interpreters, Plato starts by drawing attention to the way we classify particulars under certain concepts in everyday thought. For example, we might think that a particular object is beautiful or that two objects are equal to each other. From where do we acquire these concepts of beauty and equality? Plato, it is thought, considered such concepts to be too complex for sense-perception to provide on its own; so they have instead to come from the soul's internal resources. It is by recollection that we can apply such concepts to the world of our experience. Plato therefore breaks our mundane thoughts down into two components: those that derive from perception and those that derive from the memories of the soul.

Human understanding now comes out as the product of an interaction between the information that our senses give us about particular physical objects and the concepts, for instance, of equality or beauty, under which we classify those particulars. This makes Platonic recollection rather

At the request of the editor, I have extracted this article from parts of *Recollection and Experience: Plato's Theory of Learning and its Successors* (Cambridge, 1995), 3–80. In this article I have confined myself to passages in which Plato discusses the theory of recollection explicitly. On the relation of the theory to other issues in his epistemology (in the *Republic* and the *Theaetetus*), see pp. 80–5; on the relation between Plato's theory and theories of innate ideas in the 17th century, see chs. 9–10.

Kantian in tone, for just as Kant made intuitions and concepts the two essential sources of our empirical knowledge, Plato—according to this interpretation—uses perceptions and our innate knowledge of the forms. Of course, the recollection that we all engage in must be developed further in philosophy, but that is the next stage on, and does not upset the 'Kantian' nature of the first one.[1] In other words, everyone has achieved a dim recollection of the forms even though they may not have brought their knowledge out into the full light of day.

So much for the first interpretation, which I shall call K (for Kant). To illustrate the second, I shall follow the lead of one ancient interpreter[2] and use an analogy adapted from a story in Herodotus. In the midst of the Persian wars against Greece and with a Persian invasion of Greece imminent, the Greeks had a stroke of luck. One of their number, a Spartan named Demaratus, who lived in Persia and had hitherto been no friend of the Greeks, nevertheless decided to commit an act of spite against the Persians. He turned spy for the Greeks and warned them of the invasion. He did this by sending them a letter, a wooden tablet with wax melted on top. What he did, however, was to inscribe the message about the invasion onto the wood and then conceal it beneath the layer of wax. In Herodotus' story, Demaratus leaves the wax surface blank and the tablet is allowed to pass back to Greece, where eventually the trick is discovered; the wax is scraped away and the message underneath revealed (7. 239). For my purposes, however, I shall change the story slightly. Imagine that Demaratus had not left the surface wax blank but had inscribed upon it something innocent for Persian consumption. We would now have two messages: one obvious but unreliable, the other true but completely hidden away from view.

Certain details of this analogy force us to look at Plato's theory of

[1] It is fascinating to note, however, that one person who dissociates himself from this 'Kantian' view of recollection is Kant himself. In the *Critique of Pure Reason* he talks of the laborious process of recollection and identifies it with philosophy: see A313/B370 (ed. N. Kemp Smith (London, 1933), 310). Elsewhere, he makes recollection a very recondite affair and says that we recollect the ideas *only* with difficulty (Kant, *Reflexionen zur Metaphysik*, in *Gesammelte Schriften* (Berlin, 1928), xviii/5. 434–5). What lies behind this interpretation is his view that the ideas are not categories or concepts of pure reason, which combine with sensible intuitions to make experience possible, but intellectual intuitions of things as they are in themselves, which is a very different matter.

[2] Plutarch. His interpretation of the theory of recollection is preserved in this fragment: 'there are items of knowledge inside us, but they are concealed beneath the other things which come in from outside, like the case of the tablet sent by Demaratus' (ἔνεισιν μὲν αἱ ἐπιστῆμαι, κρύπτονται δ' ὑπὸ τῶν ἄλλων ἐπεισοδίων ὁμοίως τῇ ὑπὸ Δημαράτου πεμφθείσῃ δέλτῳ). For the origin of this fragment, see *Plutarch's* Moralia, trans. F. H. Sandbach, Loeb (London, 1969), 388–9, and L. G. Westerink (ed.), *The Greek Commentators on Plato's* Phaedo, 2 vols. (Amsterdam, 1976–7), ii. 166.

recollection from an unusual perspective. The first important detail is that a message was inscribed on the wax which made complete sense to its Persian readers; the second, that these same readers had no inkling at all that there was a message underneath; and the third, that they were deceived by the message written on the wax. What happens if we apply all these features to Platonic recollection?

In one sense we are, on this interpretation, blank tablets at birth. We rely upon external sources, perception or hearsay, to form all sorts of notions and opinions about the world around us and about morality. Furthermore—and this is crucial—we can form all these opinions without any help from our innate knowledge whatsoever. Just as the Persians could understand the surface message without being aware of the message inscribed underneath, we can make sense of externally formed views without ever drawing upon our innate resources, without even beginning to recollect. Deep in our souls, however, is knowledge of entities that exist in separation from the particulars, entities of which most people have no consciousness at all; most people would deny that there exist those entities that Plato talks of as forms. But just as the Persians were misled about Demaratus' intentions, so most people are deceived by the surface message into thinking that the world of particulars is all there is. Only the philosopher, who has become puzzled by the confusions and contradictions inherent in our external sources, takes so different a view of reality.

This reading of recollection—call it D for Demaratus—differs sharply from K on the question of what exactly is innate and what is supplied from external sources. D in fact makes Plato more generous about what the senses, for instance, are capable of giving us. They can inform us that a particular object is beautiful or that two particulars are equal without any help from our innate knowledge of the forms. He uses innateness only to explain a philosopher's knowledge of the transcendent entities, the forms, with which particulars are to be unfavourably compared.

As a result, recollection ceases to be an account of ordinary thought. Whereas K uses a cooperation between the innate and the empirical to explain ordinary thought, D allows us to make 'Kantian' sense of our experience without invoking any innate knowledge of forms at all. In other words, recollection is used to cover different stretches of intellectual development according to which interpretation one follows. K takes the broader stretch. It attempts to explain our intellectual activity from infancy through to maturity in terms of a continuous path of recollection. One theory is made to embrace the earliest glimmers of intelligence and the vertiginous heights of philosophical achievement at once. On D, Plato only uses recollection to cover the period of later or higher learning, the movement from the mundane perspective to the philosophical. The earlier stages are taken care of externally.

There is also a difference in the number of people who actually recollect. Although both theories agree that everyone has the knowledge inside them, K again takes a broader approach to the issue of who actually recollects. If recollection is necessary for conceptual thought, and if everyone engages in conceptual thought, then everyone recollects to some degree, even if few complete the process through to the end. On D, the fact that everyone engages in conceptual thought does not show that everyone recollects. Recollection only starts with the process of philosophizing, and thus only a rather limited number of people recollect. Associated with this is a further point. On D, recollection is right from the start a difficult process; on K, its first stages are automatic and easy.

This brings us to yet another important difference between the two interpretations. K allows Plato far more optimism in his approach to learning and discovery than D. Perhaps the most important aspect of Herodotus' story was that Demaratus fooled the Persians. In the D interpretation of recollection the counterpart for this feature of the story is that the opinions we derive from external sources, whether from perception or hearsay, in some way mislead us about how things really are. The Demaratus theory thus attributes to Plato a sense of gloom about the cognitive achievements of ordinary people and about the difficulty of philosophical discovery. It also entails that if the inquiry is successful we shall come to revise our earlier beliefs in quite a drastic way. The discovery will be a shock to us, just as the Persians would have been disconcerted to learn what lay under the message they had believed.

Notice that what gives D this pessimistic character is not merely the way it limits the achievement of recollection to so few. Its message is still more depressing because it says something not only about the fortunate few who recollect but about the many who do not. They are not merely missing out on something, but are in some way actually deceived. There are then two senses in which D is pessimistic.

Now in one of these senses K is obviously more optimistic than D. All human beings go through the process of concept formation and, according to K, all human beings—tyrants and sophists included—thereby recollect. But this, it might be argued, still allows for a heavy dose of pessimism in the other sense, for one could say that although ordinary thought involves recollection, it involves only a very partial recollection, only the first glimmers of truth. In completing the process of recollection the philosopher must refine and revise his earlier opinions, and the refinements that philosophy will have to make may be enormous; thus a

revisionary approach to philosophy is still compatible with K. Nevertheless, there remains a substantive contrast between D and K. Consider the
status of the opinions that arise with perception. In K these represent the
results of partial recollection and the movement from them to the final
goal is in some sense continuous. They are starting-points to be built
upon, parts of an overall picture that has to be filled in. On D, however,
things are very different. In the image of Demaratus' tablet they are messages to deceive us and are to be scraped away. We discard them, not
build on them. There is a radical discontinuity as we become aware of
the deception. This makes for an important difference between the two
interpretations.

Now that we have the two interpretations of Platonic recollection before
us, it is time to turn to the texts.[3] As we have seen, there are only three
dialogues in which the theory appears, the *Meno*, the *Phaedo*, and the
Phaedrus. A first perusal of each of these passages may well incline one
towards K. The *Meno* does, after all, say that learning and research are
wholly recollection (81d4–5). Does this not suggest that recollection must
cover the wider learning span that K advocates? On D, only *some* learning is recollections. As far as the *Phaedo* is concerned, there is quite a wide
consensus that Plato is, among other things, drawing attention to the way
in which we all recognize universals in particular sense-perceptions by
virtue of our pre-existent knowledge of the forms. Furthermore, by impos-
ing a severe limit on the number of people who actually recollect, D is
inviting the following problem: if Plato is not talking about something
everyone does, how can he prove that everyone's soul is immortal?

Perhaps the strongest evidence for K, though, is to be found in the
Phaedrus. At one point Socrates talks of the choice that the fallen souls
must make every thousand years as to what type of creature they wish to
become. Some, having once been humans, may choose to turn into animals;
others may turn back into human form after a spell as an animal. But a
soul which has never seen the truth can never take on human form, since
human beings are required 'to understand the language of forms, passing
from a plurality of perceptions to a unity gathered together by reason', and
this is nothing other than the recollection of the vision which we had before
incarnation (249b). The K interpretation rather temptingly claims that the
argument of this passage requires recollection to explain the cognitive
activity of all humans. It is the hallmark of human intelligence to classify

---

[3] For the purposes of quotation in this article, I shall be using the following translations (with
occasional modifications): for the *Meno*, *Plato: Protagoras and Meno*, trans. W. K. C. Guthrie
(London, 1956); for the *Phaedo*, *Plato's Phaedo*, ed. D. Gallop (Oxford, 1975); and for the *Phaedrus*, *Plato's Phaedrus*, ed. R. Hackforth (Cambridge, 1952).

the data of sense-perception under universals, and Plato's claim is that this would not be possible if we had not already had knowledge of general concepts. D must have a very different interpretation of this argument to offer, but it is not immediately clear what it will be.

Before we begin a more detailed look at the texts, we should take note of some problems concerning two of them. Recollection in the *Meno* is a tentative doctrine, and one should be wary of expecting too determinate an interpretation of it. Once the theory of forms has been introduced in the *Phaedo* the theory of recollection is clearer, at least in relation to the role of sense-perception, and it is possible to argue for more determinate interpretations. So it is with the *Phaedo* rather than the *Meno* that both sides in the dispute are making their strongest claims. As far as the *Meno* is concerned, I shall be limiting myself to the negative claim that it provides no evidence for K.

But if one has to be cautious about the *Meno*, one also has to be cautious about the *Phaedrus*, though for slightly different reasons. The whole passage is presented as a myth, not a proof, and so it may be objected that the text requires different treatment and cannot be used straightforwardly as evidence for a particular interpretation of recollection. So here I shall adopt a conditional strategy and argue that if one does use the myth as evidence in this way, then it is D, not K, that emerges as the most convincing interpretation of recollection. With these qualifications in mind, we are ready to begin, starting with the *Meno*.

THE *MENO*

In the first part of this dialogue Meno tries to give Socrates a definition of virtue. After three such attempts his confidence falters and, when asked for a fourth time to define it, objects: if neither of them has any idea of what virtue is, how can they make any progress towards a discovery? Socrates introduces his theory to meet this objection, arguing that discovery is made possible by our ability to revive certain memories within us. He then attempts to support his theory with the examination of the slave boy.

As presented here, there are three stages in the process of recollection:

1. The slave boy comes to realize that what he previously believed to be right is in fact wrong. Thus, after eliciting a false answer from the boy, Socrates says to Meno (82e12–13): 'Now watch how he recollects things in order—the proper way to recollect.' It is between this point and 84a2 that the first stage of recollection happens, and at the end of it the slave boy

is in perplexity, but is at least aware that he does not know, and this awareness is the result of the first glimmers of recollection.

2. In the next stage of recollection (84d3–85b7) the slave boy moves
from the mere awareness of his ignorance towards the acquisition of true
opinions. Yet when he has these opinions, he does not yet have knowledge
(85c6–10): 'So someone who does not know about something, whatever it
may be that he doesn't know, has in himself true opinions on a subject
without having knowledge . . . and at the moment these opinions have just
been stirred up in him as if he were in a dream.'

3. It is only at the final stage of recollection that knowledge is acquired,
as Socrates goes on to say in the passage immediately following the quotation. This stage is mentioned later in the dialogue, at 98a4, when Socrates
describes the difference between knowledge and true opinion. When we
have tied down an opinion with 'explanatory reasoning' we convert it into
knowledge, and this is nothing but recollection.

The examination of the slave boy shows recollection starting only after
contact with a certain type of stimulus or catalyst, in this case Socrates.
There is no evidence to show that he would have started to recollect had
he never met Socrates. In this passage recollection is only invoked to
explain the slave boy's awareness that what he originally thought was
wrong, the acquisition of certain true opinions,[4] and the movement from
these opinions towards knowledge. I do not wish to try to pin down at precisely what moment in the examination the slave boy's recollection begins;
the text is not sufficiently determinate. I am confining myself to the general
interpretation set out above in stages 1–3 and to the rejection of the
idea that recollection is used in this passage to explain how the slave
boy acquired the beliefs and concepts necessary to make sense of what
Socrates was talking about when the examination began. This is precisely
what K would have recollection do. Beginning from an analysis of propositional thought into its conceptual components, it has Plato explain the
formation of concepts that make language and thought possible. On all
such matters, however, the text itself remains completely silent.

Now for a couple of objections to my interpretation. In the first place,
it seems to be ruled out by the statement 'learning and research are wholly
recollection' (81d4–5). Nevertheless, we should be extremely wary of
taking this sentence at face value. If it is taken to imply that absolutely
everything that we learn is recollected from a previous existence, it goes
further than even the most devoted adherent of K would dare. Are we

---

[4] Notice how in 85c9–10 Socrates talks of the arousal of opinions as something that has only
just (ἄρτι) happened.

really to include *all* learning—'learning how' as well as 'learning that'? Does Plato include learning how to play the lyre, for instance? And under the label of 'learning that', do we also have to include empirical learning and discovery of individual facts? These sorts of question have, of course, already been raised by scholars and commentators who have argued for various qualifications to be appended to the sentence,[5] and they are surely right in their reluctance to take 'all learning' absolutely literally. What we have to do is to examine what Socrates says about recollection in the course of the slave boy examination in order to determine the scope of the theory.

It should also be remembered that the theory emerges from a myth, so its initial statement cannot be interpreted as if it formed part of the demonstration that begins with the interview of the slave boy. The answer to the question what qualifications we should put on the statement of 81d4–5 comes at 85e2–3, where Socrates generalizes from the slave boy demonstration to say that the boy can recollect not just geometry, but also all the other technical disciplines (*mathēmata*). Plato is interested in the acquisition of knowledge about such disciplines, of which geometry is a paradigm example.

Another objection to my view is suggested by a sentence at 82b6–7, where Socrates, before the slave boy has even opened his mouth, says to Meno, 'see whether it seems to you that he is learning from me or simply being reminded'. Should we not infer that anything that the slave boy says after this is the result of recollection, including the mistakes and false starts that lead him into his *aporia*?

The first response to this is that even if the slave boy were recollecting from the moment he begins to speak, it would not be enough to support the K interpretation, according to which recollection is meant to explain how we come by the concepts we use in everyday thought. The slave boy has acquired these before the examination began. He speaks Greek (82b4) and has sufficient conceptual apparatus to understand almost all Socrates' questions. So what happens after Socrates begins the examination is not

[5] Bluck (*Plato's* Meno, ed. R. S. Bluck (Cambridge, 1961), 9–10), for instance, argues against including experiences of a previous life into the matter of recollection. G. Vlastos ('*Anamnēsis* in the *Meno*', in J. Day (ed.), *Plato's* Meno *in Focus* (London, 1994), 97) construes recollection as '*any advance in understanding which results from the perception of logical relationships*'. See also D. Bostock (*Plato's* Phaedo (Oxford, 1986), 15), who is nevertheless one of the main proponents of K where the *Phaedo* is concerned. For an extremely severe restriction on the meaning of the word 'learn' (*manthanein*), see A. Nehamas, 'Meno's Paradox and Socrates as a Teacher', *Oxford Studies in Ancient Philosophy*, 3 (1985), 1–30: 21–2. On his view, the slave boy does not recollect at all, and would only do so if he attained knowledge, not just true opinion. If this is the case, however, it is difficult to see what the demonstration is meant to be demonstrating if not recollection in action.

relevant to questions about the ordinary learning in which K is interested. Indeed, this brings out why this whole passage was never likely to provide evidence for K in the first place. The purpose of the examination is that Meno should witness recollection actually happening. Thus there is no point in Socrates' saying anything about cognitive achievements that may have happened *before* the examination because Meno was not standing over the boy to check that such learning was genuine recollection. The only learning that Socrates is going to talk about is that which takes place within the demonstration for Meno to witness; mundane concept formation has taken place before the examination, and thus it cannot be what is at issue during the examination.

Even if it did help K's case to claim that recollection begins as soon as the slave boy begins to speak, it would be neither necessary nor at all wise to do so. The comment of 82b6–7, 'see whether he is learning from me or simply being reminded', need not apply to the immediately following section (82b9–e3) but can be taken to apply to the demonstration as a whole, in which there will indeed be some recollection. Furthermore, the consequences of making it apply to 82b9–e3, the section in which the boy gives some false answers, would be disastrous to Socrates' whole strategy in the *Meno*. This interpretation would turn recollection into something very much like the midwife story in the *Theaetetus*, where Socrates extracts from his interlocutor a number of false definitions which are 'within' him.

Now try saying that when Socrates extracts the false answer from the slave boy he is making him recollect; try saying this while at the same time remembering that Socrates is using the examination to prove to Meno that learning is recollection, as part of his programme to show that discovery is possible. Socrates' strategy in examining the slave boy is to take some subject-matter with which both he and Meno are familiar so that they can arbitrate. In the search for virtue, however, there was no one who knew, and thus no one to arbitrate. If Socrates can convince Meno that he is not teaching the boy but merely questioning him, and if Meno himself knows the answers, then he may be persuaded that when the slave boy gets it right, he is deriving knowledge from within. But if Meno sees the boy 'recollecting' false judgements, Socrates' programme is completely ruined. If we can derive from within ourselves false as well as true judgements, we shall need to decide which are which. But how are we to make this decision? Is there to be another process of recollection to help us find out? If so, we have an infinite regress on our hands.[6] If we can spare recollection from falling into these problems, so much the better; and we can—so long

---

[6] Compare this with the 'aviary' regress in *Theaetetus* 200a12 ff.

as we reject any interpretation that is not content to limit Plato's interests to the problem of how the slave boy got the right answers, but how he got the wrong ones as well.

THE *PHAEDO*

Nothing in the *Meno* suggests that recollection is used to explain the emergence of our pre-philosophical judgements. As we turn to the *Phaedo*, the focus of attention will be on the famous recollection passage at 72e3–77a5. Socrates' eventual purpose in this argument is to prove the immortality of the soul; and his precise intention at this stage is to demonstrate that the soul must have existed before birth. Using the form of equality as an example, Socrates claims that we have knowledge of the form, that we compare sensible equal objects with it, and that in order to make this comparison, we must already have knowledge of the form. He then tries to argue that we must have had knowledge of the form before we started to use our senses, and that the only time for this to have been is before birth; therefore the soul must have existed before birth. Many commentators have interpreted this passage as saying that recollection of the forms accounts for concept formation as well as the ability to compare forms and particulars.[7] For most of my discussion of the *Phaedo* I shall focus upon two closely related questions: First, what is recollection intended to explain? Second, who actually recollects? This second question arises

---

[7] It is now time to unmask some of the adherents of K in the *Phaedo*. The most articulate versions come from F. M. Cornford, *Plato's Theory of Knowledge* (London, 1935), 108; N. Gulley, 'Plato's Theory of Recollection', *Classical Quarterly*, ns 4 (1954), 194–213: 197 ff., and *Plato's Theory of Knowledge* (London, 1962), 31 ff.; J. L. Ackrill, '*Anamnēsis* in the *Phaedo*: Remarks on 73c–75c', in E. N. Lee, A. D. P. Mourelatos, and R. M. Rorty (eds.), *Exegesis and Argument*, *Phronesis*, suppl. vol. 1 (Assen), 177–95; and Bostock, *Plato's* Phaedo, 66 ff.

I have said that K interprets recollection as explaining concept formation, but just what is meant by 'concept formation' varies from one version of K to another. The most careful claims are made by Bostock, who argues that recollection accounts for our ordinary and everyday grasp of meanings of those words, such as 'equal', of which there are no paradigm examples provided by sense-perception; it should also be pointed out that Bostock gives a more linguistic slant to the issue than other commentators by talking about 'meanings of terms' rather than 'concepts'. At the other extreme, Gulley ('Plato's Theory of Recollection', 198 n. 2) thinks that the form of the argument of the *Phaedo* 'almost' implies an unlimited range of forms. This approach is more typical of commentators on the *Phaedrus*, where Plato is thought to be talking of the use of universals in language without implying any restriction whatever. Despite the differences between versions of K, I shall mount my attack on them as one body, because I am refuting interpretations which require recollection to explain any of our ordinary conceptual apparatus, however limited the range of concepts concerned.

I have argued for D in my *Recollection and Experience*. Independently, G. Fine ('Inquiry in the *Meno*', in R. Kraut (ed.), *Cambridge Companion to Plato* (Cambridge, 1992), 225 n. 41; *On Ideas: Aristotle's Criticism of Plato's Theory of Forms* (Oxford, 1993), 137–8) has argued for similar restrictions on the scope of recollection.

because Socrates frequently talks in the first-person plural and it is important to determine whether he is referring only to his circle of philosopher-friends or to people in general. But both questions are so bound up with each other that I shall treat them in tandem. If Socrates turns out to be explaining only philosophical thought, the franchise of recollection will be very limited; and if there are occurrences of the pronoun 'we' that obviously have a wide reference, the explanandum in question is likely to be a general cognitive achievement.

For most of this section I shall follow the actual course of the recollection argument of 72e3–77a5. After an introduction (72e3–73c10) containing back-references to the slave boy demonstration in the *Meno*, Socrates sets out some general conditions for recollection (73c1–74a8). In the next two parts he focuses on two cognitive achievements: the first, that we have come to think of the form of equality from perceiving the particulars (74a9–d3), and the second, that we compare the particulars to the form (74d4–75a4). This sets the stage for the crux of the argument, 74e9–75c6, where he argues that we could not have had such thoughts unless we had already known the form before we first used our senses, i.e. before birth. There is then a further stretch of argument to convince Simmias that we forget our knowledge of the form equal at birth and regain it by recollection (75d7–76d5). Socrates now thinks that he has shown that the soul must have pre-existed the body, and so brings the argument to a close, stressing, among other things, the importance of the existence of forms to the whole argument (76d7–77a5).

General conditions for recollection (73c1–74a8)

In this passage Socrates sets out four conditions for recollection. If we are reminded of *x* by *y*,

(1) we must have known *x* beforehand (73c1–3),
(2) we must not only recognize *y* but also think of *x* (73c6–8),
(3) *x* must not be the object of the same knowledge as *y* but of another (73c8–9),
(4) when *x* resembles *y*, we must consider whether *y* is lacking at all in relation to *x* (74a5–7).

All these conditions, especially the third and fourth, are to play crucial roles in the ensuing argument. We shall come back to them later.

We know what the equal is (74a9–d3)

Socrates now secures Simmias' agreement that we know what the equal is (74a9–b3):

'We say, don't we, that there is something *equal*—I don't mean a log to a log, or a
stone to a stone, or anything else of that sort, but some further thing beyond all
those, the equal itself: are we to say that there is something or nothing?'
    'We are, by Zeus,' said Simmias; 'remarkably!'
    'And do we know what it is?'
    'Certainly.'

On K, Socrates is here talking about everyone's mundane grasp of a universal concept which enables them to recognize particulars as being equal,
and underwrites their ability to use language. On D, this is not a discussion of how we originally classified the sticks and stones as equal, nor of
how it is that we understand the term 'equal' in ordinary empirical judgements about particulars. The fact that we talk of sticks and stones as being
equal is simply presupposed. Instead, Socrates focuses on the philosophical understanding of an entity very remote from most people's thoughts,
the form of equality.

An important clue to which interpretation is correct can be found in
74b1, in the way in which Simmias reacts to Socrates' claim that we say
'there is something *equal*'. Simmias uses the adverb 'remarkably' or 'amaz-
ingly' (*thaumastos*). This is a phrase very often watered down by translators into 'emphatically'. But this is misleading. Whatever Socrates is talking
about, it is an object of wonder (*thauma*), and this is hardly an appropriate way to refer to the fact that sticks or stones are equal.

Now turn back to the sentence that provoked Simmias' exclamation in
the first place. Socrates starts by specifying where his interest lies: 'we say,
don't we, that there is something equal'. This is the form of equal, some
further thing beyond all the particulars, whose very being Simmias rightly
acknowledges to be remarkable. But in the middle of this sentence and
very conveniently for us, Socrates also tells us what he is not interested in:
'. . . I don't mean a log to a log, or a stone to a stone, or anything else of
that sort . . .'. This expression is elliptical and, if filled out, would run: '. . .
I don't mean that we say that a stick is equal to a stick . . .'. This is the kind
of statement that Socrates dismisses as irrelevant to his argument, and yet
it is precisely in such statements that our humdrum grasp of the concepts
and meanings is manifested. That Socrates is prepared to dismiss such
statements so early in the argument is a good indication that recollection
is not to be invoked to explain our ordinary grasp of 'equal'.

The idea that recollection is meant to explain concept formation, moreover, is not merely absent from the text, but is also the source of acute
difficulties—difficulties that have been brought out even by the defenders
of K.[8] One problem, which Ackrill puts his finger upon, concerns the third

---

[8] See e.g. Gulley, 'Plato's Theory of Recollection', 197–8.

of the four conditions for recollection set out above.[9] Plato is right to point out that if we are to be reminded of x by y, then we must have a recognition of y that does not involve knowledge of x, otherwise we have the absurd result that in recognizing y we are already thinking of x, and so recollection of x is impossible. But if we insist that Plato is using recollection to explain concept formation, if, that is, we need to have recollected the form equal in order to recognize the stick's equality, then we invite just that absurdity. In order to recognize the equal stick we already need to be thinking of the form, and so we cannot then go on to recollect it. If, on the other hand, we have not already recollected the form, then, on the assumption that recollection is meant to explain concept formation, we cannot recognize the equal stick as an equal stick, and so, in the absence of any associative bond,[10] it cannot serve as a stimulus for recollection. Either way, recollection of forms from sensible particulars will be impossible. In fact, we find ourselves impaled on a dilemma very much like the paradox in *Meno* 80e1–5, which is a cruel irony, because that was originally the very problem that recollection was meant to solve. If, however, we do not say that reminding is meant to explain concept formation, all these problems disappear. Of course, recollection does explain concept formation of a very special kind, viz. our knowledge of Platonic forms, but not the formation of those concepts that we employ in ordinary thought.

According to D, the concepts that we need to say 'these sticks are equal' are formed by perception, and recollection has not as yet come into the picture. So not only does Plato not use recollection to explain our grasp of the equality of particulars—he actually gives his own empiricist explanation. The clearest evidence for this part of my interpretation comes not in the recollection passage itself, however, but in the 'affinity' argument of 78c10ff., and it is worth looking ahead to this passage for a moment. In this argument, Plato starts with the distinction between forms and particulars and applies a series of opposing characteristics to the two types of entity. The first pair is changing and unchanging (78d1–e5), the second perceptible and non-perceptible. Plato asserts quite unequivocally that the particulars are perceived whereas the forms cannot be. So, to use the example of the form of equality that he cites in 78e1, this implies that the sticks, their equality included, are perceptible. This goes against K's assumption that the 'stickness' of the stick is perceptible but not its

---

[9] Ackrill, '*Anamnēsis* in the *Phaedo*', 183: 'There may be a lurking danger for Plato's programme. For if reminding is to explain concept-formation, can a pre-condition for reminding be recognition or something akin to it?'

[10] On the associative bond, see 76a3–4.

equality. K would therefore have to say that in this passage Plato is being careless.

This move, however, is extremely implausible. If Plato had meant that particulars were in part perceptible and in part imperceptible, why would he not say so? It is exactly what he says about human beings. We are part body, part soul (79b1–2). We straddle the ontological divide that he is carefully building up. It would be extremely strange if he thought that particulars did the same, and yet said nothing at all about it. Furthermore, the symmetry on which so much of the argument depends would be at best thrown into jeopardy. It is far more plausible to assume that Plato means what he says. Particulars, their equality included, are perceptible.[11]

We have noticed the deficiency of the particulars to the form (74d4–75a4)

This section is particularly embarrassing for K. Throughout it the interest lies not in classification, but in something very different, namely, the comparison between form and particulars. Socrates is not focusing on the fact that we use the terms 'equal', 'good', etc., nor is he restricting himself to the claim that we recognize that equal objects are, in certain contexts, unequal. He is taking all this for granted and saying that we refer these equals to another which is never unequal, which, of course, involves having the form before our mind. Once it is clear that comparison is what is at issue here, it is easy to see the absurdity of claiming that recollection is meant to explain mundane cognitive achievements made by everyone. Platonists may go around saying that sticks and stones fall short of being like the form of equal, but who else does? If we can avoid trivializing Plato's argument by attributing to him such assumptions, so much the better; and D allows us to do this.

[11] J. T. Bedu-Addo ('Sense-Experience and the Argument for Recollection in Plato's *Phaedo*', *Phronesis*, 36 (1991), 27–60: 49 n. 35) holds that all people recollect to some degree, though their knowledge of forms is operative only subconsciously. However, apart from the fact that there is no mention in the text of any such subconscious operations, this interpretation is ruled out by the claim in the affinity argument that perception is sufficient to account for our grasp of the equality of particulars.

Apart from the affinity argument, one text which shows that the equality, for instance, of particulars is perceptible is 75b6–7. Here he talks about comparing *the equals from our sense-perceptions* to the form . . . (εἰ ἐμέλλομεν τὰ ἐκ τῶν αἰσθήσεων ἴσα ἐκεῖσε ἀνοίσειν . . .). This implies that we do grasp the equality of the particulars from the senses and it is this sensible equality that we compare with the form. The point of the phrase is that whatever we are comparing to the form comes from the senses, and it makes little sense to say that we are comparing the stick *minus* its equality with the form. Rather, the stick is deficient to the form because there is something wrong with its equality; so its equality must be perceptible.

Furthermore, there are some explicit remarks in this section of the argument that restrict the cognitive achievements in question to a small number of people. Remember again that in 74d4–75a3 Plato focuses on the comparison as his explanandum. Now at 74d9–e4 he describes this act from the point of view of the person making it: 'Then whenever anyone, on seeing a thing, thinks to himself, "this thing that I now see seeks to be like another of the things that are, but falls short and cannot be like that object: it is inferior" do we agree that the man who thinks this must previously have known the object he says it resembles but falls short of?' As Ackrill has pointed out, what is remarkable about this sentence is its use of direct first-person speech.[12] The speaker who makes the comparison is quite clearly committed to the existence of forms that act as standards for the comparison.[13] It is equally clear from a later passage in the dialogue that the majority of people, the non-philosophers, take only the corporeal to be real (81b4–5). They reject the existence of Platonic forms and therefore cannot be those who are making the comparison described at 74d9–e4. That sentence can only apply to philosophers. Throughout this passage Plato is talking about the grasp of a form as a standard of comparison which is not some mundane cognitive achievement made by everyone but something quite remarkable and achieved, if at all, only by a few.

It is undeniable, then, that only a few people have compared forms and particulars. Once this is admitted, yet another argument in favour of D comes to light. At the beginning of the passage Socrates set out four conditions for recollection. The last of these was that if one thing reminds us of another, and the two things are similar, we also compare one to the other (74a5–7). In other words, if I have been reminded of a form by a particular, I have also compared the two. Thus, if I have not compared the particular with the form, I have not been reminded of the form by the particular. But, as we have just made clear, most people have not made the comparison; therefore, most people have not been reminded of the form.

We could not have compared the forms with the particulars unless we had already known the form before we first used our senses, i.e. before birth (74e9–75c6)

Socrates has been building up his argument very carefully. By now, he has specified four conditions for recollection, and has drawn attention to two

---

[12] Ackrill, '*Anamnēsis* in the *Phaedo*', 194–5.
[13] The form is described by the speaker as being 'one of the things that are' (τι τῶν ὄντων) at 74d10.

cognitive achievements—our knowledge of the form and our comparison between it and the particulars—that will form the basis of the argument for recollection. Given the implausibility of reading K into his description of these achievements, it seems that this interpretation has been squeezed out of the argument for good. Nevertheless, the next segment of the argument, 74e9–75c5, has given some encouragement to advocates of K. In this passage Socrates starts out from the claim that we compare the form equal with the particulars (74e6–7) and then presents a very condensed argument to prove that we must have had knowledge of the form before birth. Here is the argument in full:

[1] Then we must previously have known the equal, before that time when we first, on seeing the equals, thought that all of them were striving to be like the equal but fell short of it.

[2] Yet we also agree on this: we haven't derived the thought of it, nor could we do so, from anywhere but seeing or touching or some other of the senses—I'm counting all these as the same.

[3] But of course it's from one's sense-perceptions that one must think that all the things in the sense-perceptions are striving for that which is equal, yet are inferior to it . . .

[4] Then it must surely have been before we began to see and hear and use the other senses that we got knowledge of the equal itself, of what it is, if we were going to refer the equals from our sense-perceptions to it, supposing that all things are doing their best to be like it, but are inferior to it.

[5] Now we were seeing and hearing, and were possessed of our other senses, weren't we, just as soon as we were born?

[6] But we must, we're saying, have got our knowledge of the equal before these?

[7] Then it seems we must have got it before we were born.

Some commentators have seen in this argument evidence in favour of K.[14] In their view, the reference in (5) to what we have been doing since birth makes it sound as if recollection is meant to explain early learning after all. A closer look at this passage is needed.

In the previous section Socrates has said that we come to think of the form from the particulars and that this is recollection (73c13–74d2). He then focuses his attention on the judgement comparing the form equal and the particulars (74d4–e7), thus making way for the first step in the argument just quoted: we must have known the form before we first made that comparative judgement. The next move, (2), is to state that perception is a necessary condition for thinking of the form. We need not—and should not—take this as saying that perception *instils* knowledge of the form,[15] merely that use of the senses is a necessary condition for gaining know-

---

[14] Ackrill, '*Anamnēsis* in the *Phaedo*', 192.
[15] This would clash with 65d11 ff. and 82d9 ff.

ledge, i.e. that to start the process off, we must have our memories jogged by sensible stimuli.[16] In (3) Socrates insists that it is the senses that prompted us to make the comparative judgement. It is at this point that the argument starts to become very condensed because by the next stage, (4), Socrates feels entitled to claim that we must have grasped the form before we ever used our senses. Once this is conceded it is easier to draw the conclusion, as he does between (5) and (7), that the form must have been learnt before birth. So what is it about (3) that does so much work? The assumption behind the argument is that any sense-perception that prompted us to think of the form, the process referred to in (2), would *also* prompt us to make the comparison between form and particulars, the process referred to in (3); but if this perception prompted us to make the comparison we must, according to premiss (1), have already grasped the form before having that perception. Crucial to this argument is the assumption that the *same* perception that put us in mind of the form would *also* put us in mind of the comparison and, given the prior knowledge condition implicit in (1), no perception could play both roles. So the moment of learning the form will always be pushed further back.

This seems to be the correct analysis of the argument.[17] As it stands, however, it is vulnerable to the objection that the perception that first prompted us to think of the form need not have been the same one that prompted us to make the comparison. Thus Plato does not allow for the possibility that, first, one perception merely jogs us to think of the form (2), and then, later, another perception prompts us to compare it with the particulars (3). Why, in other words, do the stages mentioned in (2) and (3) have to be simultaneous? The force of such an objection is difficult to deny, but it could never be a reason for rejecting this interpretation because Plato, as we have just seen, is clearly committed to the assumption that if one thing reminds us of another, and the two things are similar, we also think whether one is deficient to the other (74a5–7).[18]

How does this interpretation of the argument of 74e9–75c5 affect the

<hr />

[16] Socrates is perhaps referring to the necessary role of sense-perception at 83a6–7. For a convincing explanation why Plato thinks that we are dependent on the senses in this way, see Bedu-Addo, 'Sense-Experience and the Argument for Recollection in Plato's *Phaedo*', 46–8.

[17] I am indebted to *Plato:* Phaedo, ed. C. J. Rowe (Cambridge, 1993), 172–3, for this interpretation.

[18] It is, of course, a highly questionable assumption and it is unfortunate that Plato does not attempt to provide more support for it. Nevertheless, its presence in the text can hardly be denied.

A further problem for the argument of 74e9–75c5 arises from stage (2). Why are the senses necessary as a catalyst for recollection? Another possibility, one that Plato ignores, is that we grasp the form by rational intuition without any need for the senses. But see Bedu-Addo, 'Sense-Experience and the Argument for Recollection in Plato's *Phaedo*', 46–8.

decision between D and K? First, it should be clear that Plato is in no way committed to the extraordinary claim that everyone has been comparing equal particulars with the form since birth. (This claim would be doubly weird. Not only is it false that everyone makes the comparison, as we have already noted, but it is even more outrageous to say that they have been doing this since birth.) The argument is making the much more subtle point that there could not be one perception that first put us in mind of the form and another later one that first put us in mind of the comparison. But when we were first prompted to make the comparison is not stipulated in this argument. To answer that question we need to turn back to the previous passage, 74d4–75a3, to examine the way in which he describes this comparison and the thinking of those who make it (74d9–e4). As we have just seen, this passage can only be talking about a cognitive achievement occurring relatively late in a person's development, if it occurs at all.

We forget our knowledge of the forms at birth and regain it by recollection (75d7–76d6)

Having now established that we did possess knowledge of the forms before birth, Socrates takes Simmias through an argument to decide whether we retain this knowledge consciously throughout our incarnate lives or whether we forget it at birth and recollect it later on. Simmias agrees to the second of these two options. Here is the point at which he does so:

'You don't think then, Simmias, that everyone knows those objects [sc. the forms]?'
  'By no means.'
  'Are they then being reminded of what they once learnt?'[19]
  'They must be.' (76c1–5)

At first sight the way Socrates states his conclusion in these lines, 'Are they then being reminded of what they once learnt?' (76c4), suggests that everyone is in the process of being reminded of the forms, a claim that clearly rules out D in favour of K. But a more careful look at the argument of which 76c4–5 is the conclusion will show that these lines cannot be used as evidence against D.

As we have just seen, the point of the present argument is to help Simmias to decide between two alternatives. Socrates sets each of them

---

[19] An alternative translation of this line would be 'Are they then reminded of what they once learnt?' This, however, would create a needless contradiction with an earlier passage. If Socrates and Simmias are now concluding that everyone recollects, they are contradicting what they have just decided, viz. that not everyone knows the forms. At 75e5–6 it has been stated that to recollect is to regain knowledge, so if everyone recollects, everyone knows, and this is just what has been denied.

out in 75d7–11 and e2–7 respectively and then at 76a4–7 repeats the choice facing Simmias as follows:

So, as I say, one of two things is true: either all of us were born knowing those objects [sc. the forms], and we know them throughout life; or those we speak of as 'learning' are simply being reminded later on, and learning would be recollection.

In the next few lines (76a9–b2) Socrates repeats to Simmias that he must make his choice.

When Socrates sums up the choice to Simmias at 76a4–7 his language is precise and clearly compatible with D. The first option is that we all have the knowledge at birth and retain it throughout our lives, the second that 'those we speak of as "learning"' recollect. The contrast between the phrase 'those we speak of as "learning"' in the second option and the word 'all' which qualifies the first-person plural in the first option is quite marked and deliberate. So the choice that Simmias has to make is not between everyone retaining their knowledge throughout their lives and *everyone* recollecting it, but between everyone retaining it and *some people* recollecting it.[20]

What, then, has happened at 76c4? If there is to be any coherence to the argument as a whole, this line must still be referring to one of the options put to Simmias at 76a4–7. On my reading, it does, but Socrates is expressing himself in shorthand. We need to supply something like 'those we speak of as "learning"' as the subject of 'are being reminded'. Consider the consequences of not doing this. First, one would have to explain why Socrates has changed the relevant option without saying so. Second, one would have to explain away the fact that the actual argument given in favour of 76c4 supports not the reading where everyone recollects but only the one where those who learn recollect.[21] In short, the only way of giving this passage any coherence is to restrict the subject of the verb 'are being reminded' in 76c4, and such a restriction, of course, favours D.[22]

We have now examined the individual segments of the recollection argument. There are also some points to be made by looking over the argument as a whole. We can start with two further arguments against reading K into the passage.

---

[20] The option set out in 76a4–7 has already been mentioned in 75e2–7. Here the wording is compatible with K but also with D.

[21] Notice how in 76b1–2 Socrates also presents the second option in an abbreviated form. As this line comes immediately after the precise formulation in 76a4–7, it is even more implausible that he should have modified it without explanation.

[22] Hackforth (*Plato's* Phaedo, ed. R. Hackforth (Cambridge, 1955), 72), presumably aware of the mismatch between 76c4 and preceding argumentation, translates the line as '*Can* they then recollect what they once learnt?' (my italics).

The first relates to the way in which K needs the 'we' of this passage to refer predominantly to ordinary people. Although there are certain points at which the reference of the pronoun may be a matter of controversy, there are others where it must apply only to Socrates' circle.[23] One such place is 75c10–d3 where Socrates says: 'our present argument concerns the beautiful itself, and the good itself, and just and holy, no less than the equal; in fact, as I say, it concerns everything on which we set this seal, "*what it is*", in the questions we ask and in the answers we give'. This is clearly an allusion to the kind of dialectical question and answer sessions in which philosophers, rather than ordinary people, would engage. Another obvious example of Socrates' use of the first-person plural to refer only to philosophers comes a little later at 76d8–e1, where he says that 'we' are always harping on the forms of beauty and goodness and comparing the sensible particulars to them.

If we try to do justice to the fact that in such places 'we' applies only to philosophers but also insist that in other places it applies to everyone, we have to make the referents of the pronoun veer without any warning between everyone and Platonists. This is a serious difficulty for K. D, on the other hand, allows no such unsignalled shifts in reference. True, at 76a5 'we' *does* apply to everyone: 'either all of us were born knowing those objects [sc. the forms], and we know them throughout life; or those we speak of as "learning" are simply being reminded later on, and learning would be recollection'. But this is quite acceptable on D's terms. The insertion of the word 'all' is very emphatic and is contrasted with 'those we speak of as "learning"' in what follows. These latter people are those who know, i.e. the 'we' of the previous passage (74b2). Plato has generalized the results of his argument to say that if some people recollect and have known before, there is no reason why everyone cannot have the knowledge latently, though there are several good reasons why not everyone recollects,[24] and this distinction is preserved in the emphatic contrast of subjects in 76a5–7.

The second problem for adherents of K is that, as well as requiring unsignalled shifts in the reference of 'we', they have to make the verb 'know' undergo an alarming change of meaning in the course of the passage. At 74b2–3, in the passage already quoted above, it is affirmed with some enthusiasm that we know the equal:

'We say, don't we, that there is something *equal*—I don't mean a log to a log, or a stone to a stone, or anything else of that sort, but some further thing

---

[23] On this issue, it is worth taking note of 64c1–2, where Socrates sets the esoteric tone of the dialogue by saying 'let us talk among ourselves, disregarding them [sc. the majority of people]'.

[24] See e.g. 83d4 ff.

beyond all those, the equal itself: are we to say that there is something or nothing?'

'We are, by Zeus,' said Simmias; 'remarkably!'

'And do we know what it is?'

'Certainly.'

At 76b5–c3, on the other hand, Simmias agrees that it is far from true that everyone has knowledge of the forms:

'If a man knows things, can he give an account of what he knows or not?'

'Of course he can, Socrates.'

'And do you think everyone can give an account of those objects [sc. the forms] we were discussing just now?'

'I only wish they could,' said Simmias; 'but I'm afraid that, on the contrary, this time tomorrow there may no longer be any man who can do so properly.'

'You don't think then, Simmias, that everyone knows those objects?'

'By no means.'

The only way for K to deal with this is to say that at 74b2 'know' means the ordinary knowledge of a concept, whereas at 76c1–2 it means proper philosophic knowledge of the definition. Without any warning, then, Plato makes the word undergo a considerable change of meaning.

D, on the other hand, can dispense with a shift in meaning of the word 'know' altogether, and so dissolve the problem completely.[25] When Simmias admits that he knows the equal, he means that he, like other Platonists, can give an account of a mathematical form, but does not concede any more than that. Then, at 75c7–d5, the argument is broadened to include all the forms, but it is not thereby implied that Simmias has knowledge of all of these, but simply that he engages in dialectical question and answer sessions about them (75d2–3).[26] That, in fact, is all that is needed to argue for recollection, just as in the *Meno* Socrates needs only to show that the slave boy has true beliefs (as opposed to knowledge; 85c6–7), but the argument for recollection is best introduced by citing the most successful case of this dialectical activity.

---

[25] *Contra* Bostock, *Plato's* Phaedo, 67–8. He concedes that 'know' changes from the mundane to the philosophical sense between 74b2 and 76b8, but thinks that this is the more economical way of dealing with the problem. If we restrict those who recollect to philosophers, he claims, 'there must actually be three levels of knowledge in play': proper philosophic knowledge, humdrum grasp of meanings, and a third intermediate kind which is the prerogative of philosophers, but falls short of a precise grasp of the definition (68). This argument, however, fails because, according to D, the passage makes no reference to our humdrum knowledge whatsoever. This sense of 'know' is not in play in the passage.

[26] I am following Hackforth (*Plato's* Phaedo, 76), here. Gallop (*Plato's* Phaedo, 133) objects to this view because 'moral and mathematical forms are expressly said to be on a par (75c10–d2)', but the only way in which all the forms are put on a par at 75c10 is by being objects of dialectical argument, not of knowledge.

D, therefore, has none of the problems K has in keeping track of the pronoun 'we' or the word 'know' throughout the recollection passage. Nevertheless, while we are looking at the passage as a whole, we need to answer a couple of problems that do seem to arise on D. First, even if we grant that in the *Phaedo*, at least, K does not have much textual backing and in fact leads us into appalling difficulties, have we not, in replacing it with D, chosen a rather implausible theory? It seems to claim that all the concepts by which we classify our sense-experience are empirically gained, while our grasp of the forms is recollected well after we have accumulated sense-experience. But this seems puzzling. If we have these two *distinct* sources, how is it that both our empirical concept and our recollected knowledge are of 'equal'? There must be *some* connection.

There is, and it is certainly no coincidence for Plato that both the empirical concept and the recollected knowledge are of 'equal'. But the explanation for this is not that information 'leaks' from our innate source into our beliefs about particulars. The similarity between the empirical concept and the recollected knowledge stems from the similarity between the objects that are apprehended. In Plato's middle-period ontology there are two levels of entities: forms existing separately from the physical world and particular instances of those forms. The particulars resemble the forms in a limited way, and this is no coincidence: they participate in the forms. If we apprehend the forms by recollection and the particulars by perception, there will indeed be a resemblance between the contents of recollection and perception, but that stems from the ontological link and not from a cognitive one. The similarity between our concepts is thus explained indirectly. It does not arise because our beliefs about particulars draw upon our innate grasp of forms, but because, unbeknownst to most people, the particulars themselves participate in the forms. The following analogy may help. One person sees the original of a painting in a museum; another sees a very bad copy. They have similar representations in their minds not because they have communicated with each other, but because there is a similarity between the objects themselves.

The second objection that we need to answer is this. On any interpretation of the recollection passage the overall course of the argument runs as follows. Everyone has in them knowledge of the forms; this knowledge was not acquired since birth but must have pre-existed birth; so the soul must have pre-existed the body. Then, with the help of the 'cyclical' argument, Socrates infers that the soul will continue to exist after it has lost its body. As in the *Phaedo* generally, Plato eventually wants to prove that all human souls are immortal, not merely the souls of philosophers. This raises a problem for an interpretation like D that imposes such restrictions on the numbers involved at the first stage of the argument. Will not this lack of universality persist all the way through to the conclusion so that Plato will have failed to prove that all souls are immortal? If, however, he were arguing that all people recollect to some degree, his argument would have the required generality.[27]

This objection can be met in two ways. First, the claim can hardly be that Plato has a better argument if we follow K rather than D. On D he takes a limited sample and generalizes from it on the assumption that it is more plausible that all human beings are fundamentally of the same type than of two radically different types.[28] Let it be conceded that the argument of the *Phaedo* as it stands is, strictly speaking, invalid. If we follow the other interpretation and assume that Plato is proceeding from what everyone does, then the chances of him using a *valid* argument may at first look higher. But this advantage has been purchased at an absurd cost. The argument, even if valid, is based on a premiss that is absurdly false and denied explicitly in the *Phaedo*, viz. that everyone compares particulars to forms. Now, the moment advocates of K bow to the inevitable and concede that the number of those who compare forms and particulars is very restricted, they have to accept that the strict conclusion of the argument as a whole is similarly restricted. For, as we have seen, the claim that people compare forms and particulars is vital to the argument for recollection and pre-existence (74e9–75c6) and, if the number of people making this comparison is limited, so must the number involved in any conclusion validly inferred from the argument.

Second, the objection exaggerates the problems involved in restricting the scope of those who recollect; it considers it a great problem if Plato's inductive base is as narrow as D makes it. The objection only has force if it can show that Plato would have shared these worries. A brief look at the recollection passage in the *Meno* shows that this is not the case. In this dialogue he attempts to prove the theory by taking one slave boy, showing him actually recollecting, and then assuming that if he can recollect, so can everyone else. He has no qualms about generalizing from one case, and hardly expects us to respond, 'What a clever and interesting slave; I wonder if anyone else can do this.' A similar strategy is followed in the *Phaedo*. In the *Meno* Socrates' argument depended upon the true opinions that the slave boy acquired during the interview and the claim that these had not

[27] For a statement of this objection, see *Plato's* Phaedo, ed. Gallop, 120, and Bostock, *Plato's* Phaedo, 67.
[28] It should be remembered that later in *Phaedo*, 81b1 ff. (and even more in the charioteer myth of the *Phaedrus*), Plato goes to some lengths to explain why some people manifest their innate knowledge while others do not.

already been learnt in this lifetime; the *Phaedo* parallels this with philosophers' knowledge of the equal and the claim that this was not derived
purely from perception. In both dialogues these premises are used jointly
to prove recollection for one or a small number of cases, from which
Socrates then makes a tacit generalization.

Now it might be suggested here that, although Socrates is not generalizing from the widest sample in the *Meno*, he is doing so from the hum-
blest sample which will do almost as well. Since someone of such humble
origins can recollect, so too can anyone else. But nowhere in the *Meno*
does Socrates actually argue in this way. What he does make use of is the
fact that, because the slave boy has always been in Meno's household, they
know that he cannot have already learnt geometry (85e3–6). It is not so
much that he is a *slave boy* but that he is *Meno's* slave boy that matters,
as it is this that ensures that the experiment is a controlled one.

Furthermore, the objection, with its scruples about generalizing from
a limited sample, is overlooking one of the most striking features of the
Meno passage. Here there are no less than three generalizing moves. The
first, as we have seen, is from what the slave boy can do to what everyone
can do. A second is from what can be done in geometry to what can be
done in ethics. The original problem in the dialogue came from the threat
of scepticism about moral discovery, and this Socrates tries to allay by
showing that discovery is possible in geometry; he then generalizes from
geometry to cover all branches of learning (85e2–3). The third generalization lies in his assumption that, because successful recollection is possible
where the questioner knows the answers, it will be possible where the questioner does not—as will be the case in an ethical inquiry. In none of
these cases does Plato show the slightest qualms about generalizing. So the
objector needs to explain why they are attributing such qualms to Plato in
the *Phaedo*, especially at the cost of such absurdity.

It should be pointed out that there is a strategy common to both the
Meno and the *Phaedo*, namely, that Plato is inferring not from the widest
sample, but from the *best* sample. In the *Meno* he takes one of the best
disciplines available and generalizes from that. In the *Phaedo* he takes
those who have made the best progress in inquiry and generalizes from
them.[29]

We have now established that recollection in the *Phaedo* is not used to
explain mundane concept formation, which is to be accounted for empirically instead. Thus the two-source aspect of the Demaratus analogy fits
the *Phaedo* well. Also, recollection is an activity confined to a few people

---

[29] This type of strategy was to be used again by Aristotle in the *Politics* 1. 5, 1254ª34 ff.

only; most people, though they do indeed have the knowledge latently, do not manifest it. Before we leave this dialogue, we need to discuss the remaining issue implicit in the Demaratus analogy, namely the sense in which Plato's theory is pessimistic.

So far we might say our interpretation of the *Phaedo* is pessimistic in that far fewer people engage in recollection than some commentators have imagined. However, we have yet to show where the element of deception enters. True, most people rest content only with the information of the senses. But why should we say that they are *deceived* rather than merely missing out on something else? The analogy of Demaratus' tablet makes recollection out to be a deeply pessimistic doctrine. The surface message is actually deceptive and some way contradicts the message underneath. Is this right?

In fact, in stressing the element of deception, the analogy picks up on a point that is made in the *Phaedo* both before and after the recollection argument. Towards the beginning of the dialogue Socrates explains to his companions why he is so confident in the face of death. This is because death is the separation of the soul from the body and the moment when the soul no longer relies upon input from the senses. This is a benefit because, as he says at 65b4–6, there is no truth, accuracy, or clarity in the senses. The more the soul can separate itself from the bodily organs, the better its chances of attaining the truth. In this section one part of the fault attributed to the senses, or more generally to the body, has to do with the fact that they distract the soul from intellectual activity; the other part stems from the fact that they fill it with images or fantasies,[30] and in a passage after the recollection argument, Plato, with added emphasis, returns to the idea that the senses actually mislead us.

From 82d9 onwards he talks of the way in which philosophy takes over the soul and tries to release it from the prison of the body by showing the soul that 'inquiry through the eyes is full of deceit, and deceitful, too, is inquiry through the ears and other senses'. But what exactly is this deceit meant to involve? If the senses tell us that two sticks are on one occasion equal and on another unequal, Plato nowhere says that this sort of information is actually false. True, they do not tell us about the form equality, but that in itself is not deceit. However, Plato's point, developed at 83c5 ff., is that bodily experiences, such as pleasures and pains, tempt us to 'take to be real whatever the body declares to be so' (83d4–6). Because of the vividness of these experiences, we are tempted to assume that only the corporeal can be real (81b4–6). This is the point at which the senses

---

[30] 66c3 (εἰδώλων).

provide us with something that contradicts the correct metaphysic attained in recollection, and it is now easy to see how the Demaratus analogy does justice to the epistemology of the *Phaedo*. Those who attend to the surface message alone without having any inkling of the message underneath are, like the Persians in our story, simply deceived. Furthermore, the way in which the Greeks scrape away the wax to get down to the message underneath parallels a crucial feature in the *Phaedo*. What is required for any successful inquiry is that we turn away from the perspective gained from sense-perception. Philosophy is essentially discontinuous with this perspective. The other interpretation, K, mistakenly advocates not a rejection of the senses, but rather a synthesis between their message and our innate resources, and it is far from clear how, on this interpretation, the point about deception is to be understood.

THE *PHAEDRUS*

Those who interpret recollection as an explanation of concept formation have not confined their attention to the *Meno* and the *Phaedo*. There is another passage in which recollection plays an important part, the famous allegory in the *Phaedrus* (246a–257b) where Plato assimilates the experience of philosophy to the madness of love. The passage begins with the image of the soul as a winged charioteer drawn by two horses. In company with the gods, it follows a procession beyond the vault of the universe to attain a glimpse of true reality, a vision of the forms. While the souls of the gods achieve this with ease, ours do so with more difficulty (247b1–3). But such a vision is vital for the well-being of the soul and provides nourishment for its wings. Those that do attain a glimpse of the forms remain unscathed. But those that miss out on the vision may lose their wings and fall to earth (248c5–8). Here they are imprisoned in a mortal body like an oyster trapped in a shell, and in the process forget their vision of the forms. In the first incarnation after the fall, the soul must enter a human body. After its first incarnation it can choose to enter another human life or an animal one. If it chooses the latter, it can return to a human body in a future incarnation.

At this point, 249c4, Plato turns to his central topic, the nature of love, which he portrays as the highest kind of madness. This is explained partly by the contribution of the theory of recollection. A soul reincarnated as a human can, by coming into contact with a particular instance of beauty, begin to recollect its vision of the form of beauty. As it does so, as it comes to recognize the form of beauty dimly reflected in the particular, it is overcome by emotions of extraordinary power (250a6–b1). Such is the strength of these feelings that the person's whole life is turned upside-down and, in the lengths to which he will go to see his beloved and redeem his vision of the form, he appears completely mad to his fellow human beings. On recalling the form through the particular, the lover experiences pain, which Plato describes through the image of the wings of the soul regrowing, causing the kind of prickling and irritation that children have when they are first cutting their teeth (251c1–4).

Recollection is given a central role to play in the myth. But is it recollection as we have found it in the *Phaedo*, or is it as K interprets it? Throughout this passage Plato associates recollection with an experience that feels extraordinary to the person who has it and that makes him appear a madman to the majority of people around him. In my view this tells strongly in favour of D. But there is a brief passage which many have thought to point to K. Just before he begins to describe the process of recollection, Plato talks of the choice of incarnation that faces souls after their fall (249b1). After their first incarnation they may become animals. If they do this they can later be reincarnated as a human. But he adds that only a soul which has seen the forms can become a human. And it is when he spells out the reason for this that advocates of K prick up their ears:

For only the soul that has beheld truth may enter into this our human form: seeing that man must understand the language of forms, passing from a plurality of perceptions to a unity comprehended by reasoning; and such understanding is a recollection of those things which our souls saw before as they journeyed with their god, looking down upon things we now suppose to be, and gazing up to that which truly is. (249b5–c4)

Although there are a number of difficulties about the language used, difficulties that have provoked attempts to alter the text, most commentators interpret this passage in a way that clearly favours the K interpretation. Hackforth,[31] for instance, interprets the line of argument as follows:

Plato is careful to insist that the soul of an animal can pass into the body of a man only if the reverse transmigration has preceded (249b4). This has of course already been said, or implied, at 248d1, but the reason for it is now given, namely that only

---

[31] *Plato's* Phaedrus, ed. Hackforth, 91. See also Thompson (*Plato:* Phaedrus (London, 1868), 55), who says 'it is a law of human understanding that it can only act by way of generic notions ... sensibles are *per se* unintelligible'. One scholar who does not follow this line, remarkably enough, is Gulley ('Plato's Theory of Recollection', 201), who, despite his reading of the *Phaedo*, does not take the *Phaedrus* passage as an attempt to explain the possibility of reasoning from sensation to conceptual apprehension. See also T. Irwin, *Plato's Moral Theory* (Oxford, 1977), 173.

souls which have seen true being in the supra-celestial procession can possess that power of conceptual thought which distinguishes man. If it were possible to imagine a soul starting its existence in an animal, its capacity of thinking when it passed into a man's body could not be accounted for.

On this interpretation, recollection, or its first stages, is invoked to explain the possibility of conceptual thought. Taking this sentence in this way does, it has to be admitted, makes the argument of 249b–c a smooth one, and so we may be reluctant to interfere in such a way as to upset this.

Attractive as this interpretation seems, however, there are very strong grounds for rejecting it. As I have already indicated, one lies in the way Plato goes on to describe recollection in the rest of the myth. K makes at least the earlier phase of recollection something routine and something experienced by every human being. As we shall now see, this flies in the face of much that he says about recollection elsewhere in the myth.

First of all, we should keep a firm grip on the way Plato characterizes recollection. In recollecting, the lover undergoes a transition (250e2); the particular becomes the stimulus for a movement away towards the form. This shows how Plato conceives of recollection throughout the allegory as a matter of coming to see one thing through another. It also helps to explain the connection that Plato draws between recollection and the madness of love. It is because he sees so extraordinary an object through the particular that he is considered mad (249c8–d3): 'Standing aside from the busy doings of mankind, and drawing nigh to the divine, he is rebuked by the multitude as being out of his wits, for they know not that he is possessed by a deity.' A few lines later the madness of the lover is explained by his attempt to make this transition to the form (249d4–e1). It is this kind of transition that keeps recollection far apart from anything mundane or routine.

The same point emerges from the connection between recollection and the regrowth of the wings. The act of recollection, of seeing the form in the particular, nourishes the shoots of the wings and helps them to grow again. But it also causes a strange feeling of pain (251b1–c5):

by reason of the stream of beauty entering through his eyes there comes a warmth, whereby his soul's plumage is fostered; and with that warmth the roots of the wings are melted, which for long had been so hardened and closed up that nothing could grow; then as the nourishment is poured in, the stump of the wing swells and hastens to grow from the root over the whole substance of the soul: for aforetime the whole soul was furnished with wings. Meanwhile she throbs with ferment in every part, and even as a teething child feels an aching and a pain in its gums when a tooth has just come through, so does the soul of him who is *beginning* to grow his wings feel a ferment and a painful irritation. (my italics)

Plato associates recollection, even in its *earliest* stages, with the extraordinary feeling of the regrowth of the wings. Again, there is no stage of recollection that is represented as routine.

By using these associations between recollection, the madness of love, and the regrowth of the wings, Plato sets the person who recollects apart from the many. This amounts to a clear-cut distinction between two kinds of people, the lover and the non-lover, a distinction that Plato retains throughout the allegory. Here he is talking about the non-lover at 249e4:

> but to be put in mind [of the forms] by the things here is not easy for every soul; some, when they had the vision, had it but for a moment; some, when they had fallen to earth were unfortunate enough to be corrupted by evil associations, with the result that they forgot the holy objects of their vision.

Notice that when Socrates talks of those who have forgotten by falling into the wrong company, there is no suggestion that they can remember anything at all. On the other hand, they are perfectly well able to classify particulars under concepts. In other words, the knowledge that they have forgotten has nothing to do with the wherewithal for human intelligence in general to function.

Plato describes the non-lover in more detail at 250e1–5:

> Now he whose vision of the mystery is long past, or whose purity has been sullied, cannot pass swiftly hence to see absolute beauty, when he beholds that which is called beautiful here; wherefore he looks upon it with no reverence, and surrendering to pleasure he tries to go after the fashion of a four-footed beast and to beget children . . .

When such people view a beautiful object, they do not see it as a likeness of the original at all, and so treat it with no respect. The real lover, on the other hand, treats the sensibles as reminders of the vision, not as objects of desire in themselves.[32] When he recollects, he feels an emotional tug, provoked by the divine associations of the form, and his whole attitude is conditioned by this. The non-lover, however, experiences none of this, but acts like an animal (250e4–5), i.e. *as if he had never seen the form*. There is an emotional dimension that is lacking in the case of the non-lover, because the memory of the forms is playing no role in his life at all. Yet, since there is nothing to say that he cannot classify an object as beautiful, the memory of the forms is not invoked to explain such mundane acts of recognition.

So recollection, recognizing the form through the particular, is seen in the passage as a transition which inevitably involves an extraordinary

---

[32] Compare 249c7.

emotional experience and sets one person apart from the many. Because the wings begin to grow from the very start of the recollective process, all stages of recollection will be accompanied by this experience. Thus, the *Phaedrus* fits very well with D—except for the sentence at 249b6–8. K's account of this, initially attractive as it is, presents us with an anomaly in the wider context of the myth. We need, therefore, to take a closer look at the passage. The crucial sentence ran: 'man must understand the language of forms, passing from a plurality of perceptions to a unity comprehended by reasoning'.[33] Socrates then goes on to identify this cognitive achievement with the process of recollection.

There are a number of questions to be asked about this sentence. First, what level of cognition is implied by the word 'understand' (*sunienai*)? It could mean 'understand something said' in a casual sense (hence the commentators' point about generic terms essential to language and rational thought). Alternatively, we can take it as understanding of a more advanced kind (i.e. having knowledge of) an account or definition according to a Platonic form, something quite different from an innocent generic concept. So far there seems to be nothing to push us either way; the language leaves it open.

Things tilt in favour of D when we come to the word translated as 'reasoning' (*logismos*). This is a word that means 'calculation' (often in a mathematical sense), implying a deliberate, perhaps laborious activity, unlike the automatic generalizing process which K reads into the text. Furthermore, in the same part of the sentence, Plato talks about a movement away from many sense-perceptions to the form. Now K takes this to refer to the way in which we move from raw sense-data to the generic terms by which we understand them. But Plato's language corresponds much more closely to D, according to which we move away from sensible appearances in this world, leaving them behind, and go on to contemplate the form on its own. From what has emerged from our analysis of the overall context, this is clearly the point of the passage as a whole. What K is advocating, however, is not a departure from one to the other, but rather a synthesis of the two which is necessary to generate empirical understanding.

One proponent of K, Hackforth, refers us to *Republic* 476a for a parallel usage of this language of 'going to the form'. Yet if we look at that passage we do indeed find a parallel, but not one which helps K. At *Republic* 476b10–11 Socrates says that those who would be able to go[34] to the

---

[33] δεῖ γὰρ ἄνθρωπον συνιέναι κατ᾽ εἶδος λεγόμενον, ἐκ πολλῶν ἰὸν αἰσθήσεων εἰς ἓν λογισμῷ συναιρούμενον. On the translation of this sentence, see Scott, *Recollection and Experience*, 77 n. 26.

[34] Note that he uses the same verb as in *Phaedrus* 249b7 (ἰέναι).

beautiful itself would be few, and he says this to contrast the philosophers with people who do not acknowledge the form at all. At 476a4–7 he has just stated in no uncertain terms the distinction between the one form and the many particulars, which are also called appearances (thus recalling the reference to perception at *Phaedrus* 249b7–c1). So this section of the *Republic* is certainly an excellent parallel for the *Phaedrus* passage, according to D at least. In both cases, the philosopher moves away from the many objects of sense-perception to the one form which is apprehended by reasoning.

What is emerging is that the crucial sentence fits better with D than with K when examined internally. But if we now take it to be referring to the way a philosopher moves away from particulars to forms, how are we to understand the claim that humans *must* make this transition? On K, where Plato was talking about reasoning according to universals, the word 'must' had a descriptive sense: 'it is a fact of human nature that we have rational thought'. But if we take the word 'must' descriptively, and yet interpret the rest of the sentence as an account of distinctively philosophical reasoning, we end up with a blatant falsehood. It is not a fact of human nature that everyone makes the transition to the forms as a philosopher does. This problem, however, is easily solved. We take the word 'must' in a prescriptive sense: human beings *ought* to go to the form, whether we actually do or not. It is our epistemological (and hence moral) duty. This notion should already be familiar to us from the *Meno*. At the end of the slave boy demonstration, Socrates emphasizes our epistemological duty to continue to inquire: 'one thing I am ready to fight for as long as I can, in word and act: that is, that we shall be better, braver, and more active if we believe we must[35] look for what we don't know than if we believe there is no point inquiring because what we don't know we can never discover' (86b7–c2). Another parallel, this time from a very similar context to that of the *Phaedrus*, comes in Diotima's speech about the ascent to the form of beauty in the *Symposium*, 210a4 ff. Here she talks of the different stages in the movement away from particulars to the form, and at each one says how we *must* make the ascent.[36]

If the crucial sentence of 249b6–c1 refers to the duty that human beings have to ascend from particulars to forms, we are left with one final question: how is it supposed to fit into the surrounding pattern of argument? According to K, the order of argument ran as follows: all human beings reason according to universals; because this cognitive achievement

---

[35] Again, there is an important similarity of language. The word for 'must' in this line, 86b8, is the same as in *Phaedrus* 249b6 (δεῖ).

[36] From 210a4–e1 there is a string of verbs governed by 'must' (δεῖ) in 210a4.

involves recollection of the forms, a soul that has never seen the forms cannot enter a human form. On D, we do still have an argument, though a different one: human beings have an obligation to make a philosophical transition to the form; this involves recollecting the forms, and so a soul that has never seen the forms cannot enter a human form. In other words, unlike animals, human beings have the obligation to become philosophers, and—if 'ought' implies 'can'—only a soul which has seen the forms can do this and so have this obligation.

The Demaratus interpretation turns out to fit with Plato's treatment of recollection in the *Phaedrus* after all. The type of argument that K reads into 249b5–c4 initially seemed plausible, but the language of the crucial sentence actually favours D, and an argument can still be extracted on this reading. If we then recall that the context of the myth as a whole favours D, the matter is settled. The *Phaedrus*, in fact, seems to treat the theory of recollection much as the *Phaedo* does, tying it down firmly to the separation of copy and model that is one strand in the middle-period theory of forms.

I have argued that, for Plato, most people never even begin to recover from the amnesia that they suffer at birth. The *Meno* provides no evidence for the more optimistic view, K, and the *Phaedo* and *Phaedrus* provide plenty of evidence against it. Perhaps it is worth noting, by way of conclusion, that someone who defends K is like an interpreter of *Republic* 7 who thought that the prisoners at the bottom of the cave make sense of the shadows by reference to the objects outside. Curiously, although almost no one takes so bizarre a view of the *Republic*, there are several interpreters prepared to adopt the equivalent approach to recollection.

IV

LANGUAGE AND REALITY IN PLATO'S *CRATYLUS*

J. L. ACKRILL

INTRODUCTION

The *Cratylus* is a curious dialogue, and it is perhaps not surprising that it has not been a favourite among scholars or among philosophers, at least until recently. About half of the dialogue, a great chunk in the middle, speculates about the etymology of Greek words in a manner that is sometimes amusing, but often just boring. The arguments in the other half used to be interpreted in a rather narrow way, as concerned with the origin of language, or with the suitability of particular names for particular things. More recently, serious and complicated philosophical issues have been found to be raised by these argumentative parts of the *Cratylus*, though there remains dispute as to how many of the issues were in Plato's own mind, and also as to how the various parts of the dialogue hang together. The typical modern approach will regard the etymological section of the dialogue as only mildly interesting, but will discover in the rest of it material relevant to a number of important topics in the philosophy of language, philosophical logic, and metaphysics—topics carried forward in the *Theaetetus* and *Sophist*. As usual with Plato, fundamental ideas are presented in a very simple way; but it is often instructive to get back from sophisticated modern discussions to the basic essentials.

The *Cratylus* opens with a confrontation between Hermogenes and Cratylus, who hold opposed views on a *linguistic* question, whether names are purely conventional or have some natural correctness; and the dialogue mainly consists in an examination of the two rival answers to these questions. But it ends with a confrontation between two *ontological* theories, the Heraclitean doctrine of flux and the Platonic doctrine of Forms. It is not obvious that there is any correlation between the two linguistic theses and the two ontological theses. It is true that the historical Cratylus,

From J. L. Ackrill, *Essays on Plato and Aristotle* (Clarendon Press, 1997), 33–52. Reprinted with permission from Oxford University Press and the author.

presented in the dialogue as an exponent of the nature theory of language, was in fact (and is presented as) an exponent of an extreme flux view of reality; but there seems no necessary or rational connection between that theory and this view. For the one is a theory about how names name *whatever* there is; the other is a theory about what there is. Nor does Hermogenes' rival conventionalist view seem to involve the rival ontological view, the theory of Forms.

If the contrast between flux and Forms is somewhat surprising as the outcome of a discussion of the two linguistic views, it is also somewhat surprising in itself, in that the obvious alternative to the view that everything is in continuous flux is that *not* everything is in continuous flux, that there is some stability in reality. But the thesis that there are unchanging Forms goes much further than that.

In this essay[1] I discuss some of the arguments and ideas about language which the *Cratylus* contains, partly for their own interest and partly in the hope of throwing light on the question how the arguments about language are related to ontological theses.

It may be useful to give first a brief outline of the structure of the dialogue. In 383–391a Socrates argues against Hermogenes, who holds that anyone can call anything what he likes, and that there is no '*natural* correctness' of names; and the outcome of the whole section seems to be that there must be *some* such 'natural correctness', though it is not yet clear what this is.

391b–421d is a long etymological section designed to show, by analysing compound words and tracing them back to their elementary parts, what the original or basic words were, and thus to show why compound words have the meanings they have. This section leaves untouched the question why and how the elementary or 'primary' words had (or have) the meanings *they* had (or have). And this question leads into the next section.

421d–427 concerns the primary, elementary names or words, and considers the suggestion that *they* successfully and correctly do their job in so far as they imitate (or represent by *likeness*) the things they stand for—a sort of picture theory of meaning.

428e–435c attacks Cratylus' contention that there is a natural correctness of names, that only naturally correct names are names at all, and that falsity is impossible.

---

[1] This essay is based on two lectures delivered in Florence in April 1990. The lectures did not argue for a single thesis, but were designed as an introduction to the *Cratylus* and a stimulus to thought about some of the issues it raises. I hope that this published version may serve the same purposes.

435d–440 argues that knowledge of things is prior to knowledge through language, and that language and knowledge would be impossible on the flux theory, but are possible if there are unchanging Forms.

I

I shall first analyse the argument against Hermogenes and make some comments on it. In the second part of the essay I shall pick out for discussion certain main ideas from the rest of the dialogue, before finally drawing some general conclusions.

The main argument may be divided into seven sections, preceded by three short preliminary passages:

Preliminaries	(*a*) 383a3–385a	The two views
	(*b*) 385b–c	Truth and falsity
	(*c*) 385d	Hermogenes' view
Sections	(1) 385e4–386e5	Things
	(2) 386e6–387b7	Doings
	(3) 387b8–c5	Saying
	(4) 387c6–d9	Naming
	(5) 387d10–388c8	Teaching
	(6) 388c9–389a4	Name-making
	(7) 389a5–391a	Ideal names and the dialectician

Preliminaries (*a*) and (*c*) are mainly concerned with setting out the rival views. At the beginning of the dialogue (383a4–b2) Cratylus is said to hold 'that for each thing there is a correct name that belongs to it by nature: a name is not whatever any set of people have agreed to call a thing and do call it . . . but there is some natural correctness of names which is the same for all, both Greeks and barbarians'. Hermogenes, on the other hand, says (384d1–8): 'correct naming is simply a matter of convention and agreement. . . . Whatever name anyone gives a thing is its correct name; and if he then changes to another name and stops using the first one, then the new name is no less correct than the old one was, as when we rename our servants. No name ever belonged to anything by nature, only by custom and habit, that is, through people becoming habituated to its use.' Further formulations of Hermogenes' view are to be found at 385a and 385d–e3.

Hermogenes' thesis is not as precise as one would wish. Firstly, the word *onoma* (translated 'name') can cover both proper names and general or

abstract names ('dog' or 'generosity'); it can even be extended to include
adjectives, or indeed any words. So the exact scope of Hermogenes' thesis
is unclear. In what follows I shall usually speak of *names*, though many of
the examples discussed in the *Cratylus* would not usually be called names
by us, but *words*; and I shall myself sometimes speak of *words* in discussing
Plato's arguments and ideas. Secondly, there are differences, to which Hermogenes is not attentive, among such ideas as agreement, convention,
stipulation, and custom. These differences are perhaps unimportant for his
essential thesis, which is not about the exact way in which names are
initially introduced *into* a language, but about what enables them to be
correct names *in* a language. This depends, Hermogenes will maintain, on
the language-users' all *using* the names to stand for certain things, and *not*
on the existence of any *natural* relation between the names and those
things.

It *is*, however, a defect in Hermogenes' statements that they do not
emphasize sufficiently the crucial distinction between (i) the word-
introduction (whether by fiat or by agreement or in any other way) that
establishes rules for the use of a word, and (ii) the subsequent use of the
word, which is correct if it is in accordance with those rules. The clearest
expression of this distinction in the Greek is at 385d8–9, the contrast
between the past event of introducing a word (ἐθέμην) and the continuous
present custom of using it (καλεῖν). Hermogenes' thesis is not that every
subsequent use of a word that has been introduced is a correct use (i.e. a
use in accordance with the established rules for its use), but that there are
no natural constraints on what rules may be established when a word is
introduced.

The little section I have labelled (*b*), 385b–c, is an argument to the conclusion that there are true and false names. It contains a number of
difficulties, but I will make just two points, one about the content of the
passage, the other about its relevance in the dialogue.

Socrates infers from the fact that there are true and false *logoi* (sentences or statements) to the conclusion that there are true and false
onomata (names or words), on the ground that a *logos* is a whole and
onomata are its parts. This is altogether too crude as a general argument,
since wholes often have characteristics that do *not* attach to their parts.
But it does suggest an important point. Consider a standard basic statement such as 'Callias is a man'. This statement is *true* if and only if 'Callias'
is *true* of something and 'a man' is also *true* of that thing. The truth of
such statements cannot be analysed or understood without the notion of
true of which applies to names. And conversely, this notion of a name's
being *true* (or *false*) *of* requires an understanding of the whole speech-act

(e.g. the statement) of which naming forms a part. We shall meet again later (in Sections 3 and 4 of the main argument) the move from saying to naming.

But what is section (*b*) doing in the *Cratylus*? Is it put forward as in itself an argument against Hermogenes? Its conclusion is that there are both true and false names. Is Socrates implying that on Hermogenes' view there could not be false names? If so, the implication is unfair. Just as Hermogenes is not committed to the view that every use of an established name is a correct use, so he is not committed to the view that in every correct use of a name it is true of that to which it is applied.

Perhaps, however, it is wrong to regard this section as a separate argument. The point that Socrates here gets agreed is that there *is* truth and falsity of statements and so of names. This is the linguistic counterpart of the ontological point (in section 1) that will serve as the foundation of the main argument against Hermogenes, the point that *things* have independent characters of their own. The argument that then follows is designed to show that Hermogenes' thesis of absolute freedom in naming is inconsistent with there being truth and falsity and (equally) with there being things with objective natures of their own.

I turn now to the main argument against Hermogenes, and begin by giving a summary of the first four sections (i.e. up to 387d9).

Section 1 (385e4–386e5)

Socrates gets Hermogenes to reject both Protagoras' relativism—that things are just as they seem to anyone—and Euthydemus' paradox—that things both are and aren't anything whatsoever. He does this by appealing to the distinction we all draw between the wise and the foolish, the good and the bad. (Compare *Theaetetus* 152a, 161cff.) So things do have some fixed being, independent natures of their own (386e1–4).

Section 2 (386e6–387b7)

Socrates now applies this conclusion to *praxeis*, or 'doings'; for doings are themselves one kind of thing there is. They must therefore be done *according to their own nature*. For we shall *succeed* in doing this or that only if we do it according to the nature of this or that doing, and with the naturally appropriate instrument (*organon*). Otherwise we shall fail and 'get nowhere' (οὐδὲν πράξομεν).

Socrates illustrates this with the examples of cutting and burning; and with these examples it is easy to see what he means. If we want to do some cutting, it is no good trying to use a feather, we must use a knife; and if we want to cut wood, it is no use trying to do it with a butter-knife. What cutting *is*, and what the character of the candidate for *being cut* is, limit or even determine how we must proceed, and with what *organon*, if we are indeed to (e.g.) cut wood.

Section 3 (387b8–c5)

Saying things (λέγειν) is one kind of doing. So if *it* is to be achieved, it must be done in the *way* in which it is *natural* to say this or that thing (and for them to be said)—and with the naturally appropriate *tools* (*organa*).

Section 4 (387c6–d9)

Since in *saying* things we *name* this or that, naming is a part of saying. So naming itself is a kind of 'doing with regard to things' (387c6–11). Therefore we shall succeed in naming things only if we do it in the way in which it is natural to name things (and for them to be named), and with the naturally appropriate tools (387d1–8).

I will now comment on the argument so far. The idea of words as tools with which we do something seems promising, but is not Plato's comparison of naming with other activities seriously misleading?

The most obvious objection is that naming *x* is a very different *type* of 'doing' from cutting or burning *x*, and that this difference prevents the argument by analogy (which purports to show that nature dictates how and with what we must name a given thing) from doing what Socrates wants it to do. My naming *x* is not a causal transaction between me and *x*; I am indeed doing something in naming *x*, but not doing something *to x* (not effecting a change in *x*). And so my success—the effectiveness of the name I use—does not depend on the character of *x* in the way in which my ability to cut or burn something with this or that tool does depend on the character of the thing (and on my using a tool appropriate to that character).

There are of course numerous cases—indeed, kinds of case—where though φing may be counted as a doing, φing *x* is not doing anything *to x*: for example, recalling an event, buying a book, dancing a waltz, playing chess, bidding three clubs, imagining a city free of traffic. (There are also, of course, plenty of cases of φing that would be counted as doing, but where there is no x at all: walking, talking, voting, gardening.) (Note the variation in terminology between 'saying things' at 387c1 and 'a doing *with regard to things*' at 387c10. The former suggests an analogy with transitive verbs like 'burn' and 'cut'; the latter does not.)

That dancing a waltz and bidding three clubs are not activities in which one does something *to*—acts causally *upon*—a waltz or three clubs does not of course exclude the possibility that they are activities in which one does something to—acts causally upon—*something*. After all, making a marble statue is bringing a statue into being, and not doing something to a statue; yet it necessarily involves doing something to the marble. In such a case the nature of whatever *is* acted upon can determine the method and tools necessary for success in the activity.

The essential point, however, is this, that though the analogy between naming and burning (or cutting) is defective, *every* distinguishable kind of doing (as of thing) has *some* objective criteria of success, or of what counts as that kind of doing (or that kind of thing). It is not up to me to decide that I have danced a waltz or done some gardening; there are objective criteria to settle the question. So for naming also we must ask what *are* the objective criteria for success in naming things, and ask whether these criteria are such as to rule out Hermogenes' thesis.

Socrates does not in fact make *im*proper use of the argument from analogy with burning and cutting. For he does *not* say that because success in cutting x depends on using a tool naturally suited to cut x, success in naming x must depend on using a name naturally suited to name x—and that Hermogenes is thus refuted. Instead, he approaches the question about the objective criteria for success in the case of naming by asking what kind of activity it is, what we are really up to when we do it (388b8). When we shuttle, we are dividing the weft and warp. When we name we are . . . doing what? An understanding of *this* should reveal whether there are—contrary to Hermogenes' view—*natural* restrictions on what can be used as names for this or that naming task.

Before turning to Socrates' account of what we *are* doing in naming, I want to make a comment on section 4 (387c6–d9), in which Socrates moves from saying to naming. Why does he first introduce saying as a kind of doing, and then *argue* that naming is a kind of doing—on the ground that it is a 'part' of saying?

It will be helpful at this point to ask what we are to think of as a case or episode of naming (i.e. of name-using). Take a simple situation in which I point to my cat Benjamin and say to you (in an assertive tone of voice) 'cat'. What is necessary if this is to be a thoroughly *successful*

performance? One requirement is that I should convey my thought to
you; and for this to be so, I must use the word 'cat' correctly—according
to some settled usage—and you must recognize my adoption of that
usage.

Communicative success depends on shared conventions, by which one
person can come to know what another one thinks. (This point is made
later against Cratylus, 434e–435b: provided the conventions are shared,
successful communication of thoughts is possible, no matter what the conventions are.)

However, another sort of success in naming concerns *truth*. For this
success I must have used a name that does actually apply, in virtue of its
meaning, to the item to which I have applied it. In this case I have not only
expressed my thought correctly and conveyed it successfully, I have also
expressed (by my gesture and naming) a *true* thought—the same in fact as
would be expressed by the true statement 'That is a cat' (or 'Benjamin is
a cat').

This is, of course, a highly oversimplified account of one particular
naming context, but it will serve to bring into view the point I wish to make.
The use of sentences to make statements involves the use of names to
pick out or apply to things; and the point of using names to pick out or
apply to things is to contribute to the making of statements. Telling
someone something is a complex operation whose simplest form is '*S* is *P*',
and to perform this operation, we use terms '*S*' and '*P*'. If what I tell is
true, '*S*' and '*P*' must both be *true of* the same thing. (I can, of course,
as in the cat example, convey a truth using only one name—but that is
because my gesture and the context serve to pick out the subject item.)
These matters, discussed further by Plato in the *Theaetetus* and *Sophist*,
in connection with the analysis of truth and falsity, are only touched on in
the *Cratylus*; but the elements of the later discussions are to be found
here.

So much for the questions why Socrates argues from saying to
naming and why naming is a part of saying. I shall return to the distinction between the requirements for communicative success and the requirements for success in stating the truth. Meanwhile, I go on to sections 5
and 6 of the argument (387d10–389a4), which may be summarized as
follows.

Section 5 (387d10–388c8)

We shuttle with a shuttle, we name with a name. When we shuttle, we
separate out the warp and the weft; what exactly are we trying to do

when we use names as tools and do some naming?' 'We teach one another something, dividing things as they are' (388b10–11). So a name is a tool for teaching and dividing things as they are.

Section 6 (388c9–389a4)

Where do these tools, the names we use, come from? From *nomos* (law or established custom). They are therefore the product of the lawmaker (the *nomothetēs*), who must obviously—like any other toolmaker—have the necessary special skill.

Do we think self-evident, or even plausible, the thesis that the essential aim of name-using is 'teaching one another and dividing things as they are'? (I take it that the second part of this formula is intended to elucidate the first part, and is not specifying a further thing we do in addition to teaching.) Surely we use names for a great variety of purposes. However, the notion of teaching does combine two features that seem to be fundamental and essential to language: communication and truth. Of course, not every speech-act is an assertion, still less a didactic assertion intended to convey truth to another. But it may well be held that assertion is the fundamental speech-act—and an assertion certainly makes a claim to truth; and it will probably be agreed that the possibility of use in communication is essential to language. If so, the apparent narrowness of Socrates' answer to the question 'What are we doing when we use names?' will not matter. He is directing us to the two central ideas in the philosophy of language: truth and the communication of thoughts. The rest of the *Cratylus* revolves round these two ideas.

In section 6 talk of a personal 'lawgiver' or 'word-maker' carries on the analogy with ordinary crafts, but the real questions are not in any way historical, but are: what are the criteria for *being* a name (or a good name); and what (therefore) are the natural limitations or conditions upon word-*introduction* (requirements for *becoming* a name)?

Conveying truth about various things by using names requires that the names distinguish things there *are*. So here there is a 'natural necessity' which is a constraint upon name-introduction—if an essential purpose of using names is to convey truth. Names must stand for items there really are and for characteristics there really are, if we are to be able to use names to ascribe characteristics to things—and to do so truly. This is, then, a necessary condition of effective name-using, and hence a requirement for successful name-introduction: the 'lawgiver's' task is to assign names to *things there are*. This task is discussed in the next section.

Section 7 (389a5–391a)

The name-maker must, if he is to make names that are capable of doing their job, (i) identify the various real natures there are (what, for example, shuttling *is*), and (ii) express or embody each of them in a name appropriate to its nature. Whether he has done this successfully will be judged by the expert name-user, the dialectician.

The two aspects of the task here assigned to the name-maker are in effect two conditions which Plato says must be fulfilled if language is to serve its purpose, which is to communicate truth. They concern *what* is named, and *how* it is named. (i) Names must designate characters or kinds there really are, and (ii) a name must be naturally appropriate to the character or kind it corresponds to. I shall discuss these points in reverse order.

The *second* claim would seem simply to contradict Hermogenes' thesis; and surely he ought simply to reject it. He can perfectly well allow that, if language is to serve its purpose, names must designate kinds and characters there really are; but he must insist that it is up to anyone (or any group) *what* name is attached to some kind or to some character. Take the dog: it is entirely conventional (no 'natural appropriateness') whether the word 'dog' or 'chien' or 'cane' is used to stand for that kind of animal—and any other word would have done just as well. Nature may determine what kinds or properties are to be found in reality; but that is not to say that there are any natural restrictions on the names that may be introduced, and used successfully, to *stand for* this or that kind of property. For designating *x* is not a causal operation upon *x*, and a name's ability to designate *x* is not determined in any way by the *character* of *x*.

Now, Socrates' discussion of the name-maker's work contains a difficult but interesting notion in the passage 389d–390a7: a notion of *what a name really is* that distinguishes it from ordinary so-called names in particular languages. The 'name itself' or the 'form of name' is distinguished from its particular embodiments. The name itself for the species *dog* is not the English word 'dog', nor is it the French word 'chien'; these are two different expressions of one and the same name itself. Is this perhaps a manœuvre, designed to meet Hermogenes' claim that the choice of names is purely conventional by redefining what a name (really) is? But first, what exactly does the notion of a name itself amount to?

Socrates is introducing a notion of name according to which a name is to be *identified* solely by reference to the job it does—what it stands for. If 'dog' and 'cane' *mean the same*, they are to be counted as one and the same *name*, in spite of the differences of letters (and sounds). This idea, given briefly in our passage, recurs later at 394a–c. The doctor, it is there said, counts two tablets as the *same medicine*, even if they differ in shape and colour, provided that they have the same power (*dunamis*)—that is, produce the same medical effect. So, Socrates suggests, we should regard names that have the same *force* (*dunamis*) is being really the same name. (The term *dunamis* here corresponds to *eidos* and *idea* at 389e3 and 390a6.)

We might call the name identified by the idea that it expresses the *ideal* name (as opposed to the ordinary name). An ordinary name is made of particular sounds or letters; but the ideal name is a *semantically defined* unit not made of sounds or letters. It is in effect the meaning of all the ordinary names in a group of synonyms; and one might well call it the *name-as-concept*, in that what synonyms all express is *the same concept*.

So could this idea form part of an argument against Hermogenes? Surely not. If one uses meaning as the sole criterion of identity of 'names' (i.e. considers *ideal* names, or concepts), Hermogenes' original thesis is side-stepped rather than denied or refuted. For *his* thesis was about the con-ventionality of the *ordinary* words that *have* meanings (or *express* concepts), not about the meanings or concepts themselves. His thesis was that various ordinary words can be equally good for expressing a given concept (embodying a given ideal name)—and this is not contradicted by the suggestion that a concept itself is identified by what it is the concept *of*. So whatever the value of Socrates' idea about the identity conditions of concepts (or 'ideal names' or 'synonym groups'), Hermogenes' actual thesis about *ordinary* names still awaits discussion. And in fact, most of what follows in the *Cratylus* is about the sounds and letters of ordinary Greek names, and whether there is any 'natural correctness' about *them*.

Nevertheless, it seems to me that in the passages we are considering, Socrates puts his finger on a point that is essential for the understanding of language and of how it works. A primitive account of language is tempted to treat names as directly standing for things; and some notori-ous paradoxes about the impossibility of falsity arise from this assumption. So it is a matter of fundamental importance that there is a third element in the situation, an intermediary between names and things: the meaning or concept or thought. Because you know the meaning of a word I use, the

concept I express by it, you can grasp the thought I am trying to communicate to you. A common conceptual scheme is the condition of the communication of thoughts. But the question of truth depends on the relation
of concepts or thoughts to the external world, the fit between concepts or
thoughts and things. This is, of course, a very crude statement. But we are,
in the *Cratylus*, at the birth of the philosophy of language; and it would
not be helpful to use in exegesis the more sophisticated apparatus of
modern analysis. Indeed, my crude statement already goes beyond what
Plato makes explicit. In particular, it is a serious question to what extent
he himself drew a clear distinction (here or elsewhere) between concepts
and universals, and between the existence of concepts and the existence of
universals. But in any case it is certainly right to emphasize the philosophical importance of the contrast Socrates draws between ordinary
words in particular languages and the identical meanings that different
ordinary words can have.

I return now to the first of the conditions we noted: that names must
correspond to *real* characters or kinds, if we are to be able to 'teach each
other and divide things as they are'. When this phrase was first used to
describe what we are doing when we use names, it was natural to understand it in an entirely untechnical way, and to interpret the condition correspondingly. We use language to tell each other that the cat is on the mat.
This could not convey information if there were no cats or mats. We say
that lions are brave; this could not convey information if there were no
lions and no such thing as bravery.

Perhaps, however, in the section we are now considering, a somewhat
deeper meaning must be sought. For now the person said to be expert in
using names—and hence the best judge of their correctness—is the *dialectician*, 'the man who can ask and answer questions' (390c10). A surprising
assertion, and it is necessary to draw upon other dialogues to interpret it.
I summarize familiar points. The dialectician does not ask and answer such
questions as 'Where is the cat?' or 'Is the cat on the mat?' He asks after
definitions or essences: 'What *is* justice?' 'What *is* a cat?' His use of language is not identical with the ordinary use of it, but is somehow of a higher
level; it is *critical*, as it were, not of individual statements or misstatements
(like 'The cat is on the mat'), but of the language and its words in general.
One such type of criticism might direct itself to practical requirements; it
might bring out, for example, that some words are ambiguous, and therefore bad tools of communication. But another type of criticism will direct
itself to individual concepts or a group of concepts, or to the whole conceptual structure expressed in a language, which can be tested for clarity
and coherence and objective validity. If questions such as 'What is justice?',

'What is a cat?' can be answered (on this level and in this way), it is established not just that the words 'justice' and 'cat' have clear meanings, but that justice is a real, objective characteristic, and that the cat is a real natural kind. A successful language (one the dialectician commends) will be one that correctly mirrors that structure of reality.

II

The main argument against Hermogenes inferred from the fact that language-using is an activity with a definite purpose that there is a 'natural correctness' of names, but it left unanswered the question what that correctness consists in. Socrates drew an important distinction between ordinary names, made up of Greek (or other) letters or sounds, and 'ideal names' or names-as-concepts, the meanings that ordinary names (in whatever language) serve to express. It will be helpful to correlate these two types of name with the two elements in the function (*ergon*) of language. That function is 'teaching and dividing things as they are', and the two elements are communication and truth. If a language-user is to perform successfully, there are two main conditions—natural necessities—that must be satisfied. (1) The language must contain a stock of words (ordinary names) that are understood and therefore serviceable for communication of thoughts to others. (2) The words in the language must express concepts that relate to reality in such a way as to be serviceable for the communication of *truth*. This truth requirement lays a condition upon names-as-concepts. To convey truth about things and characteristics, a speaker needs concepts of qualities and other characteristics that are actually instantiated and concepts of kinds of things that actually exist.

Something more will be said about truth and reality. But in the meantime Socrates turns (in 391b–421d) to a long discussion of the ordinary (Greek) names that are the immediate tools of communication. The details of his often fanciful etymologizing do not concern us; but the main lessons derived from them, as regards conditions for having and using ordinary language, deserve some attention.

How is it possible for (ordinary) names to express and convey concepts? How might one learn such names—and learn to use them to express the concepts others use them to express? One obvious aid to rely on would be *natural likeness*. This pictorial or imitation principle is relied on as often as possible in international traffic signs; Socrates gives some basic examples at *Cratylus* 422e–433a. So one suggestion would be that ordinary names, to be effective in communication, must be learnable and teachable, and that to be learnable and teachable, they must be like what they stand for—they must *carry their meanings on their faces*.

Socrates plays with the idea that Greek names express the conceptual scheme of Heracliteans, and sets out to show how names do by their sounds imitate or represent what they stand for. The attempt breaks down in two ways. First, in more and more examples Socrates is forced to claim that, although the original words were like the things they stood for, our present words have been much changed from their original composition—letters have been added and subtracted. But if this is so, then even if names did once have a natural likeness to what they stood for, that cannot be a necessary condition of their usability now—since we successfully learn to use them for communication, even though they no longer have that natural likeness. Secondly, Socrates draws attention to a bit of vocabulary where the very idea of natural likeness is absurd—the indefinitely large number of names for numbers (435b6). The first lesson of the etymologizing is that the necessary and sufficient condition of success in communication is that the speaker and hearer have come to the custom and usage of attaching the same names to the same concepts (434e–435b). How this can be brought about is another question, which Socrates does not go into. He does, however, recognize that natural likeness is desirable as far as possible (435c2–3), since it obviously facilitates the acquisition of concepts, the learning of meanings; but it is neither necessary nor sufficient to ensure such learning.

Some words are easily intelligible to one who hears them for the first time because they are like what they stand for; but there is another way in which words may be instantly intelligible—they may be *compounds* of words already known to the hearer. Socrates offers etymologies of many compounds. He makes clear that the possibility of understanding this kind depends on there being already a common understanding of the primary words (*prōta onomata*) from which the compounds are built (425d–426a). (We may add that it is helpful in a language—it makes it easier to learn and easier to use for communication without misunderstanding—if the ways in which compounds are built are regular, so that analogies are reliable. English is notoriously unhelpful in this respect: a butter-knife is a knife for cutting butter, but a pocket-knife is not a knife for cutting pockets. But here again, although such regularity in compounds is desirable, it is neither a necessary nor a sufficient condition of the word's being understood and used successfully to communicate thought. For this a common custom or usage, however achieved, is the sole requisite.)

The core of a language, then, is a set of basic words which the language-users have learned to employ in the same customary way, to express the same concepts. This provokes two large questions, one epistemological and one ontological. (1) How is such learning possible? Can we (say, Greek-speakers) be sure that we do indeed all have the same thoughts—express the same concepts—when we use these words? And (2), supposing that we do all think of the same characters and kinds when we say '*leukon*' or '*hippos*', can we safely infer to the reality of the characters and kinds we think of? (Is it clear that you and I mean the same when we speak of 'a ghost'? And, supposing that we do, can we infer from the existence of the concept *ghost* to the existence of ghosts?)

The first of these questions, the epistemological one, is not examined in the *Cratylus*. Part of the answer, no doubt, is that we find ourselves applying the same words to the same things around us; and that we can teach and learn the meanings of many words by applying them to examples easily identified by pointing. But in other cases—and these the more important—there is dispute in applying the words and disagreement as to the identification of examples (*Phaedrus* 263a–c; *Politicus* 285d–286a). Another part of Plato's response is to be found in his doctrine of *anamnēsis*. He uses it in the *Phaedo* (73c–77a) to explain in particular our capacity to conceive universals of which we have met no actual (perfect) instance, in the *Meno* (80d–86b) to explain our capacity to see logical connections, and in the *Phaedrus* (249b–c) to explain in general our capacity to seize the universal in the particular. *Anamnēsis* is the forerunner of Locke's doctrine of innate ideas and of more recent theories of innate grammatical programmes. The ability to revive common knowledge of general ideas is presented as an innate and distinctive power of human beings. It must of course be recognized that such a doctrine cannot constitute a refutation of the sceptic who questions whether we do indeed have common ideas; it takes for granted that we do, and offers a sort of theoretical—or mythical—basis for that fact.

The second question—about the relation of concepts to reality—becomes prominent in the *Cratylus* when Cratylus, following up his thesis that names are naturally connected to the things they stand for, says that one who knows the names knows the things—and that this is indeed *the* way to know things (435d). Since our expert name-giver, competent to introduce names, attached them to things they were really like, we can infer from the names to the real things (436b12). Cratylus claims that his thesis is confirmed by the way in which Socrates has been able in his etymologizing to find a consistent theory of reality—namely, the flux theory—expressed in language (436c2–6).

The assertion that our expert name-giver correctly put into verbal form concepts that fit reality combines two claims: first, that an expert name-giver is one who is competent to introduce correct names; second, that *our* name-giver was an expert name-giver. (Put otherwise, the claims are that a good language fits reality, and that our language is a good one.) The first of these claims might be thought a necessary truth; but it is far from clear how the second is to be supported.

Against Cratylus' position Socrates makes several powerful points, which may be summarized thus. (1) It is true that in our etymologizing we found a flux theory expressed in our language. But we could just as easily have developed alternative etymologies that suggested a non-flux theory (437a–c). (2) Supposing that a language did consistently and certainly express one particular theory of reality, that would show that its word-maker had that view of reality (436d). How could we be sure that his view was correct (that he was an expert word-maker and that his language, therefore, is a good one)? (3) And how, if his view *was* correct, did *he* come to that view? (Reference to divine inspiration is a notorious dead-end.) If the name-giver was to name realities correctly, he must have been able to know realities, to grasp universals, independently of and prior to framing concepts and naming them. And so, if we ourselves are to claim that our language represents reality correctly—is a good one—we ourselves must claim an ability to grasp reality independently of language (438b5–9). Only if we know the original can we say that a picture or description is an accurate picture or description of it; similarly, in general, with realities and names (439a). Therefore, if we are to have knowledge of realities and thus the ability to see whether a given language expresses them correctly, we must have a way of studying realities not just *through* language (438d–e). What is this way? We must learn about realities 'through each other, if they are somehow related, and themselves through themselves' (438e7).

Discussion of Cratylus' views has led us right into ontology. The argument has been abstract, and has contained no conclusions about the nature of what there really is; and the prescription for studying realities ('through each other and through themselves') is far from clear. But the last pages of the dialogue notify us that the realities are Plato's Forms (439c–d, 440b6); and other dialogues can help us to interpret the prescription.

The task of the dialectician or philosopher is (according to *Phaedrus*, *Sophist*, *Politicus*, and *Philebus*) to divide reality at its natural joints, and to determine how various Forms are related to one another. He will nec-essarily—as does Plato in his examples of such dialectic—*use* language; but his enquiry is not taken to be about words or about mere concepts (the ideas and thoughts we use words to express), but about the real kinds and qualities that our concepts are (we hope) concepts *of*. But how can we be sure that our hope is realized—that if we clarify by careful discussion the structure of the conceptual scheme embodied in our language, we have thereby discovered the structure of reality? Plato himself recognizes that not every general word stands for a real kind (*Politicus* 262d–263b), but fails to tell us how to distinguish those that do from those that do not. 'How are we to distinguish the *eidos* or *genos* from the mere *meros*? This is not an easy task, and we will take it up again when we have time' (263a5–b2). Dialectical method may, by a rigorous process of question and answer, clarify and improve our conceptual scheme; but once concepts are distinguished from realities (universals, kinds, or characters), it is impossible to see how such a process can give an access to realities which is independent of the concepts, and which can therefore make it possible to see whether the concepts fit the realities.

In fact, Plato seems to rely on the idea that the skilled dialectician will eventually come to 'see' what the real kinds are. He often uses this metaphor of sight, and he speaks of *noēsis* as if it were a sort of intellectual vision (or grasp) which the philosopher achieves after methodical dialectical enquiry. He assumes that just as our eyes have the power, in good conditions, of seeing ordinary phenomena as they are, so our minds (in good conditions) can see the Forms there really are: dialectic removes confusion and fog, and enables the intellect to see reality clearly. Having so seen, the philosopher would be able to judge whether a given language or a given conceptual scheme was or was not a faithful and adequate representation of reality. It is obvious that this 'theory' of *noēsis* is in an important respect like the doctrine of *anamnēsis* referred to earlier. For it is a way of making a certain claim—the claim that we can grasp realities directly and not just through our own language and concepts; it is not a way of justifying that claim.

CONCLUSION

In conclusion I will pick out four points, not unconnected with one another, which seem to me to throw some light upon the drift of the *Cratylus* and its achievement.

1. The notion of teaching, given as the essential function of language, is well suited to move discussion from the linguistic controversy with which the dialogue begins to the ontological confrontation with which it ends, since it combines the ideas of communication and truth. Moreover, it opens the way to a dissolution—at least, a partial dissolution—of the original disagreement between Hermogenes and Cratylus: the conventionalist thesis

dwells on what is necessary and sufficient for any interpersonal communication, but the requirement of truth involves non-conventional constraints.

2. The important distinction between ordinary names and 'names themselves' assists in that dissolution. With respect to ordinary names, questions about origin, etymology, and composition can arise; and there is plenty of scope for the influence of convention and custom: the understanding of ordinary words depends on shared conventions and custom. But for the 'ideal names' no such questions arise—meanings have no etymology. Good concepts are ones that actually apply—that is, are serviceable for the grasp of objective reality; conventions and custom do not determine this.

3. The distinction between words and meanings or concepts corresponds to a distinction between two types of discourse—or two senses of *dialektike*. In ordinary discourse, people use language to talk about ordinary things. In the philosophical discourse that Plato calls 'dialectic', philosophers use language to talk about meanings or concepts (or indeed, taking the point further, about Forms).

4. The realities at which philosophical dialectic is aimed are the Forms, celebrated at the end of the *Cratylus* as things that are and are knowable. The things which ordinary talk is about, particular objects in this world, are not given a place at the end of the *Cratylus*, save perhaps by implication. Contrasted with the Forms is the (imaginary) world of complete flux, of which it is argued that in it there would be nothing of any kind or character, nothing that could be spoken of or known. What, then, of the inhabitants of our actual world, the subject-matter of ordinary discourse? The answer is no doubt that they fall, as it were, between Forms and absolute flux: they have a degree of stability sufficient to make them objects of discourse and belief (true and false), but they lack the complete stability which enables the Forms to be objects of unshakeable knowledge. This element in the Platonic ontology is missing from the last pages of the *Cratylus*, but it would suggest itself readily enough as a corollary of the dialogue, even if one did not have other Platonic texts to rely upon.

V

THE THEORY OF FORMS

T. H. IRWIN

1. SOCRATIC METHOD AND PLATONIC METAPHYSICS

Throughout the Platonic dialogues the character Socrates assumes the existence of 'forms' (*eidē*; *Euthphr*. 6d9–e1; *Men.* 72c6–d1), but most students of Plato believe that the Theory of Forms[1] is a distinctively Platonic theory, not accepted by the historical Socrates. Students who recognize a group of early 'Socratic' dialogues and a later group of 'middle' dialogues take the Theory of Forms to be introduced in the middle dialogues.

Those who accept this division between Socratic forms and Platonic Forms appeal to Aristotle's comments (*Metaph.* 987ᵃ32–ᵇ10, 1078ᵇ12–1079ᵃ4, 1086ᵃ37–ᵇ11). According to Aristotle, Plato developed his theory of non-sensible, separated Forms in response to Socrates' search for definitions in ethics, because he believed that Socratic definitions could not apply to sensible things, since sensible things are subject to change. Plato's views about change resulted (Aristotle tells us) from his early association with Cratylus the Heracleitean.

Aristotle leads us to expect, then, that when Plato argues that sensibles are deficient or imperfect, he will refer especially to change. We ought not to assume that Aristotle must be right, but it is only reasonable to examine the dialogues to see whether his claims are true, or plausible, or illuminating. To see whether he is right, we must find out what he means and how far his claim can be defended from Plato's dialogues.

The most relevant passages in the dialogues are those—if there are any—in which Plato argues for non-sensible Forms. What he says about non-sensible Forms in contexts where he assumes that they exist, or where

---

[1] This essay is derived, with some modifications, from *Plato's Ethics* (Oxford: Oxford University Press, 1995), ch. 10. I ought to emphasize that it was written as part of an account of Plato's moral philosophy, and therefore does not cover every aspect of the Theory of Forms. I use an initial capital in 'Form' and in the names of Forms ('Just' etc.) to indicate 'Platonic' in contrast to 'Socratic' forms.

he wants to raise puzzles about them, is relevant to understanding the Theory of Forms, but it is not necessarily relevant to understanding his arguments for the theory. For this reason, we may reasonably set aside the *Parmenides* and *Timaeus*; these are later dialogues that discuss Forms at length, but seem to presuppose the conception that Aristotle describes. To see how Plato forms this conception, we must look at the middle dialogues, and especially at the *Phaedo* and *Republic*.[2]

2. RECOLLECTION AND FORMS

We can see that some aspects of Aristotle's story are plausible if we turn to a development in Plato's thought that he does not mention in this context. In the *Meno* Plato examines some of the presuppositions of Socratic inquiry. He considers the conditions for an adequate Socratic definition, and he explores the distinction between knowledge and belief. He implies that knowledge of Socratic definitions must be the result not of observation, but of recollection of prenatal knowledge. In the *Phaedo* he reasserts the Theory of Recollection, but now he claims that the truths we recollect are truths about non-sensible Forms, recollected from imperfect sensible instances (*Phd.* 74e8–75a3). Since recollection is complete— according to the *Meno*—when we have a Socratic definition, Plato claims that Socratic definitions must primarily apply to non-sensible Forms. The *Republic* asserts the same epistemological and metaphysical claims; Plato argues that knowledge cannot be primarily about anything sensible, but must be about non-sensible Forms.

Plato makes it clear that he is talking about the forms that concern Socrates. He introduces the 'just itself' and all the other things that are properly called 'the *F* itself' in dialectical discussions (*Phd.* 65d4–5, 74a11, 75c10–d3, 76d7–9); these are precisely the 'beings' or 'essences' (cf. *ousias*; 65d13) that Socrates sought to define. Once he has made it clear that he is talking about the same forms that Socrates talked about, Plato claims that these forms are inaccessible to the senses (65d4–5).

What is it about Socratic forms that, in Plato's view, makes them inaccessible to the senses? We may find it easier to answer this question if we consider what Socratic forms must be like if they are to answer the questions that Socrates wants answered.

---

[2] I have discussed the order of the Platonic dialogues in *Plato's Ethics*, ch. 1.

3. SOCRATIC DEFINITION IN THE *EUTHYPHRO*

In the *Euthyphro* Socrates gradually introduces different features of forms, by telling Euthyphro what sort of answer is needed to the question 'What is the pious?' He attributes four features to forms:

1. There must be just one form of piety for all pious things (actions, people, and so on) (5d1–5).

2. It must be usable as a paradigm that we can consult to say whether something is pious or not (6e3–6).

3. It must be describable without explicit reference to properties—just and unjust, fine and shameful, good and bad—that introduce disputes (7c10–d7).

4. The single 'form' (*eidos*) or 'character' (*idea*) of piety is that 'by which all pious things are pious' (6d9). A correct description of it must describe the feature of pious things that explains why they are pious. Socrates is willing to grant that what the gods love is coextensive with piety (since he treats it as a *pathos* of piety; 11a7), but he does not agree that this description of piety answers the question he asked.

Does Socrates regard these as four distinct claims about forms? Or does he take the last three to be clarifications of the first, so that they explain what he means by speaking of one form? In saying that the form is that by which pious things are pious, he assumes that Euthyphro has already agreed with this in agreeing that there is one form (*ephēstha gar pou*; 6d11); but his original question to Euthyphro did not make this clear.[3]

In any case, two of these claims, the second and the third, seem to be primarily epistemological, and two others, the first and the fourth, seem to be primarily metaphysical. When Socrates speaks of using the form as a pattern to tell whether something is pious, and of removing terms that arouse disputes, he speaks of our cognitive relation to the form. When he speaks of explanation, he speaks of the actual relation of the form to its instances.

Why should an account of a form meet both the epistemological and the metaphysical demands? It does not seem obvious that a correct description of the relevant explanatory feature will also remove terms that arouse disputes and allow the cognitive access that Socrates demands of a paradigm.

---

[3] Perhaps 6d4–5 is meant to imply the explanatory requirement in *kata tēn anhosiotēta*.

4. SOCRATIC DEFINITION IN THE *MENO*

Does this question about the metaphysical and the epistemological aspects of forms occur to Plato? The *Euthyphro* suggests some degree of self-consciousness, especially about the difference between identification of the explanatory feature of piety and identification of something that pious things merely have in common. But we need not confine ourselves to the *Euthyphro*; for the *Meno* makes it clearer that Plato sees the difference between Socrates' demands and the different questions that they raise.

In contrast to the *Euthyphro*, the *Meno* recognizes that the demand for a single form to cover all the things that bear a given predicate is controversial. Meno supposes it is easy to say what virtue is, because he thinks he can answer the question by giving a list of different types of virtue (*Men.* 71e1–72a5). Socrates, however, suggests that there is one form because of which all virtues are virtues, and which one ought to focus on in making it clear what virtue is (72c6–d3).

Here Plato introduces the unity of the form in its many instances, and its paradigmatic and explanatory character. He may suggest that its paradigmatic and explanatory character justifies the assertion of its unity. If Meno's first suggestion were right, virtues would simply constitute a list with nothing more in common besides membership on the list. Plato answers that there is more to being a virtue than simply belonging to a heterogeneous list; virtues share some property that explains why all genuine virtues deserve to count as virtues. To recognize this property is to recognize the 'one' belonging to all of the many (*dia pantōn*, 74a9; cf. 75a7–8), something that can be attributed 'universally' to them (*kata holou*; 77a6).

These remarks present a metaphysical demand. Socrates adds an epistemological demand. He persuades Meno that the correct answer to a search for a definition must 'not only answer true things, but also through those things that the questioner additionally agrees that he knows' (75d6–7).[4] This condition—said to be characteristic of dialectic as opposed to eristic—is applied to Meno's next attempt at definition. He eventually agrees that 'whatever comes about with justice is virtue and whatever comes about without all such things is vice' (78e8–79a1). Socrates objects that if we do not know what virtue is, we will not know what any part of

---

[4] The reading *di'hōn proshomologē(i) eidenai ho eromenos* is defended by R. W. Sharples, *Plato: Meno* (Warminster: Aris & Phillips, 1985), ad loc. Some favour emending to *prohomologē(i)*, 'agrees in advance'. The MSS read *erōtōmenos*, 'the one questioned'; *eromenos* is an emendation.

virtue is; hence we will not know what justice is, and so it is illegitimate (by the standards of the dialectical condition) to mention justice in the definition of virtue (79d1–e4).

Socrates implies that we cannot know what G is if F is mentioned in the definition of G and we do not know what F is; and so, since knowledge requires definition, we cannot know what G is unless we can define F independently of G. This is not quite the same as the demand, presented in the *Euthyphro*, for the elimination of disputed terms, but it might be explained by that demand. For Socrates might argue that if G is defined by reference to F, but F cannot be defined independently of G, our initial disputes about what things are G will return when we consider what things are F.

The dialectical condition is open to question. It seems to reject interdependent definitions; but why should we reject such definitions as answers to a Socratic question? A Socratic definition identifies the genuinely explanatory property; why should it always be possible to specify this property in the terms required by the dialectical condition?

As long as Socrates accepts both the epistemological and the metaphysical demands, without saying which is more important, or how we are to decide conflicts between them, he makes the task of finding a Socratic definition significantly more difficult. Meno is as unsuccessful as both Socrates and his interlocutors have been in the early dialogues. Meno does not challenge Socrates' requirements; he believes that the difficulties he faces arise from Socrates' claims about knowledge and definition. He is mistaken in this belief; when we see that he is mistaken, we may wonder whether Socrates' other demands would make it difficult for anyone to find a satisfactory definition. In studying Plato's further reflections on the nature of forms and our knowledge of them, we might reasonably hope to find out whether Plato accepts both the metaphysical and the explanatory demands imposed by Socrates, and how he believes they can be satisfied.

5. CONVENTION AND OBJECTIVITY

The *Cratylus* clarifies some of the assumptions in the *Meno* about the unity of a form and about its explanatory character. The dialogue considers whether the 'correctness of names' (383a4–b2) is conventional or natural.[5]

---

[5] The *Cratylus* is a dialogue of uncertain date. See J. V. Luce, 'The Date of the *Cratylus*', *American Journal of Philology*, 90 (1954), 136–54; M. M. Mackenzie, 'Putting the *Cratylus* in its Place', *Classical Quarterly*, 36 (1986), 124–50.

This question divides into two further questions: (1) Is the internal character and structure of names purely conventional? (Is 'horse' a more correct name for horses than '*hippos*' is?) (2) Is it a matter of nature or convention that a particular name is the correct name for a particular sort of thing? Socrates allows that an appeal to convention may give the right answer to the first question (435a5–d3), but he rejects convention as an answer to the second question.

In Socrates' view, the conventionalist means that there is nothing about, say, horses themselves that makes it correct to give a single name to all horses rather than one name to horses and dogs encountered on odd days of the week and another name to horses and cats encountered on even days. On this view, there is nothing about external reality itself that makes it right to classify things in one way rather than another.

Socrates attacks one motive for the conventionalist view by attacking the Protagorean position that 'what things seem to each person to be like, that is also what they are like' (386c4–5). He asks Hermogenes whether 'the being (*ousia*) of things is private to each person' (385e5), or, on the contrary, things have some stability in their own right (386a3–4), so that they do not vary in accordance with variations in our views about them (386d8–e4). Socrates defends his belief in objective things and properties by arguing from the fact that we distinguish better and worse people, and in doing so distinguish wise from ignorant people (386b10–12). If Protagoras were right, we would not be entitled to draw these distinctions; for since everyone would have equally true beliefs, everyone would be equally wise, and so no one would be wiser than anyone else (386c2–d1).

Once Socrates has secured Hermogenes' agreement about different degrees of wisdom, he infers that there must be something for us to be right or wrong about, and that this must be the nature that things have in themselves, independently of our beliefs about them (386d8–e5). It follows that we speak correctly or incorrectly in so far as we do or do not speak of things as they objectively are (387b11–c5). Since naming is an action that is a part of speaking, naming can be done rightly or wrongly too (387c9–d8). The proper function of a name is to teach and distinguish the being of things (388b6–c1), and a correct name will carry out this function. Socrates suggests that a name is correct to the extent that it conveys an 'outline' (*tupos*) of its referent. The better the outline of F, the more correct the name of F; but as long as some outline of F is conveyed, the name still names F (431c4–433a2).

The assumption that some predicates are names preserving outlines underlies the discussion with Meno. For Socrates assumes that when Meno uses the word 'virtue', he preserves the outline of a genuine nature, as Socrates conceives it. Why does Socrates assume this? Presumably it is possible that some names (or putative names) are so badly correlated with reality that they preserve the outline of no genuine nature, or they combine elements of two natures so confusedly that we cannot say determinately which nature is named. Meno might argue that there is nothing that the items on his list of virtues have in common, or that all they have in common is the fact that they are conventionally recognized as virtues because they correspond to conventionally recognized roles. Alternatively, he might suggest that if some quality of a person comes to be widely admired, or admired by certain people, it is a virtue, and that this is what being a virtue consists in. This answer does not divide virtue up into many, and it does not provide a mere list. But it is not the sort of answer that satisfies Socrates. In the *Euthyphro* he considers and rejects an answer of this sort, arguing against the suggestion that piety should be defined as what the gods love.

Socrates rejects this sort of answer because he believes there is something about the virtues themselves that makes it appropriate to put them on the list of virtues. He assumes that there is some question about the objective character of the virtues that we can answer correctly or incorrectly. The *Cratylus* presents the metaphysical view of language and its underlying reality that is presupposed by Socrates' demands in the *Meno* and in the early dialogues. Socrates commits himself to the existence of real kinds and genuine objective similarities that justify our classifying things as we do. He assumes, with Meno's agreement, that there is some single standard, derived from the nature of the actions and characteristics themselves, that justifies our judgement that all the types of virtue are genuine virtues.

The demand for an objective explanatory property makes the demand for a single definition more difficult to satisfy. If Socrates were satisfied with a single description corresponding to 'F' that applies to all Fs, it would be easier for Meno to satisfy him. Since, however, he demands an objective explanatory property, he is dissatisfied with answers that do not provide the right sort of explanation.

At the end of the *Cratylus* Plato considers the implications of his conception of forms for a Heracleitean doctrine of flux. Socrates and Cratylus agree that there is such a thing as 'beautiful itself, and good [itself], and each one of the beings in this way' (439c7–d1). Then Socrates asks about the possibility of change in the forms: 'Then let's consider this very question, not whether a face, or anything of that sort, is beautiful, and all such things seem to flow. Are we not to say that the beautiful itself is always such as it is?' (439d3–6). They agree that the form itself cannot change without ceasing to be the form it is (439d8–10). They must have in mind change in respect of the property that makes the form the form it is. If triangularity were to cease to imply trilaterality, that would not be a change from one state of triangularity to another; it would be the non-existence of triangularity. Hence, if the form of beauty were to lose its essential property, such an alleged change would imply that there is no form of beauty.

We might object that this argument overlooks the possibility of saying that beauty was one thing in the Parthenon, but became something different in Chartres Cathedral, since the beauty of the Parthenon is quite dissimilar to that of Chartres Cathedral. Why should we not call this a change in beauty? Plato's answer depends on the conception of forms that Socrates defends against Hermogenes' conventionalism. The one form of beauty is the one that makes it true that both the Parthenon and Chartres Cathedral are beautiful; it has neither the specific features of a Greek temple nor the specific features of a Gothic cathedral, and hence the alleged change in beauty is not really a change in beauty itself, if there is a single form of the sort that Socrates has in mind.

While more would need to be said in a full discussion of this passage, these remarks will show how it is connected with the beginning of the *Cratylus*, and hence with questions about Socratic definition. This passage also brings us back to Aristotle's comments. For it is in a dialogue named after Cratylus; it introduces a doctrine of flux; and it insists that forms must be free of flux. Does it confirm Aristotle's comments on the origin of the Theory of Forms?

The similarities between this passage and Aristotle's comments are close enough to persuade some critics that it is Aristotle's only basis for his claim about Plato and Cratylus. Before we agree, however, we must notice some differences between our passage and Aristotle: (1) The passage does not assert that anything is in flux. The clause that refers to flux is 'and all such things seem to flow' (439d4), but this clause is part of the question that Socrates says they will not consider. (2) It does not say that being in flux has anything to do with being a sensible object. (3) It does not say that what is in flux cannot be known; it says only that if a form were in flux, it could not be known.

Despite first appearances, then, the passage does not support Aristotle; if it is his only basis for his claims, he was a remarkably careless reader. Some critics would rather embrace this consequence than allow that

Aristotle might have had some different basis for his claims.[6] But before we decide one way or the other, we should consider other evidence that might be relevant to a judgement about Aristotle.

6. ARGUMENTS IN THE *PHAEDO*

The *Phaedo* first reminds us that forms are the things Socrates tried to describe in his inquiries, and then claims that these forms have features that are not familiar to us from earlier dialogues. Plato introduces four unfamiliar claims about Forms: (1) They cannot be grasped by the senses, but must be grasped by intellect alone (*Phd.* 65d4–66a10). (2) The Form of F is different from sensible Fs because it has properties that no sensible F can have, and hence cannot be known by the senses (74a9–b7). (3) Sensible things undergo constant change, whereas Forms are completely unchanging (78c10–e4).[7] (4) Since the Form of beauty is what makes things beautiful, it cannot be identified with bright colour, or symmetrical shape, or anything else of that sort (100c9–d1).

The first task of the interpreter is to understand each of these claims about Forms. The second task is to understand whether and how they fit together; do they constitute a consistent or reasonable conception of Forms? Plato seems to intend us to understand the first claim through the second. At first he simply asserts, as though it were obvious, that we cannot grasp Socratic forms through the senses. He seems to be relying on the apparent oddity of saying that we see or hear bravery or justice. But it is not enough to agree that such claims seem odd; we want to understand why they are odd, and what it is about the senses and about Forms that makes Forms inaccessible to the senses. Plato's second claim seems to answer this question.

The third claim brings us back to Aristotle's comments on Plato's thought about Forms. In contrast to the *Cratylus*, it asserts that sensible things are in constant change, and so it tends to confirm Aristotle's comments. It falls short of Aristotle's claims, however, since it does not seem to offer flux in sensibles as the reason for believing in non-sensible Forms. Plato presents the third claim as a consequence of recognizing the Forms

---

[6] For an extreme example of refusal to credit Aristotle, see C. H. Kahn, *Plato and the Socratic Dialogue* (Cambridge: Cambridge University Press, 1996), 81–7. See e.g. p. 82: 'This attribution to Cratylus looks like an Aristotelian inference from an over-hasty reading of the dialogue that bears that name. A more perceptive reading of this same dialogue indicates that Cratylus was not someone from whom Plato thought he had anything to learn.' Compare 81 n. 20, 87 n. 30.

[7] Cf. *Rep.* 495a10–b3, 508d4–9, 518e8–9, 525b5–6, 534a2–3.

that have already been secured by the second claim. As Plato presents them, the second claim appears more basic than the third; he seems to disagree with Aristotle's account on this point.

The fourth claim is clearly relevant in the light of the explanatory role of forms. We have seen Socrates insist on this explanatory role in the *Euthyphro* and *Meno*. But its place in the *Phaedo* is puzzling. Plato gives examples (colour and shape as accounts of beauty) of unacceptable accounts of Forms, but he does not say how we are to generalize from these examples, or how this fourth claim about the forms is to be connected with any of the first three.

If we can answer some of these questions, we will have a clearer idea of the conception of the Forms that Plato develops in the *Phaedo*.

7. SENSIBLE EQUALS AND THE FORM OF EQUAL

To show that the form cannot be sensible, Plato claims that equal sticks and stones appear equal to one, and not to another, but the form cannot have these properties; the 'equals themselves' never appeared unequal, nor equality inequality (*Phd.* 74b7–9).[8]

Plato's claim about the equals raises several questions: (1) He says equal sticks and stones 'appear equal to one, not to another'.[9] Is the reference to appearing crucial to the argument? Does Plato mean that whereas sticks may appear to be equal and may appear to be unequal, the form cannot appear in these different ways? Or does he simply mean that the sticks are both equal and unequal, but the form cannot be both?[10] (2) In 'appear to

---

[8] Discussions of *Phd.* 74b6–9 include: N. R. Murphy, *The Interpretation of Plato's* Republic (Oxford: Clarendon Press, 1951), 111 n. 1; G. E. L. Owen, 'A Proof in the *Peri Ideōn*', in M. C. Nussbaum (ed.), *Logic, Science, and Dialectic* (Ithaca, NY: Cornell University Press, 1986), ch. 9; lst pub. *Journal of Hellenic Studies,* 77 (1957), 103–11; K. W. Mills, '*Phaedo* 74bc', *Phronesis*, 2 (1957), 128–47, and 3 (1958), 40–58; C. A. Kirwan, 'Plato and Relativity', *Phronesis*, 19 (1974), 112–29: 116–17; D. Gallop, *Plato:* Phaedo (Oxford: Clarendon Press, 1975), 121–2; D. Bostock, *Plato's* Phaedo (Oxford: Clarendon Press, 1986), 73–7; T. Penner, *The Ascent from Nominalism* (Dordrecht: Reidel, 1987), 20–2, 33–40, 48–52, 352; N. P. White, 'Forms and Sensibles', *Philosophical Topics*, 15 (1987), 197–214, and 'Plato's Metaphysical Epistemology', in R. Kraut (ed.), *Cambridge Companion to Plato* (Cambridge: Cambridge University Press, 1992), ch. 9, 280–3; G. Fine, *On Ideas* (Oxford: Clarendon Press, 1993), 331–2.

[9] The datives in *tō(i) men . . . tō(i) d'ou* might perhaps be translated 'in one respect . . . in another respect'. A variant text (*tote men . . . tote d'ou*) reads: 'sometimes appear equal, sometimes not'.

[10] See Penner, *The Ascent from Nominalism*, and White, 'Forms and Sensibles' and 'Plato's Metaphysical Epistemology'. The Greek verb translated 'appear' (*phainesthai*) may have a veridical sense ('evidently is', used with a participle) and a non-veridical sense ('appears to be', used with an infinitive). Since Plato uses neither participle nor infinitive with *phainesthai* here, we lack any grammatical clue to the sense of the verb.

one, not to another', 'one' and 'another' might mean either 'one (another) person' (Greek masculine pronoun) or 'one (another) thing' (Greek neuter). In the first case, Plato refers to different appearances to different people; in the second case he refers to relativity to different things. (3) What is the force of the plural in 'equal sticks and stones'? Does Plato refer to a particular pair of sticks, and mean that it appears both equal and unequal? Or does he refer to the class of sticks, and mean that it includes both equal and unequal instances?

These different questions suggest quite a few possible interpretations. Rather than examine them all, it may be useful to indicate the philosophical point that would emerge from some of those that have been favoured.

If we take 'appear' non-veridically (so that it does not imply real equality and inequality), the contrast between the equal sticks and the form lies in how they can appear. The form of equal lacks the property of possibly appearing unequal that the equal sticks have; hence (Plato argues, on this view) the form is not identical to the equal sticks. A possible objection to this argument may be seen from considering an apparently parallel argument: The number of the planets may appear to someone to be greater than nine; the number of the planets cannot appear to be greater than the number of the planets; therefore the number of the planets is not identical to nine. This apparently parallel argument is invalid; hence, if it is really parallel to the argument attributed to Plato, the latter argument is also invalid.

If we take the equality and inequality of sticks to result from relativity (so that a yardstick is equal to another yardstick but not to a foot rule), Plato is claiming that the form is non-relatively equal, so that it is equal without being equal to anything. This might well appear a nonsensical conception of an equal thing. Perhaps, however, Plato accepts such a conception because he believes we cannot understand any relative predicate without referring to, and being acquainted with, some object that bears the predicate in a non-relative sense.[11]

8. THE FORM AND THE 'MANY'

It is difficult to choose between different interpretations if we look at the passage in the *Phaedo* in isolation. But if we consider it together with other

[11] Owen, 'A Proof in the *Peri Ideōn*', C. Strang, 'Plato and the Third Man', *Proceedings of the Aristotelian Society*, suppl. vol. 37 (1963), 147–64, and Bostock, *Plato's* Phaedo, 77, 79–80, maintain that Plato's belief in Forms is a response to some sort of relativity in certain predicates. This view is criticized by N. P. White, 'Perceptual and Objective Properties in Plato', *Apeiron*, 89/4 (1989), 45–65: 45–57; Fine, *On Ideas*, 161–8.

apparently relevant passages in the *Phaedo* and elsewhere, we may find reasons for preferring one interpretation over another.

Other places in which Plato uses 'to one' and 'to another' in contrasting the form and the many suggest that he means 'to one person' and 'to another person' (*Hp.Ma.* 291d1–3; *Smp.* 211a2–5). Probably, then, he is not concerned with relativity to different things.

Nor does he seem to be concerned primarily with the possibility of appearing, as opposed to being, equal and unequal. For in apparently similar contexts he normally speaks of 'the many *F*s' appearing *F* and not-*F* in a veridical sense (*Hp.Ma.* 289b5–7; *Rep.* 479b6–7), so that different people's appearances seem to be the means of discovering a fact about the many *F*s themselves.

Plato attributes 'compresence of opposites' (as some modern writers call it), not merely compresence of opposite appearances, to the many *F*s. He contrasts the form of *F*, which cannot be both *F* and not-*F*, with 'the many *F*s' that are both *F* and not-*F*, or both *F* and the opposite of *F*. A beautiful (*kalon*) girl is also ugly (*aischron*) in comparison with gods (*Hp.Ma.* 289a2–c6). Burying our parents and being buried by our children are fine (*kalon*) in some circumstances and shameful (*aischron*) in others (293b5–e5). The many beautifuls (justs, equals, and so on) are both beautiful and ugly (*Rep.* 479a5–b10). In contrast to the *F* things that are both *F* and not-*F*, the form of *F* must be free from this compresence of opposites (*Smp.* 210e5–211a5; cf. *Hp.Ma.* 291d1–3). In the *Phaedo* itself Plato takes the argument about the equals to show that the many *F*s undergo constant change (78d10–e4), not simply that they appear to undergo change.

If equal sticks and stones are meant as examples of the many *F*s that are both *F* and not-*F*, are they particular instances or types? In one place Plato mentions the beautiful girl who is also ugly (*Hp.Ma.* 289a2–c6). In another place he mentions burying our parents and being buried by our children, a type that has different particular instances, some fine and some shameful (*Hp.Ma.* 293b5–e5). He does not mean that a particular instance of this type of action is both fine and shameful. In this case, compresence of opposites is attributed to types, not to tokens of the types.[12]

Other passages, then, do not unambiguously suggest that the argument about equal sticks must be concerned with tokens, or that it must be concerned with types. This question is important, however. For Plato does not take his argument to be confined to equals; he think it also applies to fine, good, just, and the other things that concerned Socrates in his inquiries. If he is concerned with tokens, and his argument is to be generalized to these

---

[12] On the nature of the 'many *F*s', see Murphy, *The Interpretation of Plato's* Republic, 110; Owen, 'A Proof in the *Peri Ideōn*', 174 n. 32; J. C. B. Gosling, '*Republic* V: *Ta Polla Kala*', *Phronesis*, 5 (1960), 116–28.

other properties, he must claim that every particular brave action is both brave and cowardly, every particular just action is both just and unjust, and so on. If, however, he is concerned with types, he is not committed to any such claim about particular actions.

To see what Plato is committed to, we may raise further questions about compresence of opposites: what is wrong with it, and why should the form be free of it? According to one view, anything that is both F and not F is not genuinely F after all; it is a self-contradictory entity.[13] If Plato holds this view, he turns away from sensible equals because they fail minimal logical conditions for being genuine entities at all.

It is difficult to find any basis for such an argument in Plato. He makes it clear that the compresence of opposites in the many Fs involves different respects or different relations; being buried by our children is fine in one situation and shameful in another, but it is not both fine and shameful without qualification. In *Republic* 4 Plato formulates a principle somewhat similar to the Principle of Non-Contradiction; he insists that it is impossible 'for the same thing to do or undergo contrary things in the same respect or in relation to the same thing' (436b8–9). He does not suggest that if something is F in one respect and not-F in a different respect, it is self-contradictory. All his remarks suggest that he takes the opposite properties of sensible equals, and so on, to be perfectly compatible.

Other interpreters take Plato to mean that the many Fs cannot be suitable for learning the meaning of F, or acquiring the concept of F, if they are both F and not-F. If learning a concept requires acquaintance with an unambiguous instance, and F-and-not-F things are not unambiguous instances of F, we cannot acquire the concept of F from the many Fs.[14]

This interpretation rests on two assumptions about Plato: (1) The many Fs that suffer compresence of opposites are particulars. If they were types, Plato would not be saying that particular just actions, say, are also unjust; hence they might still (for all he says) provide unambiguous instances of justice.[15] (2) He must assume that acquisition of a concept requires acquaintance with unambiguous instances.

[13] See W. D. Ross, *Plato's Theory of Ideas* (Oxford: Clarendon Press, 1951), 38; Mills, '*Phaedo* 74', Pt. 2.

[14] Bostock, *Plato's* Phaedo, 97–8, presents this argument (derived from Owen, 'A Proof in the *Peri Ideōn*') very clearly.

[15] When Bostock offers to show that, in Plato's view, we cannot find an 'unambiguous instance of courage, or beauty, or justice', he argues that paying one's debts is not an unambiguous instance, because there are circumstances in which one ought not to return what one has borrowed (*Plato's* Phaedo, 97). But this example shows only that paying one's debts—the type—has both just and unjust tokens. Nothing that Plato or Bostock says suggests that we should infer that each token of the type is both just and unjust. Hence some tokens of the type may (for all this example shows) be unambiguous instances of justice.

If we could understand the argument about equals only by relying on these assumptions, they would be reasonable. But if the argument about equals can fairly be interpreted differently, we must look at other contexts to see both whether they support these two assumptions, and whether they favour one or another interpretation of the argument about equals.

The first assumption can be dealt with briefly. Plato never asserts and never assumes (in any context apart from *Phaedo* 74, where the dispute arises) that we can infer compresence in tokens from compresence in types. Such an inference is so clearly illegitimate that we need some good reason for attributing it to Plato. We have found no good reason.

The second assumption, about Plato's views on the acquisition of concepts, needs fuller discussion. He never explicitly asserts the claim that we need unambiguous instances of *F* to acquire the concept of *F*. But we must consider alleged evidence of his relying on such a claim.

9. WHY ARE THE SENSES UNRELIABLE?

Interpreters who take Forms to provide unambiguous instances (or 'perfect samples') for the acquisition of some concepts often appeal to a passage in *Republic* 7 that discusses the connection between the senses and the compresence of opposites. When Plato describes the growth of reasoning and reflection, he especially mentions mathematical properties. These are the ones for which the senses give us unsatisfactory answers: 'In some cases the things the senses give us do not provoke thought to examination, on the assumption that they are adequately discriminated by the senses; but in other cases they urge thought in every way to examine, on the assumption that sense produces nothing sound' (*Rep.* 523a10–b4). The cases that do not provoke thought include our perception of fingers. Those that provoke thought include our perception of their largeness and smallness.

Plato explains what it means to say that the senses sometimes do not provoke thought. He makes it clear that he is not thinking of perceptual error or illusion (resulting, for instance, from seeing fingers at a distance; 523b5–e2). He is concerned only with cases in which the senses report that the same thing is large and small, or hard and soft (523e2–524a5).

To understand this passage, we need to answer two questions: (1) What contrast does Plato intend to draw between sense and thought? (2) What does it mean to say that 'the same thing' is large and small? Plato attributes to 'the same thing' the compresence of opposites that he normally attributes to the many *F*s; if we can discover what 'the same thing' is, we will have some basis for understanding claims about the many *F*s.

The first question does not allow a very detailed answer, since Plato does not say much here about the contrast between sense and thought. We might be inclined to draw the contrast so that sense by itself includes no thought; in that case the contribution of sense is the basis for a perceptual judgement, but does not itself include any concepts or judgements. This is the conception of sense that Plato accepts in the *Theaetetus*, in order to show that sense does not yield knowledge; knowledge requires the application of concepts and judgements, and the application of these is not a task for the senses (*Tht.* 184b4–186e12).

In the present passage, however, Plato does not seem to intend such a minimal conception of sense.[16] For he says that in perceiving a finger, 'sight in no case indicated to it [sc. the soul] at the same time that the finger is the contrary of a finger' (*Rep.* 523d5–6). The judgement that this thing is a finger and that thing is not a finger is attributed to sense; it is only when sense makes conflicting judgements of this sort that thought is provoked to ask questions. Plato does not say that perceptual judgements do not involve thought, but he suggests that in some cases sense 'discriminates adequately' (523b1–2) without provoking thought to examination. In some cases, the degree of thought needed for the perceptual judgement that this is a finger does not lead us into further questions about what a finger is.

If sense is not meant to exclude all thought, it may be easier to answer the second question about the passage. Plato claims that perceptual judgements about large and small, heavy and light, in contrast to perceptual judgements about fingers, provoke the soul to ask what heavy and light are. The soul is puzzled because sense indicates that the same thing is light and heavy, or (equivalently, according to Plato) that the heavy is light and the light is heavy (524a9–10). Sight shows light and heavy confused (524c3–4), so that the soul is provoked to ask whether light and heavy are one or two (524b3–5). This question arises if we cannot adequately grasp something 'itself by itself' (524d10) by sense, but can only grasp it confused with its contrary (524e2–4).

The difficulty that Plato mentions seems spurious if 'the same thing', 'the light', and so on refer to particular objects, such as this finger that we take to be both heavy and light. For the mere fact that the senses attribute

<hr />

[16] This point is made clearly by J. Adam, *The Republic of Plato*, 2 vols. (Cambridge: Cambridge University Press, 1902), ad loc.

contrary properties to one and the same object does not seem to create any special difficulty; we do not, for instance, accuse sight of confusing squareness and whiteness if it reports that a sugar cube is both square and white. Even mutually exclusive properties need not raise any difficulty. Nothing can be both red and green all over, but if sight reports that the Italian flag is red and green in different parts, it is not confusing red and green.

Equally, then, the mere fact that sight reports that something is equal and unequal, or large and small, does not imply that sight confuses these two properties. If it reports that a mouse is big next to a small mouse, but small next to an elephant, that report does not seem to confuse largeness and smallness. Nor do these perceptual judgements raise a question about whether large and small are one or two.

Plato's claim is much more plausible if we take 'the same thing', and so on to refer to properties (largeness, etc.) rather than to the particular objects (this large finger, etc.) that have the properties. This is what he means by saying that sight does not adequately see the 'largeness and smallness' of things (523e3–7). He claims that the senses confuse opposite properties, not merely that they take the same thing to have opposite properties. In saying that, according to the senses, 'the hard' is also soft (524a1–10), Plato uses 'the hard' to refer to the property that the senses identify with hardness.

Plato suggests, then, that sight counts the same things as evidence for calling something a finger in all cases, whereas it counts the same thing as evidence for attributing contrary properties in the case of large and small. If we consider what aspect of this mouse makes it big, we may mention its length—say, six inches. But if we are asked what makes it small (in comparison to an elephant that is twelve feet long), we may mention its six-inch length again. And so we are saying that the same property is both largeness and smallness.[17]

If Plato has in mind this point about properties, his position is more reasonable than if he has in mind the assumption about particulars that would lead to a demand for perfect samples. It does not follow that he must intend the more reasonable point. But at least it follows that the passage provides no evidence for the view that he demands perfect particulars. It can be explained perfectly well without assuming that he demands anything of the kind.

---

[17] This view of the passage is defended by Irwin, *Plato's Moral Theory* (Oxford: Clarendon Press, 1977), 318; Penner, *The Ascent from Nominalism*, 114–15, 142. A different view is taken by Adam, *The Republic of Plato*, ad loc.; Kirwan, 'Plato and Relativity', 121–3; White, 'Plato's Metaphysical Epistemology', 286–7.

10. COMPRESENCE AND EXPLANATION

If the second interpretation of this passage (referring to a property that is both largeness and smallness) is at least as plausible as the first interpretation (referring to a particular that is both large and small), we may ask whether Plato says anything else to suggest that one or the other interpretation captures his main reason for believing in non-sensible Forms.

We must now consider the passage in the *Phaedo* (96d8 ff.) that refers to the explanatory role of Forms. In attributing this role to Forms, Plato shows that he is concerned with their role in Socratic inquiries; for, as we have seen, Socrates wants to find the form of *F* because he wants to find 'that because of which' (*di'ho*) all *F* things are *F* (*Men.* 72c6–d1; *Euthphr.* 6d9–e1). Plato now asks what sorts of properties we must attribute to a form if it is to explain what it is meant to explain.

To clarify the explanatory requirement, Plato cites purported explanations that would be blatantly unsatisfactory. If, for instance, we tried to explain *x*'s being larger than *y* by mentioning what makes *x* larger than *y*, and we said that *x* is larger than *y* 'by a head' (*Phd.* 96d7–e1), we would have given a bad explanation, since 'by a head' explains *x*'s being larger than *y* no more than it explains *y*'s being smaller than *x*. Similarly, we cannot say that combination is what make things two, since it is equally true that the division of one thing makes it two (96e5–97b3).[18]

These are strange examples of attempted explanations. No doubt Plato means them to be strange, so that they illustrate an extreme version of the error that he means to avoid. A property *G* cannot be the explanation of *x*'s being *F* if either (1) *G* is present in *y*, but *y* is not-*F* or (2) *G* is not present in *z*, but *z* is *F* (97a5–b3, 100e8–101b2). *G* may well be present in *x* and may be connected with *x*'s being *F* (as 'by a head' plainly is, if we say that Theaetetus is taller than Socrates by a head); but if either (1) or (2) is true, *G* and *F* are not connected as they would be if *G* were what makes *x* *F*. To put it in Aristotle's terms, we cannot say that *x* is *F* in so far as *x* is *G* (that *x* is *F* qua *G*) if either (1) or (2) is true (cf. *Phys.* 196^{b}24–9; *Metaph.* 1026^{b}37–1027^{a}5).

These general claims about explanation show us why Plato focuses on the compresence of opposites. If we want to know what makes something just, and the alleged explanatory property no more makes something just

---

[18] Different views about the fault in the rejected explanations are presented by G. Vlastos, 'Reasons and Causes in the *Phaedo*', in *Platonic Studies*, 2nd edn. (Princeton: Princeton University Press, 1981), 95–102; 1st pub. *Philosophical Review*, 78 (1969), 291–325; Gallop, *Plato: Phaedo*, 172–4; Bostock, *Plato's* Phaedo, 136–42.

than it makes something unjust, we have not found the explanatory property we wanted. Plato argues that, for instance, it cannot be the fact that
the children bury their parents that makes this particular action of these
children burying their parents fine; for that fact might equally be found
in a shameful action (if, for instance, the children had murdered their
parents first).

In articulating this demand on explanations, Plato exploits some standard Socratic objections, but he develops them in a new direction. When
Charmides suggests that temperance is shame, Socrates convinces him that
this is a faulty definition because shame is good (in some situations) and
bad (in other situations), or 'no more good than bad' (*Chrm*. 161a2–b2).
He could also have pointed out to Laches, though he does not say so in
precisely these terms, that endurance is both fine and shameful (cf. *La*.
192d7–8). He does not say that shame is both temperate and not temperate or that endurance is both brave and not brave. Some of the objections
raised in the *Meno* against Meno's proposed definitions could be stated in
terms referring to the compresence of opposites (cf. *Men*. 73d6–8), but that
is not how they are stated.

None of these passages, then, states the general principle that the F
cannot be both F and not-F, whereas various candidates for being the F
are in fact both F and not-F, and therefore cannot be the F. The *Hippias
Major* comes closer to stating this general principle (291d1–3). It is
expressed most clearly in the dialogues that contrast the non-sensible
Form of F with the many sensible Fs.

Once we see why Plato contrasts the Form of F with the many Fs, we
can also see what the many Fs are supposed to be, and what an acceptable
description of the Form would have to be like. To see what he might
mean, we ought to recall what Socrates means when he implies (in the
Laches) that endurance is both fine and shameful, or asserts (in the
Charmides) that shame is both good and bad. He does not suggest that
every particular case of endurance (Leonidas' last stand, for instance) or
of feeling shame (for instance, the shame felt by a Spartan who ran
away when Leonidas stood firm) is both good and bad (or fine and
shameful). He means that some tokens of the relevant action type are good
and others are bad, or, equivalently, that the property in question (being a
case of endurance or shame) makes some token actions good and makes
other token actions bad. Equally clearly, the remark in the *Hippias
Major* about burying one's parents means not that every such action token
is both fine and shameful, but that some of them are fine and others are
shameful.

The discussion of explanation in the *Phaedo* refers primarily to properties—having a head, being taller by a head, and so on. Plato introduces a 'safe' explanation, which is safe because it does not allow compresence of opposites, and therefore is not disqualified from being an explanation. He contrasts the safe explanation referring to Forms with the defective explanations he has illustrated. The safe explanation says that beautiful things are beautiful because of the Beautiful Itself, not 'by having a bright colour or a shape or anything else of that kind' (*Phd.* 100c9–d2). Plato seems to mean the same by saying that (1) brightly coloured things, say, are both beautiful and ugly, or that (2) bright colour is both beautiful and ugly, or that (3) bright colour makes things beautiful and ugly. The third formula conveys his main point most accurately.

If this is the right way to understand the *Phaedo* on explanation, it confirms our preferred interpretation of the passage on the senses in *Republic* 7. It also suggests that we should take *Phaedo* 74 to express the same contrast between sensibles and Forms. The argument about equals, taken by itself, allows several interpretations; but the fact that Plato takes it to justify conclusions about the many *F*s in general (78d10–e5) tends to favour some interpretations over others. If he were generalizing an argument about compresence in particulars to other properties besides equality, he would be unjustified (in the light of what he says elsewhere). If he is generalizing about compresence in types, he is justified. Hence, it is reasonable (in the absence of clear contrary evidence) to suppose that he is generalizing about compresence in types.

11. THE ROLE OF THE SENSES

Now that we have seen what Plato means by his claim that the many *F*s are *F* and not-*F*, whereas the Form cannot suffer from this compresence of opposites, we ought to return to his claim that the many *F*s are sensible, but the Form is non-sensible. This emphasis on the senses is one aspect of the middle dialogues that has no parallel in any earlier dialogues. In the *Meno* Plato introduces knowledge gained by recollection, but he does not explicitly contrast it with sense-perception, and he does not discuss the role of sense-perception in the process of recollection. In the *Phaedo* and *Republic*, by contrast, the contrast between sense-perception and thought is closely connected with the contrast between the many and the one. Plato believes that in order to recollect the form of *F* that Socrates was looking for, we must distinguish it from all the sensible *F*s that suffer the compresence of opposites, and so we must grasp it by something other than the senses.

In the discussion of the senses in *Republic* 7 Plato claims that the properties making something a finger are accessible to the senses, and that the senses never take different views about what these properties are, whereas the property making something equal or large is inaccessible to the senses. How does he decide what is and is not accessible to the senses?[19]

In order to avoid judging that the same thing is both largeness and smallness, we must avoid identifying these properties with determinate lengths (or other quantities), and we must realize that whether x is large or not depends both on a comparison with other things and on reference to an appropriate standard of comparison. Why is it not within the competence of sight to take account of these features of largeness in informing the soul about what largeness is? Conversely, sense is supposed to be competent to find the features that make something a finger, and it never informs us that the same property makes one thing a finger and something else not a finger. Why is this?

Plato might argue that we can remove doubts about whether something is a finger if we observe the finger more carefully, whereas we do not remove the appearance that the same thing is largeness and smallness by further observation of the thing that has these opposite properties. If we are to understand that six inches is both largeness (in a mouse) and smallness (in an elephant), we must attend not only to this length, but also to the relevant standard of comparison and the relevant context, and these are not features that we can observe in a particular situation. If we are thinking of mice, the mouse is large; if we are thinking of inhabitants of the zoo, the comparison with mice is irrelevant and the comparison with the elephant is relevant, so that the mouse is small. Nothing in our observation of the mouse and its environment tells us that one or the other standard of comparison is the right one to apply. We would be misunderstanding the source of our mistake if we were to say that we ought to have observed the large mouse more carefully in order to recognize that it is small; we were not mistaken (we might want to say) in any of our observations of the mice, and we need to get the relevant information from some source outside our observation of this situation.

The same point comes out more clearly, as Plato intends it to, in the case of arithmetical properties. We can observe that there are three copies of a book on the table, that each has 300 pages, and that each has a binding and a dust jacket. But is there one thing, are there three things, or are there at least 906 things on the table? If we are publishers considering how many

---

[19] The inadequacy of the senses is discussed by J. C. B. Gosling, *Plato* (London: Routledge, 1973), 165–8; Penner, *The Ascent from Nominalism*, 114–16.

new titles we have published, or booksellers considering our profits, or book manufacturers considering the materials we need, a different answer is appropriate; but we do not find which answer is appropriate simply by observing these books in their present environment. The same questions arise about deciding whether something is or is not the same book or the same page as the one we were reading before; the answer seems to depend on the question we have in mind, not on something we can settle by observing the books or the pages themselves. In the cases that interest Plato, the role of contextual facts external to the observable situation implies that observation cannot provide an account of the relevant properties. What makes one situation sufficiently similar to another is an external, contextual fact that is not a matter of observation.

The relevance of context explains why compresence of opposites should be a mark of the observable instances of some properties. Being six inches long is not itself being large; it counts as being large in one context, and as being small in another. The same length may embody both properties, but which one it embodies is not determined by the length itself, but by the context (comparison with mice or comparison with animals). Plato suggests, then, that if contextual facts are essential to the nature of a property, that property is not an observable property, and observation confronts us with the compresence of opposites. This is why the senses cannot be sources of knowledge about the properties that are the normal focus of Socratic inquiry (*Phd.* 65d4–66a8, 75c7–d5).

12. THE SENSES AND THE COMPRESENCE OF OPPOSITES

Plato's claim that sensibles do not yield knowledge of forms helps to explain why Socrates did not find definitions. Socrates in the early dialogues does not speak as though his requests for definitions are unanswerable; on the contrary, he stresses the importance of answering them, and works hard to find answers. But neither he nor others are said to find answers of the sort he wants. Does he impose inappropriately stringent demands on definitions?

If we are asked to say what bravery is, we begin with our beliefs about particular brave actions and people, and we think about how we recognize them in particular situations. We observe that in particular situations brave people stand firm, temperate people are quiet, just people pay back what they have borrowed, and so on. These observations of particular situations are quite accurate, as far as they go; but Socrates points out that these observable properties (standing firm, quietness, etc.) are not the ones we are looking for, since in other particular situations we can observe the opposite properties, even though people display the same virtues, or we can observe the same properties, even though people fail to display the same virtues.

How ought we to react to this discovery? We might suppose that we have not yet found the right observable property. Socrates' interlocutors, at any rate, suppose that an account of F should mention one and the same observable feature present in every situation where something F can be observed; when they find none, Socrates points out that they have given an inadequate account of F, but he does not tell them where they have gone wrong. Does he assume that if we look hard enough, we ought to be able to find the single observable property that the interlocutors have not found?

The Socratic dialogues and the *Meno* do not actually say that Socrates assumes that observable properties are needed for a definition. But at least Socrates does not discourage the interlocutors from looking in this direction; and we have suggested, by appealing to the *Euthyphro* on disputes and measurement and to the *Meno* on the dialectical condition, that he actually requires definitions to refer only to observable properties.

Plato suggests, on the contrary, that this way of looking for a definition is sometimes misguided in principle. It is easy to see why he thinks it would be a mistake to identify largeness or smallness with observable properties; but why does he believe that moral properties are among those that cannot be identified with observable properties?

Sometimes Plato suggests that moral properties are especially likely to cause disagreement and dispute. In the *Euthyphro* Socrates contrasts moral properties with those that raise disputes that can be settled by measurement. In the *Phaedrus* he distinguishes 'gold' and 'silver' from 'just' and 'good' (*Phdr.* 263a2–b2). In cases of the first type we all 'think the same' when someone uses the name, but in cases of the second type 'we disagree with one another and with ourselves', and we are 'confused' (263a6–b5). Plato does not say that we disagree about whether this or that action is just or unjust. He says we have different thoughts about justice; he may mean simply that we have different beliefs about justice or different conceptions of justice.[20]

The division between disputed and non-disputed properties seems to be connected with that between sensible and non-sensible. The properties

[20] *Alc.* 1, 111a11–112a9 draws a similar distinction. The importance of these passages on disputed properties is rightly emphasized by Strang, 'Plato and the Third Man', 195–8.

examined by Socrates are clearly disputed properties. The *Phaedo* makes it clear that properties that involve the compresence of opposites in their sensible embodiments include moral properties.

No one would argue that numerical or comparative properties are sensible properties. When Plato mentions accounts such as 'by a head' as explanations of largeness, his point is to show how evidently ridiculous they are. In these cases there is no serious difficulty in finding an account that is not confined to sensible properties. Numerical and comparative properties are contextual, because the features that determine whether one of these properties is embodied in a particular case are features external to particular observable situations.

Something similar seems to be true of moral properties as well. Socrates often insists that each of the virtues is essentially fine and beneficial; and so facts about what is fine and beneficial must affect questions about whether this or that sort of action is brave or just. Whether an action is fine and beneficial or not may depend on (among other things) the agent's reason for doing it, the actual or expected effects of the action, and the social institutions and practices within which the agent acts. If this is so, observation of the action itself will not tell us whether it is fine and beneficial, and therefore will not tell us whether an action is brave. Bravery and justice must be essentially contextual properties.

This argument could be answered if we could show, for instance, that one moral property is sensible, so that it can be defined in sensible, non-contextual terms, and that all other moral properties can be defined by reference to this one. If we could show this, we would vindicate Socrates' suggestion that disputed terms ought to be eliminated from definitions of moral properties, and we would satisfy the dialectical condition imposed in the *Meno*. Plato's reasons for believing that moral properties are non-sensible, however, apply equally to whatever property might be chosen as the basic one—just, fine, or good. If all of these are non-sensible, we have no reason to assume that one of them must be more basic than the others. If we can define the good, the fine, and the just only by reference to each other, then we cannot hope to find an account that relies only on context-free observable properties.

If this is Plato's point, and if we have correctly understood Socrates' demands on a definition, Plato argues that Socrates' metaphysical demand for a single explanatory property conflicts with his epistemological demand. Only a sensible property would clearly satisfy Socrates' epistemological demand; but, according to Plato, no sensible property can satisfy the metaphysical demand, since no sensible property can be the appropriate single explanatory property.

13. DEFINITIONS AND HYPOTHESES

If Plato rejects an account of moral properties that reduces them to sensible properties, has he anything to say about what an illuminating account ought to be like? He comes closest to answering this question in the *Phaedo*. After rejecting the explanations that appeal to sensible properties, he offers his own preferred type of explanation. Instead of saying that things are beautiful by the presence of bright colour, or symmetrical shape, or some other sensible property, he prefers the safe explanation: whatever is beautiful is so by the presence of the non-sensible Form of the beautiful (*Phd.* 100c3–e3). This remark does not tell us what an explanation referring to the non-sensible Form will be like, or how the Form is to be described. To say that *x* is *F* because the Form of *F* is present to it is a schema for an explanatory account, not itself a satisfactory account.[21]

Plato adds something, however, to suggest how one might approach the right sort of account: we should put forward a 'hypothesis' or assumption (100a3–7, 101c9–102a1). This hypothesis is the account that we judge strongest (100a4), and we judge how strong it is by seeing whether the consequences are in accord or discord with it. The consequences of accepting the hypothesis are not merely the logical consequences of the hypothesis alone, but the total consequences of accepting this hypothesis together with the other beliefs that we accept; and so we test the hypothesis against the whole set of these beliefs. The hypothesis is to be accepted if it explains our other relevant beliefs—this is part of its function as an explanation—and if it does not conflict with them.[22]

Plato recognizes that this sort of hypothesis may not by itself provide an adequate explanation. We may have to give an account of the hypothesis. To do this, we must find a higher hypothesis, and ask the same questions about the concord or discord of other beliefs with this hypothesis. We must continue until we 'come to something adequate' (101e1). Plato does not say what counts as something adequate, but he emphasizes the importance of resorting to a higher hypothesis. It would be a sign of confusion if we mixed up discussion of a principle or starting-point (*archē*) with discussion of its consequences (101e1–3). Plato suggests that not every

[21] Vlastos, 'Reasons and Causes in the *Phaedo*', 91–2, argues that Plato's formula in *Phd.* 100c–e is meant to allude to the demand for definitions. Strang, 'Plato and the Third Man', 196, and Bostock, *Plato's* Phaedo, 150–1, deny this, but they take insufficient account of 78c10–d7, which makes it clear that the Forms are the objects of Socratic definitions.

[22] The sense of 'accord' and 'discord' is discussed by R. Robinson, *Plato's Earlier Dialectic*, 2nd edn. (Oxford: Clarendon Press, 1953), 126–36; Bostock, *Plato's* Phaedo, 166–70; J. K. Gentzler, '*Sumphōnein* in Plato's *Phaedo*', *Phronesis*, 36 (1991), 265–76.

sort of objection to a hypothesis should persuade us to abandon the hypothesis. In some cases we ought to retain the hypothesis and defend it, not by examining the consequences, but by deriving it from a higher hypothesis. Why does Plato insist on this point, and how is it relevant to Socratic definition?

We can see the point of appealing to a higher hypothesis if we consider a possible consequence of believing that Forms are non-sensible. In earlier dialogues Socrates sometimes seems to protest that if we must keep mentioning moral properties in our accounts of moral properties, our accounts will be uninformative and unacceptable (*Grg.* 451d5–e1, 489e6–8). We have seen how the *Euthyphro* and the *Meno* might support this protest. Thrasymachus makes the same protest especially forcefully in *Republic* 1, arguing that any account of the just as the expedient, or the beneficial, or the advantageous is unacceptable, and that the only acceptable definition must say what the just is 'clearly and exactly' in terms that escape from this circle of accounts of moral properties (*Rep.* 336c6–d4).[23] If Forms are non-sensible, however, circular accounts of them may be unavoidable.

To show that circular accounts are sometimes acceptable, Plato needs to distinguish different types of circular accounts. Circularity is open to objection if the circle of terms and definitions is too small. But the same objections do not necessarily apply if the circle is wider; for even if we cannot eliminate a circle of definitions, we may be able to make them more intelligible by displaying the right sorts of connections between our account of moral properties and other sorts of explanations. Plato might reasonably have this point in mind when he asks for a higher hypothesis. Circular accounts of moral properties are not necessarily to be rejected simply because each of them is uninformative by itself. We should not try to replace them with a different sort of account; instead we should place them in a theoretical context that will make them intelligible and explanatory by reference to higher and more general hypotheses.

To describe this passage as Plato's account of 'the hypothetical method' is a bit exaggerated. His remarks are too brief and too imprecise to give us a very clear impression of any specific method that he might have in mind. Still, it is useful to see how they might reasonably be connected with questions that we have seen arise in Plato's arguments for non-sensible Forms. For the more we can connect Plato's remarks about Forms and explanations with our account of his arguments, the better reason we have for confidence in our account.

---

[23] Perhaps Plato suggests that someone who raises Thrasymachus' sort of objection is a 'contradicter', *antilogoikos* (101e2), who urges against a hypothesis an objection that really needs to be evaluated by reference to some higher principle.

14. OBJECTIONS TO THE SENSES: HERACLEITUS AND FLUX

So far the dialogues confirm Aristotle's claim that Plato connects his arguments for Forms with objections to the senses. It is not so clear, however, that they confirm his claim that Plato believes in non-sensible Forms because sensibles are all subject to change and flux; for the arguments we have considered so far do not mention change, but refer to compresence of opposites. Have we, then, missed some important aspect of Plato's objections to sensible things? Or is Aristotle wrong?[24]

We have good reason to believe that Aristotle is right, once we notice that Plato himself speaks of change in sensibles and seems to regard this as a reason for denying that they can be objects of knowledge and definition.[25] These remarks tend to confirm Aristotle's claim that Plato looked at Socrates' search for definitions in the light of Heracleitean beliefs about flux. What might he have taken these beliefs to imply?

According to Plato (*Cra.* 402a), Heracleitus argues that there is more change over time than we suppose there is. The river has been replaced by a different one when we step into 'it' for the second time, because it is composed of different waters. Similarly, trees, rocks, and other apparently stable things go out of existence whenever any of their matter is replaced.

Elsewhere Plato ascribes to Heracleitus the view that everything 'is always being drawn together in being drawn apart' (*Sph.* 242e2–3). One and the same letter at the same time is both straight (if it has a straight stroke) and crooked (if it has a crooked stroke), sea water is good (for fish) and bad (for human beings), and striking a blow is just (if done by an official exacting a punishment) and unjust (if done by an individual in a private feud).

This second Heracleitean doctrine—often called 'the unity of opposites'—is evidently similar to Plato's doctrine of the compresence of opposites; some of the same examples would illustrate both doctrines. It is reasonable, then, for Aristotle to say that Plato's inspiration in formulating his claims about Forms is partly Heracleitean. But Aristotle says more than this: he says the inspiration is a Heracleitean doctrine of flux. Do Plato's claims support Aristotle on this point?

---

[24] For discussions of Plato's views on flux, see: F. M. Cornford, *Plato's Theory of Knowledge* (London: Routledge, 1935), 99; Ross, *Plato's Theory of Ideas*, 20; R. H. Bolton, 'Plato's Distinction between Being and Becoming', *Review of Metaphysics*, 29 (1975), 66–95; Penner, *The Ascent from Nominalism*, 216–21; White, 'Perceptual and Objective Properties in Plato', 58; Vlastos, *Socrates* (Ithaca, NY: Cornell University Press, 1991), 69–71; Fine, *On Ideas*, 54–7.

[25] See Sect. 6 above.

In the *Theaetetus* Socrates explains how Protagoras' belief in the truth of appearances leads to the doctrine that 'nothing is any one thing itself by itself', because, for instance, you cannot call anything large without its appearing small, or heavy without its appearing light (152d2–6). These appearances of compresence are the result of motion, change, and mingling, so that everything merely comes to be (hard, soft, light, heavy, and so on) and nothing stably is what we take it to be (152d2–e1).

According to Plato, this is a doctrine of 'flux and change' (152e8). In speaking of heavy, light, and so on, Plato clearly refers to the Heracleitean doctrine of the unity of opposites; he thinks no further explanation is needed to justify him in describing such a doctrine as a doctrine of flux. He therefore assumes that it is appropriate to speak of 'flux', 'change', and 'becoming' in describing the instability that is manifested in the compresence of opposites.

The *Cratylus* speaks in similar terms of the Protagorean doctrine. Plato claims that according to this doctrine things would be 'relative to us, and dragged by us up and down by our appearance' (*Cra.* 386e1–2). Things are 'dragged by our appearance' if we have conflicting (as a non-Protagorean would suppose) beliefs about them, so that (according to a Protagorean) contrary properties belong to them; but conflicting beliefs (of wise and foolish people) may be held at the same time. Plato does not assume that the instability Protagoras attributes to things is simply change over time; he uses terms that are appropriate for change in order to describe the instability involved in the compresence of opposites.

When Plato speaks of flux, therefore, he need not have succession in mind. If his arguments appeal only to compresence, not to change over time, we are justified in concluding that the type of flux he attributes to sensibles in arguing for non-sensible Forms is compresence.

If Aristotle sees that this is Plato's conception of flux, he does not mean to say that Plato thinks sensible objects undergo continual change over time, or that change over time is what makes them unsuitable as objects of knowledge. He may simply recognize that, given Plato's broad interpretation of flux, compresence of opposites counts as a kind of flux. We ought not to conclude, then, that Plato's argument from flux in sensibles relies on anything more than the compresence of opposites.

Once we see the Heracleitean inspiration of some of Plato's claims, we can also see where Plato disagrees with Heracleitus. In the *Cratylus* the discussion turns to the 'fine names' of 'wisdom', 'understanding', 'justice', and so on. Socrates suggests that the etymology of these names shows that the inventors of the names supposed that the underlying realities were in flux; but, in his view, they thought this simply because of their own

waverings and confusions about the nature of these things, and they transferred the instability in their own convictions to the things themselves
(*Cra.* 411a1–c5).

This remark describes a Heracleitean reaction to the compresence of
opposites. Heracleiteans may argue that (for instance) justice is returning
and not returning what you have borrowed, keeping and not keeping your
promises, and so on. In saying this they suppose that the different sensible
properties that are the focus of dispute about justice must themselves be
the only defining properties of justice.

These arguments suggest that Socrates' search for a definition of moral
properties combines incompatible demands. If we suppose that moral
properties must be identified with some sort of sensible properties, then
the assumption that there must be one form of justice, piety, and so on is
open to doubt; it seems more reasonable to identify each moral property
with a list of sensible properties. Socrates' metaphysical demand on adequate definitions is incompatible with this Heracleitean view; but if he
assumes that a definition should treat moral properties as sensible properties, he is open to the Heracleitean objection.

Against this objection Plato argues that the Heracleitean confuses different embodiments of justice in different circumstances with the property
that is embodied in these different ways, so that the Heracleitean thinks
the variation in these embodying properties is a variation in justice itself.
In Plato's view, the Heracleitean makes the sort of mistake that we would
make if we were to identify a river with the particular quantity of water
that happens to fill its banks at a particular time; on this view there cannot
be any continuing river. We might answer this Heracleitean view by pointing out that while the particular quantity of water constituting the river
changes, the river itself remains the same. Similarly, Plato argues, the compresence of opposites is confined to the sensible properties that embody
justice; since each of these is just only in its specific context, it is not surprising that in a different context it ceases to be just. Since justice itself
cannot also be unjust in a different context, it cannot be identical to these
sensible properties that embody it.

Aristotle's remarks about Socrates, Heracleiteanism, and the Theory of
Forms turn out, therefore, to be helpful, but not in the way we might at
first expect. We ought not to suppose that they refer to Plato's supposed
preoccupation with change and succession in particular sensible objects.
They refer to his reflections on Socratic definition and on the sorts of properties that might satisfy Socrates' main demands. Here, as elsewhere,
Plato's implicit criticisms of Socrates are intended to vindicate the central
and crucial Socratic doctrines.

PLATO ON THE IMPERFECTION OF THE SENSIBLE WORLD

ALEXANDER NEHAMAS

It is a commonplace, both among philosophers and among the more general public, that Plato believed that the sensible world is imperfect in comparison to the world of Forms. There is also a received tradition as to exactly how the world's imperfection manifests itself that has by now become a commonplace in its own right. I have no quarrel with the first of these two commonplaces: as stated, it is too vague to command close attention. It is only when it is interpreted in terms of the received tradition that it becomes informative enough to require consideration. And when it is so interpreted, it requires not only consideration, but, also, careful examination. For these two commonplaces, taken together, create a radically mistaken picture of Plato's view of the sensible world, and of its relation to the Forms.

In what follows, I will first set out the received tradition by means of a number of quotations, for which I ask my readers' patience: it is important to realize just how broad that tradition is. I will then suggest a view of the relation between the sensible world and the Forms which conflicts with the received tradition, and I will finally examine the merits of the two approaches.

I

Plato often tells his readers that the Forms are, in some sense, superior to the sensible objects that participate in them. He speaks of the Forms as completely and purely real at *Rep.* 477–9 (παντελῶς ὄν, εἰλικρινῶς ὄν); as perfectly and really real at *Rep.* 597 (τελέως ὄν, ὄντως ὄν). He says that particulars fall short (ἐνδεῖ τι) of being such as the Form is in which they

Reprinted with permission from *American Philosophical Quarterly*, 12 (1975), 105–17, and the author.

participate (*Phd.* 74d); that particulars desire (ὀρέγεται) to be like Forms, but fall short (ἔχει ἐνδεεστέρως) of that end (*Phd.* 75a); that particulars are inferior (φαυλότερα) to Forms (*Phd.* 75b). He makes this point forcefully at *Smp.* 210e–212a, and he also exhibits this attitude at *Rep.* 515d, *Phdr.* 247c, *Phlb.* 59d, and elsewhere.[1]

We are trying to understand what Plato had in mind when he compared sensible objects so unfavourably to the Forms. It is to this question that the received tradition has provided the answer with which I disagree.

Why are particulars imperfect in comparison to Forms? Because, writes A. E. Taylor in his *Plato*:

the pure logical concept (viz., the Form) is never fully embodied in any sensible example: two things, for instance, which at first blush appear equal, on close comparison will be found to be only approximately so; the visible diagram which we take to stand for a triangle . . . has never really the properties which we attribute to 'the triangle' in our definition; the conduct we praise as just may, on close scrutiny, turn out to be only imperfectly just.[2]

In *Plato: The Man and his Work*, Taylor writes:

the so-called equal sticks and stones we do see are not exactly, but only approximately equal . . .[3]

and expands this as follows:

The same visual sensations which suggest the notion 'straight' to me, for example, are the foundation of the judgment that no visible stick is perfectly straight. The form is thus never contained in, or presented by, the sensible experience that suggests it. Like the 'limit' of an infinite series it is approximated but never reached.[4]

Burnet, commenting on *Euthphr.* 6e4, writes:

The identical 'form' will not be fully embodied in any of the particulars, but it is the exemplar to which they more or less approximate . . .[5]

while he glosses *Phd.* 74a9 as follows:

The 'forms' are *types* (παραδείγματα) to which particular sensible things approximate more or less closely.[6]

[1] A comprehensive survey will be found in Gregory Vlastos, 'Degrees of Reality in Plato', in R. Bambrough (ed.), *New Essays on Plato and Aristotle* (London, 1965), 1–19.
[2] A. E. Taylor, *Plato* (London, 1922), 41, ch. 11. See also *Platonism and its Influence* (Boston, 1924), ch. 11.
[3] A. E. Taylor, *Plato: The Man and his Work*, 6th edn. (Cleveland, 1966), 187.
[4] Ibid. 188.
[5] John Burnet, *Plato's* Euthyphro, Apology *of Socrates, and* Crito (Oxford, 1924), 37 n. ad loc.
[6] John Burnet, *The* Phaedo *of Plato* (Oxford, 1911), 55 n. ad loc. See also Burnet's *Platonism* (Berkeley, 1928), 41–3.

W. D. Ross follows suit on this issue:

all sensible apparent equals both aspire to that which is equal and fall short of it;[7]

apparent equals are objects between which

we can detect no difference in size [while] exact instruments of measurement reveal inequalities where the eye does not detect them, and . . . in all probability we have never seen two physical objects that were exactly equal.[8]

Paul Shorey also suggests this attitude:

Experience can never give us the pure mathematical ideas which sensation and perception awaken in our minds. There are no perfect circles or equalities in nature. Yet we do conceive them, and we feel how far concrete circles and equalities fall short of the ideal toward which they strive . . . We are reminded by the imperfect copies in the world of sense of something that we have seen or known in another state of existence.[9]

And, finally, Hugh Tredennick conjectures that

Plato's reasoning may have been something like this. 'Knowledge must be possible; Socrates was sure of it, and the world makes nonsense if it is not. But the things of this world cannot be truly known, because they are changeable and imperfect, and therefore not real; for *what is* is changeless. Now in geometry [for Plato was an expert mathematician] the properties which we know and can prove to be of circles and triangles and so on are not strictly true of this particular figure which I draw, because it too is imperfect and impermanent. They are true of the "look" or Form of circle (or triangle), which exists somewhere in eternal perfection. Surely, it must be the same with everything else. The things of this world are all imperfect copies of Forms which exist eternally somewhere; which are the true and only objects of knowledge, but can only be apprehended by direct contemplation of the mind, freed as far as possible from the confusing imperfections of the physical world.'[10]

These writings cover roughly fifty years of scholarship. They range from technical commentaries to popular introductions to Plato's work. They are written by scholars on either side of the unitarian–developmental dispute about Plato's thought. Yet they all exhibit a remarkable agreement on a number of issues, examples, and vocabulary; the points agreed upon constitute the received tradition on Plato's disparagement of the sensible world. They are the following:

1. Plato was inspired to formulate the theory of Forms by his attitude towards mathematics, especially towards geometry. Geometrical truths do not concern sensible equal things, squares, or circles. Such objects

[7] W. D. Ross, *Plato's Theory of Ideas* (Oxford, 1951), 25.   [8] Ibid. 23.
[9] Paul Shorey, *What Plato Said* (Chicago, 1933), 172–3.
[10] Hugh Tredennick, *The Last Days of Socrates* (Baltimore, 1959), 14.

are only illustrations of the intelligible and unitary objects (equality, the square, the circle) about which the theorems of geometry are really formulated.[11]

2. Sensible objects only approximate the intelligible objects which they represent in geometrical contexts. They are imperfect in the sense that the definition of, say, "circle" never quite applies to any drawn circle; a drawn circle could always be closer to being the locus of points equidistant to a given point. Measurement can always be further refined, and each refinement will reveal, for example, that objects previously judged to be equal are not equal relative to the new procedure. It is in this sense that sensible equal objects are never 'really' equal, and sensible circles never 'really' circular. Geometrical illustrations, no matter how carefully they have been constructed, are always 'fuzzy'.

3. Plato, either consciously or unconsciously, applied this sense of imperfection to objects belonging to ethical and aesthetic contexts.[12] Just as geometrical illustrations are always only approximately and never exactly equal, circular, or square, so beautiful people, just actions, and healthy animals are only approximately and never exactly beautiful, just, or healthy. That is, they could always be more beautiful, more just, or healthier. It is in this sense that the Form of, say, beauty, which is perfectly (namely, exactly) beautiful is like the limit of an infinite series.[13]

---

[11] Apart from the texts quoted above, see Burnet's comment on *Phd.* 75c11, *The Phaedo of Plato*, 58, and on *Euthphr.* 5d3, 31. For a more recent statement of this view, see J. E. Raven, *Plato's Thought in the Making* (Cambridge, 1965), 69–70, 96.

The paradigm involved here is so strong that Burnet felt justified in writing this (*Platonism*, 41–2): '[The geometrician is] certainly not [speaking] of any triangle that we can perceive by the senses (for all these are only approximately triangles), not even of any we can imagine. He is speaking of what is "just a triangle" ($αὐτὸ\ τρίγωνον$) and nothing more. It is neither equilateral, isosceles, or scalene. And so it is with all other geometrical terms. It is clear from the way in which the subject is introduced in the *Phaedo* (65d4) that this was the original sense of the doctrine of "forms".'

But a glance at *Phd.* 65d–e shows that no geometrical terms or Forms are involved in that passage! Socrates directly introduces the Forms as intelligible entities by the example of *the just itself* at 65d4, and goes on to mention the beautiful itself, the good itself, largeness, health, and strength. The only vaguely 'mathematical' Form is largeness, $μέγεθος$; and there are no obvious parallels between the properties of being large (or tall) and being a triangle.

[12] That is, Plato generalized to *at least* these contexts. Some believe that he also generalized to all contexts: cf. Ross, *Plato's Theory of Ideas*, 24.

For the sake of fairness we must mention that Ross does not subscribe to the historical thesis about the genesis of the theory of Forms (ibid. 13–16). But his treatment of imperfection belongs to the same category as that of the other writers quoted above.

[13] See J. C. B. Gosling, 'Similarity in *Phaedo* 73b *seq.*', *Phronesis*, 10 (1965), 151–61. This article has been extremely helpful to me, and I draw heavily from it in what follows.

The first of these three theses is not crucial to my purpose. Already in 1912 Gillespie had cast doubts on Taylor's (and Burnet's) contention that the theory of Forms was a direct application of Pythagorean geometry by Plato.[14] Also, on this historical view, geometrical objects were thought to be unitary and Plato was supposed to have duplicated this feature in postulating a single Form for each multiplicity of objects that interested him; but this obviously conflicts with Aristotle's statement that 'mathematical objects . . . differ from sensible objects in being eternal and unchanging, and from Forms in being *many of each sort*, while each Form is itself solitary' (*Metaph. A* 987[b]16–19). Finally, this account does not explain certain crucial features of the theory of Forms, which we shall examine as we discuss in detail theses (2) and (3); for convenience, I shall refer to these two theses jointly as 'the approximation view'.

The approximation view interprets in a particular way the relation between geometrical illustrations and the 'objects' these illustrate. And it attributes to Plato both that interpretation and also a radical generalization of it to other contexts: 'Surely it must be the same with everything else.'[15] Plato's fondness for generalization notwithstanding, I find this particular instance intolerable; and, I believe, Plato himself found it unthinkable: he never made it.

On the approximation view, earthly squares and circles are fuzzy squares and circles—their outlines could always as a matter of logical possibility approximate more closely their respective ideal, which is exactly square and circular. So with justice and beauty: their earthly manifestations could always benefit from improvement along specified lines. The sensible world is imperfect because it is only approximately whatever we say it is; the Forms are perfect because they are exactly whatever we say they are. Particulars are imperfect copies of the Forms in which they participate. They are copies in that they 'strive to be like' the relevant Forms: they do possess the relevant properties. They are imperfect in that they 'fall short of being like' the relevant Forms: they possess the relevant properties only to an extent or degree. In other words, particulars resemble the Forms in which

---

[14] C. M. Gillespie, 'The Use of *Eidos* and *Idea* in Hippocrates', *Classical Quarterly*, 6 (1912), 179–203, esp. 202: '. . . Prof. Taylor's contention that Plato found the words already in current use with the specific technical sense of "simple beings," "monads," "things-in-themselves," and merely applied them to a new kind of hyperphysical monad [is unfounded] . . . My examination seems to indicate that at the time of Socrates the words *eidos* and *idea* show two trends of meaning in the general vocabulary of science. The first is mainly physical, but without mathematical associations: . . . the *form* of a bodily object . . . sometimes the outer visible form or *shape*: often the inner form, the structure, nature, *phusis*, a specially physical conception . . . The second is semi-logical, classificatory; used especially in such contexts as "there are forms, kinds" of anything, whether a substance like the "moist" or a disease or whatnot.'

[15] See the passage quoted from Tredennick above.

they participate (and this makes them copies). But the resemblance is defective in the very respect in which it holds (and this makes them imperfect). Helen is not really (perfectly, that is, exactly) beautiful, nor is Phaedo really tall, much like this page, which is not exactly rectangular, or like a portrait of Simmias, which, on this account, cannot match Simmias' complexion perfectly. 'Perfection' is explicated as 'exactness', and 'imperfection' as 'approximation'.

On this view, a Form is never manifested in the sensible objects that participate in it. This is a crucial consequence, and the proponents of the approximation thesis accept it willingly.[16] The imperfection of the sensible world consists in the imperfection of those very properties the possession of which makes it a copy of the world of Forms. This is, as Mr Crombie has put it, 'a doctrine to the effect that Helen's beauty was . . . analogous to but not identical with true beauty . . . [and] would entail the consequence that forms are to be distinguished from [the common features of actual things. It is not the doctrine] that forms are imperfectly embodied by things, [but] the doctrine that forms are imperfectly embodied in the properties of things.'[17]

II

Having given a brief characterization of the approximation view, I would like to stop for a moment and also give a brief characterization of an alternative view of the relation between sensible particulars and Forms. This is a view for which I have argued in detail elsewhere.[18] Here, I will simply restate the main points, and I hope that the subsequent discussion will make my approach slightly clearer and somewhat more plausible.

Plato, I believe, was to a great extent led to formulate the theory of Forms in the *Phaedo*, the *Symposium*, and the *Republic* out of a concern with definition springing from Socrates' unsuccessful attempts to define a number of a family of terms, attempts which Plato himself made in the early or Socratic dialogues. These terms, prominent among which are terms for the moral virtues (justice, virtue, courage, piety, temperance, beauty) and terms for properties involving measurement or comparison (largeness or tallness, equality, heat), created a peculiar problem. Although these terms did not seem to be ambiguous, not only they, but also their contraries,

---

[16] See the first quote from Taylor above.

[17] I. M. Crombie, *An Examination of Plato's Doctrines*, ii (London, 1963), 279.

[18] 'Predication and Forms of Opposites in the *Phaedo*', *Review of Metaphysics*, 26 (1973), 461–91.

seemed to apply to the same objects without obvious contradiction. Thus the same person could (in different contexts) be truly described as both beautiful and ugly, tall and short, courageous and cowardly. Further, there seemed to be no plausible single candidate to account for the application of these terms to different objects; what seemed to account for courage in one situation could also explain cowardice in another, what explained beauty in one context could equally well account for ugliness in another. No sensible object could function as the definiens of terms like 'beauty', 'virtue', or 'tallness'; for any such object, which should have explained the application of these terms and the exclusion of their contraries, also seemed to account for the application of their contraries and the exclusion of the original terms. Thus no sensible object seemed to be really or, if one prefers, essentially just, beautiful, or tall; that is, beautiful in itself, independently of whatever context in which it happened to be placed, present in all and only those objects which we might truly consider beautiful. Individual objects were beautiful only in relation to other objects and they were also, without undergoing any change in themselves, ugly in relation to still other objects. Any definitional candidate for such terms did not isolate the instances of beauty or of justice, but it applied equally well to instances of ugliness or of injustice.[19]

Predicates like these are all incomplete; they are attributive or relational. And they are to be contrasted with predicates like '. . . is a man', '. . . is a finger', or '. . . is a stick' which are complete, both grammatically and logically one-place. Objects are men, fingers, or wooden sticks in themselves, independently of any relation to other things. As long as Simmias is the same object, he will be a man, and conversely. Complete terms like these are connected with the identity of the objects to which they apply, and do not generate the paradoxes which incomplete terms seem to generate. Plato, in fact, contrasted these two classes of terms: explicitly at *Rep.* 523–5 and *Alc.* 1, 111b11–c2, and implicitly, as I shall argue below, at *Phd.* 74a9–c5.

My view is that, at least in the *Phaedo* and the middle books of the *Republic*, Plato envisaged Forms for these incomplete predicates only. In the *Phaedo* (100b–105c) Socrates distinguishes between sensible particulars, their properties or characters, and the Forms. These Forms, and all the Forms mentioned elsewhere in the *Phaedo* and in the middle books of the *Republic*, correspond to incomplete predicates. Plato is introducing a new class of objects which the soul, confused by the contradictory reports of the senses (cf. *Rep.* 524b–d), has to contemplate if it is to grasp what beauty, justice, or tallness are in themselves. Unlike sensible particulars, the Form and the characters of beauty are completely, essentially, beautiful. If a particular is beautiful, it will also be ugly in another context: that *very same* particular will be ugly, without undergoing any change. But the Form and the characters of beauty would cease to be what they are if they were ever qualified by ugliness. Socrates' language is significant: neither the Form nor the character of tallness that a tall particular object possesses, he says, 'will consent to being other than it is by remaining and accepting shortness. Whereas, remaining and accepting shortness, still being who I am, I become short without changing, it will not dare, being tall, to become short' (102e2–6). There is a clear parallel between Socrates' 'being who he is' and tallness's 'being tall', Socrates cannot cease to be a man and still be Socrates; and tallness cannot cease to be tall and still be what it is: for what it is is, in an essential way, *tall*.

By introducing this new class of intelligible objects Plato managed to resolve one of the problems of the early dialogues. We do 'mean one thing' when we call many objects beautiful, just, or tall; the terms are not ambiguous: their meaning, and reference, is the Form of beauty, justice, and tallness, respectively. Sensible objects are both beautiful and ugly, just and unjust, tall and short, because they are not *really* beautiful, just, or tall; they only participate in beauty, justice, or tallness by possessing a relevant character. And it is only the Forms and the characters which really are beautiful, just, or tall: they are beautiful, just, or tall in themselves, without qualification, in every context, and they are present in all and only those cases where we can speak of beautiful, just, or tall sensible objects.

If this view is correct, then when Plato says that sensible objects are only imperfectly beautiful or just, he does not mean that they are approximately beautiful or just. Rather, he means that they are only accidentally beautiful or just, while the Form and its characters possess the relevant property in an essential manner. Notice also that on this approach, not only the Form but also the properties of particulars (the characters) exhibit this perfection. Thus the properties that particulars possess are perfect copies of the Forms in which these particulars participate. The imperfection of the sensible world does not consist in those very properties that it shares with the world of Forms. It consists, rather, in that sensible objects possess their perfect (i.e. exact) properties imperfectly (i.e. incompletely, temporarily, accidentally). Particulars are not imperfect copies of the Forms, as the approximation view would have it; they are imperfect: that is, copies of the Forms. For we shall see, in what follows, that to be a copy for Plato is the same as to 'fall short' of, to be imperfect in comparison to, the model. The copies' imperfection does not reside in the properties that make them copies, but in the way these perfect properties are possessed. When we say that particulars are only imperfectly F in comparison to the Form of F-ness, the imperfection belongs to the 'being' rather to the 'F' in 'being F'.[20]

I am afraid that this all-too-sketchy account is all I can give here by way of exposition. Perhaps the examination of the approximation view, to which we must now return, will help to put my position in a clearer perspective.

III

The approximation view holds that, say, two particulars are equal to each other because each participates in equality with respect to the other, or that Helen is beautiful because she participates in beauty, and so on.[21] But also, on this view, no sensible object ever is equal, beautiful, and so on, because of the fact that such objects are only approximately whatever we say they are. Here, then, is a problem. On what grounds can we justify our saying that the particulars participate in equality and Helen in beauty? How can we avoid saying that our particulars really participate in inequality and Helen in ugliness? If, as Taylor says, the same visual sensations that suggest the notion 'straight' also show that nothing in the world is perfectly straight (and one can wonder at this point on what grounds this 'perfectly' was included), why does the notion of being straight ever get suggested in the first place? Why not deduce from these sensations that visible lines strive after perfect inequality? On such grounds as these, the postulation of the Forms is no more legitimate than is the postulation of material objects in order to explain the regularities of our perception, when *all* we are 'acquainted with' in perception is supposed to be only our own sense-experience. Both postulations are equally illegitimate, and both show that more than is supposed is given to us in perception.[22]

I can think of only one way in which a defender of the approximation

---

[20] See Wilfrid Sellars, 'Vlastos and "The Third Man"', in *Philosophical Perspectives* (Springfield, Ill., 1967), esp. 25–31.

[21] I leave the range of predicates for which this explanation is appropriate open, much like Socrates does at, among other places, *Phd*. 100b–c.

[22] See R. E. Allen, 'Participation and Predication in Plato's Middle Dialogues', in G. Vlastos (ed.), *Plato*, i: *Metaphysics and Epistemology* (Garden City, NY, 1971), 178: 'A crooked line is not an imperfect instantiation of straight linearity; on the contrary, it is a full and complete instantiation of the *kind* of crooked line that it is, and the kind is repeatable, though the line itself is not . . . to say that something is deficient with respect to one character is merely an awkward way of saying that it quite fully has another.'

view could try to circumvent this criticism. That would be to claim that although no two sensible objects are perfectly equal, still sensible objects participate more or less in equality. If participation were a matter of degree, then it might be argued that every pair of objects participates in equality to some extent, that we consider equal those objects whose participation in equality is very great (that is, whose dimensions yield very close measurements), and that no objects are exactly equal, although that notion is reached by approximation. But I don't think that this suggestion can work at all. First, because there is not one shred of evidence that Plato thought of participation as an ordinal relation: particulars participate in the Forms in different respects or in different contexts, but never, so far as I can tell, in different degrees. Secondly, and perhaps more importantly, because this suggestion reverses the logical relations between 'being F' and 'participating in F'. Plato introduces the relation of participation to explain the notion of, say, being equal. He says that sensible objects participate in equality because he feels that he cannot say that sensible objects are (really) equal; but his concern has nothing to do with the exactness of the instantiations of equality: it is with their accidental nature. He begins by observing that objects are equal, or just, or beautiful, but only in certain respects, or in relation to certain objects, and he introduces their participation in the Forms of account for this latter feature. And he also limits participation in the Form of F-ness only to those objects which we can, in certain respects or contexts, truly consider as F. By contrast, the suggestion we are examining takes Plato's technical term, interpreted as an ordinal relation, as basic and constructs the notions of equality, beauty, or justice as special cases of that relation.

A number of issues are involved in this question, and we shall examine them as we proceed. For the moment, we must turn to Plato's own writings and see whether the approximation view can give a reasonable interpretation of Plato's expressed position on the imperfection of sensible objects. A key passage, which has furnished the received tradition with its favourite example, is *Phd.* 72e–78b, where Socrates tries to prove the soul's immortality by appealing to the theory of recollection.

I cannot possibly give an exhaustive analysis of this notorious passage here.[23] My question concerns the adequacy of the approximation view in explaining Socrates' distinction between equal particulars and the equal

---

[23] For a detailed discussion, see K. W. Mills, 'Plato's *Phaedo* 74b7–c6', *Phronesis*, 2 (1957), 128–48, 3 (1958), 40–58. A number of references are given in this article. I will give some additional ones below, but see also R. S. Bluck, 'Plato's Form of Equal', *Phronesis*, 4 (1959), 5–11; Richard Haynes, 'The Form Equality, as a Set of Equals', *Phronesis*, 9 (1964), 17–26; and J. M. Rist, 'Equals and Intermediaries in Plato', *Phronesis*, 9 (1964), 27–37.

itself and his statement that the former are 'inferior' to the latter. On at least one problem I will be quite dogmatic: I will assume that Plato is only referring to the unitary[24] Form of equality by all three expressions that he uses in this passage, namely, 'the equals themselves' ($\alpha\vec{v}\tau\grave{\alpha}\ \tau\grave{\alpha}\ \check{\iota}\sigma\alpha$; 74c1), 'equality' ($\iota\sigma\tau\acute{o}\tau\eta\varsigma$; 74c1), and 'the equal itself' ($\alpha\vec{v}\tau\grave{o}\ \tau\grave{o}\ \check{\iota}\sigma\sigma\nu$; 74c4–5); neither mathematical intermediaries[25] nor 'things in so far as they are equal'[26] are involved in his argument.[27] I will not be quite as dogmatic, however, on the interpretation of the phrase 'equal . . . to one . . . unequal to another' ($\tau\tilde{\omega}\ \mu\grave{\epsilon}\nu\ \ldots\ \check{\iota}\sigma\alpha\ \ldots\ \tau\tilde{\omega}\ \delta'\ o\check{v}$; 74b8–9), and I will not be at all dogmatic on the interpretation of the way in which particulars 'fall short' of the Forms.

These last two points are quite distinct on the approximation view, whose reconstruction is as follows: Socrates first distinguishes equal particulars from the equal itself on the vague and incomplete grounds that 'sticks and stones, sometimes, being the same, appear equal to one, unequal to another' (74b8–9),[28] while on no occasion do 'the equals themselves appear unequal to you [viz. Simmias], or equality, inequality' (74c1–2). He then goes on to say that equal particulars fall short of equality, in that they are only approximately and not exactly equal (74d4–7). Finally, he generalizes this to all particulars and properties at 74d9–75b8.

The points are distinct because on no interpretation of the first does it follow that equal things, in contrast to equality, are only approximately equal. Whether sticks and stones appear to one *person* equal, to another person unequal; whether they appear equal to one *thing*, unequal to another thing; or whether they appear *sometimes* equal and sometimes unequal: none of these alternatives implies that their relative or temporary equality is only approximate. On the contrary, it seems to me, roughly the same predicaments, if they are predicaments, would befall things that were exactly equal. If two things were perfectly equal in this sense, then from some perspective they must appear unequal to an observer, and they

[24] Peter Geach has argued that the Form of equality actually consists of two perfectly equal objects in 'The Third Man Again', in R. E. Allen (ed.), *Studies in Plato's Metaphysics* (London, 1965), 265–77.

[25] Ross, *Plato's Theory of Ideas*, 22; R. Hackforth, *Plato's* Phaedo (Indianapolis, 1965), 69 n. 2; Bluck, 'Plato's Form of Equal', and *Plato's* Phaedo (London, 1955), 67 n. 2.

[26] Burnet, *The* Phaedo *of Plato*, 56 n. *ad* 74c1; R. Loriaux, *Le* Phédon *de Platon: Commentaire et traduction*, i (Namur, 1969), 143–6.

[27] This is also the opinion of G. E. L. Owen, 'The Platonism of Aristotle', in P. F. Strawson (ed.), *Studies in the Philosophy of Thought and Action* (London, 1968), 147–74. My conversations with Professor Owen on this subject have been extremely valuable.

[28] Or, according to the variant MSS reading (cdd. TW) '$\tau\acute{o}\tau\epsilon\ \ldots\ \tau\acute{o}\tau\epsilon$', 'sometimes equal, sometimes unequal'. This reading, however, does not introduce any new considerations, as we shall see.

must appear (and be) unequal to some things which measure differently. As to the 'sometimes' reading, we have two alternatives: we can either take it as 'they sometimes appear equal, sometimes unequal, to each other', in which case we have two only unequal things appearing to be equal on some occasions, probably because of perspectival variation; or we can take it as 'they sometimes appear equal to some things, sometimes unequal to other things'. On either alternative, the case collapses to one of the two previous possibilities; and neither of these supports the approximation interpretation of imperfection.

So, Ross's claim that in distinguishing equal things from the equal itself, Plato 'is thinking, perhaps, of the effect of perspective' cannot stand.[29] In fact, to appear equal, or square, from all angles, apart from being impossible, is also to my mind a mark of imperfection: an object which appears square from all angles cannot be a square, it must be an impossible-object construction; it would, by contrast, be a mark of the perfect square that at such-and-such a tilt, it would project exactly such-and-such a trapezoid![30]

This, then, is one shortcoming of the approximation view in interpreting Plato's argument. The distinction between particulars and Forms is quite independent of the inferiority of the former to the latter, although there should be some connection between them. Because of this, the imperfection of particulars is left undefended on this account: Socrates simply asks Simmias if this is not the case (74d5–7), Simmias immediately agrees (74d8), and Socrates generalizes his conclusion. But why should Simmias agree to such an idea? Perhaps he might have found it plausible if it concerned only squares and circles (drawn circles being only approximately circular by geometrical standards); but it doesn't. He might have been tempted, although that would have been a very mild temptation, if it concerned only equality. But Socrates proceeds to generalize to 'the larger, the smaller, and all such things'; his argument, he says, 'is not more about the equal than it is about the beautiful itself, the good itself, the just, the pious, and, I mean, about everything to which we give our seal of "that which is" in our discussions' (75c9–d3). This generalization, which Simmias also accepts without argument, certainly needs support. But before I show how Socrates does argue for it, and how the two points are connected, I

---

[29] Ross, Plato's Theory of Ideas, 23.

[30] It is instructive to compare, at this point, Plato's discussion of perspective at Rep. 597–8. The physical bed does not change, whatever the angle from which we look at it; it only appears different. Painting represents not the bed as it is, but as it appears (598a-b). Variations due to perspective have no implications as to the ontological character of physical objects, and are therefore unlikely to account for the ontological distinction which Plato is trying to draw in the Phaedo.

must discuss another difficulty for the approximation view, which was first pointed out by Gosling.[31]

Suppose the approximation view is correct, and that particulars are deficient in the very respect in which they resemble the relevant Form. Now, in this argument, Plato is trying to prove that our knowledge of equality is an instance of recollection. To this end, he specifies four conditions which cases of recollection should satisfy. Two are given at 73c6–d1: 'If someone saw, heard, or by another sense perceived something, and came to know not only that thing but also became aware of another, the knowledge of which is not the same but different, would we not be justified in saying that he remembered what he became aware of?' First, the perception of one thing must give rise to knowledge of another. All cases of recollection involve (at least) three terms: the subject who remembers, the object that reminds him of what he remembers, and the object he remembers. Secondly, the knowledge of what is remembered must be distinct from the knowledge of the reminding object. This is a puzzling condition, and Gosling takes it to mean that 'it must be possible to know or be acquainted with what we are reminded by, without knowing or being acquainted with what we are reminded of, and vice versa: I may be reminded of Simmias by his portrait, but not by Simmias himself'.[32] But I am not sure that this is right because, for one thing, such a consideration does not play a prominent role in Plato's argument; for another, as we shall see, this aspect of recollection, as stated, is covered by Plato's fourth condition.

My own view is that Plato is stating a different condition here: If A reminds me of B, then my coming to know A is not (not: need not) on that occasion sufficient for my coming to know B. For, suppose that I am looking at Simmias, who is wearing a brown tunic; can we say that (my looking at) Simmias reminded me of his tunic? No, for looking at Simmias, I am also looking at his tunic. On the other hand, I can be reminded of the tunic if my looking at Simmias when he is not wearing it brings it to my mind. Similarly, my seeing Simmias running may remind me that the bell which has been annoying me for the last five minutes signals the beginning of a lecture on ethics; even though the two events are simultaneous, one may remind me of the other if my coming to know the first does not by itself imply my coming to know the second. Notice also that on Gosling's condition, my seeing Simmias wearing his tunic could actually qualify as a reminder of the tunic, since knowing Simmias is in fact independent of knowing his tunic, and it is possible to know one without knowing the other.[33]

---

[31] Gosling, 'Similarity in *Phaedo* 73b *seq.*'.   [32] Ibid. 154.   [33] See also ibid. 159.

The third condition, given at 73e1–3, is rather loose, and not quite necessary: 'This, then is recollection: especially if it happens to someone in connection with things he has long since forgotten because of the passage of time and of not thinking about them.' Coming to know the equal itself is such a star instance of recollection. Here, too, I must disagree with Gosling, who interprets this passage as stating a necessary condition: 'I am not said to be reminded of someone or something except in some respect in which I had at least temporarily forgotten them.'[34] This is indeed true, but, as the text shows, not what Plato is saying at this point. He only wants to point out that given that the other conditions are met, and that knowledge of one thing brought to mind another, which was not there at the time (i.e. which was temporarily forgotten), we are especially justified in calling this recollection if the thing remembered has been forgotten for a long time.

The fourth condition is the most crucial one for our purposes. At 74a1–2 Socrates, having explained the general conditions of recollection, distinguishes between being reminded of *B* by *A* through some association *A* and *B* possess for the subject (as when a portrait of Simmias (73d9), or Simmias himself (73e5–6) reminds us of Cebes) and being reminded of *B* by *A* through some similarity between them (as when Simmias' portrait reminds us of Simmias himself; 73e9–10). In 'remembering through similars', Socrates now adds (74a5–7), 'isn't it also necessary that one realize whether or not what reminds him lacks something in respect of being similar to that which is remembered?' When I first read this passage, I was bewildered; eventually I came to disbelieve what I thought it said. Why should Plato make this a necessary condition for recollection, and why did he think that is was obvious, as Simmias' immediate assent at 74a8 indicates? Is it really necessary for me to realize that Simmias' portrait, which reminds me of Simmias, does not match the colour of his hair? Must I, in one breath, realize that I am looking at Simmias' portrait and that the portrait is inaccurate? Finally, why *can't* the portrait be accurate?[35]

I can see only one possible way of saying that the portrait must be inaccurate: one could argue that the colour of Simmias' hair depends on the lighting in which it is seen, and that the illumination is constantly chang-

[34] Gosling, 'Similarity in *Phaedo* 73b seq.', 154–5. A similar point is made by Aristotle in *Mem.* 451ᵃ31 ff. See Richard Sorabji, *Aristotle on Memory* (Providence, RI, 1972), 53.

[35] It is important to notice that Plato envisages as real possibilities both that the object may and that it may *not* lack anything in respect of being similar to what it reminds us of. Plato's point is, I think, very sensible. Not all similar objects are related as copy to original: two mass produced earthen jars, for example, are not. He is saving a place in his scheme for such objects in this statement.

ing; therefore, the portrait cannot capture the right colour over time. This may be thought plausible; but, by this argument, we would have to conclude that one never even sees the real colour of Simmias' hair. For the colour at any moment is different from what it has been or will be at all other moments; thus we should have to conclude that even our sight gives us an imperfect approximation to the colour of Simmias' hair. But surely this is not what Plato had in mind. And even if he did, we should note that this still would not give him (or us) good reason to say that portraits must be inaccurate. For nothing prevents the portrait from attributing to Simmias exactly the right colour of hair (or any other characteristic) at a given moment, from a given perspective, or in given conditions. The portrait's 'imperfection' does not consist in its deficiency in resembling Simmias in a given respect, but in its incapacity to capture some characteristic of Simmias in all its dimensions. This point can be made by saying that a portrait cannot possibly capture all the characteristics of its model. And this does not preclude the portrait from matching its model exactly in some characteristics (namely, those in which it resembles it). And the fact that the portrait does not duplicate all the features of its model must be clear to the spectator if he is to be aware that he is looking not at the model itself, but at a different thing, its portrait or copy, which resembles the model in certain relevant respects!

My suggestion, then, is that Plato is not maintaining the implausible idea that the approximation view attributes to him, namely, that if two things are similar to each other, and one is a copy of the other, the copy can never reproduce exactly that very characteristic which makes it a copy in the first place. Rather, Plato believes that if one thing is a copy of another then it must lack some characteristic of its model, and that one must realize this if one is to realize that one is confronted with a copy in the first place. In this way, Plato's notion of 'copy' is different from our notion of 'duplicate', and he distinguishes the two in his statement of this condition.[36] If our two similar objects share every characteristic, then we shall no longer be confronted by a copy, portrait, or image (εἰκών) and its original. Particularly, in the case of recollection, we shall not even be aware of being confronted by two distinct objects at all. But then the second condition on recollection will not have been met, and no remembering will occur: we will be seeing (hearing, etc.) what we take to be the very object which we were supposed to remember.

It is important to keep in mind in this context a passage in the *Cratylus* (432a–d), where Socrates shows Cratylus that pictures (and likenesses in

[36] Cf. n. 35.

general, including *onomata*: names or words) cannot reproduce every property of their original. If a god, Socrates says, made a likeness of Cratylus, matching not only his colour and shape, as painters do, but also made everything inside just as it is (ἀλλὰ καὶ τὰ ἐντὸς πάντα τοιαῦτα ποιήσειεν οἷάπερ τὰ σά; 432b5–6), then what we would have would not be Cratylus and his image, but, simply 'two Cratyluses'.

The implication is clear that painters can, and do, match exactly the 'colour and shape' of their subject, but that they cannot match all its properties. If they did, they would no longer be constructing a likeness, but a duplicate. Socrates completes his point by asking Cratylus if he is to aware 'how far likenesses *fall short* of being such as the things are of which they are likenesses' (ἢ οὐκ αἰσθάνῃ ὅσον ἐνδέουσιν αἱ εἰκόνες τὰ αὐτὰ ἔχειν ἐκείνοις ὧν εἰκόνες εἰσίν'; 432d1–3). The vocabulary is that of the *Phaedo*: likenesses fall short of their model—not because they cannot *exactly* reproduce *any* of its properties, but because they cannot *at all* reproduce *some* property (or properties) of their model.[37]

It is a difficult question for the approximation view how, since according to its account copies cannot match exactly any of their models' properties, we come to realize that an object is a copy of a different one in the first place. (Notice that this is the same criticism, in relation to copies and originals, that we raised at the very beginning of this section in relation to particulars and Forms.) This view appears more plausible if we think of portraits and their subjects only. For a portrait, one might say, may not match any property exactly, but it may match a number of properties approximately, and, on balance, it resembles its subject more than it resembles any other object. Even if we grant this, which is very doubtful,[38] we must still remember that portraits are only of incidental concern to Plato: his main interest is to show that sensible objects are likenesses of the Forms in which they participate. But sensible objects resemble each Form only in one respect: the only characteristic common to the equal itself and to equal particulars is that they, too, are in their way equal. And if their equality is only approximate, if, that is, it is really inequality, how can we connect them with the equal itself in the first place?[39] Since the alternative which might have applied to portraits is

[37] My debt to Gosling is obvious; he is the first to have pointed out the relevance of the *Cratylus* passage to the *Phaedo*; see 'Similarity in *Phaedo* 73b *seq.*', 157–9.

[38] I don't really agree even with this claim: how one can tell that an object is a picture of another is a much more complicated affair. But this approach may seem to some to have 'initial credibility'.

[39] Socrates' inclusion of the 'larger' and the 'smaller' in his list of Forms at 75c9 makes this point crucial. If sensible objects were all only approximately large, then they should all be small, and they would all strive to be like the 'smaller'.

no longer available to us, we should conclude that we would never realize that equal, just, or large particulars 'desire' to be like their respective Form, which we do realize, Plato says, at the very moment when we begin to employ our senses.

These, then, are Plato's conditions on recollection:

If a person, P, is reminded of B by becoming aware of A, then:
(1) A and B are distinct;
(2) Becoming aware of A was not on that occasion sufficient for becoming aware of B;
(3) In particular, we are said to recollect B especially if we have long forgotten it.

Further, if A and B are similar, then:
(4) P must realize that A is only similar to, and not identical with, B, in that it does not duplicate every property of A; in Plato's words, A must fall short of being such as B is.

Plato shows, by the example of the equal itself, that our knowledge of the Forms satisfies these conditions. First he shows that the equal itself is distinct from all sensible equal objects, which are responsible for our becoming aware of it (74a9–c10). He then states that given that equal things are similar to the equal itself, they fall short of being just like it (74c11–d8). He goes on to argue that we realize their inferiority through our senses, which we exercise from the moment we are born, and that thus our knowledge of the Forms is prior to and independent of our knowledge of equal particulars, for otherwise the comparison could not have been made (74d9–75d6). Finally, he argues in a way strongly reminiscent of *Meno* 98a2–4 and *Laches* 190c6 that, since people cannot 'give an account' (διδόναι λόγον; 76b4–9) of the Forms, their knowledge must have been lost. Our knowledge of the Forms is thus forgotten, acquired before birth and before our senses began to function (75d7–76c10). Therefore, he concludes, our soul must have existed before our birth (76c11–77a5).

IV

The approximation view fails to make Plato's theory of recollection coherent. Let us now try to show, by exploiting the suggestion made in our discussion of Plato's fourth condition, how Socrates' distinction between sensible equal objects and the equal itself supports his claim that the former are inferior to the latter.[40]

Since Socrates' peculiar claim that sensible equals are inferior to the equal itself (74d4–8) is not given explicit justification, it is reasonable to expect that it has received some support in what has just preceded it. And since what has preceded it is the distinction between these two classes of objects, our task is to read that argument in a way which will provide the support the imperfection claim needs.

What is the characteristic which allows Socrates to make the distinction? The problem is that his claim that 'sticks and stones, sometimes, still being the same, appear equal to one, unequal to another' (74b8–9) is too vague and incomplete to be understood as it stands. One alternative, older and more widely accepted than the second, has been to take the indefinite pronouns 'one' and 'another' as masculine and to render this passage as follows: 'Two stones or two logs equal in length sometimes seem equal to one man, but not to another, though they haven't changed'.[41] A number of considerations against this view, some less persuasive than others, have been given by N. R. Murphy and K. W. Mills.[42] Among them we might single out the claim that on Hackforth's interpretation Plato's second premiss appears to be irrelevant. For that premiss, stated at 74c1–2, is: 'But now, what about the equals themselves? Have they ever appeared to you to be unequal, or equality to be inequality?'[43] But what Plato should have asserted is not that the Form of equality can never appear to be unequal (or inequality) to Simmias, but that this could never happen to anyone. Antisthenes, for example, would not have been bothered by this claim, since equality never appeared to him to be anything at all. Also, Murphy argued, on this approach the first premiss is 'pointless, since we could infer only that one of the two [men] had made a mistake'.[44] Now these points have been widely discussed and, on balance, Hackforth's view and

---

[40] The interpretation of 74a9–12 is not our concern. Whether we take it to mean 'we say that something, namely, the equal itself, is equal', or 'we say that something equal exists, namely, the equal itself', the rest of the argument remains, for our purposes, unaffected.

[41] This is Hackforth's translation, Plato's Phaedo, 69; Bluck, Plato's Phaedo 67, translates as follows: 'do not stones that are equal, or pieces of wood, very often seem—the self-same objects—to one man, equal, to another, unequal?' Cf. Burnet, The Phaedo of Plato, 74 n. ad 74b8; R. D. Archer-Hind, The Phaedo of Plato (London, 1883), 77 n. ad 72e–76d.

[42] N. R. Murphy, The Interpretation of Plato's Republic (Oxford, 1951), 111 n.; Mills, 'Plato's Phaedo, 74b7–c6'. Loriaux also accepts this view, without argument, in L'Être et la Forme selon Platon (Paris, 1955), 18–19; he does argue for it in Le Phédon de Platon, 149–53.

[43] Hackforth, Plato's Phaedo, 69; cf. Bluck, Plato's Phaedo, 67.

[44] Murphy, The Interpretation of Plato's Republic, 111 n.; Mills, 'Plato's Phaedo 74b7–c6', 131–3, argues that both interpretations are subject to this shortcoming. But this is not true if the 'appears' is taken to mean, as it is taken below, 'appears and in fact is'.

Murphy's suggestion to take the pronouns as neuter and read Plato as saying 'that sticks and stones without themselves changing have contrasted predicates in different relations, but the equals themselves . . . have not'[45] have proven equally inconclusive.

I propose to bypass most of the debate and offer a different consideration that might strengthen Murphy's approach. According to Hackforth, we have a pair of objects, equal to each other in length, which, perhaps because of perspective, seem equal to some people and unequal to others. These objects, in other words, are supposed to remain in the same relation to each other while people disagree about their equality. And as long as we concentrate on this particular example, Hackforth's interpretation seems, if not confirmed, at least plausible. But surely Plato is not interested only in the predicate ʻ. . . is equal (to . . .)ʼ but also in all those predicates for which he will postulate Forms, including ʻ. . . is larger (than . . .)ʼ, ʻ. . . is smaller (than . . .)ʼ, ʻ. . . is goodʼ, ʻ. . . is justʼ, and ʻ. . . is beautifulʼ.

Let us now take one of these predicates and ask how the argument would distinguish, for example, just particulars from the just itself. According to Hackforth, Plato would claim that the same just act would appear just to some people and unjust to others. But now that perspective cannot provide the easy answer, the question why Plato would believe this becomes crucial. Plato did actually believe that people disagree about what is just, pious, brave, or beautiful. But his belief did not concern acts like returning a knife to its maniacal owner: this, he thought, was patently unjust (*Rep.* 331c–d); he did not doubt that humans are beautiful compared to apes (*Hp.Ma.* 289a); he did not question Socrates' bravery at Delion (*La.* 181b) or at Potidaea (*Smp.* 219e5–221c1). What he did doubt was that returning what one owes is always, in all contexts, just; whether a human being is beautiful no matter what that person is being compared to; whether retreating or advancing is always brave. In a specific context, Plato would not hesitate to call an action just or brave, a person beautiful or virtuous. What he did hesitate to believe was that the grounds usually given for such claims would always, in all circumstances, support the same conclusion, as he thought good grounds should.

But if this is so, then Hackforth's interpretation of our argument cannot account for its generalization, which should capture all those predicates for which Plato postulates Forms. Although a log may from a certain angle appear unequal to another log of equal dimensions, a just act will not appear unjust unless the context in which it was considered has changed:[46]

---

[45] Murphy, *The Interpretation of Plato's* Republic, 111 n; I have deleted the Greek in Murphy's sentence.
[46] Unless, that is, it is considered as an action-type to be found in many tokens.

returning a knife to its rightful owner is not just if its owner happens to be a homicidal maniac.

My claim is that Hackforth and those who agree with him have been misled by an accidental feature of the particular example that Plato used in his argument. They thus took it that Plato claims that things can appear both *F* and not *F* in the same context to different observers. But although Plato could have said this about pairs of equal things, he could not have said it about the other predicates for which he designed his argument. What he could have said, and what I think he did say, is that no earthly equal, beautiful, large, good, pious, or just object can appear equal, beautiful, large, good, pious, or just in every relation. If any did, it would be in itself equal, or beautiful, and so on. But all earthly things depended for their beauty, and their equality, on the presence of other things and on a comparison with them, and this distinguished them from the Forms which were essentially what these earthly things were only accidentally.

If we accept the idea that what distinguishes sensible particulars from Forms is the fact that particulars possess their properties only in an incomplete manner, only in relation to other particulars, while the Forms possess them completely, in themselves, not only does the general argument become coherent, but also the imperfection claim receives the support it needs. Just as Simmias' portrait matches Simmias' hair colour exactly at a given moment, so equal particulars resemble equality exactly, in relation to specific objects to which they are equal. And just as Simmias' portrait cannot match Simmias perfectly (either in all his properties, or in respect of hair colour over time), so equal particulars cannot match equality in all respects. For they are equal only to some things and not to others, and without any change in themselves (but only in their relations) they can be truly considered as both equal and unequal—while equality is always equal, and depends on nothing other than itself for this. And just as Simmias' portrait 'falls short' of being just like Simmias, so equal particulars 'fall short' of being just like the equal itself. But their imperfection does not consist in their being approximately what the Forms are exactly; it consists in their being accidentally what the Forms are essentially.

It is in this way that Socrates, in distinguishing equal particulars from the equal itself, also shows that sensible objects are inferior to the Forms. And here we have one of the reasons why the Forms that Plato postulates all correspond to incomplete predicates. His problem was that sensible objects, *still being the same*, would appear to be both equal and unequal, both beautiful and ugly, and so on. He postulated the Forms in order to show that despite their compresence these properties did correspond to distinct entities, and that the terms associated with them did have distinct, and univocal, meanings. But for this problem to even arise, the *same* sensible particulars would have to be qualified by contrary properties. And for these particulars to remain the same, there would have to be some properties which those particulars possessed in themselves, independently of their relations to other objects, properties which would allow their reidentification over time. These properties all corresponded to complete terms, they did not confuse the soul by appearing together with their opposites, they did not require the postulation of Forms, and the way in which they applied to sensible particulars actually provided Plato with the model on which he conceived of the relation between the Forms and the properties for which these Forms stood.

Plato, then, did think that the Forms have perfect instances in the sensible world (these are the 'characters' of the *Phaedo*), and that they are contained in the particulars that participate in them. What is imperfect is the way in which those perfect instances are possessed by sensible objects, an imperfection which allows us to say of everything that we consider as just or beautiful or equal that it is also unjust, ugly, or unequal. Contrary to the idea underlying the approximation view, I think that Plato was writing not so much with Pythagoras, but with Parmenides in mind. His question, as the absence of mathematical discussion in the early dialogues indicates, was not of a sort that would have taxed mathematicians. It was the question how we can even understand each other when we say that sensible objects are equal, beautiful, good, or large, since these words seemed to refer to exactly the same things to which their contraries also referred; and the question how things can both be and not be what we say they are. To these Eleatic challenges, the theory of Forms replied that none of these objects is equal, beautiful, good, or large, but that there is a whole class of different, intelligible, objects—objects which always and only are, and never are not, which we know not by the senses but by recollection, and which, by being the meanings of our words and by being instantiated by sensible objects, allow us to understand each other and to know when we are speaking truly of the changing sensible world.[47]

[47] I am very grateful to Professor John Cooper, who read a draft of this paper and saved me from some, though not all, of my errors. (Those that remain, he could do nothing about.) An older debt, acknowledged belatedly here, is due to Michael Friedman.

VII

SEPARATION AND IMMANENCE IN PLATO'S THEORY OF FORMS

DANIEL T. DEVEREUX

> But Socrates did not make the universals or definitions separate; his
> successors, however, did separate them, and beings of this sort they
> called 'Forms'.
>
> (Aristotle, *Metaphysics M* 4, 1078[b]30–2)

According to Aristotle's terse report, Plato separated Forms from sensible
particulars, and in doing so he departed from Socrates' view of the relationship between universals and their participants. Until recently, most
scholars accepted Aristotle's statement as fundamentally accurate, and
they understood *separation* to involve both the denial that Forms are
immanent in sensible particulars as well as the positive claim that they
are 'ontologically independent'—that is, they do not depend for their
existence on the things that participate in them. In the last few years
this common and familiar view has come under attack on several fronts.
As for immanence, the critics argue that the evidence is mixed; in
some dialogues, e.g. the *Symposium* and *Timaeus*, there are passages
in which Plato clearly rejects immanence, but in the *Phaedo* he seems
to regard Forms as *in* their participants.[1] It has also been claimed that
Plato's statements about Forms do not support a general commitment to
ontological independence; the most that can be said is that in some
dialogues he is committed to the independence of some Forms. Even
supporters of the traditional view sometimes claim that Plato's notion
of participation is incompatible with a strict doctrine of separation; thus

© Daniel T. Devereux 1994. Reprinted with permission from *Oxford Studies in Ancient Philosophy*, 12 (1994), 63–90, and the author.

   An earlier version of this paper was read at the University of Texas in Austin; I am grateful
to members of the audience for stimulating questions and discussion. I would also like to thank
Don Morrison for his generous help.

   [1] See G. Fine, 'Separation', *Oxford Studies in Ancient Philosophy*, 2 (1984), 31–87, and
'Immanence', ibid. 4 (1986), 71–97; R. M. Dancy, *Two Studies in the Early Academy* (Albany,
NY, 1991), 9–23.

his view may not have been as simple and straightforward as Aristotle's statement implies.[2]

I believe that Plato's views on immanence and separation are consistent and clear-cut: from the *Phaedo* on, he denies that Forms are immanent in their participants, and he is committed throughout to the claim that *all* Forms are ontologically independent of sensible particulars. Most of the following discussion will be devoted to a defence of these claims. My arguments will, I hope, improve upon the traditional view by showing that Plato's understanding of the relationship between Forms and their participants is more systematic and coherent than one might have gathered from the older discussions. Towards the end of the paper, I shall turn to the question of Plato's reasons for separating Forms from sensible particulars. Some of the arguments against Forms at the beginning of the *Parmenides* are aimed at a view of Forms as immanent in their participants, and I shall try to show that they give us valuable indications of some of Plato's reasons for rejecting immanence.

I

Aristotle implies in a number of passages that, according to the Platonic theory, Forms are not in their participants; for example, in the *Metaphysics* he says: 'But [the Forms] make no contribution to our knowledge of other things, for they are not even the essence of these—if they were, they would have been *in* them; nor do they contribute to the being of other things since they do not inhere in (μὴ ἐνυπάρχοντα) the things that participate in them (*A* 9, 991ᵃ12–14).'[3] Aristotle does not *argue* that Forms cannot be immanent; he treats the non-immanence of Forms as a well-known feature of the Platonic theory, a feature acknowledged by the defenders of the theory.[4] There are, in fact, passages in the dialogues in which Plato states

---

[2] See J. D. Mabbott, 'Aristotle and the χωρισμός of Plato', *Classical Quarterly*, 20 (1926), 72–9; W. D. Ross, *Plato's Theory of Ideas* (Oxford, 1951), 228–31.

[3] Cf. *M* 5, 1079ᵇ15–18, 1079ᵇ35–1080ᵃ2; *K* 2, 1060ᵃ10–13; *B* 2, 998ᵃ7–19; *MM* 1182ᵇ10–22; *EE* 1218ᵃ14–15. It is clear that Aristotle takes the denial of immanence to be tied to separation, for he points out a few lines down from the passage quoted that it is impossible for the substance of something to exist separately from that of which it is the substance (991ᵇ1–3); see D. Morrison, 'Separation in Aristotle's Metaphysics', *Oxford Studies in Ancient Philosophy*, 3 (1985), 134–5.

[4] Fine argues that in the *Phaedo*, at least, Plato holds that Forms are immanent in their participants, and she apparently thinks that Aristotle's assertion that Forms are not in their participants is not a *report* of Platonic doctrine, but rather a claim to the effect that, given their nature, Forms cannot be immanent (cf. 'Immanence', 94). However, there are no signs in the passages in which Aristotle says or implies that Forms are not immanent that he takes himself to be making a claim that the Platonists would dispute.

that Forms are not in their participants. For instance, in the *Symposium* Diotima says:

Nor again will the beautiful appear in the guise of a face or hands or any other portion of the body, nor as a speech or knowledge, *nor as being somewhere in some other thing*—as, for example, in a living thing or in the earth or in the heavens or in anything else; rather, it is itself by itself and with itself, while all the other beautiful things participate in it in such a way that, though all of them are coming to be and perishing, it neither increases nor diminishes, and is in no way affected. (211a5–b5)[5]

And in the *Timaeus* Forms are differentiated from their participants in the following way:

This being so, we must agree that one kind [of entity] is the Form ($\varepsilon\tilde{\iota}\delta o\varsigma$) which is always the same, ungenerated and imperishable, neither receiving into itself anything from elsewhere nor itself going into something else in some place, invisible and imperceptible by any sense, it being that which is given to intellect to investigate; a second kind [of entity] has the same name as the former, is similar to it, perceptible, generated, always being carried, coming to be in some place and passing out of existence from some place, apprehended by opinion together with perception . . . for it belongs to an image to come into being *in* some other thing . . . on the other hand that which has real being has the support of the exactly true account, which declares that, so long as two things are different, neither can ever come to be in the other in such a way that the two should become at once one and the same thing and two. (51e6–52d1)

Forms cannot be in anything else, nor can they have anything else in them. The last sentence of the passage tells us that if one thing can come to be in another, neither thing has 'real being'.

In the *Phaedo*, on the other hand, Socrates seems to speak of Forms being *in* their participants, for example, of largeness and smallness being 'in Simmias' (102b5–6); and critics of the traditional view argue that here, at least, Forms are regarded as immanent.[6] However, in the same section of

---

[5] Cf. *Prm.* 133c3–6. Notice that Diotima denies that the Form beauty is immanent and at the same time describes beautiful objects as 'participating' ($\mu\varepsilon\tau\dot{\varepsilon}\chi\varepsilon\iota\nu$) in the Form. It is sometimes thought that 'participation' is suggestive of immanence, and that the continued use of this term together with the denial of immanence is a sign of Plato's confusion about the relationship between Forms and participants; see Dancy, *Two Studies in the Early Academy*, 15, and Ross, *Plato's Theory of Ideas*, 228–31. Aristotle also couples the two when he says (in the passage quoted above) 'they [the Forms] do not inhere in the things that participate in them'; he apparently does not feel it necessary to point out, for example, that even though a thing is said to participate in a Form, the Form is not in the thing. Both Plato and Aristotle pretty clearly do not regard 'participation' as suggestive of immanence; the term is used to designate the relationship between Forms and their participants, whatever that relationship might be.

[6] See Fine, 'Immanence', 73–80, Those who hold that Plato makes no distinction between Forms and immanent characters in the *Phaedo* must also believe that he approves of speaking of Forms being in their participants; cf. Dancy, *Two Studies in the Early Academy*, 14; D. Bostock.

the *Phaedo* Socrates distinguishes between the 'largeness in us' and 'largeness itself' (or 'largeness in nature'; 103b5), and it is often thought that these expressions refer to two types of entities: immanent characters or 'Form-copies' on the one hand, and separate or 'transcendent' Forms on the other. If this is right, one might consider whether it is only the Form-copies that are immanent in sensible particulars, and not the Forms themselves; if Forms in the strict sense are not immanent, the doctrine of the *Phaedo* would be consistent with that of the *Symposium* and *Timaeus*. But the critics reply that there is no basis in the text for a distinction between two types of entities; they claim that the two expressions 'largeness itself' and 'largeness in us' refer to one and the same entity. And since this entity is said to be *in* particular individuals such as Simmias, they contend that Forms must be regarded as immanent in the *Phaedo*.[7]

The reason for thinking that Plato considers Forms and immanent characters to be distinct entities in the *Phaedo* is that Socrates seems to imply that things like the largeness in us are perishable; he says, for example, that when the largeness in us is approached by its opposite, it 'either withdraws or perishes' (102d5–103a2; cf. 103d5–104c3). If the largeness in us is the kind of thing that can perish, then it obviously cannot be identical with the Form largeness, which is imperishable. The critics' rejoinder is that Socrates does not suppose that perishing is a real possibility for the largeness in us—his view is that it must always withdraw at the approach of its opposite.[8] The reason he says it 'either withdraws *or perishes*' is that he is here laying the groundwork for the final stage of the argument for immortality: he eventually wants to apply the two alternatives 'withdrawing or perishing' to the soul, and then show that the soul cannot perish and hence must withdraw at the approach of death.[9]

However, if we look at the final stage of the argument, it becomes clear that Socrates does regard such things as the largeness and smallness in us as perishable entities. After pointing out that the largeness in us will never admit its opposite, smallness, he explains that there is another class of

Plato's Phaedo (Oxford, 1986), 186; C. Stough, 'Forms and Explanation in the *Phaedo*', *Phronesis*, 21 (1976), 1–30; D. O'Brien, 'The Last Argument of Plato's *Phaedo*', *Classical Quarterly*, NS 17 (1967), 210–13.

[7] See Fine, 'Immanence', 73 ff. According to Dancy (*Two Studies in the Early Academy* 14–18), the *Phaedo* uses the 'language of immanence' in speaking about Forms, but this way of speaking should not be taken as evidence of a firm commitment to immanence. He believes that Socrates' confession of puzzlement about the nature of participation applies to the question whether or not Forms are immanent: there is evidence for both immanent and separate Forms (the 'High Theory of Forms') not only in the *Phaedo*, but also in the *Symposium* and *Parmenides*. (See below, n. 19, for comments on the nature of Socrates' puzzlement.)

[8] See e.g. Fine, 'Immanence', 77.

[9] Cf. Dancy, *Two Studies in the Early Academy*, 17.

things with a similar property. Fire and snow are not themselves opposites, but they possess one member of a pair of opposites and exclude the other; fire is always hot, and at the approach of cold it must either withdraw or perish (103d5–12). Things like fire and snow may be called 'carriers' of opposites. Whenever one of these carriers 'takes possession of' a thing, the thing acquires both the character of the carrier and that of the opposite carried by the carrier; for example, if fire 'takes possession of' a piece of wood, the wood becomes both fiery and hot (104c11–d3). Souls, according to Socrates, are carriers of life, and when a soul takes possession of a body, that body becomes both ensouled and alive (105c9–d4). As a carrier of life, the soul must either withdraw or perish at the approach of death; it cannot admit death and remain what it is. Hence the soul is 'deathless' (ἀθάνατον) or immortal (105e6). But, interestingly enough, Socrates is not satisfied with this conclusion. He says that even if it is true that the soul does not admit death, that does not necessarily mean that it is imperishable. *Only if* the opposite carried by a carrier is imperishable will the carrier itself be imperishable—for example, if the heat carried by fire were imperishable, then whenever anything cold approached fire it would never perish or be quenched but would go away unscathed (105e10–106a10). Thus a condition is given for showing that the soul is imperishable: if the life carried by a soul is imperishable, then the soul itself is imperishable.[10]

Now, according to Socrates' reasoning, since fires *do* perish, it follows that the heat carried by fire must be perishable—if it weren't, the fire could never be quenched. Socrates assumes that most of the opposites carried by such things as fire, snow, etc. are perishable—even the opposites 'odd' and 'even', as the following passage indicates:

If the deathless [the opposite of death] is also imperishable, it will be impossible for the soul to perish at the approach of death. For, as our argument has shown, it will not admit death and be in the state of having died, just as three, we said, will not be even, and the odd will not be even, and as fire and the heat in the fire will not be cold. 'But', someone might say, 'supposing, as we agreed before, that the odd cannot become even at the approach of the even—what's to prevent it from perishing and being replaced by the even?' Now we cannot reply by saying that it does not perish, *for the odd is not imperishable*. If that *were* conceded to us [that is, that the odd is imperishable], we could easily argue that when the even approaches, the odd and

---

[10] In response to Socrates' question whether the life (or the 'deathless'—τὸ ἀθάνατον) carried by the soul is imperishable, Cebes says that since the deathless is everlasting it can hardly be subject to perishing. Socrates adds that it would be agreed by all that the 'Form itself of life', and god, and anything else that is deathless could never undergo destruction (106c9–d7). Perhaps it occurred to some of those listening to Socrates (though not to Cebes) that the 'Form itself' of heat is also imperishable, and yet, as we shall see in a moment, the heat carried by a fire is clearly not regarded as imperishable by Socrates.

three go away; and we could argue in the same way in regard to fire and heat and the rest, could we not? (106b2–c7)[11]

There are, of course, Forms for each of the pairs of opposites mentioned by Socrates: Forms for hot and cold, odd and even, large and small, etc. But he is clearly not speaking about these Forms in the passage quoted, for he says that the opposites in question are perishable.[12] So the hot, cold, etc. that are in such things as fire and snow are not Forms; they are distinct entities, subject to coming-to-be and perishing. Let us call them 'immanent characters'.

If Forms and immanent characters are distinct types of entities, we should next consider whether it is only immanent characters that are in things, that is, whether Forms themselves, according to the *Phaedo*, are not in their participants. If this turns out to be the case, Plato's position in the *Phaedo*, as we noted earlier, will not be at odds with the explicit denial of immanence in the *Symposium*, *Parmenides*, and *Timaeus*.[13]

---

[11] In speaking of 'three' and 'odd', Socrates presumably has in mind a group of three objects; when one object is added to the group, it loses its property of being three in number and odd—the oddness 'carried by' the original trio perishes.

[12] Fine suggests that what Plato means at 106c3 is not that the uneven is perishable, but rather that it does not follow from the fact that something is uneven that it is imperishable ('Immanence', 77 n. 12). This is, at the very least, a strained way of taking Socrates' words ('for the uneven is not imperishable'). We should also note that a few lines earlier (106a3–6) Socrates says that if the coldness in the snow were imperishable, then whenever anyone brought heat to the snow, it would move away, intact and unmelted. Obviously, this is not what happens, and therefore the coldness in the snow cannot be imperishable (cf. 106a8–10). In the light of 106a3–10, it seems clear that Plato means just what he says at 106c3: the 'uneven' is a perishable entity.

[13] One might wonder if there is any evidence of immanent characters in these other dialogues in which the immanence of Forms is rejected. In the *Parmenides* we find a distinction between 'similarity itself' and the 'similarity which we have' (ἔχομεν), and the latter seems to be a reference to an immanent character (130b3–4; cf. 133c8–134a1). In Diotima's speech in the *Symposium*, just a few lines before her denial that the Form of beauty is 'in anything at all', she contrasts the beauty 'in bodies' with that 'in souls' (210b6–7; cf. c3). Now this might be taken as evidence of Plato's confusion about whether or not Forms are immanent; but given the distinction between Forms and immanent characters in the *Phaedo* and *Parmenides*, it seems more likely that Diotima's reference to the beauty 'in' bodies and souls is a reference to an immanent character. Finally, in the passage from the *Timaeus* discussed above, the second type of entity is described as a 'likeness' or 'image' of the Form itself (52c2; cf. 48e5–49a1, 29b1–2); these likenesses are said to be 'carried' by something else and to come to be 'in' something else (52a6, c3–d1). Now this second type of entity could be understood as either (1) particular entities such as Socrates, who is a likeness of the Form man, or (2) immanent characters such as the character of being a man which is possessed by Socrates (cf. R. Patterson, *Image and Reality in Plato's Metaphysics* (Indianapolis, 1985), 197 n. 4). In the latter case, the likeness of the Form would be *in* a particular portion of the 'receptacle' in the sense that it would be in a particular portion of corporeal 'stuff' which, together with the likeness of the Form man, constitutes Socrates (cf. 50a4–c6); in the former, the entity, Socrates, would be *in* a part of the receptacle in the sense that he would occupy a particular location in space. An investigation of the ontology of the *Timaeus* is obviously beyond the scope of this discussion; I believe, however, that there are good reasons for preferring (2) over (1). If (2) is the right way of understanding the second type of

II

Towards the end of the argument for immortality (104b9 ff.), Socrates introduces the term 'idea' (ἰδέα) into the discussion, and some have argued that the way he uses this term shows that he regards Forms as immanent in their participants. In the passage in question he explains that whenever a carrier of an opposite takes possession of, or comes to occupy, some other entity (e.g. fire taking possession of wood), it brings to that entity both its own Form or character (ἰδέα) and that of the opposite it carries; thus, when a piece of wood catches fire it becomes both fiery and hot. Socrates speaks of the thing 'occupied' by a carrier as *having* the ἰδέα of the opposite which is brought to it (104d1–3). He also speaks of the ἰδέα being *in* the carrier: heat (106b6) or its ἰδέα (104b9–10) is said to be in fire. So when fire takes possession of a piece of wood, the ἰδέα of heat will be in the wood.

Socrates' language clearly implies that these 'ideas' are immanent in sensible objects. Now it is often claimed that the terms ἰδέα and εἶδος are used interchangeably as designations of Platonic Forms—or at least that there is no clear distinction marked by Plato's use of the two terms.[14] If this is true, we would have to agree that Forms are understood to be in their participants in the passage we have been discussing (104b–e). But some commentators have argued that Plato uses the two terms differently in this part of the *Phaedo*: he uses ἰδέα when he is speaking of the perishable entities in sensible particulars, and εἶδος when he wants to refer to imperishable, non-immanent Forms.[15] It seems to me that the latter view is closer to the truth, and that Plato, in using the term ἰδέα to refer to the opposites in (and carried by) such things as snow and fire, is not implying that these things are imperishable Forms.[16] For, as we have seen, Socrates states very

entities in the *Timaeus*, then this dialogue is in agreement with the *Phaedo*, *Symposium*, and *Parmenides*, not only in rejecting the immanence of Forms, but also in distinguishing between Forms and immanent characters as two types of entities. (For a similar view of the μιμήματα of 50c, cf. F. M. Cornford, *Plato's Cosmology* (London, 1937), 183–4; also S. Strange, 'Plotinus' Account of Participation in *Ennead* VI. 4–5', *Journal of the History of Philosophy*, 30 (1992), 481.)

[14] See D. Gallop, *Plato:* Phaedo (Oxford, 1975), 93, 236 n. 72. Fine ('Immanence', 74–5) assumes that Socrates uses ἰδέα to refer to Forms, and draws the inference that Forms must be immanent; cf. Dancy, *Two Studies in the Early Academy*, 19–20, and Bostock, *Plato's* Phaedo, 179–89.

[15] See R. S. Bluck, *Plato's* Phaedo (London, 1955), 17 n. 17; R. Hackforth, *Plato's* Phaedo (Cambridge, 1955), 150 n. 1; and Cornford, *Plato's Cosmology*, 184.

[16] The suggestion made by Bluck and Hackforth needs a slight qualification: as Gallop notes (*Plato:* Phaedo, 236 n. 72), at 104c7 εἴδη pretty clearly refers to both Forms and immanent characters. So the suggestion should be that εἶδος is used for the most part for separate Forms but sometimes for both Forms and immanent characters, while ἰδέα is used exclusively for immanent characters.

clearly that these opposites are perishable;[17] either he contradicts himself in regard to the imperishability of Forms, or the 'ideas' he is speaking about are not identical with Forms. If it is conceded that there is a difference in the use of the two terms, and that ἰδέα but not εἶδος is used when speaking of the opposites in sensible particulars, then there will be no implication that Forms are immanent; the 'ideas' of opposites are immanent, but these 'ideas' are not Forms.[18]

A good case can therefore be made that in the *Phaedo* Plato not only distinguishes between Forms and immanent characters as two distinct types of entities, but considers only the immanent characters to be *in* sensible particulars. Since this account makes the *Phaedo* consistent with the *Symposium* and *Timaeus*, we have all the more reason for accepting it. According to the proposed interpretation, sensible objects somehow 'participate' in Forms without having Forms in them. What exactly is involved in this 'participation'? The *Phaedo* provides no answer: Socrates confesses that he is 'not yet' able to specify the relationship beyond the admittedly

---

[17] Perhaps not all the 'ideas' of opposites are perishable; if Socrates' argument at 106c9–d7 is sound, then the ἰδέα of life carried by the soul must be imperishable. See above, n. 10.

[18] It is usually thought that Socrates' mention of 'the *idea* of three' (ἡ τῶν τριῶν ἰδέα) at 104d5–6 is an unambiguous reference to a Form (see e.g. Fine, 'Immanence', 75 n. 6; Gallop, *Plato: Phaedo*, 206; Bostock, *Plato's Phaedo*, 185; Dancy, *Two Studies in the Early Academy*, 20). This seems to me doubtful, but even if it is correct it would not affect the main point I wish to make—that when Plato uses ἰδέα to refer to the immanent *opposites* he is not referring to Forms (since these opposites are perishable, they cannot be Forms). There is a long-standing debate over whether Plato commits himself in this passage to the existence of Forms of 'non-opposites', e.g. Forms of fire and snow. If one holds that 104d5–6 is a clear reference to a Form of three, then it seems to me that one must also hold that Plato commits himself to Forms of fire and snow as well. For 104d1–3 implies that what is true of three applies to *all* of the intermediates that take possession of other things: just as those things of which the ἰδέα of three takes possession must be odd, so also those things of which the ἰδέα of fire takes possession must be hot. Thus if Plato is referring to a Form at 104d5–6, he must believe that there are Forms for all of the things that 'carry' opposites.
I see no compelling reason, however, to understand the ἰδέα of three as the Form of three; it could just as easily be understood as the *character* or *aspect* possessed by any group of three objects in so far as it is three in number—a character which does not exist separately from the groups possessing it. This seems to be the way ἰδέα is typically used in the *Timaeus*. For example, at 50d4–e1 Timaeus points out that the receptacle must be devoid of all those ἰδέαι which it receives; these obviously cannot be Forms since Forms are not 'received' by the receptacle (they do not enter into the receptacle). The entities received by the receptacle are images or likenesses of Forms; they are perceptible and perishable. Thus ἰδέα here refers to the perceptible character that a thing has in virtue of its participation in a Form. (For similar uses of ἰδέα, see 28a8, 35a7, 40a2, 46c8, 49c3, 71b1; cf. *Prm.* 132a3 and M. Schofield, 'Eudoxus in the *Parmenides*', *Museum Helveticum*, 30 (1973), 2 n. 9. In the *Parmenides*, but apparently not in the *Timaeus*, ἰδέα is sometimes used as a variant for εἶδος; cf. 133c8, 134c1, 135a2.) If Plato speaks of an ἰδέα of fire in the *Phaedo*, and this is understood as a character or aspect, does it follow that there must be a Form (εἶδος) of fire? (This is clearly implied by using '*Form*-copy' as a translation of ἰδέα.) It seems to me that the text does not provide us with a definite answer one way or the other. Plato may well have been ambivalent about the existence of Forms of non-opposites at the time of writing the *Phaedo*—cf. *Prm.* 130c1–4.

vague expressions 'participation in', 'being present to', or 'communion with' (100d3–8).[19]

There are other features besides non-immanence that distinguish Forms from immanent characters. (1) As we have noted, immanent characters are perishable while Forms are not.[20] (2) Immanent characters also seem subject to certain kinds of change, e.g. change of location; Forms, on the other hand, are completely free of change. (3) Further, Socrates' use of the expression 'the largeness in Simmias' suggests that there are distinct immanent characters in different objects; corresponding to the single Form largeness, there will be many immanent characters of largeness—as many as there are participants in the Form of largeness. (4) It also seems that many immanent characters can be perceived by the senses; we can see the largeness in Simmias, and feel the heat in the fire. The Forms of largeness and heat, however, can only be apprehended by reasoning. (5) Another important difference is that immanent characters depend for their existence on the particular objects that possess them, whereas the existence of Forms is independent of the objects that participate in them.[21] The ontological dependence of immanent characters comes out in the following passage: 'And in the same way, I imagine, if the "uncold" [i.e. the hot] were

---

[19] A number of commentators have noted that the expressions 'participation in', 'being present to', and 'communion with' are strongly suggestive of immanence, and that at the very least they imply that Plato took seriously the possibility that Forms are immanent in their participants; see Fine, 'Immanence', 74 (cf. p. 79 n. 16), and 'Separation', 61; Dancy, *Two Studies in the Early Academy*, 15; Ross, *Plato's Theory of Ideas*, 228; Mabbott, 'Aristotle and the χωρισμός of Plato', 74. Further, as we noted above (n. 7), Dancy claims that Socrates' confession of puzzlement about participation is naturally understood as extending to the question whether Forms are immanent. Aristotle, however, seems to have had a different understanding of Plato's attitude towards immanence and participation. Although he complains that to describe Forms as 'paradigms' and to say that other things 'participate in' them is simply a cover for confusion (*Metaph. M* 5, 1079[b]24–6; *A* 9, 991[a]20–2, 992[a]26–9; cf. *A* 6, 987[b]11–14), he does not suggest that Plato was unsure about whether Forms are in their participants; on the contrary, his assertions that Forms were not regarded as immanent by the Platonists are never hedged or qualified. Aristotle apparently believed, on the one hand, that the separation of Forms involved the rejection of immanence and, on the other, that Plato was unable to offer any clear account of what it is for things to 'participate' in separate Forms; that is, he did not take the lack of clarity about participation to extend to the question whether Forms are immanent. (See H. Cherniss, *Aristotle's Criticism of Plato and the Academy* (New York, 1962), 206 n. 123.) Aristotle's understanding seems to fit well with our findings: beginning in the *Phaedo*, Plato separates Forms from sensible particulars and takes this separation to entail the denial of immanence.

[20] It is interesting to note that Aristotle occasionally speaks of 'perishable forms'; cf. *Metaph. K* 2, 1060[a]19–24; *A*3, 1070[a]13–26; *Ph*. 1. 9, 192[a]34–[b]2. As we shall see, these entities are lineal descendants of Plato's immanent characters.

[21] This claim can be understood in two ways: (1) Forms exist independently of any particular participant or group of participants (but not independently of all participants); or (2) Forms can exist even if there are no participants (see Fine, 'Separation', 80–1). For now, we may understand the claim in the first, weaker way; I shall eventually argue, however, that Plato is committed to the stronger claim that Forms can exist even if there are no participants.

imperishable, whenever anything cold approached fire, it would never perish or be quenched, but would go away unscathed' (106a8–10). Since fires can be quenched, their heat is not imperishable; the heat in a particular fire will perish when the fire is put out—the heat cannot go on existing after the fire has been put out. Thus immanent characters like the heat in the fire and the largeness in Simmias depend on their possessors for their existence. The Form largeness, on the other hand, is in no way affected by what happens to Simmias.

III

A further indication that Plato does not regard Forms as immanent can be gleaned from his description of them as 'being themselves by themselves' (αὐτὰ καθ᾽ αὑτά).[22] In the passage quoted earlier from the *Symposium*, immediately after asserting that the Form beauty is not in some other thing, Diotima says 'rather, it is itself by itself and with itself'; the negative and positive claims seem to be two sides of the same coin. It is also clear from the following passage in the *Parmenides* that being 'itself by itself' is taken to rule out immanence:

'Socrates, I think that you or anyone else who supposes that there is an essence, "itself by itself", for each thing would agree in the first place that none of them exists in us.'
　'No, for if it did, it would no longer be "itself by itself",' said Socrates. (133c3–6)[23]

These passages clearly imply that to assert that a Form is 'itself by itself' is to deny that it is in something else.

In the *Phaedo*, also, Forms are described as being themselves by themselves (e.g. at 78d5–6, 100b5–7), but the description is not accompanied by an explicit denial of immanence. However, there are clear signs in the dialogue that Plato understands the description to imply the denial of immanence. Early in the discussion, Socrates explains that death is the separation of the soul from the body, and says that the soul can

---

[22] As Gregory Vlastos has pointed out, this expression is not found in any of the early dialogues, and seems to be applied to Forms for the first time in the *Phaedo* (see *Socrates, Ironist and Moral Philosopher* (Cambridge, 1991), 73 n. 126). We might also note that the expression is never applied to such things as 'the largeness in Simmias'.
[23] Cf. 159c6–7, where Parmenides says that 'the one' cannot be *in* other things if it is separate from them. Fine contends that 133c3–6 is an 'aporetic passage', and should not be taken to express Plato's considered view ('Immanence', 79 n. 16). However, given the way the two claims are linked in the *Symposium* (the Form beauty is 'itself by itself' and is 'not *in* anything'), and the fact that immanence is explicitly denied in the *Timaeus*, there seems little reason to doubt that 133c3–6 (and 159c6–7) expresses a view that Plato accepts.

202 DANIEL T. DEVEREUX

only achieve the state of being completely 'itself by itself' after its separation from the body.[24] The soul comes to be itself by itself when it is no longer joined to the body—when it is no longer a part of the living animal; and when the soul does exist apart from the body, it is no longer affected by what happens in or to the body. It is surely safe to suppose that Plato had something similar in mind when he applied the same description to Forms—especially given that the parallel claims are made in the same context.[25] The similar claim in the case of Forms would be that they are separate from their participants, neither existing in them nor forming part of a whole with them. A Form's separate existence from its participants is the same as its being itself by itself. And, as in the case of the soul, a Form's separate existence guarantees that it is not affected by what happens to its participants. As Diotima says, 'it is itself by itself and with itself, while all the other beautiful things partake of it in such a way that, though all of them are coming to be and perishing, it neither increases nor diminishes, and is in no way affected' (211b1–5). Forms differ from souls in that they always exist separately from their participants, whereas the soul's separate existence from the body is only intermittent.

Now it is true, as Fine points out, that the separate existence of Forms is not explicitly mentioned in the *Phaedo*. However, it is mentioned in the *Parmenides*, in an important passage in which Plato sets out the essential elements of the theory of Forms found in the middle dialogues:

---

[24] 64c4–8, 66e4–67a2. Socrates argues (at 64b ff.) that philosophers prepare themselves for death by withdrawing and separating their soul as much as possible from the body. But he indicates at several points that the philosopher in this life can only achieve at best a *partial* separation of the soul (see 64e8–65a2, 65c5–9, e6–8, 67c5–d2).

[25] According to Fine, Plato has two things in mind when he says that a Form exists 'itself by itself': (1) that each Form excludes its opposite, and (2) that a Form's nature involves nothing sensible ('Separation', 60–1). The first claim is, in effect, that the Form *F*ness is *F* 'by itself' (καθ' αὐτό)—that is, it implies a contrast between the way the Form is *F* and the way its participants are *F*; the Form equality is equal and in no way unequal, whereas sensible equals are both equal and unequal. However, in the passages in the *Phaedo, Symposium*, and *Parmenides* in which Socrates speaks of Forms being themselves by themselves, he seems to be thinking of their mode of existence, not of the way in which they possess certain properties. In regard to (2), it is clear that Plato would agree that a Form's nature involves nothing sensible since he believes that an adequate grasp of such entities is achieved by reason alone, without reliance on the senses. In some contexts he seems to use the expression 'itself by itself' to convey the purely intelligible character of a Form—for example, when he speaks of employing pure thought, itself by itself, in order to search out 'each pure reality, itself by itself' (66a1–3). But in most contexts the expression is used to describe the mode of existence of a Form, not its non-empirical character. (See e.g. 78d5–6, 100b5–7; *Prm.* 128e5–129a2, 130b7–9, 133a8–9, c3–6; *Smp.* 211a8–b2; *Ti.* 51b7–c1; cf. Vlastos, *Socrates, Ironist and Moral Philosopher*, 72–6, 261–2. Cf. also Arist., *MM* 1182ᵇ12–16: 'For the Form is separate (χωριστόν) and itself by itself (αὐτὸ καθ' αὑτό), whereas the common [character] belongs *in* all; hence the latter is not the same as the separate [Form]—for that which is separate and is by nature itself by itself could not possibly be *in* all.')

'Tell me, [Socrates,] did you come up with this distinction yourself, whereby Forms themselves are set apart from the things participating in them? And do you think there is a likeness itself existing separately from the likeness which we possess, and one and many and all the others we heard Zeno speaking about just now?'

'Yes, I do,' said Socrates.

'And also,' said Parmenides, 'a Form "itself by itself" of the just, the beautiful, the good, and all others of this sort?'

'Yes,' he replied. (130b1–9)[26]

Parmenides first asks Socrates whether he holds that there is a likeness itself 'existing separately' from the likeness in us, using the same expression (εἶναι χωρίς) that was used in the *Phaedo* in speaking of the separate existence of the soul. He then asks Socrates whether he also believes there is a Form 'itself by itself' of the just and the beautiful. Apparently Parmenides takes the question whether there is a Form existing separately to be equivalent to whether there is a Form itself by itself.[27] Further, both a Form's being itself by itself and its existing separately from its participants are understood to be incompatible with its being in its participants (cf. 133c3–6, 159c6–7).

It is natural to understand the statement that Forms exist separately from their participants as tantamount to the claim that their existence is independent of that of their participants.[28] Thus, to say that a Form 'exists separately' from its participants is to say that it has the capacity to exist even if its participants ceased to exist. But if this were true, we would have to say that the soul 'exists separately' from the body even while it is joined to it; for the soul *always* has the capacity to exist without the body to which it is joined. As the example of the soul and body indicates, separate existence for Plato is not exactly the same thing as ontological independence.

In view of this difference, one might question whether Plato actually intended to claim that Forms are ontologically independent of their participants. As Fine has pointed out, there is nothing like an explicit affirmation of this kind of independence in the middle dialogues. However, we have seen that a consequence of a Form's being itself by itself is that it is 'completely unaffected' by what happens to its participants (*Smp.* 211b1–5, quoted above, p. 202); it is natural to understand this to mean that the Form will not be affected even if all of its participants pass out of existence. Furthermore, if we consider once again Plato's treatment of the soul

[26] Cf. the use of χωρίς in 130c1, d1.

[27] See Vlastos, *Socrates, Ironist and Moral Philosopher*, 258–9.

[28] See e.g. Fine, 'Separation', 34–45, and Vlastos, *Socrates, Ironist and Moral Philosopher*, 264–5.

and body in the *Phaedo*, we can see good reasons for supposing that he intends to commit himself to the strong claim of ontological independence in this dialogue as well. Let us recall that the soul comes to be itself by itself when it is separated from the body in death. Now in order for the soul to achieve this state, it is not enough that it continue to exist after the body to which it is joined ceases to exist. For it might be a necessary condition of its continuing to exist that it be joined to some body or other; and if so, it will never be possible for a soul to exist itself by itself. Thus, to exist itself by itself the soul must be able to exist *on its own*, independently of any body. There is no reason to think that Plato believes that souls which exist on their own, not joined to a body, are still somehow dependent on bodies for their existence.[29]

Hence, even though the soul's being itself by itself is not the same as its being ontologically independent, the first attribute clearly implies the second. And if the claim that Forms exist 'themselves by themselves' is seen by Plato as parallel to the claim about souls, he must have thought that Forms do not depend for their existence on having participants.

IV

Our results so far point to a welcome consistency and harmony in Plato's various accounts of the relationship between Forms and their participants. In the *Phaedo* he is not ambivalent on the question whether Forms are immanent, and his view is not at odds with the explicit rejection of immanence in the *Timaeus*, *Parmenides*, and *Symposium*. Moreover, our results seem to agree with Aristotle's reports. In a number of places he says that the Platonists hold that Forms are not *in* their participants, and that they exist separately from them.[30] He also seems to link the separateness of Forms to their not being in their participants, in the same way that Plato

[29] Plato may not have considered the question whether souls could exist even if all bodies were destroyed. None the less, given his beliefs about the soul, it seems to me he would have had no reason to hold back from such a view. According to the 'likely story' of the *Timaeus*, although matter or the 'receptacle' has always existed, souls are created before bodies (cf. 34b–35a; also *Laws* 892a–b). Thus he seems to believe that it is possible for souls to exist even if there are no bodies. Fine concedes that there is clear evidence that Plato thought some Forms were ontologically independent of their participants ('Separation', 74–81). But why would he hold that some Forms have this attribute while others do not? And if he did believe this, why would he offer no explanation of the difference?

[30] See the passages cited in n. 3 above. (There is an unfortunate error in the Revised Oxford Translation of the *Metaphysics*: at Z 16, 1040^{b}29, Aristotle seems to refer to the Form as a 'one *in* many', but in the Greek the preposition is ἐπί, not ἐν; the translation should read 'one *over* many'.)

does in the *Symposium* and *Parmenides*.[31] Fine contends, however, that when Aristotle speaks of Forms being 'separate' he means that they are ontologically independent; and she argues that this claim is unrelated to the rejection of immanence. If so, Aristotle's understanding of separation will turn out to be somewhat different from the conception we have found in the above group of dialogues, and his reports will therefore involve some distortion of Plato's views. But it can be shown, I think, that Aristotle's understanding of the separateness of Forms is the same as Plato's, and that his reports are fair and accurate.

The question of what Aristotle means by 'separate' is complicated by the fact that he applies the term to his own favoured 'substances' as well as to Platonic Forms, and it is not clear that he has the same attribute in mind in each case. Fine argues that what Aristotle means by the claim that 'substance alone is separate' is: (1) that substances are separate from non-substances (e.g. qualities, quantities, relations, etc.), but not vice versa, and (2) hence substances can exist without non-substances, but not vice versa;[32] in other words, substances are ontologically independent of non-substances, but not vice versa. She holds that the separateness of substance is closely connected to its 'natural priority' *vis-à-vis* the other categories. If *A* is naturally prior to *B*, then *A* can exist without *B*, but *B* cannot exist without *A*. Saying that substances are separate would thus be one half of the claim that they are naturally prior to non-substances.

However, there are serious difficulties (as Fine recognizes) in the view that substances are naturally prior to non-substances. In his discussion of the different types of priority in *Metaphysics Δ* 11 Aristotle mentions that natural priority was 'used' by Plato—presumably in claiming that Forms are naturally prior to their participants (1019ᵃ1–4). When later in the *Metaphysics* he specifies the ways in which substance is prior to the other categories (*Z* 1, 1028ᵃ31–ᵇ2), he does not mention natural priority.[33] And, indeed, it is difficult to make any sense at all of the claim that substances

---

[31] See e.g. *Metaph. M* 6, 1080ᵃ37–ᵇ2; *B* 2, 998ᵇ7–9; cf. *M* 5, 1079ᵇ15–17 with 1079ᵇ36–1080ᵃ2.

[32] 'Separation', 36 n. 19; cf. 'Separation: A Reply to Morrison', *Oxford Studies in Ancient Philosophy*, 3 (1985), 159–65.

[33] According to Fine ('Separation', 35), he does; she suggests that φύσει should be substituted for χρόνῳ in 1028ᵃ33; the translation would then read 'prior in nature' rather than 'prior in time'. But φύσει is not found in any of the manuscripts, and, as we shall see in a moment, 'natural priority' does not seem to fit Aristotle's understanding of the relationship between substances and their attributes. (As far as I can tell, there are no other passages in which it is said that substances are naturally prior to non-substances.) Furthermore, it becomes clear later in *Metaphysics Z* that Aristotle does believe that there is a way in which substance is temporally prior to non-substance (see *Z* 13, 1038ᵇ26–9; *Z* 9, 1034ᵃ30–ᵇ1, 1034ᵇ16–19; cf. Morrison, 'Separation in Aristotle's Metaphysics', 136; M. Frede and G. Patzig, *Aristoteles* Metaphysik *Z* (Munich, 1988), ii. 20).

206 DANIEL T. DEVEREUX

are naturally prior to non-substances. The claim that qualities, quantities, relations, etc. cannot exist without substances is at least understandable, but what could be meant by the claim that substances can exist without any of these attributes? How could a substance exist without any qualities, without quantitative dimensions, without being related to anything? Aristotle never addresses this question.[34] Fine suggests that what he might have in mind is that a particular substance, e.g. Socrates, can exist independently of 'any given non-substance attribute' he has, and independently of *some* general non-substance attributes (he would have to have some colour or other). But this does not seem enough to justify the blanket claim that 'substances can exist without non-substances'; also, one might argue along parallel lines that a particular attribute, e.g. whiteness, can exist independently of any given substance in which it inheres, and independently of some general kinds of substances. It is significant that Aristotle links the notion of natural priority to Plato: it is just the kind of priority that Forms have in relation to their participants, but it does not seem to fit Aristotle's conception of the relationship between substances and non-substances.[35]

It is almost always taken for granted that the claim that substance is separate must be understood as the claim that it is separate *from* something.[36] Although this assumption is perfectly natural and understandable, I believe it is a mistake—a mistake that leads to much needless confusion about Aristotle's conception of substance. As has been pointed out, he

[34] He does of course consider whether matter could exist on its own without qualities, dimensions, etc., and argues that it cannot; see *Ph.* 4. 2, 209ᵇ22–3; 4. 4, 211ᵇ36–212ᵃ2; 4. 7, 214ᵃ14–16; cf. *Metaph. Z* 3, 1029ᵃ10–30.

[35] Fine also contends that, for Aristotle, any particular substance is separate from all other substances, that is, any substance could exist even if all others ceased to exist ('Separation: A Reply to Morrison', 162). In reply to the objection that Aristotle held that living things depend on the continued existence of the sun, she suggests that, if the sun were destroyed, living things could at least survive for a brief moment. There is no evidence, however, that Aristotle ever entertained the idea that substances are separate in this way. Morrison also suggests that what is meant by the claim that substances are separate is that any given substance is separate from other substances; but he does not understand separateness as ontological independence. Two things are separate if they are numerically distinct, and this comes down to their being 'outside each other's ontological boundaries' (p. 128). However, he also suggests that to be separate in the way that a substance is 'is not to be said of anything else as of a substratum' (p. 128); but to be separate in this way is not to be separate *from* anything. Morrison's second suggestion, it seems to me, is essentially right (cf. also M. L. Gill, *Aristotle on Substance* (Princeton, 1989), 36–7); what is needed is to spell out this idea, and explain why Aristotle uses the term 'separate' to characterize this feature of substance.

[36] Gill, *Aristotle on Substance*, and Ross are possible exceptions. Ross suggests that what Aristotle means by the claim is not that substance can exist without the other categories, but that 'it can exist apart' while they cannot (*Aristotle's* Metaphysics (Oxford, 1974), vol. i, p. xci). What he seems to have in mind is that non-substances depend for their existence on some underlying substratum, while substances do not.

never specifies *what* it is that substance is separate from, nor does he even say that it is separate *from something*. He does tell us, on the other hand, what it is for non-substances *not* to be separate: none of them exists on its own; all qualities, quantities, etc. depend for their existence on an underlying subject of which they are predicated.[37] If they *were* 'separate', nonsubstances would exist on their own, and would not depend on some underlying subject. This is precisely what I think Aristotle means when he says that substances are separate—they exist on their own, i.e. they do not depend on some underlying subject for their existence.[38] He is not saying that substances could exist even if something else did not exist; he is simply asserting that, in contrast with attributes that are not separate, substances do not depend for their existence on an underlying subject.[39]

If my suggestion is right—if substance is separate without being separate from something—one might reasonably complain that Aristotle's use of the term 'separate' is misleading. To say that something is separate naturally suggests that it is separate from something else. If the attribute

---

[37] See e.g. *Ph.* 1. 2, 185ᵃ31–2: 'For none of the others apart from substance is separate; for all of them are said of substance as of a substratum'; cf. 1. 7, 190ᵃ33–ᵇ1; *Metaph. Λ* 5, 1070ᵇ36–1071ᵃ2.

[38] Being dependent on some underlying subject for existence is apparently not the only way a thing can fail to 'exist on its own'; in *Ph.* 4. 2, 209ᵇ22–4 (cf. 4. 4, 211ᵇ36–212ᵃ2), Aristotle says that matter cannot exist separately 'from the thing' whose matter it is, but this is apparently not because it depends on some underlying subject. The claim that 'substance alone is separate' (*Metaph. Z* 1, 1028ᵃ33–4; cf. *Λ* 1, 1069ᵃ24) is intended to contrast substance with other categories, not with matter.

In the *Categories* we find the claim that if primary substances did not exist, it would be impossible for any of the other things (i.e. non-substances and secondary substances) to exist (2ᵇ3–6). It is natural to understand Aristotle to be implying that primary substances *can* exist independently of 'the other things'; one is then of course puzzled as to how Aristotle could hold such a view (see J. L. Ackrill, *Aristotle's* Categories *and* de Interpretatione (Oxford, 1963), 83). But it is also possible to understand the claim along the lines I have suggested: the other things depend for their existence on primary substances as their underlying subjects, whereas primary substances are not dependent on other underlying subjects for their existence. (Cf. Gill, *Aristotle on Substance*, 37.)

[39] If this is true, 'being separate' is not in general a modal notion for Aristotle—it is rather a description of the actual mode of existence of substance (cf. Fine, 'Separation', 43–4). I take Aristotle's claim that 'substance alone is separate' to be about one kind of substance, viz. particular composites of matter and form. In the *Metaphysics* he allows for other kinds of substance, or other ways of being substance—e.g. being the *substance of* an independent reality. Being substance in this way does not necessarily involve having independent existence; an animal's form can be its substance even if it depends for its existence on the subjects of which it is predicated. When Aristotle refers to the form as separate, he usually specifies 'separate *in λόγος*' in order to make it clear that he is not speaking of separate existence. However, in a few passages he raises the question whether the form of a composite is 'separate' (χωριστός), and the context makes it clear that he is asking whether the form can continue to exist after the composite substance has perished; see *K* 2, 1060ᵇ23–8; *H* 3, 1043ᵇ18–21; cf. *Λ* 3, 1070ᵃ13–26; *H* 1, 1042ᵃ29–31; *B* 4, 999ᵇ16–20. Thus, in a few isolated passages, 'being separate' seems to mean *having the capacity* to exist separately or on its own (while it is a part of the composite, the form obviously does not exist separately from it). In rare cases, then, Aristotle seems to use 'separate' to express a modal notion.

Aristotle is referring to is 'not being dependent for existence on some underlying subject', a more appropriate term would seem to be 'independence' or 'self-subsistence'.[40] However, his use of the term is understandable if it is seen against the background of the theory of Forms and the way in which Plato conceives of Forms as separate from their participants. From Aristotle's perspective, the Platonic separation of Forms involves the unacceptable thesis that Forms can exist on their own, apart from the things of which they are predicated. He argues that a universal—something by its nature predicable of a plurality of subjects[41]—is not separate from its subjects; it inheres in, and cannot exist apart from, its subjects. If this is how '*not* being separate' (or 'inseparable') is understood, it is natural to think of 'being separate' as the property of not inhering in a subject and not being dependent for existence on an underlying subject. If we bear in mind the context in which Aristotle's use of the term 'separate' evolved, we can easily understand how he might have arrived at the point of saying that substances are separate without meaning that they are separate from something else. This seems to be the most plausible way of construing his use of the term; after all, he never says that substance is separate from anything else, and it is well nigh impossible to make any sense of such a claim.

Now in speaking of the alleged separateness of Forms, Aristotle of course understands this as separateness *from* something, viz. from their participants. In this respect, there is a difference in what is meant by 'separate' when applied to Forms and to Aristotelian substances.[42] But in other respects the meaning is similar. For instance, if a substance inhered in an underlying subject, it would not be separate—that is, being separate and inhering in a subject are mutually exclusive. Similarly, a Form's being separate excludes its being in its participants, and vice versa; consider, for example, the following passage in *Metaphysics M* 5: 'But they [the Forms] make no contribution to our knowledge of other things, for they are not

[40] Cf. Morrison, 'Separation in Aristotle's Metaphysics', 132.

[41] See *Int.* 17ᵃ38–ᵇ1; *Metaph. Z* 13, 1038ᵇ11–12. The purpose of the qualification 'by its nature' is presumably to allow for the possibility that a universal may actually be predicated of only one subject. The purpose may also be to leave open the possibility of uninstantiated universals; that is, for dialectical reasons Aristotle may have wanted a definition that applies to Platonic Forms as well as to universals whose existence depends on the subjects of which they are predicated. (For a different view, see Fine, 'Separation', 39, 45.)

[42] It is true, on the other hand, that according to the Platonic theory Forms are not only separate from their participants, but they are also separate in the same way that Aristotelian substances are: they 'do not inhere in an underlying subject' (cf. *Metaph. Z* 6, 1031ᵇ15–18). Sometimes when Aristotle says that Forms are regarded as separate, he seems to have in mind the same sort of claim that he makes about his own substances, and not the claim that Forms are separate from their participants; see e.g. *Metaph. Z* 16, 1040ᵇ27–30.

the essence (οὐσία) of them—if they were, they would have been *in* them' (1079ᵇ15–17). A few lines further down he says: 'Again, it might be thought impossible for a thing's essence to exist separately (χωρὶς εἶναι) from the thing; how, then, could Forms, being the essences of things, exist separately from them?' (1079ᵇ35–1080ᵃ2). In each passage Aristotle points out a difficulty for the Platonist's claim that Forms are the essences of sensible things. In the first he says they cannot be essences since they are not *in* these things, while in the second he says they cannot be essences because they exist separately from them. These appear to be two alternative ways of expressing the same thought.

It seems, then, that Aristotle's understanding of what it is for Forms to be separate accords with the view we found in the middle dialogues: it is clear that he thinks that the separateness of Forms excludes their being in their participants. He takes separation to involve the claim that Forms are ontologically independent, but this is not a misrepresentation of his opponents' theory, for, as we have seen, Plato also understands separation to involve ontological independence. As one might have expected, Aristotle has a clear grasp of Plato's claims about Forms and their participants; moreover, his reports, though unfortunately very brief, seem not only accurate but fair and balanced. At least with regard to separation and immanence, there is no basis for the claim that he tends to fix on certain passages and ignore others, or that he portrays Plato's views as more clear-cut and definitive than they actually were.

V

At a certain point, perhaps during the course of writing the *Phaedo*, Plato made the momentous decision to speak no longer as if justice, beauty, etc. were entities existing in particular actions or persons. This was of course the way Socrates spoke about the objects of his searches in the early dialogues: for example, the Form of 'the pious' was said to be 'in' pious actions.[43] Plato came to believe that a Form (e.g. 'justice itself') was not the sort of thing that could be in particular actions or persons. He therefore made a distinction between the Form itself and particular instances of the

---

[43] See *Euthphr.* 5d1–5; also *Men.* 72c3–4, d7–e1, e6–7. I would agree with Dancy (*Two Studies in the Early Academy*, 10–14) that these and similar passages in the early dialogues do not portray Socrates as holding a particular metaphysical view about the status of the objects he is seeking to define; it is rather that his way of speaking accords with the view that Forms are immanent. (See also Fine, 'Separation', 81–5.)

Form; it is the latter entities, the 'immanent characters', that are in sensible objects. A Form (εἶδος) is not *in* anything—it is 'itself by itself', existing apart from the things that partake of it.

What led Plato to separate Forms from particulars? This question has been a source of puzzlement and debate since the time of Aristotle. In view of the different roles that Forms play in Plato's thought, it seems highly unlikely that there was a single key consideration leading to the separation. Yet those who discuss the theory of Forms often speak as if there was one factor that made all the difference. Aristotle certainly gives this impression when he suggests, in a well-known passage, that it was Plato's concern to preserve the possibility of knowledge that led to the separation of Forms from the ever-changing sensible world.[44] While it seems reasonable to suppose that this was one important consideration, it cannot have been the whole story. For the contrast between the immutability of Forms and the 'flux' of the sensible world does not figure in some of the main passages in which Forms are distinguished from particulars.[45] Furthermore, Aristotle's suggestion does not explain the specific type of separation that we find in the *Phaedo*—it does not explain why Forms are distinguished from immanent characters.

One important reason for the separation of Forms—a reason that has been neglected in scholarly discussions—is a concern to preserve the unity of a Form.[46] I shall try to show that it is this concern that led Plato to make the distinction between Forms and immanent characters in the *Phaedo*. I shall also suggest that Plato himself points to this reason for separating Forms in the first set of arguments in the *Parmenides*.

Socrates sets the stage for Parmenides' arguments by proposing that Forms are a distinct type of entity from the sensible objects that partake of them. It is clear from his initial proposal that Socrates takes Forms to exist separately from their participants. He speaks, for example, of the Form similarity being 'itself by itself'; and, as we have seen, he assumes that being itself by itself rules out being in its participants.[47] He also speaks of 'similarity itself' existing separately from the 'similarity that we have' (i.e. the 'similarity in us'; 130b3–4). In other words, Socrates rejects immanence, and draws the same distinction between Forms and immanent characters that we find in the *Phaedo*.

[44] See *Metaph. A* 6, 987ª32–ᵇ7; *M* 4, 1078ᵇ9–1079ª4; *M* 9, 1086ª31–ᵇ11.

[45] See e.g. *Phd.* 74a–c; *Rep.* 478e–479b; cf. G. E. L. Owen, 'A Proof in the Περὶ Ἰδεῶν', *Journal of Hellenic Studies*, 77 (1957), 301–11; also A. Nehamas, 'Plato on the Imperfection of the Sensible World', *American Philosophical Quarterly*, 12 (1975), 105–17. Ch. VI above.

[46] See, however, Strange, 'Plotinus' Account of Participation', 486–7.

[47] Cf. 128e6–129a1 with 133c3–6; see above, p. 201.

Given Socrates' clear affirmation of the separateness of Forms, it is quite puzzling that Parmenides' opening round of arguments against Forms treats them as immanent in their participants. He opens his attack as follows:

'Isn't it true that each of the participants in a Form must either partake of the whole of it or of a part? Or is there some other kind of participation apart from these?'
    'How could there be?' said Socrates.
    'Do you think that the whole Form (ὅλον τὸ εἶδος), being one, is *in* each of the many participants?'
    'Yes, for what prevents it from being so, Parmenides?' he said.
    'But, being one and the same, the whole of it will be in many separate things at the same time, and thus it would be separate from itself.' (131a4–b2)

In the next part of the argument the analogy of a sail over many people is introduced as a model for understanding how many participants might each partake of the whole of a Form.[48] The sail is first described as being 'over' (ἐπί) many things, but when the analogy is applied to Forms Parmenides says that the result would be that a part of a Form is *in* each participant (131b7–c7). In other words, in this opening round of arguments Parmenides is determined to understand the two alternatives as (1) the whole Form is in each participant, or (2) a part of the Form is in each participant. He does not (yet) want to consider the possibility that 'partaking' might not involve a Form's being (either as part or whole) *in* a thing at all. In the next set of arguments the preposition 'in' is replaced by 'over' (ἐπί), and Forms are not viewed as immanent in any of the subsequent arguments.[49]

As we noticed earlier, Socrates agrees with Parmenides that a Form, in so far as it is 'itself by itself', cannot be *in* its participants (133c3–6). Evidently, the separateness of Forms is tacitly ignored in the first arguments. It is as if Parmenides is thinking to himself: 'What if one takes Forms to be one in the strict sense intended by Socrates, but does not take them to be separate?' This is the view he is attacking. Given that the early dialogues often treat Forms (or the objects of definition) as being one and the same thing in many different objects, Parmenides' arguments may provide some

[48] Parmenides substitutes the analogy of the sail for Socrates' suggestion that a Form might be like the 'day', which as a whole is in many places at the same time; in the same way, a Form might be *in* many participants at the same time (131b3–6).

[49] At 132b3–5 Socrates suggests that Forms might be thoughts which exist *in* souls. Parmenides then points out that the thought will be *of* some single thing, a thing which is 'over all' (ἐπὶ πᾶσιν), i.e. a single ἰδέα (132b7–c4). In other words, he interprets the suggestion that Forms are in souls in such a way that the Form becomes a 'one over many'—just the reverse of what is done in the case of the sail analogy. At 133d ff. Parmenides uses 'in' and 'have' in speaking of the relationship between 'likenesses' (ὁμοιώματα) of Forms and the things that possess them, but not in speaking of Forms themselves.

indication of why Plato (beginning in the *Phaedo*?) rejected this way of conceiving of the relationship between Forms and their participants.

Parmenides argues that Forms cannot be in their participants, either as a whole or in part, and still have the strict unity that Socrates attributes to them. If a Form is in each participant as a whole, then it will be 'separate from itself', and this is incompatible with its being 'one and the same thing'.[50] The argument seems to rest on the principle that one and the same thing cannot exist as a whole in two distinct locations at the same time. If, on the other hand, a part of the Form is in each participant, this will mean that the Form is divisible, which Socrates admits is inconsistent with his original claim that each Form is one in a strict sense.[51] Socrates agrees that if something partakes of a Form, it must partake either of a part of the Form or of the whole Form. Hence a Form cannot be 'one and the same thing' and be in its participants—it cannot be a 'one *in* many'. (The subsequent arguments will test the hypothesis that each Form is a 'one *over* many'.) It is important to note that Parmenides' argument does not entail that if something is one in the strict sense it cannot be *in anything*; the impossible consequences follow from the hypothesis that a Form is in more than one thing at the same time; an entity could be one and the same and be in one thing, but not in more than one.

The distinction between Forms and immanent characters provides an obvious way of saving the strict unity of Forms from Parmenides' objections. According to the distinction as we find it in the *Phaedo*, neither Forms nor immanent characters are a 'one in many'; Forms are not in anything, and immanent characters are in only one thing. Once the distinction is made, the Form becomes in effect a 'one over many' (ἕν ἐπὶ πολλοῖς). It is not that Plato sees this distinction as the key to understanding the nature of participation; the problematic character of the relationship between separate Forms and their participants is admitted by Socrates, and scrutinized in detail in Parmenides' arguments against the Form as a 'one over many' (132a–135a). But the distinction does meet the challenge posed by Parmenides' first arguments; in fact, the distinction seems to fit the arguments like a glove—it is as if Plato had these very difficulties in mind when

---

[50] Cf. *Phlb*. 15b3–8; Fine, 'Immanence', 81.

[51] Socrates' requirement that a Form is one in a strict sense need not be viewed as excluding every kind of divisibility. What is objectionable, according to Parmenides' argument, is that a Form might consist of parts that are spatially separate from each other; note the use of πολλαχοῦ in 131b4 and 7. (Cf. Arist., *Metaph*. Z 16, 1040ᵇ25: 'That which is one [in number] cannot be in many places (πολλαχῇ) at the same time'; also *Ti*. 37a4–b3; *Phd*. 78c1–8.) The unity of a Form, as Socrates conceives of it, is compatible with each Form having a number of aspects or properties; the question how we are to understand a Form's relationship to its properties (or the interrelations among Forms) is not taken up in any of the dialogues we have been discussing (cf. *Sph*. 251 ff.).

he made the distinction. I would therefore suggest that the purpose of the first set of arguments in the *Parmenides* is not to attack the theory of separate Forms of the middle dialogues; if this were Parmenides' aim, he could fairly be charged with attacking a straw man. The purpose of these arguments is rather to indicate one important reason for the original separation of Forms from their participants.[52] We might then see the sequence of Parmenides' arguments as roughly corresponding to the development of Plato's conception of Forms and their relationship to sensible particulars.[53]

VI

Whether or not the *Parmenides* gives us an indication of why Plato distinguishes between Forms and immanent characters, we have seen clear evidence that such a distinction is made in the *Phaedo* as well as in other middle and late dialogues. This distinction constitutes the particular way in which Forms are separated from their participants. Plato's separation of Forms does not involve a complete abandonment of immanence. He apparently believes, for example, that Simmias' participation in the Form largeness must involve the presence of something in him—the immanent character of largeness. Immanence is thus rejected in the case of Forms, but retained in the case of immanent characters.

I shall conclude with a few remarks about Aristotle. Even though Aristotle rejects the separate existence of Forms, one can see vestigial traces of

---

[52] In other words, Plato is indicating an important reason for his departure from the practice—characteristic of the early dialogues—of speaking of Forms as *in* their participants. It is also possible that these arguments are aimed at Eudoxus' theory of immanent Forms (see Cherniss, *Aristotle's Criticism of Plato and the Academy*, 536; cf. Dancy, *Two Studies in the Early Academy*, 21–2, and Schofield, 'Eudoxus in the *Parmenides*'). This seems to me unlikely, however, in view of the fact that Parmenides makes no allusion to 'mixture', which is a crucial notion in Eudoxus' theory.

[53] In the *Phaedo*, in expressing his uncertainty about the nature of participation, Socrates speaks of the Form as perhaps being 'present to' its participants, or being 'in communion with' them; but he is not yet sure how to specify the relation (100d3–8). He does not mention the 'paradigm–copy' relation as one possible way of understanding participation. In the *Republic* and *Timaeus* Plato no longer expresses uncertainty about how to understand 'participation': the paradigm–copy relation becomes the model for understanding how Forms are related to their participants. In Parmenides' first regress argument (132a1–b2—the so-called 'third man argument') the Form is treated as a one over many but the relationship between Form and participant is left unspecified. In the second regress argument (132c12–133a3) the relationship is specified as that between a paradigm and its copy. One might speculate that here too the sequence of Parmenides' arguments reflects the development of Plato's thought about the relationship between Forms and their participants.

the distinction between Forms and immanent characters in his early works. In the *Categories*, for instance, he distinguishes between universal properties such as the colour white and particular instances of these properties, e.g. the particular whiteness in Socrates. He agrees with Plato's principle that if something is one in a strict sense (if, as he puts it, something is 'one in number'), it cannot be *in* many things; something one in number can be in one—but not more than one—subject.[54] Aristotle argues that a universal property like whiteness is naturally such as to inhere in a number of subjects, and cannot exist on its own. Thus universal properties are not one in number—that which is shared by white things in so far as they are white is a unity of form ($εἶδος$), and this form is not something numerically one. Aristotle holds, on the other hand, that the particular instance of whiteness in Socrates *is* one in number, so it can be in no more than one subject.[55]

Aristotle's 'non-substantial particulars', such as the particular whiteness in Socrates, are very similar to Plato's immanent characters. They are perishable since they depend for their existence on the perishable subjects in which they inhere. However, in view of his rejection of separately existing universals, these non-substantial particulars are an anomaly in Aristotle's system of ideas. For Plato, immanent characters have a definite explanatory role. If the explanation of Socrates' being white must include reference to something *in* him, and the Form whiteness is not in him, there must be some other entity, the immanent character of whiteness, to do the job. But for Aristotle, since the universal property of whiteness is *in* Socrates, there seems to be no need for another entity in him to explain his being white. It is hard to see what might have led Aristotle—apart from simply inheriting the apparatus from Plato—to suppose that there are two 'whitenesses' in Socrates, both of which somehow account for his being white. It is not surprising, then, that the vestigial anomaly of non-substantial particulars is sloughed off in the later development of Aristotle's ontology.[56]

---

[54] See $περὶ\ ἰδεῶν$ (Alexander, *in Metaph.* 97. 27–98. 4); cf. *Metaph.* Z 16, 1040^{b}25.

[55] *Cat.* 1^{a}20–^{b}9 (see esp. 1^{b}3–9) indicates that the only entities that are one in number are particular substances and the things that are 'in but not said of a subject', i.e. non-substantial particulars; cf. 3^{b}10–18. (The claim that non-substantial particulars can be in no more than one subject is controversial; I attempt to defend the claim in 'Inherence and Primary Substance in Aristotle's *Categories*', *Ancient Philosophy*, 12 (1992), 113–31.)

[56] In the *Categories* non-substantial particulars qualify as 'thises' since they are one in number (cf. 3^{b}10–13 with 1^{b}6–9; 8^{a}38–9, 8^{b}3–6); they are in fact the only things that qualify as 'thises' outside the category of substance. In the later works, being a 'this' becomes a mark of substance (e.g. *Metaph.* Z 1, 1028^{a}10–13; Z 3, 1029^{a}27–30, etc.); apparently Aristotle no longer believes that anything outside the category of substance qualifies as a 'this'. This would seem to count as one indication that he no longer includes non-substantial particulars in his ontology.

VIII

KNOWLEDGE AND BELIEF IN *REPUBLIC* 5–7

GAIL FINE

The *Meno* tells us that knowledge is true belief bound by an *aitias logismos*, an explanatory account (98a); the *Phaedo* tells us that all *aitiai* refer to Forms (96 ff.). It follows that knowledge of Forms is necessary for any knowledge at all. But although the *Meno* explains what knowledge is, it does not connect this account to Forms; and although the *Phaedo* tells us quite a lot about the metaphysics of Forms, it does not tell us much about their epistemological role. We must wait until the middle books of the *Republic* (5–7) for the details of how Forms figure in knowledge. Here there are two crucial stretches of text: first, a difficult argument at the end of *Republic* 5; and, second, the famous images of the Sun, Line, and Cave in books 6 and 7. Both passages are often thought to show that Plato subscribes to the Two Worlds Theory (TW), according to which there is no knowledge of sensibles, but only of Forms,[1] and no belief about Forms but only about sensibles.[2]

If Plato is committed to TW, there are, arguably, some consequences of note. First, the objects of knowledge and belief are then disjoint; one cannot move from belief to knowledge about some single thing. I cannot first believe that the sun is shining, and then come to know that it is. Second, Plato then radically rejects the *Meno*'s account of knowledge,

From S. Everson (ed.), *Cambridge Companions to Ancient Thought*, i: *Epistemology* (Cambridge University Press, 1990), 85–115. Reprinted with permission from Cambridge University Press and the author.

[1] A detailed account of what Forms are is not possible here. But, briefly, I take Forms to be non-sensible properties, properties not definable in observational or perceptual terms—the property, for example, of beauty, as opposed both to particular beautiful objects (such as the Parthenon) and to observable properties of beauty (such as circular shape or bright colour). For some discussion, see my 'Separation', *Oxford Studies in Ancient Philosophy*, 2 (1984), 31–87, and 'Immanence', ibid. 4 (1986), 71–97. See also T. H. Irwin, 'The Theory of Forms', Ch. V above.

[2] It is sometimes thought to follow from TW that Plato restricts knowledge to necessary truths; for, it is thought, all truths about Forms are necessary truths. See e.g. G. Vlastos, 'Socrates' Disavowal of Knowledge', Ch. II in this volume, p. 78. If, as I shall argue, Plato allows knowledge of sensibles, then (on the reasonable assumption that some of the knowable truths about them are contingent) he does not restrict knowledge to necessary truths.

according to which true beliefs become knowledge when they are adequately bound to an explanatory account. For the *Meno*, knowledge
implies true belief; on TW, knowledge excludes true belief.[3]

Third, Plato is then quite sceptical about the limits of knowledge;
although at least philosophers can know Forms, no one can know items in
the sensible world. No one can know, for example, what actions are just or
good; no one can know even such mundane facts as that they're now seeing
a tomato, or sitting at a table.

Fourth, this sceptical result would be quite surprising in the context of
the *Republic*, which aims to persuade us that philosophers should rule,
since only they have knowledge, and knowledge is necessary for good
ruling. If their knowledge is only of Forms—if, like the rest of us, they only
have belief about the sensible world—it is unclear why they are specially
fitted to rule in this world. They don't know, any more than the rest of us
do, which laws to enact.

Fifth, the text of the *Republic* seems to contradict TW. At 506c Plato says
that he has beliefs about, but no knowledge of, the Form of the good; and
at 520c he says that the philosopher who returns to the cave will know
the things there, i.e. sensibles.[4] Contrary to TW, then, one can have beliefs
about Forms, and know sensibles.

I shall argue that we can avoid these unattractive consequences. For
Republic 5–7 is not committed to TW. (If I had more space, I would argue
that Plato is never committed to TW: the *Republic* is no anomaly.)

Plato does, to be sure, in *some* way correlate knowledge with Forms, and
belief with sensibles—but not in a way that involves TW. He argues only
that all knowledge requires (not that it is restricted to) knowledge of
Forms; and that, restricted to sensibles, one can at most achieve belief.
This, however, leaves open the possibility that, once one knows Forms, one
can apply this knowledge to sensibles so as to know them too; the philosopher's knowledge of Forms, for instance, helps him to know (although it is
not, all by itself, sufficient for knowing) which laws ought to be enacted.

In addition to arguing against TW, I shall also, in looking at *Republic*
6–7, argue that Plato is a coherentist, rather than a foundationalist,
about justification. That is, he believes that all beliefs, to be known, must
be justified in terms of other beliefs; no beliefs are self-evident or self-
justified. I shall also suggest that knowledge, for Plato, is always essentially

---

[3] This consequence of TW is clearly noted by D. M. Armstrong, *Belief, Truth and Knowledge*
(Cambridge, 1973), 137–8. Unlike me, however, he believes the *Republic* endorses TW.

[4] Plato says that the philosopher 'will know each of the images, what they are and of what':
his use of *gnōsesthe* plus the *hatta* clause suggests he means 'know' and not merely 'recognize'.
Plato arguably explicitly admits knowledge of sensibles elsewhere too. See e.g. *Meno* 71b
97a9–b7; *Theaetetus* 201a–c.

articulate; knowledge does not consist in any special sort of vision or acquaintance, but in one's ability to explain what one knows.

REPUBLIC 5

The difficult argument at the end of *Republic* 5 is Plato's lengthiest, most sustained, systematic account in the middle dialogues of how knowledge differs from belief.[5] It is offered in defence of the 'greatest wave of paradox' of the *Republic*: that, in the ideally just *polis*, philosophers—those who know Forms—must rule (472a1–7, 473c6–e5). Plato advances this striking claim because he believes that the best rulers must know what is good; but one can know what is good only if one knows the Form of the good; and only philosophers can achieve such knowledge. He is well aware that his claim will not meet with general favour. In order to defend it, he offers a long and tangled argument, designed gently to persuade the 'sight-lovers'—people who rely on their senses and do not acknowledge Forms.

This provides us with an important constraint governing an adequate interpretation of the argument. The argument occurs in a particular dialectical context, designed to persuade the sight-lovers. If it is to be genuinely dialectical, then, as Plato explains in the *Meno* (75d), it should only use claims that are (believed to be) true, and that the interlocutor accepts; this is Plato's *dialectical requirement* (DR). Plato's opening premisses should not, then, appeal to Forms; nor, indeed, should he begin with any claims the sight-lovers would readily dispute, or that they're unfamiliar with. His conclusions may of course be controversial, but the opening premisses should not be.

The opening premisses, however, are difficult to interpret. The crucial ones are these:[6]

(1) Knowledge is set over what is (*epi tō(i) onti*) (477a9–10).
(2) Belief is set over what is and is not.

Esti (like 'is' in English) can be used in a variety of ways: existentially (is-e), predicatively (is-p), and veridically (is-v). (It can be used in yet

---

[5] I discuss this argument in more detail in 'Knowledge and Belief in *Republic* V', *Archiv für Geschichte der Philosophie*, 60 (1978), 121–39. Here I offer a brief summary of the main points. The present account occasionally differs from, and so supersedes, my earlier account.
[6] Plato also discusses *agnoia*, ignorance, correlating it with what is not (477a9–10). For some discussion, see my 'Knowledge and Belief in *Republic* V'.

further ways too—for example, for identity—but such further uses are not relevant here.) Hence (1) might mean any of (1*a–c*):

(1*a*) Knowledge is set over what exists.
(1*b*) Knowledge is set over what is *F* (for some predicate '*F*' to be determined by context).
(1*c*) Knowledge is set over what is true.

Premiss (2), correspondingly, might mean any of (2*a–c*):

(2*a*) Belief is set over what exists and does not exist.
(2*b*) Belief is set over what is *F* and not-*F*.
(2*c*) Belief is set over what is true and not true.

On the (*a*) and (*b*) readings, (1) and (2) specify the *objects* of knowledge and belief. On the (*a*) reading, one can only know what exists (there is no knowledge of, for instance, Santa Claus); and one can only have beliefs about objects that exist and don't exist (that is, on the usual interpretation, about objects that somehow 'half-exist').[7]

On the (*b*) reading, (1) claims that one can only know objects that are *F*; and (2) claims that one can only have beliefs about objects that are *F* and not-*F*. (That is, on the usual interpretation, every object of belief is itself both *F* and not-*F*—both beautiful and ugly, for example, or just and unjust.)[8]

On the (*c*) reading, by contrast, (1) and (2) specify the propositions that

---

[7] (1*a*) can be interpreted in more than one way. It might mean that (i) I can only know *x* when *x* exists; or (ii) I can only know *x* if *x* at some point exists; or (iii) I can only know *x* if *x* always exists. My own view is that of (i–iii), Plato at most believes (ii); but whatever his beliefs about (1*a*), I do not think he intends to assert any version of (1*a*) at this stage of the argument. (2*a*) is ambiguous between (i) Every object of belief both exists and doesn't exist, i.e. half-exists; and (ii) The set of objects about which one can have beliefs includes some that exist and others that don't (e.g. Santa Claus) (and perhaps some that both exist and don't exist, or that half-exist). Since (i) is the usual is-e reading, I restrict myself to it. For a defence of an is-e reading, see e.g. A. C. Cross and A. D. Woozley, *Plato's* Republic: *A Philosophical Commentary* (London, 1964). For criticism of an is-e reading, see my 'Knowledge and Belief in *Republic* V'; G. Vlastos, 'Degrees of Reality in Plato', in R. Bambrough (ed.), *New Essays on Plato and Aristotle* (London, 1965), 1–20, and in Vlastos, *Platonic Studies*, 2nd edn. (Princeton, 1981); J. Annas, *An Introduction to Plato's* Republic (Oxford, 1981), 196–7; C. H. Kahn, 'Some Philosophical Uses of "to be" in Plato', *Phronesis*, 26 (1981), 119–27.

[8] (2*b*) is ambiguous between (i) belief is about objects, each of which is *F* and not-*F*; and (ii) belief is about objects, some of which are *F* and others of which are not-*F* (and perhaps some of which are both). Since (i) is the usual interpretation, I shall not try to see how the argument goes if we assume (ii) instead. A predicative reading is favoured by Vlastos, 'Degrees of Reality in Plato', and by Annas, *An Introduction to Plato's* Republic, ch. 8. Annas correctly points out that even if Plato restricts knowledge to what is *F*, and precludes knowledge of anything that is *F* and not-*F*, TW does not follow; we could still know, for example, that this is a table, or that Socrates is a man, even if we could not know that returning what one owes is sometimes just, sometimes unjust. (Vlastos, by contrast, conjoins is-p with a defence of TW.) On the account I shall provide we can know things that are *F* and not-*F*.

are the *contents* of knowledge and belief. One can only know true propositions; one can believe both true and false propositions. Knowledge, but not belief, entails truth.

The (*a*) and (*b*) readings of (1) and (2) seem to violate DR. For both of them sharply separate the objects of knowledge and belief. But why should the sight-lovers agree to this at the outset of the argument? Plato may end up concluding that the objects of knowledge and belief are disjoint; but it would violate DR to assume so at the outset.

The (*a*) reading violates DR in further ways too. To be sure, if, for example, one takes knowledge to involve some sort of acquaintance, (1*a*) might seem plausible: I cannot know, in the sense of be acquainted with, Santa Claus, or even with Socrates, given that he is now dead. But it is unclear why we should assume at the outset that knowledge consists in or requires acquaintance with what is known. Moreover, (2*b*) introduces the difficult notion of 'half-existence'. But why should the sight-lovers agree at the outset that every object of belief only half-exists?

The (*b*) reading also violates DR in ways peculiar to it. For it claims that one can only know what is *F*; one cannot know what is *F* and not-*F*. But it is unclear how this could be a non-controversial starting premiss. Why can I not know that this pencil, say, is both equal (to other things of the same length) and unequal (to everything of any different length)? There seems no intuitive reason to suppose that Plato begins by denying the possibility of knowing that something is both *F* and not-*F*. Of course, he may end up concluding this (although I shall argue that in fact he does not); but our present task is to find suitably non-controversial *starting* premisses.

Premiss (1*c*), by contrast, satisfies DR. For it says only that knowledge entails truth, a standard condition on knowledge the sight-lovers can be expected to accept, and one Plato himself has clearly articulated before (*Men.* 98a; *Grg.* 454d6–7).

There are, however, at least two possible veridical readings of (2*c*):[9]

(2*c*i) Every proposition that can be believed is both true and false.
(2*c*ii) The set of propositions that can be believed includes some truths and some falsehoods.

Premiss (2*c*i) is controversial, since it introduces the difficult notion of a single proposition's being both true and false. We might be able to make sense of this notion: perhaps, for example, the claim is that all believed propositions are complex, and part of what each says is true, part false. But

---

[9] (2*c*i) is endorsed by J. C. B. Gosling, '*Doxa* and *Dunamis* in Plato's *Republic*', *Phronesis*, 13 (1968), 119–30. I endorse (2*c*ii) in 'Knowledge and Belief in *Republic* V' and here.

why should the sight-lovers agree that all beliefs are partly true, partly false? If we can find a more intuitively acceptable reading of the opening premisses, it should be preferred.[10]

Premiss (2cii) is such a reading. In contrast to (2ci), it does not say that each token proposition that can be believed is both true and false, but only that the set of propositions that can be believed contains both true and false beliefs. Belief entails neither truth nor falsity; there are both true and false beliefs. We cannot infer from the fact that p is believed that p is true, or that it is false, although we can infer from the fact that p is known that p is true.

If we read (1) as (1c), and (2) as (2cii), then all we have been told so far is that knowledge but not belief is truth-entailing. This of course leaves open the possibility (although is does not require) that there is knowledge and belief about the same objects (including sensibles), indeed of the same propositions. The readings of the opening premisses that best satisfy DR are thus also the least congenial to TW. Of course, later premisses might tell in favour of TW; we shall need to see. The point for now is only that at least (1–2) (if read as (1c) and as (2cii)) do not at all suggest it.

From 477b–478b Plato argues that knowledge and belief are different capacities. First he argues that capacities are distinguished by (a) what they are set over (epi) and by (b) what work they do (477c6–d5). Two capacities are the same if they satisfy both (a) and (b); they differ if they are set over different things and do different work. Plato then seems to argue that since knowledge and belief satisfy (b) differently, they are different capacities; and that since they are different capacities, they satisfy (a) differently as well.

The first inferences seems warranted; even if x and y satisfy only one of (a) and (b) differently, they seem to be different capacities. But the second inference does not seem warranted; why can't knowledge and belief do different work (and so be different capacities) even if they are set over the same things? Husbandry and butchery, for instance, do different work; but they are both set over the same objects—domestic animals.

If we favour the objects analysis, so that knowledge and belief are set over different objects, then Plato does seem to argue invalidly here. Just

---

[10] Notice, though, that (2ci) does not support TW; for there is no reason in principle why I cannot believe a proposition that is both true and false (however we ultimately explain that notion) about a Form, or know a true proposition about sensibles. On (2ci), the *propositions* one can believe and the propositions one can know constitute disjoint classes; but they could be about the same *objects*, and so TW would not yet be in the offing.

as the objects analysis seems to require Plato to violate DR, so it seems to require him to argue invalidly. If, however, we favour the contents analysis, so that knowledge and belief are not set over different objects but only over different contents, then not only are Plato's starting premisses non-controversial, but also, as I shall now argue, the present argument about capacity individuation is valid.

Knowledge and belief do different work, Plato tells us, in that knowledge but not belief is infallible (*anhamartēton*; 477e6–7). This might only mean that knowledge but not belief entails truth: that's one way (the only correct way) to read the slogan 'if you know, you can't be wrong'; and it's the only reading of the slogan that the argument requires.[11]

But how can we legitimately infer from this difference of work to a difference in what knowledge and belief are set over? My reading of (1) and (2) provides the answer: knowledge is set over true propositions; belief is set over true and false propositions. It follows from the fact that knowledge but not belief is truth-entailing, that they are set over different (though not necessarily disjoint) sets of propositions—the set of propositions one can know (true propositions) is a subset of (and so is different from) the set of propositions one can believe (true and false propositions).

Plato's inference from (*b*) to (*a*) is thus warranted after all—if we assume that knowledge and belief are set over different sets of propositions, rather than over different objects. Moreover, if we read the argument this way, then Plato leaves open the possibility (although, again, he does not require) that one can know and have beliefs about the same objects, and even of the same propositions. A valid, suitably non-controversial argument goes hand in hand with avoiding TW.

To be sure, Plato claims that what is known (*gnōston*) and what is believed (*doxaston*) cannot be the same (478a12–b2). This, however, might only mean that the set of propositions one can believe is not coextensive with the set of propositions one can know—for one can believe but not know false propositions. More weakly still, Plato might only mean that the properties of being known and of being believed are different properties. Either claim is plausible, and all that the argument, at this stage, requires.

All of the argument to 478e can be read as emphasizing this crucial point, that knowledge but not belief entails truth. At 479aff., however, Plato shifts to another point:

(3) Each of the many *F*s is both *F* and not-*F*.

---

[11] For quite a different interpretation of 'infallibility', see Vlastos, 'Socrates' Disavowal of Knowledge', Ch. II in this volume, pp. 74–5.

The many *F*s are sensible properties, of the sort recognized by the sight-lover—bright colour, for instance, or circular shape.[12] (3) claims that each such property is both *F* and not-*F*. Bright colour, for example, is both beautiful and ugly in that some brightly coloured things are beautiful, others ugly; returning what one owes is both just and unjust in that some token actions of returning what one owes are just, others unjust. Any sensible property adduced to explain what it is to be *F* (at least, for a certain range of predicates) will be both *F* and not-*F*, in that it will have some *F*, and some not-*F*, tokens. Here, in contrast to (1) and (2), 'is' is used predicatively, for 'is *F*' rather than for 'is true'. One might think that therefore (1) and (2) also use 'is' predicatively; or that Plato is confused about the differences between the predicative and veridical 'is'. But neither hypothesis is necessary. Plato shifts from a veridical to a predicative use of 'is'; but he does so without confusion. There is instead a connecting link between the two uses, as we shall see.

Plato expects the sight-lovers to accept (3); he is still speaking in terms acceptable to them. Indeed, it is because they accept (3) that they deny that 'Beauty is one' (479a4). They deny, that is, that beauty is a single property, the same in all cases; there are, rather, many beautifuls—many different properties, each of which is the beautiful. In this painting, the beautiful is bright colour; in that one, it is sombre colour, and so on.

Plato, however, accepts the One over Many assumption; there is just one property, the *F*, the same in all cases, in virtue of which all and only *F* things are *F*. If we build this assumption into the argument, then we can see how Plato finally denies the sight-lovers knowledge, and argues that all knowledge requires knowledge of Forms.[13]

The next steps in the argument are:

(4) The sight-lovers' beliefs (*nomima*) about the many *F*s are and are not (479d3–5).

(5) Therefore, the sight-lovers have belief, not knowledge, about the many *F*s (479e1–5).

Now if Plato were still concerned with the predicative reading of 'is', as in (3), one might expect him next to say:

(4′) Belief is set over the many *F*s, which are *F* and not-*F*.

---

[12] For a defence of this claim, see e.g. J. C. B. Gosling, '*Republic* V: *Ta Polla Kala*', *Phronesis*, 5 (1960), 116–28.

[13] The One over Many assumption, however, might well be thought to violate DR.

But instead of (4′), Plato says (4). Premiss (4) does not say that the many *F*s are and are not; it says that the sight-lovers' *beliefs* (*nomima*) about the many *F*s are and are not.[14] If we are now dealing with beliefs, however, then we are back at the veridical reading of 'is'. Plato is claiming that the sight-lovers' beliefs about the many *F*s are and are not true—that is, some of them are true, some of them are false. The sight-lovers have some true, and some false, beliefs about beauty; and this is so precisely because they rely on the many *F*s, on the many sensible properties. Why should this be so?

Knowledge, Plato has told us, is truth-entailing; it also requires an account (*Meno* 98a; *Phaedo* 76b; *Republic* 531e, 534b). The sight-lovers define beauty, at least in this painting, as, for instance, 'bright colour'. But no such definition can be correct; for some brightly coloured things are ugly, not beautiful. The sight-lovers cannot then know what beauty is, since their account of what beauty is—that it is bright colour—is false. Since their account is false, they lack any knowledge of beauty at all; for Plato also believes that one can know something about *x* only if one knows what *x* is.[15]

Although the sight-lovers thus lack any knowledge about beauty, they have belief, not ignorance, about it. For although beauty should not be defined in terms of bright colour, many brightly coloured things are beautiful; and so, guided by their false definition, they will be led to some true beliefs about beauty, such as that this brightly coloured painting is beautiful. These true beliefs cannot constitute knowledge, since they are not adequately explained in terms of a correct *aitias logismos*; but the fact that the sight-lovers have them shows that they are not ignorant about beauty, even if they do not know anything about beauty.

The sight-lovers thus have some true beliefs (about what things are beautiful) and some false beliefs (at least about what beauty is). Each of their beliefs is determinately true or false; Plato is not using 'belief' in a special technical sense for 'approximately correct'. Nor is he claiming that everyone who has belief, as opposed to knowledge, has some true, and some false beliefs. As it happens, the sight-lover has some true, and some false, beliefs; but other believers could have all false, or all true, beliefs.

---

[14] *Nomimon* is a general word for anything one can *nomizein*; it also conveys a suggestion of generality, and of custom or convention. It can be complemented with is-p or with is-v. In the former case it generally means something like 'customary rules or laws or conventions'; in the latter case it means something like 'customary beliefs'. That the veridical reading is intended here receives additional support from 508d8, where Plato makes a parallel point, using *doxa* (which in context clearly means 'belief') rather than *nomimon*.

[15] This is Plato's Priority of Knowledge of a Definition claim (see e.g. *Meno* 71b); like the One over Many assumption, it seems controversial.

There is, then, a well-argued connecting link between is-v and is-p. The claim is that restricted to the many Fs (is-p), which are F and not-F, one can at best achieve belief (is-v); for accounts phrased in terms of the many Fs (is-p), i.e. in terms of sensibles, will inevitably be false (is-v), thereby depriving one of any knowledge of the matter to hand.

If the sight-lovers lack knowledge, then either there is no knowledge, or knowledgeable accounts must be phrased in terms of non-sensible properties that are not both F and not-F. Plato rejects the first option and so completes the argument as follows (479e7–480a5):

(6) Knowledge is possible.
(7) There must, then, be non-sensible objects of knowledge.
(8) Therefore, there are Forms.
(9) Those who know Forms have knowledge; those who are restricted to the many Fs at best have belief.
(10) Therefore knowledge is set over (*epi*) Forms, and belief is set over the many Fs (480a1).

Conclusion (6) might seem to violate DR; the sight-lovers might protest that if they lack knowledge, so does everyone else. The inference to (7) seems to depend on the unstated assumption that knowledge requires the existence of certain sorts of objects.[16]

Is the inference to (8) warranted? That depends on how much we read into the word 'Forms'. If (as I believe) the Form of F is the non-sensible property of F, which is F and not also not-F, in that it explains the Fness of all and only the F things there are, then (8) is validly inferred. If we take Plato, in (8), to be arguing for Forms in some other sense, or for further features of Forms than their non-sensible, unitary, and explanatory nature, then the inference to (8) might be unwarranted. But there is no need to assume any other sense, or any further features of Forms, in order to understand any part of the argument. If we do not, then (8) is validly inferred.

Conclusion (9) simply summarizes conclusions that have already been

---

[16] This is not to play into the hands of the existential interpretation of the argument discussed at the outset. First, no occurrence of 'is' needs to be read as 'exists'; an existential claim is only *tacit* in the argument. (Though the use of is-e is tacit rather than explicit, Aristotle highlights it in his accounts of the theory of Forms: cf. the flux arguments recorded in *Metaphysics* A6, M4, and M9; and the second of the Arguments from the Sciences in the *Peri Ideōn* (Alexander of Aphrodisias, *Commentary on Aristotle's Metaphysics* 79. 8–11).) Second, Plato is not now claiming that knowledge is restricted to what exists—which is what (1) would claim if it were interpreted existentially—but only that knowledge requires the existence of certain sorts of objects. This reflects a realist bias about knowledge, but not one that tells in favour of TW.

validly argued for; (10), however, might seem worrying. For here Plato says that knowledge is set over—not, as we might expect, true propositions, but—Forms, certain sorts of objects; and that belief is set over—not, as we might expect, true and false propositions, but—the many *F*s. Does not this suggest either that, at this last stage of the argument, Plato falls into an objects analysis and embraces TW; or that he intended an objects analysis all along (in which case, earlier stages of the argument are invalid, and he begins by violating DR)?

We need not endorse either option. Plato has explained carefully and in detail what connection he intends between knowledge, truth, and Forms, on the one hand; and belief, truth and falsity, and sensibles, on the other. At the close of the argument he offers us an elliptical way of expressing a more complex claim. To say that knowledge is set over Forms is shorthand for the claim that all knowledge requires knowledge of Forms; to say that belief is set over the many *F*s is shorthand for the claim that if one is restricted to sensibles, the most one can achieve is belief.

I have provided an account of Plato's argument on which at least its opening premises satisfy DR; and on which it is valid and involves no equivocation on 'is'. Though it explicitly uses both is-v and is-p, and tacitly relies on an existential claim at one stage as well, there are systematic, explanatory connections between the different uses, and no crude slides or equivocations.

Nor does the argument commit Plato to TW. He argues only that, to know anything at all, one must know Forms; for knowledge requires an account, and it is only by reference to Forms that adequate accounts are forthcoming. This leaves open the possibility that once one has these accounts, one can apply them to sensibles in such a way as to know them too. Plato does not—here—explicitly say that knowledge of sensibles is possible. But his argument leaves that possibility open; so too, we shall see, does his account in books 6 and 7.

REPUBLIC 6–7

Republic 5 distinguishes between knowledge and belief as such; *Republic* 6–7 distinguishes between two sorts of knowledge and two sorts of belief. *Republic* 5 tells us that knowledge requires knowledge of Forms; *Republic* 6–7 adds that the best sort of knowledge requires knowledge of the Form of the good. *Republic* 5 considers knowledge and belief statically; it tells us how they differ, but says nothing about how to improve one's epistemological condition. In the Cave allegory in *Republic* 7, Plato considers knowledge and belief dynamically; he explains how to move from a lower to a higher cognitive condition.

Much of the epistemology of 6–7 is presented in the three famous images of the Sun, Line, and Cave. Plato apologizes for this fact; he resorts to imagery, he tells us, because he lacks any knowledge about the Form of the good (506c), whose epistemological and metaphysical role he now wishes to explain. When one has the best sort of knowledge, he later claims, one can dispense with images and speak more directly and literally (510b). Though many people are not unnaturally moved by Plato's haunting and beautiful images, it is important to bear in mind that he himself insists that he offers them only because he lacks knowledge; the best sorts of explanations and arguments, in his view, should be couched in more straightforward terms.

The Sun

Plato begins by repeating book 5's distinction between the many Fs, which are perceivable, and the Form of F, which is grasped by thought (507a7–b10). He then likens the Form of the good to the sun; as the sun is in the visible world, so is the Form of the good in the world of thought (*en tō(i) noētō(i) topō(i)*; *ta nooumena*; 508b12–c2). The sun is the cause (*aitia*)[17] of vision and of the visibility of visible objects: when one looks at visible objects in the light of the sun, one sees them; when one looks at them in the dark (unilluminated by the sun), one cannot see them, at least not well (507c–508d). Similarly, the Form of the good is the cause of knowledge and of the knowability of knowable objects (*nooumena*).[18] When one thinks about a knowable object illuminated

---

[17] *Aitia* is variously translated as 'cause', 'reason', and 'explanation'. 'Cause' is sometimes thought to be a misleading translation, on the ground that causes are entities productive of change, whereas *aitiai* are not so restricted. For some discussion of the connection between *aitiai* and contemporary accounts of causation, see my 'Forms as Causes: Plato and Aristotle', in A. Graeser (ed.), *Mathematics and Metaphysics in Aristotle* (Bern, 1987); also G. Vlastos, 'Reasons and Causes in the *Phaedo*', *Philosophical Review*, 78 (1969), 291–325 and J. Annas, 'Aristotle on Inefficient Causes', *Philosophical Quarterly*, 32 (1982), 311–26.

[18] It is striking that throughout this passage, Plato uses *nooumena*, rather than 'Forms'. Section 507b9–10 might seem to suggest that *nooumena* refers just to Forms. But it is tempting to believe that he deliberately uses *nooumena* in order to suggest, or at least to leave open the possibility, that more than Forms can be known. This suggestion is fortified by the fact that the image part of the Sun (s1 + s2: see below) contrasts two ways of looking at some one sort of entity (visible objects)—suggesting that one can have different cognitive attitudes towards a single entity. Perhaps the application part of the Sun (S3 and S4), then, also means to contrast (among other things) two ways of considering sensibles, with knowledge or with mere belief. Even if *nooumena* refers only to Forms, TW still does not follow. The point would be that one needs to know the Form of the good to have (the best sort of) knowledge about Forms. This point does not imply that one can have (the best sort of) knowledge only about Forms.

by the Form of the good, one knows it best; when one thinks about sensibles unilluminated by the Form of the good, one at best has belief about them. The Form of the good is also the cause of the being of knowable objects,[19] just as the sun causes objects to come into being and to grow.

The Sun presents an image along with its application.[20] The image contrasts two ways of looking at visible objects:

> (s1) Sight looks at visible objects in the dark, unilluminated by the sun.
> (s2) Sight looks at visible objects illuminated by the sun.

(s1) illustrates (S3), and (s2) illustrates (S4):

> (S3) The soul is aware only of sensibles unilluminated by the Form of the good (or by other Forms), and so has belief.
> (S4) The soul considers knowable objects illuminated by the Form of the good, and so has (the best sort of) knowledge.

The image (s1 and s2) contrasts two ways of looking at some one sort of entity—visible objects. The application (S3 and S4) contrasts two cognitive conditions, knowledge and belief. They are described in terms familiar from *Republic* 5: restricted to sensibles, one can at best achieve belief; in order to know, one must know Forms (and, for the best sort of knowledge, one must know the Form of the good). As in *Republic* 5, Plato does not explicitly mention two further possibilities: (*a*) knowledge of sensibles; and (*b*) belief about Forms. Neither, however, does he preclude (*a*) and (*b*). More strongly, he seems to believe they are possible. For as we have seen, he introduces the Sun image by claiming to have only belief about, and no knowledge of, the Form of the good (506c); and he says that the philosopher who returns to the cave knows sensibles (520c).[21]

Although the Sun distinguishes between the same two conditions as *Republic* 5, it adds to *Republic* 5 the claim that the best sort of knowledge requires knowledge of the Form of the good (505a, 508a5).[22]

---

[19] 509b7–8 *to einai te kai tēn ousian*. I take *kai* to be epexegetic, and both *to einai* and *tēn ousian* to refer to the being, the essence, of knowable objects.

[20] I follow T. H. Irwin, *Plato's Moral Theory* (Oxford, 1977), 334 n. 43, in using initial small letters (e.g. 's1', 'c1') for states which illustrate other states, and initial capital letters (e.g. 'S3', 'L1') for the states illustrated; and in using 'Sun' etc. for the name of the image, and 'sun' etc. for the entities mentioned in the images. My account of the Sun, Line, and Cave is indebted to his in more substantial ways as well: see his ch. 7, sects. 13–14.

[21] Moreover, (*a*) may be tacitly included in (S4), if I am right to suggest that *nooumena* may be used more broadly than for Forms; see n. 18.

[22] Sometimes Plato seems to suggest instead that all knowledge—not just the best sort of knowledge—requires knowledge of the Form of the good: see e.g. 507d11–e2, 508e3. On the interpretation assumed in the text, the Sun fits better with the Line; and Plato makes it plain that he takes the Line to be elaborating the Sun (509d–510a3). Perhaps the unclarity arises partly because Plato has not yet explicitly distinguished between the two sorts of knowledge.

Plato seems to believe this new claim because he seems to believe that the Form of the good is both a formal and final cause of every knowable object. That is, it is part of the essence of every knowable object, and in some sense what knowable objects are for. Since knowledge of a thing requires knowing its causes, full knowledge of anything requires knowing the Form of the good.

It is easy to see why Plato should believe that the Form of the good is the formal and final cause of the virtue Forms. A full account of any virtue—of justice or temperance, for instance—will explain its point, what is valuable or choiceworthy about it; and that is to explain its contribution to, its relation to, the Form of the good.

But Plato also believes that the Form of the good is the formal and final cause of all knowable objects, not just of the virtue Forms. We can best understand why if we turn for the moment to Plato's puzzling claim that the Form of the good is in some way greater or more important than other knowable objects (504c9–e3, 509b6–10), even though, unlike other Forms, it is not an *ousia*, a being (509b9–10). Usually, to call something an *ousia* is to accord it special importance. One might then expect Plato to claim that the Form of the good is the most important *ousia* of all; instead he claims that it is not an *ousia* at all.

The best explanation of this puzzling claim is that the Form of the good is not a distinct Form, but the teleological structure of things; individual Forms are its parts, and particular sensible objects instantiate it.[23] Just as Aristotle insists that the form of a house, for example, is not another element alongside the bricks and mortar, but the organization of the matter, so Plato views the Form of the good as the teleological organization of things. If we so view the Form of the good, we can explain why Plato claims both that the Form of the good is more important than other knowable objects, and also that it is not an *ousia*.

This view also helps to explain why Plato believes that full knowledge of a thing requires knowing its relation to the Form of the good. Consider Forms first. To know a Form's relation to the Form of the good is to know its place in the teleological system of which it is a part. Each Form is good in that it has the function of playing a certain role in that system; its goodness consists in its contribution to that structure, to the richness and harmonious ordering of the structure, and its having that place in the system is part of what it is. Plato believes, then, that each Form is essentially a good thing—not morally good, but, simply, good—in that it is part of what

---

[23] For this view, see esp. H. W. B. Joseph, *Knowledge and the Good in Plato's Republic* (Oxford, 1948), in particular ch. 3; J. C. B. Gosling, *Plato* (London, 1973), 57–71; and T. H. Irwin, *Plato's Moral Theory*, 225.

each Form is that it should have a certain place in the teleological structure of the world.

A similar account explains why knowledge of the Form of the good is
also necessary for fully knowing sensible objects. In the later *Timaeus* Plato
explains that the sensible world was created by the demiurge (27d ff.).
Since the demiurge is good, he wanted the world to be as good as possible; hence he tried to instantiate the Form of the good (and so the teleological structure of Forms generally) as widely as possible. Fully to
understand his creations, then, we need to refer to the Form of the good
which they instantiate.[24]

All of this embodies a crucial point to which we shall recur: Plato is a
holist about knowledge. Full knowledge of anything requires knowing its
place in the system of which it is a part, or which it instantiates; we do not
know things in the best way if we know them only in isolation from one
another.[25]

The Line and Cave

Plato introduces the image of the Divided Line in order to elaborate
the application part of the Sun image (S3 and S4). He tells us to divide
each of the Sun's two conditions—knowledge and belief—into two
(509d6),[26] thus yielding two kinds of belief and two kinds of knowledge.
The two sorts of belief—corresponding to the two lower stages of
the line (L1 and L2) are *eikasia* (imagination) and *pistis* (confidence).
The two sorts of knowledge—corresponding to the higher stages of the
line (L3 and L4)—are *dianoia* (thought) and *nous* (knowledge or
understanding).[27]

Plato initially explains each stage of the line by means of illustrative
examples. L1 is explained in terms of images of physical objects, L2 in

---

[24] I discuss Plato on teleology in somewhat more detail, though still briefly, in 'Forms as
Causes: Plato and Aristotle'.

[25] It is often agreed that Plato endorses a holist conception of knowledge in various later dialogues; but some believe that that represents a change of view from an earlier atomism. See e.g.
G. E. L. Owen, 'Notes on Ryle's Plato', Ch. XI in this volume. On the account I propose, Plato
is a holist in the *Republic* no less than in later dialogues. See my 'Knowledge and *Logos* in the
Theaetetus', *Philosophical Review*, 88 (1979), 366–97.

[26] Plato may tell us to divide the line into two unequal parts; but the text is uncertain. If the
inequality claim is made, the two likeliest explanations seem to be that (*a*) the belief part is
bigger, because more people have belief; or (*b*) the knowledge part is bigger, because knowledge is more valuable.

[27] Plato's terminology is not fixed. At 510a9, L3 + L4 are collectively called *to gnōston*; at
511a3, b3 they are collectively called *to noēton* (cf. 533e8–534a). When *to noēton* is used for
L3 + L4 collectively, *epistēmē* is sometimes used for L4 (cf. 533e8). Nothing should be made of
these terminological variations; Plato tells us (533d7–e2) not to dispute about the use of words.

terms of physical objects. At L3 one uses hypotheses, and the sensible objects imaged in L1 are in their turn used as images of Forms; mathematical reasoning is offered as a characteristic example. At L4 one uses dialectic (511b, 533c) in order to 'remove' or 'destroy' (533c8) the hypotheses of L3—not by proving them false, but by explaining them in terms of an unhypothetical first principle so that they cease to be mere hypotheses. Although Plato does not say so explicitly, this first principle is plainly the Form of the good (or a definition of, and perhaps further propositions about, it).[28] At L4 one also reasons directly about Forms without, as in L3, relying on sensible images of them.

Whereas the Line corresponds to the application part of the Sun, the Cave corresponds to its image part (s1 and s2), dividing each of its two parts into two (c1–4). It is an allegory, designed primarily to explain ways of moral reasoning (514a). Plato begins with a haunting description of prisoners who have been bound since birth so that all they have ever seen are shadows on a cave wall—shadows of artificial objects illuminated by a fire internal to the cave (c1). Strange though the image is, Plato insists that the prisoners are 'like us' (515a5). Plato then imagines one of these prisoners being released,[29] so that he can see not only the shadows but also the artificial objects that cast the shadows. When asked to say what each of the artificial objects is, he is at first confused, and thinks the shadows are 'more real' than the objects. Eventually, though, he is able to discriminate systematically between the shadows and the objects, and to see that the latter are 'more real' (c2). He learns to distinguish between the appearance or image of an object and the object, between appearance and reality.

Next the prisoner is led out of the cave. At first he sees only shadows of natural objects, then the natural objects themselves (c3), and finally the sun (c4). He learns to distinguish between appearance and reality outside the cave, just as he previously learned to distinguish between them inside the cave.

Each of Plato's three images is distinctively different from the others. The Sun describes both image and application; the Line explains the appli-

[28] Like Aristotle, Plato speaks of both propositional and non-propositional entities as being principles; I shall follow their lead. This double usage involves no confusion. One explains, or justifies one's belief in, a proposition by appealing to other propositions; but these propositions refer to, are about, various sorts of entities, which are explanatory factors one can know.

[29] I assume Plato uses the singular in order to suggest that very few people will ever undergo the transformation he describes (although he seems to believe that everyone could in principle undergo it). I hope it is not too obvious to be worth saying that Plato's picture of the release of the prisoner is an early illustration of the biblical saying 'the truth will set you free'—except that Plato believes that even the prisoners (us) can have by and large true beliefs; what the Cave really illustrates is rather the thesis that 'knowledge will set you free'.

cation further, while the Cave explains the image further. The Line is illustrated with literal examples of its cognitive conditions; the Cave is an allegory primarily about ways of moral reasoning. The Sun and Line (like *Republic* 5) describe conditions statically; the Cave explains them dynamically. Each image offers details not to be found in the others; if we interpret them in the light of one another, we can achieve a better grasp of their underlying thought than if we consider each on its own.[30]

Plato, then, distinguishes between two sorts of belief—imagination (L1) and confidence (L2)—and between two sorts of knowledge—thought (L3) and understanding (L4). One familiar way of explaining the differences between these conditions relies on an *objects analysis*: each condition is individuated by reference to its unique sort of object. Just as some argue that in *Republic* 5 there is belief only about sensibles and knowledge only of Forms, so some argue that in *Republic* 6–7 each cognitive condition has its own unique objects. On this view, one is in a belief state (L1 or L2), for instance, if and only if one is confronted with a certain sort of sensible object (images are the usual candidates for L1, and ordinary physical objects for L2). As in *Republic* 5, an objects analysis goes naturally with TW.[31]

Just as I rejected an objects analysis of *Republic* 5, so I shall reject one of *Republic* 6–7, defending again a *contents analysis*. On the contents analysis, L1–L4 are individuated, not by their unique objects (no state has unique objects), but by their distinctive sorts of reasoning (by their cognitive content). What state one is in is determined by the sort of reasoning one engages in, whatever sort of object it is about. To be sure, as in *Republic* 5, one needs to know Forms to know anything at all. Hence in a way, objects are relevant to determining cognitive level; but as we shall see, they are not relevant in a way congenial to TW.

L1: Imagination

Plato's initial characterization of L1 is quite brief. He says only that 'one section of the visible world [is] images. By images I mean, first, shadows,

---

[30] Plato plainly means there to be some correspondence between the three images; at 517b, having completed his initial account of the Cave, he tells us to apply that account 'as a whole to all that has been said', i.e. to the Sun and Line. He supplies a brief account of how to do this; but different commentators carry out his directions in different ways, and not everyone would agree with the connections I have claimed obtain. Nor would everyone agree with the account I have provided of the intrinsic nature of each image.

[31] At least, most objects analyses preclude knowledge of sensibles. However, some allow knowledge of more than Forms. For it is sometimes thought that L3 is correlated with special mathematical entities that are not Forms but which one can know. See n. 35.

and then reflections in water and on surfaces of dense, smooth and bright texture, and everything of that kind' (509e1–510a3). Similarly, at c1 the prisoners are bound, and have always been so, so that all that they have ever seen are shadows of artificial objects.

Plato might seem to be suggesting that one is at L1 if and only if one is confronted with an image of a sensible object—just as the objects analysis would have it. But if so, various difficulties arise. First, most of us don't spend much time looking at images and reflections of physical objects;[32] nor will most people in the ideal city do so. Yet Plato says that most of us are at L1 (515a5); and that most people in the ideal city would be too (517d4–e2, 520c1–d1).

Second, contrary to the objects interpretation, looking at images doesn't seem to be either necessary or sufficient for being at L1. It's not necessary because the prisoner who is released in the cave and then looks at the artificial objects (not just at their images) is at first confused; he is still at L1, even though he is confronted with an object, not just with its image. It's not sufficient because, as we noted before, Plato says that the philosopher who returns to the cave will know the images there (520c); he does not lapse back into L1 when he looks at images.

We can avoid these difficulties if we turn to the contents analysis—and also understand the nature of and interconnections between Plato's three images in the way I have suggested.

The prisoners are at L1 about physical objects not because they see, are confronted only with, images of physical objects, but because they cannot systematically discriminate between images and the objects they are of. Even if they were confronted with a physical object, they would remain at L1, so long as they could not systematically discriminate between images and their objects, and could not tell that the objects, are 'more real' than the images, in that they cause the images. They are at L1, not because of the objects they are confronted with, but because of the ways in which they reason about them. Similarly, the philosopher who returns to the cave does not lapse back into L1 about images. For he, unlike the prisoners, can systematically discriminate between objects and their images; he knows that the images are mere images, caused and explained by the phys-

---

[32] Contrast N. P. White, *A Companion to Plato's* Republic (Indianapolis, 1979), 185–6, who argues, on the basis of book 10, that most of us do, in Plato's view, spend a great deal of time looking at images of sensible objects, in that we focus only on aspects or appearances of objects, without, for example, correcting for the effects of perspective. It is also sometimes suggested that we are restricted to appearances of objects in that we are restricted to their surface features (e.g. their colour and macroscopic size) and do not know their inner structure (e.g. their atomic constitution).

ical objects. One is at L1 about physical objects, then, not just in case one is confronted only with images of physical objects, but just in case one cannot systematically discriminate between physical objects and images of them.

Moreover, one can be at L1 in other areas. When Plato says that most of us are like the prisoners (are at L1), he does not mean that most of us literally see only images of physical objects. He means that our moral beliefs are relevantly like the prisoners' beliefs about physical objects; we are at L1 in our moral beliefs (not in our physical object beliefs), just as they are in L1 about their physical object beliefs. Thus, for instance, he talks about people who 'fight one another for shadows and wrangle for office as if it were a great good' (520c7–d1)—about people, that is, who take seeming goods to be real goods, and lesser goods to be greater goods than they are. Or, again, at 517d–e, Plato speaks about contending 'about the shadows of justice'—about, that is, ordinary, unreflective beliefs about justice (cf. 493a6–c8, 515b4–c2). We uncritically accept what seems just or good as being really just or good.[33]

To be sure, the Line (unlike the Cave) is not an allegory. It describes literal examples of cognitive conditions—but they are only illustrative, not exhaustive, examples. The Line illustrates L1 reasoning about physical objects; but one can be at L1 in other areas, for example, about morality. Plato does not believe we are at L1 about physical objects (so he illustrates L1 with an example that is not characteristic of us); but we are at L1 in our moral reasoning.

Objects are relevant to the line in a way, then: if one cannot make certain sorts of distinctions between kinds of objects, the most one can achieve is a certain level of understanding about those sorts of objects. This, however, plainly allows one to have different cognitive attitudes to the same sorts of objects. L1, then, when properly understood, does not suggest an objects analysis or TW.

L2: Confidence

The prisoners advance to L2 when they are released from their bonds and gradually learn to distinguish between the images and the objects they are of. This represents the first application of elenchus or dialectic. At first the

---

[33] Many of our moral beliefs are not only unreflective, but also false. What is crucial about L1, however, is not that one's beliefs are false, but that they are accepted uncritically. Even in Plato's ideally just city, most people will be at L1, even though their beliefs are by and large true (517d4–e2, 520c1–d1).

prisoners believe they know that the images exhaust the whole of reality. Then, when they are exposed to the objects the shadows are of, and are asked to say what those objects are, they become confused and frustrated; they are at a loss. In just the same way, interlocutors in the Socratic dialogues at first believe they know the answers to Socrates' 'What is F?' questions; when cross-examined, they too are quickly at a loss. Most of the Socratic dialogues end at this aporetic stage—and so it is sometimes concluded that the elenchus is purely negative and destructive (or at best plays the modest positive role of getting people to recognize their own ignorance). Here, however, the elenchus is carried further—and so Plato shows how the Socratic elenchus can enable one to move beyond *aporia* to better-based beliefs (and, in L3 and L4, to knowledge). For the released prisoner gradually learns to discriminate between images and their objects; his beliefs become more reliable. Similarly, in the *Meno*, the elenchus with Meno's slave advances beyond *aporia*, until the slave improves his beliefs. Like the prisoner, he moves from L1 to L2, from *eikasia* to *pistis*—though in his case, of course, about a mathematical, not about a moral, belief: he (like most of us, in Plato's view) remains at L1 about morality. Because he cannot give a satisfactory account, an *aitias logismos* of the sort necessary for knowledge (98a), however, he remains at a belief state, though at a better one than he was in before.[34] Perhaps the Socrates of the Socratic dialogues would place himself at L2 about morality. He disclaims knowledge about morality, but clearly believes he is in some way better off in his moral reasoning than his interlocutors are; the difference between L1 and L2 allows us to see how this could be so. His ability to make certain sorts of systematically correct discriminations puts him in a better epistemic position than his interlocutors, even though he (believes he) lacks knowledge.

Just as L1 does not support an objects analysis, neither does L2. Plato does not mean that one is at L2 if and only if one is confronted with a physical object. He rather means that one is at L2 *about physical objects* if one can systematically discriminate between physical objects and images of them, but cannot explain their difference. This, however, allows one to be at L2 about physical objects even if one is not confronted with a physical object. Further, one can be at L2 in other areas—so long as one's reasoning is relevantly like the prisoner's reasoning about physical objects when he has reached L2.

---

[34] Though Plato adds (*Meno* 85c) that if the slave continues practising the elenchus, he will eventually reach knowledge. This claim is not further explained or defended in the *Meno*; but it is illustrated in the Cave, in showing how elenchus, dialectic, enables us to move not only from L1 to L2, but also from L2 to L3 and L4.

L3: Thought

One moves from L2 to L3—from a kind of belief to a kind of knowledge— when one emerges from the cave, from a preoccupation with sensibles, and turns one's attention to non-sensibles, that is, to Forms. As in *Republic* 5, here too one needs to be suitably aware of Forms in order to have any knowledge at all (although—again as in *Republic* 5—it does not follow that knowledge is restricted to knowledge of Forms).

Plato initially distinguishes L3 from L4 as follows:

> in one section [L3], the soul is compelled to enquire [*a*] by using as images the things imitated before [at L2], and [*b*] from hypotheses, proceeding not to a first principle but to a conclusion; in the other [L4], it [*b*] advances from a hypothesis to an unhypothetical first principle, [*a*] without the images used by the other section, by means of Forms themselves, progressing methodically through them. (510b4–9; cf. 511a3–c2)

When Glaucon professes not to understand this very abstract account, Socrates provides a mathematical illustration of L3:

> students of geometry, calculation, and such studies hypothesize the odd and the even and shapes and three kinds of angles and other things akin to these in each branch of study, regarding them as known; they make their hypotheses, and do not think it worth while to give any further (*eti*) account of them to themselves or to others, thinking they are obvious to everyone. Beginning from these, and going through the remaining steps, they reach a conclusion agreeing (*homologoumenos*) [with the premises] on the topic they set out to examine. (510c2–d3)

He adds:

> They also use the visible forms, and make their arguments (*logoi*) about them, although they are not thinking (*dianooumenoi*) of them, but of those things they are like, making their arguments for the sake of the square itself and the diagonal itself. (510d5–8)

Plato cites two key differences between L3 and an L4: (*a*) at L3 one uses sensibles as images of Forms, although one is thinking of Forms, not of sensibles; at L4 one thinks of Forms directly, not through images of them; (*b*) at L3 one proceeds from a hypothesis to various conclusions; at L4 one proceeds from a hypothesis to an unhypothetical first principle (510b)— that is, to (a definition of, and perhaps also further propositions about) the Form of the good.

L3 poses a threat for the objects analysis. For Plato makes it plain that the square itself etc. can be known in both an L3 and an L4 type way (511d); contrary to the objects analysis, then, the same objects appear at

two distinct stages of the line.[35] Moreover, L3 uses sensibles as images of
Forms; but sensibles are also in some way correlated with L2. So just as
mathematical entities appear at both L3 and L4, so sensibles appear at
both L2 and L3.[36]

Although Plato provides a geometrical illustration of L3, L3 is not
restricted to geometry or even to mathematical disciplines more generally;
any reasoning that satisfies the more general features (a) and (b) belongs
at L3. Indeed, it seems reasonable to suggest that although Socrates (in the
Socratic dialogues and *Meno*) places himself at L2 in his moral reasoning,
Plato in the *Republic* places himself at L3.[37]

The *Republic* is peppered with images used self-consciously to illustrate
something about Forms: the Sun, Line, and Cave are cases in point. Similarly, Plato partially explains the nature of justice in the soul through the
analogies of health and of justice in the city; he uses the analogy of the
ship to illustrate the nature of democracy, and so on. So the *Republic*'s
moral reasoning satisfies (a).

It also satisfies (b). Plato claims that the account of the virtues in book
4 is a mere outline that requires a longer way (435d, 504c9–e2). That longer
way involves relating the virtues to the Form of the good (a task not undertaken in book 4); and (a definition of) the Form of the good is the unhypothetical principle one advances to when one moves from L3 to L4.
Similarly, Plato offered accounts of the virtues, and justified them in terms
of their explanatory power; but the accounts were partial, and not justified
in terms of anything more fundamental.[38]

---

[35] There is dispute about whether 'the square itself', etc. (510d) are Forms; I assume they are,
but others take them to be mathematical entities that are distinct from Forms. For some discussion of this matter, see J. Annas, 'On the Intermediates', *Archiv für Geschichte der Philosophie*, 57 (1975), 146–66; A. Wedberg, *Plato's Philosophy of Mathematics* (Stockholm, 1955), ch.
3, and in G. Vlastos (ed.), *Plato*, i: *Metaphysics and Epistemology* (Garden City, NY, 1971), 28–52,
esp. app. D. The difficulty I pose for the objects analysis arises whether or not they are Forms;
for the crucial point is that, whatever they are, they can be known in both an L3 and an L4 type
way.

[36] Moreover, if Plato, in saying that L3 uses sensibles, means to suggest that sensibles can be
objects of L3 as well as of L2 epistemic attitudes, then, contrary to TW, Plato explicitly allows
one to have at least L3 type knowledge of sensibles. Even if, in saying that L3 uses sensibles,
Plato does not mean to say thereby that sensibles can be known in at least an L3 type way, we
shall see that he nonetheless leaves open the possibility that one can have L3 (and L4) type
knowledge of sensibles.

[37] For this suggestion, see also D. Gallop, 'Image and Reality in Plato's *Republic*', *Archiv für
Geschichte der Philosophie*, 47 (1965), 113–31; 'Dreaming and Waking in Plato', in J. P. Anton
and G. L. Kustas (eds.), *Essays in Ancient Greek Philosophy* (Albany, 1971); and Irwin, *Plato's
Moral Theory*, 222–3.

[38] Cf. the account of the hypothetical method in *Phaedo* 100 ff. (which is plainly not restricted
to mathematical reasoning), which the account of L3 clearly recalls. Plato's account of L3 also
recalls the *Meno*. There too Plato uses a geometrical example to illustrate a point about our
capacity for reaching moral knowledge; he again uses diagrams, but in order to make a point

Plato is often said to favour a mathematical model of knowledge. He does, to be sure, count mathematics as a type of knowledge; and mathematical studies play an extremely important role in the philosophers' education. But he places mathematics at L3—it is the lower form of knowledge. Moreover, it is just one example of L3 type reasoning—Plato's moral reasoning in the *Republic* is another example of it. Further, the higher type of knowledge—L4—is not mathematical but dialectical.

Nor does Plato praise mathematics for the reasons one might expect. To be sure, he emphasizes its value in getting us to turn from 'becoming to truth and being' (525c), that is, in getting us to acknowledge Forms. But he adds in the same breath, as though it is of equal importance, that mathematics is also of value in the practical matter of waging war (525b–c; cf. 522e, 526d). Nor does he praise mathematics for using necessary truths or for conferring some special sort of certainty. On the contrary, he believes that even if mathematical truths are necessary, they cannot be fully known until they, like all other truths, are suitably related to the Form of the good. Mathematics is not invoked as a paradigm of a discipline consisting of self-evident truths standing in need of no further justification or explanation.[39] Moreover, although mathematical reasoning may be deductive, L3 is not restricted to deductive reasoning; it includes other ways of explaining the less general in terms of the more general. Platonic moral argument, for instance, also belongs at L3, although it is not deductive in character.

It can appear puzzling that Plato counts L3 even as an inferior type of knowledge. To see why, I first need to say a bit more about what he thinks knowledge in general involves.

We have seen that Plato believes that in addition to true belief, knowledge requires an account or *logos* (*Meno* 98a; *Phaedo* 76b; *Republic* 531e, 534b). Call this KL.

It is tempting to infer that Plato is offering a version of the justified true belief account of knowledge; and many have succumbed to the temptation.[40] Recently, however, some have argued that the temptation ought to

about non-sensibles (diagonals); he insists that in a dialectical, as opposed to eristic, context, one should use claims the interlocutor agrees he knows (75d), just as here he says that the mathematicians assume that their hypotheses are obvious to everyone; and, of course, he again uses the hypothetical method.

[39] For an interesting and provocative discussion of this matter, see C. C. W. Taylor, 'Plato and the Mathematicians: An Examination of Professor Hare's Views', *Philosophical Quarterly*, 17 (1967), 193–203: 202–3.

[40] See e.g. R. Chisholm, *Theory of Knowledge* (Englewood Cliffs, NJ, 1966), 5–7; D. M. Armstrong, *Belief, Truth and Knowledge* (Cambridge, 1973), 137; and my 'Knowledge and *Logos* in the *Theaetetus*'.

be resisted.[41] For, it is argued, KL requires, not a *justification* for believing that something is so, but an *explanation* of why it is so.[42]

I agree that the sort of account Plato at least typically has in mind is an explanation. Often, for instance, he speaks, not of knowing propositions, but of knowing things. To know a thing, he believes, usually involves being able to say what it is, in the sense of articulating its nature or essence; doing this explains what the entity in question is. Even when Plato speaks instead of knowing a proposition, the sort of account he generally has in mind is an explanation of why it is so; sometimes this involves proving it, or explaining the natures of any entities it mentions.

But although Platonic accounts are typically explanations, we should not infer that he therefore rejects or bypasses a justified true belief account of knowledge. His view is rather that justification typically consists in, or at least requires, explanation. For Plato, I am typically justified in believing *p* only if I can explain why *p* is so; I am typically justified in claiming to know some object only if I can explain its nature or essence.

In addition to KL, Plato also believes that knowledge must be based on knowledge (KBK): I know a thing or proposition only if I can provide an account of it which I also know. Stating an account of something is not sufficient for knowing it; in addition, I must know the account.[43]

The conjunction of KL and KBK raises the threat of the famous regress of justification: to know something, I must, given KL, provide an account of it. Given KBK, I must know this account. Given KL, I must then provide an account of it which, given KBK, I must also know—and so on, it seems, *ad infinitum*. Plato discusses this regress in some detail in the *Theaetetus*; but it is lurking not far below the surface here as well.[44]

---

[41] See esp. M. F. Burnyeat, 'Aristotle on Understanding Knowledge', in E. Berti (ed.), *Aristotle on Science: The Posterior Analytics* (Padua: Antenore 1981), 97–139 esp. 134–5; and 'Socrates and the Jury', *Proceedings of the Aristotelian Society*, suppl. vol. 54 (1980), 173–206. We have seen before that if Plato accepts TW, that too precludes a justified true belief account of knowledge since, on TW, knowledge precludes belief; at the moment, however, I am concerned with a different challenge attributing a justified true belief account of knowledge to Plato.

[42] This is also sometimes used as part of an argument for the claim that Plato is not so much concerned with knowledge as with understanding. I consider this argument briefly below, in discussing L4.

[43] KBK is most explicitly discussed and defended in the later *Theaetetus*; but *Republic* 533c (quoted and discussed below) may endorse it as well.

[44] I discuss the regress as it emerges in the *Theaetetus* in 'Knowledge and *Logos* in the *Theaetetus*'. I argue there that Plato avoids the infinite regress by allowing justifications to be circular, if the circle is sufficiently large and explanatory. As we shall see, this is also the resolution I believe Plato favours in the *Republic*. In this respect as in others, Plato's epistemology remains relatively constant, whatever the fate of the theory of Forms.

Plato also believes, as we know from *Republic* 5, that if one knows anything at all, one knows Forms.

Can one satisfy these three conditions for knowledge—KL, KBK, and knowing Forms—within the confines of L3? And if so, how does Plato respond to the regress KL and KBK seem to give rise to? I begin by looking at KL and KBK in the abstract; I leave until later the question of whether everyone at L3 provides accounts of Forms.

Plato says that at L3 one offers hypotheses, which are then used in order to derive various conclusions. Are the hypotheses or the conclusions known at L3? At 510c7 Plato says that mathematicians offer hypotheses without giving any further (*eti*) account of them. Later he says that mathematicians can't 'see [Forms] clearly so long as they leave their hypotheses undisturbed and cannot give an account of them. For if one does not know (*oide*) the starting-point (*archē*), and the conclusion and intervening steps are woven together from what one does not know (*oide*), how ever could this sort of agreement (*homologia*) be knowledge (*epistēmē*)?' (533c1–5). Both passages may seem to suggest that KL cannot be satisfied for the hypotheses at L3. But if KL is not satisfied for the hypotheses at L3, then the hypotheses are not known at L3, since KL is a necessary condition for knowledge. Moreover, if KL is not satisfied, then neither is KBK; for one certifies that one knows something by producing an account of it.

KL might be satisfied in the case of the conclusions. For the hypotheses and proofs used to derive the conclusions might reasonably be thought to constitute an account of—an explanation of, and so an adequate justification for believing—them. But if the hypotheses are not themselves known, then KBK seems to be violated in the case of the conclusions; and so, since KBK is also a necessary condition for knowledge, the conclusions seem not to be known either.

It is thus initially unclear why Plato counts L3 as a type of knowledge. For KL, and so KBK, seem to be violated for the hypotheses; and at least KBK seems to be violated for the conclusions.

I suggest the following resolution of this difficulty. In saying that no (further) account of the hypotheses is given at L3, Plato does not mean that KL cannot be satisfied for them at L3. He only means, first, that no account can be given of them at L3 in terms of something more fundamental, such as the Form of the good; and, second, that at L3 they are used in an enquiry, in order to derive various results, before their assumption has been justified. The mathematician says, for instance, 'Let a triangle be a plane figure enclosed by three straight lines', and then goes on to derive various conclusions about triangles, without first giving us any reason to accept his account of a triangle.

None of this, however, precludes the possibility of justifying the hypotheses *in the course of* the enquiry. And it is clear how this can be done. For in using them in order to reach various results, one displays their explanatory power, shows what results one is able to achieve by using them; and showing this is one way of providing an account. In just the same way, scientists often offer speculative hypotheses, which become confirmed when they are shown to explain some variety of phenomena. One can, then, even within the confines of L3, satisfy KL for the hypotheses.

Does one then know the hypotheses? Only if KBK is also satisfied. For KBK to be satisfied, however, the conclusions must be known, for the hypotheses are justified in terms of the conclusions. But we said before that the conclusions might not be known because, although KL seemed satisfied in their case, KBK was not, because the hypotheses were not known. We seem locked in a vicious circle: we can provide accounts of the hypotheses in terms of the conclusions, and of the conclusions in terms of the hypotheses; but we do not yet seem to have reached anything that is known.

But although there is a circle here, it is not a vicious one. The hypotheses are justified in terms of the conclusions, and the conclusions in terms of the hypotheses. In providing these mutually supporting accounts, one comes to know both hypotheses and conclusions. One does not *first* know the hypotheses, and *then* the conclusions; one comes to know both simultaneously, in seeing how well the hypotheses explain the conclusions. Instead of a vicious circle, there are mutually supporting, interlocking claims.

I suggest, then, that both KL and KBK can be satisfied for conclusions and hypotheses alike, within the confines of L3. One satisfies KL for the hypotheses by appealing to their explanatory power; and one satisfies KL for the conclusions by deriving them from the hypotheses. In thus deriving the conclusions, and seeing how well the whole resultant system fits together, one acquires knowledge of both conclusions and hypotheses, and so satisfies KBK for both as well.

Now I said before that the conjunction of KL and KBK threatens a regress: to know p, I must know q; to know q, I must know r, and so on, it seems, *ad infinitum*. There are many different responses to the regress, but two of the most popular are *foundationalism* and *coherentism*. Foundationalism claims that the regress halts with basic beliefs that are not themselves justified in terms of any further beliefs; they are self-justified, or self-evident. Coherentism claims that the regress is finite but has no end; accounts can circle back on themselves. I explain p in terms of q, and q in terms of r, and so on until, eventually, I appeal again to *p*; but if the circle is sufficiently large and explanatory, then it is virtuous, not vicious.[45]

Plato has typically been counted a foundationalist. At least for L3, however, he seems to be a coherentist. For he counts L3 as a type of knowledge, and so believes that KL and KBK are satisfied at L3. But the best explanation of how this could be so appeals to circular accounts, in the way I have suggested.

One might argue that the passage cited above from 533c (cf. *Cratylus* 436cd) shows that Plato rejects coherentism,[46] but it does not. The passage does seem to commit Plato to KBK; if one does not know the starting-point, neither does one know the conclusions derived from it, because knowledge must be based on knowledge. That, however, does not show that one cannot come to know the starting-point through deriving conclusions from it, and then come to know the conclusions by deriving them from the starting-point. The passage may also suggest that consistency or agreement is insufficient for knowledge; but any self-respecting coherentist would agree. For, first, the relevant sort of coherence involves more than consistency or agreement; in addition, the consistent beliefs must be mutually supporting and explanatory, and form a sufficiently large group. And, second, not even such coherence is sufficient for knowledge, but only for justification; knowledge also requires truth.

I have suggested that if Plato is a coherentist about justification, at least for L3, then both KL and KBK can be satisfied at L3, for hypotheses and conclusions alike. One further problem remains, however. If L3 is a type of knowledge, then at L3 one must know Forms. Now Plato (who seems to place himself at L3 in his moral reasoning) seems to believe that he has at least partial knowledge of some Forms; so at least one person he places at L3 knows some Forms. But he also places the mathematicians at L3 about mathematics; yet it may seem unclear that they know mathematical—or any—Forms. At least, it seems unlikely that mathematicians explicitly recognize Forms at all; there are no entities in their ontology that they call 'Forms'. If they do not explicitly admit Forms into their ontology, is it appropriate to say that they know Forms?

This problem too can be resolved. The mathematicians offer hypotheses. These hypotheses include accounts, or partial accounts, of, for example,

---

[45] There are, of course, many different versions of foundationalism and coherentism. Not all foundationalists, for example, require self-evident beliefs, as opposed to, for example, initial warrant or credibility. Those who view Plato as a foundationalist, however, typically believe that his version invokes self-evident beliefs. For one good recent defence of coherentism about justification, see L. Bonjour, *The Structure of Empirical Knowledge* (Cambridge, Mass., 1985), part. 2, esp. chs. 5 and 7.

[46] See e.g. N. P. White, *Plato and Knowledge and Reality* (Indianapolis, 1976), 113 n. 50.

the square itself;[47] and the square itself etc. are Forms. So the mathematicians offer accounts of Forms. To be sure, they do not know that the entities they are defining are Forms. It does not follow, however, that they do not know the entities they are defining; it follows only that there are some facts about these entities that they do not know. But one can know an object even if one does not know everything about it. And Plato makes it plain that mathematicians know some crucial facts about the entities they define. Not only do they offer hypotheses, partial definitions of them. But they also know, for instance, 'that the unit should never appear to be many parts and not to be one' (525e)—the one the mathematician is concerned with is one, and not also not one; it does not suffer compresence of opposites. They may also know that mathematical entities are non-sensible (for example, 511d, 525de, 526a1–7). Perhaps this shows that mathematicians treat mathematical entities *as* Forms, even though they do not recognize that that is what they are doing.

None the less, if one can know a Form without knowing that what one knows is a Form, then the conditions for knowing Forms might seem weaker here than they did in *Republic* 5. At least, the philosopher described there seems explicitly to countenance Forms in a way mathematicians do not. Still, perhaps that is only sufficient, and not also necessary, for knowledge. Mathematicians still differ significantly from anyone at L1 or L2. For such people do not have any *de dicto* beliefs about Forms (although they may of course have some *de re* beliefs about them); but mathematicians do have some *de dicto* beliefs about Forms, as expressed in their hypotheses, even if they lack the *de dicto* belief that what they are defining is a Form.

L4: Understanding

At L4 one reaches an unhypothetical first principle (a definition of, and perhaps further propositions about) the Form of the good. When one can suitably relate the hypotheses of L3 to the Form of the good, the hypotheses are removed or destroyed (533c8)—that is, they cease to be mere hypotheses, they lose their hypothetical status and become known in an L4 type way (511d) and not merely, as before, in an L3 type way. Moreover, at L4 one no longer uses sensibles but only Forms.

In saying that at L4 one no longer uses sensibles, Plato does not mean that there is no L4 type knowledge of sensibles. He means only that at

---

[47] This is sometimes disputed; but for a good defence of the claim, see C. C. W. Taylor, 'Plato and the Mathematicians'.

L4 one no longer needs to explain the nature of Forms through images of them; one can speak of them directly, as they are in and of themselves. But once one has done this, one can apply these accounts to sensibles, in such a way as to have L4 type knowledge of them. In just the same way, Aristotle believes that one can define various species and genera without reference to particular instances of them; but, once one has done this, one can apply the definitions to particulars in such a way as to have knowledge of them.

L4 raises the following problem. At L4 one explains the hypotheses by relating them to something more fundamental (the Form of the good), which is itself known. But how is the Form of the good known? It cannot be explained in terms of something yet more fundamental—for there is nothing more fundamental (and if there were, we could raise the same question about how it is known, and then we would be launched on an infinite regress). Are not KBK and KL then violated at this later stage? The same difficulty that arose for L3 seems to arise for the Forms of the good at L4.

One answer—popular historically—is to say that both the route to L4, and what L4 type knowledge consists in, is some sort of vision or acquaintance. One knows the Form of the good, not by explaining it in terms of something more fundamental, but by a self-certifying vision, which is also what the knowledge consists in.[48] The threatened regress thus halts with a self-certifying vision that confers knowledge. This answer essentially abandons KL; for it claims that knowledge does not require an account after all, but only a vision.

However, Plato repeatedly stresses that the route to L4 (as to L2 and L3) is dialectic (511b–c, 533a–d)—the Socratic method of cross-examination, of critically testing beliefs against general principles and examples.[49] Moreover, Plato asks rhetorically, 'do you not call the person who is able to get an account of the essence of each thing "dialectician"? And will you not say that someone who cannot do this, in so far as he cannot give an account to himself and others, to that extent lacks knowledge (*nous*) about the matter?' (534b3–6).

---

[48] An acquaintance view is favoured by, for example, F. M. Cornford, 'Mathematics and Dialectic in the *Republic*, VI–VII', in R. E. Allen (ed.), *Studies in Plato's Metaphysics* (London, 1965). See also the discussion in R. Robinson, *Plato's Earlier Dialectic*, 2nd edn. (Oxford, 1953), 172–9, for a critical assessment of the acquaintance view (or, as he calls it, the 'intuition' theory).

[49] There is one difference in the practice of dialectic at L4 and at earlier stages, however: at L4 dialectic is practised *kat'ousian*; at earlier stages it is practised *kata doxan* (534c2). By this Plato means that at L4 dialectic is practised on accounts of Forms—i.e. on the hypotheses of L3 although, of course, when one begins, these are not fully satisfactory accounts—otherwise one would already be at L4); at L2 and L3, on common beliefs that fall short of knowledge and are not (except perhaps *de re*) about Forms. The method is the same, although what it is applied to differs.

Dialectic, not acquaintance, is thus the route to L4; and since L4 crucially involves the ability to provide an account, neither does it consist in acquaintance alone. KL is thus not abandoned at L4. Even if acquaintance is necessary for L4, it is not sufficient; an account is also needed. And so our problem remains: what is there in terms of which we can justify our beliefs about the Form of the good?[50]

An alternative—and I think preferable—solution appeals again to coherence: one justifies one's claims about the Form of the good, not in terms of anything more fundamental (there is nothing more fundamental), but in terms of its explanatory power, in terms of the results it allows one to achieve; and one justifies one's acceptance of the hypotheses of L3 by explaining them both in terms of their results and in terms of the Forms of the good. The Form of the good, we have seen, is the teleological structure of the world; other Forms are its parts, and sensibles instantiate it. We justify claims about other Forms and about sensibles by relating them to this general structure; and we justify claims about the Form of the good by showing how well it allows us to explain the natures of, and interconnections between, other Forms and sensibles. There is again a circle; but, again, it is a virtuous, not a vicious, circle.

But how, it might be asked, could this be so? For didn't we propose a moment ago that L3 was an inferior type of knowledge precisely because it relied on coherence? If so, how could L4's justifications also be rooted in coherence?

The answer is that it is not coherence as such that makes L3 inferior to L4, but the degree and kind of coherence. Both L3 and L4 rely on coherence for justification; but their coherentist accounts differ. The justifications at L3 are piecemeal, restricted to individual branches of knowledge—one justifies mathematical beliefs, for example, solely in terms of mathematical claims, and so on (*mutatis mutandis*) for morality and the like. At L4, by contrast, one offers more synoptic accounts, integrating every branch of reality into a synoptic whole, in terms of the Form of the good (531c6–e5, 537b8–c7)—that is, in terms of the teleological structure

---

[50] Although I have argued only that acquaintance is not sufficient for knowledge, I do no believe it is necessary either. The chief reasons for introducing acquaintance seem to be (*a*) tha it is needed to halt the regress; and (*b*) that Plato's visual metaphors suggest it. Reason (*a*) however, is false; coherence is another way of halting the regress and, as I go on to explain, believe it is Plato's way of halting the regress at L4 as at L3. As to (*b*), even if Plato's visua metaphors suggest some sort of acquaintance, they do not require it. The metaphors can as easil be interpreted in terms of understanding; when I say that I finally see the point of what yo have said, I do not mean that I have had some special vision that confers knowledge, but tha I now understand what you have said. For this point, see Gosling, *Plato*, esp. ch. 8; and M. Burnyeat, 'Wittgenstein and Augustine *de Magistro*', *Proceedings of the Aristotelian Society*, 6 (1987), 1–24; see also my 'Knowledge and *Logos* in the *Theaetetus*'.

of reality. The mathematician, for instance, provides some sort of account of the square itself; the dialectician provides an account of *each* thing (534b), and relates each thing to the Form of the good. The mathematician restricts himself to mathematical connections; the dialectician provides 'a comprehensive survey of their affinities with one another and with the nature of things' (537c)—his accounts are not restricted to individual branches of knowledge, but interrelate them, by means of the Form of the good. He shows the point and interconnection of all things.

L4 thus relies on coherence no less than does L3; but its coherentist explanations are fuller and richer, and that is why L4 counts as a better sort of knowledge. Not every sort of coherentist account is equally good; L4 is an improvement on L3, not because it appeals to something different from coherence, but because its coherentist accounts are more explanatory.

This account also helps to explain how L4 type knowledge of sensibles is possible. The teleological structure of the world is stated in general terms, in terms of properties and natural laws, without reference to sensibles. However, once this general structure is articulated, one can have L4 type knowledge of sensibles by seeing what properties and laws they instantiate, and by seeing how they contribute to the goodness of things.

Indeed, Plato's coherentism may require that L4 type knowledge of sensibles be possible. At least, it seems reasonable to suppose that Plato believes that one eventually needs to refer back to sensibles in order to justify one's belief that one has correctly articulated the world of Forms— for part of one's justification for believing one has correctly articulated the world of Forms is that it allows one to explain sensibles so well. If Plato accepts KBK, and believes one needs to refer to sensibles to justify one's beliefs about Forms, then he must allow knowledge of sensibles.

On the account I have proposed, one knows more to the extent that one can explain more; knowledge requires, not a vision, and not some special sort of certainty or infallibility, but sufficiently rich, mutually supporting, explanatory accounts. Knowledge, for Plato, does not proceed piecemeal; to know, one must master a whole field, by interrelating and explaining its diverse elements.

It is sometimes argued that if this is so, we ought not to say that Plato is discussing knowledge at all; rather, he is discussing the distinct phenomenon of understanding. For, it is said, understanding, but not knowledge, requires explanation and interrelated accounts; and knowledge, but not understanding, requires certainty, and allows one to know propositions individually, not only collectively. A more moderate version of this general sort of view claims that Plato is discussing knowledge—but an older concept of knowledge, according to which knowledge consists in or requires understanding, in contrast to 'knowledge as knowledge is nowadays discussed in philosophy.'[51]

Now I agreed before that, for Plato, knowledge typically requires explanation; but I argued too that this is only to say that, for him, justification typically requires explanation. Similarly, I agree that, for Plato, knowledge does not require any sort of vision or certainty, but does require interrelating the elements of a field or discipline or, for L4, interrelating the elements of different disciplines in the light of the Form of the good. But, once again, I do not think this shows that he is uninterested in knowledge. We can say, if we like, that he believes knowledge consists in or requires understanding. But I would then want to add that this is not so different from 'knowledge as knowledge is nowadays discussed in philosophy'. To be sure, some contemporary epistemologists focus on conditions for knowing that a particular proposition is true, or believe that knowledge requires certainty, or that justification does not consist in or require explanation. But that is hardly characteristic of all contemporary epistemology. Indeed, concern with certainty is rather in disfavour these days; and many contemporary epistemologists defend holist conceptions of knowledge, and appeal to explanatory connections to explicate the sort of coherence a justified set of beliefs must exhibit. Plato does indeed explicate *epistēmē* in terms of explanation and interconnectedness, and not in terms of certainty or vision; but we should resist the inference that he is therefore not talking about knowledge, or that, if he is, he has an old-fashioned or unusual notion of knowledge. On the contrary, in this as in other matters, Plato is surprisingly up to date.

---

[51] Burnyeat, 'Socrates and the Jury', 188. A similar view is defended by Annas.

IX

THE FORM OF THE GOOD IN PLATO'S *REPUBLIC*[1]

GERASIMOS SANTAS

> Looking into the orb of light he [Plato] sees nothing, but he is warmed and elevated.
>
> Jowett

No writer has made loftier claims for the concept of goodness than Plato makes for the Form of the Good in the middle books of the *Republic*. We are told that without knowledge of the Form of the Good we cannot know that anything else is good, and that without knowledge of this Form all other knowledge would be of no benefit to us (505–6). Further, the Form of the Good is 'the cause' of truth and knowledge. Further yet, the objects of knowledge receive 'their being and essence' from the Form of the Good, though it is not essence 'but still transcends essence in dignity and surpassing power' (509a–b). As if these intriguing views were not paradoxical enough, Plato has Socrates suggest that even the foundations of mathematics are insecure unless we have knowledge of the Good: the beginnings of geometry and arithmetic are 'hypotheses,' not known until the soul can 'ascend' from them to the Form of the Good and 'descend' back from it to them (509b–511e).

These dark sayings are not incidental to Plato's philosophy. On the contrary they are the centrepiece of canonical Platonism, Plato's ethics, epistemology, and metaphysics of the middle period. The Form of the Good is given the privileged position: it is prior, ethically, epistemologically, and ontologically to everything else in Plato's universe. In the *Republic* the

This paper was first published in *Philosophical Inquiry* (winter 1980), 374–403. Reprinted with permission of the editor and of the author. [*Editor's note*: This article has been abbreviated, but the original footnote numbers have been retained.]

[1] An earlier draft of this paper was read at the Claremont Graduate School and at the Dec. 1977 meeting of the Society for Ancient Greek Philosophy. I am indebted to several members of the audience for helpful comments, especially to Professors Charles Young, Mike Ferejohn, Charles Kahn, and Bill Jacobs.

theory of the Form of the Good represents Plato's attempt to base his ethics and politics on the theory of Forms. Probably a case can also be made that the theory is presupposed in the teleological explanation of the *Phaedo* (97–9), the 'creation' of the physical universe in the *Timaeus* (29–33), and even the theory of love in the *Symposium*.

Why did Plato assign such a supreme position to the Form of the Good? What conception of goodness did he have, which allowed him to think of the Form of the Good not only as the final cause of everything that we do, but also as 'the cause' of the knowability and even of the very being of his favourite entities, the Forms? And what connection did he see between the Form of the Good and mathematics?

As might well be expected, a considerable body of literature has been built around the relevant passages.[2] Yet, it is no hyperbole to say that we have no satisfactory or widely accepted answers to our questions.[3] In this paper I propose to re-examine closely what Plato actually says with the hope of making some progress. I think it can be shown that what Plato says about the Form of the Good is intelligible and coherent and coheres well with what is now known about his metaphysics, epistemology, and ethics of the middle period. So far as I know, the interpretation I propose has never been put forward by anyone, but it relies heavily on some of the excellent discussions about Plato's metaphysics which have appeared in the last quarter-century, especially the discussions on self-predication and the distinction between the ideal and proper attributes of Forms.[4]

I divide Plato's discussion about the Good into three rounds or (as they may well be called) three waves of paradox, and discuss each in turn. My first object is to state, on the basis of the texts, the main propositions that

---

[2] Among the older, extensive and useful discussions of the relevant texts are the following: Paul Shorey, 'The Idea of the Good in Plato's *Republic*', *University of Chicago Studies in Classical Philology*, I (1894); F. M. Cornford, 'Mathematics and Dialectic in the *Republic* VI–VII', in R. E. Allen (ed.), *Studies in Plato's Metaphysics* (London, 1965), and the relevant commentary in his translation of the *Republic* (1941); W. D. Ross, *Plato's Theory of Ideas* (Oxford, 1951), 39–69; R. Robinson, *Plato's Earlier Dialectic*, 2nd edn. (Oxford, 1953), chs. x and xi. More recent discussions include: R. C. Cross and A. D. Woozley, *Plato's* Republic (London, 1964), chs. 8–10; I. M. Crombie, *An Examination of Plato's Doctrines* (London, 1962), i. 103–33; J. C. B. Gosling *Plato* (London, 1973), chs. iv and vii. [. . .]

[3] Perhaps a fairly reliable index of the present state of affairs is afforded by Nicholas White's list of puzzling questions about the Form of the Good which remain unanswered: *Plato on Knowledge and Reality* (Indianapolis, 1976), 99–103.

[4] I am especially indebted to the following: G. Vlastos, 'Degrees of Reality in Plato', 'A Metaphysical Paradox', 'The "Two-Level Paradoxes" in Aristotle', 'Reasons and Causes in th Phaedo', 'The Unity of Virtues in the *Protagoras*', all in *Platonic Studies* (Princeton, 1973); D Keyt, 'Plato's Paradox that the Immutable is Unknowable', *Philosophical Quarterly* (1969), an 'The Mad Craftsman of the *Timaeus*', *Philosophical Review*, 80 (1971), 250–5; G. E. L. Ower 'Dialectic and Eristic in the Treatment of Forms', in G. E. L. Owen (ed.), *Aristotle on Dialecti* (1968).

constitute Plato's theory of the Form of the Good. This is completed by the middle of the second round. I then discuss the distinction between proper and ideal attributes of the Forms, which the theory seems to presuppose, the assumption of self-predication that goes with it, and some of the difficulties and implications of the theory.

I. THE FIRST ROUND: ETHICS, POLITICS, AND THE FORM OF THE GOOD

Plato's discussion of the Form of the Good occurs in a section of book 6 which is concerned with the education of the rulers (500 ff.). We are told that it is not sufficient for the rulers to learn what justice, temperance, courage, and wisdom are, according to the definitions established in book 4. These definitions do not provide a sufficient and exact understanding of these virtues. There is something greater than these virtues, and there is a 'longer way' to understanding these things, a way that culminates in 'the greatest study':

(G1) The greatest study is the study of the Form of the Good, by participation in which just things and all the rest become useful and beneficial. (505a)

(G2) If we do not know the Form of the Good, then even if without such knowledge we know everything else, it (the knowledge of everything else) would be of no benefit to us, just as no possession would be (of benefit) without possession of the Good. (505a–b)

(G3) If we know all things without knowing the Good, (this would be of no benefit because) we would not know (that) anything (is) beautiful and good. (505b)

Next, Plato rejects two hypotheses concerning the nature of the Good: (*a*) the Good is knowledge, and (*b*) the Good is pleasure. The first hypothesis is rejected on the ground that those who hold it are unable to answer the question 'Knowledge of what?' except by saying 'Knowledge of the Good', thus ending up with the circular and uninformative definition that the Good is knowledge of the Good. The second hypothesis is rejected on the ground that those who hold it admit that there are bad pleasures, and are thus compelled to admit that the same things (bad pleasures) are both good and bad (presumably a contradiction). Thus:

(G4) The Good is not (identical with) knowledge or pleasure. (505b–d)

Plato concludes this round by asserting two propositions about good things and the Good and by emphasizing the importance of knowledge of the Good for the rulers:

(G5) Many people prefer what appears to be just and honourable but is not, but no one prefers to pursue or possess what appears good but is not. (505d–e)[5]

(G6) The Good every soul pursues and does everything for its sake, divining what it is and yet baffled and not having an adequate apprehension of its nature nor a stable opinion about it as it has about other things, and because of this failing to have any benefit from other things. (505e)

(G7) Our constitution will not be perfectly ordered unless the rulers know how just and honourable things are good and they will not know this unless they know the Good. (506a–b)

This round is the least paradoxical of the three and the easiest to understand in the general setting of Plato's theory of Forms and his ethics. The main metaphysical and epistemological assertions that Plato makes here about the Form of the Good are simply instances of his general metaphysics and epistemology. Thus the second part of G1 is simply an instance of a general proposition that Plato holds, namely:

(F1) It is by virtue of participation in the Form F-ness or the F that anything which is F is F.[6]

And G3 is an instance of the general epistemological proposition that goes together with the theory of Forms, namely:

(F2) If we do not know F-ness or the F, we do not know that anything is F.[7]

---

[5] For the first part of G5, see the speeches of Glaucon and Adeimantus in *Republic* 2.

[6] The attribution of this proposition to Plato has been widely discussed in connection with the Third Man Argument; see e.g. Vlastos, *Platonic Studies*, 348. Charles Young has pointed out that, as I myself say later, the application of F1 to goodness is different for the case of the goodness of Forms and the goodness of sensibles. A Form has goodness of kind by virtue of participating in the Form of the Good; a sensible has goodness of kind (attributive goodness) by participating in the Form of that kind and that Form in turn participating in the Form of the Good. The goodness of sensibles is attributive and involves participation in at least two Forms, one of which is the Form of the Good.

[7] A Socratic version of this has been discussed by P. Geach and myself; see 'The Socratic Fallacy', *Journal of the History of Philosophy* (Apr. 1972). In *Socrates: Philosophy in Plato's Early Dialogues* (London, 1979), I find that the evidence heavily favours Geach. [. . .] In the *Republic* G3 itself is such evidence. For a more recent discussion, see M. F. Burnyeat, 'Examples in Epistemology: Socrates, Theaetetus and G. E. Moore', *Philosophy*, 52 (1977), 381–98, esp. 390.

Thus G3 and the second part of G1 do not assign to the Form of the Good any privileged position over other Forms. On the other hand, the first part of G1 (and perhaps G2 and G7) does assign to the *study* of the Good a privileged position over all other studies and to the knowledge of the Good over all other knowledge. But this privileged position, so far, can be accounted for and understood by reference to G6, another standard Socratic and Platonic ethical view. If all our actions, pursuits, and under-takings are for the sake of the Good, then knowledge of the Good would indeed seem to be the most important knowledge we can have: for without it we would never know that anything for the sake of which we did any-thing else was good (by G3). We would be like archers who lived for the sake of hitting their targets but could never see them clearly and, what is worse, could never know whether what they hit were their targets! Can we imagine anything more frustrating or less satisfying? Had Plato's asser-tions about the Good stopped here, his position would have been only mildly paradoxical and not all that different from Aristotle's; and the paradox and the difference would derive from his application of F1 and F2 to the case of goodness. We might say that the conjunction of G1, G3, and G6 assigns an ethical or practical priority to the study of the Good, and this priority might well have been thought sufficient for the paradox of the Philosopher-King.

II. THE SECOND ROUND: THE EPISTEMOLOGICAL AND ONTOLOGICAL PRIORITY OF THE GOOD

The second round is a wave of paradox indeed: Plato seems to assign to the Form of the Good an ontological and epistemological priority over all other Forms. The round (506b–509c) begins when Socrates is challenged to say what the Form of the Good is, if it is not knowledge or pleasure. Socrates implies that he does not know what the Form of the Good is, and when asked to give at least his opinion he proposes to let go for the moment the question about the nature of the Good and to speak of 'the offspring of the Good which is most like it'. He now prepares the ground for the simile of the Sun by first making the usual Platonic distinction between good things, and beautiful things, objects of vision but not thought, on the one hand, and the Good itself and the Beautiful itself, objects of thought but not vision, on the other. In the case of vision and visible things a man may have the power of vision and a thing may be visible but there may be no actual vision (seeing) if a third element is not present, namely, light which is provided by the chief of the heavenly divinities, the Sun, 'whose light makes the faculty of sight see best and visible things to be seen' (508a). Socrates now states and elaborates the simile as follows:

(G8)   As the Good is in the intelligible region to reason and to the objects of reason, so is the Sun in the visible world to vision and the objects of vision. (508c)

(G9)   The Sun (by its light) gives the objects of sight their visibility and the faculty of sight its vision; similarly, the Form of the Good gives the objects of reason their truth and to reason its knowledge of them. (508b, 508d–e)

(G10) The Sun is the cause of light and vision, and light and vision are sunlike but not identical with the Sun; similarly, the Form of the Good is the cause of truth and knowledge, and truth and knowledge are like the Form of the Good but they are not identical with it. (509a)

(G11) The Sun not only furnishes the visibles the power of visibility but also provides for their generation and growth and nurture, though it is not itself generation; similarly, the objects of knowledge receive not only their being known from the presence of the Good, but also their being and essence (reality) comes from it, though the Good is not essence but still transcends essence in dignity and surpassing power. (509b, trans. Shorey)

In Shorey's translation, Plato's next two lines read: 'And Glaucon very ludicrously said: "Heaven save us, hyperbole can no further go." '

As Socrates' reluctance and Glaucon's response indicate, the second round is far more difficult to understand and interpret than the first. Let us start by distinguishing sharply between the two rounds. The first round deals with relations between the Form of the Good and anything that is good, whether a Form or a sensible thing. But the second round deals with relations between the Form of the Good and Forms *only*: between the Form of the Good and objects of knowledge or thought, i.e. Forms. Thus it is reasonable to suppose that it is the attributes of the Forms *qua* Forms or their *ideal* attributes that are being explained or accounted for by reference to the Form of the Good; not their *proper* attributes, i.e. the attributes that each Form has by virtue of being the particular Form it is.[8] This is an important clue in understanding the second round and we shall return to it shortly. The second difference is that while the first round assigns an ethical and practical priority to the study of the Form of the Good over

[8] This point has been emphasized by Ross, *Plato's Theory of Ideas*, 40–1.

every other study, the second round assigns ontological and epistemo-logical priorities to the Form of the Good over every other Form. And it is precisely these latter priorities that have to be understood.

Essentially, the second round contains three distinct but related asser-tions: (1) the Form of the Good is 'the cause' of the knowability of the Forms; (2) the Form of the Good is 'the cause' of reason's actually knowing the Forms; and (3) the Form of the Good is 'the cause' of 'the being and essence [reality]' of the Forms.[9] Let us consider (1) and (3) together. We have a chance, I think, to understand these two assertions if we can answer the following three questions: (Q1) What constitutes the being and essence of the Forms? (Q2) What is the relation between the being and essence of the Forms and their knowability? (Q3) Given an answer to Q1, how can we understand the Form of the Good so as to make sense of Plato's view that it is 'the cause', in some appropriate Platonic sense of 'cause', of the being and essence of the Forms?

The context of the second round, the distinction between ideal and proper attributes, and Professor Vlastos's recent studies of Plato's doctrine of degrees of reality[10] make it possible, I think, to give a fairly confident answer to our first question (Q1). In a series of passages in the middle dialogues Plato contrasts Forms with the sensibles that participate in them; in these contrasts, systematically studied by Vlastos, Plato brings into relief a number of attributes which Forms have but which the sensibles that participate in them do not have. These attributes—which we may provisionally call ideal attributes of the Forms—constitute the being and essence of the Forms. Moreover—to skip for a moment to our second question (Q2)—it is precisely these attributes that make possible the knowability of the Forms or the Forms' being 'cognitively reliable', in Vlastos's phrase; so that if we can understand how the Form of the Good is 'the cause' of the ideal attributes, we will also be able to understand how it is 'the cause' of the Forms' knowability. Let us look briefly at these contrasts.

In the *Symposium* 211a–b Plato says that unlike the many beautiful sensible things that participate in it, Beauty itself always exists, it is neither generated nor destroyed, it does not increase or decrease, and it exists by itself. This is one set of Ideal attributes—'I1' for short. In addition, he says that in contrast to sensible beautiful things, Beauty itself is not beautiful in one respect and ugly in another, nor beautiful at one time and not at another, nor beautiful in comparison to one thing and ugly in comparison

---

[9] In our passage Plato does not explicitly refer to the Form of the Good as a 'cause' but later on he does, for example at 517c.

[10] 'Degrees of Reality in Plato' and 'A Metaphysical Paradox'.

to another, nor beautiful here and ugly there, being beautiful for some and ugly for others. Let us call the set of attributes of Beauty implied by this statement 'I2'.[11] Now in the *Republic* Plato tells us several times (477a, 478d, 478e, 479a–c) that the objects of knowledge, the Forms, 'are', whereas the objects of belief, the sensibles that participate in Forms, 'both are and are not'. Professor Vlastos has argued convincingly, I think, that it is not existence that is here being asserted of the Forms and both asserted and denied of sensibles, but rather perfection or complete reality; and this in turn is to be interpreted in terms of the Ideal attributes (I1 and I2) listed in the *Symposium*.[12] On this view, to say, for example, that the Form Circle 'is', whereas a sensible circle 'is and is not', is to say that the Form Circle is circular in all respects, is always circular, is circular no matter compared to what, and is circular to all who apprehend it no matter from where; whereas a sensible circle is not circular in all respects, not always circular, and so on. As Vlastos points out, Plato himself expands the 'is and is not' formula in some of these ways at 479a–c for the case of beautiful things, just things, and so on. In all these contrasts Plato surely intends to bring into relief 'the being and reality' of the Forms, and he does this in terms of I1 and I2. Moreover, in *Republic* 5 sensibles are said to be unknowable and only objects of belief precisely because they lack the ideal attributes of the Forms;[13] and this supports our answer to the second question, Q2, that it is the ideal attributes of the Forms that make possible the knowability of the Forms. In sum, and in answers to Q1 and Q2, the being and essence of the Forms consists in their ideal attributes (I1 and I2), and an object must have these to be knowable.

Let us now go to our third and more difficult question (Q3), assuming the answers we gave to Q1 and Q2. Let us first tackle part of Q3: in what sense of 'cause' can we plausibly suppose that the Form of the Good is the cause of the ideal attributes (being and essence) of the Forms? In the case of the Sun and sensible things, the Sun is presumably the (an) efficient cause of their generation and growth as well as their visibility. But there

---

[11] The implied attributes are that Beauty itself is beautiful in all respects, always, no matter compared to what, or apprehended from what point of view. These attributes clearly presuppose that Beauty itself is self-predicational or self-exemplifying. For a discussion of this assumption, see Vlastos, *Platonic Studies*, 262–3, and J. M. E. Moravcsik, 'Reason and *Eros* in the "Ascent"-Passage of the *Symposium*', in John P. Anton and G. L. Kustas (eds.), *Essays in Ancient Greek Philosophy* (Albany, NY, 1971), 296–300.

[12] Vlastos, *Platonic Studies*, particularly 62–3, 66–7, and n. 21. For discussions that disagree with Vlastos on this point, see e.g. Cross and Woozley, *Plato's* Republic, 145, and perhaps J Gosling, '*Republic* V: *Ta Polla Kala*', *Phronesis*, 5 (1960), 116–28.

[13] See the relevant parts of J. Hintikka, 'Knowledge and its Objects in Plato', and my comments in J. M. E. Moravcsik (ed.), *Patterns in Plato's Thought* (1973).

is no generation and growth and nurture in the case of the Forms, nor are the Forms probably ever conceived by Plato as efficient causes.[14] In all probability formal causation is meant via the relation of participation.[15] If so, then the Form of the Good is the cause of the ideal attributes of the other Forms in the sense that:

(G11.1) It is by virtue of participating in the Form of the Good that all the other Forms have ideal attributes.

This is our interpretation of the relevant part of G11.

We are now within sight of an answer to the more difficult part of Q3, the part concerning the nature of the Form of the Good. For it seems to follow[16] from G11.1 and the distinction between ideal and proper attributes that:

(G12) The ideal attributes of all the Forms other than the Form of the Good are proper attributes of the Form of the Good.

A host of questions now faces us. I will list and discuss them in an order that might help us answer them. (Q4) Why should Plato think that the Form of the Good, rather than some other Form or no Form at all, is the formal cause of the ideal attributes of all the other Forms? (Q5) Did Plato conflate reality and goodness, as the joining of the present interpretation with Vlastos's interpretation of the doctrine of degrees of reality would seem to imply? (Q6) What is the distinction between ideal and proper attributes, and did Plato make it or at least observe it so that we are justified in attributing G12 to him partly on the basis of it? (Q7) How is the goodness of sensible things to be accounted for on the present interpretation? These are large and difficult questions and I can only hope to indicate in outline what I think are the right answers.

We can begin to see a connection between goodness and the ideal attributes of the Forms if we assume *one* of Plato's standard ways of conceiving the Forms in the middle dialogues, that is, not as properties but as ideal

---

[14] See Vlastos, 'Reasons and Causes in the *Phaedo*', esp. 88–91.

[15] T. Irwin, in some very brief remarks about the Form of the Good, says, among other things, that 'The Good is the formal and final cause of the Forms' being what they are' (*Plato's Moral Theory: The Early and Middle Dialogues* (Oxford, 1977)). I am in agreement with the first part of this statement, but I find it difficult to see how the Good is the final cause of the Forms' being what they are since I would have thought that final causes are invoked to explain actions, activities, and movements, whereas the Forms are 'at rest'. My discussion of the first round clearly allows, though, that the Form of the Good can be the final cause of sensible things, for example, men's activities and actions. [. . .]

[16] Professor Mike Ferejohn wrote that we need at least self-participation applied to the Form of the Good for this derivation. In the last paragraph of this round I indeed allow for such self-participation or at any rate for self-predication (and in this use 'good' is not used attributively).

exemplars complete with non-Pauline self-predication.[17] On this assumption, each Form is the best object of its kind there is or can be. The Form Circle, for example, is the best circle there is or can be, the Form Justice the best (most) just thing there is or can be. Now Plato thinks, I believe, that it is by virtue of its ideal attributes that each Form (other than the Form of the Good) is the best object of its kind. Let us take the examples of Circle and Justice, a mathematical and an ethical Form, and try to see this connection with each of the four ideal attributes I2. It is the ideal attribute of being circular in every respect or part of itself that makes the Form Circle a perfect circle or the best circle there is or can be; it is precisely the lack of this attribute that makes sensible circles imperfect circles, 'in contact with the straight everywhere'.[18] Again, the ideal attribute of being circular no matter compared to what assures us that there is no circle relative to which the Form Circle is not or is less circular. On the other hand, it is more difficult, as Keyt has noted,[19] to see a connection between being always circular and the superlative goodness of kind of the Form Circle. Actually, there are connections here and there from which Plato may have overgeneralized: for example, we count durability or high degree of resistance to change as a good-making characteristic in the case of such artefacts as knives, shields, and cars. Plato himself makes a similar connection in *Republic* 380d–381b, where he argues that the better a state or condition a thing is in the less liable it is to change. And in the case of some ethical concepts such as justice the connection seems very plausible: a man who is always just is more of a just man than one who is just in some temporal stretches and not others, other things being equal. But probably, given Plato's assumption that only what is invariable can be known, the best connection we can make between the ideal attribute of, say, being always circular and the superlative goodness of kind of the Form Circle is

---

[17] The conception of the Forms as paradigms or ideal exemplars, self-predicational or self-exemplifying has been brought out by a number of authors: P. Geach, 'The Third Man Again', *Philosophical Review*, 65 (1956), 72–82; Vlastos, 'A Metaphysical Paradox'; J. M. E. Moravcsik, 'Recollecting the Theory of Forms', in W. H. Werkmeister (ed.), *Facets of Plato's Philosophy* (1976); R. Smith, 'Mass Terms, Generic Expressions, and Plato's Theory of Forms', *Journal of the History of Philosophy* (Apr. 1978). [. . .] The theory of the Form of the Good I am presenting presupposes that the Forms are self-predicational or self-exemplifying during Plato's middle period—at least in the *Republic*, the *Symposium*, the *Timaeus*, and the *Phaedo*. [. . .] By 'self-predication' I do not mean the weak version that Vlastos calls 'Pauline self-predication' but something stronger. Vlastos disambiguates the sentence (1) 'Justice is just' into (2) 'The Form Justice is itself just' and (3) 'Justice is such that anyone who has this property is (necessarily) just' and calls (3) 'Pauline self-predication'. 'A Note on "Pauline Predications" in Plato', *Phronesis*, 19/2 (1974). [. . .]

[18] See Wedberg's discussion, esp. pp. 49–50 and notes, in his *Plato's Philosophy of Mathematics* (Stockholm, 1955).

[19] 'The Mad Craftsman of the *Timaeus*', e.g. 233.

between the attributes and the epistemic value of the Form: this attribute contributes to the Form Circle's being the epistemic paradigm of its kind, the best object of its kind to know. And the same seems to be true of the fourth ideal attribute, being circular to all who apprehend it no matter from where. It seems then that the first two ideal attributes of the Form Circle contribute to its being the best circle there is or can be, and the remaining two attributes contribute to its being the best circle to know. And presumably similarly for the other Forms other than the Form of the Good. If so, we can add another proposition to Plato's theory of the Form of the Good:

(G13) It is by virtue of their ideal attributes that the Forms (other than the Form of the Good) are the best objects of their kind (or, have superlative goodness of kind).

And from G11.1 and G13, it seems that we can derive the proposition:

(G14) It is by virtue of participating in the Form of the Good that all the other Forms are the best objects of their kind and the best objects of their kind to know.

Thus the Form of the Good is, as it should be, the formal cause of the superlative goodness of kind of all the other Forms. We can see, perhaps in a short-circuit way, that this proposition is on the right track, from a Platonic point of view, on the assumption that the Forms (other than the Good) are ideal exemplars: for on this assumption the Forms have something in common, namely, their being the best objects of their kind; so it is natural that there should be a Form in virtue of which they have this in common, and in view of what this common feature is, it is natural that the Form would be the Good.

But now, having seen how it is appropriate for the Good to be the formal cause of the superlative goodness of kind of the Forms, we are faced with the question of how it is that it is also appropriate for the Good to be the formal cause of the superlative reality of kind of the Forms. For on Vlastos's interpretation of the doctrine of degrees of reality it is by virtue of (what we have called) their ideal attributes that the Forms are the most real objects of their kind. And from this and G11.1 it seems that we can derive the proposition:

(G15) It is by virtue of participation in the Form of the Good that all the other Forms are the most real objects of their kind.

The answer to our question is, I believe, that here we do have a conflation of superlative reality and superlative goodness of kind. For it is by virtue of the very same ideal attributes, it seems, that a Form is both the best object of its kind and the most real object of the same kind. Thus the superlative goodness of a given kind and the superlative reality of the same kind coincide, not only in the sense that the best and most real object of a given kind are one and the same, i.e. the Form of that kind, but also in the stronger sense that it is the very same ideal attributes of a Form that constitute both its superlative reality and its superlative goodness of kind. But here we must be careful when we speak of 'conflation': Vlastos has argued successfully, I believe, that Plato distinguishes between reality and existence, and thus the above conflation does not by itself imply a confusion of existence and goodness. It is by means of this distinction, between reality and goodness on the one hand and existence on the other, that the theory would attempt to escape a Humean objection that one cannot validly derive 'ought' (value) from 'is' (fact) alone.[20]

III. IDEAL AND PROPER ATTRIBUTES

To make further progress we need to go to Q6, the question concerning the distinction between ideal and proper attributes. This distinction is crucial to our interpretation for a number of reasons, two of which are as follows: first, we answered the question concerning 'the being and essence' of the Forms in terms of the ideal attributes of the Forms, which of course presupposes the distinction; second, we attributed to Plato G12 partly on the basis of this distinction, and G12 itself is slated in terms of the distinction, so that we can hardly understand what G12 tells us about the Form of the Good unless we understand the distinction. Moreover, one would think that, as Keyt has pointed out,[21] the distinction seems a necessary one for a logical realist like Plato to draw or observe; or at any rate a useful one to draw or observe, if he could,[22] since, for example, it would

---

[20] On the present theory, to say that a sensible exists, say, a drawn circle, is to say that it participates in the proper attributes of some Form, the Form Circle. On the other hand, to say that a sensible circle is a good circle is to say that it participates to some significant degree in the ideal attributes of the Form Circle; or, to take a simpler, comparative case, to say that some sensible circle is better than another is to say that it participates to a greater degree in the ideal attributes of the Form Circle. On this interpretation existence does not admit of degrees, whereas goodness and reality do, and the former does not imply the latter. [. . .]

[21] 'The Mad Craftsman of the *Timaeus*', 230.

[22] In 'The "Two-Level Paradoxes" in Aristotle' Vlastos argues that the distinction is incompatible with the Platonic ontology. We take up this point shortly.

enable him to disarm the two-level paradoxes often hurled by Aristotle against the theory of Forms.[23]

The distinction has been recently discussed by Owen, Keyt, and Vlastos, though the terms 'ideal' and 'proper' are used only by Keyt.[24] All three writers find the source of the distinction in Aristotle, especially *Topics* 137[b]3–13, but it is not clear that they conceive the distinction exactly in the same way, and they disagree whether Plato or the Academy ever drew or observed or could have drawn the distinction (as well as whether Aristotle ever concedes it to the Platonists). Let us first take a brief look at the ways they draw it. Owen writes:

Given any Platonic Idea, at least two and possibly three very different sorts of things can be said about it. (A) Certain things will be true of it in virtue of its status as an Idea, e.g., that it is immutable. These predicates (call them 'A-predicates') will be true of any Idea whatever. (B) Certain things will be true of it in virtue of the particular concept it represents; these (call them 'B-predicates') are sometimes held to fall into two radically different groups. (B1) . . . (B2) Other predicates belong to the idea because . . . they are simply accepted as serving to define the particular concept in question. Man, for instance is two-footed and an animal. ('Dialectic and Eristic,' 108; cf. also 119–20)

We are not interested here in B1-predicates, but only in the distinction between A-predicates, corresponding to Keyt's ideal attributes, and B2-predicates, Keyt's proper attributes. Vlastos introduces the distinction in Aristotle's terms:

sentences of the form 'the Idea of F is P' . . . are analyzed by Aristotle as true if P is predicated of 'the Idea *qua* Idea' and false if predicated of it '*qua* F' as, e.g., 'The Idea of Man is resting,' whose ambiguity is resolved by the observation that 'resting belongs to Man-himself not *qua* man, but *qua* Idea.' (Here Vlastos quotes *Topics* 137[b]6–7: *Platonic Studies*, 323)

Presumably, the predicates that belong to the Idea Man *qua* Idea correspond to Owen's A-predicates and Keyt's ideal attributes; those that belong to the Idea Man *qua* man to their B-2 predicates and proper attributes. Finally, Keyt discusses the same *Topics* text, introducing and defining 'ideal' and 'proper' as follows:

Aristotle here distinguishes two respects in which a Form may possess an attribute. The attribute of rest belongs to the Idea of man as Idea; on the other hand, the

---

[23] Ibid. and Owen, 'Dialectic and Eristic in the Treatment of Forms'. I wish to note briefly here that there will be certain two-level paradoxes against which the distinction between ideal and proper attributes of Forms is totally helpless. The Form Change provides an extreme example. [. . .] In his discussion of such paradoxes Aristotle has nothing to be ashamed about in not bringing in this distinction.

[24] Owen, 'Dialectic and Eristic in the Treatment of Forms'; Keyt. 'Plato's Paradox'; and Vlastos, 'The "Two-Level Paradoxes" in Aristotle'.

attribute of being composed of soul and body belongs to the Idea of living creature as living creature. An attribute that belongs to an Idea as Idea I shall call an 'ideal' attribute. An ideal attribute is one whose absence from a thing entails that the thing is not a Platonic Idea. This is my definition, not Aristotle's; but I hope it marks out the class of attributes he has in mind. . . .

The second respect in which a Form may possess an attribute enters into Aristotle's characterization of a proprium; what is allegedly a proprium of such and such is really a proprium if and only if (1) it is an attribute of the Form of such and such, and (2) it belongs to the Form because the Form is such and such. Thus being composed of soul and body is a proprium of living creature since it is an attribute of the Form of living creature and an attribute because the Form is a living creature (b11–13); but rest is not a proprium of man since, although an attribute of the Form of man, it is not an attribute because the Form is a man.

Noting that Aristotle here has characterized a proprium in a broader fashion than usual, Keyt introduces his notion of a proper attribute:

Taking my lead from Aristotle's temporary, broad characterization of a proprium, I shall call an attribute that belongs to a Form in this second respect a 'proper' attribute. I use 'proper' here in the sense in which it means 'peculiar' and is opposed to 'common'. Again, I suggest a definition that I hope captures the class of attributes Aristotle has in mind: a *proper* attribute of a given Form is one whose absence from a thing entails that the thing is not an instance of the given Form. Thus animal is a proper attribute of the Form of man; for if a thing is not an animal it cannot be a man. ('Plato's Paradox', 12, 13)

The first question that arises is whether the distinction between proper and ideal attributes of Forms is compatible with the ontology of Plato's theory of Forms. Vlastos seems to argue that it is not. If he is right, it can hardly be a good idea to expound Plato's theory of the Form of the Good using this distinction, as I have done. We can use a distinction an author does not explicitly make to expound and illuminate his theory, provided the distinction is compatible with the theory; Vlastos himself did so in his illuminating paper 'An Ambiguity in the *Sophist*'. But if the distinction is not compatible, we will probably end up distorting the theory. Is Vlastos then right? Well, I think he is and he isn't. The issue turns on two points: (1) whether we conceive of the Forms as ideal exemplars complete with non-Pauline self-predication, or as properties that are not self-predicational; and, perhaps, (2) on how we construe sentences of the form '*P* belongs to the Form *F qua F*'. Vlastos is right, I think, if we conceive of the Forms as (transcendent) properties that are not non-Pauline self-predicational; and he is right in the sense that, under this conception, the distinction would not apply to the Forms at all. For, so far as I can see, if the Forms are not non-Pauline self-predicational, they would have no proper attributes at all and the distinction would be at the very least idle as applied to the Forms; and Vlastos would be right in arguing, as he does

(*Platonic Studies*, 332), that while the expression 'the Idea of Animal *qua* Idea' would have a referent, namely the Form Animal, the expression 'the Idea of Animal *qua* Animal' could or would have none (for indeed the latter expression implies that the Idea of Animal is an animal). On the other hand, if the Forms are conceived as ideal exemplars with non-Pauline self-predication, the distinction is perfectly compatible with the theory of Forms and applies to Forms; under this conception, the referent of the above two expressions would be one and the same, the Form Animal. To go to point (2), the function of the word translated '*qua*' in the present context is, I think, simply to indicate the inferential basis on which the attribute is asserted of the subject. Though we need a systematic study of Aristotle's uses of this important little word (he puts it to many important uses, and the notion is crucial to some later philosophers, such as Spinoza), I believe that in its present use it is the descendant, so to speak, of Plato's 'in virtue of' and can plausibly be rendered by 'because', as Owen and Keyt often take it. Thus to say, for example, that rest belongs to Living Creature *qua* Form is to indicate the inferential basis on which the attribute of rest is asserted of Living Creature itself. The complete inference is: Living Creature itself is a Form; all Forms are at rest; therefore, Living Creature itself is at rest. Similarly, to say that being composed of body and soul belongs to Living Creature itself *qua* living creature is to indicate the inferential basis on which the attribute is asserted of the subject. The complete inference is: Living creature itself is a living creature; all living creatures are composed of body and soul; therefore, Living Creature itself is composed of body and soul. Here non-Pauline self-predication is explicitly stated on the complete inference, and is implicit in the expression '*qua* living creature'. This construction of '*qua*', essentially as 'because', begins to disarm, I think, the other objection that Vlastos has to applying the distinction to Forms. He cites *Symposium* 211a, where Plato denies that the Form Beauty 'is beautiful in one way, ugly in another', and says that 'the Aristotelian formula establishes the P-distinction at the price of losing this very feature of the Idea, allowing it to be P and not-P but in different respects, P $\hat{\eta}$ F, not-P $\hat{\eta}$ ἰδέα τοῦ F' (*Platonic Studies*, 331). But on the present interpretation of '*qua*' as 'because' I do not think that the objection is sound: to allow that the attribute *P* belongs to the Form *F qua F* but not to the Form *F qua* Form is not necessarily to allow that the Form *F* is *P* in one respect and not-*P* in another; for on the present interpretation of '*qua*' as 'because' the negation sign goes in front of the whole 'because' clause, not in front of the attribute sign *P*. What is denied is not that *P* belongs to the Form of *F*, but only that *P* belongs to the Form *F* because it is a Form; and the latter denial is perfectly compatible with *P* belonging to the Form *F*. Thus,

Plato can deny that the attribute of being composed of body and soul belongs to the Form Living Creature because it is a Form, without denying that this attribute belongs to this Form. And the *Euthyphro* shows that Plato is capable of making such a point, since there he denies that anything, including Holiness, is holy because it is loved by all the gods while allowing that Holiness is loved by all the gods. In any case, in the *Symposium* passage what Plato is denying is that the Form Beauty can be qualified in any way relative to its proper, self-predicational attributes; i.e. He wants to say that the Form Beauty is beautiful in all respects, always, etc. This point would not be compromised by his allowing that the Form Beauty is beautiful because of the particular Form it is and also that it is at rest (invariant) because it is a Form.

I conclude, then, that the distinction between ideal and proper attributes is perfectly compatible with the ontology of Plato's theory of Forms, provided that we conceive of the Forms as ideal exemplars with self-predication, and provided that we interpret '*qua*' as 'because'. Here I must make it explicit that I am not maintaining that Plato always and consistently conceived of the Forms as ideal exemplars with self-predication. I am only maintaining that sometimes he so conceived them, and in particular that he so conceived them in the middle dialogues and in conjunction with his theory of goodness in the *Republic*. We shall presently see that this conception seems indeed essential to his theory of the Form of the Good.

We are now free to take up the question whether Plato ever made explicitly the distinction between proper and ideal attributes—which he never did—or the more interesting question whether he observed the distinction in practice. This question is related to our question Q7, how the goodness of sensible things is to be accounted for on the theory of the Form of the Good as we have interpreted it. Now Keyt has produced striking evidence that Plato actually confused ideal and proper attributes of Forms:

Although Aristotle, in commenting on the theory of Forms, draws this very distinction, there is striking evidence that Plato himself overlooked it. The evidence, apart from his silence on the matter, consists of some bad mistakes that he would have been unlikely to make if he had seen it. ('The Mad Craftsman of the *Timaeus*', 230)

The 'bad mistakes' consist of certain inferences that Plato makes in the *Timaeus* from certain Forms, used as models, having certain features to their sensible copies having these features. The general context is familiar. The divine craftsman (the Demiurge), being good and unenvious, wishes to make the sensible world as good as possible; to do this he takes the Forms as his models and fashions the sensible world after the Forms as much as possible. In particular the Demiurge copies the Form of living creature. This Form, Keyt says, 'has only one feature that a sane craftsman would copy, having a soul and a body' (a proper attribute of the Form); but 'the Demiurge is not content to stop here. He notices that his model is unique, timeless, and generic, and proceeds to copy these attributes' (presumably ideal attributes; p. 232). For the argument from uniqueness, Keyt quotes *Timaeus* 31a2–5 and interprets:

Plato's argument is this: the cosmos was made according to its model; its model is unique; therefore, the cosmos is unique. If Plato accepts this argument, he should also accept the following one, which in his system has true premises and a false conclusion: the planet Mercury was made according to its model (the Form of heavenly god); its model is unique; therefore, Mercury is the only heavenly god (that is the only celestial body). (pp. 232–3)

Concerning the inference from the second ideal attribute, Keyt cites 37c6–38c3 and interprets:

Plato's argument is this: the cosmos resembles its model as closely as it can; its model is timeless, which it cannot be; so the cosmos has a feature that resembles, although it falls short of, the timelessness of its model (namely, eternal temporal duration). By the same reasoning a circle that is drawn on paper and preserved for a year would resemble the Form of circle more closely than one that is drawn with the same accuracy but immediately erased.

Keyt makes a similar point regarding a similar inference from the attribute of being generic. He also cites *Parmenides* 132c9–11 as containing a similar argument, the argument 'that since Forms are thoughts (a hypothesis momentarily proposed by Socrates) and things share in the Forms, each of these things is itself composed of thoughts', and says that this argument is 'a paradigm of the fallacy of division' (pp. 234–5). It is because he copies these ideal attributes of the Forms that the Demiurge is 'mad'. And Vlastos, in his *Plato's Universe*, understandably refers to one of these inferences of Plato's as 'a curious error' (p. 29).

We are now in the happy or unhappy position to show that, given our interpretation of the Form of the Good in the *Republic*, Plato 'had' to make these 'curious errors' and his divine craftsman had to be 'mad'. For we can show that copying the ideal attributes of the Forms, if one wishes to make sensible things as good as possible, is a direct consequence of the views that the Form of the Good is the formal cause of the being and essence of the Forms and that the being and essence of the Forms consist in their ideal attributes. We are assuming that in the *Timaeus*, when Plato was making these errors, the Forms are still conceived as ideal exemplars—the best objects of their kind—for why else would the Demiurge copy *them* if he wished to make sensible things as good as possible? And the position is happy for our interpretation since it provides evidence for it, but unhappy for Plato if the inferences are the 'bad mistakes' Keyt seems to show them to be.

To see why it is that Plato had to make the 'curious mistakes' and why his Demiurge had to be 'mad', on the interpretation we have given of the Form of the Good, let us go to our question Q7: on this interpretation how is the goodness of sensible things to be accounted for? Let us work with three kinds of examples, a mathematical Form, Circle, a 'natural kind' Form, Living Creature, and an ethical Form, Justice. To be a circle or circular a sensible must participate in the Form Circle, and this is participation in the proper attributes of the Form, namely being circular (and perhaps to all those attributes being entailed by this proper attribute, e.g. being a figure). But to be a good circle (to some degree) a sensible, on the interpretation we have given, must participate (to some degree) in the *ideal* attributes of the Form Circle: for, on that interpretation, it is the ideal attributes of the Form Circle that constitute its superlative goodness and it is by virtue of having these ideal attributes that the Form Circle participates in the Form of the Good. Participation only in the proper attributes of the Form Circle (to some degree, if degrees of participation in proper attributes is allowed) would have no tendency to show that the sensible is a good circle (to some degree), for there is not necessarily any connection between the proper attributes of this Form (or the Form Triangle, or Square, or Chiliagon, or Four or Five) and the Form of the Good. But participation (to some degree, and here degrees are appropriate) in the ideal attributes of being circular in every respect, always, no matter compared to what, and to all who apprehend it no matter from where, would show that the participant is a good circle (to some degree, or comparatively), for it is these attributes that make the Form Circle the best circle there is or can be and it is by virtue of having these that it participates in the Form of the Good. And similarly with the goodness of sensible living creatures. Thus, if the Demiurge wished merely to create or fashion a sensible living creature it would be sufficient for him to copy the proper attributes of the Form of living creature, such as being composed of body and soul. But if he wishes to create a sensible living creature that is as good as possible he can *only* do so, given the present interpretation of the Form of the Good of the *Republic*, by copying as much as possible the ideal attributes of the Form. Thus, far from being 'mad' for doing so, he would be 'mad'—or rather futile—if he didn't! Correspondingly, 'the curious mistakes' and the 'bad arguments' of Plato should begin to appear less curious and not as bad: for we are now to understand the theory of the Form of the Good in the *Republic* as an implicit premiss(es) in these arguments. For example, the argument 'from eternity' would be more complicated, roughly perhaps as follows: the Form of Living Creature is the best living creature there is or can be: it is by virtue of being eternal (among other things, or 'eternal' standing for a summary of its ideal attributes) that it is the best object of its kind and it is by virtue of this that it participates in the Form of the Good; therefore, if one wishes to fashion a sensible living creature as good as possible one must copy the 'eternity' of the Form as much as possible.[25] Of course I am speaking here to the validity of Plato's argument, not its soundness—but this is the point to which Keyt is speaking and certainly part of Vlastos's 'curious'. The soundness of the argument is quite another matter, for this depends on the truth of the theory that according to me is the theoretical backbone of the argument.[26]

Even a casual glance at the theory reveals several faults or unclarities. One fault lies in the combination of the conception of Forms as self-predicational with the theory of goodness, the theory that the Form of the Good is the formal cause of the ideal attributes of the Forms and that it is by virtue of these that the Forms are the best objects of their kind. Without self-predication this theory of goodness would collapse; for without it the Forms would not be ideal examplars—the best objects of their kind—and so there would be no motivation at all for supposing that the Form of the Good is the formal cause of the being and essence of the Forms.[27] But why is this combination faulty? One fault is that the theory seems to imply all the absurdities of non-Pauline self-predication. To be the best possible shield—the best object of its kind—a thing would have to be both a Form

[25] The other two 'bad arguments' would be more difficult to reconstruct along the lines we reconstructed the 'eternity argument'. [. . .]

[26] We may note, in addition, that Plato or his craftsman would never make the mad mistakes of some of Keyt's illustrations, for example the mistake of making a paper shield and justifying himself on the ground that his pattern (model) was of paper ('Plato's Paradox', 231). Far from sanctioning such mistakes the theory excludes them wholesale: for no sensible object is a reliable model, certainly never the best model, for making a good object of a kind; only the best objects of a kind are, the ideal exemplars, the Forms; sensible objects are copies or copies of copies. The 'paperness' of the 'model' paper shield, far from making it the best shield there is or can be, makes it one of the worst—a point we can accept. Of course Keyt was only illustrating in this passage the type of mistake he is attributing to Plato—he was not saying that Plato or his Demiurge would make this mistake. But now we can see why they wouldn't. [. . .]

[27] A similar point is brought out by Vlastos in 'A Metaphysical Paradox': 'Only when Forms assume their other role, as objects of value, and the kind of value Plato claimed for them, would the self-characterization of Forms like Beauty have any point whatever' (p. 56). The notions of Forms as ideal exemplars, self-predication, and the Form of the Good as the formal cause of the being and essence of the Forms—all these go hand in hand. In so far as Plato gave up non-Pauline self-predication in later dialogues such as the *Sophist*—and the prominence of such a Form as Change may have forced him to do it—he would also be giving up, I think, the theory of the Form of the Good of the *Republic*. [. . .]

and a shield, an immaterial shield that cannot protect![28] Another difficulty
is that it is not clear how this theory of goodness coheres with the *other*
theory of goodness we find in *Republic* 1, the theory of function and virtue.
According to the latter theory, a thing of a given kind is a good thing of
that kind in so far as and to the degree to which it performs well the function proper to things of that kind. So we seem to have two criteria of kind
or attributive goodness of sensible things: the degree to which a sensible
of a kind resembles the ideal attributes of the Form of that kind, and the
degree to which that sensible does well the function proper to its kind.
How are the two criteria related? Plato uses both, and no doubt he holds
that the theory of the Form of the Good is the more fundamental one. If
so, the view he probably holds of the relation of the two criteria is that the
more a thing of a given kind resembles the ideal attributes of the Form of
that kind, the better it performs the function proper to things of that kind.
(Or, if we like slogans, we might say that for Plato 'function always follows
form'.) So far as I am aware Plato does not give us adequate reasons for
believing that this proposition is always true. There is little doubt though
that he holds the theory of the Form of the Good to be more fundamental than the functional theory of goodness. His holding this explains well
enough his remark in the first round that the definitions of the virtues in
book 4 have not been sufficiently established; for these definitions have
been constructed on the basis of the functional criterion, and for them to
be 'sufficiently' established, Plato would have to show that they are at least
consistent with, or perhaps that they are confirmed by, the theory of the
Form of the Good. So far as I am aware, Plato never tries to do this either,
though he tells us that the philosophers who have come to know the Good
'shall use it as a pattern for the right ordering of the state and the citizens
and themselves' (540a).[29] A third unclarity in the theory is that there seems

---

[28] It is not within the scope of this paper to detail all the varieties and absurdities of self-
predication. For a recent account, see Vlastos, *Platonic Studies*, 259–65; for an earlier account,
Allen (ed.), *Studies in Plato's Metaphysics*, 43–5. In correspondence Professor Charles Young
raised the interesting question whether something less than full-blown non-Pauline self-
predication may not be sufficient for the theory of the Form of the Good, sufficient, that is, for
the Forms being the best objects of their kind. In particular, we might draw a distinction between
the *formal* attributes of sensible things and their *material* attributes; the formal attributes of,
say, sensible knives (e.g. sharpness) are those mentioned in the definition of knifehood, which
sensible knives have by virtue of participating in the Form knife; material attributes (e.g. being
made of iron) are those they have by being the particular knives they are. We can then say that
it is only those attributes that knives have as formal attributes that the Form knife has as proper
attributes (and only these would be included in self-predications). [. . .]

[29] The fact that Plato does not directly derive from knowledge of the Form of the Good any
propositions as to what is good or right is the basis of Popper's referring to the theory of the
Form of the Good as 'this empty formalism' (*The Open Society and its Enemies* (London, 1966).
i. 146). In a sense Popper is right: the Form of the Good is a 'formal' property since it is the

to be a stronger connection between certain ethical Forms and the Form of the Good than Plato's theory allows. For Plato, being a just man (or a just city) entails being a good man (or a good city). But being just is certainly a proper attribute in the Form Justice. So, in addition to the connection between the ideality of the Form Justice and the Form of the Good (a connection which is the same as that between the ideality of any Form and the Form of the Good), there is a strong entailment connection between the proper attribute of the Form, being just, and the Form of the Good. This, it appears, is as it should be—I mean there ought to be such a connection. But if so, it seems to contradict the theory of the Form of the Good we have been expounding; or, at any rate, if this is so, the Form of the Good cannot consist just in the ideality common to all the Forms. And in the latter case why should we suppose that the goodness entailed by being just is the same as the goodness by virtue of which all the Forms are the best objects of their kind, or that there is even any connection between the two?[30] [. . .]

It must [. . .] be noted that since the I2 attributes of a Form entail its proper attributes (e.g. being always beautiful entails being beautiful), there is room here for a confusion that would be vast indeed. If the Form of the Good is thought of as containing or consisting in the I2 attributes of the Forms in a concrete rather than an abstract sense, then the Form of the Good would indeed entail all the proper attributes of all the other Forms. But I seriously doubt that Plato ever thought of the matter in this way. On such an interpretation, the Form of the Good would be a vast conjunction, a wild motley indeed, of all the I2 attributes, concretely conceived, of all the other Forms. I think that Plato thinks of the I2 attributes in an abstract way in so far as they are contained in the Form of the Good: it is in virtue of participating in the Form of the Good that the other Forms are 'always the same', 'the same in all respects', 'the same no matter com-

formal cause of the ideal or formal attributes of the Forms and not of their proper attributes. But the charge that this formalism is 'empty' is probably misguided. One might as well complain that one cannot directly derive information as to what things are good from Rawls's definition of 'attributive goodness' (*A Theory of Justice* (Cambridge, Mass., 1971) 399). We have seen that the goodness of sensible things (and of Forms) is attributive goodness or goodness of kind. It is part of the notion of attributive goodness that one cannot derive, just from knowledge of what goodness is, the proposition that something is a good K: one must also know the kind K. In Plato's theory one could not derive from knowledge of the Form of the Good alone the proposition that, say, Socrates is a good man: one would also need to know the Form Man (as well as information about Socrates). [. . .]

[30] To this we may add the related and unresolved difficulty of accounting for the negative ethical forms (the unjust, the bad) mentioned by Socrates at *Rep.* 476a. This difficulty was brought to my attenion by Bill Jacobs. For a brief recent discussion, see N. White, *A Companion to Plato's* Republic (1979), 41.

pared to what', and 'the same to all who apprehend them no matter from where'. These abstract phrases, the first of which he uses quite often, are supposed to catch the idea that, for example, it is not in virtue of participating in the Form of the Good that Square itself contains four right angles, but it is in virtue of participating in the Form of the Good that it *always* contains four right angles, contains four right angles *to all who apprehend it no matter from where*, and so on. We have to think here of I2 attributes in abstraction from the proper attributes contained in them. Plato, lacking the device of variables, tries to catch this abstraction, I believe, with the above abstract phrases ('always the same', 'the same in all respects', and so on). It is important to see how very Platonic this abstraction is: these phrases attempt to catch precisely what is common to I2 attributes.

We can finally end this long discussion of the second round by some hopefully educated speculation on what the Form of the Good would be given our interpretation of the theory. G12 tells us that the ideal attributes of all the other Forms are proper attributes of the Form of the Good, and G11.1 tells us that the Form of the Good is the formal cause of the other Forms having their ideal attributes. So it would seem that the Form of the Good consists in or is constituted by the very ideality common to all the other Forms by virtue of which they are the best objects of their kind and the best objects of their kind to know. Such ideality, it would seem, would have to be conceived pretty abstractly, supergenerally as it were. For one thing, it is not ideality, superlative goodness and superlative reality, of kind, as is the case with the other Forms. The Form of the Good is not a superlatively 'good something or other', as Cooper points out; it is presumably superlatively good, period. The goodness of the other Forms is indeed superlative but also partial, the goodness of kind. Moreover, the other Forms are not in a sense self-sufficient: they are the best objects of their kind of virtue of participating in the Form of the Good, and they are the most real objects of their kind for the same reason. But the Good itself is what it is presumably by virtue of itself.[31]

IV. THE THIRD ROUND: THE DIVIDED LINE

The third wave of paradox is the simile of the divided line, especially the upper two sections (509c–511e). Though the Form of the Good is not

---

[31] 'The Psychology of Justice in Plato', *American Philosophical Quarterly* (Apr. 1977), 154. I am indebted to Cooper not only for his illuminating remarks about the Form of the Good (pp. 154–5), but also for giving me the courage to try to think seriously about this difficult topic. [. . .]

explicitly mentioned in these passages (perhaps implicitly at 509d), there is almost universal agreement that the Form of the Good is at the top of the ontological division and knowledge of it at the top of the epistemological division. Fortunately, we are not concerned here with all of the line or a general interpretation of it, but only with the relations, ontological and epistemological, between the upper two sections. The chief passages are 509b, 510c–e, 511b–d. An immense amount has been written about these passages. Here I wish only to dispute two widely accepted points of interpretation and suggest an alternative interpretation which is the natural outcome of our discussion of the second round.

The first thing I wish to dispute is that Plato's point in calling the beginning of mathematics 'hypotheses' is that they are underived, unproved, or undemonstrated. Concerning what hypotheses Plato was referring to there is much dispute; just about everything has been suggested, including the odd itself and figures themselves, propositions asserting the existence of these, axioms attributing properties to these, or definitions of the odd, figures, and angles. In this dispute I do not enter. I assume that Plato was referring to whatever the mathematicians of his day used as Euclid uses definitions, axioms, and postulates. My concern is with his point in calling these 'hypotheses'. The majority of commentators (Adam, Cornford, Ross, to mention only a few[32]) suppose that his point is that these things are unproved, underived, or undemonstrated; and of course if they were used as Euclid uses definitions and axioms, they are. But I do not believe that this is Plato's point in calling them 'hypotheses' in the present context. For one thing, while Plato calls the beginnings of arithmetic and geometry 'hypotheses' and 'hypothetical' (he uses the noun, the verb, and the adjective), he twice in these passages calls the beginning point of dialectic, that is, the Good or knowledge of it, 'unhypothetical'. Now if this is meant to be a contrast, as it seems to be, it would suggest, given the point we are disputing, that Plato meant that the Form of the Good or knowledge of it is derived or proved. But there is no evidence in our passages that Plato thought this of the Form of the Good; on the contrary, by placing it at the top of the Line he implies that it is not proved or derived from anything. Indeed from what could it be derived in the present context? Adam, making the assumption we are disputing, says that it (the Good) is 'itself proved by an exhaustive scrutiny of all noeta' (intelligibles). Just what this means—and how this would make the Good 'unhypothetical'—he does not tell us. In the second place, and aside from evidence, if one of Plato's

---

[32] See e.g. J. Adam, *The Republic of Plato*, 2nd edn.; D. A. Rees, 'Plato and the Third Man', *Proceedings of the Aristotelian Society*, suppl. vol. 37 (1963), 165–76; Cornford, 'Mathematics and Dialectic in the *Republic* VI–VII', 65–6; Ross, *Plato's Theory of Ideas*, 54–5.

complaints about mathematics were that its beginnings are underived or unproved, a defect that dialectic does not have and can remedy, he would be holding an obviously untenable position: for dialectic too has to start somewhere and no matter where it started its beginning would have the same defect. But if the interpretation of 'hypotheses' we are disputing is not correct, what is? I think Plato's point in calling the beginning of mathematics 'hypotheses' is simply that they are not known, they do not constitute knowledge. As to whether the mathematicians realize this, Plato's text is somewhat ambiguous; he says that they regard them 'as known', 'give no account of them', supposing 'they are obvious to everybody' (510c). But he seems clear that dialectic 'does not consider the hypotheses beginnings but really hypotheses' (511b). The questions why the hypotheses do not constitute knowledge—and how dialectic can be of service to mathematics—we shall take up shortly.

The second major point of interpretation I wish to dispute is that Plato holds that once we (doing dialectic) have reached the Form of the Good and have knowledge of it, we can deduce or derive from this knowledge the hypotheses of the mathematicians. This idea goes naturally with the first point we disputed, since such a deduction would remedy the alleged defect of the hypotheses of the mathematicians. The idea that Plato had such a deduction in view is also widely held, from Adam to Cornford to Ross and beyond.[33] Indeed Cornford tried to suggest how such a deduction might possibly go by introducing another Form at the top, alongside the Good, namely Unity, presumably a mathematical Form. Ross correctly pointed out that there is no evidence whatsoever for this in our texts, but nevertheless continued to hold on to the idea of such a deduction. Now this idea seems to be the height of paradox indeed. To aim at deducing all of mathematics from a few principles is an ambitious but not paradoxical ideal, one that perhaps began to be approached in this century. To suppose that all of mathematics can be deduced from a single Platonic Form may begin to sound incredible. But to suppose further that this is the Form of the Good is paradoxical indeed; for there does not seem to be even a prima-facie connection between goodness and numbers and figures; for this role the Form of the Good seems to be the wrong Form altogether. Do we really have good evidence to suppose that in our passages Plato had such a deduction in mind? The passages in which Plato briefly describes the 'descent' from the Form of the Good to other Forms are obscure and ambiguous and the meaning of his words and phrases much

---

[33] Adam, *The Republic of Plato*, 67; Cornford, 'Mathematics and Dialectic in the *Republic* VI–VII', 82–3; Ross, *Plato's Theory of Ideas*, 54–6.

in dispute. Moreover, such a view would seem to involve a vast confusion of ideal and proper attributes. For the hypotheses of the mathematicians are about the proper attributes of the Forms the hypotheses are about; they are about the proper attributes of the Forms Odd, Even, Square, Acute Angle, and so on. But the Form of the Good is the formal cause of the ideal attributes of these and all the other Forms. How then are we going to get entailment relations between the attributes of the Form of the Good and the proper attributes of these mathematical Forms? Further, the Form of the Good is the formal cause of the ideal attributes of all the other Forms. Why then should the proper attributes of (some) mathematical Forms be singled out for such a deduction? And if they are not singled out, we would have similar deductions and entailment relations between the attributes of the Form of the Good and the proper attributes of other kinds of Forms, Forms such as Living Creature, Artefact, Planet, and what have you. And in that case what would the Form of the Good be? Instead of or in addition to being the very ideality of the Forms, it would also have to be, it seems, a conjunction of several diverse kinds of Forms, mathematical, natural, artificial, and so on. I see no evidence whatsoever that Plato thought of the Form of the Good in this way in our passages. It must be admitted of course that the idea of such a deduction is a powerful one and is probably modelled on the deduction of theorems from hypotheses by the mathematicians: if the hypotheses are known, valid derivations from them of the theorems will yield knowledge of the theorems; similarly, valid derivations of the hypotheses from known things will yield knowledge of the hypotheses. Moreover, the influence of the Pythagoreans, the high esteem in which Plato held mathematics, the high place of mathematical studies in the education of the rulers, all these render general plausibility to the idea that Plato held that there is some intrinsic connection between some mathematical Forms and the Form of the Good. All the same I doubt that this interpretation is correct.

But if it isn't, what is? It seems to me that the epistemology of the upper portions of the divided line should be interpreted on the basis of the second round. An obvious clue and a solid handle is provided by the idea of the second round that the Form of the Good is 'the cause' of the knowability of the Forms. The sense we have given to this idea is that it is by virtue of their ideal attributes (I1 and I2) that the Forms are knowable entities and that the Form of the Good is the formal cause of the other Forms' ideal attributes. We have here clearly a theory of what a knowable object is: to be knowable an object must be ungenerated, indestructible, not subject to increase and decrease, must exist by itself (I1 attributes), it must always be the same, the same in every respect, the same no matter compared to what, and the same to all who apprehend it no matter from where (I2 attributes). This theory has at least one virtue: it is difficult to see how anyone who was acquainted (with 'the mind's eye') with such entities could make a mistake about them; at any rate a whole set of mistakes due to variability and spatial location have been summarily excluded (though it is difficult to see how purely logical errors have also been excluded). And this coheres well with the very strong distinction drawn at the end of book 5 between knowledge and belief in terms of their powers and their objects. Now this puts the dialectician in an epistemologically superior position to the mathematician. For unlike the latter, the former deals only with Forms: both in the ascent and descent to and from the Form of the Good the dialectician begins, deals with, and ends with nothing but Forms. Because of this and the nature of his objects, he is assured freedom from error; at any rate freedom from error as to what his objects are, the attributes that a Form can be 'seen' to have without recourse to inference. The mathematicians, on the other hand, are at best in an ambiguous epistemological position: they deal with Forms and with visible figures as images of Forms; they talk about the visible figures; but they are thinking about their models and making their hypotheses about them. Their hypotheses could be interpreted, by others perhaps, as being either about the visible figures or about their models. In so far as their thought, their mathematical intuitions, derive from the visible figures, they are not assured freedom from error (even though they may not be making any actual error). Plato says that they regard their hypotheses as known and obvious to everybody and give no account of them. What sort of being 'known' and 'obviousness' is he talking about? I think he is referring to the 'obviousness' of the visible figures; it is the visible illustrations that would make the hypotheses 'obvious to everyone'—precisely the things that, in Plato's theory, could not make the hypotheses knowledge. And what sort of 'account' is it that the mathematicians do not give of their hypotheses? I have argued that he does not mean that they are underived; and I think he does not mean that they give no definitions of the concepts they use, for surely they did construct definitions, and Euclid's *Elements* (much later of course) begins with definitions. I think Plato means that the mathematicians give no epistemological account of the sorts of objects they want their hypotheses to be about: not the visible figures but their models. They do not, for example, ask themselves and seek to answer the question what sorts of objects must the objects of our hypotheses be if our hypotheses are to be always true? They have no theory of the objects their hypotheses must (according to Plato anyway) be about if the hypotheses are to be true and to constitute knowledge. Because of their practice of using sensible figures they are liable to error, or at least are not assured freedom from error. Because of this practice they are also not in a position to 'see' the objects of their hypotheses 'in splendid isolation' from sensible figures and thus begin to appreciate their nature. And also because, as mathematicians at least, they do not raise the above type of questions, they lack a theory of objects proper to mathematics. The dialectician, dealing only with Forms, has a chance to appreciate their common nature—their nature as ideal objects possessing ideal attributes I1 and I2. And if he asks the perfectly Platonic question 'By virtue of what do the Forms have these attributes in common?' presumably he will arrive at the conception of the Good. Looking downward from the Form of the Good the dialectician would see clearly what are Forms and what are not Forms; he would never make the mistake of confusing Forms with sensible instances, for he has now grasped the nature of the Forms—the notion of what it is to be a Form. And if at any rate he has Plato's conception of knowledge, the dialectician would see that only the Forms are possible objects of knowledge, that mathematics must be only about Forms if it is to be knowledge, and that the visible figures are irrelevant to the truth or knowability of the hypotheses. It is in this sense that the Form of the Good is the 'cause' of reason's knowing the Forms, mathematical or otherwise. What the super-science of dialectic would do for mathematics is not to provide a supergeneral known basis from which mathematical hypotheses can be deduced, but rather to provide a theory of objects that mathematical hypotheses must be about if mathematics is to be knowledge. Such a theory would 'free' mathematics from sensible figures in the sense that according to it sensible figures are never evidence that the hypotheses are true or known.

V. SUMMARY

What is the moral of our story? I think it is that the theory of the Form of the Good in the *Republic* is truly the centrepiece of the canonical Platonism of the middle dialogues, the centrepiece of Plato's metaphysics, epistemology, ethics, and politics, and even his theory of love and art. The Form of the Good serves his metaphysics by bringing into relief the very ideality of the Forms, the eternal order and stability of the entities that must exist if this world is not to be a 'vast sea of dissimilarity'. It serves his epistemology by bringing into relief the knowability of the Forms, the attributes some objects must have if there is to be knowledge. The Form of the Good serves his ethics and politics, and his theory of love and art, by bringing into relief the superlative goodness of the Forms, the features that must be imitated if the imitations are to have any value. In his theory of the Form of the Good Plato was truly the first grand philosophical synthesizer. If to achieve such a grand synthesis he had to employ a few unholy combinations, such as the combination of reality, goodness, and self-predication, he may perhaps be forgiven—at least if he is understood.

A minor moral, I hope, is that when Plato looked into 'the orb of light' he really did see something. It is perhaps an ironic tribute to his artistry, so evident in the three great similes, that when many others looked into the same orb of light through Plato's telescope they were warmed and elevated even though, apparently, they saw nothing.

X

THE LOGIC OF THE THIRD MAN

S. MARC COHEN

The main problems facing the interpreter of the Third Man Argument (TMA) in Plato's *Parmenides* (132a1–b2) arise not so much from what Plato says as from what he does not say. Gregory Vlastos, in his famous paper of 1954,[1] points out that the argument is formally a *non sequitur* and sets out to discover the suppressed premisses of the argument. The literature dealing with the TMA, already large in 1954, has become enormous since then, and all of the authors I have read have followed Vlastos at least this far. But beyond a shared belief that the TMA as written is formally invalid and that in order to understand the argument we must identify its suppressed premisses, there has been little agreement among the commentators. What *are* the suppressed premisses? Is Plato committed to holding them? Is the argument, with the addition of such premisses, valid? Did Plato think it was? What does it prove? What did Plato think it proves? Radically different answers have been offered to these questions, and I do not expect to offer definitive answers to any of them in this paper. What I hope to do is to show in what way the main lines of interpretation offered to date are inadequate, and to advance a formalization of the TMA which avoids these inadequacies and seems to me better to reveal the logical structure of the argument. On the basis of my examination of the logic of the TMA I conclude that the philosophical point of the argument is different from what it has been generally supposed to be.

From *Philosophical Review*, 80 (1971), 448–75. Copyright © 1971 Cornell University. Reprinted by permission of the publisher and the author.

[1] 'The Third Man Argument in the *Parmenides*', *Philosophical Review*, 63 (1954), 319–49; repr. with an addendum in R. E. Allen (ed.), *Studies in Plato's Metaphysics* (London, 1965), 231–63. Subsequent references will be to the reprinted version, which will be cited hereafter as 'TMA I'.

276 S. MARC COHEN

I

The text, in Cornford's translation, reads as follows:

I imagine your ground for believing in a single form in each case is this. When it seems to you that a number of things are large, there seems, I suppose, to be a certain single character which is the same when you look at them all; hence you think that largeness is a single thing. . . . But now take largeness itself and the other things which are large. Suppose you look at all these in the same way in your mind's eye, will not yet another unity make its appearance—a largeness by virtue of which they all appear large? . . . If so, a second form of largeness will present itself, over and above largeness itself and the things that share in it, and again, covering all these, yet another, which will make all of them large. So each of your forms will no longer be one, but an indefinite number.

Vlastos, in his original account of the TMA, transcribes what he identifies as the first two steps of the argument in the following way:

(A1) If a number of things, a, b, c, are all F, there must be a single Form F-ness, in virtue of which we apprehend a, b, c, as all F.

(A2) If a, b, c, and F-ness are all F, there must be another Form, F-ness$_1$, in virtue of which we apprehend a, b, c, and F-ness as all F.[2]

It is obvious that (A2) does not follow from (A1), and so Vlastos concludes that 'there must have been something more in Plato's mind than the information supplied at (A1)'[3] to make the inference to (A2) seem plausible. Now the question of what was in Plato's mind at this point is admittedly a difficult one; but Vlastos is content to raise 'a more modest question: What are the simplest premises, not given in the present Argument, which would have to be added to its first step, to make (A2) a legitimate conclusion?'[4] In answer to this question he produces two premises, one to justify the antecedent of (A2) and one to justify its consequent. The two premises are the well-known self-predication (SP) and non-identity (NI) Assumptions:

(SP) Any Form can be predicated of itself. Largeness is itself large. F-ness is itself F.[5]

(NI) If anything has a certain character, it cannot be identical with the Form in virtue of which we apprehend that character. If x is F, x cannot be identical with F-ness.[6]

Given (A1), these two premises are supposed to yield (A2) in the following way. It is a commonplace that there are F things—say, a, b, c. (A1) tells us that there is a Form, F-ness, in virtue of which we apprehend these as F. (SP) tells us that this Form, F-ness, is another F thing. But (NI) tells us that the Form in virtue of which we apprehend all of a, b, c, and F-ness as F things cannot be F-ness. Hence, it must be a second Form, F-ness$_1$. And this amounts to an assertion of (A2).

---

[2] 'TMA I', 232–3. [3] Ibid. 236. [4] Ibid. [5] Ibid. [6] Ibid. 237.

But, as Vlastos himself noticed, there is something strange about the way in which these new premises operate. For it is obvious that (SP) and (NI) are inconsistent; together they entail that F-ness is not identical with F-ness, which is self-contradictory. Indeed, they are formal contradictories, as Peter Geach pointed out;[7] (SP) is the assumption that F-ness is an F thing, and (NI) amounts to the assumption that F-ness is not an F thing. But this does not discourage Vlastos from insisting upon (SP) and (NI) as being the TMA's implicit premises. For they are surely *sufficient* to generate (A2) (and hence the entire regress) just because they are inconsistent and can generate any conclusion we like. But since they are inconsistent, Vlastos feels he must conclude that Plato did not realize that these were the argument's implicit premises: 'If Plato had identified all the premises which are necessary (and sufficient) to warrant the second step of the Third Man Argument, he would not have produced the Third Man Argument at all.'[8] That the premises necessary to generate the TMA are inconsistent is thus a cornerstone of Vlastos's interpretation—for it is on this basis that he concludes that Plato did not know what premises he was using, on the charitable assumption a philosopher—or Plato, anyway—will not produce an argument whose premises are inconsistent unless he is unaware of the inconsistency of the premises. And in the case of a premiss set consisting of the formally contradictory pair (SP) and (NI), the only way to be unaware of the inconsistency of the premises is to be unaware of one or both of the premises.

It seems to me to be a matter of some importance for our understanding of the TMA to determine whether these premises *are* necessary to generate the regress. Let us be clear that we understand what is involved in the claim that (SP) and (NI) are indispensable premises. If (SP) and (NI), as formulated, were required as TMA premises, the conclusion of the argument would itself have to be logically inconsistent. A proposition is itself inconsistent if the *only* premiss set from which it will follow is an inconsistent one. But, worse still, if the conclusion were inconsistent, then it would make no sense to say that (SP) and (NI) in particular are *required* as premises—for any other inconsistent set of premises would do just as well. But is the conclusion of Plato's argument inconsistent? The conclusion, we recall, is this: 'Each of your forms will no longer be one, but an indefinite number.' I suppose there may be some inclination to regard this conclusion as logically inconsistent, for it seems to say of the Forms that each *one* is *not* one, but many. But this inclination finds no real support in Plato's text and is fostered only by a peculiarity in Cornford's

[7] 'The Third Man Again', *Philosophical Review*, 65 (1956), 72–82; repr. in Allen (ed.), *Studies in Plato's Metaphysics*, 265–77. Subsequent references will be to the reprinted version.
[8] 'TMA I', 241.

translation.[9] The conclusion of the TMA ($o\dot{v}\kappa\acute{\epsilon}\tau\iota$ $\delta\grave{\eta}$ $\check{\epsilon}\kappa\alpha\sigma\tau\acute{o}\nu$ $\sigma o\iota$ $\tau\hat{\omega}\nu$ $\epsilon\grave{\iota}\delta\hat{\omega}\nu$ $\check{\epsilon}\sigma\tau\alpha\iota$ . . .) is explicitly the contradictory of that thesis ($\check{\epsilon}\nu$ $\check{\epsilon}\kappa\alpha\sigma\tau o\nu$ $\epsilon\hat{\iota}\delta o\varsigma$) of the Theory of Forms which Parmenides cites at 132a1 and then sets out to refute in the regress argument. And the thesis that Parmenides sets out to refute is not the triviality that each Form is one (Form), but rather, as Cornford correctly puts it, that there is 'a single Form in each case'. (I will have more to say later about how the phrase $\check{\epsilon}\nu$ $\check{\epsilon}\kappa\alpha\sigma\tau o\nu$ $\epsilon\hat{\iota}\delta o\varsigma$ should be taken.) So the conclusion of the argument should read: 'And so there will no longer be *one* Form for you in each case, but infinitely many.'[10] So formulated, the conclusion no longer has even the look of a logical inconsistency.

Thus it simply cannot be true that an inconsistent premiss set—{(SP), (NI)} or any other, for that matter—is *necessary* for generating the infinite regress of Forms that the TMA purports to generate; the proposition that there are an infinite number of Forms of Largeness, for example, may be a most peculiar proposition, but it is not an inconsistent one. And if these assumptions are not necessary for generating the regress, there can be no good reason for trying to foist them on Plato. For (SP) and (NI) were introduced in the first place on the basis of their logical, not textual, credentials. And even if texts can be found which show that Plato was, after all, committed to each of these inconsistent assumptions, this will still not justify their introduction as premisses of the TMA. The TMA intrigued Plato as it has countless of his readers; and Vlastos's reconstruction of it has the defect of robbing the regress of its interest.

II

None of what I have said so far is really new. Vlastos's critics from the first have been dissatisfied with his reconstruction of the TMA for just this reason. The first and one of the most powerful of these critics, Wilfrid Sellars, proposed a formalization of the argument with a consistent premiss set.[11] Since I have argued that such a formalization is a desideratum, a look at the Sellars version will be in order.

---

[9] Cornford's reading is, of course, grammatically possible. My point is that it is not the only possible reading, and that the only reasonable way to understand the conclusion is as the denial of the $\check{\epsilon}\nu$ $\check{\epsilon}\kappa\alpha\sigma\tau o\nu$ $\epsilon\hat{\iota}\delta o\varsigma$ thesis.

[10] Vlastos's translation in his most recent TMA paper ('Plato's "Third Man" Argument (*Parm.* 132a1–b2): Text and Logic', *Philosophical Quarterly*, 19 (1969), 289–301, henceforth cited as 'TMA II'), 293. Interestingly, nowhere in 'TMA I' does Vlastos actually produce a translation of the TMA's conclusion, although there are numerous allusions to it.

[11] 'Vlastos and "The Third Man"', *Philosophical Review*, 64 (1955), 405–37; repr. in *Philosophical Perspectives* (Springfield, Ill., 1967), 23–54. Subsequent references will be to the reprinted version.

Sellars's main point is that the self-predication and non-identity assumptions do not have to be understood as contradictories. His argument turns on the question of how we are to treat the expression '*F*-ness' in the formalization of the argument. More precisely, his question is this: to what syntactic category do we assign the substituends for '*F*-ness'?[12] One possibility is to regard substituends for '*F*-ness' as proper names of Forms: 'Largeness', for example, or 'Redness'. In this case '*F*-ness' would be what Sellars calls a *representative symbol* or *representative name*. Another possibility is to regard substituends for '*F*-ness' as variables proper. To do so entitles us to quantify with respect to the substituends for *F*-ness and say, 'There is a Redness such that . . .' or 'For all Largenesses . . .', and so forth, which would be syntactically inappropriate if 'Redness' and 'Largeness' were names. Now the expression '*F*-ness' combines what Sellars calls these 'modes of variability', and is a *representative variable*. That is, '*F*-ness' stands in place of, or represents, not a class of names but a class of variables.

Looked at in this way, (SP) and (NI) are defective in that they contain free occurrences of the representative variable '*F*-ness'.[13] The defect can be remedied with the aid of quantifiers; the result is the Sellars version of the two assumptions:

(SP′) All *F*-nesses are *F*.
(NI′) If *x* is *F*, then *x* is not identical with *the F*-ness by virtue of which it is *F*.[14]

And, as Sellars correctly points out, 'the inconsistency vanishes'.

Sellars is now able to generate the regress from a consistent premiss set containing, in addition to (SP′) and (NI′), the following two premisses:

(G) If a number of entities are all *F*, there must be an *F*-ness by virtue of which they are all *F*.
(P) *a*, *b*, *c*, and so forth, particulars, are *F*.

---

[12] I use 'substituends for "*F*-ness"' here as short for the more appropriate expression: 'expressions which result from "*F*-ness" when "*F*" is replaced by one of its substituends'.

[13] Strictly speaking, the defect is this: every substitution instance of each of (SP) and (NI) contains free occurrences of the variables represented by '*F*-ness'.

[14] Sellars's formulation, (NI′), is not quite right as it stands. For (NI′), together with the other assumptions, will not generate the regress as Plato envisages it. Plato thinks of the particulars *a*, *b*, *c* as being *F* in virtue of the first Form, *F*-ness I, and *all* of these, in turn, as being *F* in virtue of a second Form, *F*-ness II. But (NI′) disallows this, since it requires that there be, for each *F* thing, such a thing as *the F*-ness by virtue of which it is *F*. Hence *F*-ness II cannot cover any of the particulars that *F*-ness I covers, and the regress will not develop. The formulation of the non-identity assumption that Sellars requires would be, rather, this: If *x* is *F*, then *x* is not identical with any of the *F*-nesses by virtue of which it is *F*.

The proof is a non-terminating sequence which proceeds in this way: (P) provides us with a stock of *F*s, (G) generates a Form by virtue of which they are all *F*, (NI′) establishes that none of the *F*s in the stock is identical with the Form (G) has generated, and (SP′) establishes that the Form just generated is an *F*. Thus our stock of *F*s is increased by one, and we are ready for new applications of (G), (NI′), and (SP′) which will generate fresh Forms, *ad infinitum*.

This argument Vlastos himself regards as 'incomparably better'[15] than an argument whose premiss set is inconsistent, as all versions Vlastos has produced have been. The only thing wrong with it, according to Vlastos, is that it is not supported by the text and so cannot be regarded as a version of the argument Plato presented. The reason it does not fit the text, according to Vlastos,[16] is that (G) represents Plato as saying that there is *at least one* Form corresponding to a given character, whereas Plato's own words, both throughout the TMA and elsewhere in the dialogues, make clear that he means to be saying that there is *just one* Form corresponding to a given character. The word 'one' ($\ddot{\varepsilon}\nu$ or $\mu i\alpha$) occurs five times in the TMA, and at each occurrence, Vlastos argues, it means '*just one*' and not '*at least one*'. And, as Vlastos further argues, in numerous other places[17] where Plato uses the phrases $\ddot{\varepsilon}\nu$ $\varepsilon\mathring{i}\delta o\varsigma$ or $\mu i\alpha$ $\mathring{i}\delta\acute{\varepsilon}\alpha$ (or their equivalent) he means '*one* Form', 'a *single* Form', not 'at least one Form'. Here Vlastos is surely correct:[18]

---

[15] 'TMA II', 293.

[16] Vlastos has located the difficulty in Sellars's account in different places at different times. In his 1955 reply to Sellars ('Addenda to the Third Man Argument: A Reply to Professor Sellars', *Philosophical Review*, 64 (1955), 438–48) he claimed that substituends for '*F*-ness' are not variables but proper names of Forms. This takes us back to (SP) and (NI) as Vlastos originally formulated them: an inconsistent pair. He now maintains that the self-predication and non-identity assumptions were defectively formulated in 'TMA I', that they are not, when properly formulated, an inconsistent pair, but that the TMA premiss set is *still* inconsistent since it must contain a version of (G) according to which 'the Form corresponding to *F* is unique' ('TMA II', 300 n. 39; cf. 292).

   That the TMA premiss set is an inconsistent triad (rather than an inconsistent pair) was first put forward, to my knowledge, by Anders Wedberg (*Plato's Philosophy of Mathematics* (Stockholm, 1955), ch. III, esp. pp. 36–7). Wedberg's premiss set is this:

   (i) A thing is *Y* if and only if it participates in the Idea of *Y*-ness.
   (ii) An Idea is never one among the objects participating therein.
   (iii) The Idea of *Y*-ness is (a) *Y*.

This premiss set has (ii), a non-self-participation assumption, in place of Vlastos's (NI). And while (ii) and (iii) are consistent (i.e. self-predication is compatible with non-self-participation) the addition of (i) produces an inconsistent set. On the inconsistency of {(SP′), (NI′), (G1)}, see n. 20 below.

[17] *Rep.* 476a, 507b, 596a; *Prm.* 131a8–9, 132b5, c3–4, 133b1–2.

[18] Another possible interpretation has been offered by Colin Strang ('Plato and the Third Man', *Proceedings of the Aristotelian Society*, suppl. vol. 37 (1963), 147–63). Strang argues that although the occurrences of $\ddot{\varepsilon}\nu$ in a1 and b2 must be taken to mean 'exactly one', the occurrences of $\mu i\alpha$ and $\ddot{\varepsilon}\nu$ in a2, a3, and a7 need only be taken to mean 'at least one'. But why should

when Parmenides concludes that there is not *one* Form in each case, but rather an infinite number, he means to be denying the ἕν ἕκαστον εἶδος thesis. So that thesis must surely be that there is *exactly* one Form in each case; if ἕν meant 'at least one', the conclusion of the TMA would not contradict that thesis. It seems to me that the best reason for trying to read ἕν here as 'at least one' would have been this: if ἕν means 'exactly one', then (G) cannot be correct as a formulation of the TMA's first premiss. Rather, that premiss would apparently have to be, as Vlastos suggests,

(G1) If a number of entities are all *F*, there must be exactly one Form corresponding to the character, *F*; and each of those entities is *F* by virtue of participating in that Form,[19]

and it is easy to see that (G1), (SP′), and (NI′) form an inconsistent set.[20]

III

We seem to be faced with the following dilemma: when Plato introduces a Form for the 'many large things' with the words μία ἰδέα, we must interpret him as meaning either 'at least one' or 'exactly one'. If we take the former reading we can generate the regress from a consistent premiss set but only at the cost of misreading the text; if we take the latter reading, we will be fair to the text but only at the cost of leaving the argument's premiss set inconsistent. Neither of these alternatives is very attractive.

Fortunately, there is a way out of the dilemma. It is to show that the second horn contains a mistake, and that we can read μία and ἕν throughout as 'exactly one' and still have a consistent premiss set. We can make a beginning in this direction by noticing that, even if we agree that μία means 'exactly one', Vlastos's (G1) is not the only alternative to Sellars's (G). Another alternative would be:

---

we assume that Plato is using ἕν equivocally in the TMA, shifting senses from one line to the next? Strang's only reason seems to be that the assumption of such a shift in senses enables him to reconstruct the TMA as a valid argument with consistent premisses and a conclusion which is the denial of the uniqueness thesis. But, as I hope to show below, it is possible to produce such a reconstruction without assuming any equivocation on ἕν. If I am right in this contention, Strang's interpretation should lose much of its appeal.

[19] Adapted from Vlastos, 'TMA II', 290.

[20] Given the assumption that there are *F* things. For suppose there are; then by (G1) there is exactly one Form—call it '*F*-ness'—corresponding to the character *F*. By (SP′) *F*-ness is itself an *F* thing and by (NI′) *F*-ness is not identical with the Form by virtue of which it is *F*. But according to (G1) *F*-ness is the Form by virtue of which *each* *F* thing is *F*, so *F*-ness is, after all, identical with the Form by virtue of which it is *F*. So *F*-ness both is, and is not, identical with the Form by virtue of which it is *F*.

(G2) If a number of entities are all *F*, there must be exactly one Form
      by virtue of which they are all *F*.

Two points should be noted about (G2). First, it is a more reasonable alternative to (G) than is (G1), since it differs from (G) *only* in that it replaces
'*an F*-ness' with 'exactly one Form', which is really all one is entitled to if
one's only objection to (G) is that (G) is based on a misreading of μία ἰδέα.
Second, (G2) does not assert that there is a unique Form corresponding
to the character *F*, as (G1) does, but only that, given a number of *F*s, there
is a unique Form corresponding to *them*, in virtue of which *they* are all *F*.
Thus (G2) leaves open the possibility, as (G1) does not, that there is more
than one Form corresponding to the character *F*. It does not *assert* this—
for, after all, that is the *conclusion* of the argument, and we should hardly
expect the conclusion itself to be baldly asserted in a single premiss—but
it does not rule it out, either. And it leaves this possibility open in spite of
the fact that it reads μία as 'exactly one' and not 'at least one'.[21]

But are there not difficulties with (G2)? (G2) seems to tell us this: (1)
if *a*, *b*, and *c* are all *F*, then there is exactly one Form by virtue of which
they are all *F*, and (2) if *h*, *i*, and *j* are all *F*, then there is exactly one Form
by virtue of which they are all *F*. The question whether the Form introduced in (2) is the same Form introduced in (1) is left open. But not for
long; for (G2) also tells us that (3) if *a*, *b*, *c*, *h*, *i*, and *j* are all *F*, then there
is exactly one Form by virtue of which they are all *F*. And now our option
to treat the Forms introduced at (1) and (2) as distinct seems to be can-
celled. For the Form introduced at (3) must be identical with the Form
introduced at (1), for it is by virtue of just *one* Form that *a*, *b*, and *c* are *F*.
But, by parity of reasoning, the Form introduced at (3) must be identical
with the Form introduced at (2). So we have one Form after all, and not
two or three. And now it seems that (G2) has been reduced to (G1), with
the result that we are still faced with the dilemma that (G2) was supposed
to get us out of.

This is one way of reading (G2), but it is not the only way. As we have

---

[21] There are good logical reasons for insisting that (G1) simply *cannot* be an indispensable
premiss. For (G1) embodies (in part) the *uniqueness* claim:

(U) There is exactly one Form corresponding to each character or property,

which is precisely what the conclusion of the TMA denies. Since not-(U) is the conclusion, (U)
cannot be required as a premiss. Vlastos's reply to Sellars ('Addenda to the Third Man Argument', 440) suggests that he would justify the inclusion of (U) in the premiss set on the ground
that the TMA is a *reductio*. But this would be to confuse the argument with its proof. If not-
(U) is a consequence of a set of premisses which includes (U), then it is a consequence of that
set with (U) deleted. Indeed, this is the leading principle of *reductio* proofs. Hence (G1), which
entails (U), cannot be *required* as a TMA premiss.

been reading (G2) it comes to this. If, say, F-ness I is the one Form corresponding to a given set of Fs, then F-ness I is the one Form corresponding to any subset of that set; members of that set participate in F-ness I and are F by virtue of that participation and they participate in no other F-ness. But it is possible to read (G2) differently; we can suppose it comes to this: if F-ness I is a Form corresponding to a given set of Fs, then F-ness I is the *only* F-ness corresponding to precisely *that* set. Other Forms might correspond to subsets of that set, but no other Form will correspond to that set itself. If we read (G2) this way, the argument of the preceding paragraph designed to show that (G2) reduces to (G1) will fail; for that argument depended on the assumption that the Form corresponding to a given set of Fs is the Form corresponding to each of its subsets.[22]

Put another way, our difficulty so far has been this: (G) and (G2), the two versions of Plato's one-over-many principle that we have been considering,[23] make reference to Fs but not to sets of Fs. Since they make no reference to sets of Fs, the force of (G) and (G2), respectively, can be given in these two quantificational versions:

(G3) For any x, if x is F then there is at least one F-ness in which x participates.

(G4) For any x, if x is F then there is exactly one F-ness in which x participates.

But neither of these is acceptable. (G3) is unacceptable for Vlastos's reasons: Plato's one-over-many principle is meant to introduce *exactly* one, not (merely) at least one, Form. (G4) is unacceptable because it is inconsistent with the introduction of a second Form into the TMA: the second Form introduced has all of the participants of the first, plus one. If we are going to come up with an adequate formulation of (G2), then, we will have to shift to a version which quantifies over sets of Fs as well as over Fs.

[22] Sellars seems to be making substantially the same point when he writes ('Vlastos and "The Third Man"', 29–30): 'as being large by virtue of participating in a given Largeness, an item is a member of a certain class of large items. Thus, a, b, c, etc., would be members of the class of large *particulars* by virtue of the fact that each participates in the *first* largeness. On the other hand, a, b, c, etc. *together with this first Largeness* are members of a more inclusive class by virtue of their common participation in the second Largeness, and so on. Thus it does *not* follow from Plato's premises that the members of *one and the same class* of large items, e.g., the class of large particulars, are members of *that* class by virtue of two different Largenesses. The latter would indeed be a gross inconsistency. . . . the regress as Plato sets it up requires that it be incorrect to speak of *the* Form by virtue of which an item, x, is large, without going on to specify the class of large things with respect to which it is being considered.' Even though his reasoning here commits him to saying that there will be *exactly* one F-ness for a given set of Fs, however, Sellars goes on to formulate his one-over-many premiss as (G), thus leaving himself open—unnecessarily—to Vlastos's objection.

[23] (G1) has already been dismissed. Cf. n. 21.

IV

We might try to formulate our set-theoretic version of (G2) in this way:

(G5) For any set of Fs, there is exactly one Form over that set.

But there is something intuitively unsatisfactory about (G5); for it intro-duces a new relation, the 'over' relation, which holds between Forms and sets of Fs, and we have, thus far, no idea of what that relation might be. It is natural to suppose that the relation of a Form to the set it is 'over' can be analysed in terms of the participation relation between that Form and members of that set. Unfortunately, there is no easy way of doing this. Suppose we try:

(G6) For any set of Fs, there is exactly one Form in which all members of that set participate.[24]

Clearly this will not do. (G6), like (G4), conflicts with the second step of the TMA. All members of the set {Mt Everest, Mt McKinley} par-ticipate in Largeness I; but they both, together with Largeness I, partici-pate in Largeness II . . . and so on. There may be more than one Form in which all members of a given set of Fs participate. We might alter (G6) to read:

(G7) For any set of Fs, there is exactly one Form in which *only* members of that set participate.

This will not do either. (G7) tells us that, given a set of Fs, there will be one Form all of whose participants are members of that set. But this seems a most unlikely assumption. Consider the set {Everest, McKinley}. There is *no* Form of Largeness whose participants are limited to the pair {Everest, McKinley}. Hence there may be no Form in which only members of a given set of Fs participate.

Perhaps we should combine (G6) and (G7), yielding:

(G8) For any set of Fs, there is exactly one Form in which all and only members of that set participate.

But this is no better. For while the objection to (G6) will not work against (G8), the objection to (G7) will; nothing in Plato's theory tells us that there should be one Form of Largeness over the set {Everest

---

[24] (G6) is essentially identical to Colin Strang's ('Plato and the Third Man') 'strong OM', the strong version of the one-over-many thesis. Strang agrees that strong OM is inconsistent with the TMA premises (giving roughly the same argument I give), but he is content to rest the TMA on 'weak OM' (essentially (G6) with 'at least' in place of 'exactly').

McKinley} and *another* Form over the set {Everest, Kilimanjaro}. Plato's one-over-many principle will have to allow for more than one Form corresponding to the predicate '*F*'; but it should not require as many Forms corresponding to '*F*' as there are sets of *F*s. Some sets of *F*s, such as the ones mentioned above, are just not interesting enough to require their own special Forms.

But some sets are—the set of *F* particulars, for example. So perhaps something like (G8) would do as a formulation of the one-over-many principle if there were some way of specifying *which* set of *F*s is involved. As a start, we might try:

(G9) For any set which is the set of *F* particulars, there is exactly one Form in which all and only members of that set participate.

But (G9), while unobjectionable as a Platonic truth, is too weak to be of much help in generating a regress. For (G9) is equivalent to:

(G10) There is exactly one Form in which all and only members of the set of *F* particulars participate.

And (G10) is silent about sets containing things other than *F* particulars, whereas it is just such a set that pops up in the second step of the TMA.

Clearly what is wanted is a more restricted version of (G8) that is not so restricted, as (G9) is, that it defuses the infinite regress. It will be my aim in the next section to produce such a version of the one-over-many principle.

V

Let me begin with a series of definitions. These definitions will be given in terms of a single undefined relational predicate 'participates in' and the schematic letter '*F*', which will serve as a dummy predicate and will play the role that 'large' does as a sample predicate in the TMA.

(D1) By an *F-object* (hereafter 'object', for short) I will mean any *F* thing (anything, that is, whether a particular or a Form, of which '*F*' can be truly predicated).

(D2) An *F-particular* (hereafter 'particular', for short) is an object in which nothing participates.[25]

---

[25] Strictly, this should be modal: a particular is an object in which nothing *can* participate. For he subsequent definition of a Form as a non-particular should have it that a Form is an object n which something *can* participate, in order to leave open the possibility of there being a Form

(D3) A *Form* is an object that is not a particular.

(D4) I will also speak of a particular as an *object of level O*.

(D5) An object is an *object of level one* if
    (a) All of its participants are particulars, and
    (b) all particulars participate in it.

(D6) In general, an object is an *object of level n* $(n \geq 1)$ if
    (a) All of its participants are of level $n - 1$ or lower, and
    (b) all objects of level $n - 1$ or lower participate in it.

I will define the level of a set of objects as the level of its highest-level member. Thus,

(D7) A set of objects is a *set of level n* if it contains an object of level n and no higher-level object. Finally,

(D8) A set of level n will be said to be a *maximal set* if it contains every object of level m for every $m \leq n$. In other words, a maximal set contains every object on every level equal to or less than the level of its highest-level member.

The one-over-many principle that seems to be operative in the TMA can now be stated. I will label it 'OM-axiom' to try to emphasize its deductive power, since it turns out to be the only assumption needed to generate not only the TMA but a number of important theorems as well.[26]

(OM-axiom) For any maximal set there is exactly one Form in which all and only members of that set participate.

(Thus (OM-axiom) is simply (G8) restricted to maximal sets.) That the infinite regress of the TMA is a consequence of (OM-axiom) can be proved formally; the proof will proceed in roughly the following way. Assume the existence of the set of particulars—that is, the set of non-Forms of which 'F' can be truly predicated; since this is a maximal set, (OM-axiom) gives us one Form over that set;[27] the addition of this Form to the set of particulars gives us a new maximal set; (OM-axiom) then gives us a new Form; and so on. Now two questions arise about the proof as just sketched. (1) How do we know that each application of (OM-axiom) gives us a 'new' Form—that is, one not identical with any of the objects introduced up to

---

which lacks participants. But no harm is done here by simplifying the definitions, since the TMA assumes the existence of particulars, which, in turn, guarantees that no Form (in this discussion) will go unparticipated in.

  [26] Except, of course, the assumption that there are particulars; we must be given a non-empty set of particulars to which to apply the (OM-axiom).

  [27] 'Over' will be used (until further notice) to abbreviate 'participated in by all and only the members of'.

that point in the proof? (2) How do we know that the addition of a Form to the set it is over produces a maximal set? It is clear that we must have answers to these questions; if we cannot answer (1) we cannot guarantee that there will be a regress, and if we cannot answer (2) we cannot guarantee that we will keep producing sets to which (OM-axiom) will be applicable. Before setting out the TMA formally, then, it will be useful to mention two consequences of the axiom and definitions which will enable us to answer these questions. They are the following two theorems:

(T1) No object is on more than one level.
(T2) There is exactly one object on each level (greater than O).

(T1) is derivable from (D2), (D4), and (D6); (T2) is derivable from (D6), (D8), and (OM-axiom). The proofs will be omitted.[28] Our formalization of the TMA can now be sketched more fully.

The TMA (first version)

1. Let α be the set of all particulars.
2. α is a maximal set (level O).   (1), (D4), (D7), (D8)
3. There is exactly one Form over α, call   (2), (OM-axiom)
    it 'F-ness I'.
4. F-ness I is of level one.   (1), (3), (D5)
5. F-ness I is not a member of α.   (2), (4), (T1), (D7)
6. $\alpha \cup \{F\text{-ness I}\}$ is maximal (level one).   (2), (4), (T2), (D7), (D8)
7. There is exactly one Form over   (6), (OM-axiom)
    $\alpha \cup \{F\text{-ness I}\}$, call it '$F$-ness II'.
8. F-ness II is of level 2.   (6), (7), (D6)
9. F-ness II is not a member of   (6), (8), (T1), (D7)
    $\alpha \cup \{F\text{-ness I}\}$.
10. F-ness II $\neq F$-ness I.   (9)

---

[28] Roughly, the proofs would run as follows.

For (T1): Suppose an object, y, to be on more than one level, say levels i and $i + j$, for some $i \geq O$ and $j \geq 1$. Then, by (D6), y participates in itself, since an object of level $i + j$ is participated in by every lower-level object and hence by any object of level i. But then y must also be on a level *lower* than i, since, by (D6), all participants of an object of level i are on a level lower than i. Iteration of this reasoning will show that y must also be on level O. But then, by (D4), y is a particular; and by (D2) nothing participates in y. Hence y does not participate in itself. But this contradicts the assumption that y is on both of levels i and $i + j$.

For (T2): To show that, for any $n \geq 1$, there is exactly one object of level n, let α be a maximal set of level $n - 1$. (This assumption is justified by the fact that it is provable that, for every n, there is a maximal set of level n.) Then by (OM-axiom) there is exactly one Form over α. But, by (D8), the members of α are all and only those objects of level $n - 1$ or lower. Hence there is exactly one Form participated in by all and only objects of level $n - 1$ or lower, which means, by (D6), that there is exactly one object of level n.

11. $\alpha \cup \{F\text{-ness I, }F\text{-ness II}\}$ is maximal (level 2).	(6), (8), (T2), (D7), (D8)
12. There is exactly one Form over $\alpha \cup \{F\text{-ness I, }F\text{-ness II}\}$, call it '$F$-ness III'.	(11), (OM-axiom)
etc.	etc.

The sequence, of course, is non-terminating; but since this is where Parmenides left off we, too, can stop at this point and examine the results.

The most important point about the argument whose proof is sketched above is the absence of explicit self-predication and non-identity assumptions. This is not to say that self-predication and non-identity are not involved in the TMA as I have presented it; they are, but not as explicit premises in the argument. This seems to me to mark the point of greatest similarity between Plato's statement of the argument and my formalization of its proof. Self-predication is *presupposed* in the definitions of 'Form' and 'object'; non-identity comes in not as a premiss but (at step 10) as a consequence of the line which is an instance of the theorem that a Form is not a member of the set it is over. It may be felt that it is perverse deliberately to conceal just those 'assumptions' that some have argued are really the ones responsible for the TMA. On the contrary, I feel that it is a virtue of this way of looking at the TMA that it directs our attention to the one-over-many principle, which has been the least discussed of the TMA's assumptions, even though it was the only one Plato explicitly formulated.

But how well does (OM-axiom) represent the one-over-many principle Plato employs in the TMA? The most glaring difference is this: Plato does not say anything that suggests that the 'many' to which the one-over-many principle will be applied must be (what I have called) a maximal set. Quite to the contrary, the text suggests that Plato is prepared to apply the principle to non-maximal sets; it is applied to πόλλ᾽ ἄττα μεγάλα, 'some plurality of large things' (Vlastos)—that is, *some* set of many large things. If Plato is prepared, as he seems to be, to start the TMA with *any* set of large things, then (OM-axiom) cannot be adequate as a formulation of the relevant one-over-many principle.

So our problem is this: if we think of the TMA as starting with some non-maximal set, we do not yet have a principle which will provide us with exactly one Form over that set, in some suitable sense of 'over'. Given (OM-axiom), the best we can do for a general one-over-many principle would be this: no matter what set we start with, there will be exactly one

Form over the lowest-level maximal set which includes that set—that is,

(G11) For any set α, there is exactly one Form participated in by all and only members of the lowest-level maximal set which contains every member of α.

The Form (G11) generates will not, however, be said to be *over*, in the sense given to that term above, the set to which (G11) is applied. For 'x is over α' has been abbreviating 'x is participated in by all and only the members of α'. And so unless α is a maximal set, the Form (G11) introduces will not be *over* α.

It should now be apparent that 'participated in by all and only the members of' does not, after all, capture the intuitive sense of 'over' ($\dot{\epsilon}\pi i$) in 'the one over the many'. For one thing, the *over* relation ought to be understood to be a one–many relation; for another, the one which is over a set of many things ought to be understood to be over each of them. Yet the *over* relation, as defined thus far, has neither of these features; it is a relation that obtains between a Form and a maximal set, and hence is a one–one, not a one–many, relation; consequently a Form cannot be said to be over each of the members of the set it is over.

VI

The formalization of the TMA proposed in the last section suffered from the defect of requiring a maximal set at step 1. Since it is at precisely that point that it seems to diverge from Plato's argument, I shall try to remedy the defect in the present section.

I shall begin by providing a definition of the *over* relation which will be closer, I think, to Plato's notion of that relation:

(D9) x is over y = df y, or, if y is a set, every member of y, participates in x.

The *over* relation will clearly not be a one–one relation. But it will not be a one–many relation, either. For to suppose it is would be to assume (G6) once again, and (G6) has already been rejected as inconsistent with the second step of the TMA. The *over* relation must—unhappily, it seems—be a many–many relation.

The *over* relation is many–many because not only is F-ness I over each of the particulars a, b, c, but so is F-ness II, and so forth. But still, it is

F-ness I and *not F*-ness II (or any of the others in the hierarchy) that makes the first appearance in the TMA. That is, it is not just *any* Form over the initial set that appears at the first step of the TMA; it is, one might say, the Form *immediately* over the initial set that appears first. The Form immediately over the particulars *a*, *b*, and *c* will be the Form whose participants are particulars only; it may be over other particulars, but it will not be over any Forms. We can make the sense of 'immediately over' more precise:*

(D10) *x* is immediately over *y* = df *x* is over *y* and *x* is over all and only those sets whose level is equal to or less than that of *y*.

Thus, while *F*-ness I and *F*-ness II are both *over* particulars *a*, *b*, *c*, only the former is *immediately* over them, for the latter is not over sets of level *O* only, being over the level one object *F*-ness I. So while the *over* relation may be many–many, the *immediately over* relation is one–many. And since it is, the one-over-many principle required for the TMA can be stated in terms of it:

(IOM-axiom) For any set of *F*s, there is exactly one Form immediately over that set.

This axiom, it turns out, is equivalent to (G11) and entails (OM-axiom);[29] hence by using it in place of (OM-axiom) we can produce a formalization of the TMA which is not open to the objections raised against that of the

---

* Since the original publication of this paper, I have discovered that the definition of 'immediately over' can be significantly simplified, as follows:

x is immediately over *y* = df *x* is over *y*, and there is no *z* such that *x* is over *z* and *z* is over *y*.

Like the more complex definition given in the text, in terms of *levels*, the revised definition has one Form being immediately over another when the first is over the second and no third Form 'intervenes' between the two. The relation between the relations *over* and *immediately over* is thus analogous to the relation between the number-theoretical relations *larger than* and *successor of*. For a deeper exploration of the parallels between Platonic Form theory and standard number theory, see S. Marc Cohen and David Keyt, 'Analyzing Plato's Arguments: Plato and Platonism', *Oxford Studies in Ancient Philosophy*, suppl. vol. (1992), 173–200. The possibility of simplifying the definition of 'immediately over' was discovered independently by Richard Patterson. See his *Image and Reality in Plato's* Metaphysics (Indianapolis, 1985), 54.

[29] That (IOM-axiom) entails (OM-axiom) can be seen as follows. Let α be a maximal set of level *n* (cf. n. 28); by (IOM-axiom) there is exactly one Form, say *x*, immediately over α; by (D10) *x* is over all and only sets of level *n* or lower; hence *x* is over α and over no higher-level set; by (D9) *x* is participated in by all members of α, and, by the previous step, participated in by nothing else; hence *x* is participated in by all and only members of α. Therefore, if α is a maximal set, there is exactly one Form participated in by all and only members of α—which is (OM-axiom).

previous section. Once again it will be helpful if we can make use of an additional theorem in our proof:

(T3) If x is immediately over y, then the level of x is one greater than the level of y.

(T3) is derivable from (D6)–(D10).[30] The formalization of the TMA follows.

The TMA (final version)

1. Let a be any set of Fs (of level n).
2. There is exactly one Form immediately over a,   (1), (IOM-axiom)
   call it 'F-ness I'.
3. F-ness I is of level $n + 1$.   (1), (2), (T3)
4. F-ness I is not a member of a.   (1), (3), (T1), (D7)
5. $a \cup \{F$-ness I$\}$ is of level $n + 1$.   (1), (3), (D7)
6. There is exactly one Form immediately   (5), (IOM-axiom)
   over $a \cup \{F$-ness I$\}$, call it 'F-ness II'.
7. F-ness II is of level $n + 2$.   (5), (6), (T3)
8. F-ness II is not a member of   (5), (7), (T1), (D7)
   $a \cup \{F$-ness I$\}$.
9. F-ness II $\neq F$-ness I.   (8)

   etc.   etc.

Once again, self-predication and non-identity assumptions are built in but not made explicit. The difference between this version of the TMA and the first lies in the different ways in which the one-over-many principle is formulated. The main advantage of (IOM-axiom) over its predecessor is that it makes clearer Plato's inclination to think that while the one-over-many principle yields exactly one Form for the set under consideration at each step, that principle is consistent with there being more than one Form over the set with which we start. This inclination comes out, I think, in Plato's use of verbs like δοκεῖ and φαίνεται to introduce the Forms at each step. Over the first set of large things *just* one Form 'appears' or 'comes into view', even though, as it turns out, there will be others. The one which appears will be the one immediately

---

[30] Proof of (T3): let y be of level n, and let x be immediately over y; then by (D10) x is over all and only sets of level n or lower; hence x is over the maximal set of level n, and over no higher-level set; by (D9) every member of the maximal set of level n participates in x, and nothing else does; hence all of x's participants are of level n or lower and all objects of level n or lower participate in x; thus by (D6) x is of level $n + 1$.

over that set. There may be more than one Form over a given set, but there would not *appear* to be someone asked to pick out the one over the many. Clearly, Plato thinks of the Form introduced at each step as just overtopping, as it were, the set of things over which it is introduced. Over the set of particulars with which, presumably, we begin there will be *just* one object of the next level. But the uniqueness of the Form on each level is insufficient to prove the uniqueness thesis in which Plato is interested—namely, that there is exactly one Form corresponding to each predicate.

All of this fits perfectly the overall structure of the TMA.[31] Plato offers the one-over-many principle (at 132a2–3) as a *reason* for holding that the Forms are unique (ἓν ἕκαστον εἶδος, 132a1).[32] The reasoning, presumably, would go like this: when you consider a set of large things, exactly one Form of Largeness will come into view, immediately over that set; so there is exactly one Form of Largeness. What Parmenides sets out to show is that this reasoning is inconclusive; indeed, it is the point of the TMA to show that the one-over-many principle, far from supporting the uniqueness thesis, leads to its denial.[33]

---

[31] The only part of my reconstruction for which there is no direct textual support is the division of objects into levels. Plato does not, of course, have a word for 'levels', nor does he explicitly divide objects in the way I have in my reconstruction. But I would defend this division on the grounds that it gives a fairly precise formulation of the logical structure implicit in Plato's argument. Any account of the TMA must, it seems to me, take very seriously the one-over-many principle, and part of doing this is to say what is involved in the claim that a Form can be 'over' its participants. It is clear that Plato thought of Forms as being on a higher 'ontological level' than particulars (cf. e.g. *Rep.* 515d, 477a ff.; *Ti.* 28a, 49e; *Phd.* 74a, 78d ff., *et passim*). The TMA seems to extend this notion by assuming, in general, that a Form is on a higher level than its participants.

[32] The importance of this line has not, I think, been sufficiently appreciated. It seems to me to show conclusively that the TMA is not, as has been generally supposed, a *reductio* argument directed against the uniqueness thesis.

[33] I have been arguing that the TMA's premiss set is consistent; hence, I am committed to the consistency of (IOM-axiom). But of course the consistency of this axiom is not independent of the sort of set theory we assume. In particular, the set theory my formalization presupposes cannot include the principle of abstraction—namely, the principle that, for any predicate, there is a set consisting of all and only objects to which that predicate applies—in formal notation:

$(\exists \alpha)(x)(x \ \varepsilon \alpha \equiv Fx).$

For if there were such a set (the universal set of *F*s) it would contain no highest-level member (there being no such thing as the *last* Form in the infinite regress) and hence it would not be a set of *any* level (cf. (D7)). But then no Form could be immediately over that set (cf. (D10)), contradicting (IOM-axiom). Even though the principle of abstraction has its own difficulties (cf. Quine, *Methods of Logic*, 249) we may still wish to retain it. In this case (IOM-axiom) would have to be altered to read:

For any set α, if α is a set of level n, for some n, then there is exactly one Form immediately over α.

VII

If my account of the TMA is, at least in its essentials, correct, then the difficulty in the Theory of Forms that is being shown up lies in the one-over-many principle. The argument of one over many, thought to be a safe route to the uniqueness thesis, has been shown to be defective. This diagnosis of the TMA, however, will be unacceptable to those who think that in *Republic* 10 Plato has shown us that he knows very well how to disable objections to the uniqueness thesis.[34] There (597c–d) Plato argues in the following way. There is just one Form of Bed (literally, 'bed in nature', ἐν τῇ φύσει κλίνην); for suppose there were two; immediately, another would crop up whose εἶδος they would both have, and it, not they, would be the Form of Bed (literally, 'what (a) bed is', ὅ ἐστιν κλίνη). The crucial move in this 'Third Bed Argument' (TBA) is a one-over-many move;[35] as soon as a second Form threatens, it is an application of one over many that saves the day. The two beds we thought were both Forms are not Forms after all; it is the Third Bed which is the *one* Form.

If the TBA shows that one-over-many reasoning does yield the uniqueness thesis, then either the TMA is invalid or my account of it is mistaken. Fortunately, the TBA does not establish the uniqueness thesis; hence it cannot provide an answer to the TMA, although TMA and TBA reasoning will jointly produce a surprising but important conclusion. The TBA shows that there cannot be as many as two Forms of Bed, for the supposition that there are two demands the existence of a Third Bed, which, the TBA assures us, is *the* Form of Bed. But suppose we add our Third Bed, TMA style, to the beds already collected. The one-over-many principle will produce a Fourth Bed, and it, not the Third, will be the Form. Clearly what the TBA shows is that there is not *more* than one Form of Bed; it cannot show that there is exactly one unless it can show that the regress described above will stop. But, according to the TMA, this is precisely what it cannot do. So while the TBA shows only that there is not more than one Form, the TMA shows that there is not exactly one Form. And if neither exactly

---

[34] e.g. H. F. Cherniss, 'The Relation of the *Timaeus* to Plato's Later Dialogues', *American Journal of Philology*, 78 (1957), 225–66; repr. in Allen (ed.), *Studies in Plato's Metaphysics*, 339–78. Subsequent references will be to the reprinted version. Cf. also Cornford, *Plato and Parmenides* (New York, 1957), 90.

[35] But cf. Vlastos, 'Addendum (1963)' (to 'TMA I'), 263, who cites the TBA as an instance where Plato employs the full-strength non-identity assumption; Cherniss, 'The Relation of the *Timaeus* to Plato's Later Dialogues', 371–3, who sees Plato here denying self-predication (on the grounds that the ἐστι in ὅ ἐστι x means '='); and Strang, 'Plato and the Third Man', 157, who correctly points out, *contra* Cherniss, that (*a*) if a denial of self-predication is involved in the TBA, Plato cannot have clearly seen it and (*b*) the TBA is 'itself ripe for the TMA treatment'.

one nor more than one, then none. The surprising conclusion of the TMA together with the TBA is that there are no Forms.[36] But Plato never put the two arguments together in this way, and hence apparently never realized that they produce this conclusion.

The one-over-many principle will not yield the uniqueness thesis. And the TBA will not safeguard that thesis from the threat of the TMA. But that principle provides only one among many routes to the uniqueness thesis that Plato might have employed. I shall briefly consider one such route, suggested by the language in which the Forms are introduced in the *Phaedo*.[37]

In that dialogue Plato claims that there is something beyond sensible F things, something he calls 'The F Itself' (74a11–12).[38] The F Itself is F without qualification (74b7 ff.);[39] it can never seem non-F (74c1–3);[40] other F things fall short ($\dot{\epsilon}\nu\delta\epsilon\tilde{\iota}$) of The F Itself (74d6–7); they are like ($o\tilde{i}o\nu$) it but inferior ($\varphi\alpha\nu\lambda\acute{o}\tau\epsilon\rho o\nu$) to it (74e1–2); they are called by the same name ($\acute{o}\mu\omega\nu\acute{\nu}\mu\omega\nu$) as The F Itself (78e2). Later in the *Phaedo* Plato starts calling such things as The Beautiful Itself and The Large Itself 'Forms' and says that other things are named after the Forms by participating in them (102b1–2).

---

[36] This conclusion can be obtained formally by altering (D3), in light of the TBA, to read:

(D3')A *Form is an object that is not a particular and does not participate in any object*,

and by substituting 'object' for 'Form' in (OM-axiom). But since every object generated by (OM-axiom) will belong to at least one maximal set, every such object will participate in a higher-level object. Then none of the objects generated by (OM-axiom) is a Form. But from this it follows that

(T3') For any *n*, if *x* is an object of level *n*, then *x* is not a Form.

[37] I owe a number of points both in the remainder of this section and elsewhere in this paper to discussions with Gareth B. Matthews.

[38] The sample predicate Plato uses is 'equal'; the phrase he uses, $\alpha\dot{\upsilon}\tau\grave{o}\ \tau\grave{o}\ \check{\iota}\sigma o\nu$.

[39] Suggested by Plato's claim that the 'sensible equals' (sticks, stones, etc.) may appear to be 'equal to this but not to that' ($\tau\tilde{\omega}\ \mu\grave{\epsilon}\nu\ \check{\iota}\sigma\alpha\ \varphi\alpha\acute{\iota}\nu\epsilon\tau\alpha\iota,\ \tau\tilde{\omega}\ \delta'\ o\check{\upsilon}$, 74b8–9). Presumably, The Equal Itself cannot appear equal to this but not to that; it is just Equal, pure and simple—the *qualifications* 'to this', 'not to that' are inappropriate. (On the reading of the datives in b8–9, cf. G. E. L. Owen, 'A Proof in the *Peri Ideōn*', in Allen (ed.), *Studies in Plato's Metaphysics*, 306, whose interpretation I follow. Even on the traditional reading of the datives as masculine rather than neuter and governed by $\varphi\alpha\acute{\iota}\nu\epsilon\tau\alpha\iota$ rather than $\check{\iota}\sigma\alpha$ it is still possible to see Plato here announcing a certain qualification of the *F*-ness of *F* particulars which does not apply to The *F* Itself. But I think Owen's reading is better.) Cf. also *Smp.* 211e; *Hp.Ma.* 289 ff.; Vlastos, 'Degrees of Reality in Plato', in R. Bambrough (ed.), *New Essays on Plato and Aristotle* (London, 1965), 1–19.

[40] The question whether $\alpha\dot{\upsilon}\tau\grave{\alpha}\ \tau\grave{\alpha}\ \check{\iota}\sigma\alpha$ can ever seem unequal is raised and answered in the negative. But it is a matter of dispute among recent commentators whether the phrase $\alpha\dot{\upsilon}\tau\grave{\alpha}\ \tau\grave{\alpha}\ \check{\iota}\sigma\alpha$ ('the equals themselves') does, in fact, refer to the Form—i.e. $\alpha\dot{\upsilon}\tau\grave{o}\ \tau\grave{o}\ \check{\iota}\sigma o\nu$. I am assuming that it does, and that the (somewhat unexpected) plural can be satisfactorily explained. Cf. Geach, 'The Third Man Again', 269; Vlastos, 'Postscript to the Third Man Argument: A Reply to Mr. Geach', *Philosophical Review*, 65 (1956), 83–94; repr. in Allen (ed.), *Studies in Plato's Metaphysics*, 279–91 (esp. 287–8, 291).

Now this way of referring to a Form (schematically) as 'The F Itself' is striking in several ways. To refer to a Form as 'The F Itself' is, first of all, to *name* the Form (to say just which Form it is). But it is also to name the Form in such a way as to make clear how it is that participants in the Form are homonymous instances of it—that is, named after it. Third, and most important, is this: to refer to a Form as 'The F Itself' makes it perfectly clear that there is just *one* Form after which F things are named. After all, it is *The F* Itself. So built into this way of referring to the Forms by their proper names are two other features: that of homonymy— particular Fs get their (common) name from the Form's (proper) name— and that of uniqueness—corresponding to the deficient, changeable, qualifiedly F things there is just *one* thing that is unchangeable and does not fall short of being F, which is hence unqualifiedly F: *The F* Itself.

What I have been suggesting is not an argument for the uniqueness thesis. That thesis is not so much argued for in the *Phaedo* as simply built into Plato's way of referring to the Forms. To refer to a Form as 'The F Itself' does not *prove* the thesis—but it does, or should, forestall any objections to it. Thus, when Parmenides, at the second step of the TMA, claims to have proved the existence of a *second* Form, what one would expect from Socrates is not a counter-argument but a charge of unintelligibility. (*Another* The Large Itself? *Two* The Larges Themselves? Whatever do you mean? That doesn't make any sense!) But no such charge is to be found in the text. Perhaps, then, Plato's willingness to press on with the TMA should indicate to us that the sort of difficulty for the uniqueness thesis which he envisaged was not one which could be palliated by appeal to a way of referring to the Forms. The text seems strongly to support this point, for, despite the fact that the TMA includes, *inter alia*, *Phaedo*-style reference to the Forms, Plato seems to take special pains to avoid having to say anything like 'another The F Itself'. The Form first introduced by the one-over-many principle is referred to canonically at 132a6 as 'The Large Itself' ($α\dot{υ}τ\dot{o}$ $τ\dot{o}$ $μέγα$), but the second Form is introduced in a specially cautious way. Parmenides asks (literally), 'will not some one [thing] once again large appear?' ($ο\dot{υ}χ\grave{ι}$ $\ddot{ε}ν$ $τι$ $α\mathring{υ}$ $μέγα$ $φανε\hat{ι}ται$). It is only after he gets assent to this, which is ambiguous as between The Large Itself making a second appearance and a second (something) making its first appearance, that Parmenides makes clear, for the first time, that the Form which has just appeared is *another* Form ("$Aλλο$ $\ddot{α}ρα$ $ε\mathring{ι}δος$ $μεγέθους$; a10). According to the reasoning of the *Phaedo* this should be unintelligible (*Another* Form of Largeness? How could it be different from the first?) but Plato does not seem to be interested in making that point.

Plato, it seems, just turns his back on the sort of reasoning which could save the uniqueness thesis.

VIII

I think it is safe to conclude that Plato in the TMA is interested not so much in the uniqueness thesis *per se* as in its relation to the one-over-many principle. What the TMA shows is that to keep uniqueness the one-over-many principle will have to be abandoned[41] or modified,[42] for it is an application of that principle to the set consisting of large particulars and The Large Itself that generates a second Form. Well, this does not seem too high a price to pay; simply modify the principle in such a way as to make it applicable only to sets of particulars. It will thus generate one Form for each predicate (which we want it to do) but no more than one. But there is no indication that Plato himself ever tried to restrict the principle in this way.[43] We can best understand and appreciate his failure thus to restrict the principle, I think, by looking at his most famous formulation of it (at *Rep.* 596a6–7):[44]

> We are in the habit of assuming one Form for each set of many things to which we give the same name.

But now recall the *Phaedo*'s doctrine of the homonymy of Forms and their participants. The things falling under a Form are *homonymous* instances of it. The general term which is applied to the many is *borrowed* from the name of the Form: they are called after the Form. That is, what makes it

---

[41] As Plato himself seems to have done. Cf. *Politicus* 262a–63d.

[42] As some members of the Academy apparently did, restricting the principle, according to Aristotle, to sets of particulars (καθ' ἔκαστα). Cf. Alex.Aphr., *in Metaph.* 80. 8 ff.

[43] There is an almost overwhelming temptation to think that the TBA depends upon a restricted one-over-many principle, for it appears that Plato is assuming, in that argument, that anything which requires a Form over it (to make it what it is) is not a Form. And does this not amount to the assumption that the one-over-many principle cannot be applied to Forms? I think this temptation should be resisted. For if the TBA really *assumed* that the one-over-many principle cannot be applied to Forms, Plato would have had to show that the two alleged Forms of Bed were not really Forms *before* he could apply the one-over-many principle to deduce the existence of the Third Bed—i.e. the genuine Form of Bed. But how could Plato show this without undercutting his own argument? If the TBA really assumed a restricted one-over-many principle, the argument would collapse. ('Suppose there are two Forms of Bed; since we can't apply the restricted one-over-many principle to Forms, we can't deduce the existence of the Third Bed; so we're stuck with two Forms of Bed!') I conclude that whereas the unrestricted one-over-many principle entails the denial of the uniqueness thesis, the restricted principle is compatible with that thesis but does not entail it.

[44] εἶδος γάρ πού τι ἓν ἕκαστον εἰώθαμεν τίθεσθαι περὶ ἕκαστα τὰ πολλά, οἷς ταὐτὸν ὄνομα ἐπιφέρομεν.

correct to call each particular F 'F' is that it is correct to call the Form under which the particulars fall 'F'. So the set of things to which we give the name 'F' will contain a Form. Yet according to 596a, the principle of collection for a set of many things to which the one-over-many principle is to be applied is that they be things 'to which we give the same name'. So it seems inevitable that Plato would ultimately include Forms in sets to which the one-over-many principle is applicable.

It is still possible to read 596a in a harmless way, even if we waive the restriction to particulars: we assume one Form for each set of many things to which we give the same name; and among those will be one thing which does not participate in that Form—namely, the Form itself. Of course, the principle could then no longer be appropriately called the 'one-over-many' (perhaps the 'one-over-all-but-one-of-the-many' would be more appropriate). This objection is not a frivolous one; for the one-over-many principle is supposed to provide an answer to questions like 'What makes it correct for many things all to be called "F"?' The answer is supposed to be that the many things all stand in a certain relation (participation) to a certain Form—the one over the many. And according to the suggested reading of 596a not all of the many things correctly called 'F' will stand in that relation. Hence the idea will have to be given up that predicating 'F' of something is, quite simply, a matter of asserting that a relation obtains between that thing and a certain Form. It is the one-over-many principle which is the metaphysical embodiment of that idea, and in the TMA, I have argued, Plato is pointing out the logical shortcomings of that principle. In so doing he has taken an important step towards liberating himself from an initially compelling but overly simple and ultimately unsatisfactory theory of predication.[45]

[45] An earlier version of this paper was presented to the philosophy department of the University of Massachusetts in Apr. 1970, as part of a symposium on Plato's *Parmenides*, and to the Institute in Greek Philosophy and Science held at Colorado College in July 1970. Among the many people of whose helpful criticism I have been the beneficiary I wish especially to thank Aryeh Kosman, Gareth B. Matthews, and Gregory Vlastos.

XI

NOTES ON RYLE'S PLATO

G. E. L. OWEN

In 1939 Gilbert Ryle broached his apparently inexhaustible cask of new thoughts on Plato. He argued in a paper and a book review in *Mind* that the *Parmenides* was 'an early essay in the theory of types'.[1] He found the same interests active in the *Theaetetus* and *Sophist*, other late dialogues which have philosophical and dramatic ties with the *Parmenides*. A year or so earlier, in 'Categories', he had paid Aristotle a modified compliment, but his Aristotle was in essentials one of those already established in the literature. He has been understood to say that in those days it looked as though Aristotle had been, for the time at any rate, pretty well surveyed while Plato still called for exploration. But there is more than that to the interest that brings him so often back to Plato. In his studies of the late dialogues it became almost an alliance. Here are some comments, inadequate thanks for the illumination and excitement that have resulted. They centre in Ryle's discussion of the dialogue which Russell in *The Principles of Mathematics* called 'perhaps the best collection of antinomies ever made'.[2]

Russell's description of the *Parmenides*, like the diagnosis I quoted from Ryle, was evidently meant for the second and last part of the dialogue

From G. E. L. Owen, *Logic, Science and Dialectic: Collected Papers in Greek Philosophy*, ed. M. Nussbaum (Cornell University Press, 1986), 85–103. Reprinted with permission of the Cornell University Press.

[1] G. Ryle, 'Plato's *Parmenides*', *Mind*, 48 (1939), 129–51 and 302–25; review of F. M. Cornford, *Plato and Parmenides*, *Mind*, 48 (1939), 536–43. The paper, but not the review of Cornford, was reprinted with an Afterword (1963) in R. E. Allen (ed.), *Studies in Plato's Metaphysics* (New York, 1965), and page references to this and other papers prefaced by '*SPM*' will be to this collection.

[2] *Principles*, 355. He also (p. 357) accepted Plato's argument from the proliferation of unity and being discussed in the last pages of this paper as proof of an infinite class, but gave this up with apparent regret in the *Introduction to Mathematical Philosophy*, 202–3, as conflicting with the theory of types.

(137c–166c).[3] Certainly there are unsolved paradoxes enough in the first part. Zeno's are merely sketched for Socrates when he tries to spell out his theory of Forms. But the systematic collection of antinomies on a large scale begins with the exercise in dialectic that Parmenides carries out in the second part. And it is immensely systematic. Many commentators from antiquity on have flagged after the early stages and offered correspondingly lop-sided interpretations. Ryle was not among them, and I imagine I have his sympathy for the obvious counter-move I must try later: drawing a map of the argument. But maps can be one-sided in other ways.

Broadly, the deductions in this part of the dialogue fall into four groups or stages, I–IV, and each stage into two movements, A and B. (For brevity I use these headings rather than Ryle's: Plato of course used none. So IA starts at 137c, IB at 142b, IIA at 157b, IIB at 159b, IIIA at 160b, IIIB at 163b, IVA at 164b, and IVB at 165e.) One movement in each stage (the 'positive' movement) professes to prove, and the other (the 'negative') professes to disprove, both members of various pairs of antithetical predicates of one and the same subject. In I and III the subject of the antinomies is *hen* or *to hen*, 'One' or 'the One' or 'Unity' according to the predilection of translators: I am inclined to prefer either of the first two versions for a reason that Ryle gives for preferring the third, viz. that Parmenides has undertaken to speak of one of Socrates' Forms, but pending comment I shall use them indifferently. In II and IV the subject of the paradoxes is everything other than One or Unity.

The first two stages are represented as starting from one hypothesis and the other two as starting from the contradictory of that hypothesis. Assuming that Plato does not, as some think, equivocate on this point, his hypothesis in I and II is that One *is* and in III and IV that One *is not*: for the present, with a caveat, I shall follow Ryle here and write the easier English 'exists' and 'does not exist'. The caveat is that some of the arguments (notably in IIIA, 162a–b) turn on the fact that Greek has only one verb at this date for 'be' and 'exist'. And this need not make for bad philosophy: it is part of Plato's *tour de force* in the *Sophist* to isolate a number of puzzles which for us cluster about non-existence, without marking off an 'existential' sense of the verb.[4]

Plato allows two small anomalies in his scheme. The first stage has an appendix (IC, 155e–157b) on the paradoxes of instantaneous change. And

---

[3] 'The dialogue': Ryle has recently (e.g. *SPM* 145) come to think the *Parmenides* a patchwork of parts from different dates. On this see the Additional Note, p. 103 below. [*Editor's note*: The additional note has been omitted. 'P. 103' refers to Owen, *Logic, Science and Dialectic*.]

[4] Cf. M. Frede, 'Prädikation und Existenzaussage', *Hypomnemata*, 18 (1967), 1–99, and my 'Plato on Not-Being', below, Ch. XVII.

in the first but not in the later stages the negative movement precedes the positive. The reason for the later ordering is no doubt mere economy: once the subject of a negative movement is shown generally incapable of carrying predicates, it is enough to refer back to the positive antinomies for all the pairs of laboriously established predicates that are now denied it. The reason for starting with the negative movement in I is probably connected, on the other hand, with some broader functions that Plato means to assign to the dialogue. Dramatically he seems to place it at the head of a group containing the *Theaetetus*, *Sophist*, and *Statesman* (as well as perhaps the *Cratylus* and *Philebus*),[5] and as an introduction to that group it might be expected to play two roles: that of marking where previous theories are suspect or superseded, and that of broaching a set of problems with which its successors will be concerned. At any rate these two tasks seem to be carried out, with some overlapping, by its first and second parts respectively; the overlap is inevitable since the new problems are largely the result of pressing dissatisfactions with the old theories. So the deductions of the second part begin with a negative movement because the general effect of that movement is to show the bankruptcy of one way of dealing with unity which had been characteristic of the theory of Forms brought up by Socrates in the first part (129a–e; cf. *Rep.* 525e). Just as a dyer's sample of vermilion might be a piece of cloth having that and no other colour, so it had been thought that in a higher world unity could be represented by a Form so paradigmatically unitary as to have no sort of plurality in it at all. The notion was helped by identifying the Form with the number 1 (*Rep.* 525e). How can 1 be another number of anything? but then how can it even be defined by any conjunction of properties? The question belongs to the lumber-room of philosophy partly because the movement IA was, *inter alia*, the necessary clearing operation.

It is this network of deductions that was designed, in Ryle's view, to show by *reductio ad absurdum* part of the difference between two sorts of concept. In the nature of the case Plato could not have had labels for them; in Ryle's labelling they are the 'formal' concepts, such as unity and existence, and 'proper' or 'specific' and generic' concepts such as squareness and largeness.

When we treat a formal concept as if it were a non-formal or proper concept, we are committing a breach of 'logical syntax'. But what shows us that we are doing

---

[5] The dramatic sequence of *Theaetetus*, *Sophist*, and *Statesman* is fixed (*Tht.* 210d; *Sph.* 216a–b; *Plt.* 257a–b); the place of the *Parmenides* in the sequence is suggested, less certainly, by *Tht.* 183e–184a.

this? The deductive derivation of absurdities and contradictions does, and nothing else can. Russell's proof that, in his code-symbolism, φ cannot be a value of x in the propositional function φx is only another exercise in the same genre as Plato's proof that 'Unity' cannot go into the gap in the sentence-frame '. . . exists' or '. . . does not exist'.

The logical apparatus of Ryle's discussion is recognizably that of 'Categories' and some of his post-war writings. The logical forms which interest philosophers are ascribed to propositions (and not, as in an earlier paper, to 'facts'), and concepts are assigned to different types which answer broadly to different roles in the formation of propositions: formal concepts 'are not subject or predicate terms of propositions but rather the modes of combining terms' (itself an echo of Russell). One and perhaps the main job of philosophers is to expose forms of speech that, without falling into blatant nonsense, misrepresent the logical powers of the concepts they employ. As a statement of grammar, ' "Unity" cannot go into the gap in the sentence-frame ". . . exists" or ". . . does not exist" ' would be false. Ryle takes it to be a statement of 'logical syntax' proved by Plato. He does not of course think that Plato argues in the formal mode. So what does he take the proof to consist in?

Here there are two points at which one would like him to have said more.

First, he speaks more than once of both the hypothesis 'Unity exists' and its contradictory as *entailing* the families of contradictions that they severally breed. As an analogy he cites Russell's use of the so-called Vicious Circle paradoxes to show that '$\varphi(\varphi\hat{x})$' is ill-formed. But he does not, of course, offer to show that Plato's antinomies follow from their first premisses as directly as those which Russell collected to argue the need for a theory of types. On Ryle's own survey of the *Parmenides* there seem to be many other premisses and assumptions intervening in the plot. The reader is left to wonder whether these interventions are systematic or perhaps just random—as they might be expected to be, for example, on Robinson's thesis that Plato 'is genuinely failing to notice the extra premisses as such'.[6] But the answer, I think, is that they are systematic. They are so arranged that the conflicts between them are the nerve of Plato's argument. If I can establish this, there will be closer analogies to Plato's strategy to be found in the classes of puzzle that Ryle discusses in 'Dilemmas'.

More particularly, unity is a paragon of a formal concept and Parmenides picks out One or Unity as the subject of his hypotheses. So once more the alerted reader might hope to be shown just where and why the

⁶ R. Robinson, *Plato's Earlier Dialectic*, 2nd edn. (Oxford, 1953), 274.

antinomies come from miscasting unity in a non-formal role—even if other paradoxes can be seen to come from a comparable miscasting of other concepts. But the comments with which Ryle intersperses his summary of the argument play coy to this expectation too. He is ready to suggest that the starting-point of the argument in IA is illegitimate because 'Unity exists' and 'Unity is unitary' are both 'bogus sentences'. But the reason he notices for rejecting the first sentence is that it couples 'exists' with what is supposed to be a proper name, so this is a mistake about 'exist' compounded with another about abstract nouns. (Thereafter, particularly on IIIA–B, he notices similar misuses of 'exist' as 'signifying a quality, relation, dimension, or state, etc.'.) The reason he suggests for calling the second sentence bogus is that it treats a universal as one of its own instances. (But if unity *were* a universal, would it not have to be one of that odd subset that instantiate themselves? Russell still thought so in *Principles*. Back to this later.) His only other detailed comment on the mistreatment of unity is: 'We may suspect that the argument [of IA] presupposes that unity is a quality.' So it does indeed: as I have said, it argues as though unity could preclude plurality as one colour precludes others. Still, extracting paradoxes from the miscasting of a non-quality as a quality is not enough to show (or show awareness) that it is a formal concept in Ryle's sense. The same miscasting was possible with any of that favoured set of incomplete predicates which seem to have provoked Plato to invent Forms as quasi-ostensive samples for them because the world, understandably, offers no such samples. The set, as any reader of the *Phaedo* and *Republic* 5–7 and the first part of the *Parmenides* well knows, is a logical mixed bag including *large*, *heavy*, *equal*, *double*, *hard*, *just*, and *beautiful* and their contraries and cognates as well as *one* and *many* and *similar* and *dissimilar*. And the miscasting not only could be but surely had been made. The Forms answering to these predicates seem to have had, among their other duties, that of being just those privileged (and logically impossible) samples in which the attributes behave as qualities.[7] When Socrates at *Prm.* 129b6–c3 says he will be astonished if the Form of unity can be shown to be plural or the Form of plurality shown to be unitary, he is arguing from the same assumptions as when he lays it down in *Phaedo* 102d6–103a2 that neither the Form of largeness nor even its proxy largeness in the individual can be or become small. Parmenides wrings a paradox from the latter claim in *Prm.* 131c–e, and most of IA together with the start of IB can be taken as addressed to the former. There is nothing in this, central as it is to Plato's emancipation from old confusions, to show a recognition that unity must be handled

---

[7] *SPM* 303–8.

quite differently from those overt or covert relatives and grade-concepts that fill up his list.

Is this to say that Ryle has no evidence for his thesis? Of course not. There are arguments, perhaps too obvious for him to have singled out, that seem designed to show the absurdity of treating Socrates' oneness as another property co-ordinate with his pallor or smallness. The two chief candidates will be interviewed later. Still it will be a question how far they can be read as proofs, even in a suitably philosophical sense of 'proof'. That Plato is at grips with the logic of formal concepts here and in other late dialogues seems to me certain, and this certainty was established by Ryle. But an interest in proving the necessary distinctions does not seem to lie central to the strategy of the *Parmenides*. As I shall represent it, the method that Plato explores with such enthusiasm is tailored not to the construct-ing of proofs but to the setting and sharpening of problems, and problems of a characteristically philosophical stamp. It is the first systematic exer-cise in the logic of aporematic and not demonstrative argument.

We shall get no further in this direction without the map I promised at the start. Here it is, as accurate as I can make it on this scale but with no claim to completeness.[8] It will help to fill Ryle's silence on the first point, for it tries to mark out, and locate conflicts between, the (or a representa-tive majority of the) cardinal theses on which Plato's antinomies turn. I number the key assumptions as Plato introduces them, trying to confine myself to those he expressly recognizes; though I have sometimes allowed myself a more general and abstract formulation when he cites only the par-ticular application, and in doing so used forms not available to him. But in using letters in a way which had not yet become part of logic I preserve his ambiguities: on occasion 'S is P' will cover identities as well as predi-cations, and there are no type-restrictions on the terms. To mark one of those conflicts between theses which seem to me to be the nerve of his argument, I shall put the sign '#' before the reference to some thesis which rejects or otherwise undermines the thesis under discussion.

Finally, to avoid encumbering the map, I relegate to a note the definitions and divisions that are introduced and not subsequently chal-lenged in the argument.[9]

---

[8] In an earlier version it has been refined and enlarged in theses by David Bostock and Malcolm Schofield, and I print it partly in the hope that it will prompt further efforts in the same field.

[9] In IA he defined 'whole' (137c; cf. *Theaetetus* 205a; Aristotle, *Ph.* 207^{a}9–10); 'round' (137e; cf. *Epistles* 7. 342b and Euclid's improvement in *Elements* 1, def. xv); 'straight' (137e; cf. Aristo-tle, *Top.* 148^{b}27 and contrast Euclid 1, def. iv); 'like' and 'unlike' (139e, 140a, and thereafter unchallenged; cf. 147c; but see *Protagoras* 331d–e; *Philebus* 13d); 'equal' and 'unequal' (140b–c, designed to cover incommensurables); 'coeval' (140e). IB takes these definitions over and adds

I. IF ONE EXISTS, WHAT CAN BE SAID OF IT?

1A (137c–142a) is negative in its conclusions. In addition to the definitions mentioned, its deductions depend primarily on nine premisses.

(1) 137c: *The One is one and not many* [# the opening argument of IB and, for a reason to be given directly, # (15)]. From this it is deduced that the One cannot have parts or members or be a whole.

(Very likely (1) depends on a confusion between the identifying and predicative uses of '*S* is *P*': One is not the same as Many and so is not many of anything. Let us call this the I/P confusion. It is surely one source of the so-called 'self-predication assumption' which characterizes the theory of Forms both in earlier dialogues and particularly in Socrates' account of the theory in *Prm.* 128e–130a. It will be challenged by the schema in (15), which distinguishes identity from participation, but the effect of (15) will in turn be spoilt by (16).)

(2) 137d: *The limits or extremities of anything are parts of that thing* [#(11)]. From this, together with the last conclusion, stem the proofs that the One cannot have limits, shape, or position.

(Throughout the deductions, save for those concerned with progress and regression in time, mathematical interests are obvious. Recall that the Form of unity had among its other duties that of representing the cardinal number 1. Here the geometrical application to points is evident, and Aristotle makes it explicit in *Ph.* 212^{b}24–5 (cf. 209^{a}7–13). Arguing that points cannot have a location because they cannot have a perimeter is part of Plato's 'war against points' (Aristotle, *Metaph.* 992^{a}19–22).)

(3) 139e–140a and ?138c, 139c: *If anything has more than one character or attribute these pluralize the thing*—or, as it is put in IB, 142d, they are *parts or members* of the thing. The attributes in question are unrestricted in type: they include unity, identity, existence, in fact anything distinguishable by the criteria in (4) below.

one of 'contact' (148e; adopted and reshaped by Aristotle, *Ph.* 226^{b}18–227^{b}2). IC defines 'combination' and 'dispersion', 'assimilation' and its opposite, and 'increase', 'diminution', and 'equalization' (156b). In addition, from IA on Plato assumes the equation between having a location and being contained in something which is standard in Greek philosophy (138a; cf. Zeno B5, Gorgias B3, and Aristotle's analysis in *Ph.* 4. 1–5). As for divisions, IA distinguishes 'shape' into 'round' and 'straight' (to which IB, 145b, adds 'mixed'), and 'change' (*kinēsis*) into 'change of quality' and 'motion' (138b–c; cf. *Tht.* 181d: there is an illegitimate conversion of one of the disjuncts in IIIA, 162e, and IIIB, 163e, though previously the division was given correctly in IIIA, 162d).

(A minor question is when this premiss is introduced. It does not occur explicitly until 139e–140a. But some think that from it, together with the conclusion given under (1), stem the proofs that the One cannot (*a*) change in quality or even (*b*) be identical with, (*c*) differ from or be (*d*) like or (*e*) unlike itself or anything else. On the other hand, and by way of showing how tentative this mapwork must be in detail, it is arguable that (*a*), and (*b*) and (*c*) with their derivative (*e*), depend only on the I/P confusion: thus (*a*) anything changing character is taken to lose its identity (138c), and (*b,c*) whatever is (identical with) One is not (not even predicatively) anything else, such as same or different (139c–d). But (*d*) is expressly represented as depending on (3) and so, in retrospect, are (*b*) and (*c*) (139e–140a). This still leaves (*a*) as dependent on the I/P confusion. In any event the argument for (*b*) imports a criterion of non-identity that finds an echo in IIB and IIIA and *Sophist* 255a–c.)

(4) 139d: *If the statement that S is P differs in truth-value* (or, in the form in which it is assumed in IB, 142b–c, *differs in sense*) *from the statement that S is Q, then P is different from Q.* (Note the extension of this in IIIA, 160c: if the statement that *S* is *P* differs in sense from the statement that *T* is *P*, even when '*P*' stands for 'non-existent', then *S* is a different thing from *T*. All such assumptions seem to be applications of the general view of words as names which appears in (17), but Plato does not draw the connection.) From the conclusions already listed under (3) it is further argued that the One is not equal or unequal to anything and that it has no temporal attributes.

(5) 138d: *Changes* (more strictly, *movements to a place*) *take time: to describe S as becoming P is to describe something temporally intermediate between an initial and a final state* [# the argument under (22), which trades on the possibility of describing the initial and final states as '*p*' and 'not-*p*' or vice versa]. From the conclusions listed under (2) it is argued that the One cannot move in one place, and then from (1) and (5) it is shown that the One cannot change place either.

(The character of one of the negative movements is becoming clear. Again Aristotle makes the application to geometrical points explicit, at *Ph.* 240^{b}8–241^{a}6).

(6) 141b: *If (when) X is becoming different from Y, it cannot be the case that Y is different from X: otherwise X would already be different from Y and not merely becoming so.* Hence it is argued that, if *X* is becoming older than itself, it is also becoming younger than itself.

But from the conclusions under (3) and (4) the One can have neither this temporal property nor that of remaining coeval with itself; hence it does not exist in time.

(Formally (6) is an argument, but I give it as a premiss. The implicit but unexpressed premiss is

(6*) *If S is becoming P it cannot yet be P*

and this is challenged by (19) in the parallel context in IB.)

(7) 141d–e: *What exists exists in time* (more exactly, *Whatever is or becomes, is or becomes at some time past present or future*). From this and the conclusions under (6) it is argued that the One does not exist (more exactly, is not in any way, is not *anything*).

(8) 141e: *If S is P, then S is or exists.* (Cited here in the particular form 'If the One is one, the One is', but in its general form the premiss recurs in IIIA, 161e, and IIIB, 163e, and it is challenged by IIIA in an argument based on the considerations under (4).) From this and the conclusion under (7) it follows that the One is not one (or not One).

(It is worth remark that even this premiss, like its predecessor, does not prove Plato's recognition of a separate existential sense of the verb 'to be'. Arguably, the logic of (8) appeared to him nearer to that of 'If Smith lies to one person, Smith lies'.)

(9) 142a: *What does not exist can have nothing related to it* [# the argument under IIIA]. From this and the conclusion under (7) it follows that the One cannot be named and that there can be neither speech nor knowledge, perception nor idea, of it at all.

IB (142b–155e) is positive and its deductions depend primarily on premisses (10)–(20) together with some from IA, viz. (1), (3), (4), (6), (7), (8), and the converse of (9). Two of these inherited premisses, (1) and (6), are challenged in the same movement. The opening arguments have no fresh premisses:

142b–143a: By (4), if the One exists its existence if not the same as its unity; hence, by (3), unity and existence are pluralizing parts of the one [#(1)]. But the same is true of each part in turn. (Here, in ascribing unity to each part, the argument seems to anticipate premiss (10); and in ascribing existence to whatever is unitary it seems to rely on (8).) Hence the One is a whole with infinite parts, and unity and existence are infinitely distributed.

143a–144a: Furthermore, if the One and its existence are differentiable they exhibit difference, which (seemingly by reliance on (4) again) is distinct from either of them. The sums and multiples of these three generate all numbers.

(10) 144c: *What is not one is nothing at all* (more strictly, *if a part were not one part it would be nothing*) [#(23)]. From this it is argued that any part of a plurality is one, that anything divisible is divisible into some number of parts, and generally that any number is a number of units.

(Here starts one of the trains of paradox which show the anomalous behaviour of unity as judged by that of squareness or heaviness. The opening arguments of IB, and the premiss (10) which they import, claim that we cannot 'abstract from' the unity or existence of a subject because unity and existence must always be reimported in talking of whatever parts or members are left. In giving a thing's properties we cannot systematically discount unity as we can systematically discount shape or weight. This is what (23) will try to challenge.)

(11) 144e–145a: *A whole contains, and so limits, its parts* [#(2), #(13)]. From this and the conclusions under (9) and (10) it is argued that the One is limited as well as unlimited.

(Here comes another trouble over unity, the unity of any limited set. The effect of (11) is to upset (2) by making the limit or limiting factor external to, and not part of, what is limited. Trouble is coming with (13).)

(12) 145b: *If X is limited X has spatial extremities.* Hence the One has shape.

(For the importing of spatial terms, cf. (14) and its temporal analogue in (7).)

(13) 145c: *If X has parts X is identical with the aggregate of those parts* [#(11)]. From the conjunction of (11) and (13) come the proofs that the One, *qua* parts, is contained in itself, *qua* whole; and also (reversing the roles) that it is not contained in itself. From this in turn flow many of the later conclusions, as that it is in contact with itself and that it is both larger and smaller than itself.

(Premisses (11) and (13) say, respectively, that the whole is an extra element over and above its parts, and that it is nothing more than the parts. In the analysis of syllables in *Theaetetus* 203e–205a these possibilities are given as an exhaustive disjunction and not, as here, as a conjunction. The disjunction is in turn superseded in the *Sophist* 252e–253c, on which more below, and Aristotle puts the moral in its simplest form in *Metaph.* 1041^{b}11–27: a syllable is a whole which is neither a heap of elements nor an extra element.)

(14) 145e: *What exists must be somewhere*, sc. (the standard treatment of location in Greek philosophy) *must be in something.* From this and the conclusions under (13) it is argued that the One must be both in itself and in another; and that, *qua* 'in itself', it is always 'in the same', and *qua* 'in another', it is always 'in something different'. From this, by way of a flagrant fallacy of relations, it is deduced that the One is static and moving and, later, that it is different from itself.

(The fallacy is that 'in the same', which began by meaning 'in the same thing as itself', is tacitly reconstrued as meaning 'in the same thing as that in which it previously was'; and 'in another' is successively construed as meaning 'in something other than itself', 'in something other than that in which it previously was', and 'in something other than that in which it now is'. Nor does Plato stop labouring the fallacy here, and this becomes a test-case for those who think him oblivious to all the component fallacies in the argument. The same misuse of 'same' and 'other', together with the I/P confusion, provides the later argument that nothing can be different from anything; and it was a comparable fallacy in IA that engendered confusions over 'getting older than oneself' and 'staying coeval with oneself'. In the *Sophist* 259c–d Plato is severe on those who commit the fallacy and produce superficial paradoxes by failing to complete the predicates 'same' and 'other'.)

(15) 146b: *Anything is related to anything in one of three ways: (a) by identity or (b) by difference or (c) as part to whole or whole to part.*

(The part–whole relation is exemplified in the sequel by 'partaking of unity' or, what comes to the same, 'being in a way (i.e. for present purposes predicatively) one' (147a). So here identity seems to be distinguished from predication. But the effect is spoilt by (16), which reimports, for negations at least, the I/P confusion.)

(16) 147a: *What is not one is related to One by (b) and not by (a) or (c).* Hence things that are not one have no unity of any sort [#(10)]; and from this, together with the conclusions under (10), they are argued to have no number at all.

(The argument is that being not *X* excludes being *X* in any way whatever: the negation is construed as denying that the subject is *X* both in the identifying and in the predicative sense of the words. So here is the I/P confusion again; it is cleared up in the *Sophist* 256a–b, but here Plato forces the issue by the challenge that is coming in IIA. Meantime the present argument is reinforced at 147a by an appeal to (1), which reappears yet once more at 148e–149a.)

(17) 147d: *Words are names, and to repeat a word is to name the same thing twice.* Here 'words' (*onomata*) covers at least all those general terms for which Plato had postulated Forms: thus it is argued that, in '*A* is different from *B* and *B* is different from *A*', the two occurrences of 'different' name a thing that *A* and *B* have in common, and thus their difference makes them alike.

(The most general Greek expression for 'word' also means 'name,' but (17) is not just a muddle reflecting this fact. It embodies the logical or semantic atomism which had shown itself in earlier writings and which probably underlies the assumptions in (4). Ryle has often argued, I think rightly, that Plato manages to recognize this linguistic model and reject it; later I shall suggest that the decisive rejection takes place when the *Sophist* moves beyond the disjunction of (11) and (13). Meantime the view in its simplest form faces the puzzle set by IIIA and IIIB jointly: even non-existing things can apparently be mentioned and distinguished from others.)

(18) 150a–d: *Smallness is small, largeness is large, etc.* (In detail: if smallness were itself equal to or larger than anything, it would be '*doing the jobs of largeness and equality, and not its own*'; and if there were no smallness in anything else, 'there would be nothing small *except smallness*.') This is put to proving that nothing but largeness can exhibit largeness, nothing but smallness smallness, etc.

(Here, explicitly and even flamboyantly introduced, is the 'self-predication' assumption which some believe that Plato was unable to recognize as a premiss of some paradoxes in the first part of the dialogue, including the notorious Third Man (132a–b). He applies it here to the very concept—largeness—which had been exploited in the Third Man, and uses it to produce still more outrageous consequences. Even if Aristotle had not recorded for us the Academy's recognition and formulation of the assumption it would take some determination to think of Plato as still reduced to 'honest perplexity' by his inability to see that largeness cannot be a large thing.)

It is now deduced from (7) that the One exists in time, and from (6) and the conclusion under it that the One is getting not only older but younger than itself.

(19) 152c–d: *If X is becoming Y, then at any 'present time' in the process X is (and not: is becoming) Y* [#(6), and esp. #(6*)]. The premiss is formulated quite generally and then applied to 'becoming older' (152c6–d4); if the One is growing older, then at any present time it is older. (Unluckily but idiomatically this is expanded into 'older than itself', and used to argue that the One is also younger than itself, but this extra fallacy of relations does not affect the main point of the conflict between (19) and (6*): see the comment below.) Subsequently, by an extension of (5) to cases of coming-into-existence, it is argued that the One is both older and younger, and neither older nor younger, than the others. And further para-doxes are wrung from the idea of becoming relatively and asymp-totically older and younger.

(Premiss (19) is plausible when applied to '*X* is in the process of becom-ing older (or taller)'; (6*) is plausible when applied to '*X* is in the process of becoming an octogenarian (or six feet tall)'. In *Philebus* 23c–27c Plato brings out part of the difference between these two sorts of filling, saying that the second but not the first sets a terminus to the becoming. Aris-totle profited from Plato's distinction in his own account of *kinēsis* and *energeia*. I take Plato to be pressing the need for such a distinction by setting up (19) as a challenge to (6), and the distinction once grasped is lethal to the simple dichotomy of 'being' and 'becoming' that Plato had inherited. Roughly, becoming is incompatible with being in (6) and entails being in (19): everything depends on the question 'Becoming *what*?')

(20) 155d: *What exists has (or can have) other things related to it.* By this converse of (9), the One can be named and spoken of and there can be knowledge, perception, and thought of it.

IC (155e–157b) is a joint appendix to IA and IB, using some conclusions from each but dropping others. It adopts those given under (1), (8), and the opening arguments of IB, but tacitly drops that under (7) on which the conclusion under (8) depends.

(21) 155e: *If S is both P and not P it is P at one time and not P at another.* From this, together with the various contradictions listed for the One, it is argued that the One undergoes various forms of change from *P* to not-*P* or vice versa.

(Here, by another I/P confusion, being both *P* and not-*P* is construed as a matter of existence and non-existence. On these terms (21) can be invoked to evade all contradictions, including that on which (24) will depend.)

(22) 156c: *There is no time in which S can be neither P nor not-P.* Hence any change, construed as a transition from *P* to not-*P* or vice versa, takes no time: it occurs at 'the instant'.

(Premiss (21) depends on the law of contradiction, (22) on the law of excluded middle; but the excluded middle seems not to apply to descriptions of 'the instant'.)

II. IF ONE EXISTS, WHAT CAN BE SAID OF EVERYTHING ELSE?

IIA (157b–159b) is positive. It depends chiefly on premiss (23), together with (10), (15), and the converse of (1) (which thus foreseeably becomes an equation). But the inherited premiss (10) is challenged in the same movement.

157b: Things other than the One are not the One (and in this sense are called 'not one'; cf. 158c). So, by an appeal to the converse of (1), they must be distinguished from the One itself by forming a whole containing parts or members; and, by (10) and the conclusions under it, each part must have unity by 'partaking in the One'.

(Here it seems initially that the argument wants to cut loose from the restrictive interpretation of 'not one' given in (16). That interpretation reimported the I/P confusion into negation by pretending that the options given under (*b*) and (*c*) in (15) were mutually exclusive. Here, things other than the One are carefully said to be 'not *the* One' before this phrase is replaced in 158c by 'not one'. Vain hope. The next move in the argument rejects (10) and the conclusions under it, and the puzzle is restored.)

(23) 158c: *If anything is related to the One by neither the first nor the third of the options under (15)*—i.e. neither is nor even exhibits unity—*it must be mere unlimited plurality* [#(10)]. Now considered in themselves ('at the time they are starting to partake of the One,' or 'abstracted in thought') the things other than the One answer to this condition and hence are bare plurality. In this way they are unlimited as well as (in virtue of the unity that accrues to them) limited; and from these contraries all others are made to flow.

(See the comment under (10). (23) and its dependent arguments propose an answer to the question 'What can be said of anything in abstraction from its unity?' as though this had the logic of 'What was he before he became a greengrocer?' or 'What sort of thing is it, apart from its shape?' (10) claimed in effect that the abstraction is impossible; and in particular, the hopeful answer that what is left is a kind of bare plurality runs against the conclusion under (10) that any plurality is a plurality of units, a conclusion repeated in IIB.)

IIB (159b–160b) is negative and relies wholly on premises already introduced. The One and the things other than the One form an exhaustive disjunction. By the conclusion under (1) it is argued that the two camps cannot be related by (c) in the schema at (15), and evidently they cannot be related by (a) either; so the other things are isolated from all unity. If IIA were right, quite a lot could still be said of them. But IIB reverts to the conclusion under (10), that any plurality is a plurality of units; so these things other than the One are not plural either [#(23)]. They have neither number nor limit nor any enumerable properties whatever.

III. IF ONE DOES NOT EXIST, WHAT CAN BE SAID OF IT?

IIIA (160b–163b) is positive and relies on premises already introduced or, in the case of (4) and (8), on more or less questionable extensions of them. By the extension of (4) noted under that premiss, it is argued that even a non-existent One can be known and mentioned and distinguished from other things; hence it has various properties and stands in various relations. Yet, by (8), if it does not exist it must lack properties and relations, from which it follows that it cannot have equality with anything; and hence, by a fallacy of negation which underlay another argument in IB (150d), it is deduced to be unequal to anything.

(The fallacy is the assumption that if something lacks a given predicate it must have some other of a family of incompatible predicates which includes the first. Perhaps the double use of 'not', to signify both bare negation and this loaded variety, is acknowledged in *Theaetetus* 183b—though not, I think, in *Sophist* 257b.)

But now, by an extension of (8), the One must exist if only to *be* non existent. From its existence and non-existence are deduced its mutability and other characteristics.

(But the detail of the argument makes it clear how far Plato is here from saying unambiguously that *S* must exist in order to have non-existence. Otherwise he would also be claiming that *S* must be non-existent *qua not being* non-existent. 'To be' and 'not to be' are run in harness here as in the *Sophist*, and that dialogue tackles its problems about not-being without giving up either the hard-won subject–predicate model for statements or the treatment of '. . . is . . .' and '. . . is not . . .' as a two-place predicate.)

IIIB (163b–164b) is negative and relies on premiss (24), together with (9).

> (24) 163c: *What does not exist cannot also 'in some sense exist'* [# the general argument of IIIA]. Hence, by (9), nothing can be said or known, etc., of the One.

(A beneficial truth about existence? But in the Greek the factotum verb 'to be' is still in play. So Plato may be calling attention once more to a misuse of negation that began in (16) and will still exercise him in the *Sophist*: the assumption that what is not *X*, in some sense or respect, is not *X* at all. He may just be anxious to discredit the notion that *not to be* is *not to be anything*.)

IV. IF ONE DOES NOT EXIST, WHAT CAN BE SAID OF EVERYTHING ELSE?

IVA (164b–165e) is positive and relies on premisses already introduced together with the relational fallacy described under (14).

If the others are other, by (9) they cannot be other than the One; so they are other than each other. But if so they must be supposed, or must seem, to have plurality and hence, by the conclusion given under (10), they must be deemed to have number, unity, and the dimensional properties inferred from these in IB.

(IVA reinforces IIIA, arguing that even if the One does not exist it must figure in discourse and conjecture, however mistaken. IVB, like IIIB, replies by an appeal to premiss (9).)

IVB (165e–166a) is negative and relies wholly on premisses previously introduced. By (10) and the conclusions given there, any plurality is a class of units; and by (15) and the conclusions drawn from it in IIA any unit must partake in the One. But by (9) this connection is now impossible, nor can the One be introduced in any connection whatever. So nothing can be said of the others at all; hence nothing exists.

Now for some morals. Two negative conclusions will help clear the way for the positive.

Sometimes the antinomies have been diagnosed as an exercise in ambiguity. The key hypotheses *hen ei estin* and *hen ei mē estin* have been thought to vary in sense between any two antithetical movements, and for a given movement the sense is to be gathered from the supporting premisses. But one thing our map shows is that the premisses which supposedly fix the sense for one movement commonly turn up in its twin as well. And some of them are both used and challenged in the same movement.[10] Again, the antinomies are sometimes branded as a professional lampoon or a school primer of fallacies. But the map makes it easier to see how often the premisses are the very assumptions which Plato puts to serious work in other dialogues of his maturity.[11]

Ryle rejected such attempts to diminish the seriousness of the work. But since a budget of unresolved paradoxes cannot be meant to expound positive doctrine, he saved the work's seriousness by reading it as a direct *reductio ad absurdum* of both one hypothesis and its contradictory—a project nearer to Kant's paradoxes than Russell's. It might be replied that in the *Sophist* Plato still seems content to have formal concepts as the subject of such hypotheses; but more recently Ryle has proposed a very late date for the second part of the *Parmenides* which would avoid this objection.[12] Even so, the map seems to show Plato far less single-minded than such a *reductio* would make him. And in particular it shows that throughout the deductions he recurs to one favourite strategem, that of setting up a conflict between a pair of premisses or between one premiss and a thesis derived from others. And these various conflicts do most to generate the major contradictions between and within movements and stages of the argument; and they are serious. They set, without solving, problems that exercise Plato in other late dialogues.

[10] The premiss (1) is used in IA and IB (and their appendix IC), and again in IIA and IIB. (3), (4), (5), (6), and (7) are used in IA and IB, and (2) after its entry in IA is implicitly subsumed under (13) of IB. (8) is used in IA and IB and again in IIIA and IIIB. (9) is used in IVA and IVB, and its use in IA is echoed by its converse in IB. (10) is used in IIA and IIB and again in IVA and IVB. (15) is used in IIA and IIB. Premisses both used and challenged in the same movement are (1) in IB, (10) in IB and again IIA, (11) and (13) and (16) in IB. And (5), which is used in IA and IB, is challenged in their appendix IC.

[11] The premiss (1) is used in *Sph*. 245a and (2) in *Sph*. 244e. (3) is used, implicitly, at any rate in *Tht*. 157b–c, 209c; (4) in *Sph*. 255a–c; (6), or the unexpressed (6*) given under it, in *Ti*. 27d–28e with which cf. *Tht*. 182c–183b and *Sph*. 248a; (8) in *Sph*. 255e–256a, cf. 256e; (9) in *Sph* 237c–239b; the disjunction of (11) in *Tht*. 203e–205a; (18) in the 'self-predicational' treatment of the Forms criticized in *Prm*. 131c–132b and later (cf. 134b6–7); (20) in *Sph*. 238a and (24) in *Sph*. 239b.

[12] See the Additional Note, *Logic, Science and Dialectic*, 103.

Here are examples: I believe a more detailed map would show others. (i) The confusion between identity-statements and predications which had beset the earlier metaphysics is brought out, with especial reference to negations, by the conflict between (16) and the argument drawn from (10) in IB and IIA, and teased out in the *Sophist* (250ff. and esp. 256a–b). (ii) Puzzles which we for some purposes can, as Plato could not, label as puzzles of non-existence, and which are taken up and transformed in *Sophist* 237b–263d, are set here by confronting (9) with the extension of (4) used in IIIA. (iii) The veteran assumption that 'being' and 'becoming' mark two different states characterizing different worlds (an assumption which the *Timaeus* appears to be trying to modify from within, without ever finally breaking the shell) is called in question by the conflict between (6) and (19), a conflict that Plato stresses by connecting it with the particular notion of 'growing older'; and the conflict and the dichotomy are sufficiently demolished by the distinction in the *Philebus* noticed under (19). (iv) The conflict between (10) and (23) is another example of the same strategy: I reserve it for a later page. (v) An abstract puzzle about the relation of a whole to its parts is set by the juxtaposition of (11) and (13). In a more concrete version (but one which is said to have quite general application; *Tht.* 204a2–3) these same premises reappear as a disjunction in the *Theaetetus* argument to which I referred under (13). It is worth while following this train of argument a little further into familiar territory, for it marks Plato's emancipation from the atomism noticed under (17) and, what is more to my purpose, it shows how the *Parmenides* sets without solving problems which Plato elsewhere offers to solve.

The *Theaetetus* (201dff.) and the *Sophist* (253a, 261d) use Plato's favourite analogy of letters and syllables to illustrate the complexity of whatever can be known and explained, and therewith the complexity of what must be said to explain it. In the *Theaetetus* (202e–206b) Socrates tries to argue this complexity away. He urges that a syllable is either just the letters that compose it or a separate single entity produced by their juxtaposition; so knowing a syllable is either just knowing each letter or knowing the new incomposite, and either way the knowledge is just of simple objects and not of complexes. After all, he pursues, the whole business of learning letters is the effort to pick out each one by itself (206a). But when the *Sophist* takes up the analogy (252e–253a) it points out that a syllable is (not an aggregate of pieces and not an extra piece, but) a nexus of constituents of different types fitted together in certain ways; and the knowledge of letters exercised in spelling is not just an ability to tell the letters apart but the knowledge of how they can be legitimately combined and how, in virtue of their different powers of combination, they differ in type. The *Philebus* (18c) points one moral: no letter can be learnt in isolation from the rest. And the *Sophist* argues that it is like this with our knowledge of the 'forms' or concepts which give our words meaning, and with our knowledge of the words themselves: they too cannot be learnt in isolation, they too are marked off by their powers of combination into different types (253a, 261d). Speaking is not stringing nouns together, and learning to speak is not, as the *Cratylus* had implied, a piecemeal business of correlating atoms of the world with atoms of language. This is a familiar enough train of argument;[13] my excuse for recalling it here is that the quandary from which it sets out in the *Theaetetus* is typically set as a conflict of theses in the *Parmenides*.

Anyone who stresses, as I have, the plurality of philosophical interests that Plato engineers into these paradoxes must ask why he tries to give some unity to the business by the architectural scheme I sketched earlier. Here is part at least of a reply. At the start of the antinomies (135d–136c) Parmenides promises that the ensuing exercise in dialectic will be an application and extension of Zeno's methods. And Zeno's hand can surely be seen in the deductions from one hypothesis, the fresh starts in the trains of argument, the consequent clusters of contradictions or seeming contradictions. But what of the extension of the argument from one hypothesis to its contradictory, and from the subject of the hypothesis to everything else; and above all what of those conflicts between theses that I have made the focal points of the enterprise?

The Zeno we need is, of course, Plato's Zeno: a defender of Parmenides who wrote one book consisting wholly of arguments against plurality (*Prm.* 127e–128e). Whether Plato's interpretation was accurate is immaterial here and undecidable anyway. Some years ago I proposed a scheme which would allow the extant arguments of Zeno to be grouped into such a book.[14]

Plato does not think Zeno proved his case and does not represent himself as taking over a method of proof. To use an anachronism, it is not the shape of the vault but the use of the buttresses that he means to

[13] There is no space to discuss Ryle's attractive suggestion ('Letters and Syllables in Plato', *Philosophical Review*, 69 (1960), 431–51, answered by D. Gallop, 'Plato and the Alphabet', *Philosophical Review*, 72 (1963), 364–76), that when Plato speaks of letters he means not the separate written characters but the 'abstractable noise-differences' which cannot be produced separately. Even if Plato means to be understood phonetically, the analogy of notes and chords that he conjoins with that of letters and syllables (*Tht.* 206a–b; *Sph.* 253a–b; *Phlb.* 17a–c) suggests that he does not have Ryle's moral in mind.

[14] See *Logic, Science and Dialectic*, ch. 3: 'Zeno and the Mathematicians'; 1st pub. in *Proceedings of the Aristotelian Society*, 58 (1957–8), 199–222.

acknowledge and adopt. To begin with he has seen that Zeno, arguing against all those who naïvely suppose the world to contain a plurality of things, proceeds by offering his opponents options. Either the kind of division that produces the alleged plurality is of a sort to end after a finite number of steps or it can be continued for an infinite number, and then on this second option either it reaches some limiting indivisibles or it can never be finished; and Zeno professes to wring an absurdity from each of these possibilities. If this is so (and I am taking my old scheme as a working assumption), such a method of trying the alternatives explains not only the variations that Plato plays on his hypothesis but other devices he adopts in the later dialogues, such as the use of logical division that he defends in the *Philebus*: division prevents hasty generalizations about a class from some unrepresentative subset.

But his acknowledgement to Zeno goes deeper than this. Zeno seems often to overpress his paradoxes by joining in one conclusion the consequences of more than one option—as when he says that the members of a plurality must be 'so small as to have no magnitude yet so large as to be boundless'. Yet these conjunctions are not arbitrary, just because each of the conflicting options is (or is made by Zeno to seem) plausible in its own right. Suppose *per impossibile* that the division of any magnitude is pushed as far as it will theoretically go, then the end-products can have no magnitude (else divisions can still be made) yet must have some magnitude if the thing divided is not to vanish into nil components; and from this he goes on to extract the conjunction already quoted. Similarly—there is a copybook example in the paradox noticed under (v) of the previous section—Plato manufactures contradictions both within and between the movements of his argument by treating both parties to one of his conflicts as forming one logical conjunction, just as at the end of the dialogue (166c) he collects all the preceding inimical conclusions into one contradiction. The training in dialectic that he acknowledges to Zeno, and illustrates in his own antinomies, is a training in the presentation of conflicts between theses each of which seems cogent in its own right. He neither adopts nor proposes any general training in the resolving of such conflicts.

Still, even if proofs are not Plato's central interest in the *Parmenides*, does he not incidentally manage to prove some differences between unity (and therewith all numbers, according to the arguments under (10)) and common properties such as size and colour?

1. Surely this is the moral of the collision between (10) and (23). He seems to be pointing to that logical indispensability that he claims for unity in the *Philebus*: its character of being presupposed by all forms and

subjects of discourse (15d4–8, 16c9, 19b6). He does it by exploring the embarrassments we run into if we try to describe any subject or congeries of subjects that has no unity and cannot be resolved into parts having any, something that happens not to be or contain one of anything at all. He proceeds as though this were a project as straightforward as describing a subject that lacks some shape or size; and then he proposes an answer that, in the fashion of the dialogue, is made to seem unavoidable under (23) and impossible under (10).

Yet here too the conflict is plainer than the moral to be drawn from it. For one thing, it is not clear that his argument allows him to mark off unity from, say, relative size and weight. The question he professes to answer under (23) is, What can be generally true of things which are coming to have but do not yet have any unity? (Cf. 158b5–9.) But consider the predicate 'large', which he takes to be typically applicable to whatever is larger than something else (not necessarily larger than a standard object or than the average of some class). A comparable puzzle seems to arise if we ask, What can be true of something which is coming to have but does not yet have any largeness? For the answer seems to be that it cannot then have any size at all, yet the question implies that it is of a type to have some size or other. Let us look for an argument that does force a distinction between 'large' and 'one', that diverse pair that had for so long rubbed shoulders in the theory of Forms.

2. Given a certain view of Plato's grasp of the issues, there is a brace of arguments that seem to force just this distinction. And they are evidence of that distribution of duties between the two parts of the dialogue that I suggested earlier. It is in the first part that, in the view of many including Ryle, Plato brings out a fallacy that had pervaded his earlier statements of the theory of Forms. He had, in Ryle's words, spoken as though universals could be instances of themselves; and he now proves, by ascribing largeness to itself, that to credit anything with both functions generates a regress, in this case a regress of largenesses that turns the supposedly single Form into an unlimited class *(Prm.* 132a–b). Notice that the regress does not depend on mistreating largeness as a quality: it is equally effective whether or not the relational nature of the attribute is recognized. That Plato was able to isolate the mistake which lies at the root of this and other troubles in the context is, I think, put beyond question by premiss (18) and the arguments under it: I refer to my note there.

Now there is a comparable regress in the second part of the dialogue, making use this time of the 'ingredience' model of predication that appears in premiss (3); and it seems designed to show the recalcitrant behaviour of such putative properties as unity and being. In IB (142b–143a) Plato argues that if unity is a part or property of something (in this case, the One) it is *one* of the thing's parts and there *is* such a part; and the same is true of the thing's being. So both unity and being have the parts or properties of unity and being, which in turn have both parts, and so *ad infinitum*. But suppose Plato to have recognized the point of his first regress, namely that the common run of a thing's properties are not to be assigned to themselves; then here is a dilemma. Either he must say that unity and being cannot be component properties of anything on the same terms as its colour and size, or he must rule that unity canot be said to be unitary or being to be. But the second alternative will not readmit them as component properties of anything, for Plato is ready to argue that any component is *one* part and there *is* such a part. He seems to be marking off the sort of concept—identity and similarity and some others as well as unity and being—that will appear as 'common' in *Theaetetus* 185c4–d3 and as the ubiquitous vowel connectives of *Sophist* 253a4–6, c1–3, concepts which must be reintroduced in describing their own behaviour as in talking about anything else (e.g. 255d9–e6, 257a1–5).

Does this settle the question? Only for those who take Plato to have come to grasp the difference between largeness and anything large, and for those others who think him incapable at any time of that confusion. There are some who still think he never saw the distinction, and the review of their reasons would take us far outside the *Parmenides*. Their Plato is a grimmer and more baffled man than Ryle's, and more baffled on these issues than Plato's immediate colleagues and successors.

What positive conclusions Plato wants to be drawn from his nexus of conflicting arguments is perhaps, like the song the Sirens sang, a question not beyond all conjecture. It seems to me more conjectural than the programme I have ascribed to him. But whether he is trying a prentice hand at a highly sophisticated kind of proof, or constructing a frame within which to set and tie together puzzles about a remarkable family of very abstract concepts, Ryle's chief point is made. These are the concepts and the problems with which Plato will so often be concerned henceforth, and Ryle was the first to turn the eyes of Plato's modern readers in this direction.

XII

KNOWLEDGE IS PERCEPTION: *THEAETETUS* 151D–184A

M. F. BURNYEAT

THE OVERALL STRATEGY OF 151D–184A

It is essential to try to get a sense of the whole discussion 151d–184a before getting stuck into its individual sections. How one reads the individual sections will depend a great deal on one's conception of the overall strategy into which they fit.

Three distinct theses are in play: Theaetetus' definition of knowledge as perception, Protagoras' doctrine that man is the measure of all things, Heraclitus' theory of flux. Protagoras' doctrine, as Plato interprets it,[12] maintains the relative truth of all appearances: however things appear to someone, things *are for this person* just the way they appear, and if they appear different to someone else, then *for that person* they really and truly *are* different. Heraclitus' contribution is the thesis that everything is changing all the time, as summed up in the famous paradox 'You cannot step into the same river twice' (cf. 160d: 'all things flow like streams').[13] Two

[*Editor's note*: At various places Burnyeat refers to Parts I, II, and III of the *Theaetetus*. These are references to, respectively, *Theaetetus* 151d–186e, 187a–201c, and 201c–210d. The selection in this volume contains most of Burnyeat's discussion of Part I, up to 184a. However, I have omitted pp. 1–6 and pp. 31–9; the latter contains Burnyeat's discussion of the Digression (*Tht.* 171d–177c). I have retained the original footnote numbers throughout; hence this selection begins with n. 12.

[12] The question how far Plato gives a faithful account of the teaching of the historical Protagoras need not concern us: see G. B. Kerferd, 'Plato's Account of the Relativism of Protagoras', *Durham University Journal*, 42 (1949), 20–6; G. Vlastos, Introduction to *Plato's* Protagoras, trans. B. Jowett, rev. M. Ostwald (Indianapolis, 1956); Jonathan Barnes, *The Presocratic Philosophers* (London, 1979), vol. ii, ch. 10. Protagoras was born early in the 5th century BC and had died some years before our discussion begins (cf. 164e, 168e).

[13] Again, there is controversy about Plato's historical understanding of Heraclitus: see W. K. C. Guthrie, *A History of Greek Philosophy*, i (Cambridge, 1962), ch. VII; Charles H. Kahn *The Art and Thought of Heraclitus* (Cambridge, 1979). The dates of Heraclitus' life are difficul' to determine, but he was probably in middle age around 500 BC.

questions arise: How, in Plato's view, are the three theses related to one another in the discussion? What in fact are the underlying philosophical connections between them? It is on the answer to these questions that the disagreement between Price and Berkeley (p. 1) depends.*

Here is one reading of Plato's strategy, which makes things come out in the manner Berkeley would wish.[14] Plato himself accepts the theories of Protagoras and Heraclitus, subject to certain qualifications: in particular the theories must be restricted (as their authors did not take care to restrict them) to perception and the world of sensible things. Sensible things are, Plato agrees, in a perpetual flux of becoming, and in perception each of us has a 'measure', i.e. an incorrigible awareness, of the sensible qualities whose coming and going constitute that flux. But Plato will then argue that this awareness, incorrigible though it be, is not *knowledge*, precisely because its objects belong to the realm of becoming, not being. It has been agreed from the start (152c) that any candidate for knowledge must pass two tests: it must be always of what is and it must be unerring. Thanks to Protagoras, perception passes the second test, but thanks to Heraclitus, in the end it fails the first. Thus the argument, taken as a whole, supports the view set forth at length in earlier dialogues like the *Phaedo* and *Republic*, the celebrated Platonic doctrine that true reality is a non-sensible realm of changeless being, the Forms, and it is in these alone that knowledge can find its objects.

To sum up this reading (call it Reading A): perception is something of which Protagoras and Heraclitus give a true account. But nothing of which these theories are true can yield knowledge. Therefore, knowledge is not perception.[15]

Now for a rival reading (call it Reading B), more in harmony with the anti-empiricist moral that Price wished to draw.[16] Plato does not accept

* *Editor's note*: The British Empiricist philosopher George Berkeley took the *Theaetetus* to favour the central claims of his own empiricist theory of knowledge, whereas the 18th-century philosopher Richard Price took the *Theaetetus* to refute empiricism. See Berkeley's *Siris: A Chain of Philosophical Reflexions and Inquiries concerning the Virtues of Tar-Water* (1744), esp. sects. 311, 347–9; and R. Price, *A Review of the Principal Questions in Morals* (1748), ed. D. D. Raphael (Oxford, 1974), 53–6.

[14] See F. M. Cornford, *Plato's Theory of Knowledge* (London, 1935). It would be fair to say that, in one version or another, this is the reading most commonly found in the scholarly literature on Plato.

[15] Readers of Berkeley may wonder how he could endorse this conclusion, for did he not himself hold that perceiving is knowing (e.g. *Principles of Human Knowledge* (1710), §§1–6)? The answer is that in *Siris* (1744) Berkeley uses 'knowledge' to mean *science*, understanding the connections between the things we perceive and (in the *Principles* sense) know. Cf. *Siris*, §§253, 304–5. So what Berkeley thought the dialogue proves is that sense-perception is not science (expertise).

[16] Sketched in M. F. Burnyeat, 'Idealism and Greek Philosophy: What Descartes Saw and Berkeley Missed', *Philosophical Review*, 90 (1982), 3–40, but originally formulated by Bernard Williams (cf. p. xiii). [Ed.: See the preface to *The* Theatetus *of Plato*.]

the theories of Protagoras and Heraclitus. Theaetetus is made to accept them because, having defined knowledge as perception, he is faced with the question, What has to be true of perception and of the world for the definition to hold good? The answer suggested is that he will have to adopt a Protagorean epistemology, and that in turn will commit him to a Heraclitean account of the world. It takes Socrates until 160e to work out with Theaetetus these consequences of the definition of knowledge as perception, after which he shows that the three-in-one theory they have elaborated (Theaetetus' first-born child) leads to multiple absurdities, culminating in a proof (179c–183c) that if the theory were true it would make language impossible. Thus the structure of the argument is that of a *reductio ad absurdum*: Theaetetus → Protagoras → Heraclitus → the impossibility of language. Hence Theaetetus' definition is impossible.

This is only the barest outline of two ways of construing the elaborate argument of Part I. They are not the only possible interpretations, but they are sufficiently opposed to one another to focus the issue of strategy. You, the reader, must now watch for the stage directions, as it were, which Plato scatters through the text to indicate how he views the three theses and their interrelations: e.g. at 151e–152c, 152e, 155d–e, 157c–d, 158e, 160c–e, 163a, 164d, 166a–b, 168b, 177c, 179c–d, 183a–c. And you must consider for yourself which construal makes a better job of threading one section to the next to shape a philosophically coherent whole.

To illustrate: a key passage, on any reading, is 160d–e, centrally and emphatically placed at a turning-point in the discussion. Socrates is summing up the whole process of bringing Theaetetus' conception of knowledge to birth before he turns to test it for soundness. He says that the three theses have been found to coincide: all three come to the same thing. In particular, he represents Theaetetus' view (160e) as the view that *since* all things change (Heraclitus) and man is the measure of all things (Protagoras), knowledge proves to be perception. In other words, he represents Theaetetus as relying on Protagoras and Heraclitus to support his definition. How are we to take this declaration?

On Reading A Socrates only says that all three theses come to the same thing because he has been making the best case he can for the definition of knowledge as perception. He will later refute 'Knowledge is perception' while retaining (some of) Protagoras and Heraclitus, so he cannot seriously think that all three stand or fall together. On Reading B this is just what he does think. Protagoras and Heraclitus provide sufficient conditions for Theaetetus' definition to come out correct (160e; cf. 183a). What Socrates has been arguing at length down to 160e is that they are the only sufficient conditions which could reasonably be devised. That means they are necessary conditions (Theaetetus → Protagoras → Heraclitus) as well as sufficient (Heraclitus → Protagoras → Theaetetus), and the three theses really do stand or, later, fall together.

That must suffice to set the question of strategy. It should whet the appetite for a closer examination of the part played by Protagoras and Heraclitus in the bringing to birth of Theaetetus' child.

EXPOSITION OF THE THREE THESES (151D–160E)

'Knowledge is perception' has a decidedly empiricist ring to it. In brief, empiricism is the doctrine that all knowledge has its source in sense-experience, although of course a bald statement like this admits of, and has been given, many different interpretations. If we may continue, nevertheless, to speak baldly and roughly, it can be said that, historically, there has been a tendency among empiricist philosophers to find the paradigm of knowledge and certainty in the immediate awareness of sensible qualities such as red or hot (Berkeleian ideas, twentieth-century sense-data). We shall find something closely similar in the *Theaetetus*, and it was this, of course, that led Berkeley to identify the *Theaetetus* theory of perception with his own (p. 321). Once a view of that sort has been adopted, it is then one of the tasks of an empiricist epistemology to explain how on such foundations we can build the rest of knowledge, or at least, if that seems too ambitious, erect a structure of more or less reasonable belief. (*i.e. not knowledge*)

Now the thesis that knowledge is perception breaks down into two propositions: (1) all perceiving is knowing, (2) all knowing is perceiving. The *Theaetetus* shows little recognition of the more generous empiricism that would result if the 'is' in (2) was changed to 'gets its content from' or, less stringently, 'is based on'. Nor is the dialogue interested in the (perhaps characteristically modern) idea that, where knowledge runs out, we may still seek reasonable belief. But the question whether the senses provide us with knowledge and certainty and, if they do, what kind of knowledge and certainty this is, goes to the heart of any empiricist programme. It is with this question that Part I of the dialogue is concerned.

However, propositions (1) and (2) are still vague. A precise meaning needs to be specified for them if philosophical progress is to be made. Socrates suggests (151e–152a) that the meaning is given, in different language, by Protagoras' doctrine that man is the measure of all things. This doctrine is expounded in terms of the example of the wind which feels cold

324   M. F. BURNYEAT

to one person and not to another, and so according to Protagoras *is* cold
for the one and not so for the other. And argument is given (152b–c) to
show that from Protagoras' Measure Doctrine we may derive proposition
(1): all perceiving is knowing. (Question: what about proposition (2)?
Could this also be derived from Protagoras? What role does (2) have in
the sequel?) All perceiving is knowing because Protagoras' doctrine of the
relative truth of all appearances enables perception to pass two tests which
any candidate for knowledge must meet (p. 321). Every perceptual appearance is shown to be the *unerring* apprehension of *how things are* for the
perceiver.

The logical analysis of the argument for this conclusion will provide a
nice task for the reader's leisure. At present we should attend to the
premiss which is accepted by Theaetetus, without argument, at 152b: 'it
appears' means 'he perceives it' or, rephrasing in the material mode, to
perceive something is to have it appear to one.

From the example of the wind it is clear that the relevant kind of appearing is that which is expressed by such a sentence as 'The wind appears cold
to me'. Recast in terms of the verb 'perceive', this will become: 'I perceive
that the wind is cold'. So in its generalized form the premiss may be stated
thus: *x* appears *F* to *a* (where *x* is an object, *F* a sensible quality, and *a* a
perceiving subject) if and only if *a* perceives that *x* is *F*. This means that
the perceiving we will be concerned with is perceiving that such and such
is the case, as contrasted with perceiving objects: '*a* perceives that *x* is *F*'
represents such constructions as 'He sees that the stone is white' (cf. 156e),
'He tastes the sweetness of wine' or 'He finds his food bitter' (cf. 159c–d,
166e), 'He perceives the lyre to be out of tune' (cf. 178d), in contrast to:
'He sees the stone', 'He hears the lyre', and the like, which incorporate no
reference to any sensible aspect the perceiver is aware of in the object
perceived, and which do not say what he perceives it *as*.

This decision on how 'perceiving' is to be taken will prove critical later
(179c, 184b ff.), when questions are raised about the role of judgement
in perception. At this stage, however, we must ask about the *status* of
the identification of perceiving with appearing. It seems to be supplementary to Protagoras' Measure Doctrine, rather than part of it, for
the Measure Doctrine, as stated, does not mention perceiving. Hence
to derive proposition (1) a supplementary premiss is needed which
does mention perceiving and identifies it with the key Protagorean
notion of appearing. Is the extra premiss one that Plato inserts because
he believes it to be true (Reading A)? Or is the thought rather this,
that Theaetetus will need to take perception this way, to assume some
element of judgement or conceptualization, or else he has no chance of

making out that perceiving is knowing (Reading B)? The text does not tell us. We must decide as we go along which answer best illuminates the whole discussion.

The next step (152c–e) brings an analogous problem. The suggestion that perhaps Protagoras taught a secret Heraclitean doctrine is not intended as a serious historical attribution—so much would now be generally agreed—but it might none the less be serious as philosophy. Reading A sees here nothing more than a humorous device whereby Plato can introduce 'a fundamental principle of his own philosophy',[17] that all sensible objects are perpetually changing (p. 321). Others, however, are not so sure that so bald a principle does accurately represent Plato's earlier views about the sensible world,[18] or if it does, that we can assume that in the *Theaetetus* Plato still adheres to it; maybe he wants to rethink his position.[19] It is important, then, that Plato could quite seriously be maintaining that all this Protagorean talk about things being what they are *for* someone is something of a riddle (cf. 155d–e, 162a), which can be clarified if it is translated into the Heraclitean idiom of becoming. Thus '*x* is *F* for *a*' gives way to '*x* becomes *F* for *a*'. On Reading B this would not be a commitment on Plato's part to a Heraclitean theory of perception and the sensible world, but a commitment on Theaetetus' part to clarify and develop the Protagorean epistemology he has just accepted.

What is gained by moving over to the idiom of becoming? Officially, it is to help with a certain problem about opposites. Opposite predicates like 'large' and 'small', 'heavy' and 'light', have the peculiar property that, when you find a thing to which one of the pair applies, it transpires that the opposite applies as well. (For the moment Plato leaves his readers to work out their own illustrative examples.) You cannot say '*x* is *F*' and leave it at that (152d: 'there is nothing which in itself is just one thing'). You must add '*x* is **F*', where **F* is the opposite of *F*. But if *F* and **F* are opposites, in some sense they are incompatible with one another. The problem is to see how a thing can manage to be both *F* and **F*.

There is no question but that this problem underlies many of

[17] Cornford, *Plato's Theory of Knowledge*, 36.

[18] e.g. Alexander Nehamas, 'Plato on the Imperfection of the Sensible World', *American Philosophical Quarterly*, 12 (1975), 105–17 [Ed.: This is Ch. VI above.]; T. H. Irwin, 'Plato's Heracliteanism', *Philosophical Quarterly*, 27 (1977), 1–13.

[19] For a now famous scholarly controversy concerning the development of Plato's views about flux in the sensible world, see G. E. L. Owen, 'The Place of the *Timaeus* in Plato's Dialogues', *Classical Quarterly*, NS 3 (1953), 79–95; repr. in *Logic, Science and Dialectic: Collected Papers in Greek Philosophy*, ed. M. Nussbaum (London, 1986), 65–84; v. H. F. Cherniss, 'The Relation of the *Timaeus* to Plato's Later Dialogues', *American Journal of Philology*, 78 (1957), 225–66; repr. in *Selected Papers*, ed. L. Tarán (Leiden, 1977), 298–339; both papers repr. in R. E. Allen (ed.), *Studies in Plato's Metaphysics* (London, 1965), 313–38 and 339–78.

Heraclitus' own paradoxical utterances,[20] but what is its relevance here? Does a Protagorean epistemology allow opposite predicates to be true of the same thing? If it does, how will the language of becoming help to make this intelligible? On any reading, the answer to these questions takes some while to emerge.

We are first (153a–d) given some general considerations favouring a Heraclitean outlook on the world. (Do a count of the jokes in this bit. With a master dramatist like Plato, the tone of a passage can be an important guide to how we should respond.) Then come some rather more argumentative considerations (153d ff.) on behalf of Protagorean relativism, culminating in the statement and analysis (154c–155c) of a pair of puzzles about the opposites 'larger' and 'smaller', 'more' and 'less', puzzles which look to be structurally analogous to the original problem about 'large' and 'small', 'heavy' and 'light'. But the analogy is also an advance, inasmuch as the new puzzles are explicitly about relative predicates (e.g. the six dice are more *than four* and less *than twelve*). Their solution can thus serve as a perspicuous model for the thoroughgoing relativization which Protagoras recommends. When you add an explicit specification of the different relations in which opposite predicates hold of the same thing, the contradiction disappears. Finally, at 155d–156a the Heraclitean explanation of all this is at last announced. It becomes clear that relativization is not the complete answer to our problem, for Socrates proceeds to a complicated account (156a ff.) of perception, perceivers, and sensible things which spells out Protagorean relativity in the language of becoming.

Let us look first at the Protagorean component of this account. It is recommended in the section 153d–154b by one of the most influential patterns of argument in the history of epistemology: the argument from conflicting appearances. It is a familiar fact of experience that the colour (taste, shape, temperature) of an object will appear different to different observers in the varying circumstances of observation. From this mundane starting-point it is inferred that the colour white, for example, is not inherent in the object, not a feature which characterizes the object in itself; white exists only in relation to a given observer, 'between' their eye and the object (154a), and it is therefore private to them (154a; cf. 161d, 166c), something of which only they can be aware.

---

[20] e.g. 'Sea is the most pure and the most polluted water: drinkable and salutary for fishes, but undrinkable and destructive for men' (frag. 61); 'The path up and down is one and the same' (frag. 60); 'As the same thing there exists in us living and dead and the waking and the sleeping and young and old; for these having changed about are those and those having changed about are these' (frag. 88).

That, in brief, is the argument from conflicting appearances as it is found in the *Theaetetus*, in the first of Berkeley's *Three Dialogues between Hylas and Philonous* (1713), in the first chapter of Russell's *The Problems of Philosophy* (1912), and in many other distinguished thinkers. The twentieth-century 'argument from illusion' for the thesis that what we perceive is sense-data (e.g. a private white), rather than whole physical objects, is a variant on the same theme, the main difference being that to call it the 'argument from illusion' presupposes we know which of the conflicting appearances is correct.[21]

It is worth pondering the argument both in the abstract and in the specific version presented here. What assumptions are required to validate the inference and how many of them does Plato make explicit? Does he need to have Socrates start from the extraordinarily strong claim (154a) that colour appearances are *never* the same between man and other animals, between one man and another, or even between one time and another within the experience of a single man? Why does Plato (unlike Berkeley and Russell, for example) couple the argument showing that white is not inherent in the object with another to show that neither is it inherent in the perceiving subject (154b)?[22] Most important of all, what (if anything) does the conflict of appearances really tell us about the nature and objects of perception?

If these questions suggest lines of inquiry into resemblances and differences between modern empiricist theories of perception and the perceptual relativism which Plato develops out of Protagoras' Measure Doctrine, they may also prompt a further thought, which the history of epistemology amply confirms. It is that you cannot go far with this sort of theory without involving yourself, as both Berkeley and Russell did, with questions about the ordinary physical objects (sticks and stones, tables and chairs) which we ordinarily think, before we start to theorize, are the things we perceive. What implications does our theory bring for them? Notoriously, Berkeley held that a stone or a table can be nothing more than a 'collection of ideas': compare 157b. In *The Problems of Philosophy*, on the other hand, Russell thought that there was something more than appearances or sense-data, viz. the physical objects which cause us to have sense-data, but that what these physical objects are like in themselves could only

---

[21] A well-known discussion of the argument from illusion is A. J. Ayer, *The Foundations of Empirical Knowledge* (London, 1940), ch. 1.

[22] There is one modern parallel for this second argument, in F. H. Bradley, *Appearance and Reality*, 2nd edn. (Oxford, 1897), 9–10, where it looks very likely that Bradley has our *Theaetetus* passage specifically in mind. However, on another interpretation (J. McDowell, *Plato: Theaetetus* (Oxford, 1973), 132) the second issue at 154b is not whether the perceiver's eye is white but whether he can be said, without qualification, to be seeing white.

be known with difficulty and by inference. If that idea seems alien to the approach followed in the *Theaetetus*, the contrast may itself serve to emphasize the extent to which the two propositions comprising Theaetetus' definition subordinate everything to the securing of certainty (pp. 323–4).

Thus, summing up the argument so far, from Theaetetus' definition we have the thesis (1) that perception, and (2) that perception alone, provides knowledge and certainty, and from Protagoras' Measure Doctrine we have a guarantee that every perceptual appearance will be the unerring apprehension of how things are for the perceiver; this secures for perception the certainty that Theaetetus requires. In addition, all through 153d–155c it has been brought home to us that what enables Protagoras to achieve this result is his strategy of relativization. And we can see why that should be so important. If there is no question of the wind being cold in itself, or not cold, but it is cold for one perceiver and not for another, then there is no question of one perceiver being right where the other is wrong about the temperature of the wind. There is no such thing as *the* temperature of the wind by which to correct, or confirm, someone who says that it is cold. There is no independent fact of the matter which they could be mistaken about. It seems reasonable to claim, therefore, that each perceiver is necessarily and incorrigibly right about all there is for them to be right about, namely, how it is *for them*. But what now becomes of the wind which we have described as cold for one perceiver and not for another, or the stone which is white for one person and a different colour for another? What about the perceivers themselves? And this coldness or whiteness existing privately for the one perceiver but not for the other? What sorts of item are these? The question is pressing, whether we take it as a question for Plato about the further development of his own theory (Reading A) or as a question for Theaetetus about the ontological basis for his Protagorean account of knowledge (Reading B). The strategy of a systematic relativization of sensory predicates makes problematic the whole nature of what we ordinarily think of as the physical world.

This brings us to the Heraclitean story set forth at 156a ff. The story teaches that there are no *things*, only processes—the world is a vast array of motions, some with active power and others passive. There are no *properties* of things either, but again only motions, produced in pairs by the pairing of an active and a passive member of the first group of motions, and distinguished from the latter inasmuch as the twin offspring are always swift motions while the parental pair are slow. As we ordinarily think of, for example, visual perception, it is a relation between two things—say Socrates or, more narrowly, his eye, and a stone—one of which has the property of seeing and the other the property which is seen, e.g. whiteness.

The Heraclitean story does away with things and properties, and would have us think instead in terms of four interacting motions:

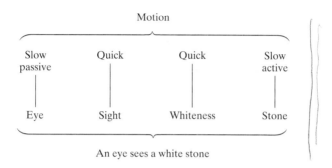

This is a remarkable theory. How exactly does it help the discussion forward?

One can interpret the theory in two very different ways, the first broadly speaking physical, the second metaphysical. To illustrate the difference, consider one detail, the description of whiteness and sight as moving through space between eye and object (156d). Is this literally meant as an account of what goes on in perception, so that we could think of colour and sight as rays of energy or streams of particles travelling from one place to another? The physical interpretation says: Yes, this is at least an outline framework for the sort of account Plato himself gives of colour vision in his cosmological work, the *Timaeus* (45b–46c, 67c–68d).[23] (The physical interpretation is thus a natural, though not perhaps an inevitable concomitant of Reading A.) The *Timaeus* account is all about particles of fire streaming out from the eye and coalescing with other fire particles emitted from physical objects, the varieties of the latter particles being coordinated with the varieties of colour seen. The *Theaetetus* story is less detailed, more of an outline than a completed theory, but it is making the same *sort* of claim and some of the same specific claims.

To this the metaphysical interpretation will reply that the *Timaeus* assumes stable objects to give off the particles and stable sense-organs to respond; the theory presupposes the notion of things having a continuing identity through time, which it is the very purpose of the *Theaetetus* story to deny.[24] Objects cannot have a continuing identity through time if every

---

[23] For elucidation of the *Timaeus* passages, see F. M. Cornford, *Plato's Cosmology* (London, 1937).

[24] For other difficulties in the project of matching up the two dialogues, see McDowell, *Plato: Theaetetus*, 139.

feature they manifest is relativized to a single perceiver and to the time of their perception, and every feature must be so relativized if perceptual awareness is to be incorrigible: stability through time, no less than objectivity between different observers, would constitute an independent fact of the matter by reference to which one perception could be counted right, another wrong. If that is the thought behind the theory, it goes well with Reading B: Theaetetus → Protagoras → Heraclitus. From this perspective it is not surprising that no mention is made of particles or stuff of a physical sort, or that no content is given to the contrast between swift and slow motions other than that the former involve two locations, the latter just one. If we stop expecting 'scientific' details of the type given in the *Timaeus*, we can take the talk of whiteness and sight moving through space between momentary eye and momentary stone as designed to bring out the point that seeing is seeing something *over there from here*, and whiteness is whiteness manifesting itself *there to me here*. Reference to two locations is intrinsic to the description of sight and colour in a way it is not intrinsic to the description of eye and stone, even though these also, on the theory, come into being, or occur, at their respective locations only as the stone acting and the eye responding at the same moment of time. We can enjoy the picturesque detail without forcing it into a scientific mould. For the Heraclitean story which Plato recounts with imaginative delight is a metaphysical projection of a world in which the Protagorean epistemology holds good.

No doubt the physical interpretation can hit back by pointing out that at the metaphysical level the *Timaeus* would agree that ordinary objects are changing all the time (cf. *Ti.* 48e–52c); Plato need see no inconsistency in combining this, his usual metaphysical view (p. 321), with the sketch of a physical theory of perception. But the reader may now be left to follow the story to the triumphant climax of 160d–e, where the three theses come together to proclaim that no perceiver can fail to be a knower of that which they perceive. On the way you will recognize the first extant statement (157e–158e) of the now classic problems, whether it is possible to determine that one is sane and not mad, awake and not dreaming: problems which were to assume great importance in the first of Descartes's *Meditations* (1641). From the absence of any clear indication by which to tell which state one is in, Descartes is tempted to infer that, for all we know, any experience might be the illusion of a dream. The conclusion drawn in the *Theaetetus* is not this radical scepticism, but it is hardly less dramatic. It is not that any experience might be the illusion of a dream, hence false, but that any experience has as much right to be considered veridical as any other; all are on a par, all true for the individual subject who has them, no matter what the conditions (dreaming, madness, etc.) under which they occur. This disarms the objection of common sense that a dreamer perceives nothing real at all, while sickness makes one liable to misperceive.

To confirm the conclusion that there is no such thing as a false perception, the discussion then moves into a tricky argument (158e–160c) for a completely universal thesis of non-identity over time. The healthy, sane, or waking Socrates who finds his wine sweet is totally distinct from the unhealthy, mad, or dreaming Socrates who finds his wine bitter, and there are two distinct wines as well. We end up conjoining, as it were, Berkeley's dissolution of physical objects into a series of ideas perceived with Hume's dissolution of the self into a series of perceptions.[25] Indeed, it is a question whether, at the end of the day, we are even allowed to construe the perceiving subject or perceived object as an aggregate of distinct perceptions–sensible qualities perceived. Compare 157b with 160b. It is clear that 'people' employ names for such aggregates, not so clear that this practice has the approval of the wise Heracliteans whose story culminates in a decree of Necessity that ties each momentary perceiver and its perceived partner to each other and to nothing else.[26] Sorting all this out will challenge the reader to reach at least an interim decision on the interpretative and philosophical issues we have been discussing.

On any account we have travelled a long way from Theaetetus' first hesitant proposal of the definition of knowledge as perception (151d–e). Thanks to Socrates' skill as a midwife of ideas, Theaetetus' original conception has proved a larger thing than he foresaw. It has grown into a whole theory of knowledge and the world, astonishing not only for its anticipations of modern empiricist themes, but even more for its own audacious combination of logical rigour and philosophical imagination. It is time to see whether the newborn child can survive in the cold light of Socrates' criticism.

CRITIQUE OF THE THREE THESES (160E–184A)

When Theaetetus' travail is finally over and Socrates turns to examine the worth of his offspring, the first, and for much of the ensuing discussion the dominant, issue is one the relevance of which is not immediately obvious:

whether the epistemology which Theaetetus has borrowed from Protagoras allows for the possibility of wisdom.

The first point to make is that the Greek word translated 'wisdom' has in this context the connotations of 'expertise'.[27] Remember also that Socrates' question 'What is knowledge?' was originally prompted by the idea that wisdom, that is, expertise, is (a matter of) knowledge (145e). The issue is not, of course, whether on the account of knowledge we have elaborated with such care there can be knowledge. The question whether there can be expertise is the question whether there can be specialist knowledge (in geometry, for example) such that one person is more knowledgeable than others, knows things that most people do not, has the truth where others are ignorant or wrong. That is how the discussion can treat the following four propositions as equivalent: (i) each man is the measure of his own wisdom (161e, 169d), (ii) everyone is equally wise (162c), (iii) there is no such thing as wisdom/no one is wise (166d), (iv) no one is wiser than anyone else (161d). If no one is wiser than anyone else, no one is wise. If no one is more expert than anyone else, no one is an expert and expertise does not exist.

On the face of it, Protagoras' relativism is incompatible with expertise. As Plato argues elsewhere, 'If wisdom and folly exist [it has been agreed that they do], Protagoras' view cannot be the truth: for one person could not be truly wiser than another if whatever seems to each is to be true for him' (*Cratylus* 386c). But in this dialogue a posthumous protest by Protagoras (162d–e) soon puts a stop to any such barefaced appeal to common sense. You cannot just assert the existence of expertise against a philosophy which is designed precisely to eliminate the possibility of genuine disagreement between people.

Still, it is a legitimate question to ask how far a Protagorean will have to go once he starts out on this line of thought. It is as a question that Socrates raises the point at 161c–162a. First, how, given his philosophy, can Protagoras set himself up to teach others? Then, more sharply, what, on Protagoras' account of truth, can be the point of philosophical discussion, including of course the present discussion of Protagoras' account of truth? We are also jokingly reminded (162c) that the young Theaetetus is supposed to be becoming more of an expert in the subjects he is learning from Theodorus, not to be already as good an expert as his teacher. There are phenomena here: teaching and learning, discussion and debate. Will a consistent Protagorean have to deny that they occur, which would seem frightfully implausible, or can he find some way of

[27] See note *ad* 145d.

redescribing them to show that they are after all compatible with his philosophy?

Essentially, the question is a challenge. So far, the strategy of relativization has been applied only to the sensory predicates involved in perception (152c), although 'good' and 'bad' were slipped in at 157d, as was the typically empiricist idea that feelings like pleasure and pain, desire and fear, are species of perception (156b).[28] But we may wonder whether language comes in neat compartments such that relativization in one area will have no consequences elsewhere. The challenge is: How much further must a Protagorean go? Just as the strategy of relativization was seen to make problematic the whole nature of what we ordinarily think of as the physical world (pp. 327–8), so also it makes problematic all those aspects of human life which involve communication. That is one possible answer to the question of relevance.

It is an answer that brings with it further questions. What right have we to discourse about human life in these terms after adopting the Heraclitean story (constant flux, universal non-identity over time) about people and things? Does this question matter? How does it affect our two readings A and B? Reading A has it that Plato is now embarking on argument to show that Protagoras' Measure Doctrine cannot hold beyond the field of sense-perception (p. 321). Reading B sees here the start of the process of bringing out the many absurdities to which Theaetetus' three-in-one theory will lead. Can either interpretation afford to ignore the questions just raised?

Whatever we decide about Plato's broadening the focus of discussion, it should come as no surprise to find that, in consequence, the application of the Protagorean formula 'x appears F to a' gets considerably extended. Instead of a sensible object appearing to a perceiver, in the following sections of the dialogue x may be, for example, a law or practice (167c) or someone's opinion (171a), a may be a whole city as well as any individual (167c, 172a), and the predicate term F may be 'just' (167c, 172a), 'false' (170d, 171a), 'persuasive' (178e). These are not sensory predicates. When we speak of a law appearing just, or an opinion false, to someone, in such cases 'it appears' means not 'he perceives it' but 'he believes it', 'it seems so to him'. If this raises in our minds questions about the relation of belief or judgement to perception, that is no doubt something Plato would wish to encourage (pp. 324–5). It should also return our attention to the second half of Theaetetus' original definition, the thesis that all knowing is

---

[28] Compare Hume, *Treatise*, I. ii. 6: 'To hate, to love, to feel, to see; all this is nothing but to perceive.'

perceiving (pp. 323, 328). If the Measure Doctrine says that however a thing appears to someone, so it is for them, and Theaetetus is brought to accept that this holds whether the appearing is to sense *or* to thought, how can he still maintain that all knowing is perceiving? Some of it must be simply believing or judging.

The stage is now set for a broad-ranging discussion of Protagorean relativism, taken in a more general form than was originally required for the elucidation of Theaetetus' definition. But first comes a section (163a–165e) which seems designed to emphasize the importance of opening up this broader perspective. It is a model demonstration of how *not* to go about criticizing the thesis that knowledge is perception, namely, by isolating the thesis from the epistemological and metaphysical concerns with which it has been connected hitherto and pointing to various sentential contexts in which 'knows' and 'perceives' are not interchangeable without loss of sense or truth. To an ear attuned to twentieth-century philosophy, one or two of the arguments are in fact quite impressive; notably some considerations after the manner of Gilbert Ryle to the effect that it is possible to see, but not to know, clearly or dimly, that it is absurd to say of knowing, what is true of seeing, that you can only do it from close by, and so on (165d).[29] But Plato makes it clear that in his view this sort of objection is no better than one which starts from the outrageous premiss that a man with one eye covered both sees and does not see the cloak in front of him (165b–c).

Readers can entertain themselves and exercise their logical wits deciding on the worth of the several objections. But you should also ask this question: Is it not a proper test of a proposed definition that it should supply a formula which is substitutable for the definiendum (in our case, the noun 'knowledge' or the verb 'to know') without loss of sense or truth? If not, why not? Is Plato really entitled to maintain that these substitution tests insist upon a too rigid and superficial verbal consistency instead of tackling the issues of substance (164c–165e, 166b–c, 168b–c)?

The issues of substance mentioned here are those that connect the definition with Protagorean relativism and Heraclitean flux (166b–c). It is Protagoras himself who, in response to this parade of 'verbal' objections, brings the discussion back to the epistemological and metaphysical implications of the definition, and Protagoras who now widens our view of these implications still further. For at 166a we embark on an important section commonly known as 'The Defence of Protagoras' in which Socrates takes on the role of Protagoras replying to the challenge, What is he to say about

---

[29] McDowell, *Plato: Theaetetus*, 163–4, feels constrained to offer a different reading just because otherwise the argument would indeed be a powerful one, which Plato should not so lightly brush aside!

The Defence of Protagoras

expertise?[30] It is proclaimed that the challenge will be met head on. Protagoras, in the mouth of Socrates, undertakes to show that expertise can exist, and the activities of experts can be described, compatibly with the relativism of the doctrine that man is the measure of all things (166d–167d). That done, he can restate relativism in the completely general form 'For each person and each city, things are what they seem to them to be' (168b).[31]

This is the passage that F. C. S. Schiller seized upon for its persuasive recommendation of the pragmatist point of view (p. 1).* Protagoras' central claim is that the expert (doctor, teacher, etc.) is one who effects an improvement in our perceptions, feelings, or thoughts. According to the Measure Doctrine, whatever we think or feel is true for each of us: so the state of mind which results from the expert's ministration is not *truer* than our previous state of mind. But it is *better* (167a–b). Schiller supposed that by 'better' Protagoras meant that one is better adjusted to life and the world around (rather as when one's eyesight is improved); and he further maintained that this is only terminologically different from the full pragmatist thesis that the true or truer state of mind *is* the one which has the most satisfactory consequences, the one which selects itself as the most serviceable to live with.

Subtract this last claim, that Protagoras is virtually reshaping the notion of truth itself, not just appealing beyond it to considerations of what is better, and Schiller's interpretation is widely shared. The meaning of 'better' is disputed: Is it that which is most in accordance with the state of mind of a healthy subject, or that which most agrees with the perception

---

[30] It is generally agreed that Protagoras must have faced this challenge, at least in regard to his own profession as educator of the young. If he answered it in writing, Plato could be making use of genuinely Protagorean material in the central portion of the Defence (166d–167d). Many scholars think that he is; the talk of plants having perceptions, for example, has an archaic ring. Others think that 168c implies the opposite, that Socrates has had to construct the Defence from his own resources, without a written statement by Protagoras to guide him; that is why later on (169d–170a) he insists that the refutation must be based on statements made in Protagoras' book. It is not much use arguing that the Defence Socrates offers must be historically sound because there is no other way Protagoras could reconcile his philosophy with his profession (Cornford, *Plato's Theory of Knowledge*, 72; W. K. C. Guthrie, *The Sophists* (Cambridge, 1971), 172 n. 1). For, as we are about to see, the text leaves us guessing which of several different reconciliations Socrates–Protagoras might be offering.

[31] Note the strict parallel between individual and city here. A modern philosopher would distinguish among relativisms between those that make truth relative to the judgement of an individual and those that make it relative to the standards prevailing in a group. The *Theaetetus* simply admits collective subjects on a par with individual ones, leaving aside questions about the relation between the judgement of the collective and the judgements of the individuals composing it.

* *Editor's note*: See F. C. S. Schiller, *Studies in Humanism* (London, 1907), ch. 2; *Plato or Protagoras?* (Oxford, 1908).

and thought of one's fellows, or that which is most advantageous to the organism, or that which will seem better in the future? All of these have had their advocate.[32] None the less, they have in common that they all provide a pragmatic, if not strictly pragmatist, test for expertise. Results are the thing, on this interpretation, not truth. It is to results that Protagoras is looking to reconcile the Measure Doctrine with the existence of expertise.

Yet there are grounds for unease. If Protagoras takes this broadly pragmatic line of defence, but stops short of a Schiller-type redefinition of truth, he compromises his relativism in two places. First, whichever of the above-mentioned senses he gives to 'better', it becomes an objective matter that one of two states of mind is better than the other. The truth of the claim that one is better is not relative to how it appears either to the expert who effects the change or to the subject whose mind he changes. Second, and consequent upon this, it is an equally objective, non-relative question whether experts exist. Schiller's suggestion that Protagoras was a full-blown pragmatist ahead of his time avoids the difficulty and secures consistency for the Defence, but unfortunately the text at 167a–b insists strongly that, as regards truth, the better and the worse states of mind are on a par. It seems that we must abandon hopes of finding the pragmatist account of truth in the *Theaetetus*. In which case, all that remains for Protagoras, if he is not to compromise the Measure Doctrine, is the following:

(D1) State of mind S_1 is better *for a* than state of mind S_2 if and only if it seems to *a* that S_1 is better than S_2.

In other words, the test is whether *a* thinks or feels himself 'better off' for the change from S_2 to S_1. From which it is but a short step to

(D2) *x* is an expert *for a* if and only if it seems to *a* that he is better off thanks to *x*.

In other words, there are experts (doctors, statesmen, and the like) just in so far as, and *for* those people by whom, they are acknowledged as such.

On this basis Protagoras could argue that he resolves disputes over who is competent and who is merely a quack, be it in medicine or education, politics or agriculture, in exactly the same way as he had earlier dealt with disputes about whether the wind is cold or not cold. It is no objection that almost anyone might be found persuasive or improving by someone in some matter or other. For one thing, Protagoras is already on record, in

[32] Respectively, John Burnet, *Greek Philosophy: Thales to Plato* (London, 1914), 116; A. E. Taylor, *Plato—the Man and his Work* (London, 1926), 322–3; Kerferd, 'Plato's Account of the Relativism of Protagoras'; Cornford, *Plato's Theory of Knowledge*, 73–4.

Plato's dialogue *Protagoras*, as maintaining that virtue is taught by every-one to everyone.[33] For another, in strict logic nothing less radical than D1 and D2 will vindicate Protagoras' claim—a claim he does seem to make (167d, 168b)—that he can save his theory without compromising its generality.

It would be nice, and the history of philosophy would be an easier subject than it is, if philosophers never wavered from the requirements of strict logic. But of course they do. In advance of a close examination of the text we have no guarantee that the Defence does not compromise Protagoras' relativism and concede the objectivity of judgements of what is better. Let us focus on the formal definition of expertise from which the argumentative part of the Defence begins: 'I call wise ... the man who in any case where bad things both appear and are for one of us, works a change and makes good things appear and be for him' (166d).

One thing this tells us is that the change to a better state of mind (described at 167a–b) is a change to a state in which better things appear and are for one. That amounts to D1 if—but alas, only if—(i) 'Better things appear and are for someone' means the same as (ii) 'Things appear and are better for him'.

It is obvious enough why the uncompromising interpretation should offer (ii) as its elucidation of (i).[34] If things appear better than they were to someone, then on Protagorean principles they *are* better *for* the person who thinks them so. As we are forcefully reminded at 167a, and again at 167d, no one can be wrong about anything, so no one can be wrong if they feel themselves better off as a result of some putative expert's intervention.

The alternative, compromising view is that 'better' in (i) refers to things that are in fact better, regardless of whether they seem so to the person whose mind the expert changes. In more technical language, 'better' belongs to the subject rather than to the complement (predicate) of the verbs 'appear' and 'are'. The point is not that *x* appears better to *a* than it did before, with the result on Protagorean principles that it is better for *a* than it was. Rather, instead of *x* appearing *F* to *a* (for some as yet unspecified value of *F*), something better than *x* appears *F* to *a*,

[33] This is the theme of his Great Speech at *Protagoras* 320c–328d. So far as concerns his own teaching, Protagoras in that dialogue sometimes seems to promise objective benefits to his pupils (318a, 318d–319a), sometimes to accept that the test of his expertise as a teacher is whether his pupils *think* themselves better off for listening to him (316c, 328b–c). Compare also *Republic* 488c.

[34] So Vlastos, Introduction to *Plato's* Protagoras, pp. xxi–ii with n. 47.

with the result on Protagorean principles that something better than x is E for a.

A nice choice. The wording of the definition of expertise quoted from 166d can be taken either way. So the next step is to consult the examples in the passage to see which construal they favour.

A doctor administers drugs which have the effect that your food tastes sweet instead of bitter (166e–167a). This fits (ii) quite well: tasting sweet instead of bitter is one way of tasting better, and on Protagorean principles a felt improvement is enough to make it true that for you the food is better. Or so the uncompromising interpretation can argue.

A politician makes wholesome things seem to a city to be just and admirable, and therefore to be just and admirable for that city, instead of the pernicious things which seemed (and therefore were for it) just and admirable before (167c). This does not fit (ii), because 'wholesome' is put on the subject side of 'seem'. The claim is not that the new conventions seem better but that better things seem just. The compromising interpretation infers, accordingly, that the improvement described here is objective: the new conventions are better whether or not they seem so. The uncompromising interpretation might think to reply that, if the new conventions are adopted because the politician has made them seem *more* just and admirable than the old, then 'wholesome' can be transferred to the predicate side of 'seem'; for seeming more just and admirable is one way of seeming better. But this looks like something the Defence ought to have said rather than what it does say. Yet another possibility would be a double application of the Measure Doctrine: things which seem and therefore are better (perhaps because they make the community's life more pleasant) come to seem just and therefore are just in that city for so long as the new convention holds.

The example of the sickly plants at 167b–c is neutral. Given the archaic belief (shared by Plato, *Timaeus* 77b, and a few modern sentimentalists) that a plant can feel better off as well as be so, there is no telling whether the improvement effected by a gardener is dependent or not dependent on the patient's subjective responses.

Shall we then declare a draw? Of the three examples described in detail, one tells in favour of compromise, one against, and the plants help neither view. If this seems unsatisfactory, the explanation might be that the indeterminacy is deliberate: Protagoras has compromised, and later (171d ff.) Plato will hammer the point home, but it would be dramatically, and perhaps also historically, inappropriate to call attention to it now.[35] Unfortunately, when we get to the later passage, which does formulate the compromising interpretation in plain terms (cf. 171d–172b, 177c–d), it turns out to be a question whether this is offered as a restatement of the Defence or as a modification of the Protagorean position.

What is at stake, philosophically, in the effort to find a satisfactory reading of this passage? Ultimately, it is nothing less than the place in human life of the notion of objective truth. Need it come in? Can a thoroughgoing relativist tell a *consistent* story about expertise, about teaching and learning, about discussion and debate, without conceding a role to objective truth? Should it come in? Can the relativist tell a reasonably *plausible* story without it? Or is Protagoras bound to compromise sooner or later, either to ensure consistency or as the price of plausibility? The Defence draws its examples from education and medicine, agriculture and politics, but are all the examples amenable to the same treatment (whatever treatment we decide is being offered)?

It could be said, for example, that D1 is a satisfactory enough principle for the medical case, since a doctor is supposed to make his patients feel better, but that the test of a politician is whether his proposals are objectively beneficial to the community. It could also be said, on the contrary, that a doctor's duty is to promote health, which is an objective benefit, whereas a good politician aims to give people a life that they themselves find satisfying. (Some years ago a British general election was won on the slogan 'You've never had it so good'—would it be obligatory to construe this as an objective rather than a subjective appeal?) What, finally, of examples which Protagoras does not mention? The presence of Theodorus is a constant reminder of the problem of mathematical expertise (cf. 169a, 170d–e). Do *any* of the interpretations canvassed above make decent sense of this? Since the question is particularly pressing for Theodorus himself, who was Protagoras' friend (161b, 162a, *et al.*) and once his pupil (164e–165a, 179a), it is worth keeping an eye on his reactions now and in the sequel (168c, 171c, 179b).

We may hope for more help on these issues as we proceed. For whereas

[35] Cf. McDowell, *Plato:* Theaetetus, 167. I add 'perhaps also historically' because it might be that the best argument for the historicity of the Defence (cf. n. 30 above) was its very indeterminacy in the face of our puzzlement: maybe one cannot expect from 5th-century work precise and sophisticated answers to the questions that we, and Plato, want to press. A. T. Cole ('The Apology of Protagoras', *Yale Classical Studies*, 19 (1966), 101–18) prefers to think that Plato misinterpreted Protagoras and was unaware that the doctor example, which preserves Protagoras' original uncompromising view, is crucially different from the politician example, in which Plato tacitly incorporates the concession to objectivity that he is seeking to establish.

in the Defence Socrates makes the statement that some people are wiser or more expert than others on Protagoras' behalf, in the next section he sets himself to derive it directly from the Measure Doctrine as expounded in Protagoras' own book *Truth* (169d–170a, 171d). But this time the interpretation of the statement is quite unambiguous. Objectivity is admitted in both the places we were uneasy about earlier (p. 336): both what experts know and that they know it are equally matters of objective, non-relative fact. We cannot, however, conclude straight away that this is a retrospective clarification of what was intended in the Defence. For the tone of the discussion undergoes a dramatic change. Socrates is no longer the polite and helpful fellow defending Protagoras against some awkward questions. He makes Theodorus strip for action (169a–c). The attack which follows leaves the old mathematician shocked and shaken (171c–d). The proposition that some people are wiser or more expert than others is now (171d) not the centrepiece of a defence of Protagoras' relativism but the ignominious outcome of its self-refutation.

The argument by which Plato tries to show that a completely general relativism is self-refuting is of considerable philosophical interest in its own right, as well as an important step forward in the investigation of expertise. The essential trick is to move the discussion up a level. Instead of asking directly 'What is expertise? How can Protagoras describe it?', the question is raised, 'What do people in general *think* about expertise?' Answer: they think there are many areas of life in which some are knowledgeable and others ignorant, the difference being that the knowledgeable ones make true judgements and the ignorant false judgements on the matter in hand (170a–b). But now, what people think and believe is the very thing the Measure Doctrine tells us about. It tells us that whatever people think and believe is true for them; no one can be *wrong* about anything. So, by way of preparation for the self-refutation to come, let us consider the belief just mentioned, the widespread belief that people are sometimes ignorant and wrong, that false judgement does occur. If people are right to think that there is false judgement, there is. But equally, if they are wrong in this belief, there is false judgement (for here is an instance of it). But Protagoras must say—must he not?—either that they are right or that they are wrong: unless he is willing to go so far as to deny that people do hold this view about each other's ignorance and expertise. To deny that, Theodorus agrees, would be quite implausible (170c). So Protagoras is caught in a dilemma. Whichever answer he gives has the consequence that false judgement occurs, which the Measure Doctrine must deny.

Ingenious. But we must be careful, both in this dilemmatic passage and in the self-refutation argument to follow, about that little qualifying phrase 'for *a*' which distinguishes the Protagorean idiom from the language of ordinary people. It is acceptable to have the ordinary man express the view that some judgements are false, without qualification. That is exactly what the ordinary man wants to say. But is it acceptable to make Protagoras comment on this view with the statement that it is right (true) or that it is wrong (false), without qualification? Should he not rather express himself as follows? 'To be sure, people believe that some judgements are false. All I need say about their belief, however, is that it is true *for them*. It does not follow that it is true *for me*. So it does not follow that it is true *for me* that, contrary to my philosophy, some judgements are false (without qualification).'

The same question arises with the self-refutation argument beginning at 170e. At a critical moment (171a–b) the relativizing qualifiers are dropped and Protagoras is made to speak of truth and falsity in absolute terms. What happens is this. We move from people's general belief that false judgement occurs to the specific belief that the Measure Doctrine in particular is false, and then on to the belief which Protagoras is committed to having *about* this belief if he believes his own theory. It is a self-refutation in that the Measure Doctrine, as a thesis about beliefs, is applied to beliefs about itself, to yield the conclusion that what it says about beliefs is not true for anybody. You need a clear head to follow the reasoning and to watch how Socrates handles the qualifiers:

Either (1) Protagoras himself did not believe the *Truth* he wrote, in which case, since no one else does, it is not (sc. the truth) for anybody at all (170e). (No naughtiness with the qualifiers here.) Or (2) he did believe it, but the majority of people do not share his opinion, in which case two consequences follow. (*a*) The more the adherents of his *Truth* are outnumbered by people who do not believe it, the more it is not (sc. the truth) than it is (171a). (Does this mean it is more false than true, absolutely, or false for more people than it is true for?) (*b*) Protagoras himself must agree (171a) that his opponents' disbelief in his *Truth* is true (query: why omit 'for them' here?), and this leads eventually (query: how?) to the conclusion (171c) that Protagoras' doctrine is not true for anybody, not even for the Sophist himself. The final conclusion of (2*b*), like the conclusion of (1), is properly relativized. The question is whether that conclusion can be fairly derived without an illegitimate dropping of the qualifiers at the point queried above (171a). If it cannot—and this has been the common verdict—we have to decide whether the faulty step is a deliberate dishonesty on Plato's part or an inadvertent slip. If it can, we have to show how the reasoning remains sound when the qualifiers are restored in the appropriate places.[36]

The issue is too complex to enter fully into here. But it is very much worth wrestling with, and one substantive aspect should be mentioned. Isn't there something inherently paradoxical about someone asserting (or believing) that *all truth is relative*? That proposition sums up the message of a completely general relativism, but when asserted it is propounded as itself a truth. The reason for this is simple but fundamental: to assert anything is to assert it as a truth, as something which is the case. (Analogously, to believe something is to accept it as true.) The relativist may reply that 'All truth is relative' is not asserted as an absolute truth, which would indeed be self-refuting, but only as a relative one: *it is true for me that all truth is relative*. This is no help. This second proposition is less interesting (because it is no longer clear that the objectivity of *our* beliefs is jeopardized if relativism is true only for the relativist), but it is still an assertion. 'It is true for me that all truth is relative' is put forward as itself true without qualification. A commitment to truth absolute is bound up with the very act of assertion.

If this is correct, we may be able to salvage something from Plato's self-refutation argument even on the more pessimistic view that the omission of the qualifiers is a fatal flaw in the text as it stands. The omission, we may decide, was a fault in the execution of a well-aimed attack. Relativism is self-refuting, and for reasons that go deep into the nature of assertion and belief. One modern philosopher who contended that any formulation of Protagorean relativism must be self-refuting was the founder of phenomenology, Edmund Husserl, and he put it like this: 'The content of such assertions rejects what is part of the sense or content of every assertion and what accordingly cannot be significantly separated from any assertion.'[37] Other philosophical traditions express the point in quite similar terms.[38] There is impressive support for the idea that Plato in this passage was on to something of fundamental importance.

We can go further and propose a general perspective on Plato's critique of Protagoras as it has developed so far. Relativism is a philosophical ten-

---

[36] I have tried to do this in M. F. Burnyeat, 'Protagoras and Self-Refutation is Plato's *Theaetetus*', *Philosophical Review*, 85 (1976), 172–95; compare S. Waterlow, 'Protagoras and Inconsistency', *Archiv für Geschichte der Philosophie*, 59 (1977), 19–36. For a logical defence of Protagoras, see M. Matthen, 'Perception, Relativism, and Truth: Reflections on Plato's *Theaetetus* 152–160', *Dialogue*, 24 (1985), 33–58.

[37] Edmund Husserl, *Logical Investigations*, 2nd edn. (1913), trans. J. N. Findlay (London, 1970), 139.

[38] See J. Passmore, *Philosophical Reasoning* (London, 1961), 67–8; J. L. Mackie, 'Self-Refutation: A Formal Analysis', *Philosophical Quarterly*, 14 (1964), 193–203. Another version in McDowell, *Plato:* Theaetetus, 171.

dency of perennial appeal. I have no doubt that many readers of this introduction find themselves drawn to it. Recognizably Protagorean themes
appear in important works of modern philosophy.[39] Of course, time and
progress have brought an immense sophistication in the working out and
advocacy of relativistic views. It would be foolish not to acknowledge this.
But the questions we have seen Plato addressing to Protagoras are still
worth asking in a contemporary context. It would be equally foolish to
presume that the *Theaetetus* no longer has anything to contribute to the
continuing debate. [. . .]*

THE CRITIQUE RESUMED: (1) REFUTATION OF PROTAGORAS (177C–179B)

The Digression over, the New Formulation** is restated in summary form
(177c–d) and Socrates turns his attention to the one element of objectivity it allows, the objectivity of judgements about what is advantageous or
beneficial. He points out that judgements about advantage are essentially
forward-looking: they concern what *will* bring about some desirable state
of affairs and so are one kind of judgement about the future (178a). (The
reader might consider how this thesis can account for a past-tense judgement like 'Your assistance was most advantageous to us'.) It follows
that any result proved for the whole class of judgements about the future
will hold *a fortiori* for judgements about advantage. The result Socrates
proceeds to argue for (178b–179b) is that judgements about the future
cannot be admitted within the scope of the Measure Doctrine; their
truth-conditions must be objective, not relative to the individual
judgement-maker.

[39] See e.g. in metaphysics and philosophy of language: W. V. Quine, 'Ontological Relativity',
Journal of Philosophy, 65 (1968), repr. in his *Ontological Relativity and Other Essays* (New York,
1969). In philosophy of science: Thomas S. Kuhn, *The Structure of Scientific Revolutions*, 2nd
edn. (Chicago, 1970). In moral philosophy: Gilbert Harman, 'Moral Relativism Defended',
Philosophical Review, 84 (1975), 3–22; B. A. O. Williams, 'The Truth in Relativism', *Proceedings
of the Aristotelian Society*, NS 75 (1974–5); repr. in *Moral Luck: Philosophical Papers 1973–1980*
(Cambridge, 1981), 132–43. In social philosophy: Martin Hollis and Steven Lukes (eds.), *Rationality and Relativism* (Oxford, 1982).

* *Editor's note*: Here I omit Burnyeat's discussion of the Digression (*Tht.* 171d–177c); this is
pp. 31–9 of his Introduction, which he calls 'The Critique Interrupted'.

** *Editor's note*: According to the 'New Formulation' of Protagoras' Defence, a 'completely
unrestricted relativism . . . has been shown to undermine itself, [so that] there must be some
area or areas in which objectivity and expertise prevail. But the self-refutation argument alone
does not determine in which area(s) the concession should be made . . . The core of the New
Formulation is a clear and unambiguous statement of the objectivity of judgements about what
is to the advantage of or beneficial for an individual or city' (Burnyeat, *The* Theaetetus *of Plato*,
31–2).

This confirms (cf. 178a), what has not previously been established, that Socrates was right to choose questions of advantage as the place to admit objectivity and the possibility of expertise in the wake of the self-refutation argument. But since the argument about the future is independent of the self-refutation, it is also an independent refutation of a completely general relativism, and is duly acknowledged as such by Theodorus at 179b. Our competing Readings A and B will draw different conclusions from this (p. 333), but the philosophical interest of the argument is by no means exhausted by that interpretative disagreement.

Consider

(1) It seems to me on Monday that on Tuesday my temperature will be feverishly hot.

To hold that judgements about the future come within the scope of the Measure Doctrine is to hold that (in the striking phrase introduced at 178b) I have within myself the criterion of what will happen tomorrow, in this sense, that from (1) we may infer

(2) It is true for me on Monday that on Tuesday my temperature will be feverishly hot.

But the Measure Doctrine also has something to say about Tuesday:

(3) It is true for me on Tuesday that my temperature is feverishly hot if and only if on Tuesday I feel feverishly hot.

Now suppose that (as the doctor in 178b predicts) on Tuesday I do not feel in the least bit hot or feverish. Then (3) tells us that it is not true for me on Tuesday that I am hot—and doesn't this contradict the conclusion already drawn at (2)?

The best way to appreciate the force of this argument is to ask what resources a determined relativist could muster in reply. Evidently the contradiction, if it is one, is due to the supposition that the Measure Doctrine vests the authority to decide how things are for me on Tuesday both with my Monday's self and with my Tuesday's self, who may disagree.[52] But now, might our relativist challenge the assumption that the two selves can disagree in this way? There are occasions when my belief that I will enjoy a feast (an example from 178d–e) *brings it about that*, when the time comes, I do; and it is not difficult to imagine a similar story for Tuesday's temperature. Could this defence be extended to the other examples? What

---

[52] Plato represents the disagreement as a disagreement on Monday between me and the doctor predicting, correctly, how it will be with me on Tuesday (178c), but for the present argument this comes to the same thing.

kind of a world would it be if *whatever* I predicted on Monday came to pass on Tuesday *because* I had predicted it? If that seems close to incoherent, we might imagine the relativist, on a different tack, exploiting the Heraclitean thought that Monday's and Tuesday's selves are two, not one and the same persisting person.

This would be analogous to a suggestion Protagoras has already made about the past. One of the 'verbal' objections to Theaetetus' definition of knowledge as perception had to do with memory: a man who remembers something he saw yesterday but does not still see now allegedly both knows (because he remembers) and does not know (because he no longer sees) that thing (163d–164b). In his Defence Protagoras offers several alternative lines of reply, one of which is to deny that it is the same person who first sees the thing and then sees it no longer (166b, picking up the Heraclitean thesis of universal non-identity over time from 158e–160c). The suggestion is not developed, but its effect is to break the objective connection we ordinarily assume to hold between memory and previous experience. And this could lead to a strongly verificationist reduction of the past to present memory experience: at any given time my past (what for me now was the case at earlier times) simply is whatever it now seems to me was the case earlier.[53] There would be no problem, on this view, if Monday's self and Tuesday's self have different impressions of what happened on Sunday (the two selves simply have different pasts), nor therefore if Monday's self and Tuesday's disagree about Monday: Monday's present does not become Tuesday's past. Now, could the relativist adopt an analogous strategy for the future? How would it work out? Are there asymmetries between past and future which would make it peculiarly difficult to transfer the strategy to the future?

If neither of these defences is satisfactory—neither collapsing the future into the present nor allowing future experience to be predetermined by present expectation—*and if* there is no other way out, the relativist is in real difficulty. There is more to it than the existence of one class of judgements for which relativism fails. In one way or another enormous numbers of present-tense judgements carry implications for the future; Plato's example was judgements about what is advantageous, but the reader will easily add more. Worse still, judgements about the near or distant future are intrinsic to action: an agent who does one thing for the sake of another typically chooses the first because it now seems to them

---

[53] A verificationist account of the past with interesting affinities to the above was put forward by A. J. Ayer in 1936. See *Language, Truth and Logic*, 2nd edn. (London, 1946), 102: 'Propositions about the past are rules for the prediction of those "historical" experiences which are commonly said to verify them.'

that the second will result. But whether it *will* in fact result or not—that, on the present argument, is something the sense of which can only be given by saying, 'Wait and see.' The very notion of the future makes us submit to objectivity. So, then, does action. That is to say, life itself. Any readers of this Introduction who still incline to relativism had better look to their guns.

THE CRITIQUE RESUMED: (2) REFUTATION OF HERACLITUS (179C–183C)

Plato has now vindicated the objectivity of truth for a significant class of judgements, and thereby has secured a vitally important condition for expert knowledge. To be sure, he wants ultimately to establish not only that judgements about the future are objectively true or false, but also (178d–e) that experts are able to give better or more authoritative verdicts about the future than other people. But the question 'Is competence in judgement just a matter of getting it right, or is there more to it than that?' is held over to Part II of the dialogue, while the ensuing question 'What makes the expert's judgement better or more authoritative?' will concern us in Part III. Meanwhile, we return to perception.

So many present-tense statements carry implications for the future that we should by now be wondering where relativism can still stand firm. It could well be argued that the only present-tense statements which do not imply anything about the future are those that report the immediate perception of sensible qualities, e.g. 'I see (something) white'. Plato does not argue this, but in the light of the New Formulation (p. 343) it is no surprise to find that such perception is in fact his next target. We are to confront at last the question whether perception, as elucidated through the theories of Protagoras and Heraclitus, is knowledge.

The section opens at 179c with Socrates meditating on whether perceptions and perceptual judgements can ever be convicted of being untrue. Our first question must be, Why raise that issue now, so late in the proceedings? Have we not supposed all along (on Reading B for the sake of the *reductio ad absurdum* argument, on Reading A because we believe it ourselves) that every perceptual appearance is true for the person who has it? Part of the answer is that we have come back to perception after rescuing the objectivity of a very large range of judgements, and objectivity is closely connected with the possibility of getting things wrong (see 178a, 179a). Only where there is something to be wrong about is there a target for objective truth. Socrates is now wondering whether the critique of Protagorean relativism can be carried further, whether the Measure Doctrine can be dislodged from the ground where hitherto it has found its firmest footing, judgements concerning sensible qualities (cf. 178d–e for an earlier hint of this development). But perhaps the terms in which Socrates expresses his question are as important as the question itself.

For notice that perceptions and perceptual judgements are mentioned separately, side by side, as distinct things. At the beginning of Part I they were not clearly distinguished but amalgamated together by the equation of perception with appearing (152b–c; p. 324). To mark off perception from perceptual judgement is to reveal that appearing is a complex notion, with these two things as its separate components.[54] Well then, if the notion of appearing is complex, the doctrine that every perceptual appearance is true for the person who has it is complex—and that complexity had better come into the open. For it will make a difference to the way perception itself is understood. And this in turn will have consequences for the relation of the Heraclitean theory of perception to the Protagorean theory of truth.

The Heraclitean theory of perception as expounded earlier certainly made provision for every sensible appearance to involve just that perceptual experience which is 'akin' (156c) or proper to the sensible quality displayed by the object perceived. The perception as such, the goings-on in eye or tongue, could hardly be convicted of being, in any sense, untrue or incorrect. But now that the other element in sensible appearances, the judgement identifying what is perceived as white, say, or sweet, has been marked off from the process of perceiving, we face a question that was not brought distinctly to our attention earlier: Does the Heraclitean theory guarantee that these judgements will always be true and correct?[55] According to Reading B they must be correct if the Protagorean-cum-Theaetetan thesis is to hold good: that every sensible appearance is a case of the perceiver knowing, in virtue of their perception, how things are for them. The provision is no less important for Reading A, according to which we want to establish that every sensible appearance is, although not knowledge, none the less an incorrigible awareness of some quality in the flux of becoming (p. 321). Now that the element of judgement has been

[54] That Plato himself believed that appearing is a compound notion is made clear at *Sophist* 264b: 'What we mean by "it appears" is a blend of perception and judgement.' This would not of course apply to the extended use of 'appears' discussed at pp. 333–4 above.

[55] Notice that Socrates in 179c speaks as if the predicates 'true' and 'untrue' apply both to perceptions as such and to the accompanying perceptual judgements, whereas at 186c we find him arguing that perception on its own cannot 'get at truth'. One of the tasks for a decision between Readings A and B is to explain this development.

disentangled from perception, let us try to pinpoint exactly what the danger is that we still need to forestall.

The Heraclitean theory is a theory according to which, as we are shortly reminded (182a–b), neither the object nor the subject of perception exists with any determinate properties of its own outside their mutual interaction. It is only within that interaction and for each other that the object can be said to be, or become, for example, white, and the subject said to be, or to come to be, seeing (159e–160c). Thus a perceptual judgement like 'I see something white' identifies and records a momentary subject's momentary perception of a momentary object's momentarily occurring whiteness, a whiteness which exists privately for that perceiving subject alone. With judgements as exiguous in content as that, nothing that happens at any other time and nothing in the experience of any other person at the present time could be the basis for a charge of untruth. So much has already been secured (on behalf of Theaetetus' definition according to Reading B, on behalf of Plato's own philosophy according to Reading A) by the contributions of Heraclitus and Protagoras respectively (pp. 329–30, 328). If there remains any basis at all for correcting a perceptual judgement, it must be found within the momentary perceptual encounter itself. This residual threat is what we still have to eliminate.

We are now in a position to appreciate that the issue at stake in the coming discussion is one that has been of the greatest importance for empiricist theories of knowledge. Socrates' question 'Can a perceptual judgement be convicted of being untrue?' is to be compared with the question often asked in modern epistemology 'Is it possible to be mistaken about one's own present sense-data?' In the quest for certainty, both ancient and modern have to decide whether 'so long as we keep within the limits of immediate present experience' (179c) our judgements are completely and in every respect incorrigible. If they are not, there is no hope for the empiricist project of founding knowledge (or a structure of reasonable belief; pp. 323–4) on a base of experiential certainty.

There is an interesting difference, however, between the Platonic and modern approaches to this question. The traditional empiricist view, of Berkeley and others, is that in naming the colour one sees there is no room for genuinely factual error. If one says 'magenta' where 'crimson' is correct, it is either a deliberate lie (hence not a mistake in one's actual judgement) or a linguistic mistake about the meaning of 'magenta', e.g. the mistake of thinking it means the colour which is in fact called 'crimson'; in the latter case one is wrong about what the colour is called, not about what colour it is. A modern discussion will take up that view and argue for or against the proposition that judgements which keep within the limits of immediate present experience can be objectively incorrect.[56] By contrast, the conclusion Plato argues for is that in naming the colour one sees any and every answer is equally correct (182d–183a). It is not, or not in the first instance, that 'I see magenta' can be wrong, but that 'I see magenta' and 'I see blue' are both correct, and so is 'I'm not seeing but hearing' (182d–e). The conclusion is then generalized (183a–b) in terms which imply that 'I see magenta' not only can be wrong but actually is wrong. Yet we are still not talking about the kind of error under discussion in the modern debate just mentioned. The point is that whatever I say is as wrong as it is right. Language is emptied of all positive meaning.[57]

This, then, is the final conclusion of the long discussion of the three theses which have been in play since the beginning of Part I. The problem for the reader is twofold: first, to see how the conclusion is arrived at, and assess the validity of the reasoning; second, to understand its significance for the three theses in general and more particularly for Socrates' question at 179c about the corrigibility of perceptual judgements. The two tasks are connected. For it will be remembered that on Reading A Plato himself accepts the theories of Protagoras and Heraclitus, so long as they are confined to perception and the world of sensible things (p. 321). He will hardly want to accept an account of the sensible world from which the conclusion follows that it cannot be described in any positive terms at all. On the contrary, within their proper sphere, perceptual judgements ought to be infallible.[58] So the task for Reading A is to show that the damaging conclusion is not derived from the theory of perception adopted earlier but from a radical extension of it which Plato introduces quite deliberately, in order to draw attention to the absurd consequence it would involve. The absurdity will demonstrate where limits must be imposed on the Heraclitean flux of becoming; within these limits the earlier theory of

[56] For: A. J. Ayer, *The Problem of Knowledge* (London, 1956), ch. 2; J. L. Austin, *Sense and Sensibilia* (Oxford, 1962), ch. 10. Against: Ayer, *The Foundations of Empirical Knowledge*, 78 ff.

[57] All positive meaning because 183b seems—half-jokingly—to leave us with the option of a language of pure denial. See Burnyeat, *The Theaetetus of Plato*, n. ad loc.

[58] So Cornford, *Plato's Theory of Knowledge*, 92 with n. 1. Note that it would not be enough to leave the phenomenal world in radical flux and claim that the situation is saved by the postulation of unchanging Forms in addition to sensible things (so Cherniss, 'The Relation of the *Timaeus* to Plato's Later Dialogues'). The unpalatable consequence of flux cannot be avoided by flux plus Forms, for it is an elementary logical truth that, if a proposition entails an acknowledged absurdity, it continues to entail that absurdity no matter what further propositions you conjoin it with.

perception can stand unimpaired, a firm Platonic basis for the proof that perception is not knowledge.[59]

For Reading B, however, denying as it does that Plato himself approves the theories of Protagoras and Heraclitus, the task is rather different: namely, to exhibit the section 179c–183c as the culmination of the long *reductio ad absurdum* which has been under way since Theaetetus' definition was first propounded (Theaetetus → Protagoras → Heraclitus → the impossibility of language). The extension of flux to the point where language is emptied of all positive meaning must be something to which Theaetetus is committed by the project of finding sufficient conditions for his definition to hold good (pp. 322–3). In relation to Socrates' question at 179c, the price to be paid for making perceptual judgements totally incorrigible is that they then have nothing to say to us. If this is the moral of the argument, its interest is not confined to a convinced Platonist. It challenges anyone who appeals to immediate present experience for the kind of certainty which can serve as a base or foundation for the theory of knowledge. And readers of this Introduction who are attracted to the empiricist programme will note that, since the argument is a *reductio ad absurdum*, its starting-point is not some alien Platonic premiss they need not bother with, but a careful analysis and elaboration of their own initial conviction that the senses provide us with knowledge and certainty.[60]

---

[59] So Cornford, *Plato's Theory of Knowledge*, 92 ff., in large measure joined on this occasion by McDowell, *Plato*: Theaetetus, 180–4, but with a disagreement as to the direction in which Heraclitean flux is extended and hence a disagreement on where limits must be drawn to save the theory of perception from the absurd consequence of extreme flux. For Cornford the extension that needs to be blocked is the extra claim that there is constant change even in the meanings of the words used to speak about perception: 'Plato's point is that, if "all things" without exception are always changing, language can have no fixed meaning' (p. 99). Similarly G. Ryle, *Plato's Progress* (Cambridge, 1966), 273. For McDowell it is the extension of change into the momentary perceptual encounter itself: 'if, as the [original theory of perception] implies, we can identify, e.g., whiteness and seeing, then it must be possible to say of each that it *is* just that' (pp. 183–4).

[60] On this understanding of Plato's argument (and subject to the qualification in n. 57 above about a language of pure denial), its closest modern analogue (noticed by K. W. Mills, 'Plato and the Instant', *Proceedings of the Aristotelian Society*, suppl. vol. 48 (1974), 91) is Wittgenstein's celebrated argument for the impossibility of a private language: *Philosophical Investigations* (1953), §§243 ff. Wittgenstein sets out to show that on certain assumptions—assumptions which are often taken to be characteristic of empiricism—statements about immediate private experience, so far from being paradigms of certainty, say nothing even to the speaker himself. The argument proceeds, like Plato's, by taking the assumptions seriously and seeing where they lead. Two of the results to which (it is argued) they lead are worth highlighting here for comparison with Plato's conclusions. One is that, when I try to name my sensation, 'whatever is going to seem right to me is right. And that only means that here we can't talk about "right"' (§258). The other, connected point is that, for all the difference it makes, the private object could be constantly changing (§293).

What evidence does the passage offer to help us decide between these two interpretations? In favour of Reading A is that some time is spent on a portrait of contemporary Heracliteans in Ionia (179d–180d). These persons, who are as unstable as everything else in their philosophy, are often supposed to be wild extremists who would actually support the extended flux doctrine. In favour of Reading B is that the extended doctrine is reached by argument. Socrates offers a reason why a Heraclitean would be committed to accepting further elements of change into the theory of perception (181d–182a). One or other of these pieces of evidence must be discounted as not serious.

It would not be quite fair to recommend on this occasion (cf. p. 326) that the way to decide is to count the jokes. The Heraclitean portrait is indeed a witty matching of the men to their philosophy. So too the materialists at 155e–156a are tough, hard fellows like the bodies they believe in, and the 'One' who is Parmenides has the unruffled composure of his one unchanging reality (183e–184a with note ad loc.). But even a humorous sketch of invented characters[61] could be a device to signal that the extended flux doctrine is an inconsequential addition to what has gone before. So let us turn to the argument of 181d–182a.

A distinction has been introduced (181c–d) between two kinds of motion or change: spatial movement and alteration (change of quality or character).[62] When the theory of perception was presented earlier, the dominant locutions were those of spatial movement, whether literally or metaphorically intended (pp. 328–31). Now the question is posed whether, when the Heracliteans say all things are in motion, they mean that everything is undergoing both spatial movement and alteration. Socrates has already expressed his opinion that they do mean this (181c). Theodorus agrees (181e), but with a hesitation which prompts Socrates to confirm the conclusion by the argument we are interested in. The argument is that if

[61] Despite the apparent suggestion that the Heracliteans in Ionia are actual people whom Theodorus might have met (180b), we have no independent evidence of these goings-on at Ephesus, and it is not certain that it is not part of Plato's joke to represent the Heraclitean philosophy by a plurality of individuals springing up spontaneously on their own, each with their own claim to knowledge (180c). How better to embody a philosophical thesis (universal non-identity over time) which denies that one ever meets the same person twice? We do know of one extremist Heraclitean of the period who 'finally did not think it right to say anything but only moved his finger, and criticized Heraclitus for saying that it is impossible to step twice into the same river; for *he* thought one could not do it even once' (Aristotle, *Metaph.* 4. 5, 1010^{a}12–15). This was Cratylus, whose view that sensible things are in flux and that there is no knowledge of them is also said by Aristotle (*Metaph.* 1. 6, 987^{a}32–^{b}1) to have been an early influence on the development of Plato's own thinking. If that sounds as though it could be helpful to Reading A (cf. Cornford, *Plato's Theory of Knowledge*, 99), a note of caution: Cratylus was an Athenian.

[62] On the terminology here, see note *ad* 181d.

they left out one kind of motion, things would be at rest or not moving as well as moving, and it would be no more correct to say 'All things are in motion' than 'All things are at rest'; to eliminate all trace of stability, they must admit that everything is in every kind of motion at once.

With this conclusion we reach the extended flux doctrine. It is the addition of alteration which leads to the collapse of language. So it is vital to know how serious the argument is meant to be.

The ground for suspicion is that the argument turns on a contradiction which is 'obviously spurious'.[63] There is no inconsistency between 'All things are in motion' and 'All things are at rest' provided it is in different respects that they are in motion and at rest. Elsewhere Plato shows himself perfectly familiar with the point (e.g. *Republic* 436c–e), which is too obvious for him or his reader to miss. Therefore, he cannot seriously mean to suggest that the extended flux doctrine is something to which a proponent of the theory of perception will be committed on pain of contradiction.

Abstractly considered, the objection appears sound enough. But Reading B will recall Socrates' question at 179c and the wider significance which the notion of stability has acquired in the course of the dialogue so far. If a thing is stable, or stable in some respect (the qualification makes no odds), that means there is an objective basis for correcting or confirming someone's judgement as to how it is, or how it is in that respect.[64] There is a fact of the matter, independent of the person's judgement. The whole point of eliminating first objectivity between persons and then identity through time was to ensure that there would be no basis in the experience of other times and other people for charging anyone with untruth. Accordingly, an element of stability within the perceptual encounter itself, although it would last for a moment only and would be inaccessible to anyone but the perceiver, would still mean that something has a determinate character independent of the perceiver's judgement about it. White is the colour I see, not pink; seeing is the perception it elicits in me, not hearing.[65] If I were to judge otherwise, I would be wrong. I would be wrong even if no other perceiver could ever be in a position to tell me so—incorrigibility by myself later and others now is not yet total incorrigibility or infallibility. Never mind what a bunch of wild Heracliteans in Ionia would

---

[63] So McDowell, *Plato: Theaetetus*, 180.

[64] Another place where the notion of stability is invoked to express the idea of objectivity is *Cratylus* 386d–e.

[65] This is McDowell's understanding of the stability to be attacked (n. 59), with a different account of why it needs to be attacked: not to show the absurd consequences from which the Heraclitean theory of perception must be protected, but to show the absurd consequences to which Theaetetus' use of that theory will be committed.

say about that. The important thing is that Theaetetus cannot allow it. Stability, even for a moment, entails objectivity, even if only for that moment. This means that a perceptual judgement could, in principle, be wrong; hence we do not yet have it absolutely guaranteed that every sensible appearance is a case of the perceiver knowing, in virtue of their perception, how things are for them (p. 348). If Theaetetus is to maintain his position, every last remnant of stability must go.

Once this is understood, it becomes clear both that the argument of 181d–182a is serious and why it was an important move at 179c to replace the compound notion of appearing by its separate components, perception and perceptual judgement. The Measure Doctrine states that things are for each perceiver exactly as they appear to them to be at the moment of perceiving. Split the notion of appearing into two components, and the Measure Doctrine itself becomes two:

(i) Things are for each perceiver exactly as they experience them at the moment of perceiving,

and

(ii) Things are for each perceiver exactly as they judge them to be at the moment of perceiving.

For the Measure Doctrine to stand firm 'within the limits of immediate present experience', both (i) and (ii) must be secured. The Heraclitean theory of perception secures (i), but (ii) requires a guarantee that perceivers will not misinterpret their experience. How is this to be secured?

There is no mechanism in the theory of perception specifically designed to prevent perceivers from misinterpreting their experience, and it would be an odd theory, to say the least, if it did in some way shackle a perceiver's judgement to match whatever perception occurred. Having one's judgement automatically determined by experience is no better than having one's future experience automatically determined to match whatever judgement of present expectation precedes (cf. pp. 344–5). Rather, the entire elaboration of the three-in-one theory takes it for granted, as do later empiricists like Berkeley, that perceivers will simply 'read off' the correct description of their perceptual experience from the experience itself. The weaknesses of that assumption will be further probed in the important concluding section of Part I (184a–186e). Meanwhile, the fact must be faced that so far there is nothing to prevent a mistaken judgement about what one's immediate present experience is. In more Protagorean idiom, 'x is/becomes F for a at time t' is itself an absolute form of statement: however momentary the state of affairs it claims to report, in principle it might fail to report correctly. To achieve total incorrigibility, therefore, we must make it impossible for *a* to be wrong if at time *t* they judge otherwise than that *x* is/becomes *F* for them.

At 182c–d Theodorus, as spokesman for the compound theory, takes the only course open to it. He accepts Socrates' argument that there must not be even a momentary stability within the perceptual encounter, lest anything remain for perceptual judgement to be wrong about: 'There is a flux of this very thing also, the whiteness, and it is passing over into another colour, *lest it be convicted of standing still in this respect*' (182d). Notice the verbal echo of Socrates' question at 179c. If the whiteness could be convicted of standing still in respect of being/flowing white, its stability would imply the possibility of convicting as untrue the perceiver's judgement about which colour they see. This is the reason for 'reimporting change into the atoms of change',[66] or rather for introducing further change, viz. alteration, within the momentary perceptual encounters which are all that remained of ordinary subjects and objects of perception when the flux story reached its climax at 160c. Without alteration the perceiver would be wrong to judge that the colour they see is not white but (say) yellow. The addition of alteration ensures that they would not be wrong.

But now, of course, to complete the *reductio*, all Socrates has to do is point out that nothing remains for judgement to be right about either (182d). Any statement is as right, or as wrong, as any other (183a).

Such is the devastating conclusion of the argument which spells out the effect on the theory of perception of adding alteration to spatial movement. There are plenty of questions to ask about the passage. Should Theodorus have allowed Socrates to go through with it? Would a Heraclitean be able to resist it? Are latter-day empiricists better placed to defend the proposition that judgements of immediate experience are incorrigible and yet meaningful? If you pursue these questions seriously, you will find yourself led back through all the philosophical and interpretative questions we have had in view during this long discussion of Theaetetus' first definition.

[66] Owen, 86.

XIII

PLATO ON SENSE-PERCEPTION AND KNOWLEDGE (*THEAETETUS* 184–186)

JOHN M. COOPER

I

Plato's argument in the *Theaetetus* (184b–186e) against the proposal that knowledge be defined as αἴσθησις[1] has, I think, not yet been fully understood or rightly appreciated. Existing interpretations fall into two groups. On the one hand, F. M. Cornford[2] and others think that Plato rejects the proposal on the ground that the objects which we perceive are not the sort of objects of which one could have knowledge: only the unchanging Forms can be known. On the other hand, there are those[3] who think Plato's argument has nothing to do with Forms but instead turns on a distinction between sensation and judgement which has the consequence that the thinking we do *about* the deliverances of the senses, and not the mere *use* of the senses, is the source of our knowledge. The interpretation which I advance in this paper belongs to the second of these two broad classes, but differs from others in providing a more careful account of the distinctions which Plato seems to be making in this passage. Much of the interest of the argument lies, I think, in the analysis of the process of perception which Plato produces by distinguishing carefully the contribution of the senses from that of the mind; but this analysis has not been given the attention it deserves.

The complexities of the argument can be usefully indicated by a brief

Reprinted with permission from *Phronesis*, 15 (1970), 123–46, and the author.

[1] An expression that might be translated by either 'perception' or 'sensation'. I shall mostly say 'perception', but the other sense should constantly be borne in mind; the ambiguity becomes important below, pp. 360 ff.

[2] In his *Plato's Theory of Knowledge* (London, 1933), 102–9. Subsequent references to Cornford's views are to this book.

[3] Cf. G. Ryle, 'Plato's *Parmenides*', *Mind*, 48 (1939), 317; repr. in R. E. Allen (ed.), *Studies in Plato's Metaphysics* (London, 1965) (hereafter abbreviated *SPM*) 136; I. M. Crombie, *An Examination of Plato's Doctrines* (London, 1963) ii. 14.

examination of Cornford's interpretation. According to Cornford Plato's argument proceeds in two stages. In the first (184b–186a1) Plato concludes that there is knowledge which is not a matter of perception, i.e. that 'percepts cannot be the only objects of knowledge' (p. 106). In the second (186a1–e12), it is further concluded that the additional objects of knowledge referred to in the first stage are in fact the *only* objects of true or real knowledge.

In the first stage Plato appeals to the distinction between, on the one hand, the use of the faculty of sensing as such, i.e. the mere presentation of an object in sensation, and, on the other hand, the making of judgements. The point of this appeal is not, however, to suggest that since only judgements are true, judging does, but mere sensing does not, exhibit a sufficient order of logical complexity to count as knowing. Rather, this distinction is introduced in order to bring out the fact that there are other objects besides sense-objects with which we are 'acquainted' (p. 106). In judgements we use such words as 'is' and 'similar', and the thought that something we are sensing exists or is similar to something else is not an achievement of mere sensing; we must bring in, and apply, the notions of existence and similarity, as well as use our senses. From this it is inferred that even if the presentation of an object of sense in sensation is an instance of knowledge, our power of making judgements shows that there is another way of being presented with objects, namely the intuition of Forms, here instanced by Existence, Similarity, and the other so-called κοινά. We could not apply the notion of existence to anything if we were not acquainted with Existence; and the knowledge of these (and other) Forms is not acquired by using the senses but by thinking—by an activity of the soul 'all by herself' (185e1), without reliance on sensation.

The argument of Cornford's second stage (186a2–e10) is apparently meant to run as follows. Existence (οὐσία) is one of the κοινά mentioned in stage one. Hence both our acquaintance with the Form Existence and our ability to formulate judgements with the help of this notion are functions of the mind independent of sensation. But it is only in attaining to existence that truth is reached; so that knowledge too first occurs at the level of the mind's independent activity, and there is no knowledge in the use of the senses at all. Cornford admits that given the context the most natural way of understanding this last point would be that sensing does not involve the use of 'is' and therefore does not amount to judging or asserting anything, so that since knowledge is necessarily knowledge of truths, sensing is in no case knowing. On this view Plato denies that to use the senses is to know anything by arguing that knowledge is the achievement of the mind's capacity to formulate judgements, which is an activity which goes beyond sensing itself. But Cornford thinks that the real point being made here relies on the other 'independent activity' of the mind referred to above—that by which it becomes *acquainted* with Forms. The Forms, taken as a group, constitute in Plato's metaphysics the realm of οὐσία and he elsewhere associates knowledge with these objects; so here too he must be making the point that since no object of the senses is a Form nothing the senses give us belongs to the realm of οὐσία. It follows that no activity of the senses, or of the mind through the medium of the senses, can amount to knowledge.

There are obvious difficulties with this interpretation. For example, οὐσία is interpreted in the first stage as naming just one Form among others, but in the second, without any textual warrant for the change,[4] it becomes the collective name of all the forms or of the metaphysical status of the Forms as a group. Again, although Cornford finds in the passage a distinction between judging and sensing, he represses this distinction at every turn in favour of the distinction between objects we are acquainted with in sensation and objects grasped by intuitive thought: with good reason, since, as Cornford admits, the former distinction points towards the activity of judging as the area where knowledge is to be found, while the Forms–sensibles dichotomy leads to the quite different, indeed incompatible, suggestion that knowledge is not a matter of judging truly, but of intuitive awareness of a certain kind of object. Cornford's attempt to combine his distinction between sensation and judgement with a reaffirmation of the doctrine that only the intuition of Forms deserves the name 'knowledge' produces a confused and inadequate line of thought.

None the less, Cornford's interpretation has met with approval in certain quarters just because it does yield the conclusion that perception cannot be knowledge because the objects of perception are not knowable. Thus H. F. Cherniss, so far as this general conclusion is concerned,

---

[4] No doubt Cornford thinks there is *some* warrant in the fact, as he thinks, that throughout this part of the dialogue Plato assumes that sense-objects are in Heraclitean flux: Plato would seem, given this assumption, to invite the interpretation of οὐσία at 186d3 and e5 as indicating the realm of Being as opposed to that of Becoming. But nothing of the kind is being assumed here about the objects of the senses: Heracliteanism is defined at 156a ff. (cf. 157b1, τὸ δ'εἶναι ἀνταχόθεν ἐξαιρετέον) as involving the refusal to say of anything that it *exists*, but at 185a precisely this *is* said by Socrates (and accepted by Theaetetus) about the objects of the senses. Cf. G. E. L. Owen, 'The Place of the *Timaeus* in Plato's Dialogues', *Classical Quarterly*, NS 3 (1953), 5 (= *SPM* 324). Cherniss's attempted rebuttal of this point in 'The Relation of the *Timaeus* to Plato's Later Dialogues', *American Journal of Philology*, 78 (1957), 244 n. 71 (= *SPM* 357 n. 1), shows that he has understood neither Owen nor Plato: in saying that Plato 'goes on to ascribe οὐσία to objects of perception', Owen obviously meant that Plato says about objects of perception that they exist, and (as just noted) Plato certainly does say this.

enthusiastically adopts[5] Cornford's interpretation, as supporting his view
concerning the unity of Plato's thought. Cherniss, indeed, goes well beyond
Cornford when he suggests[6] that not merely the general conclusion of the
passage, but even the *argument* supporting it, is borrowed from the *Republic*. In Cherniss's view *Republic* 523–5 is 'parallel' to *Theaetetus* 184–6 in
assigning to the senses the task of 'stimulating' the mind to engage in pure
thought by turning away from the sense-world towards that of the Forms.
Later on I will comment briefly on the alleged parallelism of these two
passages, but for the moment I want to concentrate on what Cornford's
and Cherniss's interpretations have in common.

   Both Cornford and Cherniss think (rightly) that the main point being
argued is that knowledge is achieved by the mind operating somehow independently of the senses. But both interpreters think that the mind's independent activity, when it produces knowledge, consists in acquaintance
with Forms. This latter point is, however, not to be found in Plato's text at
all, as I shall show in the next section. The only independent activity of the
mind discussed by Plato is that in which it applies the κοινά to the objects
of the senses, judging that some thing seen exists, is self-identical, and so
on. He never alludes to our mode of awareness of Existence, Sameness,
and so on, and does not locate our knowledge in any such awareness.
Cornford is right to emphasize the importance here of some distinction
between sensation and judgement; he goes wrong when he brings in the
intuition or contemplation of Forms in explicating what Plato says about
'judgement'.

                                 II

The passage begins (184b4–185a3) with an account of what perception
(αἴσθησις) actually is and how it comes about. If Plato is to refute the
claim that perception is knowledge he must first mark off the activity of
perception from other supposed 'cognitive' activities, so that he can then
enquire whether perception, so understood, amounts to knowledge. Earlier
in the dialogue (156a ff.) the process of sense-perception was represented
as something occurring between the sense-organ and the external object
perceived, and no account was taken of the fact that a person's *mind*, and
not merely his bodily organs, is active in perception. So Plato points out
(184d1–5) that our sensations (αἰσθήσεις; d2) are referred to the mind

   [5] *Aristotle's Criticism of Plato and the Academy* (Baltimore, 1944), 236 n. 141.
   [6] 'The Relation of the *Timaeus* to Plato's Later Dialogues', 244 n. 71 (= *SPM* 357 n. 1).

(ψυχή), and that it is not the sense-organs (or the sense-faculties) which perceive colours and sounds but the mind itself, operating *through* the organs, or, as he also says (e8, 185b8, e7), through the senses. The organs are parts of the *body* (184e5–6, 185d3), and the power of sight, touch, and the rest are capacities of the *body* (185e7). It is quite incorrect to say, as Plato himself had said in the *Republic*,[7] that the senses see this or that, or say or report this or that: it is the subject himself who perceives things *with* his mind *through* the organs and powers of the body, who says or thinks this or that on the basis of his sense-experience. In perception, then, the mind is active through the medium of the senses. Furthermore, though without arguing the point, Plato seems to limit perception to what may be called elementary sense-perception, i.e. the perception of the 'proper objects' of the five senses: colours, sounds, tastes, smells, and a supposed analogue for touch. He does not indicate how he regards seeing or otherwise perceiving a physical object, but presumably he would wish to say that this is not perception, strictly conceived, but already involves some of those higher reflective activities of mind to be introduced in a moment.

There are problems of interpretation here (particularly concerning how Plato understands the use of the mind in perception) but they are best put off until after the next section of the argument has been outlined. Here (185a–186e) Plato contrasts with the perceptual use of the mind, in which it operates through the medium of the bodily senses, a further and higher use, in which the mind works independently of the body and its senses (αὐτὴ δι' αὑτῆς; 185e1, 6). Socrates shows that such an independent use exists by reminding Theaetetus that in some cases we have one and the same thought about the objects of several senses. Thus we can think that a colour, a sound, and a taste are each of them the same as itself and different from the others; *what* we think about each of these things, namely *that it is the same as itself* and *that it is different from the others*, is the same in each case. What we are doing here is thinking something common to the objects of several senses, and Plato calls the predicates of such judgements κοινά, 'common terms'.[8] Plato explicitly includes among the κοινά existence, identity, difference, similarity, dissimilarity, being one, odd and even,

---

[7] Cf. 523c, δηλοῖ; d5, ἐσήμηνεν; e4, ὁρᾷ; 524a3, παραγγέλλει; a7, σημαίνει; a8, λέγει.

[8] Cornford, at one place (p. 105), notices that the word κοινόν here is to be understood by contrast with what is peculiar to the objects of a single sense. Yet further down the page he says κοινόν is to be understood 'in the sense in which a name is common to any number of individual things', and hence that the κοινά are 'the meanings of common names', i.e. Forms. Κοινόν is fairly frequently used in this way in Aristotle (e.g. *EE* 1218ᵃ8; *Metaph.* Z 1040ᵇ25; *EN* 1180ᵇ15), where the contexts show that it is to be understood as meaning τὸ κοινῇ κατηγορούμενον or τὸ καθόλου. But it is obvious that this is not how Plato uses the word here: since the κοινά are predicates belonging to objects of more than one of the senses, such predicates, as *white or hard*

good and bad, beautiful and ugly; all of these are properties of the objects
of several, perhaps all, of the senses. Plato argues that in applying common
terms to the objects of the senses the mind is not perceiving but doing
something else, which we may call reflecting and comparing (a term which
is meant to cover what the mind does when it is ἀναλογιζομένη, 186a10
ἐπανιοῦσα καὶ συμβάλλουσα, b8, and συλλογιζομένη, d3). His reason for
saying this is that acts of perception are always performed through one
sense or another, and what can be perceived through one sense cannot be
perceived through any other. Thus only colours can be seen, and no colour
can be heard or tasted. Hence we cannot be merely perceiving in thinking
that a sound and a colour exist: what we are then noticing about the
objects, their existence, cannot be either an auditory or a visual property
since it belongs equally to the sound and to the colour, and it is obvious
that there is no further sense through which we could perceive such
common properties. Judgements of this kind are made by the mind by itself
and without the aid of any sense or organ of sense.

It is important to realize that in his discussion of the higher, reflective
employment of the mind Plato is exclusively alluding to the activity of
judging *that* something exists, is self-identical, etc.; he nowhere raises the
question of how we become acquainted with Existence and the other terms
we apply to sense-objects in so judging. For the moment I will take this for
granted, leaving the proof until later.

In the first part of our passage, then, Plato draws two distinctions. He
distinguishes between the role played by the mind in perception and that
played by the senses, and he contrasts this use of the mind with a higher
reflective use in which it works independently of the body and its sense
faculties and judges that the objects of the senses exist and that they
possess other κοινά. Several points call for comment.

First, it should be noticed that in distinguishing between the sense
(αἰσθήσεις) as powers of the bodily organs and the mind as that which
perceives (αἰσθάνεται) Plato is in effect using the notion of αἴσθησις in two
ways. For the perceptual acts of the mind—the acts of seeing, hearing
smelling, etc.—can be called αἰσθήσεις (cf. 186d10–e2), as can the power

will not qualify as κοινά. Yet they are certainly κοινῇ κατηγορούμενα. I know of no place in Plato
where κοινόν is used in this Aristotelian sense: strictly not *Tht.* 208d7–9 and 209a10–11, to which
Cherniss (*Aristotle's Criticism of Plato and the Academy*, 236 n.) refers. By κοινόν in our passage
Plato certainly does not mean to refer to Forms generally. The κοινά may be Forms, though Plato
does not say so; but they do not include any predicates except those which are common to
objects of *several* senses.

[9] Plato finds it natural to shift from saying that the person perceives through the sensory
powers of the bodily organs (184b9, c6–7, 8, etc.) to saying (185c8, e6–7, 186b3) that the mind
perceives through the senses.

of the body which Plato says make these acts possible. αἴσθησις as act is
located in the mind, but αἴσθησις as power in the body. Now there is an
awkwardness in saying that the *mind* sees, hears, and so on (ὁρᾶν, ἀκούειν;
184c6–7, etc.), while locating the *power* of hearing, sight, etc. (ἀκοή, ὄψις;
185a2, c1–2) in the body and its organs: if the mind sees and hears, and not
any bodily part, then surely the mind and not any part of the body is
the possessor of the power of sight and hearing. But the awkwardness is
particularly acute because the thesis which Plato hopes to refute by the
analysis of perception being carried out here is put as the identification of
αἴσθησις and ἐπιστήμη (184b5). Since αἴσθησις, in the analysis, can refer
either to a power of the body or to an action of the mind, there is an initial
doubt as to what Plato is going to deny in denying that αἴσθησις is knowledge. It might be suggested, for example, that by emphasizing that the
senses are powers of the body Plato means to be saying that the *senses* do
not contain knowledge: they do no more than provide material for the
mind to act upon. It is the mind that does the knowing, and the senses are
altogether dumb and devoid of thinking: in using the senses we are not,
per se, even thinking anything, much less knowing anything. If this is going
to be his argument, Plato will only be denying that knowledge lies in the
sensory powers of the body; he will not be saying that perceptual acts of
the mind are themselves not acts of knowledge. Yet, one might object, this
last is precisely what ought to be proved. But owing to the vagueness of
Theaetetus' original definition and to the use of the word αἴσθησις to stand
for the body's powers of sensory affection, Plato might fairly claim to have
shown that on one plausible interpretation of the thesis it is false. This possibility should certainly be borne in mind, although I think that in the end
it is reasonably clear that Plato means to reject even the claim that perceptual acts of the mind are acts of knowledge.[10]

The second remark to be made at this point concerns the nature of perceptual acts, as Plato conceives them, and the distinction between these
and the higher acts of reflective judgement. Perception, as something the
mind does through the senses, is contrasted both with the sensory affection of the bodily organs and with the higher reflective use of the mind.
On close examination of the text, however, it appears that the perceptual
use of the mind is conceived of rather differently in the two contrasts. Plato
does not seem to have made a clean decision whether by perception he
means mere sensory awareness, which does not involve any application of
concepts to the data of sense, or sensory awareness plus the restricted use

[10] This seems to follow, for example, from 186d2, where knowledge is said not to reside
ἐν τοῖς παθήμασιν, which, as 186c1–2 shows, is to be understood as a reference to perceptual
acts of the mind.

of concepts which is involved in labelling the colours, sounds, etc. presented in sensation with their names—'red', 'hard', 'sweet', 'loud', and so on. This indecision on his part is of the greatest importance for the interpretation of the argument, if, as I just remarked, Plato intends to reject the claim of perceptual acts to be instances of knowing. To the extent that Plato is unclear what he includes under the notion of perceptual acts, both what he is denying and perhaps also why he is denying it will remain unclear. What he says about perceptual acts must therefore be very closely scrutinized.

In drawing the contrast between bodily affection and perception Plato is naturally interpreted as understanding by 'perception' sensory awareness by itself. Though he limits the objects of awareness to the proper objects of the five senses, saying that we perceive warm, hard, light, and sweet things (184e4–5), and even the hardness of a hard thing (186b2), through our senses, this need not imply that perception involves the awareness *that* these things are hard, light, and so on. And at one place he seems very clearly to be thinking of perceptual acts as acts of awareness only; he says they are common to men and beasts and can be performed already at birth (186b11–c2).[11] Presumably he does not imagine that beasts and day-old babies are capable of using concepts. Now if 'perception' is here sensory awareness, then one would expect the higher, independent activity of the mind to be the application of concepts to what we perceive. The line between 'perception' and reflection would then separate simple sensory awareness from the thinking, of whatever complexity, that one does *about* whatever one is presented with in sensation. On this view, the application of the concept *red* to a perceived colour would require some independent action of the mind quite as much as the application of the concept *existence*. In fact, the concepts of existence, identity and so on (the κοινά) would be in no way specially associated with the mind's independent activity;[12] the κοινά would have to be interpreted as mere examples, whose place could be taken by any other terms of any other class or category.

---

[11] Cf. also 186d2–3: παθήματα here too is naturally interpreted to mean acts of (passive) awareness.

[12] It might be suggested that οὐσία, at any rate, does occupy a special position. For, one might say, it is the one concept that is employed on every occasion on which any other concept is applied: every judgement is of the form 'A is (or is not) B'. One might attempt to argue that all application of concepts involves the use of the other κοινά as well: this is plausible for identity, difference, similarity, and dissimilarity. But it is not plausible for 'two', 'good', and 'beautiful'. In fact, however, the principle of selection for the κοινά is not their implication in all judgements, but their applicability to objects of different senses. So the supposed special position of at least some of them as regards the power of judgement is not Plato's reason for illustrating the independent activity of the mind by judgements involving them.

The fact remains, however, that the independent use of the mind is illustrated *exclusively* by the application of concepts which are applicable to the objects of more than one sense. This suggests that the independent use does not include judgements applying concepts peculiar to the objects of a single sense. And in fact, in contrasting perception and the higher use of the mind Plato does seem to contrast the application of the κοινά to objects of sensory awareness, not with sensory awareness itself but with the application of *other* concepts, namely the concepts required for the labelling of the data of sense. Not only does he not illustrate the reflective-judgemental use of the mind by the application of a concept which, like *red*, belongs to only one type of sense-object; he very clearly indicates that thinking with such concepts is not a matter of reflective judgement at all. He says (185b4–5) that we are capable of investigating (ἐπισκέψασθαι) and deciding (cf. κρίνειν; 186b8) whether a colour and a sound are similar or not, and that we do so with our minds independently of any bodily power. The same point is put (185c4–7) by saying that the mind does not operate through any sense in applying the words (ἐπονομάζεις, c6) 'exists' and 'does not exist' to things. By contrast, Plato says (185b9–c3), we investigate whether a couple of things are bitter by means of a bodily power, namely the sense of taste. This clearly means that in operating through the senses the mind applies the words 'bitter', 'red', 'hard', etc. to sense-objects: 'investigation about existence' involves the applying of the words 'exists' and 'does not exist', so 'investigation about bitterness' involves the application of the words 'bitter' or 'not bitter'. That this is so is made certain by the remark with which Socrates concludes his exposition of the contrast between the perceptual and the reflective uses of the mind: φαίνεταί σοι τὰ μὲν αὐτὴ δι' αὐτῆς ἡ ψυχὴ ἐπισκοπεῖν, τὰ δὲ διὰ τῶν τοῦ σώματος δυνάμεων (185e6–7). In order to decide whether something exists, is similar to something else, etc., one has to reflect; in order to decide whether something is red one does not need to reflect, but to use the mind at the perceptual level only.

There is thus good evidence for each of two different views as to what Plato thinks is involved in what I have called the perceptual use of the mind. He sometimes seems to have in mind sensory awareness without the application of concepts to what is perceived, but in contrasting the perceptual and the reflective uses he seems to think of the labelling of the data of sense with elementary colour, taste, etc. descriptions as itself taking place at the perceptual and not the reflective level. I do not think the evidence on either side can be explained away; the most one can do is to try to render the inconsistency palatable. The difficulty arises because Plato tries to combine two rather different distinctions, and this can be made understandable by considering how closely these distinctions are related to one another. We may begin by asking why Plato thinks that different powers of the mind are called on in deciding whether a κοινόν such as self-identity belongs to a sensed colour than are exercised in deciding whether the sensed colour is, say, red. The latter operation, the classification or labelling of the data of sense, does not indeed involve the application of a concept which belongs to objects of different senses; but why should that make any difference? In labelling a colour, surely, one is, implicitly at least, engaged in reflecting, remembering, and comparing—activities which Plato represents as distinctive of the 'independent' use of the mind (186a9–b1, b6–9). Indeed, it might be said that labelling the seen colour calls upon the power to apply some of the κοινά themselves: to recognize the colour as red one has to remember past colours, both red and non-red, and think this one *similar* to some and *dissimilar* from others. How can Plato have thought that the application of the elementary perceptual concepts could proceed without this sort of associative activity? And even if this can be managed without the use of the κοινά, why did Plato think it involves quite a different power of the mind from that exercised in thinking about existence, similarity, and so on?

A partial answer can be found, I think, in the view of thinking (διανοεῖσθαι) which Plato puts forward just a few pages later in the *Theaetetus*. Here (189e4 ff.) Plato defines the process of thinking as discourse carried on by the mind with itself.[13] On this model one might think of perceptual thought as a matter of saying to oneself, as one experiences various sensations, 'red', 'warm', 'sweet', and so on. And employing the κοινά in thought will be represented as saying to oneself 'That (i.e. that colour just labelled "red") exists', or 'that colour is the same as itself and different from this one', and so on. Now even if recognizing a colour as red requires comparison and involves the *implicit* use of various of the κοινά, it is clear that one need not *explicitly* say to oneself 'This colour is like such and such other colours I've seen and unlike such and such others, so it's red'. Anyone who possesses the colour concepts is (normally) able to apply them without any explicit process of reasoning at all. But it is an essential feature of Plato's model of what thinking is that only things which one explicitly says to oneself are counted as things that one thinks. Hence all such implicit mental activities must go unnoticed and unaccounted for so long as one retains this model. The contrast Plato draws is between labelling sense-data and *explicitly* thinking that, for example, some given colour exists, is the same as itself, different from something else, like or

---

[13] The same account appears in *Sph.* 264a–b, and the different image of writing in a mental book, which appears in the *Philebus* (38e–39a) alongside the idiom of discourse with oneself (38d1–2, 6, e1–4), is not significantly different from the present point of view.

unlike it, beautiful or ugly, and so forth. The point seems to be that the colour of a thing can simply be, as it were, read off it once one has the colour concept in question; whereas noticing the similarity of one thing to another requires explicit thinking about the other thing and overt comparison, just as in Plato's view judging that something is good requires sifting past and present against the probable future (186a1 ff.). These judgements, and all judgements involving κοινά, require that one engage in more or less elaborate *explicit* reflection.[14] It is the immediacy of the labelling function that seems to have impressed Plato, and to have distinguished it in his mind from thought employing the κοινά.

But even if Plato can by some such reasoning as this be justified in his separation of labelling and reflective judgement, what can be said in defence of his assimilation of the labelling power to simple sensory awareness? To begin with, it should be noted that the immediacy of the labelling operation is a consequence of the fact that, as it seems, one has in sensory awareness itself all the evidence one needs to justify the application of the appropriate label: I know that the colour I see is red just because I can see it. On the other hand, in order to judge that it is beautiful, just seeing it is not enough; as Plato implies, I need in addition to call to mind other objects seen on other occasions and conduct a comparison to see if this colour measures up to the appropriate standard of beauty. This means that the exercise of the labelling capacity, though of course it is different from sensory awareness, is very closely related to it. By labelling the data, it is natural to think, one merely makes explicit what was already contained in sensation. But in judgements of existence, usefulness, and so on, one goes beyond the data of sense themselves to consider their relations to one another, their probable consequences, and so on. From this point of view, then, the labelling function goes together with sensory awareness and is reasonably grouped together with it in contrast with reflective judgement. And when one adds that one crucially important step in the advance of knowledge is that from the labelling of sense-contents to explicit comparative reflection about them, one sees even more clearly why Plato, with his interest in knowledge, should tend to assimilate or confuse with one another sensory awareness and the labelling of its objects.

Now Plato's ambivalence in his characterization of perception

---

[14] Is this true of judgements of existence and self-identity? The case of existence is hard to decide because of the obscurity of Plato's examples. If 'this colour exists' means 'this is the real colour of something', then I suppose explicit reflection is required. The thought that something is identical with itself is such an unnatural thought that I have no confidence in any conjecture as to what Plato conceived was involved in thinking it; perhaps he is guided here by the thought that self-identity is not a feature of a thing that can simply be read off it in the way colours can.

complicates the interpretation of the remainder of the passage. The reason
he gives for making knowledge the outcome of acts of reflective judgement but not acts of perception turns out to lend itself to different interpretations depending on which view of perception is assumed.

But before showing how this is so, I must justify the assumption made
in the preceding discussion that in discussing the higher reflective employment of the mind Plato has in view only the power of formulating judgements involving the κοινά and not also or instead the contemplation of
the objects Existence, Identity, and so on. To do this will require a close
analysis of the passage in which the reflective employment of the mind is
contrasted with the perceptual.

The relevant section opens at 185b7 with the question 'Through what do
you think all these [i.e. the common terms] about them [viz. about sound
and colour]?' As Socrates explains, he has in mind that if you perceive that
something is red, or sweet-flavoured, you perceive these things through the
medium of a sense and a sense-organ; and he wants to know whether one
perceives something's existence or self-identity or unity through any analogous organ. At c7–8, having given this explanation of his question, he
repeats it: τούτοις πᾶσι ποῖα ἀποδώσεις ὄργανα δι' ὧν αἰσθάνεται ἡμῶν τὸ
αἰσθανόμενον ἕκαστα ('What sort of organs do you assign for all of these,
through which our sense-perceptory part perceives them?'). Here commentators begin to translate and comment as if what is in question were
'How do we become acquainted with the entities Existence, Identity, Unity,
etc.?' But it is evident that the question in Plato's text merely restates the
question at b7 and that therefore nothing is said about our becoming
acquainted with Existence; the question concerns rather our perceiving or
judging that a thing exists. This is overlooked only because the restatement
omits the phrase περὶ αὐτοῖν from the earlier statement, (b8), which would
make it clear that it is not a question of becoming acquainted with the
meanings of these common terms,[15] but rather one of perceiving or judging
that they do or do not apply to something.

That the περί phrase is to be understood with the restatement at c7–8 is
made certain by Theaetetus' reply. He adds in his answer the περὶ αὐτῶν
(d1) which was only implicit in the question: 'You mean *their* existence and
non-existence, similarity and dissimilarity, sameness and difference, unity
and other number.' But he then goes on to omit the phrase, in the same
idiomatic way, later in his reply when he in turn reformulates the question:
διὰ τίνος ποτὲ τῶν τοῦ σώματος τῇ ψυχῇ αἰσθανόμεθα [αὐτῶν] (d3–4)
('Through what bodily part do we perceive these with our minds?'). And

[15] So Cornford, p. 105.

here again translators unaccountably omit the περί phrase and misunderstand Theaetetus to be asking himself whether we become acquainted with Existence and the rest, in themselves, through any agency of the body. Cornford compounds this error by misconstruing in Theaetetus' next answer (d7–e2) the force of the phrase περὶ πάντων, which he again reimports. Theaetetus says, 'The mind itself through itself, as it appears to me, examines (ἐπισκοπεῖν)[16] for every object [whether it possesses] these common attributes' (αὐτὴ δι' αὑτῆς ἡ ψυχὴ τὰ κοινά μοι φαίνεται περὶ πάντων ἐπισκοπεῖν). But Cornford takes περὶ πάντων with τὰ κοινά, and translates 'the common terms that apply to everything', presumably thinking the phrase a variation of τὸ ἐπὶ πᾶσι κοινόν above (c4–5); but even if this is possible Greek it is obvious that περὶ πάντων ἐπισκοπεῖν is parallel to περὶ αὐτοῖν διανοῇ in the original statement of the question (b7), so that we have once again the same question about the application of these words to things and not a new question about how we become acquainted with their meanings. Other translators (e.g. Diès) take περὶ πάντων here with the verb, as its position surely dictates, but they have not, I think, seen the consequence of so doing. The consequence, to repeat, is that Theaetetus says nothing about how we become acquainted with Existence and Sameness, but rather tells us that judgements of the existence and identity of a sense-quality are not made by the mind through the agency of any sense but rather by the mind independently.

It is, then, quite clear that περὶ αὐτοῖν (185b7) is to be supplied right through to 185e whenever there is mention of grasping, thinking, or investigating κοινά. Plato himself repeats it (or a variant) as often as he decently can: the commentators' shift from the question whether we use a bodily organ in applying the κοινά to things, to the question how we become acquainted with Forms, is sheer invention. σφαλμ (A)

Nor does Plato subsequently raise this other question. In what follows (186a–c) he consolidates his position by running through the list of κοινά, adding some new ones, and obtaining Theaetetus' agreement that these are all applied to things by the mind independently of perception. Here again translators confuse the issue by taking Plato to be discussing how we arrive at our acquaintance with these common entities; and again there are very clear signs that nothing of the sort is in question.[17] Thus when Socrates

---

[16] Ἐπισκοπεῖν need not mean 'contemplate' (so Cornford; cf. Cherniss, SPM 6 and W. G. Runciman, Plato's Later Epistemology (Cambridge, 1962), 15): cf. ἐπισκέψασθαι, which is the aorist used to meet the defect in ἐπισκοπεῖν, just above, 185b5. Cf. also 161d5, e7, where both ἐπισκέψασθαι and ἐπισκοπεῖν appear and neither means 'contemplate'.

[17] Only 186a4 even remotely imports an interest in how we become acquainted with the κοινά; and its immediate sequel is quite evidently concerned not with this but with how to employ them in making judgements about αἰσθητά.

inquires whether *καλὸν καὶ αἰσχρὸν καὶ ἀγαθὸν καὶ κακόν* are among the *κοινά* about the *οὐσία* (existence)[18] of which the mind judges all by itself, Theaetetus replies in the affirmative (186a9–b1). But he goes on to add that when the mind judges about these matters it calculates within itself past and present against the future. Now this is a pretty good brief account of how one judges whether a particular person or action or situation is good or bad or honourable or disgraceful: one does have to weigh past experience and present circumstances in order to get a reasonable judgement as to a person's future behaviour or the consequences of an action, and so on. But it is precisely the *wrong* sort of thing to do in order to become acquainted with the existence and nature of a Platonic Form. Consideration of phenomena and phenomenal events is notoriously the main *obstacle* to becoming acquainted with these. It seems clear, therefore, that Socrates and Theaetetus are not discussing the question how we arrive at our knowledge of the Forms Honourableness, Disgracefulness, and the like; they are, rather, enquiring how one goes about making particular judgements about the goodness or badness, etc. of particular things.

The general point is reaffirmed once more with complete clarity in the immediately following lines (186b2–10). You perceive the hardness of a hard thing, Socrates says, through the sense of touch, and likewise the softness of a soft thing. But the existence of this hardness and this softness (or perhaps of hardness and softness in general), and their opposition to one another, and the existence of this opposition, are not discoverable by the use of the senses. For these, the mind compares things together and keeps going back over them within itself to answer its questions. Once again it is obvious that what interests Plato is the contrast between two operations of the mind, perceiving through the senses, and reflection, comparison, prediction, and in general the interpretation of the *significance* of what one perceives. Neither here nor elsewhere does he raise the question how the mind acquires its knowledge of the common terms which it employs in its interpretative activity.

Thus the difficulty noticed above (p. 357) in the first stage of the argument as Cornford interprets it is eliminated. There is no longer a conflict between the obvious implication of the sensing–judging distinction to which he appeals and the contrast between the perception of sense-objects and the contemplation of thought-objects: the latter contrast is not drawn in the argument at all. The contrast, as I have argued above, is that between

---

[18] Throughout the passage *οὐσία* seems to mean (something like) the existence of this or that: cf. 186b6, where *καὶ ὅτι ἐστόν* is epexegetical of *τὴν οὐσίαν*. At any rate, it never means the *nature* of a thing. (See below, pp. 370 f., for a needed qualification.)

elementary sensory awareness together with the labelling of its objects, on the one hand, and the supposedly more sophisticated level of thought attained in thinking that sense-objects exist, are different from one another, and so on.

III

So far, then, I have argued that Plato draws two distinctions, that between the role of the senses and the role of the mind in perception, and that between the use of the mind in perception and its use in reflective judgement involving the notions of existence, identity, and so on. The material thus provided is the basis on which Plato relies in rejecting the definition of knowledge as αἴσθησις.

The refutation Plato produces (186c6–e10) is characteristically brief and cryptic. He points out that one cannot be knowing anything when one does not grasp οὐσία (being, existence?) and truth, and then relies on the preceding analysis to show that in αἴσθησις one does not grasp οὐσία and truth. We have already seen that Cornford interprets this as meaning that it is not through the use of the senses that one becomes acquainted with the Forms, the only truly real and knowable entities. But since, as I have shown above, there is no reference in what precedes to Forms,[19] or to the process of becoming acquainted with Forms, there is absolutely no excuse for any interpretation of this kind. What Plato means by 'grasping being and truth' must be gathered from the account he has just given of perception and the employment of the κοινά in thought.

Clearly, Plato means to argue that the mind in perception does not acquire or evince knowledge, on the ground that knowledge is attained only when οὐσία is grasped, and that it is only in reflective judgement that the power to judge about the οὐσία of anything is evinced. But, because of the uncertainty about what Plato understands by 'perception', two different lines of thought, both, I think, plausible and interesting, may be proposed as interpretations of his argument here.

Let us assume first that 'perception' means sensory awareness, without conceptualization. Then it is natural to interpret Plato as pointing out that knowing involves, at least, thinking that so-and-so is the case. Knowledge therefore involves the applying of concepts and since sensory awareness

---

[19] Even if the κοινά are Forms Plato does not say they are, and for the very good reason that it nowhere matters to his argument what their metaphysical status is. See n. 8 above.

is a mental power not involving conceptualization it must be wrong to equate knowledge with sensory awareness.

There are several points in favour of such an interpretation. Foremost is the fact that Plato says that knowledge involves 'grasping truth'. This is very naturally interpreted as meaning that there is no knowledge where there is no formulation of truths, i.e. where there is no thinking *that*, no conceptualization. Secondly, Socrates in stating the conclusion of the argument seems to suggest just this contrast between sensory awareness and thinking that so-and-so is the case: he says, 'So there is no knowledge in the experiences we undergo (παθήμασιν), but rather in the reasoning (συλλογισμῷ) we do concerning them' (186d2–3). Here nothing indicates that the reasoning envisaged is restricted to any particular subject-matter (not, for example, to questions about the application of κοινά); there seems to be a blank contrast between bare seeing, hearing, etc., and thoughts, of whatever sort, about what one is seeing, hearing, and so on.

But if Plato means to say that αἴσθησις occurs without the formulation of judgements, this point must somehow be found in his assertion that in perception we do not 'grasp οὐσία'. What has the failure to grasp οὐσία to do with the non-judgemental character of perception? Throughout the argument so far οὐσία seems to have meant existence:[20] at its first introduction in the context (185c9; cf. a9 and c5–6) it seems to mean this and it does not appear to alter in meaning thereafter. Perception's failure to grasp οὐσία should therefore mean that the thought that something exists is not an act of perception. This is no doubt true, but how does this failure imply that perception is altogether non-judgemental? Judgements of existence are just one class of judgements. Does Plato mean to suggest that somehow we must always be making existential judgements whenever we make judgements of any other type? Or does he mean that before we can make judgements of other types we must be able to make existential judgements? Neither of these alternatives is at all attractive; but the mention of οὐσία here certainly seems not to be an arbitrarily chosen example illustrating a thesis which any other concept would have illustrated equally well.

Is it, however, correct to insist that grasping οὐσία must mean thinking that something exists? Even although οὐσία (and its cognates) in its earlier appearances in the passage is naturally *translated* 'existence', 'exists', etc (as in 185a9, ὅτι ἀμφοτέρω ἐστόν), it does not follow that this is what the

---

[20] So Lewis Campbell (*The* Theaetetus *of Plato*) insists: cf. his note *ad* 186c3, and p. liv n. C; also n. 18 above.

word *means* there or elsewhere in the passage. English sharply distinguishes the 'is' of existence from the copula, but Greek does not; and it is arguable, and has been argued,[21] that the Greek verb εἶναι does not have 'senses' corresponding to this distinction. It represents rather an undifferentiated concept straddling this particular distinction. If this is so, one can easily see how Plato might have thought that thinking with the concept οὐσία has a position of priority *vis-à-vis* all other conceptual thinking, and that to fail to grasp οὐσία is to fail to formulate judgements altogether. To grasp the οὐσία of something is not necessarily to think that it *exists*, but may be no more than to think that it *is F* for some predicate *F*.[22] In that case to be deprived of the use of εἶναι would mean that one was incapable of predicating anything of anything else, since the copula, which is indispensable to predication, would be unavailable. Hence, without the use of εἶναι one could not have the power of judgement, and therefore one could not have the use of any concepts at all.

In this way, assuming that by 'perception' Plato means just sensory awareness, a good and interesting argument can be found behind his assertion that since perception does not grasp οὐσία, it does not arrive at truth, and therefore cannot constitute knowledge. But although, as I have indicated, such an argument fits the text quite well in several respects, doubt must remain whether it expresses Plato's meaning. For, as I have argued in the preceding section, the neat distinction, on which this interpretation depends, between perception as sensory awareness and the higher conceptualizing power of the mind is not everywhere in the context adhered to by Plato himself. The higher power of the mind is restricted to the application of only certain concepts, namely the κοινά (which includes, besides those mentioned, also all others which belong to objects of different senses, or involve reference to objects of different senses); perception, then, includes sensory awareness and the minimum interpretation of its objects which is involved in labelling them 'red', 'sweet', and so on. The labelling process certainly amounts to using certain concepts, namely what might be called minimal perceptual concepts; and since this is envisaged as taking place without the use of εἶναι, which only comes in with the addition of the higher power of the mind, Plato cannot mean to suggest that all use of concepts requires the use of εἶναι. So one must look further to find an

---

[21] Cf. e.g. C. H. Kahn, 'The Greek Verb "To Be" and the Concept of Being', *Foundations of Language*, 2 (1966), 245–65. Cf. also G. E. L. Owen, 'Aristotle on the Snares of Ontology', in . Bambrough (ed.), *New Essays on Plato and Aristotle* (London, 1965), 71 n., for salutary remarks on Plato's use of the notion of τὸ ὄν in the *Sophist*.

[22] At 186a10, to consider the οὐσία of καλόν, etc. quite clearly means to consider whether some given thing *is* beautiful, good, etc. Here the being of a predicate is its attachment to a bject; likewise the being of a subject is (in part at least) its bearing of a predicate.

interpretation that will fit this way of understanding the distinction between perception and reflection.

If, then, 'perception' means sensory awareness plus the supposedly immediate classification of its objects, what reason can Plato be understood to be giving against the claim of perception to be knowledge? On this view, what would it be to grasp οὐσία, and why would the failure to do this entail that perception is not knowledge? The refutation of Protagoras earlier in the dialogue seems to offer a clue. Plato argues (177c–179c) against Protagoras that thinking a thing does not make it so, at least whenever prediction is involved, because in such cases the truth or falsity of the thought depends on the event; and even if each man is his own infallible judge of how the event turns out, when it occurs, the prediction, once made, is true or not depending on how things turn out (or seem to have turned out) (cf. 178d4–6). In making predictions, then, there is room for mistakes; not everyone can claim to have *knowledge* of how things *will* turn out (or even how things will *seem* to himself to have turned out). It is the expert physician who knows whether I will come down with a fever tomorrow (178c); the expert musician, and not just any layman, knows whether a lyre will be put in tune by loosening its strings (178d); and in general when one man can claim to *know* better than others how things will turn out, this claim must be based on his possession of an expertise which makes him wiser and more skilled than others in his particular subject area (179a10–b5). His prediction is not then a mere guess, as the layman's would have to be; it is founded on objectively valid principles of science or art and constitutes knowledge precisely because it is supported by such principles.[23]

This argument against Protagoras is recalled in our passage when Socrates adds καλὸν καὶ αἰσχρὸν καὶ ἀγαθὸν καὶ κακόν to the list of subject matters about which perception is incompetent to judge (186a8–b1). Judging here involves prediction, Socrates says; and in so saying he clearly refers back to what was said against Protagoras. In the argument against Protagoras, special emphasis was placed on the fact that questions o ὠφέλεια involve prediction, so that some πόλεις are wiser and more exper than others (172a, 179a5 ff., etc.); and in our passage Socrates joins ὠφέλεια with οὐσία as the two most significant matters in thinking about which w employ the higher reflective power of the mind—those of us, at any rate who are capable of having thoughts on such subjects at all (186c2–5). Th suggestion is that Plato bases his rejection of perception's claim to b

---

[23] Compare Socrates' refutation of Thrasymachus' claim that ἀδικία—and not δικαιοσύνη is a virtue and a sign of intelligence; *Rep.* 350a–c.

knowledge on the ground that knowledge implies expertise and the appeal to objectively valid principles and standards; while perception does not go beyond subjective reports of the contents of sensory experience and therefore makes no judgements to which such standards and principles are relevant. There are no experts at perception; no one can claim that his perceptual reports, as such, are more true than anyone else's; no one subjects his own or anyone else's reports to criticism by appeal to the sort of standards Plato implies are operative in the doctor's prediction of fever and the pastry-cook's of pleasure to the palate. Precisely because perception is purely subjective, because it is not open to criticism or correction (cf. ἀνάλωτοι; 179c5), perception cannot claim to be knowledge. Knowledge is always the result of directing one's thoughts in accordance with principles and standards; hence any claim to knowledge must be open to criticism by appeal to the appropriate standards. Because in perception there is no room for such criticism, perception cannot constitute knowledge.

On this interpretation the failure of perception to grasp the οὐσία of its objects would be taken to mean that in perception one notices only the colour (etc.) a thing appears to have and says nothing about what its real colour is. As I remarked above, οὐσία is an undifferentiated concept of being; but it seems naturally interpreted in this passage (at e.g. 185a9) as expressing existence. To judge that a colour exists one must engage in the kind of calculation of past and present perceptions with a view to the future which Theaetetus mentions in connection with judgements of value; and just as Plato insists that judgements of value imply the existence of objective standards which experts constantly use to guide their thought, so one must be guided by objective standards in saying how things in the world *are*. This is the work not of perception but of reflective judgement.

But if perception fails to attain to objectivity it also fails to 'hit the truth' (186c9). A thought is pronounced true or false by appeal to the standards valid for the subject-matter. Hence perception, as something altogether subjective and unguided by standards, yields neither truths nor falsehoods. Knowledge, then, must lie elsewhere; in fact, it is to be looked for in reflective judgement, where the notions of existence, identity, similarity, and so on, with their associated objective standards, enter for the first time.

I think this interpretation has much in its favour. The fact that it reads quite a lot into Plato's remark that perception fails to grasp οὐσία, and therefore misses truth too, is no objection against it; any interpretation must do the same. What matters is how one brings the context to bear on the interpretation of this final argument. In appealing to the notions of expertise and objective standards this interpretation makes good use of undoubtedly Platonic doctrines undoubtedly expressed in the context; and in understanding perception to include the classification of the contents of sensory experience it adopts what appears to be the correct interpretation of the contrast between αἴσθησις and the independent employment of the mind. And in bringing these two views together it provides a reasonable sense for the final argument.

Crombie[24] appears to reject an interpretation rather close to this one on the ground that it cannot accommodate the examples Plato gives of judgements involving κοινά other than οὐσία. Crombie thinks that on this view the 'contribution which the mind makes' consists in 'referring our sense-data to the external world'; and the difficulty then arises that one contribution of the mind mentioned by Plato is to notice that a colour and a sound are different, a contribution not plausibly interpreted as consisting in the referral of 'sense-data' to the external world. On the view I have been expounding, however, the contribution of the mind is not limited in this way. Its contribution is the appeal to objective standards, and it is only in connection with the existence of the objects of sensory awareness that the appropriate objective standards involve the referral of 'sense-data' to the external world. In other cases, e.g. those of self-identity and unity and the difference of a sound from a colour, it would seem to be a law of logic that the mind invokes, and the fact that it is *applied* to objects of sensory awareness does not make it any less something objectively valid. One cannot (let us suppose) dispute a man's report that what he sees in his visual field is a red colour and what he hears is a bang. But if he goes on to say about the colour and the noise that they are the same thing he's enunciating a falsehood; what he says at this level is subject to criticism.

Thus the upshot of the argument, on this second interpretation, is that knowledge brings with it objectivity and appeal to the sort of standard which experts employ. 'Perception' fails to be knowledge because one need not be an expert in any sense or have the use of objective standards of any kind in order to be as good at perceiving as anyone else. On this reading Plato arrives, by way of his assimilation of knowledge to expertise, at a position which gives to empirical knowledge the honorific title of ἐπιστήμη and the emphasis which he places in this connection on objectivity has the very interesting consequence that Plato's conception of empirical knowledge has a definite Kantian flavour.

Plato, therefore, rejects the claim of 'perception' (αἴσθησις) to constitu

---

[24] *An Examination of Plato's Doctrines*, ii. 15–16.

knowledge on one of two grounds, depending on which of two under-
standings of 'perception' is adopted. If 'perception' means mere sensory
awareness, then it cannot be knowledge because knowledge involves
discursive thought while 'perception' is at a lower level of logical complexity. If 'perception' means awareness of 'sense-contents', explicitly
labelled, then it fails to be knowledge because it makes no claims to objective validity. As I have already indicated, each of these interpretations is
plausible, and neither, I think, can be definitely ruled out. But on the whole
I prefer the second interpretation, because it accounts better for Plato's
emphasis on thought about κοινά in particular as marking an advance
beyond 'perceptual' thinking and into the area where we can first speak of
knowledge.

IV

But whichever of these interpretations is correct, the *Theaetetus* turns out
to contain points of great originality—points completely ignored by interpretations which, like Cornford's and Cherniss's, attempt to make the
Theaetetus merely repeat things already said in the *Republic*. The distinction between the senses as bodily powers and perception as a power of the
mind, and the identification of what is known with some subclass of judgements, constitute noteworthy philosophical achievements. They also mark
distinct advances over Plato's way of thinking about perception and knowledge in the *Republic*. Cherniss's claim that *Republic* 522–5 is parallel in
argument to *Theaetetus* 184–6 can now be seen to be an entirely superficial
view. The *Republic* passage is so far from being parallel that it actually
makes mistakes which the *Theaetetus*' analysis is intended to show up.
These are: (1) The *Republic* passage constantly speaks of the *senses* as
saying this or that, whereas (as noted above) the *Theaetetus* scotches this
misleading inaccuracy. (2) The *Republic* allows as judgements of perception things which the *Theaetetus*, in distinguishing perception from the
mind's power of independent thought, insists belong to a level of intellectual activity entirely beyond perception. Thus at 523a3 Plato speaks of the
perception that the same thing is both hard and soft, which seems to
involve a judgement of identity and so cannot be a matter of perception
in the *Theaetetus*' scheme. Cf. also 523c11 ff. (perceiving a finger), 524d9–e6
(perceiving something as a unit). Further important differences between
the two passages include: (3) The *Republic* counts both the question
whether something is hard or soft, light or heavy (524a), and the question
whether it is one (524b), as forcing the mind up to its highest level of

operation: on either subject the senses are untrustworthy witnesses (523b3–4). But the *Theaetetus* distinguishes between the two cases, and actually allows that the mind operating through the senses does judge without recourse as to hard and soft, light and heavy and the other elementary perceptual properties (185b9ff., 186b). It is only with respect to *other* questions than these that the mind's higher capacities are called into play. Hence (4) there is no resemblance at all between the function of the senses as stimulative of thought (*Republic*) and the *Theaetetus'* distinction between perception and the higher functions of the mind. Finally, of course, (5) these higher functions of the mind have nothing to do with the contemplation of Forms, as νόησις in the *Republic* does.

Furthermore, and importantly, the *Theaetetus* avoids altogether the *Republic*'s misleading analysis of knowledge by reference of the objects to which it is directed; the objects about which Plato assumes we have knowledge in the *Theaetetus* include αἰσθητά,[25] and knowledge is distinguished from other states of mind not by its objects but by how the knower is related to them. Plato's views on perception and knowledge in the *Theaetetus* are fortunately much more sophisticated than traditional interpretations make them appear. Scholars do Plato no service by trying to read into the *Theaetetus* epistemological doctrines they think they find in the *Republic*.[26]

[25] This assumption is not abandoned subsequently in the *Theaetetus*; it is very clearly reaffirmed in 201a–c (cf. Runciman, *Plato's Later Epistemology*, 37).

[26] The novelty of the *Theaetetus* is made to seem greater than it probably is by those who like Cornford and Cherniss, think that Plato in the *Republic* and other middle-period dialogues firmly denies that one can *know* anything about anything in this imperfect world. It is true that certain arguments and ways of speaking of the *Republic* imply that the things we perceive or have beliefs about are different things from those we can have knowledge about. But Plato certainly thinks that after undergoing the education he outlines his rulers will be able to govern with knowledge, and this surely means that they will *know*, for example, that a proposed course of action is right or wrong. The difference between the man who has δόξα and the man of ἐπιστήμη must, despite appearances, not entail a total difference of objects thought about. A more plausible view is that the ἐπιστήμων, because of his acquaintance with the Forms, is in a position to know things about the same objects about which the man of δόξα, because of his ignorance of the Forms, can only have beliefs. This view is in accord with the distinction between ἐπιστήμη and ἀληθὴς δόξα in *Meno* 98a, and has much else to be said for it. If this is the substance of Plato's position in the *Republic* then the *Theaetetus* in allowing knowledge of αἰσθητ does not subvert anything but unwanted implications of misleading arguments in the *Republic* the *Theaetetus* can then be seen as offering a corrected and more adequate attempt to say som of the things Plato wished to say in the *Republic*.

XIV

OBSERVATIONS ON PERCEPTION IN PLATO'S LATER DIALOGUES

MICHAEL FREDE

Ast, in his *Lexicon Platonicum*, gives the following as the general meaning of the verb 'aisthanesthai' in Plato: 'to sense, to perceive by a sense, and hence generally to perceive by the senses'. This not only seems to me to be wrong, it also seems to be seriously misleading if one wants to arrive at an understanding of what Plato has to say about perception. For it suggests that in general when Plato uses the verb 'aisthanesthai', he is relying on a common notion of sense-perception, a notion which Plato just tries to clarify. This suggestion seems natural enough. Surely, one will say, the Greeks even before Plato must have had a notion of sense-perception, and 'aisthanesthai' must have been the verb they commonly used when they wanted to talk about sense-perception. And yet it seems to me that one fails to understand what Plato is trying to do, in particular in the *Theaetetus*, unless one understands that it is only Plato who introduces a clear notion of sense-perception, because he needs it for certain philosophical purposes. What he has to say about perception has to be understood against the background of the ordinary use of the verb 'aisthanesthai' and against the background of the philosophical intentions with which Plato narrows down this common use so that it does come to have the meaning 'to perceive by the senses'.

Though 'aisthanesthai' presumably is formed from a root which signifies 'hearing', its ordinary use is quite general. It can be used in any case in which one perceives something by the senses and even more generally in any case in which one becomes aware of something, notices something, realizes, or even comes to understand something, however this may come about. There will, of course, be a tendency to use the word in cases in which it is particularly clear that somebody is becoming aware of something or noticing something, as opposed to just venturing a guess, making a con-

From Michael Frede, *Essays in Ancient Philosophy* (Clarendon Press, 1987). Reprinted with permission from Oxford University Press, and the author.

jecture, learning of something by hearsay. These will be cases of seeing, but then also cases of sense-perception quite generally. But the use of the verb is not restricted to these cases. It is used whenever someone becomes aware of something. And up to Plato's time, and often far beyond it, there is no clear recognition that there are two radically different ways in which we become aware of something, one by way of sense-perception and the other in some other way, e.g. by a grasp of the mind. Thus, there is no reason to suppose that the verb 'aisthanesthai', strictly speaking, refers only to sense-perception, but is also used metaphorically in other cases. It, rather, seems that all cases of becoming aware of something are understood and construed along the lines of the paradigm of seeing, exactly because one does not see a radical difference between the way the mind grasps something and the way the eyes see something. Both are suposed to involve some contact with the object by virtue of which, through a mechanism unknown to us, we become aware of it.

But in addition to this very general use of the verb 'aisthanesthai', we find in Plato a second, narrower use of the term, e.g. in the *Phaedo* and in the *Republic*. In this use the term is restricted to cases of awareness that somehow involve the body and that constitute an awareness of something corporeal. But even now it would be rash to assume that the verb means 'sense-perception'. For in these cases it is used almost interchangeably with 'dokein' and 'doxazein,' 'to seem' and 'to believe'. The realm of belief, as opposed to the realm of knowledge, is the bodily world with which we are in bodily contact as a result of which this world appears to us in a certain way, as a result of which we have certain beliefs about it. There is no 'doxa', no belief about the ideas, because ideas are not the kinds of things with which one could have the kind of contact that gives rise to a belief or a perception. But, just as it would be a mistake to infer from this that 'doxa' means 'sense-perception', so there also is no need to assume that 'aisthesis' means 'sense-perception', though standard cases of 'aisthesis' will be cases of sense-perception.

It is also in the later dialogues that we clearly have an even narrower use of 'aisthanesthai', in which it, indeed, does mean 'to perceive by the senses'. And it is this third sense of 'aisthesis' whose introduction I want to discuss.

Unfortunately, our main evidence for this very narrow notion of 'aisthesis' is contained in a passage of the *Theaetetus*, 184–7, whose interpretation has become highly controversial, since it involves basic claims about Plato's philosophy and his philosophical development.

In this passage Plato tries to show not only that perception is not identical with knowledge, but that no case of perception as such is a case o

[handwritten margin note: Argument: Knowledge is beyond true sort of Doubt (one?!)]

knowledge. The argument assumes that if we perceive something, a bodily sense-organ is affected, and that through this change in the sense-organ a change is brought about in the mind (186c ff., d). What the argument, as I want to interpret it, mainly turns on is that if we have a clear and precise notion of perception, we see that perception is a purely passive affection of the mind and that for that very reason it cannot constitute knowledge, since knowledge minimally involves true belief and since any belief involves an activity of the mind.

If this is correct, then it would seem that Plato's point in introducing this very narrow notion of perception is to untangle the conflation of perception, appearance, belief, and knowledge with which the main discussion of the dialogue begins in 151d ff. There perception is first identified with knowledge in Theaetetus' first definition of knowledge as perception, and perception gets quickly identified with appearance (152c11), which then throughout this section of the dialogue is treated as if it were the same as belief (cf. e.g. 158a1 with 158a2 and 185b2). But, obviously, it is useful to distinguish between these cognitive states: to perceive is not the same as to believe (though in the middle dialogues we had not paid much attention to the distinction); neither is it the same as to be appeared to, and to know is yet a fourth thing. But it is not only useful to make these distinctions, as Plato tries to make them in the *Theaetetus* and the *Sophist* (264a–b). It is necessary to make these distinctions if we want to combat a certain philosophical view that we first encounter in Protagoras, but that, in one version or another, will later be espoused by some rhetoricians, Sceptics, and the so-called Empiricists, namely the view that the beliefs which we have are just a matter of how things appear to us, how they strike us, of what impression, given the contact we have with them, they leave on us. Plato and the philosophical tradition that depends on him, on the other hand, think that we should not rest content with how things strike us, that we have to go beyond that to find out how they really are, quite independently of how they appear to us. The opponents, like Protagoras, question or deny the possibility that we ever get beyond appearance, seeming, belief. And, hence, they doubt or deny that there is any point in reserving the term 'knowledge' for something that goes beyond belief. It is in this context that I want to see the argument of the *Theaetetus*, and in particular the section from 184 to 187. Plato thinks that our beliefs and our knowledge about the physical world involve a passive affection of the mind, but he also thinks that they go much beyond this passive affection. And he wants to reserve the term 'aisthanesthai', or 'to perceive', for this passive element in our beliefs, which he was willing to grant the opponents. It is in this way that the term came to have the meaning of sense-perception.

With this as a background let us turn to the details of the argument. The conclusion that perception and knowledge are two different things is drawn in 186e9–10 on the basis of the argument in the preceding lines, 186e4 ff. It is assumed that to know is to grasp the truth and that to grasp the truth is to grasp being. But in perception we do not grasp being, hence we do not grasp truth. Therefore, to perceive is not to know. This argument has two crucial assumptions: (i) to grasp the truth is to grasp being, and (ii) to perceive is not to grasp being. It is difficult to understand and to evaluate these assumptions, since we do not know what is meant by 'to grasp being'. There is no argument for the first assumption that can shed light on the meaning of the phrase. But the second premiss is supposed to have been established by the argument that extends to 186c6. Hence, we can look at this argument to see whether it gives us a clue to what is meant by 'to grasp being'.

Now, if we look at the argument, it seems that the reason given for the assumption that in perception we do not grasp being is that the mind considers questions concerning the being of something by itself, rather than by means of one of the senses. This would suggest that the mind grasps or gets hold of being in the relevant sense when it manages to settle the question concerning the being of something which it has been considering by itself. This seems to be confirmed by the final comments on the argument in 187a1 ff. There Plato says that we have learned from the argument at least that we have to look for knowledge not in perception, but in what the mind does when it considers questions concerning being by itself (187a5–6), when it forms beliefs (187a7–8). It is because we are supposed to draw this moral from the argument that the dialogue proceeds to discuss the suggestion that knowledge is true belief (187b4–6). It is in belief that we grasp truth, if the belief is true, though, as the further argument will show, this is not yet a sufficient condition for knowledge, since knowledge requires that this truth be grasped in a particular way.

But if it is in true belief that we grasp truth, it is also in true belief that we grasp being. This suggests that by 'grasping being' Plato here means no more than that the mind in forming a true belief manages to settle the question of the being of something correctly. And it is easy to see how Plato could think this, given his views on being. For he assumes that any belief, explicitly or implicitly, is of the form 'A is F', and he thinks that in assuming that A is F one attributes being both to A and to F-ness. To assume that Socrates is just is, on this view, to attribute being to Socrates and to justice. Hence, any true belief will presuppose that one has correctly settled questions concerning the being of something.

One may, of course, think that by 'grasping being' Plato here means something much stronger than settling the question whether being should be attributed to something in this way. One may think that Plato wants to distinguish two kinds of grasps or intutions, a perceptual grasp or intuition and an intellectual grasp or intuition. Thus, one may think that Plato, having distinguished two kinds of features, perceptual features and non-perceptual or intelligible features, wants to claim that knowledge involves the intellectual grasp of intelligible features and hence that perception will never give us knowledge. But even if this should be Plato's view, this is not the way he argues in this passage. Instead of distinguishing two kinds of features and correspondingly two kinds of grasps or intuitions, he distin-guishes two kinds of features and correspondingly two kinds of questions the mind considers and tries to settle (cf. 185e6ff.). If *F*-ness is a percep-tual feature, then, when the mind considers the question whether some-thing is *F*, it draws on the testimony of the senses (cf. 185b10–12). If *F*-ness is a non-perceptual feature like being, then the mind considers the ques-tion whether something is *F* by itself. What little Plato has to say about how the mind goes about doing this makes no reference to some intellec-tual grasp. Plato is referring to comparisons and to reasonings the mind goes through to come to a judgement (186a10ff., b8ff., c2ff.), the kinds of things the mind does when it tries to decide a matter. And the fact that Plato at 187a5ff. characterizes what the mind does when it considers ques-tions by itself as 'doxazein', i.e. as coming to form a belief, certainly should warn us against assuming that some special power of the mind to grasp intelligible entities is appealed to here. All that seems to be appealed to is what the mind has to be able to do to form beliefs. And this is a great deal, though Plato here does not care to spell it out in any detail. To be able to form the belief that *A* is *F*, the mind has to have arrived at some idea of what it is to be for *A* and what it is to be for *F*-ness, or what it is to be for an *F*, and it has to find out whether *A* is such as to be an *F*. What Plato here wants to emphasize is the mere fact that the perception is a purely passive affection (cf. 186c2 and 186d2), whereas the simplest belief, even if it concerns a perceptual feature, requires and presupposes a great deal of mental activity. And he infers from this that since all this activity is needed to arrive at truth, perception itself does not give us truth and, hence, cannot be knowledge.

Now one may want to interpret the argument of 184–7 differently and argue thus: Plato distinguishes two kinds of questions, those the mind settles by itself and those the mind settles by relying on a sense. Since there are questions the mind has to settle by itself, and since, presumably, the answer to these questions can be known, we here have an argument which shows that knowledge is not to be identified with perception. But we do not have an argument, nor does Plato intend to argue, that perception never gives us knowledge. After all, there are questions for whose solution the mind relies on a sense. The answer to these questions seems to be provided by perception. It seems to me that this interpretation is wrong. Plato is quite careful never to say that some questions are settled by perception or by a sense. All questions are settled by the mind, though for some it does rely on perception. Thus, I take it that Plato wants to argue that even the question whether A is red is not settled by perception. We may be passively affected by the colour red, but to form the belief that something is red presupposes and takes a great deal of activity on the part of the mind. Hence, we perceive the colour red, but we do not, strictly speaking, perceive that A is red. Hence, knowledge, since it always involves belief, never is just a matter of perception.

The only textual evidence that seems to stand in the way of this interpretation is the following. In 186b11–c5 we are told that whereas animals and we as children perceive many things right from birth, there are other things that it takes us a long time, much trouble, and some education to grasp. Surely, one will say, to see that something is red does not take much trouble and a lot of education. It is something any infant can do. But, it may be worth remembering that even the Stoics later will deny that children, properly speaking, perceive that something is red. For perception in this wider sense presupposes a state of the development of reason that allows us to articulate a visual impression in terms of concepts and that allows us to accept such an impression as true. Thus, even the simple judgement that something is red presupposes some notion of what it is to be and some notion of what it is to be red. And this we do not have right from birth. Nor is it given to us by perception, but only by reflection on what we perceive. What we perceive, strictly speaking, are just the proper objects of the different senses, e.g. colours in the case of sight (184e7 ff.). Thus, strictly speaking, we do not even perceive the object of which we come to believe that it is red. And if this is so, it is even more difficult to see how we could be said to perceive that something is red, given this very narrow notion of perception.

Now, Plato, in restricting perception to a passive affection of the mind and in emphasizing the activity of the mind in forming beliefs, thinks of beliefs as something we deliberately arrive at after a good deal of consideration and ratiocination. As Plato puts it later in the dialogue (189e–190a), belief is the result of a silent discussion one leads with oneself. In the *Sophist* (263e ff.) and in the *Philebus* (38c–e), we get a similar view of belief. Thus, belief is conceived of as something that is actively espoused on the basis of some conscious, deliberate activity. This, no doubt, is a idealization of how we come to have beliefs. For many beliefs we just find ourselves with, and in their case there is no reason to suppose that we ever went through a process of deliberation as a result of which we espoused the belief. The Protagorean view, on the other hand, and the other views alluded to in the beginning, which are like it, assume that beliefs normally are something we just find ourselves with, which have grown on us, which we have just come by by being struck by things in a certain way. And they try to assimilate all beliefs to what they take to be the normal case. Hence, they emphasize the passive element in belief-formation. Thus, one can see why Plato should be interested in emphasizing how small the passive element in belief-formation is. To do so, he restricts the general notion of perception to sense-perception in such a narrow sense and, moreover, to such a narrow notion of sense-perception that we cannot even any longer be said to perceive that something is red. It is this philosophical motivation that underlies Plato's introduction of a narrow use of 'aisthanesthai' in the sense of 'sense-perception', a sense which the word did not have ordinarily and which it did not have in Plato's earlier writings.

XV

IDENTITY MISTAKES: PLATO AND THE LOGICAL ATOMISTS

JOHN MCDOWELL

1. My main purpose in this paper is to offer one possible diagnosis of a puzzle of Plato's. At *Theaetetus* 188a–c Socrates is made to sketch an argument which purports to prove that there can be no false judgements. Its outlines are as follows. With any given thing (e.g. Theaetetus) one either knows it or not. This applies, in particular, to things which figure in one's judgements. With two things (e.g. Theaetetus and Theodorus) there are four combinations:

(*a*) one knows both;
(*b*) one knows the first but not the second;
(*c*) one knows the second but not the first;
(*d*) one knows neither.

Now (1) it is impossible to judge that one thing is the other, whichever of these combinations obtains. Therefore (2) there can be no false judgements.

2. Even if (1) were granted, (2) would not follow. For (1) rules out judgements identifying two things, but leaves unchallenged the possibility of false judgements of at least the following kinds:

(i) false negative identity judgements (e.g. the judgement that Michael Innes is not J. I. M. Stewart);
(ii) false subject–predicate judgements involving one-place predicates, or many-place predicates other than 'is identical with';
(iii) false judgements which are not about particular things at all.

It is perhaps not surprising, in view of, for example, the *Sophist*'s account of statements, that the argument ignores the ragbag category (iii). An explanation of its passing over category (i) will become available shortly

From *Proceedings of the Aristotelian* Society, 70 (1969–70), 181–96. Reprinted by courtesy of the Editor of the Aristotelian Society and the author. © 1970.

(§7). It might be doubted that it ignores category (ii), on the ground that, in Greek at least, a form corresponding to 'x judges that one thing is another' can be used to report singular subject–predicate judgements as well as identity judgements;[1] and the argument purports to show that no statement of that form can be true. But such a doubt would be mistaken. For if the form in question is taken in the sense in which it fits subject–predicate judgements as well as identity judgements, then it fits *true* subject–predicate judgements just as well as false ones. But it figures in our argument as a prima facie plausible form for reports of *false* judgements. The idea is that if one *could* judge that one thing is another, that would indeed be to make a false judgement. We can preserve the plausibility of that idea only by supposing that to judge that one thing is another, in the sense appropriate to our argument, is to make a judgement identifying two things; and hence, that category (ii) *is* passed over. I shall not here discuss why that should have been so.

From now on I shall ignore (2), and treat the argument as if it claimed no more than (1). Even so, we have a paradox on our hands. We need to look carefully at the mechanics of the move to (1).

3. Cases (*b*), (*c*), and (*d*) go together; in each case, one fails to know at least one of the two things. And Plato seems to be working with a principle which we can state like this: if something is to figure in one's judgements at all, then one must know it.[2] Obviously that principle would rule out the supposition that one might judge that one of two things to which one was related as in (*b*), (*c*), or (*d*) was the other.

We shall need to return to the principle. For the moment, I shall mention, and shelve for later discussion (§§9, 10), its similarity to a well-known doctrine of Russell's. Russell says: 'Every proposition which we can understand must be composed wholly of constituents with which we are acquainted'; and, more specifically about judgements, 'Whenever a relation of judging or supposing occurs, the terms to which the supposing or judging mind is related by the relation of supposing or judging must be terms with which the mind in question is acquainted.'[3]

4. Now consider the remaining case. Suppose that someone judges that one thing is another, when his relation to the two things is as described in (*a*). *Ex hypothesi*, then, he *knows* both. Indeed we now have, in the prin-

---

[1] See e.g. F. M. Cornford, *Plato's Theory of Knowledge* (London, 1935), 113.
[2] See 188b8–c1; and cf. 190d7–10.
[3] 'Knowledge by Acquaintance and Knowledge by Description', *Proceedings of the Aristotelian Society*, 11 (1910–11), 117, 118; repr. in *Mysticism and Logic*, 219, 220–1. The principle urvived Russell's rejection of the theory of judgement implied in the second quotation: see *Mysticism and Logic*, 220 n. 1, and *My Philosophical Development*, 169; and cf. n. 21 below.

ciple just mentioned, an argument that if someone is to judge that one thing is another, then he *must* know both, since both figure in his judgement; i.e. an argument that case (*a*) is, so to speak, the only real starter. However, Socrates suggests,[4] the supposition that one judges that one of two things is another implies that one does *not* know the two things. Hence our putative description of a case of false judgement leads to a contradiction—the person both knows and does not know the two things—and the only real starter fails to stay the course.

5. I shall approach an account of what is going on here in a roundabout way. The first step is to derive a similar conclusion from Russell's doctrine that all true sentences of the form '*x* is *y*', where '*x*' and '*y*' hold places for names, are tautological.[5] Roughly speaking, if a sentence is tautological, then, taking syntax for granted, one need only understand its terms in order to be in a position to know that it is true. (This needs qualifying. But I think Russell would accept it for the sentences we are concerned with.) Hence if a sentence of the form '*x* is *y*' is true, then, according to Russell's doctrine, one would be in a position to know it to be true, if one so much as understood its terms. Now suppose some sentence of that form is false, and one understands its terms. Had the sentence been true, one could have known its truth straight off, simply by understanding its terms. Since its truth does not thus announce itself, one can conclude, with no further information, that it is false. So, quite generally, to understand the terms of a sentence of the relevant form is sufficient for one to be in a position to know whether it is true or false;[6] for either its truth announces itself or, by default, the sentence is revealed to be false. Now, given the assumptions (i) that one cannot judge what one is in a position to know to be false, and (ii) that one cannot correctly express a judgement with a sentence containing terms one does not understand, it follows that one cannot make a false judgement which one could correctly express with a sentence of the form '*x* is *y*'. This is at least very similar to conclusion (1) of Plato's argument.[7]

6. Here is how Russell argues for his doctrine that true sentences of the form '*x* is *y*' are tautological.

You must observe that the name does not occur in that which you assert when you use the name. The name is merely that which is a means of expressing what

---

[4] 188b3–5.

[5] *The Philosophy of Logical Atomism*, in R. C. Marsh (ed.), *Logic and Knowledge*, 245.

[6] Cf. Wittgenstein, *Tractatus Logico-Philosophicus* (1921), 4.243, and §10 below.

[7] Russell would use the doctrine of logically proper names and the Theory of Descriptions in order to represent *his* conclusion as non-paradoxical. I am doubtful whether such a move should be accepted. I cannot go into that fully here: but see §11 below.

it is that you are trying to assert, and when I say 'Scott wrote *Waverley*', the name 'Scott' does not occur in the thing I am asserting. The thing I am asserting is about the person, not about the name. So if I say 'Scott is Sir Walter', using these two names *as* names, neither 'Scott' nor 'Sir Walter' occurs in what I am asserting, but only the person who has these names, and then what I am asserting is a pure tautology.[8]

That is: it is the *bearer* of a name that occurs in what I assert when I use the name. So what I assert in saying 'Scott is Sir Walter' must be the same as what I assert in saying 'Scott is Scott'. Both contain the man, Sir Walter Scott—twice over, so to speak. But what I assert in saying the latter is a tautology. So what I assert in saying the former is a tautology too; indeed, the same tautology.

As it stands, this argument requires the difficult doctrine that when one says something about, say, a person, the person himself occurs in, or is a constituent of, what one asserts.[9] But we can capture what Russell is getting at without pressing a literal interpretation of that doctrine. We can take the argument to depend on this principle: what a sentence says (or, if you like, what is said by someone who uses a sentence to say something) depends not on its terms but on their *meanings*. Now the meaning of a proper name, according to Russell, is its bearer.[10] It follows that if two sentences differ only in that, where one has one name, the other has another name with the same bearer, then what they say is the same. In particular, any true sentence of the form '*x* is *y*' says the same as the corresponding sentence of the form '*x* is *x*'. So what such a sentence says is a tautology. Such a sentence says that a thing is *itself*.

Now this position looks like the one into which, at the beginning of 'On Sense and Reference',[11] Frege concedes that one may be tempted, if one treats identity as a relation of objects. But Frege wants *both* to maintain the legitimacy of treating identity as a relation of objects *and* to reject the view that a true sentence of the form '*x* is *y*' says the same as the corresponding sentence of the form '*x* is *x*'. He is enabled to do so, of course, by the distinction between sense and reference. What a sentence says, according to Frege, depends not on the references of its terms but on their senses. And two names with the same reference may diverge in sense. When that happens, a true sentence of the form '*x* is *y*' will say something different from the corresponding sentence of the form '*x* is *x*'.

We can perhaps describe the position like this. Frege might, with a

---

[8] *The Philosophy of Logical Atomism*, 246.
[9] The difficulty becomes apparent as soon as one considers *false* assertions. What complex, containing Scott as a constituent, could be what I assert when I say 'Scott wrote *Bleak House*'?
[10] See e.g. *Introduction to Mathematical Philosophy*, 174.
[11] *Translations from the Philosophical Writings of Gottlob Frege*, trans. P. Geach and M. Black (Oxford, 1960), 56–78: 56.

caveat about ambiguity, accept the principle on which my reconstructed Russellian argument rests, viz., that what a sentence says depends on the meanings of its terms. But he would jib at Russell's interpretation of 'meanings'. For Russell, the relevant meanings, in the case of proper names, are bearers, i.e. *references*; and Frege would insist that the required interpretation of 'meanings' is '*senses*'.[12]

Now one thing which the theory of sense and reference is meant to do is to provide an account of the behaviour of terms in certain referentially opaque contexts: very roughly, contexts involving indirect quotation. If terms are held to have their ordinary references in such contexts, there is, notoriously, a breakdown of the compelling 'Leibnizian' principle that reference-preserving substitutions in a sentence preserve its truth-value. But the theory holds that in such contexts a term has as its reference what is in ordinary contexts its sense. Hence a reference-preserving substitution, in such a context, is a substitution of a term with the same ordinary sense; and if terms with the same reference can diverge in sense, the generality of the 'Leibnizian' principle can be maintained.

Now I suggest that when we raise the question whether a true sentence of the form '*x* is *y*' says the same as the corresponding sentence of the form '*x* is *x*', we need to consider opaque contexts of the sort to which the Fregean theory is meant to apply. If a sentence is about some thing or things, it seems plausible that what it says depends on (1) what it is about, and (2) what it says about it or them. We can represent this as a slightly more precise version of the (perhaps ambiguous) principle that what such a sentence says depends on the meanings of its terms. Now my suggestion is that contexts like 'Sentence *S* is about . . .', which we need to consider in order to determine (1), and hence in order to determine what such sentences say, are opaque in the relevant way. And whether or not a precisely Fregean account of such contexts is finally satisfactory, at least it recognizes their opacity; whereas Russell's argument does not.

To illustrate this, let 'ϕa' be a subject–predicate sentence, and suppose that *a* is in fact *b*. What is 'ϕa' about? My suggestion is that if this question is meant to determine (1), and hence to determine what 'ϕa' says, the answer is '*a*'; *not* '*b*'. So what 'ϕa' says is that ϕa; not that ϕb. Similarly with two-place predicates. Let 'aRb' be a relational sentence, and again, suppose that *a* is *b*. What is 'aRb' about? Here again the answer is not '*a*', alone, or '*b*', alone (one might add, echoing the Russellian argument with which I

---

[12] Of course this is historically back-to-front. Russell thought he had disposed of Frege's position in 'On Denoting', *Mind*, 14 (1905), 483–87; repr. in Marsh (ed.), *Logic and Knowledge*, 45–51. On his arguments there, see John R. Searle, 'Russell's Objections to Frege's Theory of Sense and Reference', *Analysis*, 18/6 (June, 1958), 137–43.

began this section, 'twice over, so to speak'); but '*a* and *b*'. The *x*-argument
of the function *x*R*y* in the sentence '*a*R*b*' is *a*, not *b*; the *y*-argument is *b*,
not *a*. The function has *two* arguments, namely *a* and *b*.[13] In that case '*a*R*b*'
does not say that *a* has R to *a*, i.e. that *a* has R to itself. A sentence says
that something has R to itself only if it is of the form '*x*R*x*'; and '*a*R*b*' is
not of that form, even though *a* is *b*. For in '*a*R*b*' we have *two* arguments;
whereas a sentence is of the form '*x*R*x*' only if the two argument-places
are both filled by the *same* argument. In particular, with identity: the sentence '*a* is *b*', even if true, does not say that *a* is itself.[14] To suppose that
that is what it says, as in effect Russell does, is to miss the point about
opacity. What it says, on the contrary, is that *a* is *b*. On the other hand, the
sentence '*a* is *a*' does say that *a* is itself. So '*a* is *b*' does not say the same
as '*a* is *a*'. And, generalizing: a true sentence of the form '*x* is *y*' does not
say the same as the corresponding sentence of the form '*x* is *x*'.[15]

7. Russell, then, adopts a position about identity statements from which
a conclusion similar to Plato's paradox can be derived.[16] The position is,
essentially, that a true sentence of the form '*x* is *y*' says that something is
itself. And we can represent him as reaching that position like this. He holds
that what a sentence says depends, in part, on what it is about ((1) above).
But he reads the phrase 'what it is about' transparently: what counts is
which thing the relevant thing is, irrespective of how it is referred to in the
sentence. Whereas if we read the phrase opaquely, his position collapses,
and the paradox no longer threatens.

I suggest, now, that the line of thought about *judgements* towards which
Plato is tempted is parallel to the line of thought about *statements* which
Russell adopts. Parallel to the principle that what a sentence says depends,
in part, on what it is about is the principle that what is judged in a
judgement depends, in part, on what it is about. In this latter principle, it
is tempting to do what Russell does in the former: that is, to read 'what it
is about' transparently. But if one yields to that temptation, as I suggest
Plato is inclined to, then one has to suppose that all true positive identity
judgements about something involve judging the same thing, viz., that

[13] The opacity of the relevant contexts protects these claims from being represented, via
Leibniz's Law, as incompatible with the hypothesis that *a* is identical with *b*. No *property* is here
being *ascribed* to *a* but not *b*, or vice versa.
[14] Note the oddness of the suggestion that what the sentence says might depend on whether
it is true or false. The best argument against treating identity as a relation is undermined by the
point made in the text.
[15] Note a divergence from Frege here: this argument has 'does not' where he would say 'may
not'.
[16] But see n. 7 above.

the thing is itself. In that case all true positive identity judgements should be self-intimatingly true, in the sense that the determination of which judgement one is making leaves no further question about whether it is true. In that case, by an extension of the argument of §5, all false positive identity judgements should be self-intimatingly false. So how could anyone make them? Again, the paradox is avoided by reading the crucial phrase opaquely.

We now have an explanation of the fact that Plato's argument passes over cases like the judgement that Michael Innes is not J. I. M. Stewart (§2). My hypothesis is that Plato is tempted towards a view of *what is judged* parallel to Russell's view of *what is asserted*. And on that view, to judge that Michael Innes is not J. I. M. Stewart would be to judge that Michael Innes is not the same as himself; which seems inconceivable. On my hypothesis, it would be natural that such cases should simply not occur to Plato.

8. A principle on which Plato's argument seemed to depend (§§3, 4) was this: if something is to figure in one's judgements at all, then one must know it. Here what follows 'know' is a pronoun functioning as a bound variable; so what follows 'know' in an application of this principle would be a referring expression. This forces on 'know' an interpretation corresponding to the French *connaître* (not *savoir*), and makes it natural to paraphrase in terms of acquaintance: compare Russell's versions of this principle, cited above (§3).

Now even apart from Russell's special views about acquaintance, this principle is not very plausible. There is no good sense in which I am acquainted with Bismarck, but that does not, on the face of it, stop me making judgements about him.[17] However, plausibility is immediately restored when we turn to Russell's *argument* for his principle. In favour of the first of his two versions cited above (§3), he says, 'The chief reason for supposing the principle true is that it seems scarcely possible to believe that we can make a judgment or entertain a supposition without knowing *what it is* that we are judging or supposing about.' And about the second, he says, '*This is merely to say* that we cannot make a judgment or supposition without knowing *what it is* that we are making our judgment or supposition about.'[18] The principle stated in these quotations seems plausible enough. But it is not, as Russell claims, the same as his 'acquaintance' principle. For the 'acquaintance' principle involves *connaître*; whereas in the

---

[17] Russell manages with the fact that his principle stops him making judgements about Bismarck (see 'Knowledge by Acquaintance and Knowledge by Description'); but only at the price of insisting that many judgements are not the judgements we thought they were.

[18] Ibid. 117, 118 (*Mysticism and Logic*, 219, 221); my emphasis.

plausible principle stated in these quotations, 'know' is followed by an indirect question, and the French would be *savoir*. It looks as though Russell mistakes phrases like 'what it is that we are judging or supposing about', as they occur in the latter principle, for expressions designating the appropriate object. This would account for his taking the plausible *savoir* principle to be the same as his less plausible *connaître* principle.

The leading error in such a line of thought would be grammatical: a confusion between interrogative and relative-clause nominalizations, with (in this case) an associated confusion between interpretations of 'know'.[19] Compare:

(1) I know what you are smelling.
(2) What you are smelling is the dead cat under the floorboards.
So (3) I know the dead cat under the floorboards.

As these propositions would be ordinarily understood, such an argument would involve equivocation between the uses of 'what you are smelling' in (1) and (2), and an associated equivocation between the uses of 'know' in (1) and (3). In (2) 'What you are smelling' is a relative-clause nominalization, related to, and tantamount to, 'that which you are smelling'. It can be taken as a referring expression, and (2) can be construed as an identity statement. But in (1), 'what you are smelling' is an interrogative nominalization. It is not a referring expression. To regard (3) as licensed by substitution in (1) according to the identity statement (2) involves missing that point, and forcing on 'know' in (1) the interpretation which it must have in (3), viz. *connaître*.[20]

In the line of thought which I attributed to Russell, there are parallel grammatical mistakes. And such mistakes would import, or strengthen, a tendency to be insensitive to the sort of point about opacity which I used (§7) to dissolve the paradox. For they result in the fact that particular applications of Russell's principle look like this: if I am to make a judgement about *a*, then I must be acquainted with (know) *a*. In the consequent of this, there is no reason to regard the position of '*a*' as anything but transparent. (We can have non-transparency with 'acquaintance' idioms, but only with forms of words like 'acquainted with *a under that name*'; and there is no sign of that in Russell's principle.) Taking the formula as an application of the general principle, '(*x*) (if I am to make a judgement about *x*, then I must be acquainted with [know] *x*)', one would therefore regard the position of '*a*' in the antecedent as transparent too. In that

[19] Cf. Dennis W. Stampe, 'Towards a Grammar of Meaning', *Philosophical Review*, 77 (1968), esp. 149–54.
[20] Cf. J. L. Austin, *Philosophical Papers* (Oxford, 1970), 64–5: I have adapted an example of his.

case one would regard the position of '*a*' in 'Judgement *J* is about *a*' as transparent.[21] Hence, in the principle that what is judged in a judgement depends in part on what it is about, one would be disposed to do what I called (§7) 'reading "what it is about" transparently'. In Fregean terms, one would be disposed to limit oneself to *references*; whereas to dissolve the paradox one needs to admit opaque readings, or in Fregean terms to consider *senses*.

Note that with the *connaître* principle, if *a* is *b*, then to know what one needs to know in order to make judgements about *a* is *eo ipso* to know what one needs to know in order to make judgements about *b*. For the requirement in respect of *a* is that one know *a*. And if one knows *a* ('*a*' here occurring transparently), and *a* is *b*, then one *eo ipso* knows *b*: that is, satisfies the requirement in respect of *b*. With the *savoir* principle, on the other hand, the requirement for making a judgement about *a* is that one know that it is *a* that one's judgement is about; and the requirement for making a judgement about *b* is that one know that it is *b* that one's judgement is about. And even if *a* is *b*, the opacity of the context 'It is . . . that my judgement is about' permits these to be two different bits of knowledge.

9. Plato's argument seemed to depend (§§3, 4) on something like Russell's principle in its implausible *connaître* version. I suggest now that like Russell, Plato regards that version as interchangeable with the plausible *savoir* version. I shall offer, first, some evidence for this suggestion and, second, a partial explanation.

The evidence is that in at least two places in the *Theaetetus* (147b2 and 4–5, 196d8 and 10), Plato makes it clear that he is prepared to treat the forms (1) 'know *x*' and (2) 'know what *x* is' as interchangeable. And the two versions of the Russellian principle differ precisely in that where one has one of these forms, the other has the other.

The explanation is that Greek has an idiomatic form which is equivalent to (2) but can be literally represented by (3) 'know *x* what it is'. In occurrences of this form, what goes in place of '*x*' is the direct object of the verb, as in (1). And 'what it is' looks like an adverbial clause, of a sort which one might expect to suffer ellipsis readily. Thus there would be an easy slide from (2), via its equivalent (3), to (1).

[21] It is in fact implicit in the theory of judgement which Russell was beginning to give up by 1917 (*Mysticism and Logic*, 220 n. 1) that the position of '*a*' in, say, '*n* judges that *a* has R to *b*' is transparent; and presumably, therefore, that its position in '*n* makes some judgement about *a*' is transparent. For the former is analysed as being of the *relational* form 'J (*n*, *a*, R, *b*)'. (See 'On the Nature of Truth and Falsehood', in *Philosophical Essays*, 170–85). The retention of the acquaintance principle (see n. 3 above) means that this transparency survives the rejection of that theory of judgement.

Now if Plato concentrated on (1), he would naturally think of knowing in terms of acquaintance (*connaître*). Taking (2) to be equivalent, he would suppose that knowing there was a matter of acquaintance too. Hence, like Russell, he would be inclined to misparse phrases of the form 'what *x* is', not as interrogative nominalizations suitable to follow 'know' (*savoir*), but as designations of suitable objects of acquaintance (*connaître*).[22] As with Russell, this sort of grammatical mistake would import, or strengthen, an inclination towards transparent readings where opaque readings are required.

10. What still needs doing is to bring the line of thought which I have been discussing into closer relation with the details of Plato's argument; in particular, with the contradiction which he claims to derive from the sup-position that someone judges that one thing is another (§4). By the Rus-sellian principle (§3), such a person must know both, since both figure in his judgement. But his confusing them shows, allegedly, that he does *not* know both. So the fact that one *knows* two things is thought to imply that one cannot judge that one of them is the other. But why should such an implication have seemed plausible to Plato?

One suggestion is that he is inclined to read 'know' as 'know all about'.[23] That would indeed yield the required implication. But the drawback is that it would yield a lot more too. With 'know' so interpreted, the Russellian principle (§3) would straightforwardly 'prove' the impossibility of *any* false judgements about something, not merely those of the identity form. Perhaps, then, we should look for a less sweeping 'justification' of Plato's implication.

One such 'justification' could be extracted from the fact (§8) that with the *connaître* principle, if *a* is *b*, then to know what one needs to know in order to make judgements about *a* is *eo ipso* to know what one needs to know in order to make judgement about *b*. If *a* is *b*, and one satisfies the knowledge requirement in respect of *a* and *b*, then how (one might wonder) can one fail to notice that it is the *same* knowledge in each case? That is, how can one fail to know that *a* is *b*? And if it is obvious to one

---

[22] The supposed nature of these objects would vary according to what sort of expression is substituted for '*x*'. *What Socrates is* would presumably be, simply, Socrates. But compare *what a bed is*. It is harmlessly true that what a bed is is a bed. But misparsed, that would yield a case of 'Self-Predication'. An ordinary bed is a bed, too. But an ordinary bed (being perishable, etc.) cannot be *what a bed is* ('Non-Identity'). So an ordinary bed is not *what a bed is*, but (since both are beds) like it (cf. *Republic* 597a4–5). (For 'Self-Predication' and 'Non-Identity', see G. Vlastos, 'The Third Man Argument in the *Parmenides*', *Philosophical Review*, 63 (1954), 319–49; repr. in R. E. Allen (ed.), *Studies in Plato's Metaphysics* (London, 1965), 231–61.).
[23] See Jürgen Sprute, 'Über den Erkenntnisbegriff in Platons *Theaitet*', *Phronesis*, 13 (1968), 47–67.

that the knowledge required in each case is the same, if *a* is *b* and one has the knowledge required in respect of *a* and *b*, then if *a* is not *b* and one has the knowledge required in respect of each, ought it not to be obvious, by default (cf. §5), that the two bits of required knowledge are different? In that case, to satisfy the knowledge requirement in respect of *a* and *b*, i.e. according to this principle, to know *a* and *b*, is sufficient for one to be in a position to know that *a* is not *b*, if *a* is not *b*. And given the assumption that one cannot judge what one is in a position to know to be false, it follows that if one knows *a* and *b*, and *a* is not *b*, one cannot judge that *a* is *b*; which is Plato's implication.

Alternatively, a more logical (less psychological) 'justification' can be constructed in terms of the sort of reasoning I attributed to Plato in §7. As before, I shall begin with a parallel argument from the theory of meaning. In the *Tractatus Logico-Philosophicus*, at 4.243, Wittgenstein asks, 'Can we understand two names without knowing whether they signify the same thing or two different things? Can we understand a proposition in which two names occur without knowing whether their meaning is the same or different?' We are clearly meant to answer 'No'; and an argument for the negative answer can be constructed on lines which are by now familiar. What a sentence says depends on the meanings of its terms, i.e. in the case of proper names their bearers (3.203). So the true sentence '*a* is *b*' says the same as '*a* is *a*'. But the latter sentence, and so the former too, is degenerate, in the sense that once one has settled what it says there is no further question about whether it is true (cf. 5.5303). Thus, taking knowledge of the meaning of the identity sign for granted: if one knows the meanings of '*a*' and '*b*', and '*a* is *b*' is true, then one has sufficient information to know that it is true. Now such a sentence is either self-intimatingly true in that sense, or not; and if not, it is revealed, by default, as false (cf. §5). Thus, again taking knowledge of the meaning of the identity sign for granted: if one knows the meanings of '*a*' and '*b*', one has sufficient information to know whether *a* is *b*. Some such principle is what is suggested by Wittgenstein's rhetorical questions.

Now (by 3.203) the meaning of '*a*' is *a*, and the meaning of '*b*' is *b*. Thus to know the meanings of '*a*' and '*b*' is simply to know *a* and *b*. If we substitute accordingly in the principle just elicited from 4.243, we get this: if one knows *a* and *b*, one has sufficient information to know whether *a* is *b*. And that is, near enough, what we need for Plato's implication. For it yields this: given that one cannot judge what one is in a position to know to be false, one cannot judge that *a* is *b* if it is not.

It would be inappropriate to explain Plato's line of thought in our passage by means of reasoning which explicitly involves talk of proper names and their meanings. But we are equipped to construct a parallel argument for Plato's implication which avoids such notions. What is judged in a judgement depends in part on what it is about (cf. §7). If 'what it is about' is read transparently, it will seem that the judgement that *a* is *b* is degenerate in the sense sketched above. It follows that if one knows what judgements about *a* are about and what judgements about *b* are about, one has sufficient information to know whether *a* is *b*. But to know what judgements about *a* are about, Plato might think, is just to know *a* (cf. §9). Hence, by substitution, if one knows *a* and *b*, one has sufficient information to know whether *a* is *b*. So, as before, if one knows *a* and *b*, then, given that one cannot judge what one is in a position to know to be false, one cannot judge that *a* is *b* when it is not.

11. I have been concerned to bring out parallels between Russell's position about (some) identity *statements*, which is bound up with his doctrine about what is asserted by the use of a sentence, and involves a certain view about how genuine proper names must work; and on the other hand, a line of thought about identity *judgements* towards which I suggest Plato was tempted, which is bound up with parallel views about what is judged in judgements, and about how things figure in judgements.[24]

I shall end with a remark about what might seem an obvious objection to this allegation of parallelism between Russell and Plato. Plato's paradox, it might be said, is about things in general. That is why it is paradoxical. Russell's position, on the other hand, is restricted to logical atoms—things which are named by logically proper names. Hence, according to this objection, it is unfair to represent Russell's position as parallel to Plato's.[25]

Now it would surely be implausible to suggest that Russell *starts* with the full-blown notion of a logically proper name. Rather, he begins from a certain conception of how any genuine referring device must work; that is, of what it must be for an asserted sentence to be genuinely *about* something. We see that conception operating in arguments like the one quoted in §6. And it is that conception which, I suggest, is parallel to Plato's conception of what it is for a *judgement* to be about something.

This claim of parallelism implies that if one takes ordinary so-called referring devices (e.g. ordinary proper names) to be genuine referring devices, according to such a conception of genuine referring devices, then one will find oneself involved in paradoxes like Plato's. It is partly for

---

[24] For the parallel, cf. J. L. Ackrill, 'Plato on False Belief: *Theaetetus* 187–200', *Monist*, 50 (1966), 387: 'Socrates . . . operates with ordinary proper names as though they were logically proper names applied to simple particulars.'
[25] Cf. n. 7 above.

that reason that Russell denies that ordinary proper names are logically proper names. This denial is what prompts the objection of unfairness. But what I am claiming is that the denial itself is based, at least in part, on a conception of genuine referring devices which is wrong; and wrong in precisely the same way as the view about judgements which leads directly to the paradox.

XVI

THE DOUBLE EXPLANATION IN THE
TIMAEUS

STEVEN K. STRANGE

THE PROBLEM: αἰτίαι IN THE *PHAEDO* AND THE *TIMAEUS*

In a familiar passage of the *Phaedo* (95e–105c), Plato portrays Socrates as criticizing the kinds of explanation[1] the Presocratic philosophers had given for natural phenomena and as suggesting on the basis of this critique some different and more satisfactory sorts of accounts for them.[2] Plato makes

Reprinted with permission from *Ancient Philosophy*, 5 (1985), 25–39, and the author.

[1] The terms αἰτία and αἴτιον have traditionally been translated 'cause', but in Plato and Aristotle at least they have a much wider meaning than 'cause' does for us. They can stand for any sort of explanatory factor or entity cited in an explanation, and αἰτία can stand for the formulation of the explanation itself. In particular, they can refer to different *types* of explanation: thus Aristotle says that the different sorts of αἰτίαι are the different sorts of answers that can be given to the question, 'Why or because of what?' (τὸ διά τί; *APo.* 2. 1–2; *Ph.* 194ᵇ20). Cf. G. Vlastos 'Reasons and Causes in the *Phaedo*', *Philosophical Review* 69 (1969), 291–325: 78–81, and most recently M. Frede 'The Original Notion of Cause', in M. Schofield *et al.* (eds.), *Doubt and Dogmatism* (Oxford 1980), 221–3: other references are given in J. Annas, 'Aristotle on Inefficient Causes', *Philosophical Quarterly* 32 (1983), 311–26: 319 n. 1. The terms themselves are borrowed from Athenian legal jargon, where they signify responsibility for wrongdoing or the accusation thereof: the notion of responsibility for something is retained in the philosophical usage of the terms. They seem already to have become semi-technical in some of Plato's dialogues, particularly the *Phaedo*, *Timaeus*, and *Philebus*. I will continue to use 'cause' as the least cumbersome translation of them, as well as 'explanation'.

[2] Socrates starts by telling Cebes that they need to make a thorough general inquiry into 'the cause concerned with becoming and perishing' (περὶ γενέσεως καὶ φθορᾶς τὴν αἰτίαν; 95e9). Aristotle rightly took this to fix the subject of the subsequent discussion: this is what led him to object that the *Phaedo* makes Forms efficient causes, which they cannot be (*Metaph.* 991ᵇ3–7; *GC* 335ᵇ10–24: cf. *Metaph.* 1079ᵇ14–15). The criticism is well discussed in Annas, 'Aristotle on Inefficient Causes'. As Annas notes, Aristotle's interpretation is somewhat unfair: there are several sorts of causes, not merely efficient causes, explicitly under consideration in the *Phaedo*, and the Forms are never said to initiate becoming or perishing or to bring about participation in themselves. Moreover, Aristotle's criticism only takes account of the *Phaedo* and not the other dialogues in which Plato considers the notion of cause. Nevertheless, Aristotle does seem correct in seeing the passage as concerned with the explanation of natural phenomena in general (cf. περὶ φύσεως ἱστορίαν; 96a8), i.e. with what he calls physics (cf. *PA* 639ᵃ12). Aristotle thinks of the subject-matter of physics as sensible οὐσία (*Metaph.* 1025ᵇ18), but this

Socrates say (97b–98b) that as a young man he had become intrigued by Anaxagoras' claim that Reason or *νοῦς* was responsible for the natural world and its orderly arrangement. He had expected that Anaxagoras would go on to explain why the world is the way it is by showing how this was better than other conceivable world-orders; for, Socrates assumed, the rational principle of *νοῦς* would always order things for the best, so that showing why a particular state of affairs is best (e.g. that the earth is round; 97d) would *ipso facto* show why *νοῦς* had brought it about. The hypothesis of *νοῦς* as sole cause thus amounted, for Socrates, to the assumption of a single teleological principle of explanation in natural philosophy.

But Socrates was sorely disappointed in his expectations. When he got hold of Anaxagoras' writings he did not find this sort of explanation in them at all. The explanations that Anaxagoras actually offered for phenomena were instead like those of most other Presocratic natural philosophers— purely mechanistic ones in terms of the motions of material principles such as air, water, and *aithēr*.[3] There was no attempt on Anaxagoras' part to link these motions causally to the role of Reason in the cosmos or to show how all of them came about for the best, as his original claim that Reason was the cause of everything had seemed to promise.

Socrates says he found such purely mechanistic, non-teleological explanations completely unsatisfactory. The passage offers two sorts of reasons why he (or rather Plato) was dissatisfied with them. The first appears in an earlier part of the passage (96d–97b) where Socrates examines similar explanations offered by other Presocratics, which he also found completely unhelpful. He compares them with attempting to explain contrary facts by citing a single cause (e.g. accounting for both tallness and shortness by reference to the size of a head) or with citing something as the cause of a phenomenon when something contrary to it could equally well be cited (e.g. explaining how one thing becomes two by mentioning addition rather than division or separation).[4] Such 'explanations' of course explain nothing at all, and Socrates implies that the materialistic causes of the

---

corresponds to what Plato, in the middle dialogues at least, calls becoming or *γένεσις* and contrasts with *οὐσία* (cf. *Ti.* 29c3). Outside the *Phaedo* Plato typically links the technical notion of cause with accounting for *γιγνόμενα* and becoming: *Ti.* 28a–c, 29d–e; *Phlb.* 26e; *Sph.* 265b; cf. *Laws* 896a.

[3] By 'mechanism' I mean only the appeal to the regularities of purely material processes in explanation. This corresponds to the so-called 'Democritean' necessity recognized by Aristotle in *Ph.* 2. 9 and *PA* 1. 1: See J. Cooper, 'Hypothetical neces⁣⁣ y', in A. S. Gotthelf (ed.), *Aristotle on Nature and Living Things* (Pittsburgh, 1985).

[4] See Annas, 'Aristotle on Inefficient Causes', 314, which only mentions the latter sort of puzzle.

Presocratic physicists involve or at least do not rule out such incoherencies.[5]

But even if they managed to avoid such pitfalls, these sorts of account clearly would still not explain anything to Socrates' satisfaction. We can see this from his critique of Anaxagoras. He employs an analogy (98c–99c): suppose, he says, that someone were to claim that I do what I do on account of my reason (νοῦς) and yet try to explain the fact that I am presently sitting in prison merely in terms of physiological factors that have no connection with my reason or my concept of the good. It is rather Socrates' belief that it is better to stay and be executed rather than flee that is the *real* cause of his now sitting in prison, for without this belief he would have escaped long ago. Facts about physiology, e.g. how the configuration of his joints and sinews allows him to sit, would have to be cited in a complete explanation of his sitting, but on their own they explain nothing at all about it. Hence, they are at most necessary conditions for explanation but are not themselves causes (99b1–3). Thus, for Socrates, though Anaxagoras grasped that the real explanation of natural phenomena ought to be in terms of the teleological principle of Reason, he failed to provide such an explanation. As a result, the accounts he did offer were completely without explanatory force.

Socrates tells how his dissatisfaction with mechanistic explanations drove him to take refuge in his own favourite type of explanation by way of Forms and λόγοι (99e–105c), a type he considered 'safe' because it was not subject to the sort of incoherence mentioned above.[6] But he did not find these 'safe' causes, or the 'clever' ones he constructs from them, entirely satisfactory either—they are only a second-best sort of explanation (99c–d) because they do not explain teleologically. In short, Socrates would still prefer to be shown how the Good is cause of everything.

It is not Anaxagoras alone who is the target of the complaints that Plato has Socrates voice in this passage. The kinds of explanation Socrates objects to were ubiquitous in Presocratic physics. Anaxagoras merely presents the most disappointing case because his claim that Reason is the real cause raised teleological hopes only to shatter them. Nor need we assume

---

[5] Socrates' puzzles in *Phaedo* 96d–97b are dialectical and clearly aimed at the accounts of growth in 96c–d, which are taken as representative of the mechanistic explanations mentioned in 96a–b. Here I follow the interpretation of D. Gallop (*Plato:* Phaedo (Oxford, 1975), 171–2) against that of G. Vlastos ('Reasons and Causes in the *Phaedo*', *Philosophical Review*, 69 (1969), 291–325; repr. in *Platonic Studies* (Princeton, 1981), 95 n. 50).

[6] See Annas, 'Aristotle on Inefficient Causes', 315–16. Socrates' point seems to be that the mechanistic accounts discussed earlier, because they were incoherent, gave the wrong answer to the *same* request for explanation to which the Forms are introduced here to respond. Thus the 'second sailing' or δεύτερος πλοῦς of *Phaedo* 99c9–d1 is to the same destination as the first.

that the passage tells us anything about the historical Socrates. It is true that Socrates first introduced the notion of εἶδος or Form as cause of properties of things.[7] However, the Forms of the *Phaedo* are the Platonic separate Forms, not the immanent common characters that were the Socratic εἴδη. But the Socratic εἴδη are the ancestors of Plato's separate Forms, and we have Aristotle's explicit testimony[8] that Plato made the Forms separate when he began to apply them, as here in the *Phaedo*, to explaining the properties of Becoming and not merely to ethics as Socrates had done. That is, Plato develops the full-blown theory of Forms in application to physics and posits the Forms as causes of natural phenomena. This is even clearer in the *Timaeus*, where he gives the fullest account of the theory.

The *Timaeus* is Plato's attempt to come to grips with the problem of cosmology which was raised for him by the reflections on Presocratic physics in the *Phaedo*. Moreover, we find Plato attempting in the *Timaeus* precisely what he complains in the *Phaedo* that the Presocratics had not done—to show how Reason (νοῦς) orders nature in accordance with what is best and to account for particular features of the world from this hypothesis. In this way the *Timaeus* is a response to the challenge Socrates raises in the *Phaedo*.[9] But, as I shall argue, the *Timaeus* also shows that Plato has come to realize that the Socrates of the *Phaedo* is asking too much. According to the *Timaeus*, Reason cannot be the only real cause of phenomena; purely mechanistic accounts must also be countenanced as explanations. This raises a larger question concerning the relation between this passage of the *Phaedo* and the cosmological project of the *Timaeus*. What has happened in the *Timaeus* to the role of Forms as causes? Is the second-best sort of explanation in terms of Forms that Socrates offers in the *Phaedo* merely an inadequate alternative to the project of teleological explanation, an alternative to be abandoned when Plato comes to see how that project can be carried out? If so, what are we to make of Plato's admission of mechanistic causes as explanations in the *Timaeus*?

[7] For argument, see P. Woodruff, *Plato:* Hippias Major (Indianapolis, 1982). Woodruff calls the Socratic εἴδη of the early dialogues 'logical' causes, since they explain why predicates are true of things: this is captured by the instrumental dative in phrases like 'that *by which F* things are *F*', which occur as early as *Euthyphro* 6d, and still figure prominently in the discussion of Forms as causes at *Phaedo* 100d7–8, for example.

[8] *Metaph.* 987b1–7, 1078b17–32, 1086a35–b10. T. Irwin, 'Plato's Heracliteanism', *Philosophical Quarterly*, 22 (1977), 1–13, throws some light on the relation between Aristotle's problematic evidence and the text of Plato's dialogues.

[9] I do not want to deny that the theory of the relationship of the other Forms to the Form of the Good presented in *Republic* 6 is intended in part to do this. But this issue lies beyond the scope of this paper.

Another important connection between the *Timaeus* and this part of the *Phaedo* is that both exploit the analogy between teleological explanations of natural phenomena and accounts of intentional human action. In the *Timaeus* this analogy has two aspects. The teleological structure of nature is explained by analogy with the product of a goal-directed human activity, namely, expert craftsmanship. Goodness and order in the world are accounted for by reference to the activity of a divine craftsman who, given the nature of his materials, reproduces as accurately as possible the features of an all-good model. This amounts to an application of the familiar Socratic craft analogy to physics: in the cosmos, as in the realm of human action, goodness is construed as the product of craftsmanship. But Plato has not lost sight of the ethical applications of the analogy either. We shall see that the *Timaeus* is an ethical dialogue as well as a cosmological one. For Plato argues in the *Timaeus* that cosmology should be subordinate to ethics, not in the Aristotelian sense that it is a theoretical science that contributes to happiness as contemplation, but as a practical enterprise that promotes moral virtue. The project of physical inquiry that Plato envisages in the *Timaeus*, like the programme of studies he proposes in the *Republic*, will not be divorced from practice.

THE RELATION BETWEEN REASON AND NECESSITY

A cosmology is a general, *unified* explanation of important features of the phenomenal world. Now the reader of the *Timaeus* is faced with an initial difficulty in Plato's account: it seems incoherent. For Plato does not operate in the *Timaeus* with a single, unifying notion of cause or explanation but distinguishes two sorts of causes or αἰτίαι which he calls Reason (νοῦς) and Necessity (ἀνάγκη).[10] These two principles of explanation are ultimate in that they are themselves left entirely unexplained. Yet, though ultimate, they are not intended to be completely independent, since Plato speaks of Reason as dominating and persuading Necessity (48a).

---

[10] Things come about by two sorts of causes (46e3, 68e6)—'through the agency of Reason' (47e7) and 'from Necessity' (68e1)—and 'the becoming of this cosmos is a mixed result of the combination of Reason and Necessity' (47e5–48a2). If Plato does not mean that the causes can be *called* Reason and Necessity (and 46d8–e2, where ἡ ἔμφρων φύσις = νοῦς, and 69e4–5 seem particularly clear on this point), certainly these passages show that the two causes and the concepts of Reason and Necessity are very closely tied. (Aristotle seems to have in mind Plato's two causes, which he calls οὗ τῆς ἕνεκα and τὸ ἐξ ἀνάγκης, at *PA* 642ᵃ2–3. See below on more connections between the view of causes in this chapter of the *de Partibus Animalium* and the *Timaeus*.) Necessity is called 'the wandering sort of cause' (τὸ τῆς πλανομένης εἶδος αἰτίας) at *Ti.* 48a5–6, which seems to associate it, somewhat oddly, with chance or τυχή. See below, p. 413.

How, then, are we to understand the relation between Reason and Necessity? A first step would be to distinguish what we could call the domains of each principle, what features of the world each is supposed to explain or help explain. Plato indicates fairly clearly how this is to be done.[11] The domains do not coincide: as we shall see, Plato thinks there are some things that are to be explained by appeal to Reason alone and others that are to be explained by appeal to Necessity alone. But they do overlap, for some things are explained by a combination of Reason and Necessity.

That Plato had a clear conception of how these domains are to be demarcated is shown by the overall structure of the dialogue. It falls into three parts, with well-marked divisions between them. The first part, to 47e, is concerned with the so-called works of reason (47e4). Here, through the device of a creation story,[12] Plato explains why there is a single cosmos, why there are four physical elements, how soul is structured and how it operates, and how gods and mortal beings are arranged in the cosmos. The emphasis is on what is intrinsically good and not good merely instrumentally or with reference to the goodness of something else. Thus, the universe is one, complete, everlasting, and intelligent, because these are desiderata the all-good Demiurge takes into account quite apart from any other considerations whatsoever (Plato says, because they are features of his model, but the Demiurge uses this model precisely because it is the best possible: 30d2; cf. 29a, 30a6–7). Such facts about the cosmos fall into the explanatory domain of Reason alone. Moreover, these are features that the Demiurge is in no way impeded from realizing in his product, though in some cases certain means of realizing them impose themselves, as when he is compelled to use soul to mediate between νοῦς and body (30b). Some mechanistic accounts enter here also,[13] for instance in the passage concerning the confused state of newly incarnated souls (42e–44a), where the key notion of necessary evil first comes up in the dialogue. The explanation of vision that follows (45b–46b) is also quite mechanistic. Still, it is included with the works of Reason, apparently because observation of the revolutions of the heavens (as well as the hearing of musical harmonies

---

[11] This was seen by G. R. Morrow, 'Necessity and Persuasion in Plato's *Timaeus*', *Philosophical Review* 59 (1950) 147–63, in R. E. Allen (ed.), *Studies in Plato's Metaphysics*, International Library of Philosophy and Scientific Method (London: Routledge & Kegan Paul, 1965), 421–38. I am indebted throughout this paper to Morrow's excellent discussion.

[12] Whether the story is taken literally or is a myth in our sense will make no difference for our purposes. In any case the activity of the Demiurge represents the causality of Reason at the cosmic level. On the possibility that the Demiurge is to be identified with νοῦς, see n. 22 below.

[13] At 47e3–4 Plato says explicitly that not everything mentioned in this part of the dialogue belongs to the works of Reason.

and rhythms) first taught humans about numbers: as Plato declares, number is the source of all philosophy (47a) and, hence, ultimately of the possibility of human happiness.

The contrast in this passage between the mechanistic account of vision and the explanation of its purpose serves as a preliminary example of the combination of Reason and Necessity. Necessity is mentioned for the first time in the dialogue in what immediately follows. We are told that we must go back and begin the story again from a new starting-point. This is a fresh division of reality into three parts, instead of the two that had sufficed to treat the works of Reason: in place of the dichotomy of the intelligible world of Forms and the realm of Becoming that Timaeus had introduced at the beginning of his discourse, we now have a trichotomy of Forms, phenomena, and the Receptacle of Becoming (48–52). What follows in the second part of Timaeus' discourse concerns what comes about from Necessity (69e1). Under this heading are comprised purely material properties: elemental transformations, the random motion, structure and movement of the physical elements, the nature of compound bodies that are aggregates of the elements, and finally the affections that soul undergoes in relation to the material—pleasure, pain, and sensory qualities, including the qualitative aspects of sight and hearing as opposed to their quantitative features discussed under the works of Reason.

Plato indicates that all these things are to be explained by appeal to Necessity (69e1). This is, however, not strictly true. Reason, in the person of the Demiurge, intervenes at 53b to give regular geometric shapes to the inchoate traces (ἴχνη) of the elemental bodies in the Receptacle.[14] Timaeus insists that since the Demiurge is perfectly good, he gives them the finest shapes possible (53e1–6: cf. 53b5–6)—finest apparently because they are the simplest after the sphere and because the sphere has already been used for the body of the whole cosmos. This is a teleological explanation, involving Reason. What seems to be just necessitated and not in any way up to the Demiurge is that the elements are bodily and spatially extended (53c4–7).[15] But 48b–68d is concerned primarily with mapping the domain

---

[14] The passage 53b2–5 seems decisive against commentators who hold that the regular geometric shapes of the elements are already present in the pre-cosmic chaos. For this view, see R. Mohr, 'The Mechanism of Flux in Plato's *Timaeus*', *Apeiron*, 14 (1980), 96–114: 97 n. 32, which gives references to other literature. Mohr fails to recognize that all Plato requires for his theory of weight at 63c–e, a theory which is needed to explain the sifting of the ἴχνη according to the kinds of 52e–53a (cf. esp. 53a1–2), is that they have shapes that resemble fairly closely the regular geometric shapes the elements have in the cosmos. A persuasive interpretation along these lines is given in Mary Louise Gill, 'Matter and Flux in Plato's *Timaeus*', *Phronesis*, 32 (1987), 34–53.

[15] H. F. Cherniss 'The Sources of Evil according to Plato', *Proceedings of the American Philological Society*, 98 (1954), 23–30; repr. in *Selected Papers*, ed. L. Tarán (Leiden: Brill, 1977), 253–60: 255 n. 21) points out that *Ti.* 31b shows that corporeality is not for Plato a brute,

of Necessity alone, as 29e–47e was primarily with the domain of
Reason.

At 69a we are once more told that we must return to the starting-point,
so that in weaving and fitting together the two sorts of explanation, we
may complete the task of giving an account of Becoming. This marks the
beginning of the third part of Timaeus' discourse. Things treated here
are explained by reference to the interaction of Reason and Necessity:
the human body and irrational soul, their functioning and dysfunctions,
as well as plants and lower animals. Here teleological and mechanistic
explanations combine. These things are the work not of the Demiurge
himself but of lower gods whom he commissions for the purpose (69c–
d; cf. 41c–d). Moreover, the goods they produce are not absolutely
good, as were the works of Reason alone. Instead, they are good as instrumental means that allow the human animal to survive and pursue
happiness.

Plato has thus carefully distinguished in the composition of the dialogue
among three classes of phenomena: things to be explained by Reason
alone, things to be explained by Necessity alone, and things that come
about from a combination of the two causes, namely, the realm of mortal
living creatures. Having seen how Plato distinguished his causes through
their respective explananda, we can now go on to ask how he thinks
they are related to one another. This is treated in the transition
passages between the parts of Timaeus' discourse, at 47e–48b and at
68e–69a.

These two passages are extremely important for understanding the
explanatory structure of Plato's account. Slightly different images are used
in the two passages to illustrate the relation between Reason and Necessity. In 47e–48b Plato says that Becoming is a mixed result of Reason and
Necessity combined, but that in this mixture Reason dominates Necessity
and persuades it so as to make the greatest number of things come out for
the best. In 68e–69a Necessity is described in somewhat more positive
terms as 'helping' or 'assisting' (ὑπερητοῦν) divine Reason in the produc-

---

irreducible fact about the world. That passage makes the existence of fire and earth and,
hence, that of the intermediate elements as well, depend on the fact that the world, as corporeal,
has to be visible and tangible, i.e. perceptible. This, however, *is* a brute fact for Plato, not to
be further explained: it is one of the ἀρχαί or starting-points of Timaeus' discourse
(28a2–3, 48e6–49a1). Hence, corporeality, as a direct consequence of perceptibility, falls into
the domain of Necessity. The pre-cosmic chaos of 52d–53b would presumably be perceptible
as well, if there were perceivers to perceive it. Cf. G. Vlastos, 'Creation in the *Timaeus*: Is
it a Fiction?', in Allen (ed.), *Studies in Plato's Metaphysics*, 402–3; I. M. Crombie, *An Examination of Plato's Doctrines*, ii: *Plato on Knowledge and Reality*, International Library of Philosophy and Scientific Method (London: Routledge & Kegan Paul, 1963), 219–20. If the view
endorsed in n. 14 above is correct, the pre-cosmic chaos will also be bodily for that reason as
well.

tion of the cosmos.[16] Plato has already used this way of speaking about the relation of Reason and Necessity earlier in the dialogue, in the passage on vision. There the facts of the mechanism of vision are called 'accessory causes' (συναιτία, 46d1; συμμεταιτία, 46e6) which the creator-god uses in fitting the structure of the eye to the purposes of sight. This implies that although Reason and Necessity are co-ordinate causes in the making of the world, Reason is somehow prior or superior to Necessity, that in this context at least Necessity only counts as a cause in so far as it co-operates with Reason's purposes. On the other hand, Necessity must be a *sine qua non* for the production of at least some features of the best possible world, otherwise there would be no need for Reason to persuade Necessity. Thus far, the status of Necessity is like that of the material factors of *Phaedo* 99b, which were merely necessary preconditions for the causality of Reason. But the Necessity of the *Timaeus* is given its own proper domain of explananda: on its own, unpersuaded, it is the cause of everything dis-ordered and random (46e5). Hence, it is ranked not merely as a συναιτίον or accessory cause but as an independent kind of cause (46e3, 68e6).[17] This marks an important change from the view Socrates espouses in the *Phaedo*.

But Reason really is prior. Its priority is multiple, and not just meta-physical but epistemological and ethical as well. This is clear from state-ments in the transition passage to the third and final part of the discourse and the passage on vision. In the later passage Plato declares that after dis-tinguishing the two sorts of causes, we must always direct our inquiries towards grasping the divine kind, i.e. Reason, only examining the other kind for the sake of discovering the divine (69a: cf. 46d–e). For only by grasping the divine sort of cause (which as we have seen produces what is intrinsically good) can we attain a happy life (69a1). Here Plato seems to follow Socrates' central teaching that knowledge of the good and its causes (which Socrates identified with virtue) produces happiness; yet unlike Socrates he connects this with grasp of natural causes.[18] It seems that one

---

[16] Cornford's translation here obscures the fact that ταῦτα in 69e4 ('the causes concerned with *these things*') picks up ταῦτα in e1, the things that come to be from Necessity. Cf. [A.] Rivaud (ed.), *Platon:* Timée—Critias (Paris: Société d'Édition Les 'belles lettres', 1963), ad loc.

[17] See n. 8 above. Hence A. E. Taylor's view, 'if we could ever have complete knowledge, we should find that ἀνάγκη had vanished from our account of the world' (*A Commentary on Plato's* Timaeus ((Oxford: Clarendon Press, 1928), 301), must be rejected. What Plato objects to at 46d1–3 is not the view that material factors are causes—an objection he makes in the *Phaedo*, but drops in the *Timaeus*—but that they are causes of everything (αἰτία τῶν πάντων).

[18] I speak of grasp, not knowledge, of causes, since Plato in the *Timaeus* seems to rule out knowledge of the physical world or its causes. The investigator must be content with a best approximation to knowledge, a likely story (29c–d, 48d, 53d, 68d; cf. 51d–52a). But Plato still means to endorse the possibility and legitimacy of something like physical science, indeed, to give it a key role in the philosopher's pursuit of the best life.

must discover the operation of Necessity before grasping the work of Reason: mechanistic physics does not automatically bring with it understanding of Reason and its purposes. But Plato says that understanding of the divine causes can only be obtained through grasp of the lower kind, presumably by some process of inference. Thus, physics is prior to philosophy in the order of discovery (47a7–8), though not in the orders of explanation or value. One must study phenomena through their material causes to see how these are ordered, for only then will one be able to see how they are ordered for the best.

We have seen what can be gathered about the relation between Reason and Necessity from an analysis of the structure of Timaeus' discourse and of the crucial transition passages between its parts. Reason and Necessity have been found to be distinct principles in the explanation of the cosmos, independent in that each is sometimes invoked separately. They are coequal under this aspect but not under others. Reason is prior to Necessity in the sense that it somehow 'dominates' it; it is the real core of the explanation in cases where both causes are invoked and understanding the causality of Reason is the main factor in obtaining happiness. Necessity is prior to Reason in the order of discovery and—at least within the framework of the creation story—of time, since it 'precedes' Reason's creation of time (52d4). Necessity serves as the Demiurge's material in constructing the universe; hence, it must exist in some sense prior to the activity of Reason. It is also the first object of study for the natural philosopher. Timaeus does not take Reason and Necessity up in this order, but then the order of demonstration is not the same as that of discovery.[19] The significance of these relations will become clearer once we have a better understanding of what Reason and Necessity are in themselves.

REASON AND NECESSITY AS TYPES OF αἰτία

What sorts of explanations or causes are Reason and Necessity? It seems to me that some progress in understanding can be made by considering Plato's two causes in relation to their predecessors of the *Phaedo* and to their descendants, the four causes of Aristotle. We have already seen something of the relation of the causes of the *Timaeus* to those of the *Phaedo*. It seems reasonable to suppose that since Plato and Aristotle speak of causes in similar contexts, Aristotle's theory derives in part from Platonic

---

[19] Aristotle says that the final cause should be mentioned before the necessary cause in scientific accounts (*PA* 642^{a}31–4), apparently because it is logically prior (639^{b}14-21).

antecedents. However, any attempt to relate the Aristotelian theory to Plato's runs up against the statement of *Metaphysics* 1. 6, 988[a]7–10 that Plato used only two of the four causes, the formal and the material. (Despite Aristotle's references to the One and the Dyad in the preceding passage he probably means to include the *Timaeus* in the scope of this remark: cf. *Physics* 209[b]12–17). I will suggest in what follows that Aristotle's remark is quite misleading. But my main aim will be to illuminate the roles of Reason and Necessity in the *Timaeus* by comparing them with Aristotle's causes, and with the account of causation in the *Phaedo*.[20]

We could characterize the Reason of the *Timaeus* in Aristotelian terms as a sort of efficient causality, corresponding to the explanation of phenomena in terms of the activity of *νοῦς* or intelligent soul (soul possessing *νοῦς*).[21] At the cosmic level Reason is represented by the Demiurge, who is the rational cause of the cosmos or order of Becoming. The Demiurge always acts in the best possible way; hence, the cosmos that is his product is the best world possible (29a4–5, e2, 48a2–3). He brings this about by making his work the most accurate likeness possible of the perfect world of Forms, the intelligible Living Creature (39e). Thus, Plato represents the goodness of Reason by describing the Demiurge's activity as guided by the Forms as model.

The Demiurge is a cosmic craftsman, a divine analogue of a certain sort of efficient cause at the human level. Plato calls the Demiurge both 'father' and 'maker' of the universe (28c2).[22] Aristotle lists these two sorts of cause, the craftsman and the father, prominently among his examples of efficient causes. But Reason is a special sort of efficient cause, for it always aims

---

[20] This issue is also discussed by W. Kullmann ('Der platonische *Timaios* und die Methode der aristotelische Biologie', in K. Döring and W. Kullmann (eds.), *Studia Platonica: Festschrift für Hermann Gundert* (Amsterdam: Grüner, 1974), 139–63), who fails to distinguish, however, between the brute Necessity of the *Timaeus* and the sort of explanation afforded by Reason and Necessity combined.

[21] Three passages in the *Timaeus* suggest that the Reason-cause can be identified with the causality of intelligent soul (30b2, 37c1–5, 46d5–6: cf. *Phlb.* 30c9–10). Most recent interpreters follow H. F. Cherniss (*Aristotle's Criticism of Plato and the Academy*, i (Baltimore: Johns Hopkins University Press, 1944)) in taking these passages to imply that the Demiurge is himself a soul. But the Demiurge is said to *create* soul, i.e. to be its cause, and there is textual evidence (e.g. 39e7–9, 47e4, 48a2) that the Demiurge, like Aristotle's god, is to be identified with *νοῦς*. This was the view of most ancient commentators, and has recently again been defended by R. Mohr ('The Relation of Reason to Soul in the Platonic Cosmology: *Sophist* 248c–249e', *Apeiron* 16 (1982), 21–6: 21), who points out (correctly, in my view) that the evidence Cherniss cites need only be taken to mean that the only thing that can *contain* νοῦς is soul.

[22] At 50d1–3 the Forms are called father of *γιγνόμενα*, and the Receptacle their mother. This occurs in the passage describing the domain of Necessity. I will argue below that the Forms do in fact play an important role in Plato's conception of Necessity, not however as efficient causes.

rightly at a good goal or final cause and always achieves the best result possible. So Plato's Reason seems to incorporate the Aristotelian final cause as well. If anything in the world is good, it will be explained by appeal to Reason, either alone or in co-operation with Necessity. This is true not only of natural phenomena but, as we shall see below, also of intentional human action. Thus, Reason will be like the Anaxagorean νοῦς of the *Phaedo*, a universal final cause.

Consider the doctrine of the *Phaedrus* and *Laws* 10. According to that doctrine, all physical motions can ultimately be traced back through chains of bodily causes to the original motion of soul, which is self-motion and primary motion (*Laws* 895–7). This recalls the Reason of the *Timaeus*, which is closely connected with soul[23] and which is characterized by the activity, διάνοια, that is called 'most causal' (αἰτιοτάτη) at 76d8[24] and said to dominate the mechanistic causes of Necessity. In the *Laws* and the *Phaedrus* the self-motion of souls is the primary sort of efficient causality. But this cannot be the same sort of causality as that of Reason; for as a cause Reason is always guided by the Forms, whereas some actions of souls take place in ignorance of the Forms (cf. 44a–b). Nevertheless, the concept of self-moving soul as a sort of efficient causality seems to be shared by the *Timaeus*.[25]

The causality of Reason is symbolized in the *Timaeus*, as is the causality of soul in the *Laws*, by the dominance of rotary motion over the six kinds of rectilinear motion characteristic of the natural movement of bodies (cf. 34a).[26] This point may help clear up the apparent disharmony between the doctrine of the *Timaeus* concerning the causality of Reason and the view of the *Laws* and the *Phaedrus* that the soul's self-motion is the primary efficient cause. The problem arises for those motions of soul which are not controlled by or subsumed under Reason, motions which arise in ignorance of the Forms and so are intentional but not directed to the good. Now such ignorance, the *Timaeus* tells us, is due to the shock the soul receives when born into a mortal body. Random rectilinear motions coming through the body disturb the equilibrium of the natural rotary

---

[23] See n. 21 above.

[24] Cf. *Platon: Timée—Critias*, [A.] Rivaud (ed.), cf n16, *ad loc*. F. M. Cornford's translation (*Plato's Cosmology* (London, 1937), 301) omits all reference to διάνοια here.

[25] As Cherniss ('The Sources of Evil according to Plato', 256 n. 24) and others have noted 37b5 seems to allude to the doctrine of the *Phaedrus* and the *Laws* that soul is what moves itself.

[26] The rotational motion imparted by the World-Soul dominates the natural rectilinear motions of the elements (43a–b; cf. 63a–e), so that any apparently straight trajectory will really be an arc. On the image of rotary motion as the image of the activity of νοῦς in Plato, see E. N. Lee, 'Reason as Rotation: Circular Movement as the Model of Mind (*Nous*) in Later Plato', i W. H. Werkmeister (ed.), *Facets of Plato's Philosophy*, *Phronesis*, suppl. vol. 2 (1976), 70–102.

motions of the soul, so that they no longer control the person's actions (44a4–7) as is their nature to do (as is evident from the dominance of other motions by rotation in the cosmos as a whole). The motions of soul are distorted from smooth rotations into wobbles; hence, the person no longer has *νοῦς*, the characteristic motion of which is smooth rotation: the soul is now *ἄνους* (44a8: cf. 44a3). Plato admits that the soul's actions will still *appear* purposive in that they will still be directed by her judgements and beliefs; but these will now be false judgements (44a1–3), since true judgement requires the proper functioning of the soul's revolutions (cf. 37a–b). Only after these revolutions have been steadied from their wobblings can the soul regain its reason (44b1–7). Plato concludes from this that the ultimate responsibility for bad and foolish actions does not lie in the soul but outside it, in the random motions of Necessity that overpower the rotational motions of soul.[27]

This is why Plato refuses to hold persons responsible for their own evil actions. At 86b–d he claims that all bad and foolish actions are due ultimately to disorders or diseases of the soul, physiologically based departures from its natural condition of rationality. These are clearly the same as the physically caused perturbations of 43–4. Hence, Plato declares, every sin is excusable by reason of insanity: 'No one is willingly bad,' he says (87d7–e1). This is the well-known Socratic paradox, upheld also in the *Laws* (especially 9. 860d–862c),[28] the converse of the dictum that virtue is knowledge. Vice is due to ignorance of the Forms and is excusable because due to external causes. However, this is just one aspect of an even more paradoxical position to which Plato seems to commit himself in the *Timaeus*. For at 42e he says it is the job of the lesser gods to steer humans towards good actions, and so implies that only *bad* actions are due to the souls themselves. But if all good actions are due to divine guidance and all bad ones physiologically caused, then there seems to be nothing left for the individual soul to do—it will be the cause of none of its own actions. The obvious way out of this dilemma is to take the passage at 42e to be heavily mythical and to understand 'god' to stand for human reason or *νοῦς*.[29] This is supported by other textual evidence. At

---

[27] Cherniss, 'The Sources of Evil according to Plato', which does not deal with this passage, argues that such an explanation of moral evil is excluded by the dominance of Reason over Necessity. But it does not follow from the claim that every ultimate efficient cause is a soul-motion that every soul-motion is an ultimate efficient cause: indeed this passage is evidence that Plato holds what seems the only reasonable view, that soul's activity is subject to external influences.

[28] See the excellent discussion in R. F. Stalley, *An Introduction to Plato's* Laws (Indianapolis, 1983), 151–65.

[29] For a similar diagnosis, see ibid., 47–9.

90a2–3 the highest part of soul is said explicitly to be a god-given genius or δαίμων and at 41c7 this part of the soul is the divine element in the human constitution.

It follows that good intentional human action is also to be attributed to νοῦς or Reason, since it is guided by the same principles—the Forms—as the working of cosmic Reason, represented by the Demiurge. Thus, Reason is the universal final cause, as Anaxagoras had suggested. Plato in addition makes clear, as Anaxagoras perhaps had not, that Reason is also an efficient cause of phenomena. But, it is not the universal efficient cause, since it only produces goods. (Accordingly, Necessity must also serve as an efficient cause.) Aristotelian efficient causes characteristically aim at a good goal or τέλος (a possible exception being the natural impulses to motion of the four sublunary elements[30]). But in Aristotle the goodness of this goal or the possibility of achieving it may be merely apparent, so that the best outcome will not always result. Hence, Reason as cause is not a precise analogue of Aristotle's final cause; but it is its ancestor.

Let us now consider Necessity. It is chiefly on this point that I think previous commentators have gone astray by failing to see important connections between the *Phaedo* and the *Timaeus*. The causality of the Forms discussed in *Phaedo* 99b–105b, especially the so-called 'clever' αἰτίαι, is, I think, very close to what Plato in the *Timaeus* calls Necessity. Both the *Phaedo* and the *Timaeus* versions of this sort of causality involve the consequences for the world of Becoming of the fact that the world of Forms has a certain structure, that is, that certain Forms import certain Forms and exclude others. Forms have causal implications, as Vlastos puts it.[31] The *Phaedo* supplies simple-minded examples of this: Fire imports Heat and excludes Cold; Oneness imports Oddness and excludes Twoness. The Reason of the *Timaeus* employs the very same sorts of causal implications in constituting the cosmos,[32] and it is these very same causal implications that hinder the cosmos from being a perfect likeness of its model.

A few of the many possible examples from the *Timaeus* will serve to illustrate these points. Consider the reasoning of the god in constructing the human body out of material he has built up from the elements: bone, flesh, and sinews. At 74e–75c he is concerned with placing a layer of flesh over the human frame. Its main purpose will be to protect the body: with

---

[30] The natural motions of the elements in the *Timaeus* are similarly not to be explained teleologically, but as results of Necessity. See n. 14 above.

[31] G. Vlastos, 'Reasons and Causes in the *Phaedo*', *Philosophical Review*, 69 (1969), 291–325; repr. in *Platonic Studies*, 2nd edn. (Princeton, 1981), 105.

[32] Morrow ('Necessity and Persuasion in Plato's *Timaeus*', 427–8) speaks of reliable nature in phenomena as the Demiurge's raw materials, but does not make the connection with the 'clever' αἰτίαι of the *Phaedo*.

a view to protection, the thicker the flesh the better. But thickness of flesh will bring with it other properties which are undesirable: inflexibility and difficulty of movement as well as dullness of sensation. Because of this, two other goals the god has—ease and grace of movement and quickness of sensation—work at cross-purposes to the goal of protecting the body. The god is thus constrained by the limitations of his materials, which are due to the reflections of the Forms in the Receptacle that he has organized in a determinate way. So he is forced to choose between incompatible alternatives and he chooses as best having the body well protected by flesh only where flexibility, grace, and sensitivity, which are greater goods, are not otherwise needed. This constraint is Necessity, which can be referred to the mutual entailments and exclusions of Forms: as Plato says, the Necessity is displayed in the λόγος or account of the situation (74e4–5).[33] Consider also Plato's account of why souls must be incarnated in bodies (30a–b: cf. 42a3–4). The Demiurge knew that the cosmos, as Becoming, had to be visible and tangible and therefore bodily,[34] but also that it was better for it to contain a share of reason or νοῦς. The only thing that can contain reason is soul, so he accordingly put reason in soul and soul in body.[35]

Necessity, therefore, involves the Forms in the same way the 'clever' αἰτίαι of the *Phaedo* do. But Necessity is not merely formal causality: it seems to involve material causality as well. The craftsman of the cosmos uses the reflections or images of the Forms in the Receptacle for his raw materials, as a sculptor would use stone or other material that he knows how to cleave or mould. Necessity comes into play only when these materials are combined: it is not the properties in themselves that are incompatible with perfection but their joint embodiment.

These constraints on Reason are intimately connected with the corporeality of the physical world. This is strikingly illustrated by the passage on the pre-cosmic chaos (52d–53c). Here we are to consider the Receptacle as containing only traces or ἴχνη of the most basic Forms (Fire, Air, Earth, and Water) 'before' the Demiurge's shaping and organizing activity begins. This indicates that Plato does not think of Reason as the cause of

---

[33] Cf. Aristotle, *Ph.* 200[b]4–8. Cornford's translation (*Plato's Cosmology*, 298) of λόγος as 'cogent reason' obscures the thought. Chrysippus (*apud* Gellius, *Noctes Atticae* 7. 1 = *SVF* ii. 170) uses a similar example concerning the thickness of the bones of the skull in his explanation of how providence is compatible with the existence of necessary evil. He was very likely inspired by the *Timaeus*.

[34] See n. 12 above.

[35] Hence, there should be a Form of soul as well as of the bodily elements. This seems to be implied in calling the world of Forms an intelligible ζῷον (39e). This Form is represented by the ratios used in the Demiurge's construction of soul (35a–36b).

participation in these Forms: the Demiurge merely takes over these pre-
existing formal elements and brings them to participate in better, higher
Forms. It is these most basic formal elements which are responsible for the
uneven distribution of the elements in the cosmos. The pre-cosmic random
motion tends to sort out the elements, as particles of grain get sorted in
winnowing. Like goes to like and Fire ends up being concentrated in the
region farthest from the region of Earth, at the outside of the cosmos, with
regions of Air and Water intervening (52e–53a). The Demiurge is constrained to respect this natural distribution of the elements when he frames
the cosmos, leaving most of each element in the region where he found it.
Even if this part of Plato's story is a myth and he does not think that the
world was ever in a pre-cosmic state, it is clear that this passage is meant
to show one way in which Reason is constrained by Necessity. In fact, we
are constrained by the very same factors: what we call weight and Plato
calls 'heavy' and 'light' (63c–e).[36]

We can now get a clearer picture of what is meant by the combination
of Reason and Necessity. Reason is a cause that always makes things for
the best. It can be represented by the activity of a perfectly rational soul
oriented towards the Forms as paradigms. Necessity is a form of explanation that accounts for properties of phenomena as unavoidable consequences of the embodiment of Forms. Some things are to be explained
by appeal to one of these principles apart from the other: anything that
is either inherently good—e.g. the unity, order, and intelligence of the
cosmos—or purely material, disorderly, or bad. Other goods, which are not
valuable in themselves but contribute in some way to the overall order,
harmony, and goodness of the universe, are explained as compromises in
which Reason has persuaded Necessity. Their goodness, which Reason
provides, is dependent on certain material conditions, the contribution of
Necessity; hence, they are not good absolutely. Necessity will thus account
for all evil and imperfection in the universe (cf. *Tht.* 176a5–6), though it
will not be by nature evil nor the cause of evil, since it will also be the
cause of all things that are neither good nor evil.[37]

The *Timaeus*' distinction between Necessity operating on its own and in
conjunction to Reason corresponds closely with Aristotle's distinction
between absolute and hypothetical necessity.[38] When Reason and Neces-

[36] Cf. n. 14 above.
[37] The various sources of evil discussed by Cherniss ('The Sources of Evil according to Plato
can all be subsumed under Necessity.
[38] Cf. n. 3 above; Cooper, 'Hypothetical Necessity'; and Kullmann, 'Der platonische *Timaic*
und die Methode der aristotelische Biologie'. For argument that Aristotle's absolute or uncon-
ditional necessity is the same as the necessity belonging to a thing's essential nature (as I have
argued that the unqualified Necessity of the *Timaeus* is), see D. Frede, 'Aristotle on the Limit
of Determinism', in Gotthelf (ed.), *Aristotle on Nature and Living Things*.

sity combine, Reason 'persuades' Necessity by producing the proper ordering of the mechanical causes to give the best result. This is very like Aristotle's hypothetical necessity: the necessity that if a certain goal is to be
realized such-and-such material preconditions should obtain (e.g. sawteeth
must be hard, if they are to cut: *PA* 642ª8–14). Similarly, if the universe of
the *Timaeus* is to be intelligent, then soul must be embodied. Aristotle like
Plato will sometimes call such a necessary precondition for something a
συναίτιον (*Metaph.* 1015ª20–1) and even speak of it as Plato does as being
'used' by reason (ἡ κατὰ τὸν λόγον φύσις; *PA* 663ᵇ24). This kind of reasoning from a desired effect to its cause displays the role of Reason in
Plato's mixed sort of explanation: both Plato and Aristotle assimilate it to
the technical reasoning of a craftsman or δημιουργός.[39] Necessity, in contrast, corresponds to reasoning from cause to effect: if certain conditions
X obtain, then *Y* must also obtain (cf. *PA* 642ª33–4, 640ª3–6).[40] If in this
case *Y* is also something good, then *X* can be taken to be for the sake of
Y and we have a case of the mixed explanation. If *Y* is not a good, we have
a case of Necessity working on its own.[41] Reason working alone as cause
is an explanation solely in terms of what is best, apart from any material
conditions. This is non-instrumental reasoning, which accounts for things
merely in terms of goodness: it corresponds to Aristotle's purely teleological form of explanation. It is in Aristotle's discussion of these distinctions
in *de Partibus Animalium* 1. 1 that we can see most clearly the influence
upon him of the *Timaeus*' theory of causes.

Some important points of contact between Plato's two causes and Aristotle's formal, final, and material causes should now be clear. I have already
noted a difficulty in understanding the efficient causality of Reason, to
which I will return shortly. But Necessity is also in some sense an efficient
cause: it accounts for *disorderly* motion. It is called 'the wandering sort of
cause' (48a6–7) and is said to produce on its own the random and disordered (46e5; cf. 30a3–4, 53b2–4). This seems to connect it with τυχή or
chance (cf. *Laws* 889c1–2), which Aristotle also classifies as a sort of
efficient cause. But how can Necessity, if founded upon the reliable natures
of Forms, produce chance and disorder?[42]

[39] See also *Plt.* 281c–e.
[40] This, I think, helps account for the problematic linking at *APo.* 94ª22 of the fourth sort of
cause, normally given as the material cause with the notion of logical ground. Aristotle may be
thinking of this sort of cause, as he elsewhere does the material cause, in terms of the unqualified
necessity of the *Timaeus*.
[41] It is in this sense that Taylor (*A Commentary on Plato's* Timaeus, 301) is right to identify
Necessity with those conjunctions of properties, 'for which we can see no justification in the
form of a valuable result'.
[42] Cherniss ('The Sources of Evil according to Plato', 258 n. 40) raises this as an objection
to Morrow's interpretation of Necessity in terms of reliable natures (n. 32 above). He does
not discuss Morrow's obvious line of reply (see Morrow, 'Necessity and Persuasion in

In fact, I think it is an advantage of my interpretation of Necessity in terms of the causal implications of Forms that it allows a more satisfactory account of the connection between chance and Necessity than the one explicitly suggested by Plato's text. Plato seems just to say that as order is always a product of Reason,[43] so Necessity always produces disorder. This is the point of the statement at 46d4 that the accessory causes can contain no νοῦς or λόγος, that is, rational justification in terms of the good (cf. also 53b2–4). Plato holds that order is inherently good and so wants to account for it in terms of Reason. One problem with this is that it is implausible to claim that order cannot come about spontaneously as a result of mechanical processes, as with Aristotle's notion of the αὐτόματον. But it also does not help us see *how* Necessity produces disorder. The real reason is the complexity of phenomena. Every phenomenal object instantiates a very large number of properties, all of which have causal implications. Hence, any ordering of phenomenal properties, in particular the best one imposed by the Demiurge, will bring with it many side-effects some of which will not be goods and others of which will be positively undesirable. Plato's awareness of this is evident in his account of the coating of flesh discussed above. It is precisely these unavoidable collocations of good and bad properties that Plato would call chance.[44]

I have suggested that Plato's concept of Reason involves an intimate link between the concepts of efficient and final causality. If this can be intelligibly made out, then no problem will arise for Plato as it does for Aristotle as to *how* the final cause can act to produce phenomena. But how is it to be made out? What means can Reason employ to act on material things? The most obvious reply is that Reason as νοῦς acts through the agency of soul.[45] Now Plato does think that soul is capable of initiating bodily motion: this is what is symbolized by the dominance of rotary over rectilinear motion. But the rotary motions of soul are precisely what

Plato's *Timaeus*', 432–3), which I develop in the text, nor does he realize that such a reply is consistent with his own account of the connection between chance and Necessity: see n. 44 below.

[43] The goal of craftsmanship is always the production of order (*Grg.* 503d–e) and divine craftsmanship always succeeds in producing it. But Plato seems to make the even stronger claim I give in the text.

[44] See Morrow, 'Necessity and Persuasion in Plato's *Timaeus*', 433; Taylor, *A Commentary on Plato's* Timaeus, 301. Cherniss ('The Sources of Evil according to Plato', 258) interprets chance for Plato as the unwanted or unforeseen side-effects of the irrational motions of souls. In *Ph.* 2, Aristotle modifies Plato's scheme to bring chance or τύχη (as well as φύσις, which Plato connects with chance at *Laws* 888e–889c) under the genus of efficient causes that act for the sake of a goal (τέλος).

[45] See the texts cited in n. 21. The Demiurge is said to create soul prior to his organization of body (*Ti.* 34b–35a). Perhaps he has no alternative but must use soul to organize body.

represent the presence in it of νοῦς or Reason. Perhaps, then, the cosmic Reason acts on the world through the rotary motions of Same and Different in the World-Soul that guide the movements of the heavenly bodies. This would be strikingly parallel to the role of νοῦς in Aristotle's cosmology and suggests another way in which the *Timaeus* may have influenced him. It should be noted that this interpretation is independent of the questions (which in my view the *Timaeus* leaves open) whether the cosmic Reason is just the νοῦς of the World-Soul and whether the creation story is a myth.

But on one level the *Timaeus* is a myth. It is a myth that tells how rationality eternally confronts the world's inherent disorder and strives to bring it to order. It is not mere physiologizing: like the myths of Plato's earlier dialogues, it is a moral exhortation. The imperative is to get as large a share of reason or νοῦς as possible: to seek to understand the purposes of the universe by grasping the teleological orderings of material causes. Success or failure in doing this is the sole determinant of the human soul's fate after death (92c). Doing this will allow one to understand the nature of divine activity and by imitating it to become as much like a god as possible, which is human happiness.[46] This is why the philosopher will contemplate the motions of the heavenly bodies, which are gods (47a–c). The ultimate purpose of the *Timaeus* is thus to inspire us to undertake natural philosophy so as to learn as much as we can about Reason's purposes, so that we may harmonize the random and irregular motions of our own souls and our own lives as far as possible with the regular turnings of νοῦς.[47]

[46] Cf. *Tht.* 176b1–2, ὁμοίωσις θεῷ κατὰ τὸ δυνατόν 'becoming as much like a god as possible', a formula which later ancient Platonists took, probably rightly, as Plato's formulation of the human τέλος. It certainly seems to fit the *Timaeus*.

[47] Earlier versions of this paper were read at Tufts University and the University of Texas at Austin. I have particularly benefited from comments made on those occasions by Eugene Garver, Carl Huffman, and A. P. D. Mourelatos. Detailed criticisms by the editors of *Ancient Philosophy* of an earlier draft have also been very helpful in improving the paper.

XVII

PLATO ON NOT-BEING

G. E. L. OWEN

Platonists who doubt that they are Spectators of Being must settle for the knowledge that they are investigators of the verb 'to be'. Their investigations make them familiar with certain commonplaces of the subject for which, among Plato's dialogues, the *Sophist* is held to contain the chief evidence. But the evidence is not there, and the attempt to find it has obstructed the interpretation of that hard and powerful dialogue. The commonplaces that I mean are these:

In Greek, but only vestigially in English, the verb 'to be' has two syntactically distinct uses, a *complete* or *substantive* use in which it determines a one-place predicate ('X is', 'X is not') and an *incomplete* use in which it determines a two-place predicate ('X is Y', 'X is not Y'). To this difference there answers a semantic distinction. The verb in its first use signifies 'to exist' (for which Greek in Plato's day had no separate word) or else, in Greek but only in translators' English, 'to be real' or 'to be the case' or 'to be true', these senses being all reducible to the notion

From G. Vlastos (ed.), *Plato*, i: *Metaphysics and Epistemology* (Doubleday Anchor Books). Copyright © 1970 by Doubleday, a division of Bantam Doubleday Dell Publisher Group, Inc. Used by permission of Doubleday.

Delivered in shortened form as an Arnold Isenberg lecture in philosophy at Michigan State University in Mar. 1967. The lecture took up an older promissory note (in 'Snares of Ontology', in R. Bambrough (ed.), *New Essays on Plato and Aristotle* (London, 1965), 71 n. 1) which was accepted in its original form by G. Vlastos ('A Metaphysical Paradox', *Proceedings of the American Philosophical Association*, 39 (1965–6), 8–9). The bones of the argument were taken from a larger stew of many years' standing, familiar to seminars at Oxford and Harvard; I wish I could now distinguish the many cooks. But mention must be made not only of clarifications already published by members of those seminars but of unpublished benefactions. In the first class fall J. M. E. Moravcsik, 'Being and Meaning in the *Sophist*', *Acta Philosophica Fennica*, 14 (1962), 23–78; W. G. Runciman, *Plato's Later Epistemology* (Cambridge, 1962); and most recently M. Frede, *Prädikation und Existenzaussage*, *Hypomnemata*, 18 (1967), 1–99, and J. Malcolm, 'Plato's Analysis of *to on* and *to mē on* in the *Sophist*', *Phronesis*, 12 (1967), 130–46: the last two came too late for me to do more than signal agreement in these notes. In the second class the treatment of *kath' hauto—pros heteron* on pp. 444–5 was, I think, first suggested by a conversation with R. G. Albritton; it was reached independently by Frede.

The footnote numbering is that used in Owen's article, as it appears in his *Logic, Science, and Dialectic*. To obtain the original footnote numbering, as it appears in G. Vlastos (ed.), Plato I Metaphysics and Epistemology, add 1.

of the existence of some object or state of affairs; while in its second use it is demoted to a subject–predicate copula (under which we can here include the verbal auxiliary) or to an identity sign.[1] Plato's major explorations of being and not-being are exercises in the complete or 'existential' use of the verb. And, lest his arguments should seem liable to confusion by this versatile word, in the *Sophist* he marks off the first use from the verb's other use or uses and draws a corresponding distinction within the negative constructions represented by *to mē on*, 'not-being' or 'what is not'.[2] For the problems which dominate the central argument of the *Sophist* are existence problems, so disentangling the different functions of the verb 'to be' is a proper step to identifying and resolving them.

Since the following arguments were put together most of these commonplaces have come under fire.[3] Consequently, here the fire can be confined to one arc, the interpretation of Plato and particularly of the *Sophist*. The general syntactic claims will not come into question: we can accept a distinction between the verb's complete and incomplete uses provided we are wary of confusing the first with elliptical occurrences of the second—and this is no longer a matter of syntax (p. 443, below). The *Sophist* will turn out to be primarily an essay in problems of reference and predication and in the incomplete uses of the verb associated with these. The argument neither contains nor compels any isolation of an existential verb. Yet the problems about falsehood and unreality which it takes over from earlier dialogues do seem to be rooted in what we should call

---

[1] For the broad treatment of the verb, see LSJ s.v. *einai* and recent versions of the Oxford and Webster dictionaries s.v. 'be'; for the application to Plato, see e.g. I. M. Crombie, *An Examination of Plato's Doctrines* (London, 1962), ii. 498–9.

[2] P. Shorey, *What Plato Said* (Chicago, 1933), 298, asserted that in the *Sophist* Plato 'laid the foundation of logic' by, *inter alia*, 'explicitly distinguishing the copula from the substantive *is*'; A. E. Taylor, *Plato: The* Sophist *and the* Statesman, ed. R. Klibansky and G. E. M. Anscombe (London, 1961), 81–2, claimed that Plato 'has definitely distinguished the "is" of the copula from the "is" which asserts actual existence' and further that 'he has . . . discriminated the existential sense of the "is" from the sense in which "is" means "is the same as", "is identical with" '. So, with variations, F. M. Cornford, *Plato's Theory of Knowledge* (London, 1935), 296; J. L. Ackrill, 'Plato and the Copula', *Journal of Hellenic Studies*, 77, pt. 1 (1957), 1–5; Crombie, *An Examination of Plato's Doctrines*, ii. 499; Moravcsik, 'Being and Meaning in the *Sophist*', 51.

[3] On the general account of the verb, see C. Kahn, 'The Greek Verb "To Be" and the Concept of Being', *Foundations of Language*, 2 (1966), 245–65, who notes the difficulty of making a firm syntactical distinction between the 'absolute' and 'predicative' constructions and then argues against taking the first as 'existential'. Vlastos, in 'A Metaphysical Paradox' and 'Degrees of Reality in Plato', in Bambrough (ed.), *New Essays on Plato and Aristotle*, 1–19, holds that Plato's theory of *ontōs onta* is concerned with grades not of existence but of reality, and explores a sense of '. . . is real' which reduces it to the two-place predicate '. . . is really (sc. unqualifiedly or undeceptively) . . .'. That the *Sophist* marks off an existential sense of *einai* has been queried by Runciman, *Plato's Later Epistemology*, ch. 3, Kahn, 'The Greek Verb "To Be" and the Concept of Being', 261; and now Frede, *Prädikation und Existenzaussage*, and Malcolm, 'Plato's Analysis of *to on* and *to mē on* in the *Sophist*'.

existence puzzles, so it will need to be explained why they present themselves here in such a way as to lead to a study of '. . . is . . .' and '. . . is
not . . .'.

THE ARGUMENT FROM NOTHING

Let us begin, as Plato begins his own discussion of not-being, with
Parmenides. That philosopher had written (B2. 7–8): 'You could not distinguish, nor could you express, *what is not.*' Which of its roles is the verb
'to be' playing here? Given the conventional choice it was natural to plump
for the existential role. Not because the verb carries no complement—it is
noteworthy that scholars have been ready here to detect an unmarked
lacuna after the verb. The better reason was that Parmenides goes on to
equate 'what is not' with 'nothing'.[4] It would be absurd to think that
because a thing is not such-and-such—not blue, for example—it is therefore nothing at all; but it is natural enough to equate what does not exist
with nothing. No mermaid exists: nothing is a mermaid. Hence no doubt
the pleasing entry in my desk copy of *Webster's Dictionary*: 'Nothing:
something that does not exist'.

  Discontent about the philosophical interpretation of the verb 'to be' has
often focused on this reading of Parmenides. How can he be pinned to one
use of his favourite verb when he slides so unwarily between different
uses? For he argues first that a thing cannot be at one time but not at
another (B8. 6–21), and then takes himself to have shown that it cannot
change at all, i.e. cannot be *anything* at one time which it is not at another
(B8. 26–8). The objection can be met in this form,[5] but it returns in others.[6]
We need not pursue it: our interest in Parmenides is just that the equation
of *what is not* with *nothing* has often seemed to settle the matter. For when
Plato takes over Parmenides' topic he adopts this equation, so here too
the question has seemed, by default, to be settled. The *Republic* echoes the
familiar argument, 'How could anything that is not be known?' (477a1),
and adds a little later: 'Properly speaking, that which is not must be called
not one thing but nothing' (478b12–c1). It seems only to be emphasizing

----

  [4] 28 B8. 7–13 DK; cf. 6. 2 with 7. 1.
  [5] As perhaps in 'Eleatic Questions', ch. 1 in G. E. L. Owen, *Logic, Science and Dialectic.
Collected Papers in Greek Philosophy*, ed. M. Nussbaum (Ithaca, NY, 1986), n. 45.
  [6] Thus Kahn, 'The Greek Verb "To Be" and the Concept of Being', 251, represents the verb
as in effect an assertion sign, engrossing the 'existential' and 'predicative' uses; and M. Furth, in
'Elements of Eleatic Ontology', *Journal of the History of Philosophy*, 6 (1968), 111–32, argue-
ably that such a 'fused' use of the verb would not itself commit Parmenides to fallacy. Many
points in Furth's paper bear on my contentions here.

Parmenides' equation when it speaks of 'what is not *in any way*' and 'what *utterly* is not' (477a3–4, 478d7). And the equation with its attendant phraseology is repeated when Plato returns to the topic in the *Theaetetus* (189a6–12) and the *Sophist* (237c7–e2).[7] So it seems that in these contexts he is expressly concerned with the possibility of speaking and thinking about what does not exist. Peipers, listing what he took to be the occurrences of the 'existential' verb in Plato, remarked: 'haec nota communis est: in omnibus animo obversatur oppositio *eius quod est et nihil* (*tou ontos et tou mēdenos*).'[8]

This conclusion in turn lends a sense to another step in Plato's argument. He contends, in the *Theaetetus* (189a10–12) and the *Sophist* (237e1–6), that thinking or speaking of what is not is simply not speaking or thinking at all, and then in the *Sophist* (238d–239a) he turns this contention on itself and brands the very expressions 'what is not' and 'what are not' as ill-formed inasmuch as they pretend to pick out one or more subjects of discourse. What can this mean but that he now denies sense to any attempt to speak of what does not exist? Thus Cornford contrasted later attempts to find 'non-existent things like chimaeras' an entrée into discourse, and summed up: 'This is all [Plato] has to say about a problem that has troubled modern logicians who have discussed the thesis that "whatever is thought of must in some sense be".'[9]

As it stands, this is an ambiguous thesis. I may tell you (*a′*) 'The elves

---

[7] Notice that in *Tht.* 188e–189a the move from 'what is not' to 'nothing' is argued, not assumed: F (something)→~F (nothing)→F (one thing)→F (a thing that is), hence F (a thing that is not)→F (nothing). In the manipulation of the same counters at *Rep.* 478b–c it is assumed: F (something)→~F (nothing)→F(one thing), but F (a thing that is not)→F (nothing)→~F (one thing), hence F (something)→~F (a thing that is not). Whether it is argued or assumed in the *Sophist*'s opening puzzle depends on the sense of 237c–e and ultimately 237d6–7. Theaetetus has just agreed that, since 'what is not' cannot be said of *what is*, it cannot be said of *something* (237c10–d5); and the Eleatic Stranger then says, *either* 'Do you agree to this because you look at it in this way, that a man who speaks of *something* must speak of *one thing*?' (so e.g. Heindorf, Apelt, Cornford); *or* 'Looking at it in this way, do you agree that a man who speaks of *something* must speak of *one thing*?' (so e.g. Diès, Fraccaroli, Taylor, *Plato: The* Sophist *and the* Statesman). The second is attractive because it takes the argument forward from a proposition already agreed, that what is not cannot be something: it deduces from this that what is not cannot be even one thing and hence is nothing, and the latter proposition thus becomes a corollary and not an assumption of the argument. But the reading assumes a deviant *hoti* construction with (*sum*)*phanai*, which has no parallel in Plato (*Phd.* 64b3–4, wrongly adduced by Ast *et al.* as the single exception, is not one: the verb governs not *hoti . . .* but *eu eirēsthai . . . hoti . . .*). Back then to the first construction: the Eleatic Stranger asks why Theaetetus agrees that what is not cannot be something, and offers an elliptical argument for it which uses our proposition as an assumption: F(something) → F(one or more things) {but F (nothing) → ~F (one or more things)}, hence F (nothing) → ~F (something); {but F(what is not) → F(nothing)} hence F (what is not) → ~F (something).

[8] D. Peipers, *Ontologia Platonica* (Leipzig, 1883), 16.
[9] *Plato's Theory of Knowledge*, 208.

interrupt my typing', when there are no such creatures, or (a″) 'De Gaulle means to bribe Britain into the Common Market', when there is no such project; I may warn you (b′) 'The creatures named in (a′) don't exist' or (b″) 'The project reported in (a″) doesn't exist', and thus in different ways challenge the truth of (a′) and (a″); and in turn I may comment on the sense but not the truth of these last sentences and say (c) 'Anyone uttering (b′) or (b″) is speaking of what does not exist'. All these sorts of utterances, and others too, will fall under the rubric 'speaking of what does not exist'. Faced with such a division a defender of the established view would probably say that the *Theaetetus* is content to leave the problem of falsehood in its traditional form: it assimilates the falsehood in (a″) to the failure of reference in (a′), but it assumes without question the significance of such expressions as 'what is not'; whereas the *Sophist* turns to challenge the very use of these expressions. So it seems that in the *Sophist*, if not before, Plato expressly discounts negations of existence as unintelligible.

This reading of the argument is generally coupled with the assurance that the *Sophist* represents *assertions* of existence as wholly respectable. Cornford has his own version of this conjunction: 'Every Form exists; consequently "the non-existent" has no place in the scheme, and we have ruled out that sense of "is not".'[10] This suggests that it was a decision to talk about nothing but Forms which induced Plato to find a discussion of the status of Chimaeras unintelligible. Whether or not Cornford meant this travesty of the argument, he can at least be counted as subscribing to the common view that Plato divides positive statements of existence from their negative counterparts and welcomes the first but disbars the second.[11] There is

---

[10] *Plato's Theory of Knowledge*, 296.

[11] But there is a striking incoherence in Cornford's account. After saying that the existential sense of 'is not' has been 'ruled out' (ibid.) he goes on to write as though this sense had been not excluded but positively vindicated: he speaks of 'the preceding demonstration that "is not" has two senses—"does not exist" and "is different from"', and even of Plato's showing that 'the thing that is not' does not *always* (my italics) mean 'the non-existent' (pp. 298–9). Thereafter in translating and explaining 262c3 he reimports the sense 'does not exist' without caveat (p. 305 and n. 1: see p. 450 below). On p. 295 n. 1 (cf. 208) he concedes that at 238c '*to mēdamōs on*, "the simply non-existent", was dismissed as not to be spoken or thought of'; yet he at once dilutes this to the claim that 'there are no *true* statements saying that any *Form* does not exist' (my italics again). What is said in 238c is that *to mē on* as there construed is flatly unintelligible; what is said in 257b is that *whenever* (not, as Cornford, 'when') we speak of what is not we do not mean a contrary of what is (*hopotan to mē on legōmen . . . ouk enantion ti legomen tou ontos*)—this latter phrase representing, by Cornford's own admission, the *mēdamōs on* of 238c. This unfounded reading of the *Sophist* he subsequently applied to the interpretation of the *Timaeus* 38b2–3 (*Plato's Cosmology* (London, 1937), 98 n. 4), and a rejoinder of mine (ch. 4) which resumed the objections here set out was dismissed by an American scholar as 'brushing aside Cornford's attempt' (H. F. Cherniss, *Journal of Hellenic Studies*, 77 (1957), 18), although the scholar neither quoted nor apparently grasped the objection. He then felt able to retrieve 'is non-existent' as a 'more probable' interpretation of *to mē on* at *Ti.* 38b and yet claim that this agreed with the *Sophist*.

still room for dissension within this common view: some of its adherents
offer Plato the hospitable thesis that 'existence is a predicate of everything
whatever' or 'is necessarily all-inclusive', in a sense which will readmit
Cornford's Chimaeras.[12] Still the foundation holds firm. Plato in the
Sophist has isolated a complete use of the verb 'to be', that in which it
determines a one-place predicate and signifies 'to exist', and within this use
he rejects negative constructions with the verb as breeding intolerable
paradox. Whether Chimaeras benefit from the distinction is a matter for
scholarly debate. They and their like rear no head in the dialogue from
start to finish.

This familiar reading of the *Sophist* runs into such troubles that no
amount of ingenious patching now seems to me able to save it. I shelve
other considerations for the moment and mention two drawn from Plato's
own account of his strategy.

THE PROSPECT OF JOINT ILLUMINATION

First, Plato nowhere suggests, and by implication he consistently denies,
that he has found a use of the verb 'to be' in which only its positive occurrences have significance.

At the end of the long review of perplexities in 236d–250e, the
Eleatic Stranger says: 'Now that both being and not-being have turned
out equally puzzling, this in itself (*ēdē*) offers the hope that if one of
them can be made out to a greater or less degree of clarity the other can
be made out to the same degree' (250e5–251a1). Being and not-being have
been steadily coupled in this way in the preceding arguments (241d6–7,
243b7–c5, 245e8–246a2) and they are similarly coupled in what follows
(254c5–6, 256e2–3, 258a11–b7, and 262c3, of which more on pp. 450–1
below). After volunteering this prospect of joint illumination it would obviously be perverse to represent a positive use of the verb as luminous but
reject the negative as wholly dark. Nor would the perversity be lessened
if Plato had argued, as some of his interpreters do, that although the complete or 'existential' use of the verb makes sense only in its positive form
there is a *different* use or uses marked out in the dialogue in which negation comes into its own.[13] The hope offered by the Eleatic Stranger is that

---

[12] cf. Runciman, *Plato's Later Epistemology*, 65–6; Moravcsik, 'Being and Meaning in the
Sophist', 41; *contra*: W. Kamlah, 'Platons Selbstkritik im Sophistes', *Zetemata*, 33 (1963), 23
n. 1.
[13] Thus it will not do to suggest, as Moravcsik does ('Being and Meaning in the *Sophist*',
27–8), that when Plato says that we are now in as much confusion about being as about
not-being (250d5–e7) he means that the confusion about not-being is a puzzle about

any light thrown on either being or not-being will equally illuminate the other. And since he then sets himself to justify expressions of the form '*A* is not' only when they can be completed into '*A* is not *B*',[14] it is an incomplete use of the verb that we can expect to find vindicated in positive constructions too.

Let us call this assumption, that the one cannot be illuminated without the other, the Parity Assumption or, for short, PA. It has obvious affinities with the recommendation at *Parmenides* 135e8–36a2. And it governs the Eleatic Stranger's next proposal. 'Suppose on the other hand that we can get sight of neither: then we shall at any rate push the argument through, as creditably as we may, between both of them at once' (251a1–3). Since Campbell there has been general agreement on the sense of the words,[15] and no one is likely to explain the talk of pushing between being and not-being as a proposal to hold them apart and save only one. What is envisaged is that both may remain incomprehensible, and then the argument must get clear of both Scylla and Charybdis. (The project of dispensing with the verb 'to be' was after all an occupational temptation in Greek philosophy: witness *Tht.* 157b1–3 and Aristotle, *Ph.* 185[b]27–8.) So the PA is maintained. Logically it is the proper assumption; historically it is the appropriate reply to Parmenides.[16] It tells directly against the common

existence whereas the confusion about being is due to conflating the *other* uses of 'is' (p. 27 n. 1). It is in the lines immediately following those quoted by Moravcsik that Plato suggests that light thrown on the one will bring corresponding light to the other (250e7–251a3). Moravcsik thinks that the perplexity about being is introduced in 250a–e and not in the preceding 242b–249e because he takes the latter passage to be proving important theorems about existence. Yet one line of argument which would be integral to these 'proofs' (243c–244b) is represented by the Eleatic Stranger as identical with that which generates the puzzle in 250 (249e7–250a2). As for the Eleatic Stranger's supposed interest in proving existence to be indefinable, what he proposes, however tentatively, at 247e3–4 is a *definition* of *einai*, and not, as Cornford said (*Plato's Theory of Knowledge*, 238) and many have repeated, a 'mark' (*aliter* 'symptom', 'attempt to characterize', etc.). What he says, on the most natural interpretation, is 'I lay it down, as a *horon horizein* the things-that-are, that they are *nothing but* power'. Moreover, the context (247d2–e6) shows that he is improving on the materialists' attempt to *horizesthai ousian* (246b1), where Cornford rightly renders the verb as 'define'. For *horos* = 'definition', see e.g. *Phdr.* 237d1 (cf. c2–3), *Plt.* 266e1, 293e2; and of course the *horoi*, esp. 414d.

[14] This at least is common ground to those divided by the issue discussed on pp. 427–31 below.

[15] L. Campbell, *The* Sophistes *and* Politicus *of Plato* (Oxford, 1867), 136. Cornford (*Plato's Theory of Knowledge*, 251) objects that on this reading *hama* is redundant (251a3), and proposes to understand *amphoin* quite otherwise: 'we will force a passage through the argument *with both elbows at once*', a curiously irrelevant appeal to violence which leaves the *hama* far more nakedly redundant. The *hama* reinforces Plato's point: if both being and not-being stay intractable we must get clear of both at once.

[16] Whose project was, after all, to discount 'is-not' and retain 'is'; and his arguments are not to be met by distributing different senses of the verb between the two expressions; cf. nn. 5–6 above.

view of Plato's strategy. Some holders of that view have thought to see a way round it, but this can be blocked in the course of setting out another difficulty.

NEGATION AND CONTRARIETY

A second trouble for the received view is that Plato does not say that his problems about not-being come from understanding 'being' in a certain way; he says that they come from understanding 'not' in a certain way. On his showing, they are to be resolved, not by giving up a particular sense of the verb in negative constructions, but by giving up a confusion about negation.

Twice in setting his puzzles about not-being—once in each of the lines of argument projected in 236e1–2 and followed in the subsequent pages— the Eleatic Stranger gets his respondent to agree that what is not is the *contrary* of what is.[17] The sophist's teaching has been branded counterfeit and false. So, in the Greek idiom which is under scrutiny, he professes to deal in what is, but instead he retails and speaks of what is not (or of 'things that are not', by contrast with 'things that are'); and this is innocently equated with the contrary of what is. When the Eleatic Stranger comes to solve the paradoxes he picks on this as a cardinal mistake. When a negation sign is affixed to the verb 'to be' the expression no more signifies some contrary of being than the negation sign in 'not large' compels that expression to mean the contrary of large, i.e. small (257b1–c4). He returns to the point in his summing-up (258e6–7). So—and I shall accumulate more evidence for this later, for it is often tacitly denied—his argument is one from analogy. (In fact it is of the pattern subsequently explained in *Statesman* 277d–278e under the title of 'example', *paradeigma*.) It illuminates a troublesome case by a tractable parallel: it draws a comparison between affixing a negative to the verb 'to be' and affixing one to

---

[17] 240b5, d6–8: the puzzles are those of deceptive semblances and of falsehood, respectively. In the first statement of the puzzles (236e1–2), *alēthes* does duty for *on* in the problem of falsehood but not in that of semblances; in the development of the puzzles (cf. 240b5, d6–8) it is vice versa. Plato tries to assimilate the two lines of argument (pp. 438–9 below), so both appeals to a 'contrary of what is' are met by the reply in 257b3–c4, 258e6–259a1. Campbell (*The* Sophistes *and* Politicus *of Plato*, 96) rightly saw *tanantia tois ousi* as anticipating *tounantion tou ontos* of 256e6; Cornford (*Plato's Theory of Knowledge*, 212 n. 1) wanted to distinguish them and thereby to allow Plato's final account of falsehood to recognize 'things which are *contrary* to the facts'. But Plato's account (263b7–12) insists on the formula *ontōn hetera* and defends it by harking back to the argument of 256e–257a, which heralded the contrast between difference and contrariety.

a predicate such as 'large'.[18] Within the comparison the sense of the negated terms is not called in question. What it is designed to explain is the role of the negation sign itself.

Here again, then, Plato's diagnosis of his perplexity does not square with the usual view. But we have only the skeleton of an argument until we have explained the diagnosis, and this calls for two preliminary points to be made clear. First, I have represented Plato as concerned with affixing negatives to parts of sentences and not, as later logic accustoms us to expect, to whole sentences. This is clear from the text and needs no argument. But I have also spoken of negating the verb 'to be' and not only, as in Plato's illustration, of attaching a negative to the expression *on*, 'being'; and this needs explanation. 'Being' catches much of the Greek word's variety of use: it shifts between participle and collective noun and abstract noun in a way disheartening to philosophers. But in this context it is a participle. Plato is discussing the negating of predicates: he is comparing what it is to describe something as 'not large' with what it is to describe it as 'not-being'. And the preceding lines 256d11–257a6 show that this participial or pre-dicative use can be taken to represent other uses of the verb in which 'not' can be attached to it: to describe any thing or things as 'not-being' is just to say that it 'is not' or they 'are not'.[19] After all, the point of Plato's com-

[18] 'Whenever we speak of *not* being we don't mean some *contrary of* being; we just mean *different.*—How?—Just as whenever we call something not large: do you think then we mean *small* by our words, any more than we mean *middling*?—Surely not.' Need it be pointed out that this passage does *not* say that 'not large' means 'either middling or small', and hence does not introduce a new account of 'not', and of 'different', in terms of incompatibility? It says that 'small' has no more claim to be what 'not large' means than 'middling' has. Incompatibility has no place in Plato's explanation of falsehood either: see n. 30 below.

[19] For the purpose of this and later notes it will be useful to set out the relevant passage 256d11–e6. 'So it must be possible [a] for not-being to be, [b] in the case of change and more-over [c] in respect of all the kinds. For in respect of all of them the nature-of-difference renders each one [d] different from being, and so leaves it not-being; and thus we shall be right to describe them all, on the same terms, [e] as not-being and [f] on the other hand—since they partake in being—as being, and to say that they are ... Consequently, [g] for each of the forms *being* is multiple and *not-being* is countless in number.' The 'not-being' which appears in the singular in (d) is put into the plural in (e) and answered by the plural 'being' in (f), which is itself explained by 'that they are' (in *oratio obliqua*); so in these phrases 'being' is the partici-ple going proxy for finite uses of the verb. Moreover, since 'not-being' has been explained in the preceding lines 256d5–8 as equivalent to 'different from being', and (d) takes up this equa-tion, 'different from being' must also be understood as applying to any subject that is said *not to be.* There is a crux here. In the preceding argument change has been shown to be different from *rest*, from *the different*, and finally from *being* (255e11–14, 256a3–5, d5–8); and in these proofs of non-identity it is natural to take 'being' and the other terms as nouns, the names of abstract entities. Yet 256d–e is introduced as the immediate corollary of this passage, and the key expressions can hardly have shifted their roles so profoundly. I shall not pursue this problem beyond pointing out that the proofs of non-identity have consisted in showing the non-substitutability of *predicates* (252d6–10, 255a4–5, b8–c3, and on the interpretation given below, 256c8–d7), and that what 'being' must be in 256d–e is a *predicate.* Notice too that the conclu-sions in 256d–257a are said to apply to *all* forms, including 'being'.

parison is to clarify the perplexity about speaking of *what is not* or of *things that are not*. The verb is put in participial form here because Plato wants to draw a clear analogy with the negating of another predicate, 'large', but it is the negating of 'is' and 'are' that he is out to explain.

Moreover it is the incomplete '. . . is . . .' whose negation interests him. For the same preceding lines show that 'is/are not' and 'not-being' are being treated as fragments of predicates drawn from sentences of the form '*A* is/are not *B*' or phrases of the form 'not being *B*'.[20]

This being so, it will make for better understanding of Plato's comparison if it is reformulated by way of a distinction which Aristotle took up in his logic (*Int.* 19^{b}19–20; *APr.* 51^{b}5–10). It must be remembered that in Greek the negation sign is commonly prefixed to the verb, but that it can be shifted to precede and modify other parts of the sentence. Aristotle accordingly distinguishes (I) 'this not-is white' from (II) 'this is not-white'. The moral he draws from his distinction is unclear,[21] but Plato's point can be clarified by it. For, as applied to Aristotle's examples, I take his comparison to come to this: that in (I) the negative modifies the verb and so imports the notion of not-being, while in (II) it modifies the adjective and so imports the notion of not-white; and that just as in (II) the effect of the negative is not to produce an expression meaning the contrary of the negated term—calling a thing 'not white' does not relegate it to the other extreme, black—so in (I) saying that it 'not is' does not relegate it to another extreme from being. Thereby he clears the way for his stronger conclusion. 'Not large' does not *mean* 'small' any more than it *means* 'middling', 'not white' does not mean 'black' any more than it means 'grey'; but of course things that are not large or not white may be small or black just as they may be middling or grey. The conclusion he is leading to is that in one case this latter option is not open. With the verb 'to be' the negative construction not only does not mean the contrary (which is what the analogy was designed to show) but cannot even be applied to anything in

---

[20] See n. 19. When the *not-being* of (*a*) reappears in (*g*) it is said to be countless in number in the case of each form, and this is evidently to say that each form *is not* indefinitely many others. But (*g*) is presented as a conclusion of the preceding argument, in which change was expressly differentiated from just four other forms; so where has the Eleatic Stranger pointed out the availability of this vast range of fillings for 'not-being . . .' or 'is not . . .'? In (*c*), I think. Commonly (*b*) and (*c*) are rendered 'in the case not only of change but of all the other kinds'. But one would then expect the same preposition *epi* to cover (*b*) and (*c*); more importantly, the preposition used in (*c*) is repeated a few lines later (255a4–5) to introduce not the subject of 'is not' but the various complements for which it is true of the subject. So the argument is this: it has just been shown that change *is not* certain other kinds, and this can be generalized for the complement 'all other kinds', since the difference between *any* kind (*hekaston, sumpanta*) and any other can be established. Any 'differs from being, in respect of any other'.

[21] Cf. J. L. Ackrill, *Aristotle's* Categories *and* de Interpretatione (Oxford, 1963), 143–4.

the contrary state. For Plato, or his speakers in the dialogue, can find no intelligible contrary to being or to what is (258e6–259a1). But, he insists, this breeds no confusion in the notion of speaking of what is not. Those who try to justify the notion by searching for such a contrary, and equally those who make capital of the failure to find one, have just mistaken the sense of the negation.

This, then, is what remains to be explained in his diagnosis: the claim that there cannot be anything in a contrary state to being. His meaning is not hard to see, but one clue to it fails. Earlier in the dialogue change and rest were described as 'contrary' and 'most contrary' to each other (250a8, 255a12, b1), but it is debatable what relationship he means to hold between them. Most commentators have taken him to be denying just that the two are identical and that either is predicable of the other.[22] But these negative conditions seem to be satisfied not only by the pair large and small, which are his examples of contraries in 257b6–7, but by large and middling; and middling is his example of what is not large without being the contrary of large.

More light can be found in the treatment of large, middling, and small at *Prm.* 161d1–2. Here he exploits the familiar Greek idea of a middle state between contraries as containing something of both extremes.[23] What is middle-sized is not large, but it avoids smallness by having in it something, in a broad sense some proportion, of both large and small. And this is his point in the *Sophist*: to ascribe not-being to any subject—that is, in this context, to use 'is not' or some negative construction with the verb 'to be' in describing it—does not preclude ascribing some proportion of being to it—that is, saying that it 'is' so-and-so. Indeed, in the case of being, the negation turns out to be applicable only to subjects in the middle state. For Plato's analogy does no more than resume his previous arguments. The attempt to speak of what is not as *nothing*, a subject which is not anything at all, has broken down (237b–239b). Thereafter it has been shown, for some specimen 'kinds' of the highest rank, that there must be many things that each of them is as well as a still larger number that each is not (256e2–7),[24] and this is later assumed to hold good of all subjects of discourse (263b11–12). So those who take the negation of 'is' to import some contrary of being are those who try, hopefully or polemically, to construct a subject which for every predicate F is not F. This gives the correct sense to the expression 'is not *in any way*' which we noticed (Cornford's 'the

---

[22] Thus G. Grote, *Plato*, 3rd edn. (London, 1875), ii. 444; Taylor, *Plato: the* Sophist *and* Statesman, 53; *contra*: Moravcsik, 'Being and Meaning in the *Sophist*', 43–7.

[23] Cf. e.g. *Rep.* 478e1–5.   [24] On this difference in number, cf. pp. 443, 448 below.

totally non-existent' seems unintelligible), and relevance to the Eleatic Stranger's reply that any subject 'is in many ways as well as not being in many others' (259b5–6; cf. 237b7–8, 260d3).[25] What he has shown, in short, is that a subject must be identified and characterized as well as differentiated; and for Plato this presents itself as an exercise in the incomplete use or uses of 'is'.[26]

THE REDUCTIVE THESIS

Before interim conclusions are drawn, there is an objection to be met. Perhaps Plato does not wish to exploit an analogy between the variant elements in the sentences (I) and (II) which we borrowed from Aristotle. Perhaps his whole object in 257b1–c4 is to reduce (I) to (II) without remainder.

This reduction appears, unargued and at full strength, in Mr Crombie.

The view that negation signifies not 'the opposite' but 'the different' is the view that all statements assert that their subject partakes in existence, the function of negation being to locate the subject in some region of existence other than that part of it specified by the negated term. We might put this by saying that 'not' is logically hyphenated, not to the copula, but to the rest of the predicate; and that is what Plato almost does say in 257c when he speaks of 'not' signifying the opposite of the words to which it is prefixed and then goes on to take examples such as 'not large'.[27]

A footnote tries to make amends:

One cannot say that Plato actually makes the point which I say he almost makes, for the copula commonly is one of the words to which the 'not' is prefixed.[28]

Commonly indeed: the point is that it is so prefixed in *this* passage, both to the copula and to its proxy the participle. But let us shelve difficulties for the moment and notice how this reading of Plato's argument offers a way round the Parity Assumption.

Those who think that Plato is preoccupied with an existential sense of 'to be' in which the verb cannot be intelligibly negated might well claim,

---

[25] 'But if "*X* not-is" is elliptical in this way, surely a subject can exhibit the contrary of being: a black thing unqualifiedly-not-is white for instance.' In respect of white the black thing has the partial not-being which marks the lack of some attribute, to whatever degree; it cannot, in virtue of its relation to any predicate, have the total not-being which marks the lack of all attributes.

[26] Or in the vowel form 'being', one of the connectives which bring other forms into combination (253c1–2).

[27] *An Examination of Plato's Doctrines*, ii. 512.   [28] Ibid., n. 1.

on these terms, to acknowledge the PA. They might agree that, when we are led to expect a joint illumination (or joint eclipse) of being and not-being, it is the same concept of being that we can expect Plato to illuminate in positive and negative statements; but then, with one proviso, they might claim this to be just the concept represented by their non-negatable verb. The proviso is that in negative statements the negation sign is to be understood as detached from the verb and attached to one of its complements. Rewrite 'A isn't (sc. not-is) a greengrocer' as 'A exists as a non-greengrocer', and both assumptions seem to be saved. True, so far as Plato's argument is concerned the verb must now give up its connection with a one-place predicate. It must be read as '. . . exists as . . .' in negative statements and so, if even lip-service is to be paid to the PA, in positive statements too. But then we shall find that the one-place predicate was always a red herring. And in settling for the syntactically incomplete use as the existential verb this interpretation does avoid the absurdity (which I believe no commentator has entertained) of suggesting that A's failure to be a greengrocer is a sort of *non*-existence for A.

This reductive thesis will not do. Plato means his analogy and is ready to leave the negation sign annexed to the verb but, as he hopes, disarmed. But before seeing the thesis founder we must salvage what is true in it. It is true and important that, in the pages before Plato introduces his analogy, he has been showing on what terms something can be described as 'not-being' and has done so by proving the thing *different from*, and so *not*, various other things. He has confined his operations to certain 'greatest kinds' or, in practice, to the predicate expressions representing these kinds, and he has proved their non-identity mainly by the experiment of substituting the predicate expressions in context.[29] Subsequently, when he moves on from such negations of identity to considering falsehood in predicative statements, he builds on this earlier account of 'not-being' as grounded in difference-from-some-*X*. 'Theaetetus flies' says what-is-not about Theaetetus because what it says of him, viz. . . . *flies*, is *different from* all the predicates he does have—or, in the locution that 263b echoes from 256e, different from 'the many things that are with respect to him'.[30] So

---

[29] Cf. n. 19 above.

[30] This remains the simplest interpretation, requiring no shift in the sense of 'different' such as is sometimes found in 257b (cf. n. 18 above). To be sure, if it were taken as a rule for verifying or falsifying statements it would make falsification an interminable business, but this is not its function. If *X* is not beautiful, all *X*'s predicates fall into the class different-from-beautiful introduced at 257d4–e11. (For 'nature-of-the-beautiful' in this passage as equivalent to the predicate '(the) beautiful' and not to the abstraction 'beauty', cf. 257a9, 'the nature of the kinds' = 'the kinds' and similar periphrases at *Rep.* 429d; *Phdr.* 248c; etc.)

difference-from-some-X always is, or is contained in, the grounds on which Plato admits any subject as 'not-being'.

But it is never a ground on which he proposes to transfer the negative construction from the verb. The subject 'must be described as different from other things and consequently, in respect of all those other things, it *not-is*. For in *not-being* them it is its own single self but at the same time *not-is* all those countless others' (257a1–6, taken up more emphatically in 259b1–6: the subject, treated as representative of all the others, is Being or What-is). By such arguments he tries to show that 'not-is' calls for completion, and on what terms the completion is to be supplied. But he never professes to cut his knots by relieving his key verb of its negation sign. Otherwise his argument would be over by 257a instead of culminating, as it does, in the carefully worked analogy of 257b–259b. And its conclusion would be different and, considered as a device for saving existence propositions and disarming their negations, a distinct anticlimax.

Before mounting some larger objections to the reductive thesis it is worth noticing how it gets illicit help from Cornford's version. He renders the Eleatic Stranger's warning at 257b9–c3 correctly enough: 'So, when it is asserted that a negative signifies a contrary, we shall not agree, but admit no more than this: that the prefix "not" indicates something different from the words that *follow*—or rather from the things designated by the words pronounced *after* the negative' (my italics). Yet throughout the context he translates *to mē on* by 'what is not', reversing Plato's ordering of the last two words. So the innocent reader is led to suppose that Plato is concerned not at all with the negation sign as preceding and hence modifying the verb but only with its role in such sentences as (II).

But Plato's interest in his analogy is proved by more than the text that Cornford misdepicts. For we have seen, first, that he has a stronger conclusion in view: 'not-X' not only does not *mean* 'contrary-of-X' but in one case, that of the verb 'to be', cannot even be applied to a contrary, since no subject can be intelligibly relegated to a state contrary to being. But if 'not-being' is always to be recast in the form 'being not-X' there will be plenty of contraries to being. Finding them will be merely a matter of finding a contrary to the negated term. When *not-being* is *being not-large*, *being small* is the desiderated contrary.

Further, it is the analogy between negating 'being' and negating such terms as 'large' and 'beautiful' that governs the next stretch of the argument (257c5–258c5). The Eleatic Stranger observes that 'not beautiful' and 'not large' each mark off a real class on the basis of a particular difference: the first marks off what is other than beautiful, the second what is other than large.[31] He generalizes this for an indefinite range of values of 'not *X*' (258a4–10); and then he applies the generalization to the case of 'not-being' (258a11–b3).[32] The pattern of argument is brought out clearly in his conclusion (258b9–c3): 'We must have the nerve then to say that not-being certainly is something with its own nature, just as we agreed that large is large and beautiful is beautiful, and the same with not-large and not-beautiful: *in just the same way*, not-being *too* has turned out to be, and is, not-being—*one* sort of thing to be counted among the many sorts of things that are' (cf. 260b7). The being or reality ascribed here to sorts and classes will be taken up later. Our present business with the argument is that it shows Plato still pursuing his parallel. It is the effect of attaching a negation sign to the verb 'to be' that he wants to explain, and he is still explaining it by analogy with, and not by reduction to, the negating of any grammatical complements the verb may carry.

So the non-negatable use of 'to be' is nowhere in view, and the Parity Assumption is not diluted to accommodate such a use. Our interim conclusion stands firm: Plato's account of his strategy tells directly against two theses basic to current views of the dialogue. The one is that he wants to signal a sense of the verb in which it cannot be straightforwardly and intelligibly negated; the other is that he represents his troubles about not-being as due to taking the verb in a certain sense rather than (as in fact he does)

---

[31] At 257e2–4 *allo ti* is often construed as the interrogative *nonne*, but a question answering another question does not need such a prefix (e.g. 257d6–7) and the sentence does not then lead directly to the conclusion in 257e6–7, that 'not beautiful' represents a contrast between two things-that-are: so the antithesis must be *allo ti tōn ontōn—pros ti tōn ontōn*. Again, it is often assumed that what not-beautiful is 'marked off from' (*aphoristhen*) is the same as what it is 'contrasted with' (*antitethen*), which leaves a pointless repetition; what it is marked off from is the whole class *different* under which it falls (cf. 229c1–3, 231b3–4, 268d1–2; so too 257c11); what it is contrasted with is *beautiful*. Thus 'One of the things that are, marked off from a given class (the different) and moreover contrasted with one of the things that are (the beautiful)— is this what the not-beautiful turns out to be? ... So the not-beautiful turns out to be a contrast between one thing that is and another thing that is.' I have shifted between the predicate expression 'beautiful' and the class description 'the beautiful': for the not-beautiful to be is for it to be marked out by a particular difference, viz. from the beautiful, and this comes to more than saying (though it certainly includes saying) that the sense of the predicate 'not beautiful' is given by this difference: Plato is also assuming that the predicate has application (cf. pp. 447–8 below).

[32] Since he is still concerned with the effect of negating the verb we are not to supply *moriou* with Campbell (*The* Sophistes *and* Politicus *of Plato*) at 258b1: that is the reductive thesis. Similarly at 258e2 *hekaston* is better taken with *morion* (cf. 257c11: so Diès *et al.*) than with *on* (Campbell), but interposing *hekaston* between article and noun is poor practice. Accordingly I accept the *hekastou* of all MSS. (Stallbaum's often repeated claim that Simplicius 'preserved the correct reading, *hekaston*' is quite misleading: Simplicius, *Ph.* 238. 26 reads *hekaston* but the first transcription at 135. 26 has *hekastou*). The sense here is: 'that part of the different which is contrasted with the being of any subject is not-being': '*X* is . . .' expresses *X*'s being, and the negation of this imports that part of the different which is contrasted with *X*'s being. For some complement, *X* is different-from-being . . .

to taking the negation in a certain sense. In short, there is no hint that any sense of the key verb must be dropped or modified between positive and negative constructions, or between the opening puzzles and the subsequent explanations. What then of the commentators' existential verb? Plato's clarifications of 'not-being' are a study in the syntactically incomplete 'is', and so long as the reductive treatment of the negation sign was taken to be part of his strategy it was possible to read the 'is' as 'exists'. But it is not part of his strategy; he does not offer to detach the negative from the verb it modifies, only to show grounds for its attachment and bring out its sense by parallels. And I assume without more argument that no one will read these exercises in 'not-being' as an attempt to explain the *non*-existence of motion and rest and the other kinds. So the concept of being that he takes himself to be elucidating here is not that of existence. By Parity, it cannot be an existential sense of 'to be' that he means to isolate and explain in positive constructions either. If the Chimaera rears its head in the dialogue, it is in the shape of the familiar interpretation from which we set out. It is time to reconsider our original reason for accepting that interpretation: the equation of 'what is not' with 'nothing' in Plato's puzzles, which persuaded us that by 'what is not' he here meant 'what does not exist'.

THE SUBJECT NOTHING

(*a*) Plato equates 'what is not' with 'nothing'; (*b*) 'nothing' is equivalent to 'what does not exist'. Can either claim be upset?

1. Perhaps too much weight was put on (*a*). The Eleatic Stranger sets out his puzzles about not-being in five stages, and of these only the first makes any play with 'nothing'. But the first is the puzzle of falsehood in its old form, using 'what is not' without suggesting that its very use is logically incoherent. That suggestion is argued through the second and third stages, but by that time 'nothing' has left the scene. So the equation plays no part in the argument it was used to interpret.

This objection fails, but it is prompted by a distinction of the first importance. I discuss it by way of making that distinction clear.

Briefly and provisionally, the stages of the Eleatic Stranger's puzzle are as follows; I shall come back to the assumptions which control them later. (i) 237b7–e7 is a version of the familiar paradox.[33] 'What is not' stands for nothing, hence speaking of what is not = speaking of nothing = not

---

[33] But the version already contains the seeds of a transformation, cf. pp. 433–4 below.

speaking at all. (So, if speaking falsely is speaking of what is not, there is no such speaking as false speaking; but the application is not made here.) (ii) 238a1–c11 tries for conclusions that have *what is not* as their express subject. Since what is not cannot have any actual attributes, it cannot have any number nor therefore be one or many of anything, yet to speak or think of it we have to refer to it in the singular or the plural; so it eludes our references and cannot be spoken or thought of. But by this reliance on the material mode (ii) undermines itself. (iii) 238d1–239c8 points out that according to (ii) the argument and conclusion of (ii) cannot be consistently formulated. If it proves anything, it proves that no subject of discourse can be introduced under the description 'what is not' or 'what are not'. So the Eleatic Stranger's inquiry has no subject and threatens to vanish without trace.

The remaining two stages (239c9–240c6, 240c7–241b3) bring no new arguments for the incoherence of 'what is not'. With them the strategy shifts, in a way reminiscent of the second part of the *Parmenides*, from negative arguments terminating in philosophical frustrations and silence to a positive display of contradictions which must somehow be swallowed if sense is to be made of counterfeits and falsehoods.[34] These are not our present business.

What is the connection between (i) and the two stages which follow it? First, it is obviously not the job of (ii) to challenge (i) in the way that (iii) upsets (ii). No doubt (i) deserves challenge: it interprets its thesis, that 'what is not' stands for nothing, simply as allowing the substitution of 'nothing' for 'what is not' while keeping both expressions in use.[35] So it seems open to the charge of attempting what it claims to be impossible—speaking of what is not. But (ii) also keeps 'what is not' in use and indeed makes its role as a referring expression central. Its claim to deal with the 'very basis of the argument'[36] means that it picks out *what is not* as its formal subject, where (i) had framed its conclusion in terms of *speaking of what is not*. About this subject it seems to argue for much the same conclusion as that which (i) had reached by its equation between 'what is not' and 'nothing'.

But if (ii) does not challenge (i), it does not seem to build on it either: and this is what suggests that (i) is merely superseded in the argument. (ii) leaves the important equation in silence, and (iii) follows suit: it makes no

---

[34] In the *Sophist*, unlike the *Parmenides*, these stages lead to the positive proposal to disarm the paradoxes (241d1–242b5). This seems the correct moral to draw for the *Parmenides* too.

[35] 237e4–6 is not of course a recommendation to drop the expression 'nothing', but a claim that speaking of nothing is not speaking at all.

[36] *Peri autēn autou tēn archēn*, sc. *tou logou* (cf. 237e7): at 233e1–3 Theaetetus fails to understand *tēn archēn tou rhēthentos* because he does not understand the subject of discussion, *panta*.

play with 'nothing' and concentrates its attack on (ii). The effect is to make (ii) and (iii) appear a self-contained pair, providing between them all the material for the *Sophist*'s new problem: the problem, namely, whether sense can be made of those expressions 'what is not' and 'what are not' which had been so artlessly used in describing and debating falsehood. (ii) introduces them as carrying a reference, (iii) replies that on (ii)'s interpretation of them no reference has been made. This is what prompts the notion that the treatment of the key verb which leads to the impasse in (iii) is not to be explained by drawing on (i). 'To be', as any account of the dialogue shows, is a versatile source of mischief; in (i) the Eleatic Stranger pays respect to one veteran puzzle which can be got from negating the verb, and it is common opinion that this is a puzzle about non-existent subjects of discourse. But if it is quietly shelved in stating the new paradox, we need not assume this or its solution to turn on an existential use of the verb. And if such a switch of sense seems violent, the objector has a defence. After all, the conventional interpretation requires Plato to drop the existential sense of 'what is not' between the puzzles and the solution. It is only an improvement on this to suggest that the sense is dropped in the course of the puzzles and before the substantial problem is set at all.

I said that this objection would serve to introduce a major distinction. What it grasps or half-grasps is that the argument which culminates in (iii) has transformed the old perplexity about speaking of what is not: that it is an anachronism to read the *Sophist* as answering the *Theaetetus*' problem in the *Theaetetus*' terms. Even the *Euthydemus* and the *Cratylus*, which debate the possibility of falsehood expressly in terms of fitting words to the world, use such locutions as 'what is not' without ever asking whether *these* are capable of coherent use.[37] The *Sophist* by contrast proceeds on the view that if and only if we can understand the proper use of 'what is not' and some related expressions, we shall understand—understand philosophically—the situations those expressions are commonly invoked to explain. When it turns to query the tools which had been taken for granted in constructing the old puzzles, it carries the mark of Plato's maturity. It ranks with, and because it offers solutions it goes beyond, the study of 'participation' in the *Parmenides*.

It is also true that the first stage of its argument reads in part (237e1–6) like a mere echo of the old puzzle. If speaking of what is not is speaking of nothing, it is not speaking at all: why? The *Theaetetus* has already

---

[37] The *Cratylus* at 429d, unlike the *Euthydemus*, uses *mē to on* (and not *to mē on*) *legein*, but he other expression is implied by 385b10.

supplied one analogy (188e3–189a14): seeing nothing is not seeing, hearing and touching nothing are not hearing or touching (188e2–189a14).

Beyond this the objection miscarries. No doubt (i) ends by settling for a version of the old paradox, with the key expressions still unassailed; but it begins by asking the *Sophist*'s question, and the answer it gives controls the following stages. 'Suppose one of this company had to give a serious and studied answer to the question, *What is the proper application of the name "what is not"*? Of what thing and what sort of thing should we expect him to use it, and what would he point out to his questioner?' (237b10–c4, recalled at 250d7–8).[38] And the answer, that 'what is not' = 'nothing', is only verbally absent thereafter. It is surely this equation that (ii) is designed to reinforce by its independent proof that what is not cannot be one or more of anything (238a5–b5). The puzzle is converted into one about reference when (ii) deduces that, since what is not (*i.q.* nothing) does not give us even one thing to mention, it is unmentionable (238b6–c10). And it is the incoherence of this conclusion, and therewith of the original answer, that is shown by (iii).

So the first of the two claims stands firm. The equation with 'nothing' cannot be dislodged from the puzzles. We must shift to the second: the claim that 'nothing' is equivalent to 'what does not exist' or, more exactly, that Plato could not set and solve puzzles about the former without supposing that his puzzles were about the latter. We have a distinction in hand now that will defeat this second conjunct.

2. Let us try adapting a Platonic argument to show that the non-existent is not the same as nothing. If I talk or think of centaurs I am not talking or thinking of nothing, for then I should not be talking or thinking at all. If I tell Theaetetus he has taken wing I speak of a non-existent flight, but not of nothing. Plato's discussion of 'is not' in the *Parmenides* (160b6–161a5; countered at 163c2–d1) suggests that he has an approximation to this distinction in view. But as a help to grasping his intentions in the *Sophist* it is open to objection, and it is worth distinguishing objections from two different points of view. One, to put it broadly, is that of the *Theaetetus*, the other is that of the *Sophist*.

The form of the puzzle which is found in the *Theaetetus* seems to depend on obliterating just this distinction. Speaking of something is not distinguished from saying something, and the speaking is compared to seeing or touching, as though the words had content to the extent that they made contact with the actual situation (189a3–10). In falsehood the speaker does not touch anything: where there should be the flight ascribed to

---

[38] A syntactically confused text; but the sense is not in question.

Theaetetus,[39] there is no such object for the words to hit. There are primitive assumptions about language in Plato which reinforce this view from a consideration of words rather than of speakers. Words are given their purchase on the world by being used to name parts of it, and names, or the basic names to which others are variously reducible, are simple proxies for their nominees.[40] Thus falsehood at its simplest, for instance in the presence of the falsifying situation, becomes as vacuous as calling 'Stetson!' when Stetson is not there, or pointing at vacancy.[41] These assumptions have been too often studied in Plato to need expansion here, and I take them to be modified at an essential point in the *Sophist*. In due course I shall argue (pp. 450–3 below) that the modification does not make use of an existential sense of 'to be': it does not need an existential sign. But there is no blinking the fact that for us Plato's puzzle in the *Theaetetus* seems to consist just in the non-existence of what falsehoods speak of, and that this is apparently what he expresses there by the phrase 'speaking of nothing'.

Now the *Sophist*. Is it true that if I talk or think of nothing I do not think or talk at all? I seem to be able to do the first without ceasing to talk, for I have just done it: I have been asking whether *nothing* is to be identified with *what does not exist*. To meet the *Theaetetus* puzzle we needed a distinction between the case in which there isn't anything being talked about and that in which what is talked about is a fictitious animal or an imaginary situation; now we seem to need a distinction between the case in which there isn't anything being talked about and that in which there is something that is talked about, viz. nothing. Let us for the moment, with Plato's leave, assume these distinctions: let us say that we can speak of mythical centaurs or chimerical flights (which I think Plato does not wish to deny), and that we can also speak of nothing without ceasing to speak (which I take him to be denying). How shall we show that these do not come to the same thing?

---

[39] Or perhaps the flying Theaetetus or the fact-that-Theaetetus-flies: the original puzzle notices no such distinctions, but the suggestion that the false statement says what-is-not *about* something (*Tht.* 188d2, 9–10) implies that what is missing is the flight. This squares with the implication of *Tht.* 190b2–4 that if *X* is beautiful and I call it ugly what I do is misidentify the *beautiful*; what misfires is the predicate word 'ugly'. For an interesting attempt to reimport Theaetetus-flying, on the strength of a construction with some verbs of perceiving (though not with 'touching', and not with verbs for saying or believing), see D. R. P. Wiggins's paper 'Sentence Meaning, Negation, and Plato's Problem of Non-Being', in G. Vlastos (ed.), *Plato*, i (Garden City, NY, 1971), 268–303. See too Furth's discussion, 'Elements of Eleatic Ontology', 123–4.

[40] Thus e.g. *Tht.* 201e1–202b5 and the thesis pursued in *Cra.* 391a–428e.

[41] At *Cra.* 429e ff. Socrates accepts the 'Stetson' analogy and offers to vindicate falsehood on these terms, but in effect he does so by distinguishing the conditions for making a reference (looking towards, pointing, etc.) from the actual use of the name; I shall argue that the *Sophist*'s final account of falsehood is a more sophisticated version of this distinction (pp. 451–2 below).

Well, we can describe our centaurs. They have hooves, not fishtails; they are made of flesh and blood, not tin; and they are fictitious, not found in Whipsnade Zoo. Similarly with the flying done by Theaetetus: it can be described, and indeed must be if we are to know what we are rejecting as false. But suppose we are asked to describe the *nothing* that we have been talking about: then there seems to be no description at all available for it. It is not (to put an instance) a horse, for it can't be added to another horse to make two of them. In discourse the function of 'nothing', like that of 'nobody' and 'nowhere' and 'never', is just to indicate that there isn't as much as one of whatever it may be. This is a point that Plato drums home for his *what is not* when he equates it with *nothing* in the *Republic* (478b) and in stage (i) of the *Sophist*'s perplexity, and (ii) reinforces it. It can seem an unremarkable point or, as Plato makes it seem in the *Sophist*, astonishing and indeed unintelligible. It is unsurprising if we reflect that expressions such as 'nothing' were coined to block gaps that would otherwise be filled by references to one or more of whatever sort of thing is in question. It becomes baffling if we insist that if Nothing can be spoken of it must conform to the rules for those subjects of discourse that it is designed to displace: that is, if we ask Plato's question 'What is the application of this name, "what is not"? Of what and of what sort of thing should we expect a man to use it?' and then identify What is not with Nothing. For this is to require that if Nothing is to be mentionable it must establish its credentials as a logical subject, identifiable and describable: we must be able to say that it is a so-and-so, and which so-and-so it is. Yet the more we miscast Nothing as such a subject and ignore its role as a subject-excluder, the more we run into those paradoxes flagged by Plato and after him by Frege and Quine.[42] We find ourselves unable to say, not only that it is one or more of anything, but what it *is* at all (238e5–239a2).

Plato's question, then, sets strong conditions for reference. Naturally it produces (anyhow temporary) bafflement when it is applied to Nothing. The word seems to flout the basic requirements of accidence: a singular term, framed to exclude singular reference. But if this were the sole claim of the paradox on philosophers' interest it could long ago have been stored with the other phlogiston of the subject. 'Nothing', we could say, is only parasitically singular, taking the size of the gap it blocks; it dissolves into 'not even: one thing'. If in consequence its role in the language cannot be

---

[42] *Translations from the Philosophical Writings of Gottlob Frege*, ed. P. T. Geach and M. Black (Oxford, 1955), 83: 'The answers "never", "nowhere", "nothing" . . . to the questions "when?", "where?", "what?" . . . are not proper answers but refusals to answer, which have the form of an answer.' They are not of course refusals either; merely designed to show that there is no answer.

explained as a name or description under which references can be made, so much the more reason for seeking other models of explanation. But in fact the paradox has no independent importance in Plato's argument. His aim is to show that when 'what is not' is correctly understood the *Sophist*'s question *can* be answered. The impression that it cannot is produced by identifying, as the sophist tries to, 'what is not' with 'nothing'; and I have argued that Plato's subsequent diagnosis makes it certain, for the *Sophist* at least, how he wants to understand this identification. It introduces not a special sense of the verb but a special mistake about negating it. It comes to equating 'what is not' not with 'what does not exist' but with 'what is not anything, what not-in-any-way is': a subject with all the being knocked out of it and so unidentifiable, no subject. As the scope of the negation is cleared up, so it becomes clear that anything can and must 'be many things as well as not being many others'. The answer to the *Sophist*'s question— the original question, let me insist: not an impostor smuggled in by switching the sense of the verb—is not 'nothing' but 'anything whatever considered as differentiable from other things'. And the answer (or part of the answer) to the sophist's puzzle about falsehood is that his diagnosis imports an unintelligible term: but not the term on which the commentators pitched.

How much or little do these considerations prove? They prove, I think, that it is possible to raise puzzles about Nothing without confusing them with puzzles about non-existence. They show that the *Sophist*'s question brings these puzzles to the fore of the discussion so as to lead naturally to that study of subject–predicate syntax and of the connective '. . . is . . .' which Plato does undertake. They leave the way open to the sole interpretation I can find which squares with the evidence already canvassed and does not accuse Plato of grossly missing or misrepresenting his own strategy.

And they leave Plato's argument a piece of successful pioneering in its chosen territory and not a lame attempt to evade a problem about non-existence by, in Cornford's phrase, 'ruling out' an accepted sense of a word in one construction. Teachers of logic generally spend time explaining how substitution instances are supplied for the constituents of the formulae (Fa) and (Ra,b) before they introduce $((\exists x)Fx)$ or $((\exists G)Ga)$ or any expressions for individual existence. Nor do they mention existence among the requirements for the terms of such elementary propositions. Plato's study is earlier than formal logic and concerned with far more than the construction of formulae, but it can be read as the earliest exercise at the level of those initial explanations. It is essentially preliminary to, and not based on, the isolation or construction of the difficult notion 'exist'.

Before following out this suggestion it may be as well to make one disclaimer. I am not arguing that Plato never, or never in the *Sophist*, uses the verb *einai* in such a way that 'exist' is a natural English translation. No doubt he does. What I hope to show is that the central arguments and explanations become broken-backed if they are read as containing an implicit or explicit separation of such a sense of 'is' from others. But so far the interpretation leaves a good deal of unfinished business. I proceed to detail what seem the main difficulties it faces and then, as best I can, to meet them.

EXISTENCE REIMPORTED

1. It can be argued on the following grounds that the problem set in the central section of the dialogue can be solved only by isolating an existential use of the verb.

The sophist, unless he is that mere sophist whom Dr Peck regarded as deserving only treatment in kind,[43] might well feel that a substantial child has gone with the bathwater. Given greater articulateness he might complain that it is all very well to save the locution 'speaking of what is not' by proving it capable of carrying an intelligible reference at the point where the sophist's translation of it is not. But how was he ever induced to suppose, or to try to say, that false speaking is speaking about a non-subject? Surely because what it speaks about does not exist because there just is not the correlate in the world for the false words to express?

And the Eleatic Stranger's puzzles recognize this existential concern. They have been under-described until all the assumptions and problems are set out. In particular, consider the assumption on which (ii) relies to prove that what is not is nothing, i.e. not one or more of anything. It lays it down (238a7–9, c5–6; cf. 241b1–3) that something that is cannot be attached to what is not, and interprets this to mean that what is not cannot have any of the attributes that are, such as number. What is this but the hatstand model of predication: actual hats cannot be hung on non-existent pegs?

Again, stages (iv) and (v) await description. The sophist has been denounced for offering only semblances of the things he claims to purvey, and making false claims in doing so (cf. 236e1–3). So he both purveys, and

[43] A. L. Peck, 'Plato and the *Megista Genē* of the *Sophist*: A Reinterpretation', *Classical Quarterly*, NS 2 (1952), 32–56: my 'sophist' is no doubt a fiction but represents positions that (*pace* Dr Peck) Plato takes seriously and tries to meet.

states, what is not instead of what is. But in both cases this contrast between what is and what is not can be made problematic. (iv) (239c9–240c6) discusses semblances, and its language (esp. the recurrent *alēthinon* in 240a7–b8) makes in natural to interpret the verb 'to be' here as 'to be real'. What distinguishes a semblance of *A* from *A* itself? Well, *A* is real, the semblance is not (in fact 'in no way real, the *contrary* of real'). Yet surely it really is what it is, a semblance? A real unreal, then, which upsets the incompatibility of what is and what is not which we seemed to assume in denouncing the sophist. (v) (240c7–241b3) discusses falsehoods. False thinking is thinking that what is is not (in fact 'the contrary of what is'), and vice versa; but this diagnosis has to mention what is not as though it had being (241b1–2). Or, to supply the usual interpretation, it professes to refer to just that non-existent state of affairs which the man with false belief supposes to exist.

'To be real', 'to exist': such a confusion is one which Plato has the terminology to avoid, for 'real' can be turned by the word *alēthinon* as it is in (iv), and this word does not naturally go proxy for other uses of the verb 'to be'. Instead Plato seems to do what he can to strengthen the confusion, stretching the same formula to cover the paradoxes of both (iv) and (v) (240c3–5, 241b1–2, d6–7) and ultimately reducing the problem of unreality to that of falsehood (264c10–d5). The conflation can be left as a puzzle to those who believe that in his metaphysics Plato must and can readily divide reality from existence.[44] It does not weaken the point I have to meet. The picture of the argument just given seems to show that its assumptions and problems do not hinge on the connective '. . . is . . .' which carries no expressly existential sense but serves as copula or identity sign. The senses of the verb that seem to be required are those conventionally associated with the one-place predicate '. . . is'. So it is surely this use of the verb, in which it signifies existence or reality, that Plato must pick out for scrutiny if he is to dissolve his puzzles about not-being.

The same moral can be drawn from the puzzles about being which succeed them (242b–250e); for now an enquiry is broached into the number and nature of real things (242c5–6). We have seen that the two lines of perplexity are linked in 250e5–6. So it is the same use of the verb that asks to be picked out and clarified here.

2. Next, it will be argued that not only Plato's problems but his positive conclusions compel him to distinguish this use of the verb. For (*a*) it is

[44] Vlastos, 'A Metaphysical Paradox' and 'Degrees of Reality in Plato'. Since Plato here conflates 'to be' with 'to be real' and since Vlastos takes the second in Plato to mark a two-place predicate distinct from existence, the interpretation I shall propose can be read as a corollary of his thesis.

surely the existence (or else the reality) of change for which he is contending in 248e6–249b3, and which he thereafter assumes (250a11–12, b9,
254d10, 256a1). And (*b*) it is surely the existence (or reality), first of the
not-beautiful and not-large, and then of what-is-not itself, which is the
burden of the argument in 257d12–258e5. And finally (*c*) there is the explanation of falsehood itself (261d–263d). It seems common doctrine that here
he 'assumes that, whatever statements are about, if they are about anything they are about something that exists'.[45] Is not this, after all, the moral
of the exercise: that to speak falsely is not to make the vain attempt to
mention what does not exist, but rather to mention something that does
exist and ascribe to it real properties which are, however, different from
the real properties it possesses? Is not this his way of satisfying the 'hatstand' assumption which controls stage (ii) of the first puzzles?

3. That Plato does expressly mark off the existential use of the verb
which his reasoning should force him to recognize has been argued in this
way.[46]

First, he seems prepared to distinguish two *incomplete* uses of the verb,
that in which it couples subject and predicate ('this is fragile') and that in
which it marks an identity ('that is Socrates'). The section of the dialogue
in which the distinction is drawn is introduced by a puzzle to which it is
directly relevant (251a5–c2). Some opsimaths have failed to understand
how one thing can have various appellations, for instance how anything
can be called not only a man but good; and the common and plausible
diagnosis of their confusion is that they have mistaken the different predications for different and competing statements of identity.[47] The appropriate distinction is then made in 256a7–b4. The Eleatic Stranger proposes
to explain how we can say that a thing is *F* and yet is not *F*, when by the
first arm of the statement we mean to ascribe an attribute to it and by the
second we mean to deny that it is identical with the attribute ascribed. His
explanation is that in the first case the thing 'partakes of *F*' whereas in the
second it 'shares in (*i.q.* partakes of) difference which severs it from *F*'.

---

[45] Moravcsik, 'Being and Meaning in the *Sophist*', 41.

[46] Most explicitly by J. L. Ackrill, 'Plato and the Copula', 1. Disagreement with Ackrill's
express conclusion, that Plato wants to mark off different senses of 'is', does not at all carry disagreement on his substantial issue, that Plato succeeds in distinguishing predications from statements of identity.

[47] To this it is irrelevant whether 'man is man' and 'good is good' are the sole legitimate forms
of statement in their object language or whether these are the sole forms admitted in their meta
language to justify some analysis (e.g. atomistic) of their object language. It is irrelevant too
(though important for other issues) whether they had any grasp of such distinctions (cf. G
Prauss, *Platon und der logische Eleatismus* (Berlin, 1966), 184). What they reject, wittingly or
unwittingly and on some level of discourse, is predication: 'they do not allow anything to be
called another thing by sharing in the other's character' (252b9–10).

These formulae are not expressly proffered as analyses of the verb 'to be'; still it seems reasonable to infer that Plato regards the verb in its copulative use as requiring the analysis 'partaking of . . .', but in its identifying use as requiring the analysis 'partaking of identity relatively to . . .' (or, in the negative form discussed by the Eleatic Stranger, 'partaking of difference relatively to . . .').

If this is so the context seems to give us yet a third way of analysing or paraphrasing out the verb. At 256a1, for instance, the Eleatic Stranger remarks that 'change is, by *partaking in being*' (*esti dia to metechein tou ontos*). Since this formula did not occur in the previous analyses and since unlike the others it seems to make '. . . is' a one-place predicate, it arguably should represent a third sense of 'to be'. What can this be but the existential sense?

4. Finally, the existential meaning appears to be marked off once more at 255c8–d8, where the Eleatic Stranger is distinguishing being from difference.

I think you agree that there are two ways in which we speak of 'things that are': in some cases we call them so in their own right (*auta kath' hauta*), in some cases we call them so with reference to other things (*pros alla*); but 'the different' is only ever so called with reference to something different (*pros heteron*). This would not be the case if being and difference were not quite distinct things; if difference partook of both characters as being does, the class of different things would sometimes contain a thing that was different but not relatively to something different from it.

It is commonly said that here Plato is representing being as both 'absolute' and 'relative', while difference is only 'relative';[48] and that what he means is just that, while the description of a thing as 'different' is always an incomplete description, awaiting some further reference to complete it, the description of something as 'being' or as 'what is' does not in one use of that expression call for any completion. And this latter use, the use in which one can say of something that *it is* and leave it there, is surely the existential use.

So far as I know, and as forcefully as I can put them, these are the considerations which have led scholars to ignore the troubles attending any version of the established interpretation. I must try now to show that they are misleading. Of the four heads of argument, (1) and (2) profess to prove that Plato could not help but notice the importance to his discussion of

[48] For the list of those who have said so, from Wilamowitz on, see now Frede, *Prädikation nd Existenzaussage*, 22; he could have gone back to Campbell, *The* Sophistes *and* Politicus *of lato*, 152. An old comment of mine to the same effect ('A Proof in the *Peri Ideōn*', ch. 9 in *ogic, Science and Dialectic*, 172 n. 25) has been taken as supporting evidence by Moravcsik nd Runciman *inter alios*, and pp. 444–6 below, are addressed to them by way of apology. The mment was retracted in 'Snares of Ontology'.

picking out an existential sense of the verb 'to be'. (3) and (4) profess to show that he expressly made this distinction. So (3) and (4) make the stronger claim, and I take them first.[49]

THE EXPLICIT DISTINCTION

*3. The appeal to the expression 'partaking in being' can properly be met by the reminder that Plato also uses 'partaking in not-being' (*metechein tou mē ontos*, 260d7; *koinōnein tou mē ontos*, 260e2–261a1) and plainly does not mean this to signify non-existence or mark a one-place predicate.[50] But without reliance on Parity the same point can be proved of the positive expression. When it occurs in the *Parmenides*, for instance, it is evidently not pre-empted for existential being.[51] And (lest this be set down as another chicanery of the *Parmenides*) we can bring it home to the *Sophist*. That the phrase can be used of that connective '. . . is . . .' which I have alleged to be at the heart of Plato's investigation is proved by 259a6–8. The Eleatic Stranger sums up his argument about the Different: it 'partakes in being, and is by virtue of that partaking—but not the thing of which it partakes but something different'. The verb in the last clause must be supplied from its predecessor, and the verb supplied is the incomplete 'is'. (To be sure, the reductivists hoped to save an existential sense for the incomplete 'is' without engaging Plato in a study of denials of existence. But their thesis depended on displacing the negative, and that is a past issue.)

Now consider the formula 'partaking in being' as it occurs at 256a1. It is embedded in a stretch of reasoning (255e8–256e6) whose results are summarized, with the help of the same formula, at 256d11–e6. The reasoning was sketched under (3): it consists in showing, for various general terms P, that with a certain proviso a specimen subject (in this case Change) can be said both to be P and not to be P. The proviso is that the pattern of analysis of 'This is P' varies in the two cases: in Plato's examples, the positive statement is predicative and the negative is a denial of identity. The Eleatic Stranger concludes:

[49] They have now been ably debated by Frede, *Prädikation und Existenzaussage*, 55–9 an 12–29, but I retain my own replies as making a few different points of controversial interest.

[50] What it does mean to say that *logos* partakes in not-being is obscure until *logos* is replace by *to legomenon* (much as *kinēsis* and *stasis* had to be replaced in the non-identity proo by *kineitai* and *hestēke* or *kinoumenon* and *hestos*; 250c6–d2, 252d6–10). *What is said*, in falsehood, *is not*: that is, about some subject one says what is not in the sense explained abov (p. 428 and n. 30 above).

[51] Among many occurrences, note 141e7–14, 161e3–162b8, 163b6–d1, 163e6–164a1.

So not-being necessarily *is* in the case of change, and with respect to all the kinds,[52] for with respect to them all difference makes each one different from what is, and so makes it what is not. Hence it is in just the same way that we can correctly describe them all as 'not being' and on the other hand (since they partake of being) say that they 'are' and describe them as 'being' ... So, [the Eleatic Stranger goes on] in the case of each of the forms, the being is multiple and the not-being is countless in number.

'The being is multiple, the not-being is countless': I shall come back to this distinction in number, but a little must be said of it now. Briefly, the Eleatic Stranger has been arguing concerning a specimen subject that it is, predicatively, many things, but that it is not identical with these things. So it *is not*, as a matter of identity, all those things which it *is* predicatively. But in addition to this it is not, as a matter of identity, countless things which it is also *not* predicatively. (Greed is one of the things which change is not identical with, but neither is it a possible attribute of change.) So if 'This is *P*' is understood predicatively and 'This is not *P*' is understood as a denial of identity, there are countless more things that anything is not than that it is. That the Eleatic Stranger has been dividing the positive and negative occurrences of the verb in this way seems clear enough, and I shall suggest a reason later. Meantime the distinction does not affect our argument. The use of the verb 'to be' on which the Eleatic Stranger rests his conclusion is the connective use, distributed between identity and predication. So he can fairly claim that 'it is in just the same way (*kata tauta*, i.e. by finding an appropriate complement) that we can correctly describe them all as "not-being" and—since they partake of being—as "being"'. And to clinch his meaning the Eleatic Stranger at once refers to the multiple being and countless not-being of any of the forms he has been discussing. He means that (as Cornford's version paraphrases it) 'there is much that each *is* and an indefinite number of things that it *is not*'.

So to extract any express recognition of a substantive or existential use of 'is' from this passage would not square with the argument. The formula 'partaking of being' is not used to mark this distinction in the summary of the discussion at 256e3 (or therefore in the preceding lines 256d8–9). Nor, as we saw, is it so used in 259a6–8. It cannot therefore have this task in the argument's opening move at 256a1. Whether the words 'change is' are read as a fragment of the preceding 'change is different from rest' (255e11–12)[53] or as elliptical for 'change is with respect to something' (i.e. is instantiated, the converse of participation: 256e5, 263b11–12, and p. 447 below), fragmentary or elliptical they surely are in Plato's view.

---

[52] On the interpretation of this, see nn. 19–20 above.
[53] cf. Frede, *Prädikation und Existenzaussage*, 56–7.

'Partaking in being', then, is not pre-empted for ascribing unqualified being to any subject. But once it is put in this way no reader of Plato should cavil. Participation was shaped as a technical device to meet just those cases in which a thing is qualifiedly P but also qualifiedly not P.[54] Consider the uses of 'partaking' in our context: each thing is different, by partaking in the form of difference (255e4–6); each is identical, by partaking in identity (256a7–8); and each thing is, by partaking in being. The question remains what something differs from, what it can be identified with, and, quite generally, what it is.

A particularly illuminating parallel is the treatment of unity in the *Parmenides*. There (129c4–d2) Socrates explains how he can be both one and many: he is many parts, and in this way partakes in plurality; he is one man, and thus partakes in unity. It would be absurd to suggest that Plato views these partakings as endowing Socrates with some kind of unqualified unity and plurality: on these terms, Socrates would still be the subject of a contradiction and Zeno's paradoxes could never be cleared up. In other words, Plato does not represent the situation as analysable into 'Socrates is one & Socrates is many & Socrates is human & Socrates has parts'. To say that Socrates is one and many is to say something elliptical, not to isolate two independent conjuncts from a longer conjunction: 'one' and 'many' are completed by specifying 'in what respect and in what relation' (*Rep.* 436d).[55] Similarly, then, with participation in being and not-being.

*4. The second argument for presenting Plato with the explicit distinction of existence from other sorts of being can be more quickly met.[56] In 255c12–d7 he does indeed draw a distinction between different uses of the verb 'to be'; but these are almost certainly its incomplete uses, in statements of identity and of predication.

First, when the Eleatic Stranger marks off difference from being he does not say, as the commentators make out, that to call X 'different' is to give a *relative* or *incomplete* description of X (*pros ti*). He says that it is to give a description which must always be filled out by reference to something *different from X* (255d1, 7). By contrast, when we describe things as 'being'

[54] See 'A Proof in the *Peri Ideōn*'.

[55] This gives added point to Parmenides' query whether Socrates wants a Form of Man, and to Socrates' hesitation (*Prm.* 130c1–4): for to admit this *would* seem to commit him to analysing 'I am one man' as 'I partake in unity and I partake in humanity'. In fact it does not: the essential incompleteness of 'one' and 'many' and 'same' and 'different' and 'is' and 'is not' is well brought out by paradoxes in the *Parmenides* (e.g. 146d5–e4, 147a3–8, 161e3–162b8), and for them the original model of participation holds good.

[56] Cf. Frede, *Prädikation und Existenzaussage*, 12–29. See also Additional Note at the end of this chapter.

(i.e. say that they are) it is only in some instances that what we say must be completed by reference to something other than the subject (*pros alla*; 255c13);[57] in other instances things can be said to be 'themselves in their own right' (*auta kath' hauta*, 255c12–13). Now it is in predication that the complement of the verb 'to be' imports something different from the subject: on this the Eleatic Stranger hangs a major argument at 256a3–c10, and it was of course a thesis basic to the theory of Ideas.[58] In identity statements, on the other hand, the expressions which flank the verb cannot designate different things; indeed in this context they seem to be regarded as typically of the form '*A* is *A*' (254d15, 257a5, 259b3–4).

Secondly, the language with which the Eleatic Stranger makes his contrast at 255c–d (*kath' hauto . . . heteron, allo*) has already been introduced, at the start of this section of the argument, to mark the distinction between identity statements and predications. The opsimaths whose theory commits them, wittingly or unwittingly,[59] to leaving only the first sort of statement standing are said to 'debar anything from sharing in the condition of another and so being called that other' (*mēden eontes koinōniai pathēmatos heterou thateron prosagoreuein*; 252b9–10); and then in producing the identity statements that are essential to stating their case they are said to couple the expressions *einai . . . chōris . . . tōn allōn . . . kath' hauto* (252c2–5). So the commentators who gloss our passage by the distinction between *kath' hauto* and *pros ti* or *tini* in the *Philebus* (51c) or the *Theaetetus* (157a–b) have looked too far afield and brought back the wrong dichotomy.[60]

Thirdly, it is this interpretation that explains, as the older one cannot, why the Eleatic Stranger needs a different argument (255b8–c7) to distinguish being from *identity*. For 'same' is a grammatically incomplete predicate, no less than 'different'; what makes the argument inapplicable to it is just that it cannot be supposed to mark a relation between different things (cf. 256b1).

Fourthly, the Eleatic Stranger at 255c10 introduces his distinction between uses of 'to be' with the words 'I think you agree' (and not, as translators on the received interpretation generally feel impelled to turn it, 'I think you will agree'). Why assume that he already has Theaetetus' assent?

---

[57] That Plato does not mean to distinguish between *heteron* and *allo* here (Deichgräber *apud* Frede, *Prädikation und Existenzaussage*, 12 n. 1) is proved by 256c5–6, 257a1, b4 and 10, and in the essential anticipation at 252b10, c3.

[58] It is a premiss of the Third Man paradox, Alex.Aphr., *in Metaph.* 84. 21–85. 12.

[59] Cf. n. 47 above.

[60] The distinction as here interpreted also leads naturally to Aristotle's division between *to kath' hauto legomenon* and *to heteron kath' heterou legomenon*.

Simply because he has just followed his review of the opsimaths' theory with an argument to show their mistake (252d–254d): predications are possible and necessary, even though in abstract contexts it takes philosophical expertise to determine what can be predicated of what. And Theaetetus has agreed: predication is as necessary as identification.

This plea, that the distinction be read as arising from its context, can be made broader. Just as it is the division of identification from predication that the Eleatic Stranger needs to settle the opsimaths' confusion, so it is this that he requires to explain the general paradox about being which precedes it (249c10–250e4: see p. 449 below) and to disarm the paradoxes which follow (255e8–256c10; cf. 259b8–d7). The division that is not made, and not relevant to these problems, is one between a complete or existential use of 'to be' and an undifferentiated parcel of incomplete uses.

There is another moral to be drawn from these answers. Even in performing the valuable and essential task of disentangling predicative and identity statements which carry the verb 'to be',[61] Plato can hardly have seen his project as that of displaying different senses of the verb. His comments upon its syntax are taken to mark out the different tasks, or different possibilities of combination, of a single undifferentiated form, being. For if (*3) shows that the expression 'partaking in being' is not used to identify a special sense of the verb it becomes the less likely that the other expressions quoted in (3) are meant to paraphrase the verb in other senses; no such role is claimed for them in the text (256a10–b4).[62] And the matter seems to be clinched by the argument just discussed. If Plato took himself to be distinguishing senses of 'being' he would surely have to conclude from his reasoning in 255c8–d7 that he had managed to distinguish difference from only one of the concepts falling under that name, i.e. from the sort of being which is not *pros allo* (or, on the older interpretation, *pros ti*). One proof that being remains for him a unitary concept is that he concludes directly to his distinction between being and difference.[63]

In the *Sophist*, then, Plato does not (in Shorey's words) 'explicitly distinguish the copula from the substantive *is*'. Does his argument nevertheless compel him to set apart an existential use of the verb?

---

[61] The brunt of Ackrill's argument, 'Plato and the Copula'.

[62] Indeed, 256a11–b4 (where the supposedly central verb 'to be' is merely left to be understood from the previous sentence) is more easily read as offering different analyses of 'the same': in 'change (is) the same' it signifies 'partaking in the form Identical', in 'change (is) not the same' it signifies 'the form Identical'. If *ouch homoiōs eirēkamen* (256a11–12) promises paraphrases these are the readier candidates, but a phrase that often promises paraphrases in Aristotle must not be assumed to in Plato (cf. p. 453 below).

[63] It remains the vowel form, being (n. 26 above); but I cannot here pursue the conceptual distinctions embodied in the 'communion of forms' or the role of *methexis*.

THE PARADOXES

*1. Consider again the assumptions which govern Plato's puzzles about not-being (236d–241b), and his treatment of those assumptions. The paradoxes are represented as all in various ways dependent on one veteran and protean hypothesis, that *being can have no connection with not-being* or, more at length, that what-is-not cannot be in any way and what-is cannot not be in any way (cf. 241b1–2, d6–7). Understandably, in view of its ambiguity, the hypothesis takes various forms: in (i), that 'what is not' cannot designate anything that is (237c1–7); in (ii)–(iii), that an attribute that is cannot be attached to a subject that is not (238a7–9, c5–6); in (iv), that it is paradoxical that what really is not (or is not real) should really be (or be a real) anything at all (240b12–c3, Badham's text); in (v), that it is paradoxical, in the case of believing what is not, that what is believed should also have being (241a3–b3). In addition, (i) assumes the identity of what is not with nothing,[64] and (iv) and (v) take what is not to be the contrary of what is (249b5, d6–9).

I believe it will be agreed that Plato's understanding of these skeletal assumptions must be gathered from his subsequent treatment of them. On this point the traditional interpretations seem curiously ambivalent. There is an evident wish to retain the second assumption, construed as meaning that only existent subjects can have actual attributes (see (2*c*) on pp. 439–40). Otherwise the assumptions are regarded as an intractable set of dicta about non-existence which Plato drops in favour of some innocuous ones exploiting a different sense of the verb 'to be'. But neither of these reactions is Plato's. He offers to *contradict* them all, to refute them and prove their negations (cf. *ton elenchon touton kai tēn apodeixin*; 242a7–b5). He takes them (though he cannot yet allow himself the luxury of the word) to be, straightforwardly and sense unchallenged, false.

Thus the first is contradicted by showing that, given the appropriate complements, 'what is not' and 'what is' must be applicable to the same things (256e2–7) and indeed to any subject of discourse (263b11–12). The third, i.e. the claim that 'real' and 'unreal' do not cohabit, can evidently be rebutted in the same manner, and the Eleatic Stranger's formulation of the reality puzzle (240b9–13) seems tailored to this solution: the semblance is not the real original but it certainly is the real semblance.[65] But in the end he simply reduces the problem of unreality to that of falsehood (264c10–d5).

---

[64] Cf. n. 7 above.
[65] On this as an element in Plato's standard view of reality, see Vlastos, 'A Metaphysical Paradox' and 'Degrees of Reality in Plato'.

Nor, of course, is the second assumption smuggled out of this general rebuttal. It is contradicted by the same passages which prove the contradictory of the first. What is not (sc. not so-and-so) must nevertheless have attributes that are—viz. 'are with respect to it', are its attributes (256e5–6, 263b11–12). On these terms an attribute can evidently be said both to be and not to be, belonging to some subjects but not others: the incomplete 'is' in one more role, introduced (but not paraphrased) to mark a relation just the converse of participation.

Here, however, there is a complication which helps to explain the course of Plato's argument. Some forms—being, identity, and difference *imprimis*—can be attributed to anything whatever. So how can these be said 'not to be' with respect to any subject? Well: they can, provided this is understood as a denial of identity. This I take it is why Plato, discussing these all-pervasive concepts, is ready to explain the 'multiple being' which belongs to a subject in terms of the predicates which are true of it, but turns to non-identity to explain its 'countless not-being' (cf. p. 443 above). And it is why, when he shifts to such unpervasive attributes as flying and sitting, this asymmetry seems to be quietly given up: the not-being of these attributes is extended to the case in which they are not truly predicable of some subject (263b11–12). But the tacit extension is not a slip: no doubt Plato feels entitled to adapt his analysis to these cases on the ground that non-identity is still central to it. If flying 'is not with respect to Theaetetus', the non-identity holds now between flying and any and all of the attributes which do belong to Theaetetus, which 'are' for him (p. 428 above). And thus he prepared his ground for contradicting the assumption used in (v) to extract contradictions from falsehood. The man who speaks or thinks falsely does after all and without paradox ascribe being to what is not, or not-being to what is: he counts among X's attributes one which 'is not with respect to X', i.e. which differs from any of X's attributes; or he counts among attributes of the second class one which 'is with respect to X'. The distinction seems to be that between positive and negative falsehoods, and Plato deals expressly only with a falsehood of the first class (263a1–d5); but his language implies that he is ready for the others (240e10–241a1; cf. *apraxian* (non-action), 262c3).

There is no need for more words on the remaining assumptions, that what is not is *nothing* and is *contrary to what is*. The sophist is nowhere advised that his puzzles over not-being and falsehood employ a special concept of being or a sense of the key verb which will not stand negation. He is instructed in the proper scope of, and safeguards on, the 'is' and 'not is' that he mismanaged. He will look in vain for any recognition here of the baffling unavailability of what false statements try but fail to mention.

Let us leave him unassuaged for the moment and notice that the sub-sequent paradox about being (242b6–250e4) is equally ill adapted to forcing a recognition of 'exists' as a distinct sense of 'is'. As the Eleatic Stranger forecast, the accounts of 'is' and 'is not' go hand in hand.

This section of the dialogue is designed to culminate in a paradox (the *aporia* of 250e1–2) whose diagnosis is generally agreed.[66] It depends on con-fusing identity statements with predications. This is why the Eleatic Stranger moves at once to the opsimaths (251a5–c6) and proposes to give one answer to both difficulties (251c8–d2). On the way to his problem he has shown that previous attempts to characterize being (or 'what is' and 'what are') were unduly restrictive: those who say that being is a plurality or else that it is only one thing, that it is corporeal or that it is immutable and non-perceptible, are all rebuked for leaving something out of the inventory (242c4–249d8). Thus he reaches a proposal (A) that seems to leave nothing out: 'being is whatever is changed and (whatever is) unchanged' (249d3–4). He comments that the disjunction 'changed–unchanged' is surely exhaus-tive (250c12–d3), and in fact any other exhaustive dichotomy would serve the paradox equally well. For now he repeats an argument which saw service earlier against the pluralists: being is neither change nor rest—it is this dif-ferent thing, being (250c3–4). And this is at once restated (B) in the form: 'by its own nature being neither rests nor changes' (250c6–7). So (A) seems to be in conflict with (B).

It is commonly agreed that (B) is proved by an illicit move from 'X is not identical with either Y or Z' to 'X is not characterized by either Y or Z'; and that subsequently the Eleatic Stranger blocks this move by distin-guishing identity statements from predications and showing, for some ubi-quitous predicates (being, identity, difference), that a subject which is not identical with one of these still cannot help being characterized by it. So this problem is set and solved as an exercise in the logic of identity and predication, not of existence. True, commentators have hoped to find Plato arguing positive truths about existence in his prefatory review of older theories of being.[67] Given his general strategy in the section, such truths could be no more than parenthetical. For my part I doubt that Plato is pressing even such parenthetical doctrine on the reader: it is enough to read this study of 'things that are (or are not)' against the *Parmenides*' study of 'things that are one (or not one)' for the essentially elliptical character

---

[66] Even when existence is thought to be the topic of the introductory pages: n. 13 above.

[67] On this, see Malcolm, 'Plato's Analysis of *to on* and *to mē on* in the *Sophist*', who finds no existential sense of the verb distinguished in it; and notice that Plato takes no care in these pages to restrict the verb in its critical appearances to one grammatical role. It varies from adverb to connective and from these to roles in which no explicit complement is supplied.

of these descriptions to be clear. Plato's arguments about being are, what he represents them to be, prefatory to a paradox. What they show (at best) is the incoherence of certain claims that, for some favoured value of *F*, *to be* is just *to be F*. They lead to the proposal that *to be* is *to be either or both F and not-F*; and thus they set the scene for the puzzle described above.

THE APPROACH TO FALSEHOOD

*2. In the Eleatic Stranger's scheme, the being of an attribute such as change or not-being carries at least the requirements that it be unproblematically identifiable and instantiated. That is, to say that 'it is' promises two sorts of completion: that it is *A*, 'having a nature of its own', and not *B* (cf. 258b8–c3); and that it is 'with respect to' other things *C*, *D*, . . . (pp. 447–8 above). Similarly with any subject of attributes: to say that 'it is' is to face the *Sophist*'s question 'Is what and what sort of thing?' What then of the requirement, supposedly fundamental to Plato's final analysis of true and false statement (261c6–263d4), that the subject of any statement must exist?[68]

Evidently the requirement can no longer be defended as satisfying the 'hatstand' assumption discerned in stage (ii) of the puzzles. The Eleatic Stranger has contradicted the assumption governing that stage, and in such a way as to show that it was not understood as existential. But consider the analysis itself.

What is striking is that, while Plato insists that a statement must be *about* (or *of*, or must *name* or *belong to*) something, he does not use the verb 'to be' in any existential sense to bring out the nature of this thing. He says that a statement must be about *something* (262e5) and not *nothing* (263c9–11), and he has spent a long argument explaining the terms on which the first but not the second can be made a subject of discourse; but when he uses the verb in this connection he speaks of the subject as 'what is or what is not' (262c3). This last phrase has understandably troubled the defenders of the received view: they have tried to deny that it applies to the subject of a statement, and even construed it as making a broad distinction between positive and negative assertions.[69] But the context defeats them. Plato is arguing that any statement requires the coupling of a subject and predicate expression. Without marrying some such expression as 'a

[68] Moravcsik, 'Being and Meaning in the *Sophist*', 41.
[69] Ibid. 63 n. 1; cf. Campbell, *The* Sophistes *and* Politicus *of Plato*, 173 ad loc.

lion' to one of a different family such as 'runs', it is not possible to declare 'the action or non-action or being of what is or what is not' (*oudemian praxin oud' apraxian oude ousian ontos oude mē ontos*; 262c2–3). Just as 'action or non-action or being' characterizes what the predicate expression contributes,[70] so 'what is or what is not' picks out the contribution of the subject phrase.[71] Plato wants to provide for such subjects as 'the not-beautiful' (or 'what is not beautiful') as well as for 'the beautiful' ('what is beautiful'). Otherwise he would have disallowed some of his own conclusions as candidates for a truth-value. As it is, when it is most important for the received interpretation that he should pick out the subject by an existential use of the verb, it is the connective 'is' and its negation that he leaves entrenched.[72]

It remains to show how the sophist's puzzle is finally diagnosed within this scheme of concepts, which lacks or ignores an expression for 'exist' and makes no attempt to isolate such a 'kind' or 'form' as existence. The *Theaetetus*' analogy between speaking and seeing or touching is not recalled: that was only a symptom.[73] What is taken up is the premiss from which the *Euthydemus* started its paradoxes about falsehood, that things (*pragmata*) can be spoken of only by expressions which belong to them. The Eleatic Stranger accepts this—too hospitably—in the form that any statement having a truth-value must belong to something, viz. to what it is 'of' or 'about', the *pragma* that it 'names' (cf. 263a4–5, 262e12–13). Let me call this relation between a statement and what it is about the 'A-relation', and notice two points in Plato's treatment of it. First, he illustrates but does not offer to analyse it: evidently he assumes that it has been elucidated by the whole study of subject–predicate relations which he now recalls in the dictum 'There is much that is with respect to each thing and much that is not' (263a11–12). Secondly, it becomes clear from 262e12–263a10 (esp. 263a4–10) and c5–d1 that he takes the intuitively plausible view of the relation: he holds that 'Theaetetus sits' and 'Theaetetus flies' are both about just one thing, Theaetetus. There is no suggesting that they are about (or name, or belong to) *sitting* or *flying*. Of course statements about sitting and

---

[70] And the 'being' cannot be represented by the traditional interpretation as existence without committing Plato to explaining in the sequel how existential statements can be false but significant. On the whole phrase, Apelt, *Sophista*, ad loc.; on *ousia*, n. 72 below.

[71] So Diès, 'ni action, ni inaction, ni être, soit d'un être, soit d'un non-être'; and Taylor, *Plato: The Sophist and the Statesman*: 'the action, inaction, or being of anything that is or is not'.

[72] The *ousia* of 261e5 is of course the 'being' studied in the preceding arguments: the texts cited in n. 51 above prove that it is not confined to existential contexts, and the other occurrences in the *Sophist* can be explained on the same terms.

[73] Such non-intensionally transitive verbs as 'hitting' and 'kicking' seem equally appropriate to conveying the sophist's demand for a verbal contact between statement and situation. On one view that (some) verbs of perception are especially important to the analogy, see n. 39 above.

flying are possible, including some which are equivalent to those just quoted: 'Sitting is with respect to Theaetetus', for example. But from what Plato says it seems that these are not the same statements: they would not be characterized as being about the same subject (262e5–6).[74]

It is this A-relation, then, that gives the sophist the connection he demands between the words and the actual situation described: the verbal contact, or the verbal 'belonging'. (It is what Austin called the demonstrative component in the statement; what is often called the reference.) The sophist is allowed his claim that if this relation does not hold, no truth or falsehood has been uttered. But then it is explained that he has exaggerated the scope of the relation. It is a necessary condition of both truth and falsehood, but it is not a sufficient condition of truth. The mere naming— even the stringing together of names (262a9–10)—does not 'complete the business' (*perainein ti*) or achieve a truth-value (262b9–c7): that comes only when something is *said about* what the statement is about,[75] and for this one needs to import an expression with quite another function, such as '. . . sits' or '. . . flies'. Once the place of 'what is not' in the diagnosis has been vindicated, it is in the A-relation that Plato seems to locate the residual mistake in the sophist's picture of falsehood. Falsehood had appeared an abortive attempt to mention something, like an unsuccessful effort to touch or to hear; and this confused the conditions for naming with the conditions for truth.

I need not dwell on this familiar and, I think, satisfactory account of Plato's reply.[76] My argument concerns the way in which the relation of aboutness is introduced. Doubtless it needs (and is currently receiving)

[74] This brings out the irrelevance of representing Plato as meeting the sophist's puzzle by the explanation that 'Theaetetus flies' mentions (= belongs to, is of or about) two things, the falsehood consisting in mentioning together things not found together in fact; or of looking for some 'correlate' with which the false sentence as a whole makes verbal contact. The expressions used at 261e4–6 and 262e10–11 are innocuous preliminaries to the point insisted on in 262e5–6, 262e10–263a10, c5–11.

[75] That the *peri* in 263b4–5 is to be coupled with the *legei* and not merely with the *onta hōs estin* is certified by 263d1 and generally by the requirement that the *logos* must be *tinos* or *peri tinos* (262e5–6, 263a4).

[76] But since I have implied that it is novel with the *Sophist* I must notice the unitarian suggestion that the solution is already recognized in the *Euthydemus* (284c) and *Cratylus* (385b), which characterize true speaking as speaking of things that are, as they are, and false speaking as speaking of things that are, as they are not. The first half of the conjunction is echoed in the *Sophist* (263b4–5). But (i) the description of falsehood is not echoed in the *Sophist*—understandably, since it is at least ambiguous and its ambiguity is used to generate unresolved paradoxes at *Euthd.* 284c–e, 285e–286b. (ii) The echo of the truth-description in the *Sophist* has a quite different sense: the *Euthd.* makes it clear that the 'things that are' are subjects of the statement (see examples in 284d–e), whereas in *Sph.* 263b4–5 they are equally clearly predicates and the sense in which a predicate 'is (or is not) with respect to' a subject has had to be established earlier (256e5–6, recalled here at 263b11–12).

harder analysis before it will carry any more ambitious study of statement structure; but Plato's exploration of the ways in which something can be unparadoxically differentiated, assigned and denied attributes, is a necessary and for his purpose an adequate introduction. The requirement that the subject should exist is neither: witness the insoluble and irrelevant query whether he wants to make room for centaurs.

'But the requirement that the statement should be about *something* and not *nothing* just is the requirement that the subject should exist; for Plato, *to be* is *to be something*,[77] and surely this is an account of existence.' Two last remarks on this.

I have tried to characterize the scheme of concepts within which Plato studies 'nothing' and its twin, 'something', as possible subjects of discourse. For such a study of subject–predicate structure an account of existence is neither a presupposition nor a part; but it might well be a further outcome, much as a logic without existential presuppositions can be made to yield a formula for individual existence.[78] This is, I think, what it became in Aristotle's metaphysics. But notoriously Aristotle complains of Plato for not taking this step, for ignoring the consequent distinction of senses in 'is' and remaining content with his unitary concept, being.

As for the equation '*to be* is *to be something*', the negation of 'to be something' is 'not to be anything' or 'to be nothing', which Plato holds to be unintelligible; and then it would follow from the equation that 'not to be' makes no sense. But Plato recognizes no use of the verb in which it cannot be directly negated. He holds indeed that *to be in no way at all* is a merely paradoxical notion; but he argues with all possible emphasis that this is not the legitimate negation of *to be*. To discount this is to fall into the embarrassments of the traditional account: to saddle Plato with an argument which first sets puzzles about non-existence, then offers to refute the assumptions on which the puzzles depend, and finally backs down and recommends that direct negation be prudently reserved for other uses of the verb 'to be'.

Additional Note
(see n. 56 above)

The preceding argument (255b8–c7) distinguishes being from identity, and since it discusses being without specifying any complement for the verb 'to be' it is often

[77] In the earlier passage in 'Snares of Ontology' cited in the first uncued note above I used the expression '*to be* is *to be something or other*' in describing Plato's theory, and now think this unperspicuous for reasons given here. The familiar idiom *einai ti* is of course used in the *Sophist* (e.g. 246e5) as elsewhere in Plato.
[78] J. Hintikka, 'Studies in the Logic of Existence and Necessity, I: Existence', *Monist*, 1 (1966), 55–76.

understood as dealing expressly with existence. But it follows the argument of
255a4–b6, in which change and rest (C and R) are distinguished from identity and
difference on the ground that, while both C and R can be called either identical or
different, C cannot be said to rest nor R to change. Thereafter being is distinguished
from identity on the ground that C and R can both alike be said to be, but not said
to be identical (*tauton*). Throughout both arguments the complements to 'identical'
and 'different' are left unspecified. So in the first argument the ascription of identity to C and R is tacitly understood as meaning that C is identical *with C*, and R
with R, while in the second it is tacitly understood as meaning that they are the same
as each other. (The use of the singular *tauton* as a joint predicate in 255c1 helps the
shift, but is itself illegitimate: the counterpart predicate from the verb 'to be' would
be *on*, which cannot be a joint predicate at all.) What the arguments show, if anything, is that for some subject in whose description 'the same' and 'different' can
properly occur (sc. with some undeclared complement), neither expression can be
replaced in the description by 'changing' or (in the alternative case) by 'at rest'; and
that, for some subjects in whose joint description 'being' can properly occur, that
expression cannot be replaced by 'identical' (again with some undeclared complement). Patently the argument loses none of its force if we write: 'for some subject
in whose description "being" can properly occur (*with some undeclared complement*)'; the argument systematically discounts complements.

XVIII

BEING IN THE *SOPHIST*:
A SYNTACTICAL ENQUIRY*

LESLEY BROWN

Plato's *Sophist* presents a tantalizing challenge to the modern student of philosophy. In its central section we find a Plato whose interests and methods seem at once close to and yet remote from our own. John Ackrill's seminal papers on the *Sophist*,[1] published in the 1950s, emphasized the closeness, and in optimistic vein credited Plato with several successes in conceptual analysis. These articles combine boldness of argument with exceptional clarity and economy of expression, and though subsequent writers have cast doubt on some of Ackrill's claims for the *Sophist* the articles remain essential reading for all students of the dialogue.

Among the most disputed questions in the interpretation of the *Sophist* is that of whether Plato therein marks off different uses of the verb *einai*, 'to be'. This paper addresses one issue under that heading, that of the distinction between the 'complete' and 'incomplete' uses of 'to be', which has usually been associated with the distinction between the 'is' that means 'exists' and the 'is' of predication, that is, the copula.

I

Those who hold that there is a sharp distinction in ancient Greek between the complete and the incomplete *esti* may take one of the following stances *vis-à-vis* the *Sophist*:

This is a lightly revised version of an essay which was first published in a volume of *Oxford Studies in Ancient Philosophy* dedicated to John Ackrill. The new version expands Sects. V(c) and V(d), and makes some reference to recent publications. New footnotes are cued with an asterisk.

[1] '*ΣΥΜΠΛΟΚΗ ΕΙΔΩΝ*', *Bulletin of The Institute of Classical Studies of the University of London* (1955), 31–5; 'Plato and The Copula: *Sophist* 251–9', *Journal of Hellenic Studies*, 77 (1957), 1–6; both repr. in J. L. Ackrill, *Essays on Plato and Aristotle* (Oxford, 1997), 72–9 and 80–92.

(1) The *Sophist* contains a clear statement of the distinction, which is just what is needed to help solve the philosophical problems raised in the dialogue.

(2) The *Sophist* needs a statement of the distinction (since it contains at crucial points both complete and incomplete uses), but, alas, it lacks it.

(3) The *Sophist* lacks a statement of the distinction, but this is no ground for lamentation since it would be irrelevant to the philosophical issues addressed by the dialogue.

(3) represents Owen's position in his 1971 article, which has received widespread acceptance.[2] His central claims are the following:

(i) that the *Sophist* is an essay in problems of reference and predication [and *not* of existence] and in the incomplete uses of the verb *to be* associated with these and

(ii) that the argument neither contains nor compels any isolation of an existential verb.

It is on the first claim that this article will focus, though some discussion of the second will naturally be involved. I argue that the distinction between syntactically complete and incomplete uses of the verb *einai* needs careful examination before dispute about Plato's overall position or about individual passages can be fruitfully pursued.[3] I distinguish two different ways of characterizing a complete use, and argue that the one that Owen presupposes, in his *Sophist* article, is the less plausible. In its place I offer an alternative characterization of a complete use, whose effect is that the distinction between the syntactically complete and incomplete uses is less sharp than it has traditionally been conceived to be. With the new understanding of *complete*, many centrally important uses of *esti* in the *Sophist* can be reinstated as complete. Provided that we recognize the continuity between the complete and the incomplete (predicative) uses, there will be no harm in regarding the complete use as weakly existential in force. But it is a consequence of the continuity between the two that distinguishing one from the other is not and could not be part of Plato's

---

[2] Ch. XVII of this volume.

[3] R. Heinaman, 'Being in the *Sophist*', *Archiv für Geschichte der Philosophie*, 65/1 (1983), 1–17, disputes Owen's claim that Plato's discussion in the *Sophist* concerns syntactically incomplete uses of *einai*. Though some of his points against Owen are well taken, he appears to accept the traditional account of the distinction, which I shall dispute, and does not pause to define the crucial terms *complete* and *incomplete*. Some of Heinaman's arguments are discussed in Sect. V below. For a critique of Heinaman, see now J. Malcolm, 'Remarks on an Incomplete Rendering of Being in the *Sophist*', *Archiv für Geschichte der Philosophie*, 67 (1985), 162–5.

answer to the problems he inherited from Parmenides. To this extent, then, I accept Owen's thesis, but I believe that a misconception of the nature of the complete use of *esti* led Owen to the implausible views that the problems of the *Sophist* do not concern existence and that the central uses of *esti* in the dialogue are to be construed as incomplete.

II

In this section I outline those parts of Owen's position which are relevant to my discussion. Those familiar with his paper may proceed direct to Section III.

Owen opens with a rehearsal of some—up to that time—accepted commonplaces (416–18). These include two theses about the Greek language and a third about the *Sophist*. The theses about Greek are

(*a*) a distinction between two syntactically distinct uses of the verb *to be*: a complete, substantive use in which it determines a one-place predicate, and an incomplete use determining a two-place predicate;

(*b*) answering to the syntactic distinction, a semantic one: in its substantive, complete, use the verb signifies *exist*; in its incomplete use it is the copula or identity sign.

(*c*) The commonplace about the *Sophist* is that here Plato marks off the first use of *esti*—complete, existential—from its other, incomplete uses, and similarly for the negative construction represented by *to mē on*; for (the commonplace runs) the problems which dominate the central arguments of the *Sophist* are existence problems, so that disentangling the different functions of the verb *to be* is a proper step to identifying and resolving them.

Owen's paper confines its attack to commonplace (*c*); he explicitly accepts the first point, the syntactic distinction.[4] In place of (*c*), Owen's central theses include the two quoted above in Section I. He accepts that there is a distinction (which he does not define) between a complete and an incomplete *esti*, but argues that Plato's interest in the *Sophist* is exclusively in the incomplete uses.

---

[4] 'The general syntactic claim will not come into question: we can accept a distinction between the verb's complete and incomplete uses provided we are wary of confusing the first with elliptical occurrences of the second' (p. 417 above). Thus Owen accepts that *esti* has complete uses, but he argues that putative candidates in *Sph*. are incomplete elliptical. His attitude to the second commonplace, the semantic distinction, is not clear from the article, for he does not make clear what semantic force (whether existential or some other) a 'complete' use of *esti* would have.

Owen's reasoning for the desirability of his interpretation can be reduced to four main steps. (1) It is agreed on all hands that the troublesome concept Not-being or *to mē on*, whose discussion was forbidden by Parmenides' strictures, and which gave rise to a clutch of paradoxes at the beginning of the central section (236–41), is legitimized in the following way. Far from being disallowed as not true of anything (as had at first appeared) *to mē on* is reinstated as true of everything, for everything *is not* countless other things. Not-being is thus equated with difference and shown to be one of the all-pervasive kinds which occupy so much of the central section of the *Sophist*. Everything, then, *is not* countless other things: the vindication of *to mē on* is squarely of its incomplete use—not being is always not being something or other: there is no trace of a legitimization of not-being as a negative existential. (2) That being so, it would be feeble of Plato to raise puzzles about not-being in its other, complete, use, given that his 'solution' ignores such a use. (3) It would be worse still if we should find him explicitly pointing to such a distinction among 'ises', when (as established at step (1)), he forgets or suppresses the distinction as applied to 'is not'. (4) What is more, Plato explicitly tells us that (in Owen's words) 'any light thrown on either being or not-being will equally illuminate the other' (p. 422). This dictum, which he dubbed the Parity Assumption, Owen derived from 250e, and made it a governing assumption of his interpretation. Now it is accepted (step (1)) that the only illumination cast on not-being, on 'is not', is on its incomplete use: by the Parity Assumption, then, we should expect to find only the incomplete use (or uses) of 'is' illustrated. So not only would it be unfortunate if Plato were to allow a use of 'is' while disallowing the corresponding use of 'is not', here he explicitly tells us (if we press the so-called Parity Assumption) that he will not do so.

So much, then, for the broad canvas of Owen's argument, which might be described as tailoring Plato's problem to fit the solution offered. In addition, of course, Owen examines the text passage by passage, hoping to show that in each case where a complete or existential 'is' had been assumed, or argued for, an incomplete 'is' was either mandatory or at least possible. Some of these passages I review in Section V below.

III

First a closer look at the complete–incomplete use distinction. Neither of the pair of terms is explicitly defined by Owen, though he uses the terms *one-place* and *two-place* predicate as apparently equivalent to *complete* and *incomplete* (see (*a*) in Section II above).[5] I therefore take as the definition of an incomplete use that in McDowell's commentary on *Theaetetus*,[6] which seems to state in an admirably clear and precise way what Owen intended by his use of the term: 'an incomplete use, i.e. a use in which a subject expression and the appropriate form of the verb requires a complement in order to constitute a complete sentence, though in an elliptical sentence the complement may be omitted'.

Two crucial points emerge: (1) in an incomplete use a complement is *required*, and (2) an 'is' lacking an explicit complement may yet be an incomplete 'is'. In such a case, presumably, the hearer or reader has not correctly understood the sentence unless he is able to supply the missing complement. A clear example of such a use occurs at *Sophist* 233c6–8 in the course of the attempt to define the sophist as an image-maker who imparts false beliefs to his pupils. Sophists, says the Eleatic Stranger, appear to their disciples to be wise in all things: *panta ara sophoi tois mathētais phainontai.* (*Theaetetus*: Yes, indeed.) *ouk ontes ge*: though they are not [wise]. Here the reader has not understood the phrase *ouk ontes ge* unless he supplies *sophoi*, wise, from two lines before. Let us acknowledge the existence of such uses and dub them IE, for incomplete elliptical. How important and frequent they are in the *Sophist* remains to be seen (Section V).

How should we characterize a *complete* use? I offer two possibilities: a complete use of *esti* is

(C1) a use which neither has nor allows a complement;
(C2) a use where there is no complement (explicit or elided) but which allows a complement.

I believe that commentators have, implicitly or explicitly, assumed a C1 characterization of *complete*, but that C2 is preferable.

I illustrate the difference between the two, and in particular the meaning of 'allows a complement', with a comparison with verbs other than the verb *to be*. (Naturally the definitions C1 and C2, with their reference to a complement, cannot be applied directly to other verbs, but I hope the point of the comparison will be obvious.) Consider these pairs of sentences:

(1*a*) Jane is growing tomatoes.
(1*b*) Jane is growing.

[5] Owen also employs the contrast between a 'substantive' and a 'connective' use. I believe this terminology is misleading, for the complete use (as I define it) is *potentially* connective, and the incomplete use is often *substantive*, if by this is meant that it can have semantic force over and above its role as a copula (see Sect. IV, p. 465).
[6] J. McDowell, *Plato:* Theaetetus (Oxford, 1973), 118.

(2*a*) Jane is teaching French.
(2*b*) Jane is teaching.

It is, I hope, uncontroversial to say that in (1*a*) we have a transitive, in (1*b*) an intransitive, use of 'is growing'; equally that (1*a*) contains a two-place or dyadic use, (1*b*) a one-place or monadic use. Since this latter terminology is standardly used to explicate the incomplete–complete distinction it would be natural to say that (1*a*) contains an incomplete, (1*b*) a complete, use of 'is growing', between which there *is* a sharp syntactic and semantic distinction. Pair (2) is clearly rather different, in the following ways (*inter alia*): (i) while (1*a*) neither entails nor is entailed by (1*b*), (2*a*) does entail (2*b*); (ii) while (2*b*) entails 'Jane is teaching something', (1*b*) does not entail 'Jane is growing something'; (iii) (a corollary of (ii)) one who heard (1*b*) and asked 'growing what?' would reveal misunderstanding of (1*b*), while the follow-up question to (2*b*), 'teaching what?', is perfectly proper. Though (2*b*), like (1*b*), contains an intransitive, complete use of its verb (for 'is teaching' in (2*b*) is certainly not elliptical, though the use no doubt derives from (2*a*)-type uses), it is far closer semantically to its transitive, incomplete partner than (1*b*) is to its partner.

Returning to the rival characterizations, C1 and C2, of a complete *esti*, the meaning of 'allows a complement' is, I hope, clear from these analogies: just as 'is teaching' in (2*b*) is complete but allows an object (it would not be a solecism to ask 'is teaching what?'), so a C2 complete *esti* is one that allows a complement, that is, it is not a solecism to ask 'is what?' An incomplete and a C2 complete *esti* would bear a closeness analogous to that between the uses of 'is teaching' in pair (2). Many other verbs have complete and incomplete uses like those in pair (2): *fight, eat, breathe.* As Kenny has shown,[7] verbs, unlike relations, can exhibit variable polyadicity; it is therefore misleading to assimilate verbs to relations and characterize their uses as one-place, two-place, etc. If we compare the Greek verb *to be* with verbs of variable polyadicity, we shall avoid the pitfalls that arise from this practice.[8] My suggestion, then, is that the complete *esti* should be characterized as C2 rather than C1, that is, as complete but allowing further completion.

That Owen understood C1 as his characterization of 'complete' is shown

---

[7] A. Kenny, *Action, Emotion and Will* (London, 1963), ch. VII. I am indebted to Kenny's chapter, and to discussions with Michael Woods, for suggesting an account of *einai* along the lines of Kenny's verbs of variable polyadicity. Kenny correctly insists that sentences such as 'Plato taught' are not elliptical.

[8] Witness, for instance, M. Matthen, 'Greek Ontology and the "Is" of Truth', *Phronesis*, 28 (1983), 122: 'Let us call a use of "is" *monadic* if it must be completed by exactly one term to form a sentence, *dyadic* if it requires exactly two.' Such regimentation fails to do justice to the nature of verbs in general, and of *einai* in particular.

by his discussion of 259a6–8, one of the passages where Plato uses *esti* without explicit complement, and offers the paraphrase or analysis *dia to metechein tou ontos*, 'because it shares in being'. It was the glossing of 'is' by 'shares in being' that earlier commentators (e.g. Ackrill[9]) had taken to be Plato's way of marking off the existential *esti* from other uses of *esti*, which do not receive this paraphrase. In several places in the *Sophist* it is said of one kind or another that it is, because it shares in being, and it was perhaps natural to see this as marking off an existential, complete use. (These passages are discussed in Section V(*c*) below). At 259a6–8 the Eleatic Stranger sums up his argument about the Different thus: partaking in being, it is by virtue of that partaking—but not the thing of which it partakes but something different:

τὸ μὲν ἕτερον μετασχὸν τοῦ ὄντος ἔστι μὲν διὰ ταύτην τὴν μέθεξιν, οὐ μὴν ἐκεῖνό γε οὗ μετέσχεν ἀλλ᾽ ἕτερον.

'The verb in the last clause' (Owen continues—namely 'but not the thing . . .') 'must be supplied from its predecessor, and the verb supplied is the incomplete "is"' (p. 422).

Owen argues that since a subsequent clause adds a completion, the verb in the clause to which it is added cannot be complete. And this piece of reasoning shows that Owen must understand by a 'complete' use one which (not only does not require but also) *does not allow* further completion. The success of Owen's argument at this point thus depends on understanding 'complete' as C1. If we define it, as I shall argue that we should, as C2, it will not follow from the fact that a completion is added in the second clause that the verb in the first was not complete, so that we could read 259a6's first clause as containing a complete *is* (glossed as *metechei tou ontos*) notwithstanding that the second clause promptly specifies what *heteron* is, or rather, is not. Compare 'My sister is still teaching, but not French these days, only Spanish'.

The effect of understanding the complete *esti* as C2 rather than C1 is that the distinction between the incomplete and complete uses is far less striking and clear-cut.[9*] In suggesting that it should be so understood, I take issue not only with Owen but also with Vlastos, who in his important

---

[9] 'Plato and the Copula', 82.

[9*] N. White, *Plato: Sophist* (Indianapolis, 1993), p. xxiii, uses the terms *uncomplemented* v. *complemented* uses of 'is', where Owen (whom I have followed) uses *complete* v. *incomplete*. White (p. xxvii) shares my view that for Plato there is no sharp distinction between the two uses. But I have reservations about his claim that complemented being ('is . . .') stands to uncomplemented being ('is' *tout court*) as 'heavy, in comparison to *X*' stands to 'heavy' (*tout court*), at least in so far as it seems to suggest that the uncomplemented use of 'is' is prior in understanding to the complemented use.

462 LESLEY BROWN

article 'A Metaphysical Paradox'[10] writes of 'the difference between the "is" in *Troy is famous* and in *Troy is*', implicit knowledge of which 'even a Greek child would have had'. (Vlastos's chief interest is in the question how we should understand Plato's descriptions of the forms as *ontōs on*, 'really real', and so forth; he insists that these uses of 'to be' are to be sharply distinguished from those in which 'to be' means 'to exist'.) His choice of example suggests that he takes as one aspect of the distinction the fact (presumably supposed to be well known to the Greek child) that

(3a) Troy is famous   does not entail
(3b) Troy is,   hence, is consistent with
(3c) Troy is not (i.e. does not exist).

Vlastos's remarks suggest that he believes there is a sharp syntactic and semantic distinction waiting to be articulated, such that only a paradox-monger could trade on an equivocation between them. I discuss this further in the next section, but remark here on a difficulty which must strike all readers of the *Sophist*: if so sharp a distinction existed (as sharp as that between the use of 'is growing' in (1a) and (1b)) and if, as Vlastos insists, Plato faithfully *observed* it, then the *Sophist* of all places was the dialogue where the distinction ought to have been explicitly stated. But not only does Plato not, according to present consensus, explicitly mark the distinction, he does not even *observe* it to the extent of allowing that a sentence of form (3a) can be true while one of form (3b) is false. He nowhere allows that *X is F* does not entail *X is* but is consistent with *X is not*. Indeed he allows no role to the complete *is not*, and this is what prompted Owen to deny that Plato's problem concerned existence (i.e. the complete *esti*) at all, for if it had done, Plato could not have failed to delineate both the 'is' of existence and the 'is not' of non-existence. But if, as I shall suggest, the syntactic distinction (at least) is not as sharp and clear-cut as Vlastos assumes, then Plato's failure to exploit it is more explicable.[11]

IV

But it may be claimed that we *do* find paradox-mongers exploiting precisely this equivocation on the two distinct *estis*. I now consider the little

[10] G. Vlastos, 'A Metaphysical Paradox', *Proceedings of the American Philosophical Association*, 39 (1965–6), 5–19; repr. in *Platonic Studies*, 1st edn. (Princeton, 1973), 47. Vlastos agrees with Owen that the *Sophist* does not contain an explicit statement of the distinction between the 'is' of existence and other uses of 'is'.
[11] In Sect. V(d) below I concede that the proof at 255c–d does invoke a distinction between the complete and incomplete uses of *einai*, but, though it can be used for that purpose, it did not form a major plank in Plato's answer to Parmenides.

sophism at *Euthydemus* 283c–d. Socrates and his friends want young Kleinias to get an education, that is, they want him to become wise, which he now is not. So, they are told,

(1) Ὑμεῖς δέ, ἔφη, βούλεσθε γενέσθαι αὐτὸν σοφόν, ἀμαθῆ δὲ μὴ εἶναι.
(2) Οὐκοῦν ὃς μὲν οὐκ ἔστιν, βούλεσθε αὐτὸν γενέσθαι, ὃς δ' ἔστι νῦν, μηκέτ' εἶναι.
(3) ἐπεὶ βούλεσθε αὐτὸν ὃς νῦν ἐστιν μηκέτι εἶναι, βούλεσθε αὐτόν, ὡς ἔοικεν, ἀπολωλέναι.

(1) 'You want him to become wise, and not to be ignorant,' he said.
(2) 'You want him to become what he is not, and to be no longer what he is now.'
(3) 'Since you want him, who is now, to be no longer, you want to destroy him apparently!'

A standard diagnosis of the fallacy would be to see an equivocation on *esti*: in (2), which is *true*, it is the two-place copula; in the *false* protasis of (3), it is the one-place existential. But the correct diagnosis is different; it is that the fallacy depends on a syntactic ambiguity in the clauses *hos esti nun* and *hos nun estin*. In (2) it means '(you want him no longer to be) *what he now is*', where *hos* is the equivalent of *hoios* and the complement of *estin*. But in (3), 'you want him, *who now is*, no longer to be' *hos nun esti* is a relative clause dependent on *auton*; *hos* is the subject of *esti* which is left without a complement, as is the infinitive *einai*. Now it is true that the effect of lopping off the complement of *einai* is to make 'you want him no longer to be alive', or '. . . to exist' a natural translation. But I do not think we are forced to postulate a radically different use of 'is' or 'be' here.

To show this I suggest the following, parallel, argument. Socrates and his friends try to rescue a child from a smoke-filled room; that is, they want him no longer to breathe what he is now breathing (namely smoke). The wily sophists exclaim 'You want him no longer to be breathing what he's now breathing'—(Yes)—'So you want him, who is now breathing, no longer to be breathing'. Once again Socrates and friends want the child to die—they want him no longer to be breathing.

Now no one, I think, would try to argue that the fallacy involved a shift in uses of the verb 'breathe', simply because in one clause an object is specified and in another it is not. Whenever '*X* is breathing' is true, it will also be true that *X* is breathing something—oxygen normally. Conversely '*X* is not breathing' will normally mean the same as '*X* is not breathing anything'. But for all that, we should not say either that '*X* is breathing' is elliptical, or that the use of the verb where it has an object is significantly different from the use where it has no object. Of course, that in itself is a difference, but not involving an important shift in the verb's sense. And exactly the same may be said of the original argument with the verb *to be*:

lopping off the complement produces a falsehood but need not be seen as yielding a sharply different ('one-place, existential') use of *esti*. Rather, 'They want him not to be' will be equivalent to 'They want him not to be anything at all', just as 'They want him not to breathe' will be equivalent to 'They want him not to breathe anything at all'. Contrast the lopping off of the object in 'You want her to stop growing tomatoes', which yields 'You want her to stop growing': here the effect of lopping off the object *is* to produce a sharply different use of the verb.

The sophism in the *Euthydemus*, then, need not be understood as relying on an illicit shift between two uses of the verb *to be* which are syntactically and semantically distinct. The inference from *X is not F* to *X is not* (the move which results from the change in role of the subordinate clause in the sophist's argument) is illicit whether the complete *is* is understood as C1 or as C2, that is, whether or not a 'new' use results. It is only in connection with an inference from *X is F* to *X is* that the two characterizations give divergent answers: with a C2 use, the inference is as straightforward as that from (2*a*) to (2*b*), while a more complex story has to be told if a C1 use is envisaged. So the *Euthydemus* passage cannot be used as evidence for a sharp syntactic–semantic distinction known implicitly to all Greek speakers and exploitable by paradox-mongers. For all that that little argument shows, the continuity between the complete and the incomplete *esti* is as strong as that between complete and incomplete uses of the variably polyadic verbs listed above (p. 460).

It is, I believe, this continuity between the apparently complete and the incomplete use of *esti*, *on*, etc. in the *Sophist* that has led Owen and others to claim that (contrary to appearances) only incomplete uses play any important role in the dialogue, and to interpret those uses without explicit complements (which I read as C2 complete) as incomplete but elliptical. They may urge that this IE use has been found in a very important role elsewhere in Plato, in his discussion of the Form *F* and the many *F*s, where claims about the being of the Form and the being-cum-not-being of the many *F*s require us to supply a complement: the Form *F* is perfectly, unqualifiedly [*F*], the many *F*s are and are not [*F*].[12] If the IE use is well attested and important elsewhere in Plato, why should I baulk at Owen's detection of it in the *Sophist*?

My answer is this: that if we take the notion of an ellipse seriously,

---

[12] This way of understanding claims about the being of the forms derives from Vlastos's influential articles 'A Metaphysical Paradox' and 'Degrees of Reality in Plato'; repr. in *Platonic Studies*. Though I have reservations about aspects of Vlastos's position (see p. 462 above and Sect. V(*b*) below), accepting it will not affect my argument that the *Sph.* passages discussed in Sect. V(*c* below are *not* elliptical.

we may detect an ellipse in the assertion that *X is* only where the context supplies the elided complement. In English these uses are extremely common: 'Is he tall? Yes, he is', 'Who is coming? Jane is'. But such 'everyday' ellipses are far from commonplace in ancient Greek.[13] Only in a narrow range of contexts do we find a true ellipse of the complement after 'is', and these are the well-known contrasts, between being and becoming (*F*); between being and merely seeming (*F*); or the comparison between a thing's *being* so and so, and what it is *said* by some speaker or *logos* to be. In all of these cases the verb *to be* is more than the mere copula, but gets a meaning of its own by contrast with its partner: *becoming*, *appearing*, etc. We should be chary of detecting an ellipse unless the context supplies it or gives us reason to look for one. And though this is sometimes the case in key passages in the *Sophist*, there are very many other central passages which both Owen and Frede[14] have read as incomplete uses where no elided complement can be supplied from the context. These are, I submit, best understood as what I have called C2 complete uses.[15]

V

I now turn to the *Sophist* and examine selected parts of the central section (236–64) in the light of the foregoing discussion.

(a) The Paradoxes of Not-Being (to mē on): 236–41

Though the topic gets introduced by the description of the sophist as a pedlar in illusions and falsehood—both of which seem to call for description involving *to mē on*—the scrutiny of the phrase that follows does not

---

[13] It appears that in Plato, at least, the interlocutor's reply *esti* never echoes the *mere* copula; the plain *esti*, as opposed to the very frequent *esti tauta* ('that's so'), may mean 'it is possible' (*Cratylus* 430c1; *Sph.* 225a7). An interesting case, where what we have is the *is* of definition and not the plain copula, is Theaetetus 152b12: *ΣΩ. Τὸ δέ γε "φαίνεται" αἰσθάνεσθαί ἐστιν; ΘΕΑΙ. Ἔστιν γάρ.*

[14] M. Frede, *Prädikation und Existenzaussage, Hypomnemata* 18 (1967), 1–99.

[15] C. H. Kahn, *The Verb 'Be' in Ancient Greek* (Dordrecht, 1973), 240, draws the syntactic distinction between an absolute and a predicative construction of the verb *be*. (His well-known thesis is that the absolute construction of *einai* by no means always bears an existential meaning; indeed he suggests the Greeks did not have our notion of existence.) The absolute construction is defined as one where 'there is no nominal or locative predicate and no other complement such as the possessive dative, nor even an adverb of manner. An absolute construction may however admit adverbs of time'. In a later article ('Some Philosophical Uses of "To Be" in Plato', *Phronesis*, 26 (1981), 131 n. 20) he emends the above to allow expressions such as *to pantelōs on* to count as absolute, adding 'perhaps the notion of an absolute construction has a clear sense only by contrast with the nominal and locative copula, and does not admit of more precise definition'.

confine itself to a scrutiny of its role in the description of images and false-hood. Rather the phrase *to mē on* itself comes under scrutiny in the opening section of the paradoxes, 237b–239c: what can we apply it to? and what can be applied to it?—with the paradoxical result that it has no application, nor can anything that is—number, for example—be applied to it. So it is unsayable, unthinkable, etc.—but in so saying we contradict ourselves—we apply being and number to it.

Confining my attention to this opening paradox (237b–239c, labelled stages i–iii by Owen (p. 431)), I argue for understanding *to mē on* as a C2 complete use, and proceed by examining Owen's position and Heinaman's arguments against Owen. In brief, Owen claims that *to mē on*, here equated with *to mēdamōs on* (237b7; cf. c2) cannot mean the non-existent, and cannot be a complete use, but means 'that which isn't anything at all', that is, that which for no *F* is *F* (see below). Heinaman counters that it cannot mean the latter but must mean 'the non-existent', and must be a complete use. I argue that their shared assumption, that we must choose between the two interpretations, depends on a faulty understanding of the contrast, and that no such choice is necessary if *to mē on* represents the negation of a C2 complete use, for as such it will be equivalent to 'that which isn't anything at all' without being elliptical or incomplete. If we take *to mē on* to be the negation of a C2 complete *esti*, we can understand it as *both* 'that which isn't anything at all' *and* 'the non-existent' and we are not forced to treat these as rival inter-pretations.

First, Owen's position: the paradoxes, he writes, arise from the assump-tion that *to mē on* is the *contrary* of *to on* (n. 18); that is, they treat the phrase *to mē on* as one that attempts to pick out a subject 'which for every predicate *F* is not *F*'. Following Heinaman, let us call this 'that which is predicatively nothing'.[16] We may agree with Owen that the paradox, as sketched two paragraphs above, proceeds by stipulating that nothing that is may be applied to what is not (*to mē on*), nor may the latter expression apply to anything that is (238a7–8, 237c7–8), which amounts to treating *to mē on* as that which isn't anything at all, that of which no statement of the

---

[16] Cf. J. Malcolm, 'Plato's Analysis of τὸ ὄν and τὸ μὴ ὄν in the *Sophist*', *Phronesis*, 7 (1967), 137: '[*to mē on*, here = *to mēdamōs on*] may be read, literally, as "that which "is not" in all pos-sible respects' or 'that which in no way at all may be said to be. . . . On this reading *to mēdamōs on* is stronger than "non-existence".' I take it that what Malcolm means is this: Plato refuses to allow anything the description *to mēdamōs on*, while he would have had to allow that, for example, Pegasus qualifies for the description 'non-existent'. But this shows only that *to mēdamōs on* is 'stronger than' *our* notion 'non-existent'. It remains possible, and indeed likely, that Plato's failure to make the 'Pegasus point' is due not to a lack of interest in 'existence prob-lems' (as Owen would have it), but to the fact that he cannot distinguish non-existence from not being anything at all.

form 'It is . . .' is true.[17] But we can accept this point and still read *to mē on* as a C2 complete use, for, as I have argued in Section IV, the negation of the C2 complete *esti* is equivalent to 'is not anything at all'. And there are good reasons for doing this, and for saying that *pro tanto* the paradox is about *to mē on* in the sense of the non-existent. For (i) when a puzzle is raised about the applicability of the term *to mē on*, about whether *to mē on* can be thought about, etc., it is natural to take this as an early member of that long-lived and far-flung family of puzzles about how one can think of, speak of, or refer to the non-existent. Not the earliest, of course: and in recalling Parmenides we have another reason to expect a puzzle about non-existence. (ii) When in the course of the argument it is said that nothing that is, no *on*, can be applied to *to mē on*, with the result that number, which is *in primis* an *on*, cannot be applied to it (238a7–b1), what is here said about number is surely that it is a thing that is, i.e. exists, not that it is [some unspecified complement], which is how the incomplete reading would have to take it if it is to treat *on* and *mē on* in the same way.

Heinaman attacks this interpretation of *to mē on* as what is predicatively nothing, correctly pointing out that it does not fit 240e.[18] His argument does indeed show that Owen's interpretation of *to mē on* and *to mēdamōs on* as *that which is predicatively nothing* does not fit the 240 passage, but Heinaman concludes that Owen's reading must be wrong *passim* and that the only alternative is to read *to mē on* as the non-existent.[19]

But while Heinaman does show that Owen cannot claim support for his interpretation of *to mē on* at 237 from the 240 passage, he, like Owen, is assuming that the phrase has the same role in the two passages, which need not and indeed cannot be so.[20] In fact Heinaman's own candidate, 'the

---

[17] See McDowell, *Plato: Theaetetus*, 200, for this formulation.

[18] I here abbreviate Heinaman's argument ('Being in the *Sophist*', 4–6): at 240e false judgement is described as (*a*) one which judges *pōs einai ta mē onta* (or, the line before, *ta mēdamōs onta*), (*b*) one which judges *mēdamōs einai ta pantōs onta* (describing positive and negative false judgements respectively). If *ta mē onta* (= *ta mēdamōs onta*) = that which is predicatively nothing, then by parity of reasoning *ta pantōs onta* would have to be things which are predicatively everything, an absurdity.

[19] Heinaman ('Being in the *Sophist*', 20) dismisses another possibility, the veridical *esti*. I agree that *to mē on* and *to mēdamōs on* in 237–9 cannot consistently be read as veridical, in spite of the introduction of the topic of not-being at 236e via the mention of falsehood, and the allusion at 237a3–4 to the characterization of false speaking as *legein to mē on*; cf. 260c3–4.

[20] Malcolm, 'Remarks on an Incomplete Rendering of Being in the *Sophist*', 164 n. 3, concedes that he was wrong to invoke the 240e passage in support of his interpretation of *to mēdamōs on* as absolute (predicative) non-being. He continues to defend the latter as an interpretation of 237–9; my only disagreement with him is over his insistence that this is to be distinguished from an interpretation in terms of non-existence.

non-existent', fits 240e no better than Owen's, while in the original paradox (Owen's i–iii) we do not need to choose between them. We can say both (A) that a complete (C2) use figures in that paradox and (B) that the heart of the paradox is an understanding of *to mē on* as that which isn't anything at all. This yields a reading which is more satisfying both than Owen's which denies (A) and Heinaman's which denies (B). And if it be objected that on this reading we can draw no distinction, on Plato's behalf, between the non-existent and that which isn't anything at all, I reply that this is merely to be faithful to Plato. Had the possibility of the distinction been implicit in his knowledge of Greek, his failure to avail himself of it (by saying that 'does not exist' has a legitimate application, while 'isn't anything at all' has none) would be inexplicable. However we should understand his 'solution' to the paradox concerning Not-being,[21] it is clear that it dismisses as a wholly absurd notion that Not-being which is the simple *negation* of the complete *X is*,[22] allowing only *X is different from being* and *X is not F, [G, etc.]* as acceptable.[23] As noted above (in Section II), it was because Plato's *solution* does not countenance the negation of the complete *esti* that Owen reconstructed the original *problem* to exclude it. But, as I have argued, we can preserve Owen's insight that the original paradox gets its force by treating *to mē on* as 'that which isn't anything at all' within a framework of seeing it as a (C2) complete use; and, as I am about to argue, the complete use is prominent also in the sequel to the paradoxes.[24]

---

[21] A question too complex to be considered here. For some recent discussions, see D. Keyt, 'Plato on Falsity', in E. N. Lee, A. P. D. Mourelatos, and R. Rorty (eds.), *Exegesis and Argument*, (*Phronesis*, suppl. vol. 1) (Assen, 1973), 285–305; F. A. Lewis, 'Plato on Not', *California Studies in Classical Antiquity*, 9 (1976), 89–115; J. McDowell, 'Falsehood and Not-Being', in M. Schofield and M. Nussbaum (eds.), *Language and Logos* (Cambridge, 1982); D. Bostock, 'Plato on "Is Not"', in *Oxford Studies in Ancient Philosophy*, 2 (1984), 89–119; Job van Eck, 'Falsity without Negative Predication: On *Sophistes* 255e–263d', *Phronesis*, 40 (1995), 20–47.

[22] 258e7–259a1.

[23] For the former, *X is different from being*, see 256d5–8, d11–e2; for the latter, *X is not F, G, etc.*: this may be either a negative identity-statement or a negative predication. Whether and how Plato distinguishes these is a vexed question, since he appears to have but one analysis, '*X* is different from *F*'. For denials of identity, see 257a3–5, but 256e6 may mean to include negative predications as well as negative identities in the 'countless not being with respect to each form', i.e. the countless truths of the form '*K* is not . . .'.

[24] The puzzle that immediately follows, 239d–240c, where an image is defined as that which οὐκ ὂν ὄντως ἐστὶν ὄντως ἥν λέγομεν εἰκόνα ('something which is not really but really is what we call an image'), does seem to contain (elliptical) incomplete uses of *esti* and cognates. That this is so is shown by the context: the contrast between the genuine, *alēthinos* (e.g. horse) and the thing that is like, *eoikos*, but isn't really (a horse). The difficulty with this little puzzle is to see how it could be thought to engender paradox once the missing complements are supplied.

(b) The Theories about Being (to on), 242–50

I shall discuss this section briefly and dogmatically, extracting some points important to my thesis.[25] (1) Plato discusses philosophers who had something to say about being (*to on*, or *ousia*; used interchangeably, e.g. compare 248c2 with 247d6). The assertions he ascribes to them (that hot and cold are, that only one thing is, that only that which offers resistance to touch is, etc.) must for the most part be construed as containing syntactically complete uses of *esti*. (2) Most of the theories discussed are about *what there is*, and most of the relevant uses of *einai* look exceedingly like existentials, and call for the translation *exists* (see e.g. 246a10, 247b1, e3). (3) However, while the theories of the dualists, monists, and materialists are naturally described as theories about what exists, about what there (really) is, in that each can be seen as offering a reductive account of all existents to their favoured candidate(s), the Idealist theory, ascribed to 'Friends of the Forms' is rather different. In allowing *ousia* only to forms, and relegating perceptible, changeable objects to the status of *genesis*, it is *not* reducing all things to forms, but rather according forms a special status among things that exist. Thus Plato does not hesitate to include among theories of *to on* both theories about what exists *and* the 'Friends of the Forms' theory about what is real. This casts further doubt on Vlastos's claim (referred to above, p. 462) that Plato observed a sharp distinction between the two senses of *esti*. (4) In places (e.g. 246e–247b) the argument uses the absolute *einai* interchangeably with *einai ti*, to be something, which is just what is to be expected if the former is a C2 complete use (as illustrated in Section III). (5) Though the discussion makes heavy use of the complete *esti*, (1), which is by and large to be understood as existential, (2), one of Plato's chief interests in this whole section is in scrutinizing the role of a predicate expression, preparatory to his discussion of the late-learners' difficulty. (The late-learners refuse to admit statements which predicate one thing of another (an *other*)—they won't allow you to say that a man is good or to apply anything except 'man' to man. And this position, the refusal to take seriously the role of a predicate expression, lies behind the fallacious refutation of the dualists at 243d–244a; cf. 250a–e.) The predicate expression chosen for scrutiny, *esti*, is to that extent representative of all predicates, and Plato need not be interested in pursuing the complete *esti* for its own sake, but in order to draw some morals about the correct understanding of an ascription of one thing to another. Once again

---

[25] The whole section on theories of being is virtually ignored by Owen. Malcolm, 'Plato's Analysis of τὸ ὄν and τὸ μὴ ὄν in the *Sophist*', holds that in this section *to on*, *einai*, etc. may but need not be taken as complete and therefore existential.

we can accept this without having to accept that the complete *esti* has no role in this section. It is important for what follows that we have in this section just what we seem to have: theories about what is, where that 'is' is a complete use.[25]*

(c) The Communion of Kinds (252–9)

We have finally arrived at the heart of the *Sophist*, the section in which five *megista genē*, greatest kinds, are identified and proved to be distinct from one another, and their interrelations plotted. Our path lies through a minefield of difficulties, which cannot be here discussed. I shall concentrate my attention on those passages where Plato asserts of some form or other that it *esti dia to metechein tou ontos*, that it is because (or, in that) it shares in being, and argue for a traditional understanding of them as containing complete uses.

Before turning to these, I sketch briefly the aims and achievements of the important section 255e–256e, a section in which Ackrill claimed that Plato distinguishes the 'is' of identity from the 'is' of predication (as well as the 'is' of existence, which I discuss below). Like Owen, I believe that Ackrill was right to hold that this stretch of argument aims to distinguish predications from identity-statements, but wrong to say that Plato's way of doing this is to distinguish two uses or meanings of 'is'; I argue for this in the next paragraph. The section contains four groups of statements about change, tracing the connections between change and the four other kinds, rest (*stasis*), the same, different, and being. I return shortly below to the first group, which discusses change and rest, and which contains the claim that change is, because it shares in being.

The remaining three groups all follow the same pattern. Starting with change and the same, it is argued (1) change is different from the same, so (2) change is not the same but (3) change is the same, because (4) change shares in the same. The apparent contradiction in the conjunction of (2) and (3) is mirrored in what follows with 'change is different and is not different' (256c8), and finally 'change is being and is not being' (256d8–9). Plato makes the Stranger explain away the apparent contradiction in (2) and (3) by saying (256a11–12) that 'when we said [it is] the same and

[25]* I have discussed the section on theories of what is in Lesley Brown, 'Innovation and Continuity: The Battle of Gods and Giants, *Sophist* 245–249', in Jyl Gentzler (ed.), *Method in Ancient Philosophy* (Oxford, 1998). In exploring the *gigantomachia* there, I examine the '*dunamis* proposal'—the suggestion that to be is to be capable of affecting or being affected (*dunamis tou poiein kai paschein*). Whatever the correct interpretation of the *dunamis* proposal, and whether or not Plato endorses it—both highly debated issues—it is manifest that it offers an account of what it is to be, where 'to be' is understood in a complete use.

not the same, we were not talking in the same way', i.e. by pointing to an ambiguity. Now many scholars read Plato here as distinguishing an 'is' of identity in (2) *change is not the same*—i.e. change is not the kind *sameness* (as proved earlier at 255a–b), from the 'is' of predication, the copula, in (3) *change is the same*.[26] But a grave difficulty for this interpretation is that in the vital lines explaining the ambiguity (256a10–b4), Plato does not even use the verb to be, let alone draw attention to it (though it has to be supplied in the sentence, as my translation indicates). However, as Owen noted (n. 47), we may and should credit Plato with distinguishing predications from statements of identity in this section, even though the text does not allow us to credit him with a distinction between an alleged 'is' of identity and one of predication.[26*] Distinguishing predications from statements of identity is just what is needed to defuse the late-learners' difficulty of 251a–c, for they, we are told, did not allow one to say that a man is good, but only that the good is good and the man is a man. They did not understand how a thing can be what it also is not, but in discussing the communion of kinds Plato shows how even a kind can be (predicatively) what it is not (i.e. what it is not the same as, what it is different from). Solving this difficulty does not require distinguishing an 'is' of identity from an 'is' of predication; it is sufficient for Plato to do what he here does, viz. draw the distinction between a predication and a statement of identity without 'pinning the blame' on the verb to be.

After that excursus into passages where the incomplete 'is' is found, I now turn to the locution *esti dia to metechein tou ontos* (it is, because it shares in being). I shall argue that it does offer an analysis of a complete *esti*. I fully accept, however, two important points. The first is that a major aim of this section (as just described) is the distinction of predications from identity-statements, each of which contains an *incomplete* 'is'. The second is that, though the phrase *dia to metechein tou ontos* (because of sharing in being) analyses a complete 'is', this use is not seen as importantly distinct from incomplete uses of 'is'. Indeed, this is part of my thesis about

---

[26] Ackrill, 'Plato and the Copula', 82–4, followed by Vlastos, 'An Ambiguity in the *Sophist*', in *Platonic Studies*, 288 n. 34. Doubters include Owen, Ch. XVII, n. 46; pp. 445–6; F. A. Lewis, 'Did Plato Discover the *Estin* of Identity?', *California Studies in Classical Antiquity*, 8 (1975), 113–43; Bostock, 'Plato on "Is Not"'.

[26*] Where does Plato locate the ambiguity, if not in the 'is'? Two answers suggest themselves: (i) he notes that the term following the 'is' is an adjective in (3), i.e. used predicatively, but an abstract noun in (2) or (ii) he notes that the sentence form '*A* is (not) *B*' allows interpretation both as a predication and as an identity-sentence, without pinning the ambiguity on any one element of the sentence. Each of these explanations is as satisfying an account of the ambiguity as one invoking the alleged ambiguity between an 'is' of predication and one of identity.

the complete, C2, use. Nevertheless, it is important to argue, against Owen and Frede,[27] that the locution *esti dia to metechein tou ontos* offers an analysis of a complete use of *esti*.

There are three main passages to be considered:

(i)   256a1
(ii) 256d8–e6
(iii) 259a4–b1.

Owen considers these passages in reverse order, arguing that since neither (iii) nor (ii) can be construed as containing a complete use of *esti*, (i), despite appearances, cannot either (pp. 442–4). I shall take them in their natural order.

(i) forms part of a series of propositions about the sample kind *kinēsis*; it comes in the pair *Kinēsis is not stasis* but *Kinēsis is, because it shares in being*.[28] How should we understand the claim that *Kinēsis is, because it shares in being*? One would have to have very good reason for rejecting the view that this is a syntactically complete, existential 'is', given what has led up to this. *Kinēsis* is one of five distinct kinds. It was one of the first to be postulated. In the course of the proof of the non-identity of the kind *being* with either *kinēsis* or *stasis* (254d10) we have the premiss *to de ge on meikton amphoin*, being mixes with (i.e. is predicable of, as it transpires) both—*eston gar amphō pou*—for both, presumably, are. Again, one would have to have good grounds for denying that this is a complete, existential use. And this is reinforced by going back again to 250a–b where it is agreed that *kinēsis* and *stasis* both are (250a11). Now 250a–b is the culmination of the discussion of theories of being, discussed above (Section V(b)). I insisted that these are theories of what there is, while conceding that ontological questions were not, for all that, Plato's chief target.

A connection can be traced between the three passages 250a11, 254d10, and 256a1, which all make the same assertion but with increasing technicality of expression: at 250a11 we have simply, *kinēsis* and *stasis are*; at 254d10 the same assertion, accompanied by the claim that being mixes with both (*to de ge on meikton amphoin*); finally at 256a1 the fully technical version: *kinēsis esti, dia to metechein tou ontos*. This, then, is the argument for taking 256a1 as analysing a complete use of *esti* and *pro tanto* making

---

[27] Frede, *Prädikation und Existenzaussage*, argues that all three passages to be discussed contain *incomplete* uses.

[28] This pair of statements has a different form from the next three (*K* is and is not *tauton*, is and is not *heteron*, is and is not *on*), because *stasis* is not even predicable of *kinēsis*.

an existence claim: it is naturally connected with the two earlier passages, each of which contains a complete use.[29]

(ii) 256d8–e6. This much-discussed passage has often been cited to show that *esti, dia to metechein tou ontos* cannot analyse a complete use.[30] I argue that if we take a complete use to be C2, the argument has no force.

The passage is the culmination of the discussion of the interrelations of *kinēsis* with the other kinds. It is here said that *kinēsis* is not being (since it is different from being) but *kinēsis* is being, since it shares in being (*epeiper tou ontos metechei*). The result is then generalized for all the kinds, and the following conclusion drawn:

Περὶ ἕκαστον ἄρα τῶν εἰδῶν πολὺ μέν ἐστι τὸ ὄν, ἄπειρον δὲ πλήθει τὸ μὴ ὄν.

In the case of each of the forms, then, there is much that it is and indefinitely much that it is not.[31]

There is thus an inference from

(1) Each kind shares in being (256e3)   to
(2) There is much that each kind is (e5).

And this, in Owen's view, shows that 'the use of the verb [*to be*] on which the Eleatic Stranger rests his conclusion is the connective use, distributed between identity and predication. . . . So to extract any express recognition of a substantive or existential use of *is* from this passage would not square with the argument' (p. 443). With the second sentence we may agree, if by 'a substantive or existential use' is intended a use seen as discrete from the incomplete use. The passage does indeed show that Plato saw an intimate connection between (1) and (2), but this is quite consistent with taking (1) to contain a complete, C2, use. Compare the inference from *Jane is teaching* to *Jane is teaching something*. Once again, we can preserve an important insight, in this case into Plato's perception of the relation between

[29] Frede, *Prädikation und Existenzaussage*, 56, claims that 256a1 is contained in 255e11: *Kinēsis is altogether different from stasis* (1). (1), he argues, contains both subsequent assertions; both (2) *(Kinēsis) is not stasis* (a14) and (3) *Kinēsis is, because it shares in being*. If this means that (3) is an *ellipse* of (1), this cannot be right. That would be to treat it like the exchange 'Courage is different from foolhardiness'—'It is indeed'. Here we have true incomplete elliptical use, but such a use would, I submit, not be permissible in Greek. If it means that (3) is an *inference* from (1), then we need not hold that because *is* in (1) is incomplete, so must *is* in (3) be. We need not, because we have an alternative account, in terms of a C2 use (in (3)), and an analogy with the inference from 'Caesar is fighting the Gauls' to 'Caesar is fighting').
[30] e.g. by Owen, pp. 442–3 above; Malcolm, 'Plato's Analysis of τὸ ὄν and τὸ μὴ ὄν in the *Sophist*', 143; cf. Malcolm, 'Remarks on an Incomplete Rendering of Being in the *Sophist*', 165.
[31] I prefer this to the alternative translation proposed, for his own reasons, by McDowell: 'in the case of each of the forms, what is (it) is multiple and what is not (it) is indefinite in number' 'Falsehood and Not-Being', 125).

(1) and (2), while rejecting the implausible view that (1) is an incomplete (i.e. elliptical) use.[32]

(iii) 259a4–b1. This passage has already been discussed, in Section III (p. 461). Owen's argument against this passage containing a complete use was there shown to depend on understanding a complete use as one which *does not allow* a completion. If we understand a complete use as one which allows but does not require a completion, the sentence presents no difficulty for the view that *esti, dia to metechein tou ontos* (and the variant here found: *metaschon tou ontos*; 259a6) represent a complete use.

To sum up my discussion of the passages containing the key phrase *esti, dia to metechein tou ontos*: there is every reason to take passage (i) as containing a complete use. Since passages (ii) and (iii) repeat the phrase, this gives us good grounds for interpreting them in the same way. But passages (ii) and (iii) suggest a C2 understanding of complete, rather than C1; that is, a use connected to the incomplete use in the manner explained in Section III. This being so, we can agree with those who deny that distinguishing the complete from the incomplete use was an important part of Plato's strategy, while insisting that the phrase in question does analyse a complete (C2) use. Plato has no idea of solving the problem of not-being by allowing that *X is F* need not entail *X is*, no wish to allow that only a subclass of things that are *F* are things that are (i.e. exist). But though it is not part of his overall strategy to draw a distinction between the complete and the incomplete use, he does, I believe, employ it as an occasional tactic, to wit, in his proof of the non-identity of the kinds *being* and *different*.

(d) 255c–d: The Proof of the Non-Identity of Being and the Different

This proof proceeds by invoking a distinction, said to be familiar to Theaetetus (255c12), in the way things that are are said to be:

Ἀλλ' οἶμαί σε συγχωρεῖν τῶν ὄντων τὰ μὲν αὐτὰ καθ' αὑτά, τὰ δὲ πρὸς ἄλλα ἀεὶ λέγεσθαι.

But I think you agree that some of the things that are are said to be 'themselves by themselves', while some are said to be in relation to other things.

In contrast, that which is different is always said to be different in relation to something different (*to de ge heteron aei pros heteron*).

What is the distinction alluded to? One line of interpretation, A, takes

---

[32] Heinaman, 'Being in the *Sophist*', 7–8, suggests that in this passage Plato either 'slides from *Each form is (i.e. exists)* to *each form is (predicatively) many things*, or infers the latter from the former. My view is the second; the inference is a straightforward one if a C2 use is involved in (1). Malcolm, 'Remarks on an Incomplete Rendering of Being in the *Sophist*', 165, resists this interpretation on the grounds that such an inference would be 'flagrantly fallacious'.

it to be between uses of *esti*: according to A, the proof points out that *esti* has both a *pros allo* use and an *auto kath' hauto* use, while *heteron* has only the former. The other line, B, denies this.[33] Those who favour A differ over whether the distinction is, A(i), between the complete (*auto kath' hauto*) and the incomplete (*pros allo*) uses,[34] or A(ii), between distinct incomplete uses which these labels pick out.[35] Like many others, I believe A(i) is correct, since it makes a clear and correct point, using fairly familiar terminology. The clear and correct point is this: that 'is' can be said of something on its own (as when one says, for instance: *change is*), and also in relation to something else, as when one says, for instance, *change is the opposite of rest* or *Socrates is wise*. But any use of *X is different* must be completed, with a reference to what *X* is different from. In Plato's usage elsewhere something said 'itself by itself' (*auto kath' hauto*) is typically something said with no qualification, not in relation to anything. So when the first way things can be said to be is labelled 'themselves by themselves' it is natural to understand this to mean uses of 'is' which stand on their own, i.e. complete uses. Which kind of complete use is meant I discuss below. The second way things can be said to be is characterized as 'in relation to something else' (*pros allo*, then *pros heteron*); this is understood as those uses of 'is' which have some completion, i.e. where 'is' is followed by another term. On this interpretation, then, Plato uses a familiar contrast (between non-relative and relative) to designate complete and incomplete uses of 'is' respectively.

But critics of A(i) disagree, using an argument from the choice of the expressions *pros allo* and *pros heteron*, where the more usual term is *pros ti* ('in relation to something') for the second term of the familiar contrast described above. They argue that Plato cannot have intended to include all incomplete uses of 'is' with the designation 'things said to be *pros allo*', since in some incomplete uses the completion picks out the *same* thing as the subject term (as in *Change is change*, or *The beautiful is beautiful*), not something different. So, they argue, we should not discern here the familiar contrast between non-relative (i.e. complete uses of 'is') and relative (i.e. incomplete uses), but should look for a different one, one which does justice to the choice of the expression 'in relation to something different'. Here Owen and Frede offer different alternatives, though both argue

---

[33] Heinaman, 'Being in the *Sophist*', 14: 'the passage is standardly interpreted as drawing a distinction between non-relative or complete predicates such as *man* and relative or incomplete predicates such as *equal*'. See e.g. A. E. Taylor, *Plato: The* Sophist *and the* Statesman (London, 1961), 161, for this view.

[34] e.g. J. M. E. Moravcsik, 'Being and Meaning in the *Sophist*', *Acta Philosophica Fennica*, 14 (1962), 48.

[35] Owen, pp. 444–6 above; Frede, *Prädikation und Existenzaussage*, 12–29.

against interpreting *auta kath' hauta* uses as complete, and both interpret the first use as well as the second as an incomplete use. Owen suggests that the contrast involved is that between the 'is' of identity ('is *auto kath' hauto*') and the 'is' of predication. Frede, followed by Meinwald,[35*] holds that the use of 'is' labelled *auto kath' hauto* is one in which we say what something is *of itself* or *by itself*. Examples would include 'White is a colour', 'Not-being is not-being', and 'The beautiful is beautiful'. The second use, on Frede's reading, picks out ordinary predications. In sum, those who believe that interpretation A(i) does not do justice to Plato's choice of terminology at 255d–e agree in denying that the first use of 'is' should be read as a complete 'is', but disagree in what alternative contrast Plato is signalling. Owen holds that the contrast is between the 'is' of identity and the 'is' of predication, while Frede holds that it is that between 'of itself' predication and ordinary predication, as explained above.

How serious is their objection from Plato's choice of the expression 'in relation to something else', in place of the more familiar 'in relation to something'? It can easily be answered, I believe. First, elsewhere Plato uses the two expressions interchangeably.[36] Second, given that he apparently regards them as interchangeable, the choice of the less usual *pros heteron* is easily explained by the contrast the Stranger is drawing between 'is' and 'different', since the natural way to say that different only has relational uses (what is different is always different *from something*) is to say that the different is always so-called in relation to something different.

So the objections to A(i) are easily answered. The rival interpretations of Owen and Frede, however, each suffer from the drawback of invoking a quite unfamiliar interpretation of the label *auta kath' hauta*.[36*]

[35*] Frede, *Prädikation und Existenzaussage*, and, for a more recent and much briefer treatment, M. Frede, 'The *Sophist* on False Statements', in R. Kraut (ed.), *The Cambridge Companion to Plato* (Cambridge, 1992); C. Meinwald, *Plato's* Parmenides (Oxford, 1991) and (a briefer discussion) 'Goodbye to the Third Man', also in Kraut (ed.), *The Cambridge Companion to Plato*.

[36] At *Philebus* 51 Plato draws the contrast between non-relative and relative, when discussing the beauty of shapes, pictures, and sounds. He uses both phrases, 'in relation to something' (*pros ti*)—at 51c6—and 'in relation to something different'—at 51d7—evidently to make one and the same contrast, between things beautiful relative to something, and things which are beautiful *auta kath' hauta*, just in themselves. See Bostock, 'Plato on "Is Not"', 92–4, for further arguments against Owen's view and in favour of the view I have labelled A(i).

[36*] Owen (n. 61) appealed to the division in Aristotle between *to kath' hauto legomenon* and *to heteron kath' heterou legomenon*. Frede (*Prädikation und Existenzaussage*, 27) appealed to a fragment of Aristotle to defend his interpretation of the expression in terms of what a thing is said to be *of itself, by itself*, or *in relation to itself*. Meinwald (*Plato's* Parmenides, and 'Goodbye to the Third Man') accepts Frede's reading of the distinction at *Sph.* 255c–d, and uses it to explicate a problematic contrast in *Parmenides* (an earlier work) between predications said to be *pros heauto* and those *pros ta alla* (in relation to itself versus in relation to the others). Meinwald ('Goodbye to the Third Man', 381) suggests that the starring role accorded to the distinc-

I conclude, therefore, that in this passage Plato makes the Stranger draw a distinction between two uses of 'is', the first of which is the complete or absolute use, the one we have met often already in the *Sophist*, and which gets glossed as 'shares in being' in the passages cited in (*c*) above. That being so, we may ask: is the complete (*auto kath' hauto*) use to be understood as C1 or as C2?

There seems to be no objection to taking the distinction to be between an incomplete (*pros allo*) use and a use which *does not need* a completion, that is, a C2 use. Plato's point would then be that every use of *heteron* requires a completion while some uses of *esti* do not require a completion. To make his point Plato needs only the C2 understanding of an *auto kath' hauto* use: he does not have to claim that there are some uses of *esti* which additionally do not *allow* a completion (C1). Indeed the traditional explication of the *auto kath' hauto–pros ti* distinction is phrased in precisely C2 terms (Diogenes Laertius 3. 108: 'things which are said *kath' heauta* are such as do not need anything additional in their interpretation').

I believe that this proof does invoke a distinction between a C2 complete and an incomplete use of *esti*. But there is no inconsistency in maintaining both of the following: (i) in this passage, 255cd, to achieve a proof of the non-identity of the kinds *being* and *different*, Plato points out that *esti*, unlike *heteron*, has a complete (C2) and an incomplete use; and (ii) the relation between the complete (C2) and the incomplete use is such that the distinction between them cannot form part of his overall strategy in solving the problems of not-being.

CONCLUSION

I have argued for a new understanding of the distinction between the syntactically complete and incomplete use of *esti*, supplanting the traditional understanding in terms of *monadic* and *dyadic*. A consequence of the proposed characterization, which I labelled C2, is that the complete and incomplete uses are related as follows: *X is* (complete use) entails *X is something* and *X is F* entails *X is*. *X is not* (complete use) is equivalent to *X is not anything at all*. Understanding the complete *esti* thus allows us to

---

tion in the *Parmenides* explains why Plato relied on it at *Sph.* 255c12 without explaining it or even drawing attention to it. But a major difficulty for Meinwald's identification of the two distinctions is the difference in terminology, for while the expression used in the *Parmenides* (*pros heauto*) does mean 'in relation to itself', it is far harder to understand the *Sophist*'s expression (*auta kath' hauta*) in that way, especially when it has a more familiar meaning which fits the context well.

say (*contra* Owen) that the *Sophist*'s problems about not being are stated in terms of the complete *esti*, but also to see why Plato found no role for *to mē on or to mēdamōs on* where that is the negation of the complete *esti*. We can also agree that at 255c–d Plato draws attention to the distinction between the complete and incomplete uses of 'is', while denying that this amounts to the discovery of a fundamental distinction between existence and the copula.

I hope to have shown that understanding the relation between the complete and incomplete uses of *esti* in the way proposed yields a satisfying reading of the *Sophist*. I believe that this proposal for the *Sophist* can be extended to, and supported by consideration of, other works of Plato and indeed Aristotle.[36**] Aristotle's well-known insistence (*Analytica Posteriora* 92^{b}4–8) that it is necessary to know *that* a thing is in order to know *what* it is (in other cases, as with 'goatstag', one can know only what the name signifies) is well explained if we pursue the analogy between *einai* and verbs such as *teach*: compare 'it is necessary to know that *X* is teaching in order to know what *X* is teaching'. And though Aristotle explicitly recognizes that *What is not is thought about* does not entail *what is not is* (the very point which the *Sophist* requires but which Plato fails to make), his discussion of the point does not suggest that he finds a clear semantic and syntactic distinction between the *estis* in that pair of sentences.[37]

[36**] See Lesley Brown, 'The Verb "To Be" in Greek Philosophy: Some Remarks', in S. Everson (ed.), *Language*, Cambridge Companions to Ancient Thought, iii (Cambridge, 1994) for a fuller treatment, which discusses Parmenides, Plato, and Aristotle.

[37] For a defence of this, see ibid. Among key texts are: *de Interpretatione* 21^{a}31–2; *Sophistici Elenchi* 166^{b}37–167^{a}4; cf. 180^{a}32–4. In the second passage the fallacious inference is put under the general heading of fallacies παρὰ τὸ ἁπλῶς τόδε ἤ πῆ λέγεσθαι καὶ μὴ κυρίως and is treated analogously to that from *the Indian is white in the tooth* to *the Indian is white*. Each involves the illicit removal of a qualifier (is white *in the tooth*, is *thought about*). Far from showing that Aristotle has here recognized two distinct senses of *esti*, his discussion of the fallacy suggests that he assumed a single sense to be involved, as with *white*. His point would then be that just as being white in the tooth is not really a way of being white, being thought about is not really a way of being. So that although he points out that 'it is not the same thing to be something and to be *haplōs*', this does not seem to be an express recognition of a clear-cut distinction such as Vlastos believed to be latently known to every speaker of Greek.

NOTES ON THE CONTRIBUTORS

J. L. ACKRILL was, until his retirement in 1989, Professor of the History of Philosophy in the University of Oxford and Fellow of Brasenose College. He is also Fellow of the British Academy. He is the author of *Aristotle:* Categories *and* de Interpretatione (translation and notes) (1963), *Aristotle the Philosopher* (1981), and *Essays on Plato and Aristotle* (1997), and the editor of *A New Aristotle Reader* (1987).

LESLEY BROWN is Centenary Fellow in Philosophy at Somerville College, Oxford. She is the author of several papers in ancient philosophy, and is working on a Clarendon edition of Plato's *Sophist*.

M. F. BURNYEAT is Senior Research Fellow in Philosophy at All Souls College, Oxford, and Fellow of the British Academy. He has also been Laurence Professor of Ancient Philosophy in the University of Cambridge. He is the author of *The* Theaetetus *of Plato* (1990), the editor of *The Skeptical Tradition* (1983), and co-editor of *Doubt and Dogmatism* (1980) and *Science and Speculation* (1982).

S. MARC COHEN is Professor of Philosophy at the University of Washington. He is the author of several papers in ancient philosophy, and co-editor of *Readings in Ancient Greek Philosophy from Thales to Aristotle* (1995).

JOHN M. COOPER is Stuart Professor of Philosophy at Princeton University. He is the author of *Reason and Human Good in Aristotle* (1975) and of *Reason and Emotion: Essays on Ancient Moral Psychology and Ethical Theory* (1999), and the editor of *Plato: Complete Works* (1997).

DANIEL DEVEREUX is Professor of Philosophy at the University of Virginia. He is the author of many articles in ancient philosophy.

GAIL FINE is Professor of Philosophy at Cornell University. She is the author of *On Ideas: Aristotle's Criticism of Plato's Theory of Forms* (1993) and co-author of *Aristotle: Selections* (translation and notes) (1995).

MICHAEL FREDE is Professor of the History of Philosophy in the University of Oxford and Fellow of Keble College. He is the author of *Prädikation und Existenzaussage* (1967), *Die stoische Logik* (1974), *Essays in Ancient Philosophy* (1987), co-author of *Aristoteles* Metaphysik Z (text, translation, and commentary) (1988), and co-editor of *Rationality in Greek Thought* (1996).

T. H. IRWIN is Susan Linn Sage Professor of Philosophy at Cornell University. His books include *Plato's Moral Theory* (1977), *Plato:* Gorgias (translation and notes) (1979), *Aristotle:* Nicomachean Ethics (translation and notes) (1985), *Aristotle's First Principles* (1988), *Classical Thought* (1989), *Plato's Ethics* (1995), and *Classical Philosophy* (1999). He is also co-author of *Aristotle: Selections* (translation and notes) (1995).

JOHN MCDOWELL is University Professor of Philosophy at the University of Pittsburgh. His books include *Plato:* Theaetetus (translation and notes) (1973), *Mind and World* (1994), *Mind, Value, and Reality* (1998), and *Meaning, Knowledge, and Reality* (1998).

ALEXANDER NEHAMAS is Edmund N. Carpenter II Class of 1973 Professor in the Humanities, and Professor of Philosophy and Comparative Literature at Princeton University. He is the author of *Nietzsche: Life as Literature* (1985), *The Art of Living: Socratic Reflections from Plato to Foucault* (1998), and *Virtues of Authenticity: Essays on Plato and Socrates* (1998).

G. E. L. OWEN was Laurence Professor of Ancient Philosophy at the University of Cambridge from 1973 until his death in 1982. He also taught at the Universities of Oxford and Harvard. His papers are collected in *Logic, Science and Dialectic* (1986). He also edited *Aristotle on Dialectic* (1968), and co-edited *Aristotle and Plato in the Mid-Fourth Century* (1960) and *Aristotle on Mind and the Senses* (1978).

GERASIMOS SANTAS is Professor of Philosophy at the University of California at Irvine. He is the author of *Socrates: Philosophy in Plato's Early Dialogues* (1979) and of *Plato and Freud: Two Theories of Love* (1988).

DOMINIC SCOTT is Lecturer in Philosophy at the University of Cambridge and Fellow of Clare College. He is the author of *Recollection and Experience* (1995).

STEVEN K. STRANGE is Associate Professor of Philosophy at Emory University. He is the author of several papers in ancient philosophy, and of *Porphyry's On Aristotle's Categories* (translation and notes) (1992).

GREGORY VLASTOS was Stuart Professor of Philosophy at Princeton University until his retirement in 1978. He then became Mills Professor of Philosophy at the University of California at Berkeley. He died in 1991. He is the author of *Socrates, Ironist and Moral Philosopher* (1991). Many of his essays are collected in *Platonic Studies* (1973, 1981), *Socratic Studies* (1993), and *Studies in Greek Philosophy*, 2 vols. (1995). He was also the editor of *The Philosophy of Socrates* (1971), and of *Plato, i: Metaphysics and Epistemology* (1971) and *Plato, ii: Ethics, Politics, and Philosophy of Art and Religion* (1971).

SELECTED BIBLIOGRAPHY

This bibliography lists some works that might be useful to readers who wish to pursue the topics discussed here further. It is far from being comprehensive. I have focused mainly on fairly recent work, and on work in English. The essays reprinted in this anthology are not listed here, nor have I listed all the sources they cite.

Abbreviations

CCP   R. Kraut (ed.), *Cambridge Companion to Plato* (Cambridge: Cambridge University Press, 1992).

EA   E. N. Lee, A. D. P. Mourelatos, and R. M. Rorty (eds.), *Exegesis and Argument: Studies in Greek Philosophy Presented to Gregory Vlastos* (Assen: Van Gorcum, 1973).

EPS   H. H. Benson (ed.), *Essays on the Philosophy of Socrates* (New York: Oxford University Press, 1992).

FA   C. Gill and M. M. McCabe (eds.), *Form and Argument in Late Plato* (Oxford: Clarendon Press, 1996).

LL   M. Nussbaum and M. Schofield (eds.), *Language and Logos: Studies in Ancient Greek Philosophy Presented to G. E. L. Owen* (Cambridge: Cambridge University Press, 1982).

LSD   G. E. L. Owen, *Logic, Science and Dialectic: Collected Papers in Greek Philosophy*, ed. M. Nussbaum (Ithaca, NY: Cornell University Press, 1986).

MAP   J. Gentzler (ed.), *Method in Ancient Philosophy* (Oxford: Clarendon Press, 1998).

Plato i G. Vlastos (ed.), *Plato*, i: *Metaphysics and Epistemology* (Garden City, NY: Doubleday Anchor, 1971).

PS   G. Vlastos, *Platonic Studies*, 2nd edn. (Princeton: Princeton University Press, 1981).

SPM   R. E. Allen (ed.), *Studies in Plato's Metaphysics* (London: Routledge & Kegan Paul, 1965).

Texts and Translations

The Greek text of Plato is collected in five volumes published by Oxford University Press (Oxford Classical Texts—OCT), edited by J. Burnet (1900–7). These are gradually being replaced with new editions, the first volume of which has appeared, edited by E. A. Duke, W. F. Hicken, W. S. M. Nicoll, D. B. Robinson, and J. C. G. Strachan (1995). The Greek texts, with facing English translations, are available in the Loeb library; the translations are of varying quality. The Budé texts are also worth consulting; they contain a Greek text with facing French translations, and short notes. The Clarendon Plato series provides generally accurate translations along with detailed notes. The books in this series include:

Gorgias, ed. T. H. Irwin (1979).
Phaedo, ed. D. Gallop (1975).
Philebus, ed. J. C. B. Gosling (1975).

Protagoras, ed. C. C. W. Taylor (1976, 1991).
Theaetetus, ed. J. McDowell (1973).

Translations of all the dialogues and letters, by various authors, can be found in:

Plato: Complete Works, eds. J. M. Cooper and D. S. Hutchinson (Indianapolis: Hackett, 1997).

Some of these translations appear in separate volumes, with introductions and notes;

Plato: Cratylus, ed. C. D. C. Reeve (1998).
Plato: Parmenides, eds. M. L. Gill and P. Ryan (1996).
Plato: Phaedrus, eds. A. Nehamas and P. Woodruff (1995).
Plato: Philebus, ed. D. Frede (1993).
Plato: Sophist, ed. N. P. White (1993).
Plato: Symposium, eds. A. Nehamas and P. Woodruff (1989).
Plato: Timaeus, ed. D. Zeyl (1999).

Another widely used collection is:

The Collected Dialogues of Plato including the Letters, eds. E. Hamilton and H. Cairns, Bollingen Foundation (New York: Pantheon, 1961; Princeton: Princeton University Press, 1971).

The reader new to Plato might begin with:

BENSON, H. H. (ed.), *Essays on the Philosophy of Socrates* (New York: Oxford University Press, 1992). Cited as *EPS*.
IRWIN, T. H., *Plato's Ethics* (New York: Oxford University Press, 1995). (This is a significant revision of *Plato's Moral Theory*, which is listed separately below. Though both books are primarily concerned with Plato's ethics, they both discuss metaphysics and epistemology.)
KRAUT, R. (ed.), *Cambridge Companion to Plato* (Cambridge: Cambridge University Press, 1992). Cited as *CCP*.
OWEN, G. E. L., *Logic, Science and Dialectic: Collected Papers in Greek Philosophy*, ed. M. Nussbaum (Ithaca, NY: Cornell University Press, 1986). (Difficult but rewarding.) Cited as *LSD*.
VLASTOS, G., *Platonic Studies*, 2nd edn. (Princeton: Princeton University Press, 1981). Cited as *PS*.
——*Socrates, Ironist and Moral Philosopher* (Ithaca, NY: Cornell University Press, 1991).
——(ed.), *The Philosophy of Socrates* (Garden City, NY: Doubleday Anchor, 1971).
——(ed.), *Plato*, i: *Metaphysics and Epistemology* (Garden City, NY: Doubleday Anchor, 1971). Cited as *Plato* i.
WHITE, N. P., *Plato on Knowledge and Reality* (Indianapolis: Hackett, 1976).

Readers interested in the chronology of Plato's dialogues might look at:

BRANDWOOD, L., *The Chronology of Plato's Dialogues* (Cambridge: Cambridge University Press, 1990).
——'Stylometry and Chronology', in *CCP* 90–120.
YOUNG, C., 'Plato and Computer Dating', *Oxford Studies in Ancient Philosophy*, 12 (1994), 227–50.

See also the provocative remarks by Cooper, in his introduction to *Plato: Complete Works*.

There is dispute as to whether the dialogues that are generally taken to be early represent the thought of the historical Socrates. For the view that they do, see:

VLASTOS, G., *Socrates, Ironist and Moral Philosopher* (Ithaca, NY: Cornell University Press, 1991).

For a more sceptical assessment, see:

KAHN, C., *Plato and the Socratic Dialogue: The Philosophical Use of a Literary Form* (Cambridge: Cambridge University Press, 1996).

NEHAMAS, A., 'Voices of Silence: On Gregory Vlastos' Socrates', *Arion*, 3rd ser., 2 (1992), 156–86.

For another recent discussion of the 'Socratic problem', see:

TAYLOR, C. C. W., *Socrates* (New York: Oxford University Press, 1998).

On the question of why Plato wrote dialogues, see:

FREDE, M., 'Plato's Arguments and the Dialogue Form', in J. Klagge and N. Smith (eds.), *Methods of Interpreting Plato and his Dialogues*, *Oxford Studies in Ancient Philosophy*, suppl. vol. (Oxford: Clarendon Press, 1992), 201–19.

This topic is also touched on in:

IRWIN, T. H., 'Plato: The Intellectual Background', in *CCP* 51–89.

KRAUT, R., 'Introduction to the Study of Plato', in *CCP* 1–50.

For discussion of literary and historical aspects of the dialogues, see:

RUTHERFORD, R., *The Art of Plato: Ten Essays in Platonic Interpretation* (Cambridge, Mass.: Harvard University Press, 1995).

The rest of this bibliography lists, first, books that cover a fairly broad range of topics and/or dialogues, and then various other works, listed under the name of the dialogue or topic with which they are primarily concerned. Material already mentioned above is not repeated below. I list most works just once; some works, however, are relevant to more than one section.

General Books

ALLEN, R. E. (ed.), *Studies in Plato's Metaphysics* (London: Routledge & Kegan Paul, 1965). Cited as *SPM*.

ANTON, J., and KUSTAS, G. (eds.), *Essays in Ancient Greek Philosophy* (Albany: State University of New York, 1971).

—— and PREUS, A. (eds.), *Essays in Ancient Greek Philosophy*, ii (Albany: State University of New York, 1983).

———— (eds.), *Essays in Ancient Greek Philosophy*, iii (Albany: State University of New York, 1989).

CROMBIE, I. M., *An Examination of Plato's Doctrines*, 2 vols. (London: Routledge & Kegan Paul, 1963).

DENYER, N., *Language, Thought and Falsehood in Ancient Greek Philosophy* (London: Routledge & Kegan Paul, 1991).

GENTZLER, J. (ed.), *Method in Ancient Philosophy* (Oxford: Clarendon Press, 1998). Cited as *MAP*.

GILL, C., and McCABE, M. M. (eds.), *Form and Argument in Late Plato* (Oxford: Clarendon Press, 1996). Cited as *FA*.

GOSLING, J. C. B., *Plato* (London: Routledge & Kegan Paul, 1973).

GROTE, G., *Plato and the Other Companions of Socrates*, new edn., 4 vols. (London: John Murray, 1888).

GUTHRIE, W. K. C., *A History of Greek Philosophy*, iv (Cambridge: Cambridge University Press, 1975).

——*A History of Greek Philosophy*, v (Cambridge: Cambridge University Press, 1979).

HARDIE, W. F. R., *A Study in Plato* (Oxford: Clarendon Press, 1936).

IRWIN, T. H., *Plato's Moral Theory: The Early and Middle Dialogues* (Oxford: Clarendon Press, 1977).

KLAGGE, J., and SMITH, N. D. (eds.), *Methods of Interpreting Plato and his Dialogues*, Oxford Studies in Ancient Philosophy, suppl. vol. (Oxford: Clarendon Press, 1992).

LEE, E. N., MOURELATOS, A. D. P., and RORTY, R. M. (eds.), *Exegesis and Argument: Studies in Greek Philosophy Presented to Gregory Vlastos* (Assen: Van Gorcum, 1973). Cited as *EA*.

MCCABE, M. M., *Plato's Individuals* (Princeton: Princeton University Press, 1994).

NUSSBAUM, M., and SCHOFIELD, M. (eds.), *Language and Logos: Studies in Ancient Greek Philosophy Presented to G. E. L. Owen* (Cambridge: Cambridge University Press, 1982). Cited as *LL*.

PENNER, T., *The Ascent from Nominalism: Some Existence Arguments in Plato's Middle Dialogues* (Dordrecht: Reidel, 1987).

PRIOR, W., *Unity and Development in Plato's Metaphysics* (London: Croom Helm, 1985).

ROBINSON, R., *Plato's Earlier Dialectic*, 2nd edn. (Oxford: Clarendon Press, 1953).

ROSS, W. D., *Plato's Theory of Ideas* (Oxford: Clarendon Press, 1951).

SANTAS, G., *Socrates: Philosophy in Plato's Early Dialogues* (London: Routledge & Kegan Paul, 1979).

SAYRE, K., *Plato's Analytic Method* (Chicago: University of Chicago Press, 1969).

——*Plato's Late Ontology: A Riddle Resolved* (Princeton: Princeton University Press, 1983).

SCOTT, D., *Recollection and Experience: Plato's Theory of Learning and its Successors* (Cambridge: Cambridge University Press, 1995).

The Early Dialogues

ALLEN, R. E., *Plato's* Euthyphro *and the Earlier Theory of Forms* (London: Routledge & Kegan Paul, 1970).

BENSON, H., 'The Problem of the Elenchus Revisited', *Ancient Philosophy*, 7 (1987), 67–85.

——'Misunderstanding the "What is *F*-ness?" Question', *Archiv für Geschichte der Philosophie*, 72 (1990), 125–42; repr. in *EPS* 123–36.

——'The Priority of Definition and the Socratic *Elenchos*', *Oxford Studies in Ancient Philosophy*, 8 (1990), 19–65.

BEVERSLUIS, J., 'Does Socrates Commit the Socratic Fallacy?', *American Philosophical Quarterly*, 24 (1987), 211–23; repr. in *EPS* 107–22.

BRICKHOUSE, N., and SMITH, T., *Plato's Socrates* (Oxford: Oxford University Press, 1994).

BURNYEAT, M. F., 'Examples in Epistemology', *Philosophy*, 52 (1977), 381–98.

GEACH, P. T., 'Plato's *Euthyphro*: Analysis and Commentary', *Monist*, 50 (1966), 369–82.

GUTHRIE, W. K. C., *Socrates* (Cambridge: Cambridge University Press, 1971); first pub. as pt. 2 of *A History of Greek Philosophy*, iii (Cambridge: Cambridge University Press, 1969).

IRWIN, T. H., 'Coercion and Objectivity in Plato's Dialectic', *Revue Internationale de Philosophie*, 40 (1986), 47–74.

KRAUT, R., 'Comments on Gregory Vlastos, "The Socratic Elenchus"', *Oxford Studies in Ancient Philosophy*, 1 (1983), 59–70.

LESHER, J. H., 'Socrates' Disavowal of Knowledge', *Journal of the History of Philosophy*, 25 (1984), 275–88.

MACKENZIE, M. M., 'The Virtues of Socratic Ignorance', *Classical Quarterly*, NS 38 (1988), 331–50.

NEHAMAS, A., 'Confusing Universals and Particulars in Plato's Early Dialogues', *Review of Metaphysics*, 29 (1975), 287–306.

PENNER, T., 'The Unity of Virtue', *Philosophical Review*, 82 (1973), 35–68; repr. in *EPS* 162–84; and as Ch. III in Vol. ii of this work.

PRIOR, J., 'Plato and the "Socratic Fallacy"', *Phronesis*, 43 (1998), 97–113.

REEVE, C. D. C., *Socrates in the* Apology: *An Essay on Plato's* Apology *of Socrates* (Indianapolis: Hackett, 1989).

SANTAS, G., *Socrates: Philosophy in Plato's Early Dialogues* (London: Routledge & Kegan Paul, 1979).

TAYLOR, C. C. W., *Socrates* (New York: Oxford University Press, 1998).

VLASTOS, G., Introduction to *Plato:* Protagoras (Indianapolis: Bobbs-Merrill, 1965).
—— 'The Unity of the Virtues in the *Protagoras*', *Review of Metaphysics*, 25 (1972), 415–58; rev. in *PS* 221–69.
—— 'What did Socrates Understand by his "What is *F*?" Question?', in *PS* 410–17.
—— 'Is the Socratic Fallacy Socratic?', *Ancient Philosophy*, 10 (1990), 1–16; rev. in *Socratic Studies*, 67–86.
—— *Socratic Studies*, ed. M. F. Burnyeat (Cambridge: Cambridge University Press, 1994).

WOODRUFF, P., 'Plato's Early Theory of Knowledge', in S. Everson (ed.), *Companions to Ancient Thought*, i: *Epistemology* (Cambridge: Cambridge University Press, 1989), 60–84; repr. in *EPS* 86–106.

Meno

BLUCK, R. S., *Plato's* Meno (Cambridge: Cambridge University Press, 1964).

DEMAS, P., 'True Belief in the *Meno*', *Oxford Studies in Ancient Philosophy*, 14 (1996), 1–32.

FINE, G., 'Inquiry in the *Meno*', in *CCP* 200–26.

MORAVCSIK, J. M. E., 'Learning as Recollection', in *Plato* i. 53–69.

NEHAMAS, A., 'Meno's Paradox and Socrates as a Teacher', *Oxford Studies in Ancient Philosophy*, 3 (1985), 1–30; repr. in *EPS* 298–316.
—— 'Socratic Intellectualism', in J. Cleary (ed.), *Proceedings of the Boston Area Colloquium in Ancient Philosophy*, ii (Lanham, Md.: University Press of America, 1986), 275–316.

SHARPLES, R. W., *Plato:* Meno (Warminster: Aris & Phillips, 1985).

THOMPSON, E. S., *The* Meno *of Plato* (London: Macmillan, 1901).

VLASTOS, G., 'Anamnēsis in the Meno', Dialogue, 4 (1965), 143–67.
——'Elenchus and Mathematics', American Journal of Philology, 109 (1988), 362–96; repr. in Socrates, Ironist and Moral Philosopher (Ithaca, NY: Cornell University Press, 1991), 107–31; and in EPS 137–61.
WHITE, N. R., 'Inquiry', Review of Metaphysics, 28 (1974), 289–310.

Cratylus

ANNAS, J., 'Knowledge and Language: The Theaetetus and the Cratylus', in LL 95–114.
BARNEY, R., 'Plato on Conventionalism', Phronesis, 42 (1997), 143–61.
BAXTER, T., The Cratylus: Plato's Critique of Naming (Leiden: E. J. Brill, 1992).
FINE, G., 'Plato on Naming', Philosophical Quarterly, 27 (1977), 289–301.
KAHN, C., 'Language and Ontology in the Cratylus', in EA 152–76.
KETCHUM, R., 'Names, Forms, and Conventionalism: Cratylus 383–95', Phronesis, 24 (1979), 133–47.
KRETZMANN, N., 'Plato on the Correctness of Names', American Philosophical Quarterly, 8 (1971), 126–38.
MACKENZIE, M. M., 'Putting the Cratylus in its Place', Classical Quarterly, NS 36 (1986), 124–50.
SCHOFIELD, M., 'The Dénouement of the Cratylus', in LL 61–81.
SILVERMAN, A., 'Plato's Cratylus: The Naming of Nature and the Nature of Naming', Oxford Studies in Ancient Philosophy, 10 (1992), 25–72.
SPELLMAN, L., 'Naming and Knowing: The Cratylus on Images', History of Philosophy Quarterly, 10 (1993), 197–210.
WILLIAMS, B. A. O., 'Cratylus' Theory of Names and its Refutation', in LL 83–93.

Phaedo and the Theory of Forms

ACKRILL, J. L., 'Anamnēsis in the Phaedo', in EA 177–95.
ANNAS, J., 'Aristotle on Inefficient Causes', Philosophical Quarterly, 32 (1982), 311–26.
BOLTON, R., 'Plato's Distinction between Being and Becoming', Review of Metaphysics, 29 (1975), 66–95.
BOSTOCK, D., Plato's Phaedo (Oxford: Clarendon Press, 1986).
CHERNISS, H. F., 'The Philosophical Economy of the Theory of Ideas', American Journal of Philology, 57 (1936), 445–56; repr. in SPM 1–12; and in Plato i. 16–27.
FINE, G., 'The One over Many', Philosophical Review, 89 (1980), 197–240.
——'Separation', Oxford Studies in Ancient Philosophy, 2 (1984), 31–87.
——'Forms as Causes: Plato and Aristotle', in A. Graeser (ed.), Mathematics and Metaphysics in Aristotle (Bern: Haupt, 1986), 69–112.
——On Ideas: Aristotle's Criticism of Plato's Theory of Forms (Oxford: Clarendon Press, 1993).
GENTZLER, J., 'Sumphōnein in Plato's Phaedo', Phronesis, 36 (1991), 265–76.
GOSLING, J. C. B., 'Similarity in Phaedo 73b seq.', Phronesis, 10 (1965), 151–61.
HARTMAN, E., 'Predication and Immortality in Plato's Phaedo', Archiv für Geschichte der Philosophie, 54 (1972), 215–28.
IRWIN, T. H., 'Plato's Heracleiteanism', Philosophical Quarterly, 27 (1977), 1–13.
KEYT, D., 'The Fallacies in Phaedo 102a–107b', Phronesis, 8 (1963), 167–72.
KIRWAN, C., 'Plato and Relativity', Phronesis, 19 (1974), 112–29.

MALCOLM, J., *Plato on the Self-Predication of Forms: Early and Middle Dialogues* (Oxford: Clarendon Press, 1991).

MATES, B., 'Identity and Predication in Plato', *Phronesis*, 24 (1979), 211–29.

MATTHEWS, G., and BLACKSON, T., 'Causes in the *Phaedo*', *Synthèse*, 79 (1989), 581–91.

——and COHEN, S. M., 'The One and the Many', *Review of Metaphysics*, 21 (1968), 630–55.

MILLS, K. W., 'Plato's *Phaedo* 74', *Phronesis*, 2 (1957), 128–74; 3 (1958), 40–58.

NEHAMAS, A., 'Predication and Forms of Opposites in the *Phaedo*', *Review of Metaphysics*, 26 (1973), 461–91.

——'Self-Predication and Plato's Theory of Forms', *American Philosophical Quarterly*, 16 (1979), 93–103.

OWEN, G. E. L., 'A Proof in the *Peri Ideōn*', *Journal of Hellenic Studies*, 77 (1957), 103–11; repr. in *SPM* 243–312; and in *LSD* 165–79.

ROWE, C. J., *Plato:* Phaedo (Cambridge: Cambridge University Press, 1995).

SEDLEY, D., 'Teleology and Myth in Plato's *Phaedo*', in J. Cleary and D. Shartin (eds.), *Proceedings of the Boston Area Colloquium in Ancient Philosophy*, 5 (Lanham, Md.: University Press of America, 1991), 359–83.

VLASTOS, G., 'The Third Man Argument in the *Parmenides*', *Philosophical Review*, 63 (1954), 319–40; repr. in *SPM* 231–63.

——'Degrees of Reality in Plato', in R. Bambrough (ed.), *New Essays on Plato and Aristotle* (London: Routledge & Kegan Paul, 1965), 1–18; repr. in *PS* 58–75.

——'A Metaphysical Paradox', *Proceedings and Addresses of the American Philosophical Association*, 39 (1966), 5–19; repr. in *PS* 43–57.

——'Reasons and Causes in the *Phaedo*', *Philosophical Review*, 78 (1969), 291–325; repr. in *Plato* i. 132–66; and in *PS* 76–110.

WHITE, N. P., 'Forms and Sensibles: *Phaedo* 74bc', *Philosophical Topics*, 15 (1987), 197–214.

——'Perceptual and Objective Properties in Plato', *Apeiron*, 22 (1989), 45–65.

——'Plato's Metaphysical Epistemology', in *CCP* 277–310.

WIGGINS, D., 'Teleology and the Good in Plato's *Phaedo*', *Oxford Studies in Ancient Philosophy* 4 (1986), 1–18.

Republic

ADAM, J., *The* Republic *of Plato*, 2 vols. (Cambridge: Cambridge University Press, 1902).

ANNAS, J., *An Introduction to Plato's* Republic (Oxford: Clarendon Press, 1981).

BURNYEAT, M. F., 'Platonism and Mathematics: A Prelude to Discussion', in A. Graeser (ed.), *Mathematics and Metaphysics in Aristotle* (Bern: Haupt, 1987), 213–40.

CROSS, R. C., and WOOZLEY, A. D., *Plato's* Republic: *A Philosophical Commentary* (London: Macmillan, 1964).

FINE, G., 'Knowledge and Belief in *Republic* V', *Archiv für Geschichte der Philosophie*, 60 (1978), 121–39.

FOGELIN, R., 'Three Platonic Analogies', *Philosophical Review*, 80 (1971), 371–82.

GOSLING, J. C. B., '*Republic* V: *Ta Polla Kala*', *Phronesis*, 5 (1960), 116–28.

——'*Doxa* and *Dunamis* in *Republic* V', *Phronesis*, 13 (1968), 119–30.

JOSEPH, H. W. B., *Knowledge and the Good in Plato's* Republic (Oxford: Clarendon Press, 1948).

KARASMANIS, V., 'Plato's *Republic*: The Line and the Cave', *Apeiron*, 21 (1988), 147–71.

MURPHY, N. R., *The Interpretation of Plato's* Republic (Oxford: Clarendon Press, 1951).

REEVE, C. D. C., *Philosopher-Kings: The Argument of Plato's* Republic (Princeton: Princeton University Press, 1988).

STRANG, C., 'Plato's Analogy of the Cave', *Oxford Studies in Ancient Philosophy*, 4 (1986), 19–34.

TAYLOR, C. C. W., 'Plato and the Mathematicians', *Philosophical Quarterly*, 17 (1967), 193–203.

WHITE, N. P., *A Companion to Plato's* Republic (Indianapolis: Hackett, 1979).

WILSON, J. S., 'The Contents of the Cave', in R. Shiner and J. King-Farlow (eds.), *New Essays on Plato and the Pre-Socratics*, *Canadian Journal of Philosophy*, suppl. vol. 2 (Guelph: Canadian Association for Publishing in Philosophy, 1976), 111–24.

Symposium *and* Phaedrus

BURY, G., *The* Symposium *of Plato*, 2nd edn. (Cambridge: Cambridge University Press, 1932).

FERRARI, G., *Listening to the Cicadas: A Study of Plato's* Phaedrus (Cambridge: Cambridge University Press, 1987).

HACKFORTH, R., *Plato's* Phaedrus (Cambridge: Cambridge University Press, 1952).

HEATH, M., 'The Unity of Plato's *Phaedrus*', *Oxford Studies in Ancient Philosophy*, 7 (1989), 151–73.

——'The Unity of the *Phaedrus*: A Postscript', *Oxford Studies in Ancient Philosophy*, 7 (1989), 189–91.

MORAVCSIK, J. M. E., 'Reason and *Eros* in the "Ascent"-Passage of the *Symposium*', in J. Anton and G. Kustas (eds.), *Essays in Ancient Greek Philosophy* (Albany: State University of New York, 1971), 285–302.

ROSSETTI, L. (ed.), *Understanding the* Phaedrus, *Proceedings of the Second Symposium Platonicum* (Sankt Augustin: Academia Verlag, 1992).

ROWE, C. J., 'The Argument and Structure of Plato's *Phaedrus*', *Proceedings of the Cambridge Philological Society*, 32 (1986), 106–25.

——'The Unity of Plato's *Phaedrus*: A Reply to Heath', *Oxford Studies in Ancient Philosophy*, 7 (1989), 175–88.

——*Plato:* Phaedrus (Warminster: Aris & Phillips, 1986).

Parmenides

ALLEN, R. E., *Plato's* Parmenides: *Translation and Analysis* (Minneapolis: University of Minnesota Press, 1983).

CORNFORD, F. M., *Plato and Parmenides* (London: Routledge & Kegan Paul, 1939).

FINE, G., 'Owen, Aristotle, and the Third Man', *Phronesis*, 27 (1982), 13–33.

GEACH, P., 'The Third Man Again', *Philosophical Review*, 65 (1956), 72–82; repr. in *SPM* 265–77.

MCCABE, M. M., 'Unity in the *Parmenides*: The Unity of the *Parmenides*', in *FA* 5–47.

MEINWALD, C., *Plato's* Parmenides (New York: Oxford University Press, 1991).

——'Good-bye to the Third Man', in *CCP* 365–396.

MIGNUCCI, M., 'Plato's Third Man Arguments in the *Parmenides*', *Archiv für Geschichte der Philosophie*, 72 (1990), 143–81.

MORAVCSIK, J. M. E., 'The "Third Man" Argument and Plato's Theory of Forms', *Phronesis*, 8 (1963), 50–62.

PETERSON, S., 'A Reasonable Self-Predication Premise for the Third Man Argument', *Philosophical Review*, 82 (1973), 451–70.

—— 'The Greatest Difficulty for Plato's Theory of Forms: The Unknowability Argument of *Parmenides* 133c–134', *Archiv für Geschichte der Philosophie*, 63 (1981), 1–16.

RYLE, G., 'Plato's *Parmenides*', in *SPM* 85–103.

SCHOFIELD, M., 'Likeness and Likenesses in the *Parmenides*', in *FA* 49–77.

SELLARS, W., 'Vlastos and the "Third Man"', *Philosophical Review*, 64 (1955), 405–37.

STRANG, C., 'Plato and the Third Man', *Proceedings of the Aristotelian Society*, suppl. vol. 37 (1963), 147–64; repr. in *Plato* i. 184–200.

VLASTOS, G., 'The Third Man Argument in the *Parmenides*', *Philosophical Review*, 63 (1954), 319–49; repr. in *SPM* 231–63.

—— 'Plato's "Third Man" Argument (*Parm*. 132a1–b2): Text and Logic', *Philosophical Quarterly*, 19 (1969), 289–91; repr. in *PS* 342–65.

Theaetetus

ACKRILL, J. L., 'Plato on False Belief: *Theaetetus* 187–200', *Monist*, 50 (1966), 383–402.

ANNAS, J., 'Knowledge and Language: The *Theaetetus* and the *Cratylus*', in *LL* 95–114.

BOLTON, R., 'Plato's Distinction between Being and Becoming', *Review of Metaphysics*, 29 (1975), 66–95.

BOSTOCK, D., *Plato's* Theaetetus (Oxford: Clarendon Press, 1988).

BURNYEAT, M. F., 'The Materials and Sources of Plato's Dream', *Phronesis*, 15 (1970), 101–22.

—— 'Plato on the Grammar of Perceiving', *Classical Quarterly*, NS 26 (1976), 29–51.

—— 'Protagoras and Self-Refutation in Later Greek Philosophy', *Philosophical Review*, 85 (1976), 44–69.

—— 'Protagoras and Self-Refutation in Plato's *Theaetetus*', *Philosophical Review*, 85 (1976), 172–95; repr. in S. Everson (ed.), *Companions to Ancient Thought*, i: *Epistemology* (Cambridge: Cambridge University Press, 1989), 39–59.

—— 'Examples in Epistemology: Socrates, Theaetetus, and G. E. Moore', *Philosophy*, 52 (1977), 381–98.

—— 'Socratic Midwifery, Platonic Inspiration', *Bulletin of the Institute of Classical Studies*, 24 (1977), 7–16; repr. in *EPS* 53–65.

—— 'Conflicting Appearances', *Proceedings of the British Academy*, 65 (1979), 69–111.

—— 'Socrates and the Jury: Paradoxes in Plato's Distinction between Knowledge and True Belief', *Aristotelian Society*, suppl. vol. 54 (1980), 177–91. (Reply by J. Barnes, 193–206.)

—— 'Idealism and Greek Philosophy: What Descartes Saw and Berkeley Missed', *Philosophical Review*, 90 (1982), 3–40.

—— *The* Theaetetus *of Plato*, trans. M. J. Levett, rev. and introd. Burnyeat (Indianapolis: Hackett, 1990).

CORNFORD, F. M., *Plato's Theory of Knowledge: The* Theaetetus *and* Sophist (London: Routledge & Kegan Paul, 1935).

DANCY, R., 'Theaetetus' First Baby: *Theaetetus* 151e–160e', *Philosophical Topics*, 15 (1987), 61–108.

FINE, G., 'False Belief in the *Theaetetus*', *Phronesis*, 24 (1979), 70–80.

—— 'Knowledge and *Logos* in the *Theaetetus*', *Philosophical Review*, 88 (1979), 366–97.

—— 'Plato on Perception', *Oxford Studies in Ancient Philosophy*, suppl. vol. (1988), 15–28.

—— 'Protagorean Relativisms', in J. Cleary and W. Wians (eds.), *Proceedings of the Boston Area Colloquium in Ancient Philosophy*, 10 (Lanham, Md.: University Press of America, 1996), 211–43.

—— 'Conflicting Appearances: *Theaetetus* 153d–154b', in *FA* 105–33.

HOLLAND, A. J., 'An Argument in Plato's *Theaetetus*: 184–6', *Philosophical Quarterly*, 23 (1973), 97–116.

KANAYAMA, Y., 'Perceiving, Considering, and Attaining Being (*Theaetetus* 184–186)', *Oxford Studies in Ancient Philosophy*, 5 (1987), 29–81.

KERFERD, G. B., 'Plato's Account of the Relativism of Protagoras', *Durham University Journal*, 42 (1949), 20–6.

KETCHUM, R., 'Plato and Protagorean Relativism', *Oxford Studies in Ancient Philosophy*, 10 (1992), 73–105.

LEE, E. N., 'Hoist on his Own Petard', in *EA* 225–61.

LESHER, J. H., '*Gnōsis* and *Epistēmē* in Socrates' Dream in the *Theaetetus*', *Journal of Hellenic Studies*, 89 (1969), 72–8.

LEWIS, F., 'Foul Play in Plato's Aviary', in *EA* 262–84.

—— 'Two Paradoxes in the *Theaetetus*', in J. M. E. Moravcsik (ed.), *Patterns in Plato's Thought* (Dordrecht: Reidel, 1973), 123–49.

MATTHEN, M., 'Perception, Relativism and Truth: Reflections on Plato's *Theaetetus* 152–60', *Dialogue*, 24 (1985), 33–58.

MODRAK, D., 'Perception and Judgment in the *Theaetetus*', *Phronesis*, 26 (1981), 35–54.

MORROW, G., 'Plato and the Mathematicians: An Interpretation of Socrates' Dream in the *Theaetetus* 201e–206c)', *Philosophical Review*, 79 (1970), 309–33.

NEHAMAS, A., '*Epistēmē* and *Logos* in Plato's Later Thought', *Archiv für Geschichte der Philosophie*, 66 (1984), 11–36.

RUDEBUSCH, G., 'Plato on Sense and Reference', *Mind*, 104 (1985), 526–37.

RYLE, G., 'Letters and Syllables in Plato', *Philosophical Review*, 69 (1960), 431–51.

—— 'Logical Atomism in Plato's *Theaetetus*', *Phronesis*, 35 (1990), 21–46.

SILVERMAN, A., 'Plato on Perception and "Commons"', *Classical Quarterly*, NS 40 (1990), 148–75. (Also discusses the *Timaeus*.)

TIGNER, S., 'The "Exquisite" Argument at *Theaetetus* 171a', *Mnemosyne*, 24 (1971), 366–9.

WATERFIELD, R., *Plato:* Theaetetus (Harmondsworth: Penguin Books, 1987).

WATERLOW, S., 'Protagoras and Inconsistency', *Archiv für Geschichte der Philosophie*, 59 (1977), 19–36.

WILLIAMS, C. J. F., 'Referential Opacity and False Belief in the *Theaetetus*', *Philosophical Quarterly*, 22 (1972), 289–302.

Timaeus

CHERNISS, H. F., 'A Much Misread Passage in Plato's *Timaeus*', *American Journal of Philology*, 75 (1954), 113–30.

——'The Relation of the *Timaeus* to Plato's Later Dialogues', *American Journal of Philology*, 78 (1957), 225–66; repr. in *SPM* 339–78.

CORNFORD, F. M., *Plato's Cosmology: The* Timaeus *of Plato* (London: Routledge & Kegan Paul, 1937).

DRISCOLL, J., 'The Platonic Ancestry of Primary Substance', *Phronesis*, 24 (1979), 253–69.

FREDE, M., 'Being and Becoming in Plato', *Oxford Studies in Ancient Philosophy*, suppl. vol. (1988), 37–52. (Reply by A. Code, 53–60.)

GILL, M., 'Matter and Flux in Plato's *Timaeus*', *Phronesis*, 32 (1987), 34–53.

KEYT, D., 'The Mad Craftsman of the *Timaeus*', *Philosophical Review*, 80 (1971), 230–5.

KUNG, J., 'Why the Receptacle is not a Mirror', *Archiv für Geschichte der Philosophie*, 70 (1988), 167–78.

——'Mathematics and Virtue in Plato's *Timaeus*', in J. Anton and A. Preus (eds.), *Essays in Ancient Greek Philosophy*, iii (Albany: State University of New York, 1989), 303–39.

LENNOX, J., 'Plato's Unnatural Teleology', in D. O'Meara (ed.), *Platonic Investigations* (Washington: Catholic University Press of America, 1985), 195–218.

MILLS, K. W., 'Some Aspects of Plato's Theory of Forms: *Timaeus* 49c ff.', *Phronesis*, 13 (1968), 145–70.

MOHR, R., *The Platonic Cosmology* (Leiden: E. J. Brill, 1985).

MORROW, G., 'Necessity and Persuasion in Plato's *Timaeus*', *Philosophical Review*, 59 (1950), 147–64; repr. in *SPM* 421–37.

OSBORNE, C., 'Topography in the *Timaeus*', *Proceedings of the Cambridge Philological Society*, 34 (1988), 104–14.

OWEN, G. E. L., 'The Place of the *Timaeus* in Plato's Dialogues', *Classical Quarterly*, NS 3 (1953), 79–95; repr. in *SPM* 313–38; and in *LSD* 65–84.

——'Plato and Parmenides on the Timeless Present', *Monist*, 50 (1966), 317–40; repr. in *LSD* 27–44.

PATTERSON, R., 'The Unique Worlds of the *Timaeus*', *Phoenix*, 35 (1981), 105–19.

REED, N. H., 'Plato on Flux, Perception and Language', *Proceedings of the Cambridge Philological Society*, 18 (1972), 65–77.

SILVERMAN, A., 'Timaean Particulars', *Classical Quarterly*, NS 42 (1992), 87–113.

TAYLOR, A. E., *A Commentary on Plato's* Timaeus (Oxford: Clarendon Press, 1928).

VLASTOS, G., 'The Disorderly Motion in the *Timaeus*', *Classical Quarterly*, 33 (1939), 71–83; repr. in *SPM* 379–99.

——'Creation in the *Timaeus*: Is it a Fiction?', in *SPM* 401–19.

——*Plato's Universe* (Seattle: University of Washington Press, 1975).

ZEYL, D., 'Plato and Talk of a World in Flux: *Timaeus* 49a6–50b5', *Harvard Studies in Classical Philology*, 79 (1975), 125–48.

Sophist

ACKRILL, J. L., '*Sumplokē Eidōn*', *Bulletin of the Institute of Classical Studies*, 2 (1955), 31–5; repr. in *SPM* 199–206; and in *Plato* i. 201–9.

——'Plato and the Copula: *Sophist* 251–59', *Journal of Hellenic Studies*, 77 (1957), 1–6; repr. in *Plato* i. 210–22.

BLUCK, R. S., *Plato's* Sophist: *A Commentary* (Manchester: Manchester University Press, 1975).

BOSTOCK, D., 'Plato on "is-not" (*Sophist*, 254–9)', *Oxford Studies in Ancient Philosophy*, 2 (1984), 89–119.

BROWN, L., 'Innovation and Continuity: The Battle of Gods and Giants, *Sophist* 245–259', in *MAP* 181–207.

CAMPBELL, L., *The* Sophistes *and* Politicus *of Plato* (Oxford: Clarendon Press, 1867).

FREDE, M., *Prädikation und Existenzaussage, Hypomnemata,* 18 (Göttingen: Vandenhoeck & Ruprecht, 1967).

——'Plato's *Sophist* on False Statements', in *CCP* 397–424.

——'The Literary Form of the *Sophist*', in *FA* 132–51.

HEINAMAN, R., 'Self-Predication in the *Sophist*', *Phronesis*, 26 (1981), 55–66.

——'Being in the *Sophist*', *Archiv für Geschichte der Philosophie*, 65 (1983), 1–17.

——'Once More: Being in the *Sophist*', *Archiv für Geschichte der Philosophie*, 68 (1986), 121–5.

KETCHUM, R., 'Participation and Predication in the *Sophist* 251–60', *Phronesis*, 23 (1978), 42–62.

KEYT, D., 'Plato's Paradox that the Immutable is Unknowable', *Philosophical Quarterly*, 19 (1969), 1–14.

——'Plato on Falsity: *Sophist* 263b', in *EA* 285–305.

KOSTMAN, J., 'False Logos and Not-Being in Plato's *Sophist*', in J. M. E. Moravcsik (ed.), *Patterns in Plato's Thought* (Dordrecht: Reidel, 1973), 192–212.

LEE, E. N., 'Plato on Negation and Not-Being in the *Sophist*', *Philosophical Review*, 81 (1972), 267–304.

LEWIS, F., 'Did Plato Discover the *estin* of Identity?', *California Studies in Classical Antiquity*, 8 (1975), 113–43.

——'Plato on "Not"', *California Studies in Classical Antiquity*, 9 (1976), 89–115.

McDOWELL, J., 'Falsehood and Not-Being in Plato's *Sophist*', in *LL* 115–34.

McPHERRAN, M., 'Plato's Reply to the "Worst Difficulty" Argument of the *Parmenides*: *Sophist* 248a–249d', *Archiv für Geschichte der Philosophie*, 68 (1986), 233–52.

MALCOLM, J., 'Plato's Analysis of *to on* and *to mē on* in the *Sophist*', *Phronesis*, 12 (1967), 130–46.

——'Remarks on an Incomplete Rendering of Being in the *Sophist*', *Archiv für Geschichte der Philosophie*, 67 (1985), 162–5.

MORAVCSIK, J. M. E., '*Sumplokē eidōn* and the Genesis of *Logos*', *Archiv für Geschichte der Philosophie*, 42 (1960), 117–29.

——'Being and Meaning in the *Sophist*', *Acta Philosophica Fennica*, 14 (1962), 23–78.

NEHAMAS, A., 'Participation and Predication in Plato's Later Thought', *Review of Metaphysics*, 36 (1982), 343–74.

PELLETIER, F. J., *Parmenides, Plato, and the Semantics of Not-Being* (Chicago: Chicago University Press, 1992).

PRIOR, W., 'Plato's Analysis of Being and Not-Being in the *Sophist*', *Southern Journal of Philosophy*, 18 (1980), 199–211.

REEVE, C. D. C., 'Motion, Rest, and Dialectic in the *Sophist*', *Archiv für Geschichte der Philosophie*, 67 (1985), 47–64.

ROBERTS, J., 'The Problem about Being in the *Sophist*', *History of Philosophy Quarterly*, 1 (1986), 229–43.

VLASTOS, G., 'An Ambiguity in the *Sophist*', in *PS* 270–322.

WIGGINS, D., 'Sentence Meaning, Negation, and Plato's Problems of Not-Being', in *Plato* i. 268–303.

Statesman

ACKRILL, J. L., 'In Defense of Platonic Division', in O. P. Wood and G. Pitcher (eds.), *Ryle: A Collection of Critical Essays* (Garden City, NY: Doubleday Anchor Books, 1970), 373–92.
MORAVCSIK, J. M. E., 'The Anatomy of Plato's Divisions', in *EA* 324–48.
—— 'Plato's Method of Division', in J. M. E. Moravcsik (ed.), *Patterns in Plato's Thought* (Dordrecht: Reidel, 1973), 158–80.
OWEN, G. E. L., 'Plato on the Undepictable', in *EA* 349–61; repr. in *LSD* 138–47.
ROWE, C. J. (ed. and trans.), *Plato:* Statesman (Warminster: Aris & Phillips, 1995).
—— (ed.), *Reading the* Statesman, *Proceedings of the Third Symposium Platonicum* (Sankt Augustin: Academia Verlag, 1995).
—— 'The *Politicus*: Structure and Form', in *FA* 153–78.
SKEMP, J. B., *Plato's* Statesman (London: Routledge & Kegan Paul, 1952; 2nd edn. Bristol: Bristol Classical Press, 1987).

Philebus

BURY, R. G., *The* Philebus *of Plato* (Cambridge: Cambridge University Press, 1897; repr. Arno Press, 1973).
COOPER, J., 'Plato's Theory of Human Good in the *Philebus*', *Journal of Philosophy*, 74 (1977), 714–30; repr. as Ch. XV in Vol. ii of this work.
DANCY, R., 'The One, the Many, and the Forms: *Philebus* 15b1–8', *Ancient Philosophy*, 4 (1984), 160–93.
DAVIDSON, D., *Plato's* Philebus, Harvard Dissertation Reprint (Cambridge, Mass: Harvard University Press, 1949).
—— 'Plato's Philosopher', *London Review of Books*, 7/14 (1985), 15–17; repr. in T. Irwin and M. Nussbaum (eds.), *Virtue, Love and Form: Essays in Memory of Gregory Vlastos*, Apeiron, 26 (Edmonton: Academic Printing and Publishing, 1993), 179–94.
HACKFORTH, R., *Plato's Examination of Pleasure* (Cambridge: Cambridge University Press, 1945).
HAMPTON, C., 'Plato's Late Ontology: A Riddle Unresolved', *Ancient Philosophy*, 8 (1988), 105–16.
—— *Pleasure, Knowledge, and Being: An Analysis of Plato's* Philebus (Albany: State University of New York Press, 1990).
MEINWALD, C., 'One/Many Problems: *Philebus* 14c1–15c3', *Phronesis*, 41 (1996), 95–103.
—— 'Prometheus's Bounds: *Peras* and *Apeiron* in Plato's *Philebus*', in *MAP* 137–80.
MORAVCSIK, J. M. E., 'Forms, Nature and the Good in the *Philebus*', *Phronesis*, 24 (1979), 81–104.
SHINER, R., *Knowledge and Reality in Plato's* Philebus (Assen: Van Gorcum, 1974).
—— 'Must *Philebus* 59a–c Refer to Transcendent Forms?', *Journal of the History of Philosophy*, 17 (1979), 71–7.
—— 'Knowledge in *Philebus* 55c–62a: A Response', in F. J. Pelletier and J. King-Farlow (eds.), *New Essays on Plato*, Canadian Journal of Philosophy, suppl. vol. 9 (Guelph: Canadian Association for Publishing in Philosophy, 1983), 171–83.
STRIKER, G., *Peras und Apeiron*, Hypomnemata, 30 (Göttingen: Vandenhoeck & Ruprecht, 1970).

Taylor, A. E., *Philebus and Epinomis* (London: T. Nelson, 1956).
Waterfield, R., 'The Place of the *Philebus* in Plato's Dialogues', *Phronesis*, 25 (1980), 270–305.
—— *Plato:* Philebus (Harmondsworth: Penguin Books, 1982).

INDEX OF NAMES

NOTE: Page numbers in **bold** refer to main sections by the commentator.

INDEX OF PLATONIC PASSAGES, VOL. 1

512   INDEX OF PLATONIC PASSAGES, VOL. 1